THE MONOTHEISTS

THE MONOTHEISTS

JEWS, CHRISTIANS, AND MUSLIMS IN CONFLICT AND COMPETITION

VOLUME II

The Words and Will of God

F. E. Peters

Princeton University Press   **Princeton and Oxford**

Copyright © 2003 by Princeton University Press
Published by Princeton University Press,
41 William Street, Princeton, New Jersey 08540

In the United Kingdom: Princeton University Press, 3 Market Place,
Woodstock, Oxfordshire OX20 1SY

Second printing, and first paperback printing, 2005
Paperback ISBN-13: 978-0-691-12373-8
Paperback ISBN-10: 0-691-12373-X

The Library of Congress has cataloged the cloth edition of this book as follows

Peters, F. E. (Francis E.)
The monotheists : Jews, Christians, and Muslims in conflict and competition / F. E. Peters.
p. cm.
Includes bibliographical references and index.
Contents: v. 1. The peoples of God—v. 2. The words and will of God.
ISBN 0-691-11460-9 (v. 1 : alk. paper)—ISBN 0-691-11461-7 (v. 2 : alk. paper)
1. Judaism—Relations—Christianity—History. 2. Christianity and other
religions—Judaism—History. 3. Judaism—Relations—Islam—History.
4. Islam—Relations—Judaism—History. 5. Islam—Relations—Christianity—History.
6. Christianity and other religions—Islam—History. I. Title.
BM535 .P32 2003
291.1'72—dc21 2002042462

British Library Cataloging-in-Publication Data is available

This book has been composed in Janson
Printed on acid-free paper. ∞
pup.princeton.edu

Printed in the United States of America

3 5 7 9 10 8 6 4 2

For

Peter Paul Peters,

good man, great son

Contents

Preface   xvii

Introduction   xxi

1. THE SCRIPTURES: BIBLE, NEW
   TESTAMENT, AND QURAN
   Three Sacred Books   2
   People of the Book   3
   The Bible   4
   Sacred Tongues   5
   On Translations   7
   Scriptural Criticism   8
   Who Wrote the Bible?   10
   Explaining Revelation   11
   High Prophetology   14
   Heavenly Books   15
   The New Testament: Notion, Text, and Canon   16
   The Biblical Canon   18
   The Inspiration of Scripture   20
   Contingency and the Constraints of History   21
   Humanist Critics of Scripture   23
   The Old Testament and the New   24
   The Arrangement of the Quran   25
   The Composition of the Quran   27
   The Editing of the Quran   29
   The Collection of the Quran   30
   Qere and Ketib   32
   Interpolation and Abrogation   33
   Closure   34

2. UNDERSTANDING THE WORD OF GOD
The Seal and the Silence   35
Biblical Exegesis   36
Midrash   37
An Unfolding Tradition   38
Philo Rereads Scripture   40
Evangelical Exegesis   41
The Senses of Scripture   42
Marcion Reads the Scripture   43
Why Don't We Understand?   44
Fathers and Other Authorities   45
The Glossa Ordinaria, Christian and Jewish   46
The Quran Reads the Bible   46
Quranic Ambiguities   48
The "Occasions of Revelation"   49
Tabari Enthroned   50
Plain and Allegorical Exegesis in Islam   51
The Muslims Struggle with Revelation and Reason   52
Shiite Tafsir   54
Learning from the Muslims   55
Two Medieval Jewish Commentators:
    Ibn Ezra and Rashi   56
The Great Debates   57
The Reform of Christian Exegesis   60
Control of the Book   61
A Closer, and Different, Look at Scripture   62
Exegesis and Hermeneutics   63

3. SCRIPTURE AND TRADITION
The Great Tradition   65
Rabbinic Judaism   66
"How Many Torahs Do You Have?"   68
Making the Mishnah   69
Mishnah and Gemara   70
Validating the Rabbis   71
Attacking the Tradition: Sadducees and Karaites   71
Jewish Reform   73
The Beginnings of a Christian Tradition   74
The Deposit of Faith   74
Apostolic Tradition and Apostolic Succession   75
Sola Scriptura   76
The Tradition Debate   78
The War of the Historians   79

The Sunna of the Prophet   80
Hadith Criticism   82
The Canonical Collections   83
Quran and Sunna   84
The Shiite Hadith   85

4. GOD'S LAW AND ITS OBSERVANCE
Purity and Defilement   87
Biblical Law   88
The Lesson of Qumran   89
The Tradition from the Fathers   90
The Mishnah and the Two Talmuds   91
Two Jewish Codes:
    Mishneh Torah and *Shulkhan Aruk*   92
The Purpose of the Law   94
The Administration of Jewish Law   94
The Rabbis   95
The Instruments of God's Justice   96
Jesus and the Law   96
Christians and the Law   97
A Law for Christians   98
The Sources of Christian Law   99
The Codification of Church Law   101
The Beginnings of Western Canon Law   101
Gratian   102
Catechesis and Catechism   103
An Islamic Catechism: The Pillars of Islam   105
Sharia, the Muslim Way   106
From Prophetic Tradition to Law   108
The Administration of Justice in Islam   109
The Qadi   110
The Qadi's Justice   111
Responsa and Fatwas: The Mufti   112
The Qadi and the Mufti   113
The Schools   114
Shiite Law   115
Ijtihad   116
The Closing of the Gate   117
The Hierarchization of the Ulama   118
Ijtihad Unchained   120
Customary Law and Governance in Islam   121
Qanun: The Sultan's Law   122
Jewish Rabbis and Islamic Ulama   123

5. GOD'S COMMANDMENTS AND
   HUMAN MORALITY
   Values and Value Systems   127
   Whence Evil?   129
   The Diabolic, the Demonic   130
   The Jinn, Shaytan, and Iblis   132
   Sin and Atonement in Israel   133
   Acquittal   134
   Jesus' Moral Teaching   135
   Pauline Morality   136
   Original Sin   137
   Manichaeism   138
   Augustine as Moralist   139
   Augustine and Pelagius   140
   Penance and the Sacramental System   141
   Purgatory and Indulgences   143
   Who Will Be Saved?   145
   The Absolute Will of God   146
   The Disputed Question of Nature and Grace   147
   Justification   148
   Doubly Saved and Doubly Damned   149
   The Council of Trent on Justification   150
   The Magisterium Restored   151
   A Conference on "Aids"   152
   The Crisis in Catholic Morality   153
   Jansenism   155
   From Pascal to Alfonso di Ligouri   157
   Muhammad as Moral Exemplar   158
   Islamic Morality   160
   Free Will and Predestination in Islam   162
   A Rationalist Solution   163
   Acquiring Responsibility   164
   Consensus on Matters Moral   165

6. DIVINE WORSHIP
   Shekinah/Sakina   168
   Sacrifice   169
   The Jesus Sacrifice   170
   The Jewish Priesthood   171
   The Synagogue   172
   The Eucharist   174
   Liturgies Eastern and Western   175

Eucharistic Issues: Who, When, and How?   177
The Reform Liturgy   178
Christmas   178
Muslim Prayer   179
Friday Prayer and the Mosque   180
The Hajj   180
Intercalation Prohibited   183
The Enshrinement of Jerusalem   184
Christian Pilgrimage   185
The Western Wall   187
Popular Devotions in Christianity   188
The Cult of Mary   189
From Piety to Dogma: An Immaculate Conception and
    Prophetic Impeccability   190
The Veneration of the Saints   192
Canonization   193
Eucharistic Devotions   194
Popular Devotions in Islam   195
The Friends of God   197
Three Dramatic Narratives: Passover, Passion, and
    the Death of Husayn   198
Idols and Images   200
Emperor Portrayal, Christian Style   202
Christian Images   203
Christian Iconoclasm   204
Stripping the Altars: Images and the Reform   206
Islam and the Graven Image   207
The Word as Decoration   208

7. THINKING ABOUT GOD
Mythos and Logos   211
The Theology of Philo of Alexandria   213
Athens and Jerusalem   215
Theology and Creeds: Nicaea to Chalcedon   217
The Muslims Encounter Aristotle   219
Falsafa   220
Talking about God: The Muslim Beginnings   222
Learning to Speak Dialectically   223
An Islamic Inquisition   225
Kalam Matured   226
Muslim Creeds   228
Reason and Revelation in Islam   230

God Supreme: Islamic Occasionalism   232
Ibn Rushd   233
The Voice of Conservative Islamic Orthodoxy   235
Jewish Kalam   236
A Guide for the Perplexed   237
Falsafa and Kalam   238
Received Wisdom   238
Sacred Theology, Western Style   240
Thomas Aquinas   241
Scholasticism   242
Latin Averroism   244
The Two Faces of Truth   244
The Reformation and Christian Systematic Theology   246
The Wisdom of Illumination   247
The School of Isfahan   249

8. FROM DESERT SAINTS TO MUSLIM SUFIS
The Way of the World   251
The Issue of Jewish Asceticism   252
The Desert a City   254
Obedience of the Spirit   255
The Saints in the City   256
The Rule of St. Basil   257
Benedict and the Benedictines   258
Benedictine Experiments: Carthusians and
     Cistercians   260
Canons Regular and Other   261
The Mendicant Friars: Franciscans and Dominicans   262
Is Perfection Possible? The Franciscan Controversy   265
Military Orders, Christian and Muslim   267
The Rise and Fall of the Society of Jesus   270
The Holy Mountain   273
The Personal Life of Muhammad   274
This World and the Next   275
The Beginnings of Muslim Asceticism   276
Sufi Convents: Khanqah, Ribat, Zawiya   278
The Sufi Orders   279
Sufis in the Service of Islam: Chishtis and Bektashis   282
The Chinese Rites   284
Christian and Muslim Religious Orders   285
Suppression   286
Jewish Brotherhoods in Galilee   287

Saints without Rules: The Hasidim   288
The Apostolic Succession in Eastern Europe   290
The Habad   291

9. LEAPING FROM THE DARK INTO
   THE LIGHT: MYSTICISM
   Face to Face with God   293
   The Beginnings   294
   The Adepts of Qumran   295
   The Celestial Chariot   295
   "Four Who Attempted to Enter Paradise"   296
   God's Love, God's Body   297
   The Palaces   297
   The *Book of Creation*   298
   From Christian Asceticism to Mysticism   299
   Approaching the Unknowable   301
   The Jesus Prayer   302
   Hesychasm   303
   God's Energies and God's Essence   305
   Spirituality, Eastern and Western   306
   The *Spiritual Exercises*   306
   Muhammad Cleansed, and Rapt   308
   Did Muhammad See God?   309
   The Sufi as Mystic   310
   The Growth of Sufi Theory   311
   Sufism and Gnosticism   313
   Sufis and Shiites   314
   Al-Hallaj   315
   The Sufi Way   317
   Practical Sufism   318
   Spiritual Hierarchies   320
   The Apotheosis of Ali: The Alawis   320
   The Fathers of Islamic Theosophy:
      Ibn Sina and Suhrawardi   321
   Defender of the Faith   324
   Making Sufism Safe for Islam   326
   Spiritual Resurrection   327
   On the Edge: Ibn Arabi   327
   The Seal of the Saints   329
   The Teaching and Its Opponents   330
   The Beginnings of Kabbalah   333
   The *Zohar*   334

The World of the Sefiroth   335
Isaac Luria   336
Kabbalah for Everyone: Hasidism   337

10. THE LAST THINGS
End Time Scenarios   339
After Death, What?   341
Death and Judgment   342
The Particular Judgment   343
The Resurrection of the Body   343
The Seed, the Statue, and the Conjunction
      of Materia and Forma   345
In the Meantime . . .   346
The Cosmology of the Other World   347
Mapping Paradise and Hell   349
A Heavenly Journey   350
Living High: The Angels   351
Angels in Arabia   353
The Vision of God   354
With a Little Help from the Creator   355
Paradise Lost: Maimonides (and Others)
      on the World to Come   356
Salvation   358
Religious Zionism: Hurrying the End   359
Political Zionism and Eretz Israel   360
The Birth Pangs of the Messiah   362
Realized and Futurist Eschatology in Christianity   363
A Christian Apocalypse   364
Millennialism/Chilianism   365
The Reign of the Spirit: Joachim de Fiore   366
Abraham the Intercessor   368
The Muslim Dead   369
The Quranic Eschaton   371
Intercession in Islam   371
A Savior Returns   372
The Mahdi   375

END THOUGHTS
People of the Book, and of the Covenant   377
Odium Theologicum   377
The Religion of Abraham   378
Who Is the Heir?   379

The True Israel   380
A Fractious Family   381
The Rivals' Charms   383
Faith and History   384

Index   387

Preface

IN 1982 I WROTE a small book called *Children of Abraham*. In it I attempted to put the three monotheistic faith communities of Jews, Christians, and Muslims in a comparative context. The work was undertaken before the appearance of my annotated collection of texts, *Judaism, Christianity, and Islam: The Classical Texts and Their Interpretation*, and my repeated use of this latter book in the classroom. I have taught a course on the combustible mix of Jews, Christians, and Muslims in every academic orbit for more than twenty years, and have lectured on one or another aspect of the subject in a variety of venues across the country. I have learned a great deal not only from my own research and study but from listening to student and audience reactions, and even on occasion from listening to myself since I too have had the not uncommon teaching experience of hearing myself say things I didn't realize I knew or understood. I have tried to put something of what I have learned into this new book.

Another fruit of the classroom experience is my attempt here to be somewhat fuller in my explanations. My first essay was much too condensed in its matter, too telegraphic in its style. The present effort may still suffer some of those same ills because the complexity of this subject has managed to stay well ahead of my understanding of it. The reader must just be patient: I shall do better the next time.

I have also become more venturesome and extended the time frame of the story, as far as Christianity is concerned, to somewhere beyond the Reformation. A similar decisive moment does not occur in Judaism until the nineteenth century, and I have had something to say at least about Hasidism. One of Islam's defining experiences seems to be occurring in the very immediate present, but I have done no more than touch on it.

For all that, this remains an introduction rather than a history, a guide to some of the notions and practices shared by the three monotheistic communities, notions that have also been sources of contention among them. The hard realities of politics and economics are never very far removed from this probe into issues, ideas, and institutions. Who was in charge or who possessed the power at this time or in this place is always a basic ingredient mixed into the relations, and the perceptions, of Jews, Christians, and Muslims. Sometimes these are explicit and apparent in the text; at other times they glare darkly from between the lines. But they are always there.

The intent of this work is not to make peace or to stir up war, or even ill feelings, among the three religious communities, but simply to lay out their common roots, their evolution over time, and what I see as their striking resemblances and their equally striking differences. I am not so foolish, however, as to think this is a value-free exercise. Comparisons can of course be read as invidious; certain resemblances can be parsed as reductive, or relativizing, particularly among believers who are characterized by their conviction of their own unique destiny, as these three certainly are. But this same approach can also broaden understanding in quite remarkable ways. It is a little like experiencing one's own personality in one's offspring, where traits may appear far less endearing and charming than we imagine them in ourselves. It is one of the more salutary effects of forcing these three particular siblings to pose, however briefly, for a family portrait.

A caution for the reader: As everyone since Thales has discovered, it is considerably easier to talk about complex phenomena if we essentialize or reify them into a single, and relatively simple, "thing." It is difficult to imagine more complex phenomena than the three "things" here called—not for the first time, of course—Judaism, Christianity, and Islam. We know but sometimes forget that there really are no such "things." There are only Jews, Christians, and Muslims, billions of them, whose common marks we try to make sense of here. They have collected themselves in communities and answer to those names, and a book like this is an attempt to answer why. It is assuredly easier to get and compare the answers if we attend to what is called the "high tradition," the thoughtful literary works of educated Jews, Christians, and Muslims who, like us, are looking for the forests, instead of scrutinizing the scattered records carved on the individual trees. The latter records are assuredly there, thin in some times and places, thick in others, telling which Jews were mixing their milk with their mutton and which not, how many Christians were sleeping in on Sunday mornings, and why this Muslim woman wore a veil and that one chose not to. The argument can be made that *this* is really what those three "religions" are all about, and not what Maimonides or Augustine or Ibn Khaldun thought they were. Perhaps, but these forests, for all their subversive nonexistence, are not yet so clearly charted that we can all fall to counting trees. Hence, this essentialist guide to three very thickly wooded, and essential, patches of the human experience.

Each of these volumes has been indexed separately in the hope of saving the reader some thumb-wrenching acrobatics, and there are abundant cross-references to carry one back and forth between the two. Finally, some paragraphs of these volumes, notably those having to do with Islam, have appeared in somewhat different form, and in a quite different context, in my work *Islam: A Guide for Jews and Christians* (Princeton, 2003).

In my earlier work I gave abundant thanks to my academic colleagues for their help and inspiration. The gratitude is still academic, but this time it is for all the winning young men and women who have paid quite extraordinary sums of money to sit on the other side of the desk and listen, after a fashion, to what I have had to say. They may not have always understood what the gentleman leaning on the podium and rattling on about Rambam and plenary indulgences was exactly up to, but they listened, most of them, and they talked back on occasion, some of them, though always in good humor. They likely taught me a great deal more than I taught them, and I take this occasion to thank them all for giving me a couple precious months of their lives.

Introduction

FROM WHAT WE READ in the recorded history of his devotees, the god who created the universe had shown some earlier, generally benevolent interest in what he had brought into being. Then, at a given moment in historical time, he addressed himself to one Abram, the sheikh of an extended family of Near Eastern sheep nomads who were camping in what is today called the Negev. Worship me, the god said, and I will make you and yours a great people. It was not a unique or a solitary voice: we know from plentiful evidence that there were other, many other, gods on that landscape and in the minds of Abram's contemporaries. Abram, however, limited his worship to this one deity, and the god in turn granted his favor to Abram, or Abraham, as he was henceforward called.

The story continues—in the Bible and in the countless books that derive from it—with an account of how Abraham's descendants, the "Sons of Israel," were drawn into Egypt, where there were gods in great abundance, figured in almost every form of human and beast. The Israelites eventually escaped under divine guidance and the shrewd and courageous leadership of Moses. On their long trek across Sinai, their god, who revealed that his name was Yahweh, unfolded his will to Moses and the Israelites. From atop a mountain in Sinai, he unmistakably asserted what was already perhaps implicit in the dialogue with Abraham: I am your Lord; you will worship no other but me.

This was an assertion of divine primacy; the god was *primus inter impares*, though in this instance Yahweh did not explain in what his primacy consisted, whether the other deities were his offspring, his consorts, his messengers, or perhaps just too minor to matter. He simply ignored them, though his worshipers assuredly did not on occasion. What was truly revolutionary in the covenant offered to Abraham, and then in more detail to Moses, was its exclusivity clause. The tribe of Israel was to worship no other god, to pay no dues, to give no respect, honor, or even acknowledgment to the deities of other peoples. This appears to us, who define monotheism as the denial of belief in any god save one, as at best henotheism, the recognition of a primary god above all others. But it is in practice, true monotheism. Where it really counted, in sacrifice and invocation, the Israelites were required to behave as if there were only one god. It would take centuries for that radical liturgical disregard of the other gods to be fully conceptualized into a denial of their very existence, a process immeasurably aided by the fact that this god, astonishingly, had no image or effigy. Boldly, Yahweh could only be imagined.

Yahweh would have it no other way. He was, in his own words, a "jealous god" whose very first commandment to Moses on Sinai had to do with his own exclusive rights to the gifts and rituals that were the dues of a god. Jealous and phobic: in the biblical account that sets the tone and terms for all who subsequently worshiped him, Yahweh demanded that all forms of "impurity" be kept at a very safe distance from him, away from his throne and his house, away from his city, away from his land. We are puzzled by the exact nature of this terrifying impurity that runs broadly and somewhat erratically through Yahweh's own creation, which he had earlier praised as "good." But the "abomination of abominations," the Mother of all Impurities, was an altar set up to one of those other gods in Yahweh's own Jerusalem sanctuary. Finally, and with extraordinary consequence, what was abominable to Yahweh was also to be abominable to the Israelites, who thus became morally identified with their god.

These are the beginnings of monotheism, a way of acting toward, thinking about, and, eventually, of believing in this deity known as (but not readily called) Yahweh by the Israelites, as God the Father by others, and as Allah by still others. Whatever the name, he is the same God worshiped by Jews, Christians, and Muslims as the creator and sustainer of the universe, the supreme and unique Deity from whom all proceeds and in whom all ends. Why there are three distinct communities of his believers and how and why they worship and think about him (and one another) as they do is the subject of the following pages.

The three communities have had a long, complex, and profoundly imbricated history, and I have here divided it, to grant some intermission, into two volumes. The first, *The Peoples of God*, describes how the three communities came about, evolved, identified and organized themselves. The first volume has a great deal to do with externals of community formation, whereas the second, *The Words and Will of God*, is given over to what might be called the internal or spiritual life of the monotheists, the working out of God's will in the lives, hearts, and minds of his believers. Running through both volumes is the enormously interesting and increasingly vital question of how Jews, Christians, and Muslims have dealt with one another. In another book I used the metaphor of the family to describe that relationship—these are the "Children of Abraham"—and the figure is still useful in understanding them, as I attempt to spell out in the end thoughts of each volume.

Before we begin, some simple cautionary remarks may be in order. Whatever may be thought of it, Christianity is by now common intellectual and spiritual coin in the West, and Judaism only somewhat less so. But for many Western readers, "Islam" and "Muslims" are still exotic or even somewhat baffling terms and concepts. The notions surrounding Islam will be unfolded in detail in the pages that follow, but a few sentences on the terms themselves will help at the very outset. "Islam" is an Arabic term that broadly means "submission," in this context, submission to God; thus, a "Muslim," a derivative from the same root, is "someone who has submitted." Though "Islam" and "Muslim"—as well as "Quran"—are all Arabic in origin, not all Muslims are Arabs by a long shot, and a great many Turks, Iranians, and Afghans, and millions and millions of Pakistanis, Indians, and Indonesians are properly upset when they are thought to be Arabs because they are Muslims. If all Muslims are not Arabs, neither are all Arabs Muslims. Many Palestinian Arabs are Christians, for example, and so too are very many Lebanese Arabs. Christians too can be of any ethnicity, and how the Jews identify themselves will emerge as we go along.

The reader will already perhaps have noted a discrepancy between an anticipated "Moslem" and the somewhat less familiar spelling of "Muslim." There is much of the same ahead. The more common Englished "Koran" will appear in these pages as "Quran," and even though I have used only one of them, there are almost as many English versions of "Muhammad" in circulation as there are of "Hanukkah." The reason is that both Arabic and Hebrew use their own, non-Latin scripts, and they do not normally insert vowels in writing their words. Thus, when these words are transcribed into a Latin script that must represent both the consonants and English vowel sounds, some transcriptions reflect what is written and others what is heard. In any event, I have tried to be both consistent and helpful rather than baffling or just downright quirky. But, as the Muslims say, God knows best.

To pass from simple orthography onto the more slippery terrain of the theology of names, which the monotheists take extremely seriously, as already noted, the name of our subject deity will here be referred to throughout simply as "God"—with apologies to those who prefer an even more reverential but somewhat distracting "G-d." And no effort will be made to conceal God's unmistakable—to his earliest devotees—masculine gender, even after worshipers came to believe he had no body at all.

As some will doubtless note, the punctilious rubric "is understood" or "is believed," or the less polite and more pointed "says you," will be omitted throughout—though the reader may supply it as liberally as is thought necessary. The descriptive and argumentative statements in the text will be presented, unless otherwise noted, as they are accepted and understood by the monotheist community in question.

The present work is more about faith than about history, more about the faith communities than about the various tribes of historians who have studied them. At stake here is not what *really* happened, even if that were possible to ascertain, but rather what Jews, Christians, and Muslims *believe* happened. I do not forswear analysis; indeed, there is a good deal of it here. But it will be used principally to elicit the similarities and differences among the three faiths and so render their comparison intelligible, not, in the manner of the critical historian, to weigh and verify or discard. Some things are ignored here from economy or perhaps simple inadvertence; nothing is discarded. The contents of every page of this book, like every line of the Scriptures and traditions on which they are based, have been the subject of intense critical scrutiny and equally intense argument among historians who are believers, nonbelievers who are historians, and generations of believers caught between the two.

Finally, in everything that follows, "Bible" always means the Hebrew or Jewish Bible. Although the Christians certainly reckon their own Scriptures as part of the Bible, these will always be called here the "New Testament" or the "Gospels." "Old Testament," which is an argument rather than just a name, will be reserved for the quite different version of the Jewish Scriptures preferred and used by the Christians.

Note: It is my unhappy but inevitable duty to say something about calendars since they have been the source of both mischief and misunderstanding. Jews, Christians, and Muslims reckon time in different ways, so here all years will be recorded as B.C.E. (before the common era) and C.E. (common era). A distinction must be made between *where* people begin counting time and *how* they count it. The Jews begin with Creation, which they put at 3760 B.C.E., and count straight onward without a break. Thus, our portentous year 2000 fell quite innocuously across the years 5760–5761 in the Hebrew calendar. Christians too begin with Creation, except their traditional date for that event is 4004 B.C.E. They count downward from there to the end of 1 B.C., when they reverse at this watershed year of Christ's birth (A.D., *anno Domini*), which marks the beginning of the Christian era. Thenceforward they begin numbering upward toward the end of the world, the day or the hour of which no one knows. For Muslims, the years from Creation to the Hegira, Muhammad's migration from Mecca to Medina, in 622 C.E. are simply lumped together as "the era of ignorance" (*al-jahiliyya*). In 622 begins the Muslim era proper, generally designated by A.H., *anno Hegirae*, "year of the Hegira."

How the three communities count is another matter. Jews and Muslims use lunar calendars made up of 12 months of 29+ days for a total of 354 days. This puts the lunar year 11 days behind the solar cycle of our

(*continued*)

calendar. Jews address the discrepancy (and thus keep their festivals in step with the seasons) by intercalation, the practice of adding an extra month seven times in every cycle of 19 years and adding a single day at other shorter intervals. The Quran (9:36–37) strictly forbade Muslims to intercalate (as they had in pre-Islamic days), and so their lunar year falls 11 days behind the solar cycle each year. By their reckoning, the solar year 2000 c.e. spanned the lunar years 1421–1422 a.h. Christians follow the solar calendar commonly used in the West.

I

The Scriptures: Bible, New Testament, and Quran

JUDAISM, CHRISTIANITY, AND ISLAM are all scriptural religions, that is, they affirm the existence of a divine revelation in written form. "The Sacred Writings," "The Scripture," and "The Book" are practically interchangeable terms among the three communities, and their adherents can all be identified, as we shall see, as People of the Book, which the Muslims in fact call them. The three Scriptures show marked differences, however. In the Jewish—and Muslim—view, God gave and Moses wrote down a distinct and discrete multipart book, the Law or Torah. But although the Torah holds pride of place in Jewish revelational history, God's direct interventions were in one manner or another continuous between Moses and Ezra, and thus the Jewish Bible is a collective work that includes, under the three headings of Law, Prophets, and the miscellany called Writings, all of God's revelation to his people.

This was certainly the Jewish view in Jesus' day, and there is no reason to think that Jesus regarded Scripture any differently. He produced no new Writings or Book of his own, and so Christian Scripture is formally quite different from what the Jews thought of as such. The Gospels are accounts of Jesus' words and deeds set down, in approximately a biographical framework, by his followers. In the eyes of Christians, Jesus did not bring a Scripture; he was himself, in his person and message, a revelation, the "Good News." His life and sacrificial death sealed a "New Covenant" that God concluded with his people, and so the Gospels and the accounts of the deeds and thoughts of the early Christian community recorded in the Acts of the Apostles, and the letters of various of Jesus' followers came to be regarded by Christians as a New Covenant or Testament to be set down next to the Old—that recorded and commemorated in the Jewish Bible.

Muhammad may have had a somewhat different understanding of this complex process. Though he commonly refers to the Jewish revelation as *Tawrat*, the Prophet of Islam was certainly aware that there were other Jewish prophets, and so possibly revelations, after Moses. But he never mentions a New Testament; his sole references are to a singular "Gospel," in Arabic *Injil*, and he seems to have thought of it as a sacred book that Jesus had brought or written, much as Moses had the Torah.

Muhammad had a strong sense of the prophetic calling and the line of prophets that had created the Judeo-Christian tradition; and after some brief initial hesitation, he placed himself firmly within that line. He too was a prophet, and when God's earlier revelations had become distorted at the willful and perverse hands of the Jews and Christians, God had given to him, no less than to Moses and Jesus, a revealed Book. Or so it was in its final, codified version. What God himself had instructed Muhammad to call "The Recitation," in Arabic *al-Quran*, was in fact a series of messages delivered to Muhammad by the angel Gabriel over twenty-two years. Each part was already identified as Scripture during the Prophet's lifetime, and the Book was finally closed only with Muhammad's death.

Of the three sets of Scriptures, only the Quran enjoys a self-conferred canonicity: it anoints itself as Scripture. In contrast, both the Bible and the New Testament underwent a long (and largely invisible) process to achieve a status that was, in the end, conferred by the community.

Three Sacred Books

Thus there came into being three sacred books, each in some sense the Word of God. Each collection has traditionally been regarded by its faith community as a complete, authoritative, and universal statement regulating the role and conduct of humankind vis-à-vis its Creator. History suggests something different, however, Direct challenges to Scripture are by and large a very modern phenomenon, but even in traditional settings each community implicitly contested the completeness of Scripture by attempting to open other channels of continuing revelation (see II/3); by struggling to wrest the authority of the words of Scripture into the hands of its interpreters (see II/2); and in more recent times, by setting next to the universality of Scripture the notion of its historical conditioning—that it was expressed in a cultural milieu that to a greater or lesser extent determined its moral parameters. Each Scripture was, furthermore, the birthright and charter for a community that had not existed before. Each community lived in the profound conviction that God had spoken to it for the last time: the Jews, for the first and final time; the Christians, for the second and final time; the Muslims, for the third and final time.

The Bible, New Testament, and Quran, though looked on as emanating from the same source, are very different works. The Bible is a complex and composite blend of religious myth, historical narrative, legal enactments, prophetic admonitions, cautionary tales, and poetry composed over a long period and edited at some point into a single Book. The time span for the composition of the New Testament is considerably shorter, a half century perhaps, but it too has a very mixed content of quasi biography, community history, letters, and, in some versions, an apocalyptic Book of Revelation. The Quran, as we have seen, is absolutely contemporary to its revelation, twenty-two years in the lifetime of the Prophet.

There is nothing but God's own Word in the Quran, as Muhammad himself could assure the community of believers, though there were a great many of Muhammad's words circulating outside Scripture and with great consequence (see II/3). In Jewish and Christian circles, however, there were assuredly circulating other writings that had some claim to being God's Word but are not found in the Bible or the New Testament. Both these Scriptures represent, then, a deliberate decision by someone to designate certain works as authentic or canonical Scripture and to exclude others from the authoritative list that is called the canon. That decision was essentially theological, and the exclusion of the noncanonical writings, generally called Apocrypha from the Jewish or Christian Scriptures does not render them any less interesting or important from a historical point of view. The Books of Maccabees never made it into the Jewish canon, for example, nor the Gnostic gospels into the Christian, but each tells us something of the events and attitudes of the time that produced them.

People of the Book

For the Quran and Muslims generally, the phrase "People of the Book" refers to those peoples—Jews, Christians, Muslims, and latterly some others—who were recipients of a revelation in the form of a sacred book. Although the source, God, and so the truth of the Books is identical, the Scriptures themselves differed—witness their different names—not only from the beginning but particularly after the Jews and Christians began tampering with their Books, as the Muslims believe.

The Jews would deny flat out the assertion that there was more than one People of the Book, to wit, themselves: there were no further revelations after the closure of the biblical canon. Christians would agree that both they and the Jews were indeed People of the Book, in that their faith was rooted in the Bible, the only Scripture the earliest Christians knew. When the early Christians spoke of "Scripture," they meant the Jewish Scriptures or *Tanak* (see below), and it took some time (and a major separation from Judaism) for them to begin the process of assigning their own writings about Jesus to the same category of sacred Scripture. But eventually the Christians too came to regard their own books as Scripture, that is, "a Book" on a par with the Hebrew Bible, though in this case it records the New Covenant or Testament that God had concluded with his people (see below). Jesus' redemptive act was decisively effective for all humankind, however, and so there would be no future revelations before the End. Finally, Muslims see themselves as People of the Book par excellence, since the Quran has superseded the two earlier Scriptures, which were, nonetheless authentic. (On the Muslim political implications of the essentially theological concept of People of the Book, see I/8.)

The Bible

The Bible (from Greek *biblia*, "books") is really a collection of twenty-four separate books recognized by the Jews as the authentic record of God's dealing with them. It is often called Tanak, an acronym for its three major divisions. *Torah* (Law) is the five books (Pentateuch) of Moses—Genesis, Exodus, Leviticus, Numbers, and Deuteronomy. *Nebiim* (Prophets) includes both the former prophets (what we might regard as books of history), namely Joshua, Judges, then Samuel and Kings (both of these latter in two books, though counted as one), and the latter prophets, that is, Isaiah, Jeremiah, Ezekiel, and the twelve minor prophets (again counted as one book). The mixed collection called *Ketubim* (Writings) includes such diverse works as the hymns called the Psalms and the Song of Solomon; the moral stories of Job, Ruth, and Esther; the wisdom of Proverbs and Ecclesiastes (or Qohelet), the threnody of Lamentations, the apocalyptic Daniel, and the historical Ezra-Nehemiah (counted as one book) and Chronicles (again, two books counted as one).

Even when they returned from Exile, the Jews were losing their native Hebrew and adopting Aramaic, the Semitic language that served as the lingua franca of the eastern Mediterranean. Parts of the latest books of the Bible were actually written in Aramaic, as were later legal works like the Talmuds (see II/3). Diaspora Jews eventually adopted the Greek "common tongue" (*koine*) as their ordinary language (Hebrew never entirely disappeared as a learned language), and later spoke, and wrote, in everything from Arabic to English and a number of patois between. So there was need for the Bible to be translated. This need produced assorted Aramaic translations (called targums), which often paraphrased rather than simply translated the Bible. A Greek translation done at Alexandria in the mid–third century B.C.E. gained great currency among Diaspora Jews like Philo and Paul, and then universally among Greek-speaking Christians; it is called the Septuagint ("Seventy") from the myth of its making.

> **Note:** The prevalence of Greek-sounding titles (Genesis, Deuteronomy, Ecclesiastes, etc., and the very word Bible) in a collection of Hebrew books is attributable to the fact that they were most commonly cited in the literature at large by Christians, who from the beginning used the Greek Septuagint. In Hebrew the books are universally cited by the opening words of each book's first line. Thus what is commonly referred to as Genesis is called in Hebrew *Bereshit* ("In the beginning...").

What eventually drove the Septuagint out of circulation among Jews was precisely the ever-increasing Christian use of this rather loose translation, with its elastic canon (many of the Apocrypha like Judith, Wisdom of Solomon, Ben Sira, and 1 and 2 Maccabees were included in the Septuagint and so became part of the Christians standard Old Testament until the Protestant Reformers reverted to the Hebrew canon of twenty-four books) and the Christians' even looser interpretation of it for their own theological purposes. In the second and third centuries c.e. the Jews opted for a series of more literal Greek translations and effectively discarded the Septuagint. Jerome (d. ca. 420) used the Septuagint as the basis, though with corrections from the Hebrew, of his own Latin translation of the Old Testament, called the Vulgate, and so it passed in this form into Christian currency in Western Christendom.

Sacred Tongues

One element in understanding Jesus' significance is that his intentions were finally recalled in the form of biography, the Gospels, rather than as a mere collection of his sayings. Originally both forms may have been in competition, the narrative biography as witnessed by Mark's Gospel, for example, and a sayings collection like the noncanonical Gospel of Thomas or the famous "Q" that modern scholarship has reconstructed out of the identical, but non-Marcan, verses shared by Matthew and Luke. But it was the Marcan-type biography that quickly prevailed in the churches and constituted the "Good News" for Christians. This triumph of biography over sayings may also have influenced the easy and very rapid transition from the native Aramaic of Jesus and his followers to the Greek of our New Testament, which does not appear to be a translation. It was not important, at any rate, that Jesus' own words be recalled in their original language, and the few times that Jesus' actual Aramaic is set down in the Gospels (e.g., Mark 5:41; 7:24), they give the impression that those who recollected them thought they were sacred formulas or even magical incantations rather than a historically authentic speech.

The issue of a sacred language thus scarcely arose among the Christians, and the New Testament quickly passed into a variety of vernaculars: Egyptian Coptic, the Syrian Aramaic called Syriac, Latin, Slavic, and eventually the entire range of European and Asian tongues. In Western Europe the Latin translation done (or supervised by) Jerome finally gained currency as the *versio latina vulgata* or, in English, simply the Vulgate.

Note: The Vulgate translation, like the Septuagint among the second- and first-century Jews, gained a status among medieval Christians close to the inspiration of Scripture itself. Its accuracy required increasingly spirited defense, however, against the doubts raised on purely scholarly grounds by humanists like Lorenzo Valla (d. 1457) and Desiderius Erasmus (d. 1536)

> (*continued*)
>
> (see below) and by the increasing number of vernacular translations varying in understanding of what was being translated. Luther's own translation of the Scriptures—beginning in 1522 and often revised during his lifetime—went behind Jerome to newly available and more reliable editions of the original: Erasmus's of the New Testament (1519) and the Soncino edition of the Hebrew Bible (1495). The Roman Church responded at the Council of Trent, which affirmed the authority of Jerome's version but at the same time called for a new critical edition of the Vulgate. This was not achieved until 1590, and had almost immediately to be revised (1592–1598). The most famous of the early English translations, the King James, appeared in 1611.

If Jesus' Aramaic quickly disappeared behind other linguistic versions of his teachings and work, the careers of the languages of the Jewish and Muslim Scriptures had quite different trajectories. Both Hebrew and Arabic were, and are, the working language of clerical elites in Judaism and Islam (as was Latin in European Christianity). Jews at large, however, began losing their Hebrew as a vernacular sometime after the Exile and increasingly spoke whatever language prevailed where they lived. It is not surprising, then, that if a German- or Arabic-speaking Jew of the Middle Ages fancied becoming a rabbi, he had perforce to learn Hebrew, just as a Persian or Turk who wished to study sharia did so not in his native tongue but in Arabic. The tension in Muslim countries between the secular vernaculars and the religious Arabic is graphically illustrated in both the Turks' 1924 abandonment of Arabic script in their desire to create a new secular republic and in the 1979 Constitution of the Islamic Republic of Iran's mandating the study of Arabic for high school students.

The connection between religious learning and language is obviously dictated by the language of the sacred text itself, or, to put it more pointedly, by the language of the Words of God, one version of which is found in Hebrew and the other in Arabic. Jewish and Muslim clerics have been equally enthusiastic in praising each of the two tongues as "the language of God" or "the language of the angels," but there is a very distinct difference in the relationship of each to the Book in which it is found. First, the Bible is not entirely in Hebrew: parts of the canonical books of Ezra and Daniel were written in Aramaic, and those other near-canonical extensions of God's intent for his people, the Mishnah and the two Talmuds (see II/3), show a growing mixture of Aramaic and Hebrew in the recorded rabbinic discussions. But more fundamentally, the Bible is not merely God's direct speech—indeed, direct discourse forms only a small percentage of the whole—but a composed narrative framework within which actions as well as speech unfold, and most often it is the speech of mortals. The Jews understood that the biblical books had authors, and to that extent they were linguistically conditioned, though nonetheless inspired.

The Quran, in contrast, seems to present itself as the *ipsissima verba* of God, and in "manifest" or "convincing" Arabic (Quran 16:103, etc.). It has no framing narrative however, no authorial signature or presence. In the Muslim view, Muhammad is not even a transmitter; he merely announced with absolute accuracy what he himself had heard. The consequence, then, is that the Quran contains the precise words of God, without human intervention or conditioning of any sort; that God had spoken, and Muhammad had heard and reported, Arabic speech.

Finally, both Jews and Muslims use the text of Scripture as the essential base for their liturgical prayers. Though the Mishnah (Sotah 7:1) explicitly allows the use of the vernacular ("any language") for the central liturgical prayers, the pull of the original tongue is strong among Jews. Among Muslims the practice of using Arabic in liturgical prayer is almost universal.

On Translations

The Bible was, then, originally composed in Hebrew—though, as already noted, some of the later passages are in Aramaic—and it is available in various English translations, either alone or in combination with the New Testament. It is notable that where once sectarian differences among Jews, Catholics, and Protestants created marked discrepancies in their respective translations, the differences have presently narrowed to so few words or passages that it is possible for Jewish and Christian scholars, Catholics and Protestants, to cooperate on collaborative translations.

There had been earlier collaborations on scriptural translation. As we shall see, in 1142 Peter the Venerable (d. 1156), abbot of the monastery of Cluny, conceived of a project to assist in the conversion of Muslims. Among other pieces it was to contain a translation of the Quran, into Latin, of course. In the mid–fifteenth century, the Quran was translated again, on this occasion to save the fading tradition of the ancestral faith of the Moriscos, the converted Muslims of Spain. The Muslims of the northern parts of Spain, who had early passed under Christian sovereignty as Mudejares, eventually spoke, wrote, and read a Romance tongue rather than Arabic. They attempted to compensate, at least symbolically, by writing Romance texts in Arabic script, the practice known as Aljamiado, since the writing as well as the language of the Quran was regarded as God's gift. But the loss of the language meant they could no longer read the Quran itself. Between 1456 and 1462 the Muslim cleric who was head of the Mudejar community in Segovia produced not only a Castilian Quran but a kind of Islamic primer for the benefit of Muslims who were rapidly descending into religious illiteracy.

In 1698 Europe got its first printed translation of the Quran, a learned version by Ludovico Marraci, once again in Latin. Although there were professors of Arabic at both Cambridge and Oxford in the 1630s—a considerable work on

Islam by one of them, Edward Pococke (d. 1691), whose Arabic tutor in Syria said knew the language "as well as the Mufti of Aleppo," was still in Latin—the first English translation of the Quran directly from Arabic did not appear until 1734. It was the work of George Sale (d. 1736), an English lawyer who learned Arabic privately from tutors in London. The incentive may have come from the British Society for the Promotion of Christian Knowledge, which enlisted him to translate the New Testament and Psalms into English. Sale had access to a range of standard Muslim commentaries (perhaps from Pococke via Marraci), which he used to explain the text. Even more remarkably, the translation was prefaced by a long "Preliminary Discourse" that gave English readers a detailed explanation of the Arabian background to the rise of Islam as well as a life of Muhammad. Sale's version was the standard English translation of the Quran until well into the second half of the nineteenth century.

Muslims, for their part, have been far more reluctant to translate, and so transform, God's own dictation. Even where the Quran has been translated by Muslims for the benefit of other Muslims without Arabic, like those living in the West, for example, the effort has sometimes been modestly disguised as a paraphrase or summary of the sacred book's contents. A few English translations of the Quran are in print, also commonly though somewhat less properly spelled Koran. The diction of the Quran is extremely elliptical, and any English version of it will, of course, sound far more alien to Western ears long attuned to the familiar rhythms and images of the Bible and the New Testament.

But it is more than familiarity that makes both Bible and Gospels better served by their translations than is the Arabic Quran. God's message to Muhammad was delivered in the highly charged, affective images of the sacred poet. It is allusive rather than explicit, a great body of warning, command, injunction, and instruction delivered against a background of people and manners as barren to our eyes as the steppe itself. We feel Sinai and Canaan in the Bible; Palestine, its houses, mountains, rivers, and lakes, its towns, cities, and the men and women who lived in them are all present in the Gospel narrative. In the Quran, however, we search without success for Mecca, for the profane but vividly commercial life of the Quraysh, for Muhammad's family and companions. In its pages there is the voice of God alone. When it was heard, it overwhelmed hearts, as it still does in its written form, but it leaves the historian attending vainly, and deafly, for context.

Scriptural Criticism

Almost from the beginning, each of the Peoples of the Book has studied its Scripture seriously and in detail but always with the respect and veneration owed to the Word of God. In European academic circles of the nineteenth century, a new approach began to be followed. It differed from earlier study of the same texts in that it regarded the Scriptures—Bible, New Testament, Quran—merely as documents, no different from Homer's *Iliad* or Livy's *Histories*. This critical method, as it was called, was not directed solely at Scripture; indeed, it made its formal debut as a way of studying early Roman history. The results there were startling, as long-held assumptions about the age and validity of our Latin sources began to totter on their venerable foundations, pushed over in some cases, propped up in others, by the new science of archaeology. Once the same techniques were employed on the Scriptures, people were not merely startled; they were scandalized as the results of the new critical investigations began to trickle down into popular consciousness. The faith itself seemed under attack, as perhaps in many cases it was.

Note has already been made of scriptural criticism in discussing the lives of Jesus and Muhammad. It will not otherwise be much on display here since the point of the present undertaking is principally to understand the beliefs of the communities in question as the believers understand them, not how scholars think they got to be believed in the first place. But the "higher criticism," as it was called, is important on two scores. First, its roots run deep back into the three religious traditions that were exposed to earlier and equally potent strains of rationalism and had to react or adapt to them. Second, the critical method is now ignored only by the most radically conservative members of the three monotheistic communities. Many of the findings of scriptural criticism have been incorporated into the traditions themselves for their own use or else the communities have devised mechanisms to respond to them.

Scriptural criticism deals generally with two interrelated issues, the text itself of Scripture and its composition. Textual criticism asks questions about the preservation and transmission of the actual text of Scripture, from manuscript to print, in order to establish the most reliable and authentic version of that text. It obviously implies the collection and comparison of as many manuscripts as possible, the dating and sorting of them into "families," an understanding of when and how they were copied, the kinds of errors that scribes make, and the kinds of things they were likely to put in or leave out of the text before them, even a text of the Word of God. The end of all this labor is either the publication of the very best manuscript (with corrections, as they may seem necessary) or, in the case of Scripture where there is a proliferation of manuscripts, the production of a critical edition, wherein the editor "creates" out of the available evidence a text that seems closest to the original, although with all the editor's choices and variant possibilities noted for the reader's own judgment. There are critical editions of both the Bible and the New Testament, though none as yet for the Quran since the collection and comparison of manuscripts of the latter Scripture is nowhere near complete.

Historical, literary, and redaction criticism all address the actual composition of the text. Historical criticism investigates the date, time, place, authorship, and circumstances of composition—of Paul's letters, for example, or the Book of Daniel—and, crucially here since these texts are thought to derive from God, the sources used by the author(s). Literary criticism studies both the language of the text—all three communities did this almost from the beginning—and the literary form(s) of either the whole work or its parts, the parables, for instance, in the Gospels or the oaths with which many chapters of the Quran open, and this in the light of what we know from elsewhere about the rules governing such forms. Finally, redaction criticism attempts to understand the editorial processes that led to final production of the work as we have it, how its apparent strands came together to form our Genesis, or what Matthew and Luke did to Mark's Gospel in producing their own.

Who Wrote the Bible?

There are two types of answers to who wrote the Bible. One is complex but highly responsive and comes from Jewish tradition. It knows precisely who wrote each book of the Bible. Indeed, some authors still have their names on their books, like Joshua, Samuel, Jeremiah, Ezra, and Nehemiah. Others are rather easy to figure out: Moses the Pentateuch, David the Psalms. But still others can only be deduced, which the rabbis adroitly did. Moses also wrote the Book of Job, and Samuel also authored Judges and Ruth; Jeremiah wrote Kings and Lamentations besides his own book; Ezekiel and his group wrote Isaiah, Proverbs, and the Song of Songs; the men of the Great Synagogue wrote Ezekiel, the books of the twelve minor prophets, Daniel and Esther; Ezra also wrote Chronicles.

The other answer, which comes from modern biblical criticism, runs in precisely the opposite direction: we have no idea who composed the Bible. Nor can we, since the biblical books we possess are all the work of anonymous editors, or even "schools" of editors, who over a long period assembled these books out of older, equally anonymous materials. Even the prophetic works, which have the straightforward look of compositions of single authorship, turn out to have numerous interpolations and additions. The prophet the tradition knows simply as Isaiah turns out to have lived circa 742–701 B.C.E. and to have written only chapters 1–39 of that book; chapters 40–55 belong to a later Exilic second Isaiah (ca. 587–539 B.C.E.) and chapters 56–66 to a third Isaiah who wrote sometime after the Exile. Where the going gets extremely sticky, of course, is in the Bible's opening cluster of five books, the Torah or Pentateuch. The tradition calls them the "Books of Moses"; the "Yahwist" did it, responds the critic, or the "Elohist" (see below), and both with a lot of editorial help.

As even the casual reader may observe, the Torah repeats stories, the creation of Adam, to cite but one famous example, with different and often conflicting details, and sets down different versions of the Ten Commandments in Exodus 20 and Deuteronomy 5. The fact was early on noted and explained—or explained away—in assorted ingenious ways that left the question of Mosaic authorship untouched and untroubled. But one astute medieval exegete, the commentator Abraham ibn Ezra (d. 1164) (see II/2), proposed a more economical, if somewhat more dangerous, solution. When the laws differed, he explained, it was because one version came directly from God and the other from Moses. By the nineteenth century, however, God's claim to authorship had been disallowed by the critics, and it simply remained to identify the human hands responsible for such anomalies in the Torah.

In 1883 Julius Wellhausen, in his *Prolegomena to the History of Israel*, offered a solution to the composition of the Torah, plus Joshua, the so-called Hexateuch, or "Six Parts," that explained those anomalies. This "documentary theory," as it is generally called, remains, in one form or other, the prevailing critical theory on the Torah's composition. The issue of authorship may be dismissed immediately: the Hexateuch as we have it was assembled out of various older materials in the fifth century B.C.E., after the return from Exile. It was the origin and nature of these "older materials" that Wellhausen undertook to demonstrate. He showed on linguistic and stylistic grounds that different strands of material run through our Hexateuch. By way of hypothesis, he called the two oldest authors/editors the "Yahwist" and the "Elohist" because of their habit of calling the deity "Yahweh" (in German, *Jahweh*, hence the abbreviation J) and "Elohim" (E), respectively. Wellhausen thought both originated in the divided kingdom that followed Solomon's death, J in the early days of the southern kingdom of Judah (870 B.C.E.?) and E in the northern kingdom of Israel (770 B.C.E.?). Their work may have been combined sometime about 680 B.C.E., and then the D material (the Deuteronomist Source) was added under Josiah, the king of Judah who in 621 B.C.E. discovered and promulgated a "book of law" discovered in the temple (2 Kings 23:8–10) that is thought to be the central core (chapters 5–28) of Deuteronomy. The writing up of the last source, P, or the Priestly Source, which is responsible for most of the ceremonial laws in the Torah, explanations of things like circumcision (Gen. 17:9–14), and the dietary laws (Gen. 9:4), was in this hypothesis begun after the Exile and continued down to the point when it was finally combined with the work of J, E, and D to form the Torah, perhaps about 450 B.C.E.

Explaining Revelation

In the context of our discussion thus far, revelation has appeared to be a matter of a book or writing, in short, of Scripture. But there lay beneath the sacred text what is, by general agreement, an oral-aural foundation. God spoke and the messenger heard, whether that latter was Moses or Muhammad. Revelation, then, at least in its Jewish and Muslim versions, has three distinct moments: God's oral communication with his messenger; the messenger's public pronouncement of God's message, generally understood to be in oral form, though in Moses' case at least God managed his own publication by providing Moses with a summary copy of his laws written in God's own hand on tablets of stone (Exod. 32:15–16); and finally, the committing of God's pronouncements to writing so that the community might continue to possess them in the form of a book.

All three stages of the process just described are subject to some degree of authentication. The believers must be assured that it was in fact God who spoke to the messenger and thus what was coming from the latter's mouth was truly oracular, not the product of some malign spirit or self-delusion, as was alleged by some in Muhammad's audience (see I/3). The so-called Thirteen Principles of Judaism formulated by Maimonides (d. 1204) address all three of these propositions. His seventh principle is the affirmation by all Jews of the fact of Moses' prophetic powers (and their priority to all others'). The eighth affirms that the Torah is indeed from God—the Mishnah (Sanhedrin 10:1) had already denied a share in the Afterlife to "the one who says the Torah is not from heaven"—and the ninth asserts that "the Torah is precisely transcribed from God and no one else." Muslims affirm the same. The shahada or Islamic profession of faith has as the second of its two clauses the statement that "Muhammad is God's messenger," an affirmation that implicates the divine authority of the Quran.

The messenger or prophet and the sacred text that comes down from him are the foci of most subsequent discussions of authenticity. The first, the question of the messenger, was principally a matter of the "proofs of prophecy," as the Muslims called an entire literary genre devoted to it: how the messenger demonstrated to his immediate audience, and so to later generations of believers, that he was indeed the bearer of God's Word. It was only much later, and almost certainly under alien cultural pressure, that the believers also had to fashion for themselves a rationally adequate explanation of how that communication took place between God and his prophet.

The preeminent proof of prophecy is the miracle. The prophet can invoke, or God can merely unbidden provide, some visible demonstration of supernatural intervention. Moses had to convince the Pharaoh that he was the bearer of God's Word, a task he doubted he could perform (Exod. 6:30). God assured him, however, that he would provide a demonstration (7:3–4; 10:1–2), which he did in part in the dramatic contest with the Pharaoh's wizards (7:7–8; cf. Quran 7:103–137) and by the spectacular plagues he sent upon the land and its people (Exod. 7:14–12:36). Once out of Egypt, the Israelites began to have their doubts, doubts regularly assuaged by Moses' being miraculously able to provide food and drink, for example (16:2–17:7). The Quran told the same stories and others about earlier prophets and their authentication through miracle (40:78), but when Muhammad's audience not unnaturally demanded similar signs from this self-proclaimed prophet (6:37; 13:7; 21:5), he refused. The Quran was his miracle; let anyone who doubted it produce another Quran (2:23; 10:38; 11:13). It is the Quran's inimitability that at base validates

Muhammad's prophethood. Even so, the later biographies of Muhammad adduced a full range of more traditional miracles to buttress the Quran.

God speaks to Moses almost continuously from the opening of Exodus to the end of the Torah. The reader is left with little doubt that the laws that fill up most of the last four of the five books of the Pentateuch originated with God and that Moses is by and large reporting what he has received from on high. But Genesis has a far different ring to it, as do the narrative sections of Exodus and the rest of the Bible generally from Joshua onward. Here the tradition designates human authors—Moses, Joshua, David, the men of the Great Synagogue, and so on—not God. The post-Pentateuchal books may be about God or, more accurately, about God's Chosen People, but they are not from or by God in the same sense as the laws in the Torah. God spoke to Moses "face to face, as one man speaks to another" (Exod. 33:11). Did he also speak thus to Joshua, David, Isaiah and Jeremiah, Ezra and Nehemiah?

The answer is obviously nuanced. God did speak to Jeremiah—"I put My words in your mouth" (1:10)—as he did to Isaiah, after that prophet's lips had been cleansed with a hot coal (6:6–9). And "the word of the Lord" came to the other prophets as well. Joshua, however, and David, "the singer of Israel's psalms" (2 Sam. 23:1), to cite but two examples, stand well behind their ascribed works. Here we are in the presence not of oracles but of distinctly authorial acts—editorial acts according to modern scholarship—where God's role is not asserted but must be assumed. We are even on occasion given a glimpse of the author at work. In the introduction to his wisdom work, Ben Sira explains the care and toil he put into his writing and asks that the reader overlook any imperfections there might be. The author of 2 Maccabees does the same: he did his best and assumes responsibility for whatever shortcoming the work has (2:24–33).

Believers make many different assumptions about Scripture, in this case the Hebrew Bible, which arose in stages we cannot always trace. The divine origin of the Law is asserted in the Bible itself, but the conviction that the contents of the *whole* Bible are relevant and important—why else would the rest be collected and preserved together with the venerable Torah?—came much later, and very gradually, insofar as we can see. By the first century B.C.E. all of Scripture was cited as authoritative, even though what precisely was in Scripture had yet to be determined. By then what was believed of the works of Moses and the other prophets was extended, in some analogous fashion, to that of all the biblical authors: the authors of Judges and Kings were prophets no less than Jeremiah and Isaiah, and David's privileges were extended to the authors of Proverbs, Ruth, and Esther. Thus, a divine provenance certified the work of authors from Moses to Ezra: their books were sacred as well.

The earliest Christians, who were fond of citing it, provide a privileged view of how the Bible (loosely defined; see below) was regarded. Jesus himself calls the entire Bible "Scripture" (*graphe*) and asserts that "it cannot be put aside" (John 10:34–35). The authors of the New Testament likewise consider the Bible nothing more nor less than the Words of God (Heb. 1:5–13; Rom. 5:9–12). The author of 2 Timothy, referring to the Bible, declares that "all in-spired Scripture has its use for teaching the truth and refuting error, or for the reformation of manners and discipline in right living, and also that the man of God may be capable and equipped for good work of every kind" (3:15–16); 2 Peter sums it up as follows: "It was not on any human initiative that prophecy came; rather it was under the compulsion of the Holy Spirit that people spoke as messengers of God." There is no discernible difference between these views and Josephus's first-century summary, for the pagan world, of how the Jews regard their Scripture: "It is an instinct with every Jew, from the day of his birth, to regard them [the Scriptures] as the decrees of God, to abide by them, and, if necessary, to die for them gladly" (*Against Apion* 1.8.42).

Islam did not have, or did not recognize, an author or a multiple-author problem. God had spoken in this instance to one sole messenger, Muhammad, and the Quran is, in effect, his Torah; it is, in its entirety, the ipsissima verba of God, without the addition of either Kings or Job. Muslims, moreover, will distinguish rather sharply the "inspired" Muhammad, whose word was Torah, from the man of Mecca and Medina who offered explanation, advice, and wise counsel. These latter were not in the Quran but were collected in a kind of deuterocanonical form in the *hadith* (see II/3). Nor did Muslims much con-cern themselves with how precisely the communication with Muhammad took place except to note that its form was oral/aural, as a number of stories attest, and that it was, in the manner of late antiquity's embrace of divine messengers and intermediaries (I/1), not directly from God but through the agency of his angel, Gabriel (Quran 2:97).

> **Note:** Some non-Muslims have argued that these hadith are a kind of Muslim apocrypha, the sayings pool out of which the Quran was se-lected and anointed as revelation, but the vocabulary, style, and content of the great body of hadith are so different from what we have in the Quran as to make that possibility highly unlikely. The hadith belong to another world. They had their origin in Muhammad's own inspired, but decidedly human, head and heart, according to the Muslims, or in the fertile but tendentious imaginations of eighth- or ninth-century lawyers, according to most non-Muslims.

High Prophetology

What urged, or perhaps constrained, Jews and Muslims to give more deliber-ative thought to the modes of revelation was their exposure to larger cate-gories of epistemology, when they had to accept (or reject) the prophet as the possessor of the same intuitive knowledge that occurred in more spacious theories of knowledge. Philo, for example—the Hellenized Alexandrian Jew who had at his disposal several sophisticated theories of how knowledge is achieved—undertook to explain how Moses knew God's truths by invoking the two Hellenic models of the philosopher and the legislator. Moses grasped the "realities" in the intuitive manner of the Platonic philosopher; what set him apart was his ability, as a supreme legislator, to translate those transcendent truths into a concrete code of conduct for his people.

By adopting these Hellenic cognitive categories, Philo could explain Moses' prophetic knowledge in an intellectually satisfactory way, as did the later Muslim aficionados of Greek learning, though at the perhaps fatal price of vacating any claim to Moses' or Muhammad's unique status as a prophet. This is what might be termed "high prophetology." The prophet's highest cognitive faculty is illumined by or becomes identical with an even more transcendental intelligence outside himself. For many Greeks this was the so-called agent intellect, which is "always in act"; for the monotheists it was an angelic intelligence, traditionally Gabriel's. Its only miraculous quality is perhaps God's choice of a Moses or a Muhammad; the actual process of prophecy uses all the subtle cognitive machinery already in place in Greek theories of intellectual cognition. It is set against the "low prophetology" of the Bible's account of God speaking to Moses "man to man" and the Muslim biographical tradition that has Gabriel sitting on Muhammad's chest and reciting the Quran to him. Each explanation was preposterous to adherents of the other, the first for its secular and reductive quality, the second for its blatant anthropomorphism.

Heavenly Books

It was not enough to authenticate God's prophets; the books they promulgated had also to be verified. So strong was the conviction of authenticity that sometimes it could simply be asserted, as Josephus did in his tract *Against Apion*; "although long ages have now passed, no one has dared to add, remove, or change a syllable [of Scripture]" (1.8.42). But there were also strong external props to support it. One was quite traditional: both the Bible and the Quran were thought to have eternal and invariable heavenly prototypes, a belief that directly addressed their authority as *books*. This idea is very old in the Middle East, and the Jews and Muslims were not the only ones to believe in the existence of an eternal heavenly book in which divine decrees, and so the fate of humankind, were inscribed. That notion is expressed in passing in the Bible (e.g., Ps. 139:16), in the New Testament's Book of Revelation 5–6, and most insistently of all, in the Quran (e.g., 69:19,25; 82:10–12, etc.). But that was not the same book given to Moses or Muhammad. The heavenly books in this instance are the archetypes of the Torah and the Quran, in the Jewish case, created before the universe, and, in the Muslim one, uncreated (for the debate on this matter, see II/7). The Torah's claims to a transcendental existence as well as an earthly one with its bestowal on Moses were put forward in post-Exilic days in the wisdom literature popular at the time (see I/1) and reached their apogee in the rabbinic era, when the Torah had become the central focus of Jewish life. The Quran, in contrast, advances its own claim: behind the Quran revealed by Muhammad stands the "Mother of the Book" (43:3–4), a "hidden Book" (56:78) accessible only to God.

For the Jews, the sacredness of Scripture opened another issue. Scripture, like all sacred objects, was the source of ritual taboo—what is sometimes called "ritual impurity"—a state that is possible to transfer by contact. The rabbis determined early on that "all the scrolls (of Scripture) render the hands unclean" (Mishnah Kelim 15:6)—that is, transfer their taboo quality to those who handle them. A section of the Mishnah titled "Hands" (Yadaim) is given over to determining precisely which books and what physical parts of those books constituted Scripture and so were holy enough to "defile the hands" (3:4–5). Even the original Aramaic snippets in Ezra and the Aramaic sections of Daniel qualify, but not translations of Scripture (Yadaim 4:5). Nor do the Bibles of the Christians: there is no sanctity there (4:5–6).

The New Testament: Notion, Text, and Canon

The New Testament is at once an idea and a collection of texts thought to both describe and embody that same idea. The idea is one of the basic elements of the Christians' construction of a self-identity in the years following Jesus' death. Like much else in that construct, it was a Jewish idea. "Covenant," here called "testament" by way of the Septuagint's Greek rendering of Hebrew *berit* as *diatheke* (Lat. *testamentum*), is the Abrahamic cornerstone of the Jewish self-identification as God's Chosen People. God's Covenant with Israel underwent frequent renewals and rethinkings in the long history of that people, but for the Christians a critical recasting of the Covenant was announced by Jeremiah (31:31–33), who said, "The days are coming when I will make a new covenant with the house of Israel and the house of Judah. It will not be like the covenant I made with their ancestors. . . . I will place My law within them and write it upon their hearts. I will be their God and they will be My people." Early on, this theme began to be echoed by Jesus' followers (2 Cor. 3:6; Gal. 4:24–26) and may even have been introduced by Jesus himself since the phrase "a new covenant"—which was to be sealed by his blood—occurs in his own reported words on the occasion of his eucharistic supper the night before his execution (Mark 14:4 and parallels). Thus a new covenant or new testament is a theological notion, and the Christians used it to bundle together the body of texts thought to describe (as in the Gospels) and explain (as in Paul's letters) how the events of Jesus' life, both his actions and his teachings, make it certain that through him God had indeed initiated the new covenant/testament of prophetic promise.

Theological ideas invariably create theological collections of texts, and such indeed is the Christians' New Testament, as certainly as is the Jews' own Bible. Like the Bible, the texts collected by the Christians as their covenantal brief included some that presented themselves purely and simply as some type of history. As we have already seen, the two volumes by Luke, his Gospel and the Acts of the Apostles, are quite formally works of history. Other pieces finally included in the New Testament, notably the letters of Paul, although more concerned with the meaning of Jesus' life rather than its discrete events, also contain bits and pieces of what appears to be historical information.

The bundling of the New Testament into a single package was neither immediate nor uniform. The works eventually included were written sometime between 50 and 150 c.e., but only in the second century did the designation "New Testament" first appear. Before and after that moment different churches had different ideas of what constituted the New Testament dossier. One such idea, that put forward in Rome by a certain Marcion (d. ca. 160), was so narrow in scope—on ideological grounds it limited Christian Scripture to Paul's letters and an edited version of Luke—that the Church was driven to make explicit exactly what constituted this New Testament. The present collection of four Gospels (Matthew, Mark, Luke, John), the Acts of the Apostles, the letters of Paul, Peter, James, John, and Jude, and, finally, the Book of Revelation, an apocalypse attributed to John, did not entirely stabilize until the fourth century when all the churches of both the Greek East and the Latin West reached a consensus on what constituted their New Testament.

Although this Church-wide consensus did not emerge until the fourth century c.e., numerous prescriptive lists of "received works" already existed in most if not all the Christian assemblies (*ekklesiai*) we call churches. Such lists were later called canons (Gk. *kanones*, "measures," "standards"), so named because of their association with certain criteria of authenticity known by somewhat later Christian writers as the "earmarks of canonicity." This weighing of sacred writings also owes something to the process of judging and winnowing, of "canonization," practiced among Greek academic literary critics who centuries earlier had compiled authoritative lists of the "received" tragedians, lyric poets, and so forth that ended up as the literary benchmarks of most of Western culture.

The earmarks of canonicity were both theological and historical. For inclusion a work had to pass a test of orthodoxy: was it congruent with the "rule of faith" followed by the church in question and, somewhat more generally, was it "apostolic" in origin? It seems doubtful that the churches looked on the latter notion as a strictly historical criterion whereby "apostolic" meant only and exclusively "eyewitness"—the apostolic designation more likely spoke to the spiritually guaranteed probity of the witness than to the mere act of witnessing—but it carried with it an assurance that the document was in fact early, and hence more reliable.

The canon of the New Testament, which may originally have been designed to *include*, ended by *excluding* from "official" consideration a broad range of writings circulating among Christians from at least the second century onward. Some of them were gospels, that is, narrative-framed discourses on the life and sayings of Jesus, whereas others were simply collections of the Savior's *logia* or sayings. From a theological point of view, such writings were thought to be beyond the pale, useful, perhaps, in some instances for edification or entertainment, but generally of suspicious orthodoxy. For many centuries, for all their occasional effect on popular piety—the "Infancy Gospel of James," for instance, supplied many of the popular notions in the celebration of Christmas—the "excluded" or "apocryphal" (Gk. *apocrypha*, "hidden") gospels had little role in either the construction of Christian belief or an appreciation of the historical dimensions of Jesus. Even when the quest for the historical Jesus took a decidedly secular and skeptical turn in the nineteenth century, the early Christian Apocrypha continued to labor under their explicit theological (and implicit historical) derogation. In the most recent Jesus scholarship, however, the apocryphal gospels, like that of Thomas, are undergoing considerable historical rehabilitation.

The Biblical Canon

The word "canon" in the context of sacred writings was, then, a Christian usage, borrowed from an earlier Greek literary practice to describe works that were "received" by Christian congregations and so constituted the New Testament. The New Testament itself, when speaking of the Bible, simply refers to "the Scripture" or, as in 2 Timothy 3:15, to the "sacred writings," identical to the common Jewish way of referring to the same material. But, the word apart, did the Jews too hold, by decree or common consensus, that a closed body of writings constituted the Bible? Apparently so, at least by the first century C.E., since Josephus (d. ca. 100 C.E.) describes a collection of writings regarded by the Jews as "decrees of God" that has remained unchanged since their composition. There are, he tells his Gentile audience, twenty-two such works, five composed by Moses, thirteen prophetic compositions, and four others containing hymns and moral precepts; altogether they cover the period from Moses to the death of Shah Artaxerxes I (424 B.C.E.).

Josephus's testimony speaks to a common Jewish conviction that there was a closed canon of divinely inspired Scripture divided into three parts akin to the later division of Tanak, but he provides no clue as to how the process of acceptance took place or why. In rabbinic times, the criterion, or rather, the sign of inclusion among the Words of God, was whether or not a book "defiled the hands," that is, partook of the taboo of the sacred. We do know, however, that other religious writings that enjoyed some degree of prestige and authority circulated among Jews, though they were not regarded as Scripture. Josephus himself, for example, does not tell us whether he is using "canonical" or other books when paraphrasing Jewish history in his *Antiquities*, and the Essene library discovered at Qumran contains a wide range of religious texts that are not in the standard Hebrew Bible yet are cited authoritatively and without prejudice. The New Testament too, the product of a first-century Jewish milieu, used a variety of writings it regarded as still possessing authority among Jews. Finally, the books called 2 Esdras, roughly contemporary with Josephus, describe Ezra as redictating, under divine inspiration, the entire collection of Scripture, which had been destroyed by fire. According to that account, the finished product comprised twenty-four works for general circulation—presumably the "canon" mentioned by Josephus—and seventy additional books for the exclusive use of "the wise among your people." These latter are apparently the Apocrypha, which were also believed, it appears from this story, to have been composed before Ezra's time.

All this evidence speaks to the Bible as a whole and suggests that in the first century c.e. Tanak was a more or less open body of text, at least as far as the category called Writings (Ketubim) is concerned, and that the rabbis continued to discuss the canonical status of some books well into the second century. There is reason to think, however, that the Mosaic Pentateuch was much earlier recognized as a closed scriptural unit. As we have already seen, Deuteronomy, the last of those five books, was "discovered," it appears, in 621 b.c.e., during Josiah's reign, and so closed at least the initial redaction of the Pentateuch canon. This is supported by the fact that the Samaritans, who broke away from their southern brethren in the fourth-century b.c.e. at the latest (see I/1), recognized only the Pentateuch as Scripture, that is, Prophets and Writings were added sometime after that schism. But we have also seen that Jews were willing to accept certain works as authentic revelation perhaps as late as the mid–second

> **Note:** The Old Testaments read by Catholics and Protestants are markedly different. Catholic Bibles have 73 books in all, 46 of them in the Old Testament and 27 in the New. Protestant Bibles have 66 books since they include only 39 books in the Old Testament. The books omitted from the Protestant versions are Tobit, Judith, Baruch, Wisdom, Sirach, 1 and 2 Maccabees, and parts of Esther and Daniel. These books are called "Deuterocanonical" by the Catholics, who do include them, and "Apocryphal" by the Protestants, who do not. The difference dates back to Luther, who relegated those seven books to an appendix in his translation of the Bible. They continued to be printed as an appendix in most Protestant Bibles until about 1826, when they were omitted altogether.

century, when the Bar Kokhba revolt showed the danger of appeals to apocalyptic scenarios and messianic hopes that filled some of these later books. The rabbis, then, pruned down the list of what was circulating as Scripture: a great many books once implicitly accepted as Scripture were then explicitly excluded and the present Hebrew Bible came into existence. The voice of prophecy, a dangerous voice as recent history had shown, was now stilled. But perhaps, from the Jewish perspective, this occurred just a bit too late.

The Inspiration of Scripture

For Jews and Muslims Scripture is revelation; for Christians revelation is *in* Scripture, or to put it in more current terms, Scripture is where the Christian encounters revelation. That revelation is Jesus Christ, and although Christians continue to debate the relative roles of his teaching, his life, and the event of the resurrection, or whether the Christian encounters revelation *outside* Scripture as well—the issue between Catholics and Protestants—the equation itself remains fixed. Thus, the "proofs of prophecy" take on a different quality in the instance of Jesus, where they become the "proofs of messiahship" or, in a more elevated Christology, "proofs of divine Sonship."

Scripture itself is somewhat more problematic among Christians than among Jews and certainly among Muslims. Both those other Scriptures are dominated by the prophecy model, where God delivers a message to a privileged but human messenger for public proclamation. Although Jesus was thought a prophet by some of his contemporaries (Matt. 16:14), and the Quran identifies him as a prophet to whom a Scripture had been revealed in the manner of Moses and Muhammad (5:46), Christians have rejected Jesus' identification as a prophet, first in favor of Messiah and finally of Son of God.

At first the Christians knew only one Scripture, the Jewish Bible, which they used in its expanded and Greek translated Septuagint version. Their own writings, like some books of the Bible, had authors' names attached to them, but whoever else they were—"witnesses" is a characterization that recurs in the early discussions—these New Testament authors were not prophets. None of the four evangelists was either a Moses, who brought the Law, or an Isaiah, who brought God's warnings and promises to Israel. Mark was merely a reporter; Matthew and John were supposedly eye witnesses to events, the latter somewhat more personally involved; and Luke apparently fancied himself an actual writer, a historian. Paul was a struggling and distraught letter-writer (1 Cor. 1:17), who dictated his work (16:21).

When the Christians bethought themselves to explain the exaltation of biography and letter-writing into sacred Scripture—the authors of Enoch, Baruch, and the Wisdom of Solomon had at least borrowed some distinguished names—they had at hand an extensive repertoire of literary terms in Greek and

Latin that might be used to describe the "creative" aspect of poetry, for example. Thus "God-breathed" (*theopneustos*) and "God-possessed" (*theophoretos*) were available to describe divinely assisted composition, terms that had already been applied by Christian writers to the Jewish Scripture (2 Tim. 3:16; 2 Pet. 1:21, already cited). The Latin provided *afflatus*, "blowing into," and similar terms. Among them, the Greek *epipneia*/Latin *inspiratio*, "breathing into," which both Philo and Josephus had used in connection with the Bible, finally became the Christian commonplace description of God's action on the human authors of Scripture, whether of the Old, or now, the New Testament: they were "inspired."

In late antiquity a definitive formula was enunciated, for the first time by Pope Gregory I (called "the Great") (r. 590–604), and often repeated thereafter. God was the author (*auctor*) of Scripture, man its writer (*scriptor*); or as Thomas Aquinas later put it, somewhat more technically, the Holy Spirit is the principal author of Scripture, men the instrumental authors. How this actually worked was a somewhat more delicate matter. Greek cognitive theories had already provided a kind of dual model of inspiration. In the first, the human intellect of the prophet/author becomes illumined by the higher divine (or divinelike) intellect. In the second, they become identical: the prophet's own faculties are suspended, and the Spirit takes over and speaks through him. Some Jews and Muslims were attracted to this latter model of prophetic inspiration—it proved far more dangerously attractive to all three in a mystical context—but the Christians, except for the occasional brief flirtation, would have none of it. The authors of the New Testament were enlightened by the Holy Spirit, not possessed by it.

Contingency and the Constraints of History

But if God is, in some profound sense, responsible for Scripture, and if the latter was intended to be an authoritative guide to salvation, how to explain the apparent errors in Scripture? What of the self-contradictions, between John and the synoptic Gospels, for example, and the scientific and historical inaccuracies? Should Scripture not be inerrant? The ancient and medieval answer was "yes"; the more modern one is edging ever more closely to "no."

If "yes," the apparent discrepancies in Scripture must be explained, which they were (and are) with considerable ingenuity and elegance in the practice of exegesis or scriptural interpretation (see II/2). What opened the possibility of "no" was the recognition, from the outset, that a human agent was involved, as remote as Moses, as present as Paul or Muhammad. Indeed, an oral revelation, an act of speech, immediately invokes a question of language and draws further attention to the fact that revelation is in reality conditioned— that is, whatever God's intent, the actual revelation was given in these words to this man in this time and place. It has in the first instance to be comprehensible to him, appropriate to his intelligence and understanding, which the theory of inspiration had addressed. But the conditioning did not stop there. The message, as delivered, had to be intelligible and consequential to an audience also limited in language and the skills of understanding—to newly nomadic Israelites wandering somewhere in Sinai, or to the fishermen and farmers of first-century Galilee, or to the illiterate townspeople of remote, seventh-century Mecca.

Almost from the beginning, Christians seemed willing to make some concession to the human element in the composition of Scripture. The Greek Father Origen attempted to draw a distinction between the words of revelation the authors had received from the Holy Spirit and what they chose to say about them, their own commentary, in a sense, though both are included in Scripture, and in the latter they might indeed err. Augustine, who strongly insisted on the divine inspiration of the Scriptures, gave their human authors even greater latitude. They could not change the subject matter, which is from God, but the choice of words and modes of expression were theirs, and in this they might indeed fall short of perfection.

> **Note:** Augustine himself thought that Scripture was dictated, and in the scriptural debates that took on new fire in the Reformation, both sides availed themselves of the theory. Calvin (d. 1564) used it consistently to explain the composition of Scripture, although apostolic scribes could err. On the Catholic side the dictation theory is enshrined in a decree of the Council of Trent in 1546, which was repeated verbatim by the First Vatican Council in 1870.

Christianity has come slowly to consider the implications of a human element in the production of Scripture. One of the primary motive forces was the rise of textual criticism, with its discovery of thousands of variants in the manuscripts of the New Testament. Which were the "inspired" ones? Verbal inspiration could no longer be thought about the same way. The Church was driven too, rather than led, by the parallel movement of historical criticism that since the early nineteenth century has insisted on treating the Gospels as human documents rather than the work of the Holy Spirit. The human author was gradually moved to the front of Scripture, to a position of responsibility, and it became important as never before to know who he was, when and where he wrote, and, most radical of all, for whom. The religious tradition in all three faiths had always stressed the universal character of Scripture; in the twentieth century there came a growing realization that these books were written for specific historical communities and that the needs and aspirations of those communities shaped the works that lie before us.

What has been said about the conditioning, the human parameters that have been called the "constraints of history" that operate on the Bible and the New

Testament, is obviously true of the Quran as well. But only if those same assumptions regarding inspiration are made—assumptions Muslims do not make. Muslims continue to maintain—as do a number of conservative or traditionalist Jews and Christians regarding their own Scriptures—what has been called the theory of "plenary verbal inspiration," that every word of the Quran is directly inspired by God, with the result that (1) it is quite literally the word of God; (2) every word is true; and (3) the truth of revelation rests in propositions of the Quran, not in the events of history. Muhammad, in this view, which represents Muslim orthodoxy, was in no sense the author of the Quran; at most he was its transmitter. The Quran is eternal and unconditioned.

Humanist Critics of Scripture

With the beginning of the European Renaissance, and its rediscovery of the Greek and Latin classics, the human, and so the conditioned and perhaps problematic, aspects of Scripture appeared in a new light. In the fifteenth century graduates of the arts faculties of the European universities, where the literary classics of antiquity were being newly appreciated and scrutinized, turned their attention to the classics of Western Christianity, notably the Latin version of Scripture produced by Jerome a millennium earlier with papal approval. The best known among these scholars was probably Lorenzo Valla, who taught at the universities of Pavia and Rome. His intellectual career was marked by a series of challenges (which anticipated the later Reformers' own) to several of the Church's traditional positions: he denied the spiritual preeminence accorded to the monastic orders over ordinary Christians, preferred the early Fathers to the scholastic theology that was almost exclusively studied in his own day (see II/7), and had grave doubts that faith could in the end be reconciled with reason. He was, in addition, one of the first to contest the authenticity of the Donation of Constantine, the document that provided the foundation for the Church's political possessions in Italy (see I/7).

Valla's work on Christian Scripture is summed up in his *Collation of the New Testament*, a series of textual and literary observations on the Vulgate, Jerome's famous Latin translation prepared in Rome in 383–384 at the request of Pope Damasus. By Valla's day the Vulgate shared some of the aura of inspiration granted to the Greek originals, and was in 1546 formally declared the authentic version for "public reading, disputations, sermons and explanations" by the Council of Trent—although the council also called for a new critical edition of the text, which did not appear until 1590. Valla's notes were a first step toward that critical edition a century before Trent, but they also pointed out in grim detail the all too human inaccuracies, ambiguities, and errors in Jerome's own work and so seemed to call into doubt one of the scriptural pillars of Western faith.

Valla's Spanish counterpart was Antonio de Nebrija (1441–1522), who learned his humanism in Italy and taught it at Salamanca as a professor of grammar, at least until he applied his philological skills somewhat too enthusiastically to the Bible. Despite the criticism, and the fact that he was a layman, not a cleric, he was chosen by Francisco Cardinal Jiménez de Cisneros, the Franciscan confidant of Isabella who became archbishop of Toledo, primate of Spain, and, in 1507, inquisitor-general of Spain (see I/5), to collaborate on a new multilingual Bible known as the *Polyglot Complutense* after the city of Alcalá (Lat. Complutensis), where it was published in 1521. The finished version printed in parallel columns the Greek Septuagint and Latin Vulgate texts, as well as the Hebrew text of the Old Testament and the Syriac text of the Pentateuch. But it did not correct the Latin from either the Hebrew or the Greek texts, which was Nebrija's understanding of the project and, in his mind, its most significant contribution, and so he withdrew from the work before its completion.

The Old Testament and the New

It is reductive to say "Old Testament" is merely the Christians' slightly disparaging term for the Hebrew Bible. In a sense it is true. The Covenant made by God with Abraham and his descendants is recorded and its history described in the Hebrew Bible. That Covenant is replaced by that made with the Christians through Christ and whose witness is found in the Christian writings that they too eventually came to regard as Scripture. But the Jewish Bible was not simply discarded, as some Christians suggested be done in the second century; it still served an important Christian purpose, as we shall see. But it was not the same work. Materially and formally the Hebrew Bible of the Jews and what the Christians began to call the Old Testament were and are two very different books.

First and most obviously, there is the matter of language. Jews read or, more accurately, Jews *expound* a collection of books written almost exclusively in Hebrew. The Christians, with a few exceptions like Origen and Jerome, read, understand, and interpret the Old Testament on the basis of either a Greek (Septuagint) or Latin (Vulgate) translation where the words have quite different resonances and often carry quite different implications than those in the Hebrew. But even more tellingly, the Jews and Christians are reading different books in their Bibles, ordered in a different way as well. As already remarked, the anonymous second-century rabbis who finally determined what was to be in the Bible rejected several books that earlier generations of Jews, including Jesus, his followers, and even the next generation of Christians, regarded as authentic prophecy. Those books—Wisdom, Ben Sira or Ecclesiasticus, Baruch, and 1 and 2 Maccabees—survived into the Christian canon of the Old Testament. Although the Protestant Reformers' desire for historical correctness led them to purge the texts in the sixteenth century—they are still present in Roman Catholic versions of the Bible—those same books were, for a millennium and a half, an essential part of Christian thinking about the biblical past.

Besides differences on which books to include, the Christians arranged their Old Testament books in a significantly different way from the Jews. The last works in the Tanak's Writings are Ezra-Nehemiah and Chronicles, and so the Hebrew Bible ends with the disaster of the Exile and the elegiac return and attempt at a restoration. The Christian Old Testament, in contrast, whether in its Protestant or Catholic version, has four divisions rather than three. The Hebrew Nebiim is broken up into historical books (the former prophets, Joshua et al.) and prophetic books (the "latter prophets, Jeremiah et al.); the Christian Old Testament ends with Prophets. This final placement is patently theological. The Old Testament does not close; it is continuous with the New and the prophets lead directly to Jesus.

Americans and Britons are two peoples divided by a common language, Oscar Wilde once famously remarked. With equal justice, though considerably less originality, it has also been said that Jews and Christians are two peoples divided by a common book, the Bible. The two versions, the Hebrew Bible of the Jews and the Old Testament of the Christians, not only read differently in terms of their language, content, and structure; they are also read differently by the two communities. Rabbinic Judaism of the mishnaic and talmudic eras, called in more modern times the Orthodox tradition, understands the Bible overwhelmingly in legal or halakic terms, whereas Christians from the beginning took the story, the haggadic elements of the Bible, and let the halakah go (see II/2).

The Arrangement of the Quran

As already remarked many times, the founding document of Islam is called *al-Quran*, "The Recitation." It also calls itself a "Book," although that word is to be understood in its symbolic sense, in much the same way we use "Scripture." These revelations, the Quran asserts, are a Book in the same sense that the Jews and Christians possess a Book, a Scripture. That Book came from God, it is made clear, was delivered to Muhammad and pronounced by him, but the actual physical book in the sense of pages within covers came later and was produced by human beings. The latter, which in length is roughly the size of the New Testament, is a collection of 114 suras further subdivided, like their counterpart "chapters" in the other Scriptures, into verses (*aya*; pl. *ayat*) of varying length.

The sacred content of the Quran—our copies have various editorial additions like titles and other brief indications—comprises a series of revelations given to Muhammad between 610 and his death in 632. They were delivered orally, in diverse circumstances, and, as it was explained, through the medium

of the angel Gabriel. These God-sent communications were repeated verbatim and publicly by Muhammad over the twenty-two years of his ministry,
first at Mecca between 610 and 622, and then at Medina from 622 to 632 (see
I/3). Thus the Quran is literally the Words of God, repeated, without error,
by his "envoy" or "messenger" (*rasul*), as he is called in the Quran, and as
every Muslim must believe.

The suras as we now have them in *our* version are arranged, after a short introductory prayer (the *Fatiha*, or "Opening"), roughly in descending length.
This arrangement, whose original purpose we cannot fathom, obviously tells
us nothing about the order in which they were actually revealed to Muhammad, but it is possible, based on their changing style and differing content,
among other things, to discern somewhat generally their original chronological
sequence.

From the point of view of prayer, ritual, or meditation, the chronological
order of the suras is of no concern whatsoever to Muslims, who recite the
work in its present nonchronological order, either by selecting passages
deemed suitable for special occasions or in a monthly cycle. For this latter
purpose, the standard edition of the Quran is divided, just as the Hebrew
Bible is for an annual reading cycle, into thirty sequential "portions" of
roughly equal length—they are generally marked in the printed text—to be
recited as an act of piety, half a portion at the morning, half at the evening
prayer, over the course of a month. But some Muslims *were* interested in the
historical order of the revelation—even the original editors had affixed
"Mecca" or "Medina" at the head of the suras. These were chiefly lawyers and
exegetes for whom it was important to establish the context of each revelation, the so-called occasions of revelation, so that the exact legal implications
of each enactment might be understood. As we shall also see, there was the
doctrine of "abrogation" that held that a later verse of the Quran might nul-
lify an earlier one, a view that obviously puts the historical order of the suras,
and even their verses, in play. Finally, later historians desired to provide a
biography of Muhammad, for which the Quran was an important if elusive
source.

The Muslims had, then, good reason to attempt to arrange the suras in
their chronological order—though never to publish the Quran in that form,
as is sometimes done in the West. The standard edition of the Quran, the
present version of the book, has become in effect almost as canonical as the
Book itself. Non-Muslims embarked on the enterprise of rearranging the
suras only in the mid–nineteenth century as part of the general Enlightenment project to treat even sacred books, whether Bible, Gospels, or Quran, as
documents rather than as Holy Writ. The results were not very different from
what medieval Muslim scholars themselves arrived at: the Meccan suras can
be divided into "early," "middle," and "late," whereas the long suras dating from

the Medina period of the Prophet's activity, many of which are composite, defy much further categorization.

With these admittedly tentative results in hand, we can begin to trace the trajectory of Muhammad's ministry. Many of the suras that appear to be early show a manner and elevation of style not unlike that of the Jewish prophets, as they admonish humans to reform, or warn of the judgment of eternity. The later suras are longer and contain detailed regulations for the conduct of the already converted. Little wonder. At Mecca Muhammad was chiefly engaged in converting pagans, persuading their submission to the One True God. At that early stage submission meant primarily daily prayer, almsgiving, and a strict commitment to worship only Allah, a deity well known to the Meccans—who nonetheless associated other gods, his so-called daughters, with him. Muhammad warned his fellow Meccans that in the past God had visited terrible punishments on those who ignored the prophets—many of the examples are drawn, as has been noted, from Bible history—God had sent to them. To no avail. Driven from Mecca to Medina in 622, Muhammad began to gain a more favorable hearing, and the Medina suras show him now addressing a Muslim rather than a pagan audience. Both the background of his revelations and what is implied by submission are now spelled out in greater detail. Muhammad, we discover, stands at the end—there will be no other after him—of a line of prophets that began with Adam. Three of these prophets were notably entrusted with a public revelation in the form of sacred books—Moses the Tawrat, Jesus the Injil and Muhammad the Quran—illustrating God's continuing mercy toward a wayward humanity. The present revelation is, in a sense, the most fundamental of the three since it goes back to, and revives, the religion of Abraham, which had managed to survive at Mecca in a disfigured form for centuries. That is why Islam still venerates the Kaaba built by Abraham and Ishmael—toward which Muslims now pray—and must continue to practice the ritual of the hajj (pilgrimage) begun in Abraham's day (see II/6).

The Composition of the Quran

We have already touched on the complex question of the inspiration of Scripture: how the task of producing Holy Writ was shared by God, whom all believers agree somehow to be the source of its contents, and his human agents—Moses, Mark, or Muhammad—who were chosen to mediate those contents to their contemporaries and beyond. As we have also seen, the inspiration thought to lie behind the Quran is straightforward: God, through the agency of the angel Gabriel (how precisely this occurred is not entirely clear; see below), relayed the text verbatim, and thus in Arabic, to Muhammad, who then reported it to the people on various occasions of revelation.

On the evidence of the final product, the Quran could have been composed either orally or in writing, but when we examine the text more closely, the issue becomes far more complex. Long sections of the Medina suras might well have been composed in writing: they are made up of long periods, are prosaic in diction and didactic in manner. Those ascribed by Muslims and non-Muslims alike to the Meccan period, in contrast, bear many signs of oral performance, and even, the non-Muslim might argue, of oral composition. The diction is poetic, indeed rhymed; the style is emotive, rapid; the expression brief, colorful, often abrupt. There are repetitions of the type we have come to expect of oral poetry. And finally, Muhammad's own contemporaries identified what they were *hearing* as poetry and Muhammad as a poet (Quran 21:5, etc.). He denied the charge (36:69), as well he might since none of the preserved pre-Islamic poetry has as its subject God, salvation, or resurrection.

But Muhammad may have seemed like a poet nonetheless, certainly by his diction and perhaps also in his manner. We do not know and cannot imagine how those suras came forth from his lips; the Meccan suras have none of the sometimes chatty tone of Jesus' Sermon on the Mount nor the pedantic assurance of Leviticus or Numbers. God seems often to shout in the Quran, and we can only assume that Muhammad did so as well on occasion. Did he in fact appear jinn-possessed, as some of his contemporaries thought (52:29)?

It is now an almost dogmatic belief of the hardened Muslim historical tradition that the "clear Arabic" of the Quran (16:103; 26:195) was in fact the Meccan dialect of the Quraysh. It does not seem so, however. Although there is no unanimity on the subject, a substantial number of scholars are convinced that the Arabic of the Quran is expressed in a kind of art-speech, a poetic *koine* that was the linguistic currency of the poet and comprehensible throughout Arabia. That fact too may have convinced Muhammad's Meccan audience that they were listening to a poet, albeit a rather odd one who spoke not of love or the deeds of war but of God's justice and mercy and the Afterlife. Nonetheless, the argument may be taken as closed. We can grant Muhammad his denial that he was a poet; at the same time, what is heard and read in the Meccan suras of the Quran is assuredly poetry.

The composition of the Medina suras presents a far more serious problem. They smack of prose and of the pen, more of reflection than of intuition, and yet we know with certainty that Muhammad lacked the skill to write much less to compose in writing. The Medina suras were perhaps dictated, carefully and thoughtfully. That process would explain the style and diction of the later parts of the Quran, but we may also suppose there were at the agricultural oasis of Medina near-professional scribes capable of writing down, in the highly defective Arabic script of that day, what the Prophet spoke to them. The supposition is not impossible, merely discouragingly implausible in that setting. It remains, however, our best guess.

The Editing of the Quran

As already noted, the suras in our copies of the Quran vary widely in length, from the two verses of the early Meccan sura 112 to the 286 verses of the Medina sura 2. In addition, many of the suras are transparently composite. If we take the very early Meccan sura 74, for example, we note that verse 26 affirms that one of Muhammad's opponents will be flung into "the burning." This is apparently a new word or usage, since it is immediately followed (v. 27) by the stereotyped quranic phrase used to signal an explanation: "What will explain to you what 'the burning' is?" There quickly follow verses characterizing "the burning" for the audience. The last of these (v. 30) says, "over it are nineteen." Nineteen what? And why nineteen? The same questions must have occurred to others in Mecca, and perhaps in Medina as well, since verse 31 is a long, rambling, and quite combative rejoinder to those who had made an issue over "nineteen." The verse is obviously intrusive, a later insertion wholly different in style from what precedes and follows. At verse 32 there appears to be a seam, a series of oaths that typically begin the early Meccan suras and so here probably represent what was once the beginning of a new pronouncement.

Thus, many of what we have called the Quran's "chapters" are in fact composites and raise the larger question of the work's authorial unity and the variety within it. The whole Quran is, on its own testimony, certainly to be thought of as constituting a book, like those of the Jews and the Christians (3:3–4). Yet, again by its own witness, it was delivered piecemeal (17:106). Sura 25:32 famously states: "And the disbelievers say, 'Why is not the Quran revealed to him all at once?' It is revealed thus that We may strengthen your [i.e., Muhammad's] heart thereby. And We have measured it out in measured stages." At first glance we might think those "measured stages" refer to the suras, the Quran's 114 well-marked divisions. But almost everywhere in the Quran occur the same abrupt changes of subject, diction, rhythm, and rhyme that unmistakably signal a paste-up of Muhammad's pronouncements. There are, in short, more than 114 revelations in the Quran, a fact apparent to Muslim as well as non-Muslim students of the text, although they disagree on who is responsible for such editing. One Muslim tradition from Ibn Abbas (d. 687), a nephew of the Prophet, has Muhammad instructing his scribe after the revelation of some verses to "put those verses in the sura in which such-and-such is mentioned." The report thus shows Muhammad as his own editor, counter to the general Muslim tradition, which was, as we shall see, that the Quran was assembled as a whole well after Muhammad's death.

Among Western critics—the Muslims' own theological aesthetic of the Quran's inimitability (see II/7) bars them from this type of analysis—the general judgment that many of the suras are pastiches is by no means unanimous.

A case has been made that at least the Meccan suras represent structured uni-
ties, and that their composition as such was the work of Muhammad. The latter point seems correct: it is difficult to imagine any scribe or collector, even at
the bidding of a caliph, "editing" the Word of God, unless there was Muhammad's own precedent to encourage him. Regarding the suras' unity, both sides
in the debate—those who wish to dissolve them into small pieces, a couple of
verses at most, and those who argue for some degree of intrinsic unity among
the suras—may be correct. Even if we except the clear interpolations, the
early revelations do give the appearance of having been assembled, though
without a great deal of regard for logic or consistency. Two motives suggest
themselves. The first is liturgical. Very early on, in sura 73:1–5, Muhammad
himself is instructed to spend part of the night "reciting The Recitation in
measured fashion." The injunction does not refer here to the public announcement of the Quran—it is, after all, nighttime—but rather to a liturgical action. Even more clearly, Meccan sura 29:45 commands Muhammad to
"follow what has been sent to you of the Book by inspiration and establish
prayer." The first command appears to refer to the public promulgation of
God's revealed message, and the second to its use in liturgical prayer. In short,
the early Muslims prayed the Quran after they had heard it preached, and for
this purpose some of the pronouncements may have been joined to make
units appropriate for liturgical repetition, where neither internal logic nor
consistency is demanded.

The second motive has left no such telltale signs in the text itself, but we
know with some certainty that large parts of the Quran were memorized—
tradition assures us some individuals had memorized it in its entirety—and to
accomplish this, or at least facilitate it, some assemblage was required. The
smaller units must have been joined together in some rough fashion to form
larger ones with a degree of internal integrity. In both instances, whether
for liturgical purposes or for memorization, the "editor" was doubtless
Muhammad. He too later inserted prose clarifications or annotations into
some of the already assembled units.

These are essentially editorial questions posed in connection with the earliest
compiling of the Quran, a process that lasted most of Muhammad's prophetic
career. His death inaugurated a new process: an attempt, or perhaps attempts,
at collecting all the suras created by the Prophet and arranging them in some
kind of order that had not existed theretofore.

The Collection of the Quran

Although its content authentically represents the revelations given to
Muhammad, the finished Quran as we have it is surely not the work of the
Prophet himself: other hands collected the suras. If Muhammad himself was

not responsible, these same hands may even have joined some of the suras together since many of them, as we have just seen, appear to be composite, made up of more than a single revelation. What those near-anonymous editors certainly did was arrange the suras in their present order, which is generally in descending length, longest to shortest, and assign them the names—"The Opening," "The Cow," "The Abundance," and so forth—by which Muslims generally cite them.

Systematic study of the Quran as a canonical document began in Islam in the late eighth or early ninth century. Western scholarship has been trying for somewhat more than a century to restore the original order and understand the editorial process that began at Muhammad's death and led to the Quran that is before us. The task has not been easy. The Quran as it stands is a very complex and often opaque text, and we know remarkably little about what was happening in the Muslim community in the crucial first century of its existence. Almost all the sources of our information about the earliest community of Muslims, their concerns and accomplishments, date from after 750, or even later, better than a century after Muhammad's death.

The Bible and the Gospels are filled with many of the same themes and images as the Quran, but in the former books they are surrounded by a body of narrative that provides a context that smoothes the way to comprehension. The Quran, in contrast, has no narrative framework. It is not that God's utterances are totally disassociated from contemporary events; it is simply that we do not always, or even often, know what he is talking about, though Muhammad and his audience apparently did. Where the revelation does take the form of a story, in the "Joseph" sura (Quran 12), for example, the narrative is so allusive and disjointed that one can only assume that the Meccan and Medinan listeners were already somewhat familiar with the matter.

The Quran's literary style has been characterized as "referential rather than expository." The audience, we must assume, caught the references, but there is somewhat more to it than the listeners' privileged position. The ellipses and repetition of themes in the text, the abrupt shifts in the narrative point of view from first to second to third person, the great number of hanging pronouns whose antecedents are uncertain also point to a text that was orally composed—or, to be more theologically correct, orally recollected and orally delivered. Seventh-century western Arabia was an overwhelmingly oral society, and whatever knowledge of writing existed was surely limited to a very few practitioners and to a few occasions. Nobody suggests that Muhammad himself wrote down the Quran, though there is strong evidence that he edited it. Muslim sources do insist that, while many were memorizing the Quran as it was delivered, parts at least were written down by others during Muhammad's lifetime. We know not what to make of this. The orality of the culture and the deficiencies of Arab script at that time and place—its signs could only very imperfectly distinguish one letter from another: initial *y*, *b*, *t*, *th*, and *n* would all appear identical, for example—make it seem highly unlikely that such was the case. But the Muslim tradition says it was so, and Muslims accept this.

At Muhammad's death, there were Muslims who had memorized the Quran, while others, like his wife Hafsa, the daughter of the later caliph Umar, possessed written "copies." The tradition goes on to assert that under the early caliphs there were three separate attempts to collect and codify these various testimonies to the Quran. The first was under Abu Bakr (r. 632–634) immediately after the Prophet's death; the second, under Umar (r. 634–644); and a final, definitive effort under Uthman (r. 644–656). All three attempts seem very similar, with respect to motive—the fear of the multiplication of different versions and the death of "reciters" who knew the full text by heart—and even procedure. To accomplish their task, a committee was assembled, generally under the direction of the Prophet's "secretary," Zayd ibn Thabit, to collect all the available evidence, to "debrief" the reciters, and to assemble and collate the various written versions of the Quran. So it was done, and a standard edition was produced. Copies were sent to all the Muslim centers, with the order that older versions be destroyed. The latter might seem an impossible task in an early medieval society, and so it evidently was since modern scholars have identified in the remains of ancient commentaries and newly discovered manuscripts various somewhat different readings of quranic lines and verses. None of these variants challenges the basic meaning of the received text, but there are enough of them to cause us to believe that differing versions of the Quran were in circulation long after 650, and to suggest to others the even more radical position that the Quran as we know it, at least in the form we know it, did not come into existence until well into the eighth century.

Qere and Ketib

The Hebrew Bible and the Arabic Quran show a marked textual affinity. Both are written in Semitic languages where scribal custom was to write merely the consonantal text and to leave unmarked the short vowels that determine the exact pronunciation. Thus in both Scriptures there is a difference between what is written and what is actually read, in Hebrew, between the *qere* and the *ketib*. The sacred text was too important for that vocalization to be left to chance, and so both Jewish and Muslim scribes began to mark the short vowels in written texts of Scripture with a series of diacritical marks. In the biblical tradition, where from early on the Scripture was both written and read, the scribal experts who supplied the diacritical coding were called *Masoretes*, and the vocalized text (*masorah*) they sought to protect from the vagaries of both script and pronunciation is called in English the Masoretic Text. To this they appended voluminous critical annotations—which are never included in Torah copies used for liturgical purposes in synagogues—a large pool of qere variants in which later Bible commentators could fish at their pleasure. The work of these virtuosi did not produce a single uniform Masorah, however. Tradition remembered there were a number of such, chiefly stemming from Palestine, Babylonia, and—the one that since about 1000 has enjoyed preeminence—Tiberias.

In Islam, the emphasis was and is quite different. The preservation and transmission of the Quran has been overwhelmingly oral in nature, and so experts in the Book have been reciters (*qurra*) rather than scribes (*kuttab*). Thus there have been no Masoretes jealously guarding a textual tradition and, in the process, noting the slightest variants. Among the Jews the effort was to preserve a properly written text, whereas the Muslims have been more concerned with a properly remembered text. The objective has certainly been achieved. There are remarkably few variants in the preserved manuscript copies of the Quran and so even fewer in the printed versions: almost all printed copies of the Quran reflect the text printed in Egypt in 1924, which stems from the line of transmission attributed to Abu Umar Hafs ibn Sulayman (d. 796). But the Muslims have their own tradition of differing ways of reciting the text (*qira*). Seven such were thought to have gone back to the earliest days of Islam—some maintained that they all derived from the Prophet himself—and they received community and scholarly approval in the Middle Ages. But absent a masoretic tradition among Muslims, the variants on the quranic text—as there certainly must have been with the early defective Arabic writing system that scarcely distinguished some consonants, much less vowels—have largely disappeared, and those that have survived are largely inconsequential to the text.

Interpolation and Abrogation

It is a commonplace belief in the three communities that Scripture interprets itself, that later verses sometimes elucidate and explain earlier ones. The Quran, however, introduces a radical form of scriptural reinterpretation. The notion of inspiration, coupled with the conviction that God is both omniscient and unchanging, strongly argues that God's Words are totally and simultaneously true, and the three monotheistic communities have generally regarded them as such. Apparent contradictions or inconsistencies between two passages could be ironed out by careful application of a harmonizing exegesis (see II/2). But at two points in the Quran (2:106 and 16:101), God allows that on occasion he himself has substituted one verse for another, thereby abrogating or canceling the earlier verse. Besides serving as a powerful inducement for Muslims to attempt to discover the actual chronological order of the suras— the later verse would presumably abrogate the earlier one—the notion led to considerable speculation about whether any of the abrogated verses were still in our Quran and why such action was necessary in the first place.

On another occasion (22:52–53) the Quran says that Satan has inserted certain verses in the Quran, which God eventually cancels, in order to test the believers' faith. The remark is baffling, but it may go back to a historical incident in which Muhammad, yielding to a satanic temptation to appease the Quraysh, allowed that the "daughters of Allah" had some intercessory power with God. As we have already seen (I/3), these so-called satanic verses occurred after Quran 53:20, but God soon intervened—exactly how soon or under what circumstances is not said—and the offending verses were canceled and our present 53:21–23 were put in their place.

The Muslims recognize that both the Torah and the Gospels originally represented true and authentic revelations from genuine and esteemed prophets, Moses (Musa) and Jesus (Isa). But subsequently Jews and Christians tampered with the texts—they removed predictions of Muhammad, for one—and so their present versions are generally unreliable. They are not, in any event, either required or even recommended reading for Muslims. Within Islam, Shiites have accused the Sunnis of tampering with the Quran by removing the pronouncement of Ali's appointment as Muhammad's successor.

Closure

The canonization of Scripture marks its closure. God's final words have been uttered, the Book closed and sealed. The process is unmistakable in Islam. The Quran was God's revealed Word delivered to humankind through the agency of his prophet, Muhammad. At Muhammad's death the revelation was completed, as was the Quran, the Book, heavenly and earthly, that contains it. It will not be reopened or continued through another prophet. The Quran uniquely announces its own canonization. Muhammad is the "seal of the prophets" (33:40); there will be no other. The matter is not so clear-cut in the case of the Jews and Christians. Both the Bible and the New Testament are constituted of a series of books, the overwhelming majority of them independent of one another, and their contents are not always sequential in the manner of Exodus-Joshua-Judges-Kings or Luke-Acts. There is no reason, then, why there should not be more such books, another prophet in the Bible, for example, or another gospel in the New Testament. Indeed, John's Gospel unself-consciously announces that "There is much else that Jesus did. If it were all to be recorded in detail, I suppose the whole world could not hold the books that would be written" (21:25). There were in fact such books, but just as the Muslim community refused authorization to those who claimed prophethood after Muhammad, so the Jews and Christians in the end denied those other books all claim to the title "Word of God." The canon was closed by consensus among the Jews and Christians, by Muhammad's death for Muslims.

2

Understanding the Word of God

IF GOD'S DISTINCT VOICE was stilled with the closure of Scripture, it was not rendered completely inaudible. Each of the People of the Book thought it could catch richly nuanced echoes of those original words beneath the surface of Scripture and, even more consequentially, in what was believed to be an ongoing stream of "secondary" revelation within the community itself. The first conviction leads to a discussion of how the Jews, Christians, and Muslims proceeded to unpack the rich contents of the scriptural revelation; the latter, to an inspection of the notion of tradition (see II/3).

The Seal and the Silence

All who believe in a purposeful God are assured that the divine purpose is manifest in the world. God's providential care and purpose are visible in various signs of nature, and the Creator is thought to have occasionally intervened directly in the affairs of his creatures for the benefit of his favorites among them. What sets the three monotheistic communities apart, and unites them as People of the Book, is their shared conviction that God has also directly and verbally revealed his will to his Chosen People, and, through them, to all humankind. That revelation, moreover, has been successive: across the books of the Bible; for Christians, from the Old to the New Testament; and for Muslims, from *Tawrat* to *Injil* to *Quran*. For Christians and Muslims, those revelations have also been progressive, one following another toward a foreseen end. The divine plan in this serial revelation was more apparent to Christians than to Muslims perhaps. For Christians, the biblical revelations were preordained to end with Jesus, the promised Messiah who was in his own person the revelation and fulfillment of a New Covenant. Although Muhammad and the revelation entrusted to him are the climax of what had been sent down before, he is merely asserted to be the end or "seal" (Quran 33:40) of a series of prophets speaking for God. Even less determined was the end of the prophetic (and so the revelational) tradition in Israel: although there was considerable speculation on the subject, the Jews were unsure why God had fallen silent after Haggai, Malachi, and Zechariah.

In the silence after the seal, while Christians looked forward to the new messianic age inaugurated by Jesus, Jews and Muslims turned inward, back to the already revealed words of God in the Torah and Talmud. The great age of scriptural scholasticism had begun. The Word was now text—not until the nineteenth century did it become for some merely a document—and the process of unpacking its infinite content was under way. What is now figured as "unpacking" was once more soberly known as exegesis (Gk. *exegesis*, a "drawing" or "leading out")—in Hebrew *midrash*, "inquiry," in Arabic *tafsir*, a "disclosure" or "explanation"—a name for the general process of extracting the meaning from a text, in this case, Scripture.

Biblical Exegesis

There is no getting at the beginning of biblical exegesis. In the present version of the Book, it is clear that the Bible was already interpreting itself, the later books reflecting on the earlier. Indeed, the whole work is like a commentary on the Covenant made with Abraham or the promises confirmed to Moses, with the Torah as text and the Prophets and Writings as midrash. As for attempts at interpreting Scripture from outside the text, there are first of all what are obviously scribal additions and explanations that have become part of the text itself. Bethel, we are told, was once called Luz (Gen. 28:19), and the foreign term *pur* is glossed as "lot" in Esther 3:7. Indeed, the anonymous scribe's explanatory additions to Isaiah 29:10, "Namely, the prophets" and "(namely,) the seers," appears to have changed the sense of the passage.

Nor are these the only kind of explanation. Jeremiah 17:21–22 enlarges the Sabbath prohibitions found in the Pentateuch, to which the Septuagint translation added its own extension. Furthermore, there is a great profusion of enlargements, extensions, and retellings of scriptural material in the Jewish literature between the Exile and the end of Second Temple times, in which the Bible accounts are often pulled, shaped, and tweaked for transparently sectarian purposes. Some of those works are anonymous, like *Jubilees*, while other pieces are disguised as the work of some venerable figure from the past. Enoch, Baruch, and Ezra all served here to mask and presumably give authority to those contrived (and eventually judged noncanonical) pieces of Jewish antiquity called the pseudepigrapha, just as the names of Thomas and James did for equally sectarian (and equally noncanonical) gospels in early Christian times.

The Jewish pseudepigrapha are not commentaries in any formal sense, that is, a piece-by-piece or verse-by-verse treatment of a text, but the sectaries at

Qumran came far closer to writing exactly that. They too could compose biblical paraphrases, the *Genesis Apocryphon*, for example, but they were also capable of producing more direct readings of a text. Their "explanations" (*peshar*; pl. *pesharim*) are exactly that, although their attention is limited to prophetic texts. The preserved pesharim on Psalms and Habakkuk are devoted to showing, much as Jesus' contemporary followers were, that past prophecy was merely reflecting—they cared little for the original settings of such prophecies—the present and future reality.

All scriptural exegesis—Jewish, Christian, and Muslim—is, of course, committed to discerning both what the text means in its literal intelligibility and, more specifically, what its behavioral imperatives are for us, the community of believers, and for me and thee, the individual believers. But how the text is approached, with what methods and what assumptions, differs considerably within the faith communities. The earliest scribal tradition in Israel, and the first to address the study of the Torah in a systematic fashion, appears to have been motivated chiefly by lawyerly and didactic concerns, the same that led to the collection and canonization of Scripture by those same professionals. The objective was to keep a people in a rapidly changing world—even Hebrew, the very language of revelation was disappearing—in touch with and observant of the community's foundation traditions. There may have been a mimetic element at work as well: the Israelites' was not the only scribal tradition in the ancient Near East nor was the Torah the only sacred book.

Whatever their origins, the existence in the post-Exilic Jewish community of a class of professional scribes or bookmen (*soferim*) like Ezra suggests that by then the expounding of Jewish Scriptures for learned and laity alike was already well under way. The task itself and some of the literary works that embody it are called generally midrash, and midrash may be the single most characteristic act of post-Exilic Judaism. The root from which the word derives means simply to "study" or "expound," but when connected with Scripture, the task took on for many Jews the quality of a liturgical act.

Midrash

From the available evidence we can conclude that in the decades following the return from the Exile two exegetical processes were going on among the Jews. In their own "study houses" (*bet ha-midrash*), the soferim were extracting, comparing, and combining the legal precepts (*halakoth*) they had derived from Scripture, a work that came to term in the Mishnah (see II/3, II/4). In more general places of community assembly, perhaps the forerunners of the later synagogues, these same and other scriptural texts were adduced and expanded, in the manner of a homily (*haggadah*), for purposes of moral formation, edification, and piety.

This latter hortatory or homiletic approach to Scripture, called haggadic midrash or sometimes simply midrash, makes its appearance in many different contexts. Translations of the Bible are a prime locus for exercise of the midrashic method, for example. The language of post-Exilic Judaism was changing from Hebrew to Aramaic in the immediate pre-Christian centuries. Since large numbers of the laity could no longer understand Scripture in its original form, the Bible was translated into the common Aramaic tongue of Palestine, just as it was turned into Greek at Alexandria for the Greek-speaking Jews living there and elsewhere in the Diaspora. The Alexandrian Greek version, the Septuagint, whose origins are surrounded by stories calculated to guarantee its authenticity, was a relatively straightforward but rather free translation (see II/1), but the Aramaic translations, called targums, were even freer. They are often closer to paraphrases than to translations, and approach commentaries in their homiletic manner of expanding the text. There is little wonder in that since the targums were principally used in a homiletic setting, namely for liturgical recitation in the synagogue service.

The targums are obviously midrashic in type but they are still expansions of a text rather than free-standing haggadic commentaries on a text in the formal, literary sense. The earliest preserved examples of these latter midrashim are the already noted sectarian commentaries found at Qumran and the works of the rabbis of the talmudic era. These latter rabbinic midrashim fall into two general categories. The first are commentaries in the ordinary sense of the word, except that not surprisingly they reflect Scripture as read by a lawyer. These purely expository commentaries settle into a standard method of approaching Scripture in the order of its verses, each verse expounded by an appropriate tale or parable. The second type are the straightforward homiletic midrash, which differ from the expository midrash not only in preference for an edifying, and often legendary, rather than a legal approach to the Bible, but in mechanics: the homiletic midrash treat Scripture according to its liturgical divisions, that is, the Torah selections that are read daily in the synagogue over a cycle of three years or else the "section" (*pesiqta*) reserved for Sabbaths and special festivals.

An Unfolding Tradition

The development of Jewish exegesis is not unlike the history of logic. There is a kind of logic in almost all forms of human thought, but only after arriving at a certain degree of self-consciousness about the process were the "rules" governing such thought first formulated. Aristotle did not invent logic; he simple abstracted and formalized an operation many could perform but few could as yet describe. The post-Exilic scribes too must have been practicing midrash without formalizing the process, though their growing self-consciousness is already reflected in the encomium of the scribe and his work in the second-century B.C.E. Wisdom of Jesus ben Sira (39:1–8). Tradition, however, grants Jesus' contemporary Hillel the glory of being the Aristotle of Jewish midrash. Some of Hillel's rules for elucidating the meaning of a text were by then commonplace in the Greek and Roman rhetorical and philosophical schools of the era, so commonplace, perhaps, that there was no need to "borrow" them in any formal sense of that word. Hillel simply used what was at hand for reading a text.

After 70 C.E. Scripture was the sole foundation stone left to support the identity of the Jewish people. State and cult had disappeared, and the Jews now gathered about the Torah as their guiding and identifying principle. The Sadducees, the bearers of priestly thinking, were rendered functionally impotent, the Essenes and Zealots were destroyed, and the followers of Jesus went, or were pushed, into another place. The Pharisees became the rabbis, the expositors and guardians of the law and the authoritative interpreters of Scripture. At this point Scripture had become a closed body of texts to which nothing could be added or subtracted. As a result, the ongoing task of community formation could be accomplished only by exegesis, by reopening Scripture through interpretation, which the Pharisees proceeded to do, relying for their authority on the notion of the "Twin Torahs." They held that besides the written Torah another, equally authoritative deposit of faith had been given to Moses on Sinai and then eventually passed to the Pharisees, who were now its guardians (see II/3).

The earliest rabbinic midrashim, as already remarked, had as their object extracting legal material from Scripture by applying this midrashic method. Such are *Sifra* or *The Book* written on Leviticus, the *Sifre Zuta* devoted to Numbers, and the *Mekilta* on the legal material (chaps. 12 to 23:19) in Exodus. Examples of purely expository midrashim are the *Bereshit Rabba* on Genesis and the *Midrash on Lamentations*. Among the oldest homiletic midrash works are the *Pesiqta of Rab Kahana*, the *Tanhuma*, and the *Pesiqta Rabbati*. All these midrashim carry within them the stuff of Jewish legends and tales that are used to fill out, magnify, and illumine the biblical text, sometimes in ways startling to the modern reader.

Note: These haggadic expositions of Scripture have been called "a popular mythology of the Jewish universe," a characterization that applies equally well to the very similar material we find in the Muslims' "Tales of the Prophets" and their quranic commentaries generally. This latter material obviously originated in a Jewish milieu, but since the exact dating of the haggadic midrashim is almost impossible to determine, it is difficult to say which direction the influence was flowing, from eighth-century rabbis to eighth-century Muslim writers, or vice versa.

As we have just seen, Hillel, a Pharisee, was credited with codifying the rules of exegesis, possibly because the Pharisees could not claim the priestly authority of the Sadducees and their scribes in interpreting of Scripture, and so if they wished to depart from the literal sense (*peshat*), as the Sadducees refused to do, they had to justify their midrash carefully on technical grounds. But the Pharisees were not the only ones to "apply" the Scripture to their own point of view. The community at Qumran did the same in their pesharim, as did Jesus' followers, although the former did it on the basis of the Hebrew text and the latter on that of the Greek Septuagint. Pharisaic midrash, and the rabbinic midrash that grew out of it, both aimed at extracting of a deeper understanding (and a wider application) of the legal and ethical principles inherent in Scripture. The Essenes and Christians had quite different interests: to read in the Scriptures the foreshadowing of events in the future that was now present or in the future that would be the End Time.

Philo Rereads Scripture

The exegetical technique of both the Essenes and the Christians involves a kind of allegorizing: its premise is that although Scripture is talking about one thing (the present), it is really referring to something else (the future). The allegorical reading found its broadest extension in Philo of Alexandria (d. ca. 50 C.E.), whose understanding of "the other" was the whole body of contemporary Greek philosophy. Philo understood well enough the value of the plain sense, where a great deal of law lay, and he could also compose moral midrash in the best Palestinian style. But his chief contribution to scriptural exegesis was his application of the peculiar Greek sense of *allegoria* (other-referent) and *hyponoia* (under-thought) to the Bible.

That there might be depths beneath the surface of the text was new to neither the Jewish nor the Greek traditions in which Philo was raised. Already the earliest rabbis, those who seem to be Philo's contemporaries, were asserting of the Bible that "all is in it" (Mishnah Aboth 5:22) and using various techniques to draw it forth. For their part, the Greek philosophers, particularly the Stoics, had already allegorized Homer and other poets, for much the same reason Jewish exegetes later "interpreted" patriarchal polygamy and incest: the stories, of the Olympian gods in the Greek instance, of Israel's patriarchs in the other, were morally offensive and yet they occurred in a context of divine inspiration. Philo did not allegorize on quite the same moral grounds, but rather because of his conviction that Scripture and philosophy were speaking of the same truths, though in different forms of discourse. The Scriptures themselves invited allegorization, somewhat the way the poets did, by presenting things in a manner that made the literal interpretation unlikely, offensive, or absurd to a later generation with different sensibilities. With the Bible before him, Philo retold the story from Creation onward in a way that made sense to an assimilated Jewish Platonist of the first century.

Evangelical Exegesis

If Scripture for the earliest Christians was nothing other than Jewish Scripture, Tanak, their understanding of those same texts was likewise Jewish. Indeed, the Jesus movement as a sectarian form of Judaism and then Christianity as a different and distinct *religio* were born of exegesis. That Jesus was the Messiah was demonstrated in the first instance not by miracles but through a privileged understanding of Scripture, a Jewish understanding of Jewish Scripture. The argument begins to unfold in the opening lines of the Gospels and never leaves off: Jesus by his words and deeds fulfilled what the Jewish prophets had said of the one who was to come. This exegetical approach to messiahship may have been Jesus' own—"Today, in your hearing, this text [Isa. 58:6; 61:1–2] has come true," he is reported to have said publicly in the Nazareth synagogue (Luke 4:21)—but it was eagerly taken up by his followers. Matthew's Gospel in particular relies heavily on the "messianic exegesis" of Jewish Scripture.

The early Christians swiftly followed the Gospels in reading the past as the future and turning the biblical prophets from moral scolds into prognosticators pure and simple. It seems fair to assume that other first-century Jews who heard or read this type of exegesis of Scripture found nothing objectionable, or perhaps even unusual, in it, however much they may have disagreed with its conclusions. To us, who prefer to interpret texts historically and contextually, these Christian readings appear willfully free and the texts themselves either wrenched out of context or pieced together quite arbitrarily. The "virgin" in Isaiah 7:14, for example, on whom the entire weight of Jesus' virginal conception seems to rest in Matthew 1:22–23, means nothing but "young girl," and the expression "Son of Man" in Daniel 7:13, which is read as a messianic title in the Gospels (Mark 2:10, etc.), is the lowercase Aramaic "son of man," that is, a human. But what disturbs us did not disturb Jesus' contemporaries, and the evidence of how Scripture was being read by Jewish sectaries, those at Qumran, for example, makes the early Christian way of handling Scripture not only possible but even commonplace in first-century Jewish circles. And for long after as well. No examples of Rabbi Akiba's midrash have been preserved, but we may be assured that his recognition of Bar Kokhba (Num. 24:17) as Messiah was buttressed by his own collection, and understanding, of the apposite scriptural texts.

The Senses of Scripture

Paul pioneered the notion that Jewish Scripture foreshadowed the events of the Christian dispensation. Adam was the analogical "type" of the coming Messiah; the sin of the first foreshadowed the redemptive act of the second (Rom. 5:14). The Israelites' experiences in Sinai happened "typically" to teach the results of Christians' resistance to God (1 Cor. 10:11). Succeeding generations of Christians brought this foreshadowing or typological exegesis of the Bible to a very sophisticated level and ensured, in the process, that the Old Testament would be forever bound to the New, the prefiguring to the prefigured reality. But tied to the Bible, Christians could not always abide by it. Paul had already cast away the Law in the case of the new Gentile Christians, who were, as it soon turned out, to constitute the bones and flesh of Christianity.

Many of those same Gentiles were trained in allegorical exegesis—it was a staple of a rhetorical education, the humanities major in the ancient university—and it proved to be the perfect instrument for freeing the Christian from the ceremonial and dietary laws of the Torah, much the way Paul had already "spiritualized" circumcision for his Gentile converts, while holding on to moral precepts like the Ten Commandments. The second-century *Letter of Barnabas*, likely the work of a Jewish Christian, is a prolonged allegorization of the Bible's dietary laws. For the ancients, animals were already a kind of moral paradigm—Aesop's *Fables* and the popular medieval bestiaries are examples of how zoology could be read in both an entertaining and an instructive fashion—and the author of the *Letter* turns this to exegetical use. The prohibition against eating swine's flesh, he argues, is not intended literally but rather is an allegorical warning not to behave swinishly. In this fashion he proceeds through the Torah's entire menu of prohibited foods and demonstrates that in each case certain kinds of behavior, typified by the animal in question, are being forbidden to the Christian.

Over time the Christians lost their audience of Jews or Jewish converts. As a result they turned away from the methods of rabbinic midrash, which was more and more engaged in the legal exegesis of Scripture, to the broader allegoria of Philo, which addressed the narrative. The Christian Fathers seem to have known Philo's allegorical method very well, and whether or not they read Philo themselves, the new Christian intelligentsia received ample instruction on allegorical interpretation from those who had, notably, two Alexandrian Christians of the early third century, Clement and Origen. All these scholars—Philo, Clement, Origen, and their Greek and Latin successors—tried their hand at formalizing *allegoria* by subdividing it in one way or another. There was general agreement that both a literal and a "spiritual" sense of Scripture existed; the latter was commonly divided into a moral sense, which was not very different from rabbinic haggadic midrash, and a Philo-type allegoria that penetrated into the deeper, that is, the philosophical truths embodied in the sacred book. Occasionally the older eschatological sense was added, Scripture viewed in the light of the now distant but still inevitable End Time.

Thus, the most influential Christian exegetes of Scripture, Clement (d. ca. 215) and Origen (d. ca. 254) in the Greek East, Augustine (d. 430) and Gregory the Great (d. 604), all recognized that assorted figurative or allegorical readings might complement, or even override, the literal sense of the Bible—allegory, Augustine remarked, teaches us that something should not be taken literally—and each had attempted to reduce them to some order. Origen took as his point of departure the tripartite division of the human person into body, soul, and spirit and advanced the notion that the literal sense of Scripture was like the body, the moral sense, its soul, while the highest human faculty, the spirit, was represented by the spiritual sense of the sacred book. Augustine thought there might be four divisions: "what things are related as having been done," the literal or historical sense of the text; "what things are foretold," a prophetic or typological sense; "what eternal things are intimated there," a spiritual reading of the text; and "what we are instructed to do," or Scripture as a source of moral guidance.

Augustine's fourfold division became popular throughout Latin Christendom, although there was no unanimity on what precisely the elements were. In subsequent discussions there was little disagreement about the nature of Scripture's literal sense; the historical truth of the Bible, and more so of the New Testament Gospels, had to be taken seriously, and the moral sense remained the staple of both preaching and contemplation. Typology became less important in time since it was no longer necessary to argue the cause of Jesus as Messiah to Christians who now accepted the New Testament as irrefutable evidence for Christ as Savior. The spiritual sense of Scripture became the reading of choice for the Church's mystics and theologians, as it did for their Jewish and Muslim counterparts, all of whom found there divine truths closed to the ordinary believer.

Marcion Reads the Scripture

Although the Christian Fathers paid lip service to the Old Testament's literal-historical sense, they did not expend a great deal of exegetical energy explaining it. This is not surprising, perhaps, by a community that had quite explicitly rejected most of the Bible's prescriptions. One who did take the Jewish Scripture seriously and who, as a Christian, was led to conclude that it was not Scripture at all, was Marcion. Whereas a Jewish-Christian author like Barnabas managed to embrace the Jewish Bible by allegorizing it almost beyond recognition, Marcion quite simply rejected it. Marcion was rejected by the Church in turn—he was excommunicated at Rome in 144 C.E. Most of the Christian Fathers followed the example of the Gospels themselves and offered a typological interpretation of what they called the Old Testament, or else they followed where Philo had led, converting a Mosaic philosophy into a Platonic one.

Why Don't We Understand?

Exposure to literary Hellenism—and the growing difference of opinion on Scripture's *meaning*—taught the Christians (and Jews and Muslims) more than just exegetical methods. It forced them to confront the very meaning of exegesis, what was later called hermeneutics (see below). Why, for example, if God is all-knowing and all-powerful, did he express himself in ways that could be, and were, misunderstood? With so much at stake, why should the Word of God be opaque or ambiguous? The answer, the Christians felt, lay in Eden. Original Sin had not only deranged humans' moral faculties (see II/5); it had closed their understanding as well. When God spoke to Adam and Eve in the garden, they grasped his meaning exactly. It was only after they had sinned that they failed to understand, and act, on God's command to love him and serve him.

The argument is taken up at this point by Augustine, Christianity's most astute and influential mediator on the events in Eden, in his work *On Christian Doctrine*. Just as God condescended to save humankind from sin through the death of his son, he also lowered himself to speak in the halting tongue of Adam and Eve's descendants. Revelation is cast in human speech, not God's, and like human speech it is material, concrete, and disturbingly plain, as Christian stylists sometimes complained. In revelation God is operating in time but talking about eternity; it is the mortals' responsibility to press beyond Scripture's time-bound language, which God has mercifully chosen to use for our sake, and try to find there the alien and difficult language of eternity. God's truths are not in the words, although they may be fitfully visible there, but in what lies beneath.

For all its biblical underpinning in Augustine, this theory of the depths of Scripture, not only had Jewish (and later Muslim) resonances but was available in the critical thinking of later Hellenism as well. For the Greeks and Romans, no less than for Muhammad's contemporaries, the poet, the *vates*, was divinely inspired. The Alexandrian exegetes, when they undertook to explicate the text of Homer, for example, thought they were doing theology and read the work before them in a highly allegorical fashion. Homer's reputation as a theologian was fashioned not merely from his lengthy descriptions of the doings of the Olympian gods but from the conviction that he was, like all poets, god-possessed. "Poetic inspiration is divine," Plato said, though he was gravely suspicious of the truths they fashioned. Beneath the tales of the gods, many of them so morally reprehensible as to coerce us to seek another, deeper truth, we cannot but think that the "words are veils and the truth is beyond speech," as one Latin literary critic put it.

Fathers and Other Authorities

Christians, no less than Jews and Muslims, were committed to the total and simultaneous veracity of Scripture. God's Words occurred in highly complex texts, however, and the challenge of reading and understanding them aright was daunting. Until the Reformation few counseled the Christian to take on Scripture alone, and even fewer gave that advice among the Jews and Muslims, who still mostly read Scripture—as opposed to reciting it—with a long and deep tradition peering over their shoulders, or, more literally, from the margins of the text. Exegetes in all three faith communities expended enormous energy over the centuries discussing and smoothing the rough spots and harmonizing the apparent contradictions that presented themselves to readers of Scripture.

As time passed, the task of the Christian interpreter was rendered both simpler and more complex by an ever growing body of authoritative exegesis that began to collect around the New Testament. In the fourth century Christian authors began referring to the "Fathers," an elastic category designed to include older authorities and, more specifically, to the "Fathers" gathered at the Council of Nicaea in 325. Later councils referred somewhat more formally to those earlier conciliar Fathers to support their own decrees, and eventually, with the sense of a growing separation from the pristine state of Christianity—a sentiment quite visible in Europe in the ninth century—the "Fathers" came to designate the orthodox authorities (and some, like Origen and Tertullian, who were not so orthodox) of that earlier, ill-defined era. In the East the "age of the Fathers" is generally reckoned from the apostolic era to that of John of Damascus (d. 749)—the last great Christian authority in the pre-Islamic Middle East—and in Latin Christianity, to Gregory the Great (d. 604) or perhaps Isidore of Seville (d. 636), two figures thought to be on the cusp of the now disappeared ancient world. Collectively, they are known as the Church Fathers, and they represent a kind of "framing authority" that was thought to embody, and explain, the apostolic tradition in its most authoritative sense.

> **Note:** The Muslims too relied on the notion of "the Fathers," in Arabic *al-salaf*, or "the Ancestors." Consensus (*ijma*) is an important hermeneutic tool in Islam, and although how far that consensus extended was debated, all recognized that agreement on a matter of belief or behavior by the "Companions"—Muhammad's contemporaries who stand in the same functional position as the Christians' Apostles—and by Muslims of the two generations immediately following constituted an indisputable norm for the community. See further II/3, II/4.

The Glossa Ordinaria, Christian and Jewish

Their Scriptures came to learned Christians and Jews virtually wrapped in exegesis. The texts of the Latin Vulgate, for example, almost always bore some version of Jerome's prologues to each sacred book. These explanatory summaries were useful for what Latin Christianity came to regard as one of its clerics' primary tasks, *praedicatio*, the preaching of God's Word to the faithful. To do this well, the preacher required preparation, and this was achieved, in an ideal and literate world perhaps, by two of the main preoccupations of medieval Christianity's religious elite. The first was the *lectio*, the reading or study of Scripture, which necessarily included a commentary, whether this was read off the margins of the biblical text itself (always the Latin Vulgate, of course) in the form of notes (*glossae*) or heard in the lectures of one of the masters of the "sacred page." The second was the *disputatio*, a deeper, more detailed, and more complex discussion of the difficulties in Scripture.

The eleventh and twelfth centuries were an orderly and exacting time in Western Christendom. Digests were produced, curricula arranged, and, an effort was made to go through the Fathers and collect the most pertinent, illuminating, and authoritative clarifications on any given text in Scripture. Thus there slowly came into being, by consensus and not by ecclesiastical fiat, what came to be known as the *glossa ordinaria*, or "standard notes," which were eventually found as both interlinear and marginal comments in most copies of the Bible. The work had no single author, although the chief hands on this widespread and deeply influential exegetical aid seem to have been Christian teachers and scholars in France. By the mid–twelfth century, in any event, every book of both the Old and the New Testament came enveloped in the glossa ordinaria.

The Jews too read the Bible with "the Fathers" peering over their shoulders. In medieval times there appeared, again by accretion and consensus rather than by decree, the *Mikraoth gedoloth* or "Great Readings"—sometimes called the "Rabbinic Bible"—which presented the reader, on each page, with not only the standard Hebrew text (*masorah*) of Tanak but one or more Aramaic targums (see II/1) and various medieval Hebrew commentaries. The number of commentaries varied according to the size of the page but they invariably included the work of the most profoundly influential medieval commentator, Solomon ben Isaac, also known as Rashi (d. 1105) (see below).

The Quran Reads the Bible

The Quran too "read" the Bible or, to put it more accurately from a Muslim perspective, God "reinterpreted" his earlier revelations in this, his latest, and last, version of The Book. Events and personalities recounted or described in

the Bible and New Testament are reintroduced in the Quran and most frequently in an exegetical setting. That setting is often somewhat different from
the earlier scriptural presentation of the same event. While there is a gentle
and very occasional nod to the prefiguring sense of the Jews' and Christians'
revelation (so Quran 61:6), the quranic emphasis rests heavily on what the
Christians' called the moral sense. Biblical accounts of the prophets take on,
in their retelling, a distinct moral tone. Some, like those connected with the
people of Noah (e.g., 11:25–48) or of Lot (e.g., 15:57–77) or the Pharaoh
(e.g., 54:45–48), are "punishment stories" purely and simply, but throughout
the Meccan period the Quran tells and retells stories of the sufferings of former biblical prophets with one eye cocked obviously and deliberately on
Muhammad and his beleaguered followers. There are moral lessons too in the
long, edifying story of Joseph (sura 12), who is rewarded for his virtue, and of
Mary, Jesus' mother, also falsely accused and vindicated (19:16–34).

Thus far the question has been the Quran's own exegetical use of the former Scriptures. Behind it lies another question, albeit one not entertained by
Muslims since it inquires about the Quran's sources. The Quran knows a
good deal about the Bible and somewhat less about the Gospels, but none of
that knowledge appears to be textual. There is, in other words, little evidence
that Muhammad, his informants, if such there were, or his listeners had any
knowledge of the text of either Scripture. None was available in Arabic in any
event, and none would be for perhaps two centuries after the Prophet. The
religious culture of Muhammad's Arabia was overwhelmingly, if not exclusively, oral, and, at least among Arab speakers, midrashic rather than textual.
Except for certain liturgical uses, the Bible had been replaced by Bible history,
stories derived from the Scriptures but then enlarged, enhanced, and illumined in the manner of the haggadic midrashim. Those midrashic tales of the
prophets and of Jesus and Mary had passed through Jewish and Christian
hands and come to rest in the Quran, some, undoubtedly, with one final
homiletic turn from the Prophet himself.

The Quran's citation and understanding of selected passages from the Bible
and the New Testament became, for a very long time, the Muslims' only access to those earlier revelations: first, because the Quran had superseded them
and second, because the Jews and Christians had either concealed part of their
sacred books or else tampered with them, rendering them useless not only to
those other communities but to the Muslims as well (see II/1). This essentially
theological point of view, which the Quran invokes to explain why the Jews in
particular had not accepted Muhammad's prophethood, long narrowed the
field of discourse between Muslims and the other monotheists. The polemic
from the latter was often directed at the Muslims' misunderstanding of their
Scriptures, and the Muslims, if they chose to address the accusation directly,
were hampered by their unfamiliarity with the full texts of either the Bible or
the New Testament in Arabic. Even when such translations were finally in

circulation among Jews and Christians in the ninth and tenth centuries, Muslims seem not to have used them and as late as the fourteenth century learned Muslim authors still apparently preferred using oral (and inaccurate) accounts of the scriptural texts from converts among the People of the Book.

Quranic Ambiguities

The Quran openly warns of its own ambiguities (3:7), and so Muslims have not hesitated to attempt to unravel the sacred text's obscurities and have devoted enormous energy to the task of tafsir in all the same types practiced by the Jews and Christians. These exegetical efforts eventually ranged from detailed and sophisticated study of the lexicographical and syntactical problems posed by the Quran to driving its meaning into the sometimes remote regions where sectarian preferences or mystical longings wished it to go. But not perhaps from the very beginning. Since the Quran was not a historically conditioned revelation, but rather was thought to reflect an eternal heavenly archetype composed of the very same words, the Mother of the Book, the Muslim approach to its exegesis was initially quite different from that pursued by the People of the Book. The Quran did not easily suffer either translation or paraphrase. On the Christian premise, Jesus was his own revelation: he could teach its significance with authority and pass on that teaching to his disciples in a formal and imperative fashion. Muhammad, in contrast, was the conduit of God's revelation, much as Moses was, and during his own lifetime there was no question that he and only he was the authoritative interpreter of that revelation for the Muslim community.

Some of Muhammad's exegesis is to be found in the Quran itself. The Prophet had twenty-two years in which to refine, edit, or explain the revelation—as well as the undoubted authority to do so—and what are clearly editorial glosses became part of the text. In sura 74, for example, which some think may be the oldest in the Quran, Muhammad explains in verses 27 onward an odd or unusual term, *saqara*, used in verse 26. That gloss was done on the fly, so to speak, and the rhythm of the text is not broken. Verse 31, as already remarked, contains a long prose explanation of the term "nineteen" used in the preceding verse. It bears all the intrusive signs of a later addition, yet, like the many Jewish and Christian examples of the same phenomenon (Gen. 32:32; Mark 7:19), it is part of the text. It is revelation itself no less than the word it seeks to explain.

Far more of the Prophet's understanding of the sacred text he himself had revealed lies outside the Quran, however, in the vast body of "Prophetic reports" (*hadith*) that form the basis of the Muslims' legal exegesis of the Quran (see II/3). According to one such report, there was an early prohibition against the very act of interpreting the Quran. If authentic, the prohibition was not very closely observed, and the earliest identifiable types of quranic exegesis were very similar to the familiar forms of Jewish homiletic or haggadic midrash, and show some of the same motives: to fill in gaps in quranic narratives, and to assist in the construction of a genuine Islamic piety. Most of the narratives in question were stories about biblical prophets and what befell those who did not heed them. According to the Muslim tradition itself, details for their elaboration were supplied by new converts with a particular knowledge of the Jewish tradition, especially the popular, legendary, and edifying material known under the common name of haggadah.

A common form of Muslim commentary on the Quran is the explication of the very words of the text, a procedure that presumes the existence of an authoritative canonical text, the one, we are assured, prepared at the direction of the caliph Uthman sometime between 644 and 656. The language of the Quran was, of course, Arabic, a "manifest Arabic speech," in the Scripture's own words (16:103; 26:195). If quranic Arabic was "clear" to Muhammad's audience at Mecca and Medina, as it surely must have been to some degree, it was apparently less so to second- and third-generation Muslims, many of whom did not have Arabic as their native tongue. They turned in a somewhat unexpected direction for help in explicating the text, to the works of the otherwise reprehensible pagan pre-Islamic poets, the only historical tool available for understanding the Arabic of the Quran. What that poetry could teach about the language of the Quran was, however, limited: in the eyes of Muslims, the holy book was inimitable not merely in content but in language and style. Nor was the poetry of much help with the Quran's content. Pre-Islamic poetry operated in a different field of notion and sensibility from the Quran and showed little interest in religion or religious issues. Pre-Islamic poetry did supply an enormous lexicon of Arabic roots, the same pool of etymons that underlies the Quran's own Arabic. Muslim exegetes were thus empowered to explain in purely etymological terms the considerable number of quranic words that are foreign-derived, from Syriac Aramaic, Ethiopic, Hebrew, and Greek, among others, a borrowed vocabulary that served to render precisely the Quran's religious ideas.

The "Occasions of Revelation"

The extant early biographies of Muhammad, which are arranged in traditional chronological order, often gloss events in his life by reference to specific verses in the Quran, most notably 93:6–8 on his preprophetic days and 53:1–18 on his visions. The connection is of course equally effective in the opposite direction: the biographical event inevitably illuminates the quranic verse by providing the sorely needed context—the Quran provides none of its own—in which the verse was sent down. These latter stories, taken discretely, constituted an entire genre of Arabic literature. The "Occasions of Revelation"—its most famous example is a work of that same name by al-Wahidi (d. 1075)—find themselves midway between biography and exegesis. Standing separately, as they did in the "Occasions" collections, they are clearly intended to explain scattered, though by no means all or even most, verses in the Quran. Arranged chronologically with a linking narration, they become the stuff of a "Life" of the Prophet.

As exegetical devices, the anecdotes dubbed "Occasions of Revelation" served both halakic and haggadic ends, that is, to illumine behavioral prescriptions and prohibitions or to enlarge, for any of various reasons, a quranic pointer into what remains in the sacred text a dark corner. In the first instance, the Quran's assorted injunctions against drinking wine are explained in the "Occasions" through a series of anecdotes in which one or a number of Muhammad's followers come drunk to prayers or commit other improprieties, which then provokes the sending down of the verse. Thus, it becomes clear that wine is forbidden not because it is impure or unclean, like the prohibited flesh of swine or carrion, but because it causes intoxication, which in turn leads to impropriety.

The haggadic occasions are more diverse since their end is not so much practical as informational or devotional. Many of the verses of sura 2, for example, are explained in terms of Muhammad's confrontation with the Jews of Medina in 622–624. In another approach, Quran 2:116 notes (with disapproval) that "They say, 'God has taken a son. Glory be to Him!'" without, as often, bothering to identify "they." Al-Wahidi, in his *Occasions*, explains, not entirely helpfully, that "they" in this verse refers to "the Jews when they said Uzayr [Ezra?] is the son of God and the Christians of Najran when they said the Messiah [that is, Jesus] is the son of God, and the polytheists among the Arabs who said the angels are the daughters of God." The verse, then, is expanded either from an independent source or, far more likely, from what seems plausible to either al-Wahidi or other practitioners of the genre.

Tabari Enthroned

Many of the developments in Islamic exegesis are traditionally attributed to the second-generation Muslim Ibn Abbas (d. 687), but like many other such attributions in early Islamic history, its object may have been to confer antiquity on something that occurred a century or more later. We know for certain that most of what was done in the earliest Islamic attempts at explaining the Quran was assimilated into the *Collection of Explanations for the Exegesis of the Quran*, simply called *The Exegesis*, composed in the 880s or 890s by Muhammad Ibn Jarir al-Tabari (d. 923), and which from his day to this has held pride of place in Muslim exegesis. Tabari's enormous commentary—in its original form it had thirty parts and its early printed edition ran to fifteen volumes—proceeds majestically through the Quran sura by sura, indeed, word by word, combining legal, historical, and philological explanation of great density. Each word is taken and turned over in his hand, this way and that, and its every lexicographical and grammatical feature noted and often explained, as already indicated, by reference to the pre-Islamic poetry of the Arabs, which was used continuously by Muslim exegetes, somewhat in the manner of an etymological dictionary of Arabic with which to unpack the text of the Quran.

But Tabari was also a historian; his equally monumental and influential *Annals* were composed after The *Exegesis*. Just as he often provided alternative versions of an event in his history, so Tabari offered the reader of his commentary on the Quran a variety of narrative interpretations of a given quranic text. Each of these was supported by a chain of authorities going back to Muhammad's own contemporaries, the famous Companions of the Prophet (see II/3), and particularly to the most influential Muslim of the very first generation after Muhammad, Ibn Abbas, whom the Muslim tradition recalls as the author of one of the oldest and authoritative works of tafsir. These chains of authorities, which may have originated in legal texts to give authenticity to the Prophetic traditions to which they were attached, became almost as pervasive, if somewhat less formal in their structure, in history writing and exegesis. Here too they conferred both authenticity and an authority that reached back to the men and women of the first generation of Muslims who had seen and heard the Prophet in the flesh. The result in exegesis is to confront the reader with an invitingly open quranic text. Even though a commentator like Tabari may signal his preference among the various interpretations he cites, none is foreclosed since each is, in a sense, authoritative. The Christian Church too appealed to a "traditional" reading of Scripture in the same historical sense as Muslims did, but that historical tradition was in the end guided and shaped by the magisterium. This never occurred in Islam, where the glossa ordinaria remained, thanks to Tabari and his kind, an open and flexible hermeneutic field.

Plain and Allegorical Exegesis in Islam

Since he occasionally addressed himself to the question, it appears from Tabari's commentary that in his day there was already understood to be another distinction in exegetical approach that cut across the categories just discussed: that between *tafsir, or* "plain" exegesis, and *tawil*, which is often understood as allegorical exegesis. The distinction may go back to the Quran itself (3:7), which seems to suggest that there are two kinds of verses in Scripture: those whose meaning is clear and those that require some kind of explanation. The explanations that followed have been no more than the application of personal reasoning (*ijtihad*) or some mildly critical research to the text, as opposed to the acceptance on authority of the plain meaning—a distinction that was current, and debated, in legal circles. Most of the commentators and commentaries discussed to this point operated within a tradition that regarded the body of prophetic hadith as the primary exegetical instrument for understanding the Quran, particularly on legal matters, much the way the Talmud served the rabbinic exegetes in Judaism. On that understanding, the difference between tafsir and tawil was not, then, between exoteric and esoteric passages but rather between clear and ambiguous ones. Where tawil took on its allegorical association was when exegetical principles began to be used to elicit from Scripture dogmatic and mystical understandings of which both Muhammad and the Quran were at first totally innocent.

The Quran was not a historical document in Muslims' eyes, nor was Muhammad a historian. Since the Enlightenment secular critics have looked on the Bible, the New Testament, and the Quran as documents of their times (see II/1). The believers, in contrast, see in those Scriptures a point of contact with God himself. Each of the three communities continues to take its Scripture seriously as history, of course, first in the sense that it was revealed at a fixed moment of human history, and then, in that its behavioral prescriptions refer to ongoing human life, in all times and all places, and have historical relevance. But Philo, as we have seen, attempted to peer beneath the Bible's historical surface into the timeless riches beneath. He thought he could discern there the truths of which the Greek philosophers also had some presentiment, or may even have borrowed from Israel. The Christians peered through the same aperture Philo had opened, as did the Muslims after them, and all saw in their Scriptures the same perennial truths. But some looked even more deeply, into the profound heart of Scripture where God himself dwelled. This is the Scripture of the mystics, the Torah of the Kabbalists, the New Testament of Bernard of Clairvaux, and the Quran of Ibn Arabi, a presence contained not only in the whole of Scripture but also, without distinction of importance, in each verse and even in every word and letter.

The Muslims Struggle with Revelation and Reason

Early Islam witnessed a profound struggle for its soul and its identity. On one side were the "partisans of tradition" (*ahl al-hadith*) who longed for a Quran- and prophet-oriented society whose image was slowly emerging, in a highly idealized version, in the enormous collection of hadith, the Prophetic traditions that purported to define and describe the community's earliest days (see II/3). The Quran was viewed in those circles as an object as holy as God himself, and their reading of the text, as is common among religious conservatives, remained reverentially close to the plain meaning. Opposition to these "traditionists" came from the "partisans of dialectic" (*ahl al-kalam*); (on *kalam* or dialectical theology, see II/7), particularly from the group known as the Mutazilites. It is not known whether these latter rejected the hadith or, as seems more likely, merely took a more hypercritical view of them than was common in most Muslim circles. Certainly they preferred to ground their Muslim sensibilities in the Quran. But they read the Book like rationalists: the gross anthropomorphisms of the simple-minded pietists were not for them. But the Mutazilite dispute with the traditionists went deeper than this. The latter's veneration for the ipsissima verba of the Quran and the Mutazilite insistence on using dialectical methods of analysis came to term in the profound and profoundly disruptive debate on whether the Quran was created, and so, by implication, conditioned, as the Mutazilites held, or whether it was eternal, coeval, and coequal with God.

For the Mutazilites, an uncreated Quran was a theological affront to a unique God as well as a manacle that chained human reason and conscience to a text, however revered that latter might be. In traditionist eyes the uncreated Quran was a mysterious embodiment of the sacred, an almost sacramental link between a transcendent God and his earthly creation. In a verbal struggle in which all the weapons belonged to the dialecticians, it is difficult to piece together the nuances of the traditionist position, but out of the ahl al-hadith came two Islamic "schools," those of Ahmad ibn Hanbal (d. 856) and Dawud ibn Kalaf (d. 884), from which a coherent stance can be derived. Both groups insisted on the evident (*zahir*; Dawud's followers were called Zahiris) sense of both the Quran and the hadith—on pious, conservative grounds, to be sure, but almost as surely as a reaction to a Mutazilite exegesis of the sacred text that was based on somewhat freewheeling analogy (*qiyas*) and critical investigation of its meaning.

Exegesis lay at the heart of the debate over the conflicting claims of faith and reason in the domain of revealed religion. The rationalizing theologians wrested some of the rights of exegesis away from the lawyers because they were more skillful in allegorical exegesis. Traditionists were tied by their own legal premises to literal interpretation of Scripture, a connection that committed them in nonlegal passages to certain gross anthropomorphisms the dialecticians could devour with arguments. More, the theologians permitted themselves a far wider exegetical range, and could apply both learning and imagination to the text of Scripture, whereas the traditionists were largely limited to rhetoric and philology. Just how attractive a carefully wrought theological tafsir might be is demonstrated by the position won among all segments of the Islamic community by the monumental quranic commentary *The Unveiler of the Realities of the Secrets of Revelation*, by the Mutazilite Zamakhshari (d. 1144), and by the fact that Philo's discredited allegorical exegesis found a new audience once Jewish theologians under Islam rediscovered philosophy.

Later the philosophers of Islam would make even bolder claims than the early partisans of tradition. For the dialectical theologians who came after the Mutazilites, rational discourse, whether in exegesis or elsewhere, was complementary to and defensive of the higher truths of revelation, but the philosophers, the Muslim Avicenna or the Jewish Maimonides, regarded philosophy's claim as the higher one. Scripture figured truth for the unphilosophical masses; philosophy uttered its very name. There can be no conflict, however. Where Scripture appears to conflict with the conclusions of demonstrative reasoning, it is a clear sign that Scripture's literal meaning must be interpreted allegorically, not by the lawyer or the theologian, whose powers of reasoning are undermined by faulty premises, but by the philosopher, who alone possesses truly rigorous scientific knowledge.

Shiite Tafsir

If the philosophers imagined they had a privileged understanding of the Quran, they were not the only Muslims to make such claims. As already noted, the Quran makes quite explicit that Muhammad is but one of a line of prophets that stretches back to Adam. But that line closes with Muhammad, and however hard some sectarians like the Bahais and Ahmadis attempted to pry it open once again (see I/5), the main body of Muslims has resisted: Muhammad was indeed the "seal of the prophets" (Quran 33:40). But if prophethood was a closed way, there was another route that led, almost as effectively, through exegesis. The Shiite Muslims believe that Muhammad was followed by a series of divinely appointed Imams who are God's vicars and infallibly guide the community (see I/8). One of their powers is understanding the "hidden" sense of the Quran.

All the varieties of Shiites share a belief in the Imam as the head of the umma, but the group called the Ismailis, who possessed actual Imams longer than any of the other groups, developed an elaborate theory of prophecy and of exegesis. According to them, each of the prophets—or "speakers," as the Ismailis preferred to call the traditional prophets of the Quran—was entrusted with the "outer" or "obvious" (*zahir*) sense of the sacred texts. But each was followed in turn by a "deputy" (*wasi*)—Aaron for Moses, for example, Peter for Jesus, and, of course Ali for Muhammad—who was privy to the inner (*batin*) and so more profound meaning of revelation. Ordinary Muslims practice their tafsir on the literal sense of the Quran, which produces the standard practices and beliefs of what we call Islam. But Ismaili exegesis is not reading but interpretation (tawil). It fits within the broad category of what we have called the allegorical interpretation of the sacred text. Its specific differences are, first, that it is hidden—that is, from the mass of Muslims—and thus esoteric; and second, that it is guaranteed, in this instance by the authority of the infallible Imams. (On the content of the Ismaili tawil, see II/9.)

Learning from the Muslims

The preferred rabbinic approach to Scripture was, as we have seen, the process called midrash, from the root meaning "to seek." The earliest form of it is still visible in texts like Jeremiah 21:1–2, where the prophet is bidden to "seek from the Lord on our behalf." The rabbis too were seeking from the Lord on behalf of the people, though in the rabbinic instance the sacred text itself was being queried. Scripture was subjected to the most minute scrutiny, although chiefly in a formal sense: peculiarities of spelling, word order, and style were all carefully dissected by the rabbis to elicit the deeper significance that lay behind the plain sense.

The midrashic method is richly represented in the rabbinic midrashim of both the legal (halakic) and homiletic (haggadic) types, and its results lie open for inspection in the Mishnah and the two Talmuds. But in the tenth century, under the unmistakable influence of their Muslim environment, Jews adopted a new way of understanding the Bible. The first known proponent of this new approach was Saadya ibn Yusuf (d. 942), the Egyptian-born scholar who became the head of the Babylonian academy, which had by then been transferred from provincial Sura to metropolitan Baghdad, the seat of the caliphate (see II/4). Saadya produced a pioneer Arabic translation of the Hebrew Bible for the benefit of the now Arabic-speaking Jews in Mesopotamia, but more importantly for our present purpose, his translation was accompanied by an extensive commentary on the text that set Jewish biblical exegesis on a new track.

The rabbis engaged in midrash had never much concerned themselves with context. Their gaze was fixed on the text itself, or, more accurately, on its words: what they were thought to have said (or not said) and, perhaps more significantly, what they intended. An astonishing variety of verbal clues were read with the same virtuoso perspicacity that the ancient augurs devoted to reading the entrails of animals. Muslim commentators on the Quran looked on their text differently. In the face of their firm conviction of the Book's divine origin, they read it as a literary product, not of Muhammad, of course, but of God, yet a product nonetheless. Thus the Quran was open to—indeed, required—the same kind of literary and rhetorical analysis as the Arabs' rich (and profane) poetical tradition. Muhammad denied being a poet, but the Quran was undoubtedly poetry, and of the highest order. Again, quite counterintuitively, the Muslim commentators read the heavenly book, with its almost defiant lack of historical context, as a historical document. As we have seen, the "Occasions" set down verses of the Quran in very concrete circumstances in Muhammad's life and understood them precisely in that context.

Beginning with Saadya, the rabbis began to do likewise with their own Scripture, employing the method that became known as peshat, sometimes called the "plain" or "literal" reading of the Bible but which is rather a profoundly contextual address of the text. The rabbis may have had little choice perhaps. It was not their Muslim contemporaries who led them down this exegetical path but fellow Jews who were resisting both the rabbis' freewheeling interpretation of Scripture and their construction of its results into the imposing edifice of tradition. These were the Karaites (see II/3), and it was their assault on midrash with the weapon of contextual exegesis that drove Saadya and the rabbinic establishment of Iraq to defend themselves with the Muslim-inspired instrument of peshat.

The Jews may have had the advantage over their Muslim models. The latter generally had only Arabic at their exegetical disposal (which was thought to be enough in the light of the Quran's own insistence that it was in "manifest Arabic"), whereas Jewish scholars had not only Hebrew, biblical and rabbinic, but Aramaic, and now, of course, what had become their vernacular Arabic. By Saadya's lifetime Arabic was already a highly analyzed and systematized language that had moreover developed into a supple and elegant literary tool capable of expressing everything from the most tender lyric to the most dauntingly technical prose, whether in law, mathematics, or philosophy, where it was already being used to translate Plato and Aristotle.

The Jews learned all this—Saadya wrote a groundbreaking Hebrew grammar on the Arabic model—and put it to good use. As they continued to interpret Scripture, the peshat or contextual method became widespread among the Jews of Muslim lands. The Jews also pursued philosophy and the sciences in Arabic—here again, Saadya was in the lead (see II/7). Most startling of all, they resurrected Hebrew as a literary medium, which the Jews of Muslim Spain, the Sephardim (see I/6), used to produce an extraordinary body of quite secular poetry.

Two Medieval Jewish Commentators: Ibn Ezra and Rashi

Two European commentators, the Spaniard Abraham ibn Ezra and the French rabbi Solomon ben Isaac, better known by his acronym Rashi, illustrate the full flowering of both the peshat and the midrash method of reading the Bible. Although younger, Ibn Ezra (d. 1164) logically comes first since his work carried the contextual method, with its concomitant language skills, outside the Muslim world, where it was widespread among the Sephardim, to the Jewish commentators of Christian Europe, who knew nothing of the Arab tradition of a close philological and contextual approach to Scripture. Born in Spain, Abraham ibn Ezra traveled extensively across the Abode of Islam from Morocco to Egypt. But in 1140 his son's conversion to Islam persuaded him, or forced him, into Christian exile. From then until his death he traveled widely in Italy, France, and even, on one occasion, England.

Like Saadya, Ibn Ezra was a polymath, but he was also a poet, indeed, one of the last representatives of the golden age of Hebrew poetry in Spain. He was also, in a sense, a cultural historian, and two of his Hebrew writings in particular, a Hebrew grammar and a history of the development of Hebrew linguistic studies, offered Jewish scholars throughout Christian Europe a convincing and attractive introduction, in Hebrew raiment, to the poetics and philology of Muslim Arab Spain. Ibn Ezra wrote multiple, often boldly innovative (see II/1), commentaries on Scripture often on the same text from different perspectives. One of his sets of comments on the Song of Songs, for example, examines the language of the Hebrew text in the manner of the Arab philologists, while another deals with the work's literary qualities as poetry. A third demonstrates that he can present midrash as well as any rabbi: the Song of Songs is unfolded as an allegory of God's love for Israel.

Rashi (d. 1105) was born in Troyes, where he was a vintner as well as a rabbi of remarkable contemporary reputation and, after his death, the exegete par excellence in the Jewish tradition. Rashi commented on the entire Bible, Chronicles alone excepted, and this renowned work—his commentary on the Pentateuch was in 1475 the first Hebrew work ever printed (without the biblical text)—generated hundreds of supercommentaries over succeeding generations. Though a pioneer in using the vernacular in biblical exegesis—he often translated difficult or technical Hebrew terms into contemporary vernacular French—Rashi was not an exegetical innovator. He passed on, in concise and comprehensible fashion, the standard rabbinic interpretation of the text, to wit, "what the Written Torah means is what the Oral Torah [the Talmud and the midrash] explains." The oral Torah explained a great deal, but Rashi kept it down to the essentials and saved his detailed remarks for difficulties in wording or expression in the biblical text.

The Great Debates

A major change took place in the scope and manner of Latin Christian exegesis in the thirteenth century. Spain had long been a place where Christians, Muslims, and Jews were in direct, sometimes cooperative, sometimes confrontational, contact (see I/5). By the 1230s, however, the political tide there had shifted in favor of the Christian kingdoms, and what had once been convivencia or "getting along" was replaced by an unmistakable sense of Christian triumphalism. The Church, from the papacy down through its bishops and preachers, could now entertain the possibility of converting the Muslims and Jews.

The thirteenth-century conversion projects took different trajectories. Since the Muslims had their own Scripture, they had to be approached from another angle. Reason was a terrain shared by Christians and Muslims, a generous

philosophical landscape first explored by Plato and Aristotle, whose charts
had come, via translation, into the hands of both the Arab Muslims and the
Latin Christians (see II/7). Reasoned discourse, then, might be the means,
some thought, to convince the chief Muslims, their rulers and "doctors," to
recognize the truth of Christianity. "Truth itself compels us," Thomas
Aquinas had written. Indeed his *Summa contra Gentiles* (1270–1272)—the
"Gentiles" in question being the infidel Muslims—was written for the express
purpose of laying out the rational arguments, without recourse to Scripture,
that might "compel" a thoughtful Muslim to Christianity.

The Jews were a different matter, however. They too shared the rational
landscape inherited from Hellenic antiquity—both Saadya and Maimonides
built noble structures there (see II/7)—but since they and the Christians had
a common Scripture, the Bible/Old Testament, and the Christians had built
their "case" on it, medieval discourse between Christians and Jews often took
the form of a debate about the reading of Scripture, whether the Jews read it
aright or the Christians. The debates were not the Jews' idea, nor were they
in any position to arrange them even if they were so inclined. Mostly, the Jews
were summoned, the general Jewish population and Muslims too, if there
were any living in the place, to attendance at sermons in the local church,
whenever the bishop or visiting Franciscan or Dominican preachers (see I/5)
thought it would be a good idea. Attendance was mandatory. According to a
decree issued by King James of Aragon in 1242, "Our officers, if they want
to obtain our favor, shall, heedless of excuse, compel them [the Jews and
Muslims] to do this."

James sponsored one of the most famous examples of public debate or disputation with Jewish experts. Here the central issue was invariably—as invariably as in the required sermons and most of the polemical literature generated
by the conversion program—exegesis, Christian and Jewish, of the Bible generally and of the messianic prophecies particularly. These disputations were a
somewhat awkward and even dangerous enterprise: for the Jews, obviously,
because they were fated by circumstance to be declared the losers, and for the
Christians because their Jewish opponents seem rather often to have had a
better command of the Bible, especially of its literal meaning, than their own
champions. We have preserved handbooks prepared by both sides for some of
the less skilled disputants. They seem designed chiefly to avoid surprises; the
critical texts are all put on the table, together with the appropriate responses.

The chief point of exegetical contention was the Christians' typological
understanding of the Old Testament and the Jews' literal reading of the same
texts. The Jewish disputants, who were necessarily cast as defendants, were
often at a loss in the face of the Christians' pervasive "foreshadowing," but
eventually they received help. In the mid–thirteenth century, Joseph ben
Nathan Official, the financial consultant of the archbishop of Sens and the
student of one of the participants in a Talmud "trial" in Paris in 1240 (see II/3),

wrote his *Book of Joseph the Zealot* to serve as a guide for Jews attempting to refute the Christians' interpretation of the Bible. A little later the more specialized *Book of the Old Polemic*, which took the prospective disputant verse by verse through the Christians' favorite typological passages of the Old Testament, appeared.

James of Aragon, meanwhile, summoned Jewish experts to debate his Dominicans in his presence at Barcelona in 1263. The chief participants were, on the Jewish side, Rabbi Moses ben Nahman, or Nahmanides, and, on the Christian, Friar Pablo Christiá, or Paul Christiani, a Jewish convert to Christianity.

> **Note:** Nahmanides (d. 1270) was born in Gerona in Catalonia, a town that had passed from Muslim to Christian hands in 1015. Like the younger Maimonides—in the acronymic style of the times, the first was known as "Ramban," the second as "Rambam"—Nahmanides was a Spanish physician and an authority on Jewish law who turned to other pursuits as well. With Maimonides, it was to the somewhat dangerous business of philosophy on the Aristotelian model current in Muslim circles (see II/7), whereas Nahmanides, who wrote in Maimonides' defense, was attracted to the Kabbala or mystical Judaism popular in many Sephardic circles (see II/9), and he later composed his biblical commentaries from that perspective. After the disputation of 1263, he was forced to leave Spain, but whereas Maimonides, himself an exile from Muslim Spain, spent the rest of his career at the royal court in Cairo, Nahmanides chose migration to Eretz Israel, where he attempted to open a school for the wretchedly poor community there. He passed the final years of his life in Palestine and died there, apparently still hoping to be able to return to Spain.
>
> Considerably less is known of Paul or Pablo Christiani. A man of some learning—one Christian report calls him "a learned cleric in the Mosaic law"—he was a convert from Judaism, possibly in Italy, and later became a Dominican friar. He brought to the task of persuading the Jews to convert enormous zeal and knowledge of the Scripture in Hebrew as well as of the Talmud and midrash. Later he appeared at the French court, where he persuaded Louis IX to require Jews to wear identifying badges and to allow him, Paul, to preach to the Jews in their synagogues.

Paul undertook to prove "through authoritative texts of the Law and the Prophets as well as through the Talmud" that the Messiah had come. Nahmanides took up the challenge—"You do not understand Torah and halakah," he at one point said to Paul, "and only a little haggadah." The discussion ranged widely over the familiar passages, some identifying a suffering Messiah, others asserting that the scepter would not pass from Israel. The disputation was later followed by sermons in church, one of them delivered by Raymond of Peñaforte, the Spanish Dominican in the forefront of the thirteenth-century conversion efforts directed at both Jews and Muslims, and another by the king himself, with a circumspect response again by Nahmanides.

It matters little who "won" these encounters, which were not intended, in any event, to settle anything but patently to convert the Jews of Aragon. They signaled that the Christians' free allegorizing of the Bible might suffer in the face of Jewish scholars' rather more sophisticated grasp of the text and its literal sense. Paul himself indicated part of the remedy. A knowledge of Hebrew was increasingly available from rabbis, but Jewish converts would be willing to instruct Christians not only on the Talmud's contents (see II/3) but on the peshat or contextual method of dealing with a text that the Jews had learned from the Muslims. The results are fully on view in the work of Nicholas of Lyra (d. 1340), who more than any other sums up medieval Christian exegesis. This Franciscan from Normandy, a professor at the Sorbonne for most of his career, wrote numerous works on theology but is best known for his enormous *Postillae* or *Notes* on the whole of Scripture, which was probably the most widely consulted text on exegesis in pre-Reformation Christianity and the first to be printed. Nicholas was critical of his predecessors, first because they were often misled by the Vulgate, which at times departed from the Hebrew—he was himself quite expert in Hebrew and showed considerable familiarity with Rashi—and second because they indulged in allegorical exegesis without paying sufficient attention to the literal sense of Scripture. His commentary sought to remedy that, and he had considerable and expert help. Nicholas, it is clear, had carefully read Rashi's biblical commentaries and put the Jewish scholar's learning and approach to good use.

The Reform of Christian Exegesis

The foundations of traditional Christian and Jewish exegesis received their first real textual shocks in the fifteenth century, when humanists like Lorenzo Valla in Italy and Antonio de Nebrija in Spain cast critical eyes on the textual accuracy of Jerome's Latin translation of Scripture (see II/1), followed by the historians' scrutiny of the same texts in the sixteenth century, climaxing in major rationalistic assaults on Scripture in the seventeenth. Martin Luther was well acquainted with the traditional exegesis of the Church, and though he never doubted the divine inspiration of Scripture, he began to recoil from the Church's free and abundant use of allegorical exegesis. He admired the literal approach of Nicholas of Lyra, whom he called "a fine soul, a good Hebraist and a true Christian." "The Holy Spirit," Luther contended, "is the plainest writer and speaker in heaven and earth and therefore His words cannot have but one sense, and that the very simplest sense, which we call the literary, ordinary, natural sense." All heresy, he went on, arose precisely from ignoring the plain, literal sense, "unless," he added, "the particulars of the words compel us not to do so." He then invoked the standard Christian teaching of when precisely the metaphorical sense of a scriptural passage was to be preferred.

Luther was also concerned with the contradictions between the various parts of Scripture, particularly the theological ones, and in some instances was unconcerned to reconcile them. The Letter of James, for example, has a quite different view of the relationship of faith and good works toward salvation, different from the way Luther read Paul and different from Luther's own understanding of the issue (see II/5). As a result, he cast doubts on James's apostolic authenticity (as well as on Revelation, though for different reasons) and relegated it to a kind of apocryphal appendix in his German translation of the New Testament.

The Council of Trent issued the Church's riposte. In its decree of 1546 it defended the authenticity and authority of both Scripture and tradition. Both the Old and the New Testament, as well as the oral tradition that had come down from the Apostles (see II/3), were "accepted and received by the Church with equal piety and reverence." The Reformers were not silenced, however. Luther's successors were insistent that historical context was crucial to a true understanding of Scripture. But these writings remained nonetheless the inspired Word of God, and hence all contradictions remained, for the time being, more apparent than real. Protestants, no less than Catholics, were content to measure the correctness of their interpretation of a given passage in Scripture by its "agreement with faith."

Control of the Book

At stake here was the control of Scripture, the foundation stone on which Christianity, everyone's Christianity, in some manner rested. Before Luther scriptural exegesis was firmly in the Church's hands, and the Christian was bound to follow it in the name of the Church's teaching authority, the posture of acceptance that the Muslims called taqlid. If the Reformers were going to reread Scripture in a different way, some defense had to be made for departing from the traditional way. The Reform slogan *sola Scriptura*, "Scripture alone," meant not only that Scripture was the sole source of revelation but that the new Reformed Christian did not need the Church's prescriptive advice in order to understand the Word of God. What it did *not* mean was that each could read Scripture as he or she wished. Early in the Reform the problem of individual, eccentric, or radical readings of Scripture had arisen, and most of the leaders needed little convincing that if the unity of the community, of the Church, was to be maintained, there had to be a guide. One such guide was the Church itself, as the Catholics maintained, but now more narrowly, and authentically, defined by the Reformers back to the Fathers and the first councils: it was the "modern" Church, the one located in "Babylon," to use a favorite Reformer trope, that had betrayed the truth of Scripture.

Generally speaking, the Reformers preferred history to tradition in the matter of exegesis. That principle was laid out in some detail in the *Key to Sacred Scripture*, a work written in response to the Council of Trent by Matthias Flacius Illyricus (d. 1575). His Latinized name gives him an antique air, but the vernacular name concealed beneath Flacius, Vlacich, places him somewhere in the mosaic of modern "Yugoslavia" on the eastern, Slavic frontier of Latin Christendom. Vlacich was the Reform's pioneer hermeneutical expert and a church historian of considerable acumen (see II/3).

In the opening tract of the *Key*, "On the Proper Way to Understand Holy Scripture," Vlacich lays down the principles of exegesis, or, as it would be called today, hermeneutics (see below). In it he advances the argument that the literal or "grammatical" sense is the proper one yet should be set aside, with grave misgivings, when it makes no sense, and the possibilities of allegoria should be addressed. This is in part a reaction to the broad Catholic use of those "other" readings to give a scriptural basis to its beliefs and practices, and in part an optimistic confidence in the philological tools newly fashioned by the Renaissance humanists. Those humanists now read their classical texts "in context," and Vlacich argues that it is no different—Erasmus, the humanist, had insisted that it was *very* different—with a scriptural text: to understand it, one must understand its historical context or "life situation" (*Sitz im Leben*), as it came to be called by a later generation of investigators.

The way of close textual inspection opened by Matthias Vlacich was broadened still further by the Catholic cleric Richard Simon (d. 1712), though to entirely different ends. Vlacich argued that close analysis could lead to understanding almost all problem passages; Simon demonstrated that such close analysis, which he commended, revealed even more difficulties in understanding and showed that without the traditional teaching of the Church, one could never hope to understand what God was trying to say through his human instruments. Neither of these positions was comfortable to either the Reformers or the Catholics. Both sides were committed to the notion that the sacred texts were divinely inspired and that they could not, correctly understood, mislead the believer. How, then, correctly to understand? Traditional teaching was one answer, narrowly defined by the Reformers, broadly by the Catholics. The infallibility of faith, claimed the Reformers, a quality in the believer, was matched by a "clarity" (*perspicuitas*) in the Scripture; the infallibility of the Church and its tradition, replied the Catholics, alone guaranteed a true understanding.

A Closer, and Different, Look at Scripture

The Renaissance had opened European minds backward onto the old but intellectually vibrant landscape of Greco-Roman antiquity, traditions that appeared learned and at the same time humane and so were regarded with esteem. They were skeptical traditions as well, with a highly relativistic view of religion that was a natural outgrowth of the Greeks' and Romans' polymorphous paganism and their highly rationalized natural philosophy. Some Christian scholars now began to look on their own ecclesiastical tradition through those same somewhat skeptical humanist eyes, emboldened perhaps by the new pluralistic religious world created by the Reformation "settlement" and equipped with a new expertise in languages and history.

In exegesis the fruits of the new learning and new attitudes boldly appear, as we have just noted, in the French Catholic cleric Richard Simon, whose *Critical History of the Old Testament* (1678) is the first modern critical study of Scripture. It created a furor in Christian circles and the Church fairly successfully suppressed it. But Simon was not intimidated. He followed it with a series of works on the text and earlier Christian commentaries on the New Testament, where for the first time the text of the Gospels was subjected to close critical scrutiny, and the authority of the earliest exegetical authorities on the Christian Scriptures was weighed and often found wanting. Though Simon was a theologian, and made no attempt to disguise the fact that his work was primarily a refutation of Protestant claims about Scripture, he came to the Bible and the New Testament with the methods and sensibilities of a historian. The Dutch Jew Baruch Spinoza (d. 1677) was perhaps more a philosopher than a theologian, but like Simon he saw in Scripture a human document—he specifically denied Mosaic authorship—and, in the case of the Bible, a history of a people rather than a record of God's dealings with that people. His theories on the Bible, set out in detail in his *Tractatus theologico-politicus*, led in the end to his excommunication from the Amsterdam synagogue.

Both Simon and Spinoza stand at the beginning of the modern Western treatment of Scripture as a human document, a piece of writing subject to the same conventions of composition as a work of literature and the same rules of authentication as a work of history. Two broad approaches to Scripture developed. Theologians continued the task of exegesis, of extracting God's meaning from the sacred text, but henceforward they were accompanied by—and often heeded—historians and literary critics who thought they detected, in those same pages, the voices of the human authors who had in fact composed them.

Exegesis and Hermeneutics

If exegesis addresses the text, hermeneutics addresses the very notion of exegesis. In its broadest understanding, hermeneutics (< Hermes, the messenger, and so the interpreter, of the Greek gods) signifies interpretation, and Aristotle's treatise on logical meaning is called "Concerning *Hermeneia*." The word retained this broad acceptance for a long time, with the further understanding that it was more about theory than practice. Indeed, one common way of both linking and distinguishing hermeneutics and exegesis was to describe the latter as the practical application of the principles of the former.

Several developments upset that easy systematic relationship of the two terms. First, the humanists of the European Renaissance were learning to read the texts of Greek and Latin authors in closer and more sophisticated ways. Second, the Protestant Reformers, as we have seen, made an important issue of how Scripture was to be read: while the Catholics continued to sustain a broad allegorical approach to the Scriptures, the Reformers tended to stress a more literal and "historical" reading of the texts. But the matter was by no means that simple. The traditional Church from Origen onward had produced commentaries *ad sensum*; the Reformers for their part never left off insisting, with the Catholics, and against the Jews who continued to protest that the plain sense of the Bible was being violated thereby, that the Old Testament was to be read Christologically, or what we have called typologically. As for the New Testament, there was a major dispute among the Reformers on precisely how literally one was to understand the most extreme and explosive of all literal texts, Jesus' well-attested words "Take this and eat; this is my body" (Matt. 26:26, etc.). The Catholics understood it *ad literam ipsam*; some Protestants did, others did not.

Despite the mixed results, the larger issue of how exactly—and why—Scripture should be read, the issue of hermeneutics, had been raised and has never disappeared. The Reformation–Counter-Reformation debate may have been largely fueled by partisan polemics, but later hermeneutics has been drawn into the orbit of philosophical and literary studies and then sent back to the theologians and scriptural exegetes with new and troubling questions attached. The father of modern hermeneutics, and perhaps of modern theology as well, Friedrich Schliermacher (d. 1834), argued that the books of Scripture were not tracts of systematic theology but the products of human intuitions fashioned in particular historical circumstances, an insight that continues to dominate modern readings of Scripture. Hence, one must deal not only with the text in terms of its linguistic expression but also with the mind and intent of the author. These are two of the primary elements of modern hermeneutics: the text as a kind of speech act, and the mental history of the author. To understand the latter, Schliermacher maintained, the reader must somehow transform himself into the author, a task he thought was possible.

That exactly the opposite is likely true was the insight of Martin Heidegger (d. 1976), the German existentialist philosopher who argued that the reader does not find truth in the text—or in the world generally—but in himself. Meaning occurs when a subject encounters an object, in our case, Scripture. The point had a profound impact on the Protestant theologian Rudolf Bultmann (d. 1976). For Bultmann, the truth of Scripture lay in the believer's experience of Christ, the Christ who is in Scripture. But the encounter cannot take place until the reader can get through the contingent elements of the authors' expression. The exegete must, in short, "demythologize" the sacred texts, or, as Bultmann once put it, "to distinguish what is said from what it means and measure the former by the latter."

3

Scripture and Tradition

IF EXEGESIS IS a method of prying open the firmly closed Book of God and finding in its depths solutions to more contemporary problems of behavior and belief, tradition provides the community of believers with an instrument with which to prolong revelation itself, as in fact the three Peoples of the Book have done. What came to be normative Judaism was no more simply a matter of the Bible than traditional Christianity was of the New Testament or Islam of the Quran alone. Each group believed there was more—that certain other texts spoke with the authority of the Book or that certain latter-day people spoke with the same authority as the canonical prophets. And in the end Jews and Christians at least had to face powerful waves of dissent to the existence of a kind of second or supplementary revelation as authentic and authoritative as the first. That same issue continues profoundly to divide both bodies of believers to this day.

The Great Tradition

All three communities of Scripturalists understood the notion of a continued or continuing form of revelation, whether in texts or voices, as received from an older and indubitable source, and so it is fair to describe it as "tradition" (< Lat. *traditio*; Gk. *paradosis*), something handed down or handed over. In English the word is used in the singular to describe a whole range of concepts, from a cast-in-stone practice, to authoritative counsels or exemplary guidelines, to mere customary action, with a semantic inclination toward the latter end of the scale. It is a social tradition, for example, for almost everyone to shake (or kiss) a hand in greeting, and even for atheists to utter "God bless you" at a sneeze. Little survives of the doubtless religious origins of the latter act, but there remain an abundance of genuine religious traditions understood as such. It is (or was) a tradition in this sense for a Muslim to begin formal pronouncements with the Quranic formula "In the name of God, the Compassionate, the Merciful"; for some Christians to incline their heads at the mention of the name of Jesus; and for Jews to avoid even mentioning, or writing, the name of God by inscribing "G-d" or even "g-d" or "g-dess" on the page before them. Major (nonscriptural) holy days like Hanukkah, Christmas, and the Birthday of the Prophet (Mawlid al-Nabi) are chock full of such sometimes pious, sometimes casually secular traditions (see II/6).

Tradition is also used as a collective plural in English, to describe, for example, the sum of customs, laws, rituals, and institutions that constitute the identity of a given group. Neither use, singular or plural—although they have their place in Jewish, Christian, and Muslim society—covers exactly what is mean by "tradition," or perhaps better, "The Tradition" in the context of the three Peoples of the Book. Rather, it may here be defined as a nonscriptural pronouncement, derived from an authoritative source, validated by trustworthy eye- or earwitnesses, transmitted by an authenticated chain of reporters and so absolutely binding on believers as a standard of belief or conduct. This is the Great Tradition of the three monotheistic communities, a foundation stone in the construction of what we call Judaism, Christianity, and Islam. Adherence to it as a standard of belief is part of what constitutes orthodoxy, and, as a standard of action, orthopraxy. Indeed, tradition in this sense—and it is used in this sense throughout—is so much a part of orthodoxy and orthopraxy that the great reform movements in Christianity, and Judaism, which essentially attacked both the authority and authenticity of the Great Tradition, ended by recasting not only the content of prescribed belief and behavior but also the manner in which orthodoxy and orthopraxy are to be defined.

The authority of this elemental religious tradition derives in the first instance from its source. Scripture was primary in this matter. There were traditions before Scripture, at least in Judaism and Christianity, but once the Book was established as the revealed Word of God, it enjoyed what appeared to be an absolute authority for believers: it was what the Quran calls "The Guidance." Tradition, which, as remarked, antedated Scripture and may in fact have eventually produced it, had in the end to carve out its own place in the face of this apparently unique claim of Scripture. In Judaism, and later in Islam as well, tradition is thought to have arisen at the side of Scripture and to have been transmitted through the same source. As the matter was understood by a later generation of rabbis, Moses received two revelations on Sinai, one of which he was commanded to write down, which is our book called Torah, and another, the same but not identical, which was passed on orally and constituted for countless generations of Jews as authoritative a guide to conduct and belief as the Bible itself. A similar conviction arose, as we shall see, in Islamic circles.

Rabbinic Judaism

The double Roman destruction of Jerusalem in 70 and 135 c.e. radically affected the course of Judaism and set it on its path from "politics to piety," as it has been described. Both the temple and even the dreams of state were gone, and out of the doctrinal and cultic diversity of barely a century earlier survived only the Pharisees and their program. The temple priesthoods were rendered moot by their functional impotence. After the year 70 the kohenim were blacksmiths in an automotive world; Hellenistic Judaism and its spirit of accommodation fell into increasing disrepute; militant nationalists were swept away by the Romans; and new messianic claims, whether pacific or militant, fell on deaf ears. The Pharisees escaped the debacle. Note has already been taken (see I/2) of a widespread story of how the chief of the Pharisees, the famous Yohanan ben Zakkai, whose tomb is still reverenced in Galilee, was carried out of the city concealed in a coffin just before the end and reconstituted a Pharisaic "school" first at Yabneh or Jamnia near the coast and finally at Tiberias in Galilee.

The Pharisees, as we have seen, are familiar figures from Josephus, who admired them, and the New Testament, which vilified them. Indeed, the Gospels may be our best source on the Pharisees after 70. Though purporting to describe Jesus' lifetime, the portrait of the Pharisees in Matthew and Luke in particular may be based on their relations with the Jewish Christians in the 80s or 90s, when the Gospels were written. If so, they suggest that at that point Jesus' Jewish followers were experiencing increasing difficulties with the Jewish authorities and that those latter were the Pharisees, who by the end of the first century were in firm and full control of the community.

Although the evidence is spotty and there are anomalies—the rabbis describe what they call the *perushim* (Pharisees?) as a group (somewhat) different from themselves—it still seems safe to assume that the earlier Pharisees had become the rabbis of the post-200 era. If we look back from the perspective of the Talmud, we note the presence, from the Hasmonaeans onward, of an important institution, the Sanhedrin, governed by two collegial heads, the senior *nasi*, who served as its president, and the junior *ab bet din*. This body took responsibility for the community's moral well-being and adjudicated cases of law and conscience that fell within the general competence of the Mosaic Law (see II/4).

The later Jewish tradition recollected the holders of these two chief Sanhedrin offices as "pairs" (*zugoth*), but it is vague on the details of their functions and rulings until about the time of Jesus, when the "pair" of Hillel and Shammai filled the offices and developed distinctive attitudes toward interpreting the Law. The "schools" of Hillel and Shammai dominate legal discussions down to 70, when the Sanhedrin had necessarily to leave Jerusalem and reconstitute itself elsewhere under the leadership of Yohanan ben Zakkai.

These were difficult days for the Jews, and remain so for the modern historian attempting to trace events as dim as they are important. Cultic or temple Judaism, which had its unique center in Jerusalem since the days of David and Solomon, disappeared after the debacle of 70, and the priests, who for long centuries had guided the religious life of Jewish society, were replaced by others.

The community's new leaders, most of whom appear to have been religious scholars rather than political figures or rich landowners, had to rebuild a shattered community on a new foundation.

The new foundation was the Law. It is one of the oldest parts of Judaism's structure, and had long been explained and administered by the priesthood—who also presided over the other foundation stone of Jewish life, the temple ritual. Since the return from the Exile, the Law was being promoted by many, the scribes and Pharisees chief among them, as a central concern of the Jew. Now, however, it became the unique standard of Jewish identity and solidarity. Or nearly so: in these new circumstances the Torah was supported, expanded, and explained by another source of growing authority, the oral Torah or Mishnah.

"How Many Torahs Do You Have?"

We cannot tell exactly when the notion of an oral tradition arose among the Jews. All religious communities seem to have such, and almost from the beginning, but those same communities tend to ascribe greater antiquity to their "tradition" than documentary evidence justifies. The Pharisees were already talking about a "tradition of the fathers" in Jesus' day, and though the contemporary Sadducees denied any authority to such, it is not clear what Jesus' position on such an "oral law" was, if any. Not until "rabbinic Judaism," the religious profile developed by the Jews in the era after 200, do we receive justification for honoring such tradition: it comes down to us in the form of a "foundation story" explaining the existence and authority of this other Torah. Two Torahs were revealed to Moses on Sinai, we are told, one to be written down (our present Torah) and the other an "oral Torah," which was not to be committed to writing and which was eventually thought to contain everything the community would ever need for its information and guidance. This latter Torah passed, still in oral form, from Moses to Joshua, then, according to an account in the Mishnah itself (Aboth 1:1), through various more or less anonymous groups down to the earliest identifiable figures of Second Temple times. This oral Torah was finally written down around 200 and stands behind the particular Mishnah of Rabbi Judah ha-Nasi (d. ca. 217), "the Prince"—there were apparently other mishnahs—which soon gained canonical status equal to the Torah's own (see II/4).

The contents of our Mishnah do appear to represent an oral tradition, edited, arranged, and set down in writing. The trouble is, it does not appear to be an oral Torah, not, at least, in the same sense as the preserved written Torah we call Scripture. The Mishnah is constituted of neither laws embedded in a narrative in the manner of our written Torah, nor a law code in the sense of an organized collection of statutes, nor even an organized commentary on the written Torah's laws. Rather, it seems to be a discussion among lawyers about disputed points of religious law and some of its current interpretations. The time, setting, and circumstances are all unspecified, but the lifetimes of the authorities mentioned stretch back to about 100 B.C.E. There is no preamble in the Mishnah, no mise-en-scène; indeed, the Mishnah begins abruptly in medias res, and the reader—it is doubtful the work was ever intended to be "read" in our sense of the word—has the uncomfortable feeling of entering on a complex discussion already well under way. The discussion sometimes reaches conclusions and at other times simply states opposing positions, often those of the two rabbinical schools of Hillel and Shammai.

Making the Mishnah

Although the Mishnah has been described as the writing down of the oral law, it is probably incorrect to think of it as a written book in the modern sense, not at least at the outset, since none of the sages who commented on it ever refers to a written document. It is perhaps more accurate to suppose that from the time of Rabbi Akiba (d. ca. 135) onward there were in circulation written legal statutes (*halakoth*), some of them fully articulated as such and many inchoate, still embedded in ongoing discussion and debate. When this material had been collected and arranged, it was committed to memory by professional "reciters," the *tannaim*, they were called collectively, and once the whole had been memorized and recited, it was regarded as "published," that is, it possessed a canonical authority. Subsequent additions were made down to the time of Rabbi Judah, the prestigious leader-scholar, who, as stated above, made a new, definitive edition of the Mishnah.

There is some evidence of what did and did not go into Rabbi Judah's Mishnah and why. Statutes cited by Judah's successors but not included in his Mishnah are known generically as *baraita*, or "additional material," and there is, moreover, a rather formal collection of such material in what is called the *Tosefta*, or "Supplement." The author of this latter work is anonymous and his purpose unclear, but the arrangement of the legal material within and its manner of dealing with it presupposes the Mishnah's existence. When we compare the considerably more diffuse baraita with the Mishnah, we can observe what Judah, and probably Akiba before him, had done: compress, abbreviate, and refine a great body of legal argument and discussion.

As we possess it, Judah's Mishnah is divided into six "orders" (*sedarim*) devoted to the most minute details of the laws governing (1) "Seeds" (agricultural produce and the shares of it owed to the priests and Levites); (2) "Festivals" (the prescribed holy days); (3) "Women"; (4) "Damages" (property, damages, and penalties); (5) "Holy Things" (temple paraphernalia); and (6) "Purities" (ritual purity and impurity). To the secular eye, the Mishnah is an extraordinarily detailed casebook compiled by lawyers for their own use and instruction. It deals chiefly with ceremonial practice, much of it already irrelevant to Jewish life in the new Diaspora, and has little to say on matters of ethics, theology, and devotion, with which Jews of that and later ages also concerned themselves. But it must not have appeared incomplete to its editors, who preserved its contents as a testament to a tradition they regarded, in the best Pharisaic manner, as the normative heart and essence of Judaism. The Covenant was the Law, and the Mishnah was the pledge of fidelity to both by a new generation of Jews.

Mishnah and Gemara

We have little idea why particular opinions on precise subjects in the Mishnah were preserved. Presumably they enjoyed some authority—an authority conditioned by the preservation and transmission of other, divergent opinions—in the world in which they were written down. Whatever the case, they quickly did gain authority in the immediately subsequent generations of rabbis, the *amoraim*, or "speakers," who were now concentrated in schools in Galilee—Jews were banned by the Romans from Jerusalem in the wake of the insurrection of 132—and in Babylonia, as modern Iraq was then called in Jewish circles. The amoraim we can identify stretch from Rabbi Judah's immediate successors in the beginning of the third century to the last distinguished members of the declining academies at the close of the sixth century. The body of legal statutes, whether drawn from the exegesis of Scripture or, as in the case of the Mishnah, from recourse to the oral tradition, was now regarded as closed and complete.

Note: Western Christian ignorance of the Talmud and its contents ended in the thirteenth century when converts from Judaism began to reveal its contents to their Christian coreligionists and to suggest that the Talmud's pages abounded in statements blasphemous of Christian beliefs. Consequently, Pope Gregory IX (r. 1227–1241) dispatched warnings to various Christian rulers bidding them to seize the Jews' books and hand them over to the Franciscans and Dominicans (see II/8) for investigation. At the subsequent "trial" of the Talmud held in Paris in 1240, two main charges were leveled at the Jews: first, that they preferred the teachings of the rabbis (the Talmud) to the Words of God (the Bible), and second, that they slandered Christ and Christianity. The charges were sustained by the ecclesiastical court and the Jewish books were publicly burned. In 1247, however, Innocent IV reconsidered the Church's position. Since the Jews had long been granted official toleration by the Church (see I/5), and since their sacred books, including the Talmud, were essential to their faith, they should be permitted to keep and use them, but only after the passages offensive to Christianity had been excised.

The Mishnah, accompanied by its two respective *gemaras*, or "completions," took final form as the two Talmuds, the Babylonian (Judah's Mishnah surrounded on each page by the gemara of the Babylonian amoraim) and the Jerusalem or Palestinian (Judah's same Mishnah, though now embedded in the gemara of the amoraim of Tiberias), the former of which gained a preeminent position of authority. With the Christian appropriation of the Bible—in its Greek Septuagint or Latin Vulgate versions (see II/1)—Jews eventually came to think of the Talmud as their distinctive scriptural mark, not merely because of its increasingly normative authority but by reason of its not being a text shared with the Christians.

Validating the Rabbis

At some point the rabbis of Palestine had begun to formalize the delegation of their powers through the ritual known as "ordination" (*semika*). The semika came to be understood as not merely the delegation of powers but their actual transmission. The handing down of the oral tradition was ritualized, as it had been from Moses to Joshua, by the "laying on of hands" (Num. 27:18). With the textualization of the Mishnah, semika became the extension of that passage to the generations beyond the Mishnah, but once the "chain" of rabbinic ordinations was broken in the fourth century, as all agreed it had, the rabbis' authority changed. The office had appeared to be evolving in the same direction as the Christian episcopate—whose own "succession" crisis did not occur until the Reformation—but then in the fifth and sixth centuries it took a new turn into something quite different. The authoritative rabbinic magisterium became, in the attenuated ordination of posttalmudic times, merely a certification, or licensing, of rabbinic competence (see II/4).

Attacking the Tradition: Sadducees and Karaites

If "Sadducee" means "Son of Zadok," a high priest of the Davidic era, then the Sadducees were likely a priestly party of some sort. Josephus's brief remarks about the Sadducees characterize them as a group that rejected any law not explicitly contained in the Torah. This was a direct denial of the Pharisees' tradition of the fathers. For the Sadducees the Torah alone was revelation, and it should be interpreted in a direct, literal fashion; all else was at best speculation and at worst innovation. This was not an attack on the Law—the priests were, after all, the chief guardians and interpreters of Torah almost from the beginning—but a defense of priestly prerogatives against the Pharisaic extension of the Law via the notion of an "oral Torah" over which they could then exercise control.

We hear this charge once again in Judaism, there urged by a group called the Karaites against Babylonian rabbis of the eighth century. The Karaites were literally "readers"—their name is etymologically linked to "Quran"—who confined their reading to Scripture and attempted to live according to its commandments (*mitzvoth*) and those alone. We do not know how the Karaites managed this in a society already remote from the mores and manner of life of the patriarchal age. Literalism brought freedom from the "derived laws" (*halakoth*; see II/4) of the rabbis, it is true, but many of these latter were not the "burden" sometimes suggested by Christian sources. Rather, they effectively brought the biblical commandments into line with local custom and evolving circumstances, much as the hadith did in Islam. The Karaites' danger to Jewish life as it had evolved in the eighth century was the threat they posed to the power of the rabbis, who by then were the uncontested authorities among the Jews in both the Christian and the Muslim world.

It is doubtful whether the Torah could indeed have served in its literal sense as a normative code for an eighth-century Jewish community, and the version of a Torah society put forward in Iraq in the 760s by the Karaite leader Anan ben David may have foundered on its own literalism. A later generation of Karaites under Benjamin al-Nihawandi, a disciple of Anan, and Daniel al-Qumisi (d. ca. 900) took a different path; they granted each Jew the privilege of being his own rabbi, to construct his own Talmud out of a commonly held Torah. It was, once again, an attractive possibility, and Karaism spread far beyond its Babylonian place of origin to Jewish communities all over the Abode of Islam and beyond. The Karaite intellectual leadership turned away from a discussion of the biblical mitzvoth in what at first seems like an unexpected direction, to philosophical speculation and the allegorical interpretation of Scripture. They may have been following an Islamic lead. As the early Muslim theologians known as Mutazilites had shown (see II/7), Scripture could be controlled as effectively by rational inquiry as by an appeal to tradition. The rabbinic response was, as we have seen, Saadya's appropriation of another weapon in the Muslim arsenal: the contextual interpretation of Scripture.

In Islam there are distinct parallels to the Karaite position in the early Islamic partisans known as the Kharijites (see I/5). This ill-defined group—one hardly knows whether to call them a sect or a political party—attempted to establish a Muslim community and a Muslim way of life based on the Quran, without resort to the "interpretation" of the plain meaning of the text. Again like the early Karaites, they took a severe view of associating with those who did not share their views. The Kharijites put forward their views late in the seventh century, well before the imposing body of hadith and its derived prescriptions were in place, and so they were likely reacting to what they construed as worldly and non-Islamic behavior rather than to an oppressive tradition.

Jewish Reform

In the nineteenth century, in the wake of the European Enlightenment and the Jews' emancipation from the crippling discriminatory legislation that had marked most of their history there, some European Jews attempted to bring their own religious beliefs in line with the new liberal Protestant versions of Christianity. Traditional rabbinic Judaism seemed to many to have sunk beneath the weight of its own tradition. Doubts were cast on the heart of that tradition, the absolute authority of the halakoth and so of the oral tradition generally. These were, the reformers argued, man (i.e., rabbinic) made prescriptions, useful in their own day but retrograde in the enlightened culture that typified nineteenth-century Europe. Reform Judaism began early in the nineteenth century in congregations in Germany, and was carried by many migrants to America later in the nineteenth century.

Other Jews—Eastern Europeans from the shtetl communities of Poland, Russia, and the Ukraine—migrated to America as well. In the New World the contrast between the liberal and enlightened Reform Jews, who appeared very much in the American mold, and the less affluent, less educated, and decidedly more ethnic "Orthodox," as the Reformers disparagingly called them, was even more striking. Reform Jews founded Temple Emanu-El in New York City in 1846—Reform Jews prefer to call their place of worship a temple rather than a synagogue—for their place of worship and the Hebrew Union College in 1875. The Reform program included far more than rejecting the authority of the oral law, of course, and its heart was set out in eight paragraphs in the "Pittsburgh Platform" of 1885. The Reform asserted that the Jews constituted a religion, not a nation, and so rejected Zionism. Like the Christians before them, they accepted the moral laws of the Torah while rejecting most of the dietary and purity regulations. But unlike the Christians and Muslims, they refused to accept a vision of the Afterlife accompanied by reward and punishment.

The Jewish Reform generated its own reaction. "Conservative" Judaism began not as another separation from the rigors of Orthodoxy but as a reaction to the Jewish Reform. It began in Germany in the 1840s over the Reformers' stringent curtailment of Hebrew in the liturgy, which in the minds of some was to push Reform, which seemed to be carrying Western European Judaism by storm, to a point where it was no longer continuous with the Jewish past. For Conservatives, Hebrew was and remains one of the great threads that binds Jews together across the centuries. The dissenters did not disavow the project of Reform—they agreed, for example, that the oral Torah had human origins and that the Bible should be studied critically—but at the same time they undertook to conserve the Jewish ideals set forth in the Law. What authorizes the Law, according to the Conservatives, is the *kelal Israel*, what may loosely be called "catholic Judaism," that is, the consensus of the Jewish people, a notion explored by the great Conservative paradigm Solomon Schechter (d. 1915), professor of Hebrew at Cambridge University (see I/5).

Conservative Judaism, like the Reform itself, found its true identity in the brighter light of America, where all the religious contrasts among of European Jews grew sharper, particularly after the Reformers' radical profession of faith in the "Pittsburgh Platform." Conservative Jews once again had to distinguish themselves from the Reform. It was no simple matter: in 1880, all but twelve Jewish congregations in the United States were Reform. They could have rejoined Orthodox Judaism, an option they formally rejected in 1880; instead, the Conservatives struck out on their own. In 1902 they founded the Jewish Theological Seminary of America—Schechter was an early president—from which flowed a stream of schools that carried Conservative learning and tradition across America.

The Beginnings of a Christian Tradition

Christianity was born and evolved in the same cultural and religious environment that debated the oral law and eventually produced the Mishnah. The Pharisees in fact made the traditions of the fathers a principal element in their definition of what it was to be a Jew. Jesus himself had more than once debated the Pharisees on the authority of the oral tradition, and though he does not appear to have denied the premise, Jesus consistently substituted his own authority for that of the fathers. Thus Jesus was proposing himself as the source of a new tradition (*paradosis*) handed on to his followers and confirmed by the Holy Spirit on the day of Pentecost.

The view that there was a specifically Christian "handing-down" distinct from the Scriptures may have begun with the early Jewish Christian understanding of Scripture as synonymous with the Bible—the Gospels were not paid serious exegetical attention until the end of the second century—whereas the new Christian "tradition" was constituted by Jesus' teachings and redemptive death, both of which Jesus himself had placed in their true "scriptural" context. Thus, even when parts of Jesus' teachings and actions had been committed to writing in the Gospels, and so began to form a new and specifically Christian Scripture, the distinction between Scripture in the biblical sense and tradition in the Christian sense continued to be felt in the Christian community.

The Deposit of Faith

It is clear from the Gospel narratives that Jesus had a distinctly defined—in the sense that everyone knew there were twelve—circle of "apostles" ("those sent forth"), who had, besides their eschatological role of presiding over the restored Tribes of Israel, the more pastoral assignment of spreading the "Good News." They were dispatched to this task by Jesus himself (Matt. 10:5–42). Among the Twelve was a smaller group of three—Peter, James, and John, the latter two the sons of Zebedee—signaled out to be present on special occasions, like the Transfiguration (Matt. 17:1–8). Finally, there was a larger, ill-defined group of "disciples" or followers outside the Twelve (Matt. 8:18, 21). Their number included women—if "were with him" signifies membership in the group, as seems likely—and they supported the movement out of their own resources (Luke 8:3).

Some of these same Gospel texts depict Jesus giving his disciples—which in this context seems to refer to the Apostles—special instruction on the meaning of his teaching, on the significance of the parables, for example. Though Jesus describes that private instruction as "the secret of the Kingdom of God" (Mark 4:11), as that privileged teaching is presently laid out in the Gospels, the parables are explained in what seems a quite ordinary fashion (so Mark 4:14–20), and Jesus' teaching generally shows no signs of genuine esoteric qualities. In any event, the early communities of Jesus' followers looked to the Twelve for authoritative guidance, whether because of their station or because of the understanding they were thought to possess of Jesus' teaching. Christians soon looked on the Apostles somewhat in the manner of Moses on Sinai, in that they had been entrusted with all the knowledge and understanding necessary for salvation, the sum total of what a somewhat later generation was to know as the "deposit of faith."

Apostolic Tradition and Apostolic Succession

The transformation of the Apostles into bishops, from Jesus' eschatological Twelve designated to assume authority over the restored Tribes of Israel into the "overseers" (*episkopoi*) eventually found at the head of each Christian community, is a shadowy and ill-defined process (see I/6), though there can be no doubt it occurred. In the view of those early Christian communities, everything that had come to be called in the second century "the rule of faith" or "the rule of truth" was, in the words of the bishop Irenaeus of Lyons (d. ca. 200), "received from the Apostles and guarded in the Church by the succession of presbyters." This is a clear and forthright statement of the so-called apostolic tradition, which included the correct interpretation of Scripture as well as certain prescribed forms of behavior, and it was explicitly tied to the bishops' being the direct spiritual descendants of the Apostles. This notion of apostolic succession was already formalized about 175 c.e.

The Christian bishops spoke, then, with the authority of the apostolic tradition behind them. At times their voices were single—that of an Ignatius, an Irenaeus, a Basil, or a Chrysostom—but there was also a broad consensual tradition that manifested itself by the bishops sitting in synods or, from the fourth century, in the ecumenical councils of the Great Church, and pronouncing on matters of faith and morals. The bishops in council might refer to Scripture in their decrees, but Scripture was not their justification. And though their common pronouncements were cast in the form of dogma, literally "something decided," the voice was actually that of the apostolic tradition and so of Jesus himself. Once expressed, it suffered no appeal, no change.

By the later Middle Ages, the thirteenth and fourteenth centuries, the Church's theologians had formally recognized three authoritative sources of Church teaching. First was Scripture and what could be directly derived from it. Second were those long-standing beliefs and practices, which, though not found in Scripture, were judged by consensus as going back to the early Church and so might properly be regarded as "apostolic" in the sense of "justified by their universally accepted existence in the apostolic era". Finally, there were the decrees of the Church, what constituted ecclesiastical tradition. In a sense all three had become Scripture since the notion of "inspiration" or divine guidance had been extended, from a very early date, to cover not merely Scripture proper but also the early Church Fathers, the ecumenical councils, and the ordinary teaching of the Church, its magisterium (see II/5), and carried with it the related concept of infallibility. In the end, it was no great stretch to put papal decrees on the same inspired terrain as the New Testament.

Sola Scriptura

Well before Luther there were calls for reform from within the Western Church. Most of these reforming challenges based themselves on Scripture, or, more precisely, they called for a return to the New Testament in the face of practices that seemed to have no scriptural warrant. Pierre Valdès, or Waldo, was a merchant of Lyons who sometime after 1160 had undergone a personal conversion, embraced a life of evangelical poverty and preaching, and commissioned vernacular translations of the Bible and the Fathers. He and his followers, the Waldensians, broke with the Church authorities, who were concerned and frightened by the rising tide of Catharism in southern France (see I/5). The Waldensians appealed to the Gospel as the warrant for their way of life and practices, to which Pope Alexander III replied in 1179 with a reminder that Scripture must be read "according to the Fathers"—that is, in the light of the Church's tradition. From the Frenchman Waldo to the Englishman Wycliffe to the Bohemian Hus there is a straight line with a common theme: less of the Church and more of Christ—the Christ, of course, of the Gospels, not of the theologians and canon lawyers. At first this was a protest without a theology and without protective political cover, but John Wycliffe

(d. 1384) provided the theology, and Jan Hus (d. 1415) faced the Roman Church with the support of a great many fellow Bohemians. Luther in the end had both, a powerful theological voice and the political muscle of the German princes.

Almost from the beginning of his academic career, Luther based his arguments, even in defense of fairly conservative positions, on what he found in Scripture. It was only as his thinking progressed and his positions became more radical that he took to arguing Scripture against tradition. There is no obligation to believe what is not asserted in Scripture or proven by revelation, he maintained, a posture he used to argue against the Church's sacramental system (see II/5). Tradition for Luther lacked the capitalization that has been supplied here: "Tradition is nothing else but the traditions of men," he wrote. In Luther's view Scripture was the sole instrument of salvation since its content is nothing other than Jesus Christ and the Holy Spirit alone is the principle of its understanding.

Far more radical than Luther in adhering to the principle of *sola Scriptura*, "Scripture alone," was the Swiss Ulrich Zwingli (d. 1531), a priest of the Zurich cathedral, who in 1519 resolved to preach solely on the basis of the Bible. He quietly attracted a circle of followers who in 1522 went public with their program of scriptural reform and openly and defiantly ate sausages during the abstinence period of Lent. There was no license for Lent in the New Testament, the reformers argued, nor for the entire iconic apparatus of Catholicism. In 1524 all pictures and statues were removed from the churches of Zurich, and in 1525, the Mass, for which Zwingli also thought there was no scriptural justification, was abolished in the Swiss city where Zwingli now ruled like a prince.

But the early Reformers' position was far from being the sloganized sola Scriptura. They all recognized the decrees of the early general councils—the first six perhaps in Luther's own case—as authoritative Christian doctrine. The Reformers took as authoritative the teachings of the Fathers—it is difficult even to imagine a Luther without an Augustine—but only, they insisted, insofar as those teachings were in accordance with Scripture. Whatever was not in Scripture could be rejected, as in fact was done with the sacraments of Confirmation and the Last Anointing, the tradition-based doctrine of Purgatory (see II/5), prayers for the dead, Church feasts, the cult of images (see II/6), monastic vows, and more.

The Reformation, town by town, city by city, was not merely an attack on tradition and a return to the "pure Gospel" free of the structure of both dogma and canon law that had been erected on it; it also took up arms against the Church's institutions, particularly those seen as enriching the clergy at the expense of the population at large. Benefices, endowed masses, and indulgences all came under attack. Church lands were confiscated, monasteries dissolved, and the payment of Church tithes refused, all, obviously, where they occurred, with the approval of both princes and magistrates, who themselves stood to gain by what was in many German cities an enormous redistribution of wealth. Finally, the Reformers turned on the clergy themselves, their rights, privileges, and exemptions. The Reformation had a strongly egalitarian flavor that in many instances rose from below and in the end affected the Reform princes almost as much as it did the Church.

The Tradition Debate

The Reformation began among university theologians as a reaction, generally speaking, to the intrusion of philosophical discourse into the matter of theology (see II/7). The matter of theology, the Reformers argued, was the scriptural witness, the Gospel of Jesus Christ. The content of that Gospel had become submerged under a language that had subverted it—witness the teaching on transubstantiation—and by an authority that had illegitimately extended it beyond its scriptural limits—witness the teaching on indulgences and the very notion that we the living can alter the state of the souls who now rest at the feet of God's mercy or justice.

On 8 April 1546 the Council of Trent issued its decree "On the Canonical Scriptures," which also addressed the sources of the Church's teachings. It affirmed that the Gospel of Jesus Christ, which is humankind's salvation, is contained in the sacred Scriptures *and* in "the unwritten traditions, which, received by the Apostles from the mouth of Jesus or transmitted by the Apostles themselves under the inspiration of the Holy Spirit, have come down to us, as though passed on from hand to hand."

Bracketing Scripture and tradition was not the council's initial inclination. The original draft of the decree spoke of "the truth (of faith) contained in part in the written books and in part in the unwritten traditions," which would seem to make Scripture and tradition two independent and parallel sources for the rule of faith. The bishops and others at Trent may have been reluctant to do so, hence the changed language, but the Catholic Church later proceeded to do exactly what the earlier draft had envisioned, though never denying the link between the two.

Martin Chemnitz (d. 1586), whose reply to Trent is the most authoritative statement of what constituted Lutheran orthodoxy, admitted seven different types of tradition were in accordance with Scripture. They ranged from the actual message of Christ and the Apostles as a whole down through primitive forms of the creed and ancient rituals to consensus among the Fathers. What Trent seemed to grant, and Chemnitz denied, was the existence of tradition as a formal principle different from Scripture. For Chemnitz in particular and the Reformers in general, tradition had no basis unless formally identical with explicit scriptural testimony.

The War of the Historians

Luther's basic thesis was that much of what passed as the Church's tradition was fabricated by humans and had progressively corrupted the true message of Scripture. Luther and the other Reformers professed to retrieve the true meaning of God's salvific Word by their own rereading of the text, and it fell to the aforementioned Matthias Flacius (see II/2) to systematically demonstrate the truth of the corruption thesis. Vlacich undertook the task in his *History of the Church of Christ*, later called *The Magdeburg Centuries* (1559–1574), whose thirteen volumes were dedicated to tracing the Church's history, century by century, from its origins to 1300. He went even further. His *Catalogue of the Witnesses of the Truth* attempted to demonstrate a line of doctrinal continuity between the apostolic age and Luther. To do so, Vlacich had to find a thread that led through other earlier opponents of Roman ecclesiastical authority, a task that prompted the edition of the works of earlier heretics and the rehabilitation of their reputations. His line of attack occurred on two fronts: he criticized Roman doctrinal authorities like Gratian and Peter Lombard (see II/4, II/7) as overlearned and oversubtle lawyers and theologians who had distorted the sentiments of the Fathers—a bow toward the simple and often illiterate "popular" heretics of the earlier Middle Ages—and at the same time extolled some of the latter, most notably the Waldensians, as more learned than the Church authorities were willing to portray them.

Vlacich had an eminent predecessor, of course: Eusebius of Caesarea (d. ca. 340), biographer of Constantine and author of the groundbreaking *Church History*. One of the points of the latter work was precisely to show the continuity of the dogmatic tradition by tracing the episcopal succession in the various sees of the Church. Vlacich, for his part, was not interested in continuity; his heuristic principles were decline and corruption, which he found on an ascending scale as the Church moved from its pristine era toward its current manifestation.

The *Magdeburg Centuries* and the *Catalogue* gave the Reformers ample historical documentation with which to assail the "tradition" the Council of Trent was offering as an additional or at least a supplementary source of revelation to Scripture. The Catholic riposte to this damaging attack came in an almost identical form, the *Ecclesiastical Annals* of Caesar Cardinal Baronius (d. 1607). Baronius attempted to be as stringently documentary as Vlacich and thereby to demonstrate exactly the opposite thesis—that there was a reliable continuity in the development of the Church's teachings and institutions. The *Annals* was a popular work, much printed. To counter its effects, the Calvinist scholar Isaac Casaubon (d. 1614) produced his *Counter-Baronial Operations*, in which, in the humanist tradition of the times, he attacked Baronius's Latin, Greek, and Hebrew learning in an effort to undermine the entire work.

It is impossible to tally the final score of this historiographical contest except to say the Reform seized and held a considerable piece of the historical high ground. Its more lasting effect, however, may be that all these works put in the hands of preachers everywhere a rich weaponry of historical argument to hurl against the other side in the popular trench warfare where the Reform was fought with particular ferocity.

The Sunna of the Prophet

Muhammad, like Jesus, spoke with authority, not his own, to be sure, but God's and, in this instance, with God's very own words. The Quran was understood by Muhammad's followers as the ipsissima verba Dei, and we must assume that in this case too God's Prophet both volunteered and was requested to explain the sometimes opaque meaning of God's words and will, even to give direction in other matters that were treated more generally, or perhaps not at all, in the Scripture. Muhammad, it is not difficult to believe, was Islam's first and most authoritative exegete and jurisprudent. Nor is it unreasonable to imagine that his respectful and perhaps awestruck contemporaries remembered his words of personal guidance and explanations with some of the same fervor and fidelity as they remembered his announcement of the words of God.

There was in circulation a century or so after Muhammad's death in 632 a growing body of reports (hadith—in English the Arabic term is increasingly used as both a singular and a collective plural) that purported to record a saying or act of the Prophet. Though distinctive in form, they appear in very varied contexts, as the building blocks in what has become the biographical tradition concerning Muhammad, for example, as bits and pieces of the Muslims' earliest attempts at interpreting the Quran, and finally, and very consequentially, as a guide to Muslim behavior. Taken together, these latter hadith were understood to constitute the custom or customary behavior (*sunna*) of the Prophet in the same manner that individual tesserae are assembled to constitute a single mosaic. By the end of the eighth century the "sunna of the Prophet" was being put forward as nothing less than the archetype of Muslim behavior.

In the Muslim context, a hadith or (Prophetic) tradition may be defined technically as a report handed down, generally though not exclusively orally, by trustworthy witnesses concerning a saying or an action of the prophet Muhammad and so providing an authoritative guide to permitted and forbidden action or belief. Such a tradition is normally made up of a "chain" (*isnad*) of transmitters and the text (*matn*) of the matter being transmitted.

Once the hadith began to be accepted as common currency in the lawyers' attempts at fashioning a body of Islamic law—recourse to the custom of the Prophet began to carry as much weight as the Quranic proof-texts themselves—such traditions not unnaturally began to multiply: supply went out to meet demand. Collectors fanned out across the entire Abode of Islam in search of these precious nuggets and returned to the great legal centers in Iraq, Syria, and Arabia with their heads crammed with hadith. The enormous amount of material collected on these "hunting expeditions" was obviously quite inconsistent in quality. There were mutually contradictory traditions, those with incomplete chains of transmitters, and others with multiple weaknesses. The reports themselves contained material that ranged on occasion from the trivial to the superstitious, or was transparently Jewish or Christian in origin. A great many were overtly and outrageously political in their inspiration, like the hadith that have Muhammad praising his uncle Abbas, a very late convert to Islam but, more consequentially, the ancestor of the then reigning dynasty in Baghdad.

Note: The need to authenticate the hadith by investigating their isnads and establishing at least the possibility that the tradents named in that chain transmitted the report in question, one to the next, led to the collection of a staggering amount of biographical information and the creation and growth of one of Arabic literature's most prodigiously rich genres, the biographical dictionary. The earliest of them, Ibn Saad's (d. 845) *Book of Classes*, shows the initial impulse behind such works. The lives in it are all of transmitters of hadith and are arranged according to the "classes" of the title, each representing one generation after the Prophet. The work opens with a biography of the Prophet himself, then moves on to the Companions of the Prophet, and proceeds down to the author's own day, with the later, ever larger classes sorted by the place of their activity. This is a large work, with more than 4,250 entries, and the biographical data was patently arranged for the benefit of the isnad investigator since each tradent in the chain was thought to represent a single and successive generation.

From Ibn Saad the genre quickly expanded to embrace almost all conceivable categories of Muslims, from poets to physicians to famous natives of Baghdad. In the ninth century Ibn Saad's somewhat cumbersome class organization yielded to a more coherent alphabetical principle, at least to the extent that all transmitters of the same first name were grouped together. Not until the thirteenth century was full alphabetical order observed, although the Muhammads were often put first. As might be imagined, these biographical dictionaries, taken as a whole, preserve an enormous amount of information on Muslims from one end of the Abode of Islam to the other and represent an unexploited database of inestimable historical value.

Many in the ninth century began to criticize the rising tide of hadith that was threatening to drown Muslim jurisprudence. Some resorted to mockery, while others, like the new rationalists in Islam who accepted the Quran as revelation but were averse to an authoritatively traditioned explanation to revelation (see II/7), lodged even more trenchant criticisms against the hadith. To resolve the obvious difficulties of the tradition system, scholars devised a critical method for studying hadith that would enable them to sort out the "sound" from the "weak" hadith.

Hadith Criticism

In their earliest form the hadith appear to have been offered with little more validation than "I heard it said that the Prophet, upon whom be peace . . ." or "I heard from X, to whom it was reported that the Prophet . . ." With the multiplication of Prophetic reports, however, and the consequent jostling over their recognition as a basis of Law, credentialing hadith became more explicit and the Prophetic traditions were eventually cited with a fully articulated chain of transmitters that extended from the most recent tradent, or transmitter, one who "hands down" (< Lat. *tradere*), backward to an eye- or earwitness among Muhammad's own contemporaries, the generation later canonized as the *sahaba*, or Companions of the Prophet.

Were the Companions of the Prophet and the other tradents in those chains reliable reporters? The question sounds historiographical, and to some extent it was: were X and Y in the same place at the same time, to enable them to pass on the story? Those and similar historical questions could be and were answered in some considerable detail.

> **Note:** The Companions who stand at the eyewitness base of every hadith have been defined as any adult Muslim—though some wished to remove the qualification of adult—who had some sort of contact with Muhammad. The total number varies widely. One authority tallied them at 100,000, while Ibn Hajar (d. 1448), the Cairene scholar and judge who devoted himself to collecting every shred of evidence on the Companions, published critical lives of 12,267 individuals who qualified, 1,522 of them women. The number of Companions to whom sound hadith are actually attributed amounts to no more than 1,060, however. Even this figure is misleading. Five hundred related only one such report, and only 123 are credited with having witnessed twenty or more. At the very top of the list is a certain Abu Hurayra, whose chief claim to fame is that he related 5,374 hadith. Close by is Muhammad's wife Aisha, who is credited with 2,210.

When the medieval Muslim spoke of reliability, he was referring as much to moral probity as to circumstances of time and place. Was the tradent the sort of person who was trustworthy in this important matter of Prophetic reports?

The consensus among Muslims was that the entire first generation of Muslims, the Companions of the Prophet, enjoyed that probity *as a class*, that they were in fact absolutely trustworthy witnesses to and reporters of the hadith (see II/7). The Companions of the Prophet may have enjoyed an ex post facto infallibility in the eyes of later generations of Muslim lawyers, but they were in fact and in theory mere eyewitness reporters of the words and deeds of the Prophet. There was no Pentecost and no laying on of hands at this critical point in the Islamic tradition.

The Canonical Collections

Criticism concentrated, then, principally on the isnad, and by the mid–ninth century the investigation had proceeded to the point where the newly authenticated hadith could be brought together for lawyers' use. That they were in fact designed for lawyers is manifest in the earliest collection, that by al-Bukhari (d. 870), called *The Sound Collection*. All the hadith in it—2,762, discounting repetitions, of an alleged 600,000 investigated—are certified as sound with respect to their isnads and so usable in matters of law. To that end they are arranged according to their applicability to the categories of jurisprudence, ninety-seven in all.

> **Note:** Non-Muslim Western scholars first encountered the hadith in the nineteenth century when they took up critical-historical investigation of Muhammad's life. The Muslim biographies of the Prophet are composed at base from hadith, though here they are historical rather than legal in content and are arranged chronologically rather than categorically. From the outset, there were doubts about their authenticity and soon Western scholarship turned its full critical attention to the question, particularly of the legal hadith which had reportedly been sifted free of forgeries. The results were and remain overwhelmingly negative: according to Western critics, the great bulk of the hadith, "sound" or otherwise, appear to be forgeries and there is no reliable way of determining which, if any, might be authentic historical reports from or about Muhammad. This judgment may be the single most important bone of contention between modern Muslim and Western scholarship on the origins of Islam.

Bukhari's collection was soon accorded canonical status in Islam and was followed over the next decades by the work of a scholar named Muslim (d. 875) and four other similar and equally authoritative collections. Taken as a whole, the six collections of hadith represent the body of traditions accepted as authentic, and so juridically binding, by Muslim legal experts of the second half of the ninth century. In them the description of the sunna of the Prophet, and so the blue-print for a Muslim life, was essentially complete. Beyond these canonical hadith the Muslim had to be guided by advice, his piety, or his sectarian leanings.

Of the authors of the canonical collections of hadith, Muslim is the most forthcoming in explaining his methods in separating the reports before him into various categories of acceptability. The first are the sound, whose trans-mitters are both morally upright and intellectually skilled; their transmitted hadith show no signs of contradiction or misrepresentation. The second class, generally called good, are those transmitted by individuals of equal character but somewhat lesser learning. Finally, there are the suspect hadith, also called weak or infirm, whose content gives them away because they totally diverge from what reliable tradents have passed down. These transmitters have not discriminated in passing on their received material—consequently a good deal of forged or even heretical material has entered the hadith corpus—or else they have yielded to the temptation of enhancing a report.

Quran and Sunna

Eventually the authority of the Prophet's sunna, and so the hadith that trans-mitted it to succeeding generations, came to be protected in another, quite extra-ordinary manner. We have already seen in the Jewish tradition how Moses was thought to have been given two Torahs on Sinai, the written one that became Scripture and an unwritten or oral one that formed the foundation of the Mishnah and thus of normative rabbinic Judaism. Something similar occurred in Islamic circles. Here too the point of departure was a remark in Scripture. Quran 3:164 announces that God has conferred a great blessing on the believers by sending them a prophet "to teach them the Book and the Wisdom, whereas previously they had been in manifest error." One strain of the Muslim tradition saw in the distinction between the Book and Wisdom the difference between the written tradition that was the Quran and the oral trad-ition that was the sunna. In fact, one hadith says quite explicitly that Gabriel revealed the sunna to Muhammad and taught him its meaning just as he had the Quran. The sunna was, in effect, revelation as surely as the Quran was.

> **Note:** The possibility of Jewish influence on hadith's elevation to the status of the Quran has been raised, by non-Muslims needless to say. Muhammad himself may have been aware—and disapproving—of the Jewish oral Torah tradition, or so Quran 3:78 can be read. The second caliph, Umar (r. 634–644), is reported by Ibn Saad to have prayed an en-tire month on whether to allow the hadith to be written down and then

> (*continued*)
>
> to have said, in what is almost certainly a reference to the Jews: "I re-
> member a people who wrote down a writing and they turned to it and
> forgot the Book of God." The early (unavailing) warnings against writ-
> ing down the oral tradition were, in any event, equally strong in both
> traditions.

As might be imagined, the consequences of equating the sunna and the
Quran were considerable. They were tersely and strikingly summed up in a
famous Muslim legal aphorism of the early ninth century: "Sunna decides
Quran; the Quran does not decide sunna," or, even closer to the bone, "The
Quran needs the sunna more than the sunna needs the Quran." Both sentiments make perfect sense: the reports credited to Muhammad in the hadith
would necessarily explain or complement verses already revealed in the Quran,
and hence this interpretation, the Prophet's own, not some other imagined
exegesis of the Book, should be followed. Shafii (d. 820), the most influential
of the early Muslim jurists—it was he who first glossed "Quran and the Wisdom" (Quran 2:129, 151, 231, etc.) as referring to the twin pillars of Quran
and the sunna of the Prophet—tried to express this in legal terms. A hadith
may simply reaffirm or complement what is already in the Quran. Or it may
render specific what is in the Quran only in general terms, the exact times of
prayer, for example, or the precise terms of the alms-tithe. Finally, and here is
where Quran and sunna are treated equally as revelation, there is the case
"where the Prophet establishes a sunna (a custom) about which no part of the
Quran has been revealed."

If the sunna of the Prophet, which is normative in the matter of the Law
(see II/4), unfolded in word and deed at Mecca and Medina under divine
guidance, it follows that the hadith that severally express it must be regarded
as a form of revelation. Generally, traditional Muslims have not shrunk from
this identification, though some have attempted to distinguish between the
Quran's direct and verbal "revelation" (*wahy*) and the more subtle and suggestive
"inspiration" (*ilham*) given the Prophet in other circumstances. If nothing
else, the stylistic and lexical difference between the Quran and the hadith
is unmistakable. It remained a distinction without a difference, however. In
legal terms, the sunna of the Prophet was a full partner with the Quran in
prescribing Muslim behavior.

The Shiite Hadith

Among the Shiites the Tradition in the technical sense in which it is used here
has been as important as in Sunni Islam—albeit with a profound methodological difference. In the Sunni view, the hadith transmit only the sunna of the

Prophet, whereas for Shiites the category broadens out to include not only the Prophetic hadith but also those instructions and illuminations attributed to the twelve Imams chosen by God to guide the community as "executors" after the Prophet's death (see I/8). These Imams were part of the Prophet's earthly family—through the marriage of the first of them, Ali, to the Prophet's daughter Fatima—but also his spiritual descendants. Each of them possessed a share of what later, somewhat more esoteric Shiites called the "Muhammad Light" and so represented a type of ongoing revelation in Islam.

With the concealment of the twelfth Imam in the ninth century, the teaching power among the Shiat Ali had passed into the more mortal hands of certain of that last Imam's surrogates and, more consequentially, into the hands of a new Shiite class of jurisprudents who set about constructing their own version of Islamic law (see II/4). Their chief building materials were the hadith or reported sayings of their Imams. The Shiites reject a number of the Sunni hadith because they were transmitted by the same unreliable Companions of the Prophet who chose Abu Bakr over Ali as the head of the umma; they prefer the dogmatic utterances of the various Imams. Indeed the Prophet's hadith and those of the Imams appear together, and so are given parity, in the Shiite collections.

Shiite Imam traditions, which have much the same form (isnad and matn) and quality as Muhammad's own, multiplied as rapidly, and as suspiciously, as had the Prophet's, and Imam hadith were eventually subjected to the same kind of critical scrutiny as the Sunni hadith. Just as in Sunni Islam, there emerged from this scrutiny what came to be regarded as canonical collections of sound traditions, that is, those whose chain of transmitters had stood up to the investigation of biographers and historians. The four principal tenth-century collections, when there was a Shiite-leaning dynasty of sultans "guiding" the Sunni caliph in Baghdad, are those of al-Kulayni (d. 940), Ibn Babuya (d. 991), and two by al-Tusi (d. 1067), all of which became canonical for Shiites. The best known was probably al-Kulayni's *Sufficiency on the Science of Religion*, which presented the Shiites with a basic collection of some sixteen thousand hadith that provided the groundwork for a Shiite jurisprudence.

4

God's Law and Its Observance

THE TRADITION OF A SOCIETY governed by law is very old in the Near East, and where societies were governed by rulers whose powers were intimately bound up with divine descent, designation, or approbation, the distinction between secular and religious law is not easily or even profitably made. The Israelites were unusual in that their law came directly from God and not from some god-king: Moses was simply a prophet. But otherwise, the oldest parts of the Bible contain legal codes similar in detail to those found among the Babylonians and Canaanites.

Purity and Defilement

The Israelites, whose obligation to the God of Abraham had previously been limited to his exclusive worship, manner unspecified, and the circumcision of every male on the eighth day after birth, were given a detailed code to regulate almost every aspect of their lives. It was called Torah and was given to Moses on Sinai, the Bible tells us, in the summary form of ten commandments on two stone tablets, and then, over the remainder of Exodus and the entirety of Leviticus, Numbers, and Deuteronomy, in quite extraordinary detail, though with overlaps and repetitions. God now described precisely how he wished to be worshiped, when, where, and through whom (see II/6). There were extended lists of foods that might not be eaten. Crimes and their punishments were described. And finally, the Israelites were commanded to render themselves holy (see I/4), chiefly by keeping holy the Sabbath, avoiding ritual defilements or taboos incurred by physical contact with impure objects—the so-called fathers of impurity (e.g., a corpse) or persons (e.g., a leper)—or being the subject of certain almost inevitable but nonetheless defiling acts like menstruation, bloodshedding, and intercourse, most of which seem to have to do with the willing or unwilling "leakage" of vital fluids.

Ritual impurity, for all the attention devoted to its avoidance, is not, however, sin; indeed, the most common occurrences of it are contracted by activities that are obligatory like burying the dead, praiseworthy, like childbirth and intercourse, or natural and unavoidable, like menstruation. None of these cases suggests the slightest moral taint. And even though some defilements can be contracted by deliberately immoral acts, like eating certain fats or blood (Lev. 7:22–27), or having sex with a menstruating woman (20:18), ritual impurity is more of a taboo, a dangerous state, it has been suggested, because in some fashion it threatens God. People in that state were under the strictest injunction not to enter the temple (Lev. 12:4; 15:31; Num. 19:13).

Though many such taboos were removed with "the setting of the sun," that is, the end of the day, the most common method of freeing oneself from ritual impurity was washing. The ritual bath reserved for such purposes is called a *miqveh* (Lev. 11:36), which in the Bible is simply a "collection" of water, though its modalities were later explored at length by the rabbis. The paradoxical nature of the taboo is perhaps best illustrated by the fact that the fairly common impurity arising from contact with a corpse could be removed only by a complex procedure involving the slaughter and burning of a "red heifer" whose ashes were mixed with water, then poured over the person with the corpse pollution. The person so "washed" was rendered clean, but everyone connected with the preparation of the ashes was rendered impure.

Violations of these rules of purity and defilement were subject to severe punishments including banishment from the community and even death, though these were generally commuted to something less drastic by the rabbis. Expiation for the offense could be made by certain prescribed sacrifices ("sin offerings").

Biblical Law

Biblical law is, like all other law, a pattern of prescribed behavior. It differs from its secular counterparts because these prescriptions and prohibitions are believed to have come from God, notably in the revealed Scripture. In the Jewish case, the sending down of the law to Moses on Sinai completed the Covenant that had been made long before between Yahweh and Abraham on behalf of the latter's descendants. But although religious law comes from God, it is not limited to what is explicitly expressed in God's words. Jewish law, collectively called Torah and sometimes Halakah, is of two general types. The first comprises the mitzvoth, the explicit commandments set down in Scripture, all 613 of them, in the form of both positive commands and negative prohibitions. The second is the halakoth, the laws "extracted" or "derived" from Scripture. The latter are always thought of as drawn forth from revelation, never as human-made, since in all three religious traditions only God can "make" law. In Judaism the halakoth are derived chiefly by rabbinic exegesis and are justified either by the theory of the double Torah (see II/3) or by the conviction that later Jewish juridical bodies inherited Moses' authority—just as the bishops did the Apostles' (and thus Jesus') in Christianity. But unlike what occurred in Islam (perhaps because of very different political circumstances), the rabbis themselves did not hesitate to make a third kind of law called either a "decree" (*gezerah*) to "protect" already existent mitzvoth or halakoth or an "enactment" (*taqqanah*) framed for commemorative purposes or to advance the common good.

> **Note:** A modern example of a gezerah is the prohibition posted at the access ramp to the temple mount in Jerusalem advising Jews of the chief rabbi's ruling that entry into the area is forbidden. Presence in the temple precincts required varying degrees of ritual purity, including the very highest in the Holy of Holies; since it is no longer certain where those zones begin or end, it has been judged prudent that no Jew enter in order to protect the sanctity of the whole. A taqqanah, in contrast, permits members of the Israel Defense Force to enter that same area for security purposes, a particularist but understandable parsing of the common good and one previously explored in granting permission to fight on the Sabbath.

It may have been Deuteronomy, the last of the great legal tracts included in the Bible, that was reported to have been "discovered" in the temple in 621 B.C.E. during Josiah's reign (2 Kings 22:8–23:3). There was almost certainly some editorial retouching of the codes after the Exile, but the text of the pentateuchal Torah was by then effectively complete, and it was generally understood that there would be no more absolute scriptural ordinances or mitzvoth in the post-Exilic era. What we have thereafter in place of the direct written testimony of the earlier period is circumstantial evidence for continued legal activity among the Jews, namely, the obvious existence of a functioning society; presence in it of a class of scribes (*soferim*) devoted to the study of Scripture, part of whose activity must surely have been legal in nature; and the existence from Maccabean times onward of the popular and influential sect of the Pharisees, whose chief ideological and behavioral preoccupation was the Mosaic Law. But for all this we know of no derived laws or halakoth that can be unhesitatingly attributed to either the scribes or the Pharisees.

The Lesson of Qumran

In attempting to understand the Jewish legal tradition between the Exile and the beginnings of the Talmud, one might turn in two other directions: to Philo and to whatever legal evidence can be elicited from the Dead Sea

Scrolls. Not much can be gleaned directly from Philo, the Hellenized Jewish intellectual of Alexandria, since he was not much interested in the halakoth as such. Yet his life's work was a commentary, from his own Hellenized philosophical standpoint, on the legal books of the Bible, and so it is possible to understand at least something of his view of the Law's positive precepts—those concerning the Sabbath, for example. His practice, or rather, his preaching, seems altogether unexceptional: Philo appears to have shared the general Jewish understanding of biblical law and its observance. The Dead Sea Scrolls, in contrast, have provided a new and unexpected glimpse into the evolution of Jewish law. Although the community was admittedly sectarian—most identify them with the Essenes of Philo and Josephus—there was probably no truly "normative" Judaism in the centuries just before and after the beginning of the Christian era (see I/1). The Qumran Covenanters, and so their view of halakah, may fruitfully be compared with other contemporary Jewish views of the Law and its derived positive prescriptions.

The Qumran community, like most other Jewish groups, derived its laws from an exegesis (midrash) of Scripture (see II/2), yet made no reference to or use of a theory of oral law like that (later?) proposed by the rabbis. Indeed, the Essenes at Qumran did not hesitate to write down and publicly promulgate their exegetically derived halakoth. When it came to exegesis, they did, however, draw an interesting distinction. In the Qumran view, all law was contained in Scripture, including the Prophets, and though some precepts flow from a plain understanding of the text (peshat), other "hidden" precepts can be derived only by the special understanding possessed by the Sons of Zadok.

Like the Essenes of Qumran, the contemporary Pharisees were deriving legal prescriptions by recourse to another principle, the tradition of (or from) the fathers, or the oral Torah (see II/3 and below). But the oral Torah was knowledge in the public domain, whereas the privileged exegesis of the Sons of Zadok stood closer to a *gnosis*, a secret understanding granted only to a few adepts (see II/10). As will be seen, many Sunni Muslims operated on the Pharisaic model of law derived from a public "tradition" rather than on the Essene one; the knowledge possessed by the Shiite Imams stood much closer to the "understanding" enjoyed by the Sons of Zadok. And yet, the community at Qumran showed little actual divergence from what we know of contemporary Jewish practice, just as Shiite law in practice differs little from its Sunni counterpart.

The Tradition from the Fathers

Post-Exilic Judaism is absolutely consistent in deriving its positive law directly from Scripture, narrowly from the Torah, and somewhat more widely, on occasion, from the Prophets as well. Essenes, Pharisees, and Hellenizers, as later the rabbis and still later the Karaites, all turned to God's revealed Word for instruction on the good to be done and the evil to be avoided. They differed, of course, on how literally or broadly the scrutiny (midrash) of Scripture should range, but not on the fact that Scripture was the fount and origin of the Law. Fundamental disagreement arose over whether there was any *other* source from which religious law might be derived. The Sadducees, Essenes, and Karaites denied that there was; the Pharisees, followed by the rabbis and the main body of medieval and later traditional Judaism, affirmed the existence of a tradition from the fathers that was an equally authoritative matrix of halakoth.

The genesis and evolution of this tradition is overgrown, like much else in the study of revelational religions, with claims of absolute antiquity: "from the fathers" meant at base from Moses and so, in consequence, directly from God. The claim for such was being advanced in the first century by the Pharisees, as both Josephus and the Gospels bear witness, yet was denied explicitly by the contemporary Sadducees and implicitly by the Essenes. It has long been assumed that the Pharisees' tradition from the fathers was in fact the unwritten Torah subsequently alluded to in the Talmud (see II/3). The notion of an oral Torah that claimed to reproduce the exact words of halakic prescriptions given to Moses may have been, as some have thought, the creation of the rabbis who reconstituted the foundations of Jewish life in the dark years after 70 c.e. It does not follow, of course, that those legal traditions have no claim to antiquity, although how ancient they might be we cannot guess. We are on somewhat firmer ground in tracing the redaction of those traditions from oral to written form as the Mishnah.

The Mishnah and the Two Talmuds

As we have seen (III/3), the Mishnah is a collection of discussions concerning the halakoth or derived laws that was assembled, according to tradition, by Rabbi Judah ha-Nasi and put into circulation sometime around 200 c.e. It is sometimes referred to as a code of Jewish law, but it fits into that category only with difficulty. A law is *codified* when it has been arranged according to some principle of order, for example, when all the statutes on one subject (blasphemy, purity, divorce) are collected together. It appears that several different law codes, like the "Holiness Code" in Leviticus 17–26, were integrated into the opening five books of the Bible (the Pentateuch or "five [not so easy] pieces," as it has been called).

Beneath its general divisions into orders, the Mishnah's further organization often seems haphazard and arbitrary; it lacks the kind of logical arrangement one expects in a legal code. More, the lawyers' discussions incorporated in the Mishnah are free-flowing and often not conclusive. Objections and variant opinions unfold in what gives more the appearance of the minutes of law professors' debates than the record of legislative opinion, or perhaps an extraordinarily detailed casebook compiled by lawyers for their own use and instruction.

As we have seen, the Hebrew Mishnah received two separate sets of Aramaic commentary (*gemara*) in the generations following Rabbi Judah, one at the hands of the newly emergent schools in Babylonia, and another in the Palestinian academies. The sages who labored over the gemara were known, in contradistinction to the earlier reciters (*tannaim*), as speakers (*amoraim*). Their function was essentially to explicate, reconcile, and expound the inner logic of the halakoth enunciated by their tannaitic predecessors.

Though neither of the two Talmuds was intended to be, nor ever became, the final word on Jewish law, the respect given to both derived from the fact that they were the products of a scholarly and legal consensus at a time when the academy (*yeshiva*) and the religious court (*bet din*) guided the fortunes of Judaism without peer or rival. But no matter how great its authority, neither Talmud was a legal code; they were rather shorthand transcriptions of convoluted discussions concerning legal questions that occupied lawyers from the second to the sixth century of the Christian era.

Two Jewish Codes: Mishneh Torah and Shulkhan Aruk

The disengagement of the halakoth from the surrounding discussion, debate, and speculation did not occur until well into the Islamic period of Jewish history. The procedure was taken up and continued among scholars who lived in the rapidly expanding Jewish community outside the Abode of Islam, and at a time when the former paramount authority of the Near Eastern academies was flowing to new centers and new scholars. Only two examples need be cited here. The *Mishneh Torah* of Moses Maimonides, written in Cairo and completed in 1190, although not the first such, is a genuine code produced by a scholar who belonged to a larger intellectual tradition than that of the Talmud. Maimonides was a first-rate philosopher and theologian schooled in both Greek rationalism and Islam's sophisticated legal traditions. His *Mishneh Torah* reflects both those strains in its introductory discourse on the modes of knowledge and the foundations of Judaism, its logical arrangement of the halakoth and its exclusion of what Maimonides judged to be irrelevant or nonlegal material.

Maimonides' view of the Law was to a large degree determined by his political theory, much of which derived from the Muslim philosopher al-Farabi (d. 950), and through him from Plato. For Maimonides no less than for al-Farabi, the prophet was both philosopher and lawgiver. By his surpassing intelligence, he had attained—or been granted (there are important nuances here)—eternal truths, and by the power of his imaginative faculty, he converted them into law. Law, then—the revealed Law—had the twofold aspect of regulating life and society, just as human law did, and of embodying the same absolute truths that the philosopher struggled to achieve.

The Torah, in Maimonides' view, possessed this same double purpose: to order society and to bring humans to an understanding of the highest truths. It had, in sum, an ethical and a religious purpose. To concentrate exclusively on the first, as many talmudic scholars did, was simply to enter the grounds of the royal palace without going inside. To understand the Torah's second and more profound intent, Maimonides argued, one must penetrate deeper into the mysteries of revelation through allegorical exegesis; this is one of the purposes of his *Guide for the Perplexed* (see II/7). Elsewhere, Maimonides is far more direct, and presents in dogmatic form the articles of faith necessary for salvation, thereby formulating the nearest thing Judaism had to a formal creed (see I/5).

Maimonides provides some guidance on the Torah's ethical intent as well—guidance that must have sounded alien indeed in a traditional yeshiva. In a remarkable passage in the *Guide* (3.32), he compares God's indirect yet purposeful working through natural causes in the universe with his similar activity for moral ends among humankind. Moses was given the Law to modify pagan custom for the better, and so provide a bridge from idolatry to a belief in the unique God. Maimonides supports his contention with considerable documentation, since he had available what passed in his day for an authentic description of pre-Abrahamic Aramaic paganism. The Law appears, then—and most clearly in its cultic and sacrificial aspects—to be a transitional and ameliorative instrument rather than final and perfect, at least when viewed from a historical perspective.

This was not a widely shared view, but even among the traditionalists the Talmud was not looked on as a legal system frozen in permanent stasis. A generation before Maimonides a French scholar, Rabbi Solomon ben Isaac (d. 1105), now generally known as Rashi, had written an immensely learned and exhaustive commentary on the Talmud that cast new light on its meaning and interpretation (see II/2), and other scholars continued to render legal *responsa* to Jewish communities all over the European continent and the Islamic empire. Maimonides had ignored much of this new legal material in his somewhat idealized version of the Law, but other, later attempts at codification were more responsive to the changing circumstances of Jewish life. One such code eventually gained a position of almost absolute authority, the *Shulkhan Aruk*, or *The Table Set*, of Joseph Karo (d. 1575), the eminent lawyer and Kabbalist of Safad (see II/9). But no authority was absolute in the face of the Torah and the Talmud, and the *Shulkhan Aruk* underwent its own revisions, chiefly in the form of deferential glosses and commentaries.

The Purpose of the Law

The ongoing Jewish attempts at codification may have been in part affected by
contact with the sophisticated codification tradition of Roman law. But an
even earlier generation of Jews, the first to come in contact with Hellenism in
the centuries just before the common era, had been prompted by similar contact with an alien tradition to concern themselves with the *purposes* of the Law.
Then as now, rationalists thought they could discern behind God's Law some
purpose useful or necessary for humankind. The dietary laws and circumcision
were favorite topics for such speculation, that the former, for example, really
embodied principles of good nutrition and the latter served as both a protection against disease and a curb on sexual desire, a view particularly attractive to
Christian moralists. Others were not so sure and thought that at least some of
God's commandments, like his order to Abraham to sacrifice Isaac, had no
purpose other than to test human obedience. The Sabbath regulations—and
the Ramadan fast when Muslims began to concern themselves with the
same issue of purpose—were thought to fall into that category, though more
modern sensibilities have found a day of withdrawal from ordinary cares
psychologically useful and a month of fasting salutary for the health.

The Administration of Jewish Law

We know far more about the content of Jewish law than we do about its application and the administration of justice among Jews. There was always in
post-Exilic Judaism an authoritative body, generally called the Great Sanhedrin,
that both legislated and judged. Its head was the nasi, who both before and
after the destruction of the temple possessed extensive legislative powers in
his own right (see I/6). Even after the Pharisees introduced the notion of an
oral legal tradition whose validation went back to Moses, the nasi did not
cease enacting the positive legal prescriptions called gezeroth and taqqanoth.
The first had, in fact, a Pharisaic justification in that such positive enactments
provided "a fence for the Torah"—that is, by surrounding the Torah with additional prescriptions, they guaranteed the observance of the explicit Torah
commandments or mitzvoth. But eventually a gezerah came to mean any
"tightening" legal enactment that was not a traditional rabbinic legal prescription (halakah), whereas the taqqanoth referred more properly to "loos-
ening," the creation, for example, of new institutions whose purpose it was to
improve the conditions of social, economic, and religious life.

The legislative and judicial process was not confined to the nasi and his
court. He could by "ordination" (*semika*) delegate his powers to individual
rabbis so that they too could adjudicate disputes at law and issue binding

enactments. There was no such ordination among the Babylonian Jews, and if some of the early Babylonian rabbis went to Palestine for ordination, the result was to strengthen the authority of the yeshivas where they taught and not that of the Babylonian exilarch, who was their nominal leader. With the disappearance of the Palestinian patriarchate in 425 c.e. under Christian pressures, the Babylonian model began to prevail in Palestine as well: the rabbis could adjudicate and legislate on their own authority.

The Rabbis

We have noticed the contest between kings and priests for leadership in the community after the Jewish return from the Babylonian Exile. The contest was rendered moot, however, by the destruction of both the temple and the kingdom by the Romans in the first century c.e. Thereafter the rabbis, the spiritual and methodological descendants of the earlier scribes and Pharisees, without serious competition from within—at least not until the rise of the Hasidic movement (see II/8)—controlled the religious and social life of Jewish communities within both Christendom and the Abode of Islam.

Functionally speaking, the rabbis were a relatively small group of "religious virtuososi" who administered Jewish law for Jewish communities that had been granted a certain degree of self-government by their political sovereigns, the Romans in Palestine and the Sasanians in Iraq. This law, like its later Islamic counterpart, the sharia, had chiefly to do with personal status, and dealt with matters of marriage, inheritance, and the transfer of property. But the writ of the rabbis did not end there. In legal matters their word was law, and by their carefully cultivated prestige they influenced a broad range of religious and ethical matters.

It is difficult to underestimate the rabbis' importance for the continuity of the Jewish tradition. Judaism was precisely tradition, the handing down, in both spirit and letter, of the Covenant. The biblical account of that process smoothes over, perhaps, the enormous difficulties in both establishing and maintaining Jewish continuity. We do, however, have graphic evidence of the difficulty when the Bible account ends and the historian can confront unedited testimony to the bewildering variety of Jewish sects and factions that prevailed in Palestine and the Diaspora in the years that followed the Maccabees, the Herods, and the Romans (see I/1). The collapse of Jewish political expectations and the destruction of the Jews' unique place of liturgical worship were events of extraordinary magnitude in the life of the community.

Some Jews turned, as we have seen, to more radical expectations in this world or the next, to zealot nationalists, messianic claimants, Gnostic reflexes of eschatological hope or historical despair, or the attractions of Hellenic assimilation. Not the rabbis: quietly, patiently, they rebuilt a shattered Judaism on the foundations of the Law. The historian may cast a doubtful eye on their claim to represent an unwritten tradition going back to Moses himself, but that claim was accepted in the end by the great body of Jews, and the rabbis used its authority to expand, modify, and define the Torah for a new age.

The Instruments of God's Justice

There were good biblical grounds for the appointment among the Jews of both religious courts (*bet din*) and judges to sit in them. Note has already been made of the Sanhedrin, which in its juridical functions was known as the "Great Bet Din" and was presided over by the ab bet din. There were lesser courts as well, whose members were probably originally appointed by the Sanhedrin. When the Great Court, which had met in the temple, moved to Galilee in the post-70 era, authorities there maintained some control of the judicial process through the ritual laying on of hands to signify the delegation of their powers, including their judicial functions, to others. The power of such delegation rested solely with the rabbis of Eretz Israel. As the prestige of the Palestinian community declined—hastened, no doubt, by the Roman withdrawal of their recognition of the patriarch (nasi) as the head of the Jewish community early in the fifth century—ordination eventually ended and the dispersal of rabbinic authority began, to the advantage of the rabbis of Babylonia.

With the end of ordination, the rabbis began to assume an immediate authority of their own, namely the permission to teach, somewhat in the manner of the later masters in European universities. The rabbi's power now lay not in appointment or delegation but in his acknowledged mastery of the Law. The yeshivas became the centers where competence was assured and so power bestowed. Rabbis now possessed the magisterium, and with it went, since there was no other competent office, the authority to judge. Thus, in the end, the rabbis administered justice but only in their respective communities and more by consent than by statute, by the consent of their own Jewish constituents and the tacit or explicit consent of their sovereigns, whether Christians or Muslims.

Jesus and the Law

To return to the first century, the Gospels present Jesus as an observant Jew in a manner that was probably common to most Jews of his day: he kept the Sabbath, for example, participated in the temple liturgies, and likely observed the dietary laws. But these same accounts also portray a Palestinian Jewish milieu in which the Pharisees' preoccupation with the halakoth is very much in the foreground. Jesus clearly did not share some of the Pharisees' more detailed views on how close Torah observance should be: whether one may violate the letter of the Sabbath rest to perform an act of compassion (Mark 3:4–5), for instance, or whether ritual purity was a higher value than winning souls to belief. These are debatable questions, surely, but a more profound question lingers of how the messianic Jesus or his movement stood generally with respect to the Torah. We cannot be sure if the question arose in this form during Jesus' own day or, equally likely, if it was prompted by his later disciples'— most notoriously Paul's—suggestion that the Torah belonged to the past, but Jesus is made to answer it rather precisely. He had come not to abolish the Law but to complete it and, as he explained, "not a letter, not a stroke will disappear from the Law until all that must happen has happened" (Matt. 5:17–20).

The matter was far from simple, however, since the context of Jesus' remarks on the matter of Torah is often messianic. Different norms prevailed or, as his followers later realized, *were* already prevailing, rendering the historic Torah problematic. When asked why his disciples were not fasting, for example, Jesus famously replied, "Can you expect the bridegroom's friends to fast when the bridegroom is with them? As long as they have the bridegroom with them, there can be no fasting" (Mark 2:19–20). The remark strongly suggests at least some degree of Torah suspension in the light of the messianic era. Yet that apparent suspension of the Law has to be matched against other passages where Jesus seems to be issuing his own mitzvoth. "You have learned that they [the Israelites] were told, 'Do not commit adultery.' But what I tell you is this, if a man looks upon a woman with a lustful eye, he had already committed adultery" (Matt. 5:27–28) extends the sin from the act to the intent. When asked if it was permissible for a man to divorce his wife, Jesus answered that Moses had permitted divorce "because your minds were closed." But there was a more profound commandment, Jesus announced: "What God has joined together, man must not separate" (Mark 10:2–9).

Christians and the Law

Not all Jesus' followers construed the advent of the messianic age as abrogating either the mitzvoth or the halakoth—witness the example of James and the Jewish Christians in Jerusalem—but Paul did. In his Letter to the Romans and elsewhere he argued fiercely and at length, occasionally with personal ambivalence, that the establishment of a New Covenant meant that the Mosaic Law both as a general concept and as a collection of specific precepts was no longer binding on the Christian who had found his manumission from sin not in observance but in redemption.

In his Letter to the Romans, Paul worked out a fairly systematic understanding of Jesus' death as a salvific event. The sacrifice of the Son of God on the cross brought freedom to humankind (Rom. 5:12–7:25): freedom from death and sin (5:12–21), freedom from the old self (6:1–23), and finally, freedom from the Law (7:1–25). In Galatians (3:19–25) Paul had offered a preliminary attempt at resolving the Jewish Christian's relationship to the Torah. Before their faith in Jesus, such Jews were "prisoners in the custody of the Law." And then, changing the figure, "The Law was a kind of tutor (*paidagogos*, a slave attendant) in charge until Christ should come, when we should be justified through faith; and now that faith has come, the tutor's charge is at an end." The teacher is no longer required; he has been discharged. In Romans he takes a closer and more nuanced look. Again, the argument is part judicial, part analogical. The law, any law, binds only the living; the Christian has died in Christ. Switching roles, the Christian has become like a widow who, at the death of her husband, is freed of her marriage obligations. She has found a new spouse in Christ, and a new obligation: "to serve God in a new way, the way of the spirit, in contrast with the old way, the way of a written code"—the Torah (Rom. 7:1–6).

The musings continue, though now, somewhat oddly, in the first person: "Except for the Law I should never have become acquainted with sin" (7:7). The Law gave form and shape to sin, even a kind of life: "Sin found its opportunity in the commandment," since what was previously only a (dim?) matter of conscience now became fully explicit. But the trouble is not in Torah; it is in humankind. The human will agrees with the Law, but "I do not what I want to do but what I detest." The Law is spiritual but humankind is not. "In my inmost self I delight in the Law of God, but I perceive that in my bodily members there is a different law, fighting against the Law that my reason approves and making me a prisoner under the law that is in my members, the law of sin" (7:21–23). For Paul, the conclusion is clear: "What the Law could never do, because our lower nature robbed it of all potency, God has done by sending His own Son in a form like that of our own sinful nature and as a sacrifice for sin" (8:3).

A Law for Christians

The Gospels are a form of early Christian preaching that preserve Jesus' teachings on various matters of general morality—in a Jewish context, of course—as well as specific behavioral precepts. Given the circumstances, Jesus could teach rather than prescribe, but thereafter, and soon thereafter, the Church that followed had to organize and regulate what was emerging in the first generation of Jesus' followers as a Christian life. Whatever confessional form the Church has taken, its activities from that day to this have been devoted in large measure to the same end, to converting Gospel into a way of life that, in its external behavioral aspects, is Law.

Jesus' sacrificial death, as Paul declared, bought freedom from sin and from its necessary corollary, the Law. But though ontologically "saved" by Jesus' redemptive death, the Christian still had to live in the world and in the end to appear "before the tribunal of Christ, to be repaid with good or evil for the life he has lived" (2 Cor. 5:10). That life is governed, as Paul says, by "the law of Christ" (Gal 6:2; 1 Cor. 9:21), and throughout his letters he attempts to lay down both guidelines and statutory halakoth of this "law of Christ" that must now govern a Christian life. Many of Paul's instructions list virtues to be pursued and vices to be avoided by the Christian (e.g., Gal. 5:19–23; 1 Cor. 5:10–11, etc.), and differ little from what can be found among Greek moralists and contemporary Jewish teachers. There is no revolutionary social teaching here (1 Cor. 7:20–24); Paul's radical side appears in his instructions on sexuality and marriage. Finally, the elders and overseers of the early Christian community, like Timothy and Titus, were urged to show the same dual concern for faith and morals. Faith there must be, but faith alone would not suffice. The Christian, no less than the Pharisee, had to hold himself apart from the practices of the pagan world that surrounded him, to live, as Paul was ever fond of saying, "in Christ."

As Jews, Jesus' earliest followers seem oddly unconcerned, in the Acts of the Apostles, for example, with either their own relationship to the Torah—how persuasive were Paul's arguments?—or with formulating a new behavioral code of their own. Their own eschatological expectations may have reduced the urgency of such concerns. But norms and rules did eventually emerge, particularly as the anticipated end of the world receded into the more remote future, and what may have been the original community's short-term eschatological ethics were gradually replaced by the long-term institutionalization of praxis that has been termed Early Catholicism. As we have seen, Paul had contented himself with setting down some general guidelines under the heading "don't behave like the pagans," but a formal Christian society did not appear until after the third-century persecutions that had forced many Christians underground. Constantine and his successors legislated paganism out of existence—the last indigenous *pagani* ("hillbillies," "outbackers") disappeared from the Roman Empire in the sixth century; thereafter all the pagans were outside the frontiers, where the Church pursued them with missionaries. At the same time, the Church's bishops—or perhaps they were Constantine's— who convened at Nicaea in 325, and who were understood to possess the magisterium, undertook on a grander, Church-wide scale what had already begun in local episcopal synods. They issued decrees called "canons," behavioral yardsticks to regulate the actions of both the clergy and the laity of the Church.

The Sources of Christian Law

This emerging law of the Church derived from a number of different sources. There was in the first instance Scripture, with its guarantee of divine authority. In some instances behavioral prescriptions were stated as such in the Christian Scripture, whether as a mitzvah by Jesus himself, in the matter of divorce, for example, or by one of the other "apostolic" authorities, notably Paul, collected in the New Testament. There were many additional commands and prohibitions, of course, in the Jewish Bible, what the Christians now called the "Old Testament," but not all were binding in the new Christian dispensation. Paul had made no distinctions in his dismissal of the Torah as the no longer pertinent Old Law, and so one of the earliest and most difficult tasks of Christian exegesis was disengaging from the biblical text what remained, pace Paul, in force in the Church and what did not.

The authority of Scripture extended forward beyond the New Testament onto the earliest Christian writers, the authors whose orthodoxy was unquestioned and whose understanding of the apostolic tradition was recognized by all. These came to be regarded as the Church Fathers, accepted in both East and West (see II/2). Their theological writings were combed in search of normative teachings that might be incorporated into the Church's statutes. The authors of these latter statutes were groups or individuals whose authority derived not from their understanding of the apostolic tradition but their collective or individual office. Collectively the chief "legislative" instrument for making the Church's statute law—though they would never have confessed to "making" law but merely to enunciating it—were the bishops sitting in council, whether locally, regionally, or, more persuasively and authoritatively, as a conclave of the whole Church—the ecumenical councils that began at Nicaea. These bishops represented the "orthodox consensus" that prevailed throughout Christendom down to at least the sixth century. They promulgated canons as well as doctrinal norms in their creeds, and though they might cite Scripture or the Fathers in support of their pronouncements, their authority came from the understanding that they operated, like the Evangelists themselves, with the guidance of the Holy Spirit.

At the same time the ecumenical councils were meeting and regulating belief and behavior for Christians, the emerging authority of the bishop of Rome (see I/6) prompted the appearance of a new notion in the Latin Church: the decrees of the councils, whether provincial synods or ecumenical councils, were not authoritative until approved by the pope. The popes accepted decrees of many local councils, local in the sense that they included only Western bishops under the jurisdiction of the bishop of Rome, and they too began to be regarded, at least in the Latin Church, as "great councils."

Papal authority was most formally expressed in a bull, so called from the Latin *bulla*, "seal," since the document in question was sealed in a particular way. Originally it was sealed in wax with the papal ring, but later various leaden or wax seals were used. The document itself was an official declaration of the pope on a doctrinal matter affecting most or all of the Church. It was usually named from the first two or three words of its Latin text. Somewhat less formal was the decretal, a papal letter that generally expressed a papal ruling on some matter of Church discipline. The collection of the decretals, some of them dating back to the fourth century, is one of the foundations of canon law (see below) in that these decretal letters expressing the papal will constitute precedent for all future rulings.

The Codification of Church Law

The legal material produced by the councils continued to accumulate with each new synod, but not until Emperor Justinian (r. 527–565) sponsored an authoritative codification of Roman law in his *Corpus juris* did the Church attempt to put its own juridical house in order. The Antiochene lawyer John, later the patriarch of Constantinople (r. 565–577), drew up his *Collection of Ecclesiastical Canons*, the antecedent of all later codes of canon law, in which the conciliar enactments were arranged by subject matter rather than chronologically by council. As a further innovation, he introduced into his collection certain patristic regulations, canons drawn up by St. Basil, for example. Somewhat later John brought together all those civil laws of Justinian that pertained to religious matters.

Justinian's translation of religious questions into civil law was in no way extraordinary. The process had begun as early as Constantine, who had legislated on the Sunday rest, celibacy, and divorce. Far from usurping the Church's judicial prerogatives, Justinian's legislative work openly and officially recognized the parity of civil and canon law in a Christian Roman Empire: aphoristically put, whatever the ecclesiastical canons forbid, the civil statutes also forbid. The Church was accepted as a legislative partner of the state, just as earlier bishops had been granted the right to hear certain civil law appeals. Indeed, by the time of Justinian, the Christian bishop had became a major administrative official, and was frequently used as a check on the unscrupulousness of secular functionaries at all levels of provincial administration. The bishop had the power to force officials to perform their duties, and he had to be rendered an account of public funds. He reported to the emperor on local conditions, and in his own community the bishop was an ex officio member of the election board and one of the group of four notables whose task was to supervise baths, granaries, aqueducts, and bridges.

The Beginnings of Western Canon Law

Very early on the bishop of Rome had begun issuing his own statutes in the form of written responses to inquiries or requests for judgment from other bishops. These papal responsa, sometimes to individual bishops, sometimes to regional inquiries, were, as stated above, called decretals. The earliest dates from 385. With the pope's growing authority, they too began to be regarded, along with the conciliar canons, as a source of Church law. Thus there grew up in the West a body of statute law that constituted the basis for a legal tradition: books of collected canons and decretals, schools in which to teach them, and lawyers produced by those schools to explicate and enlarge them.

The canons collected under Justinian were merely the first step in a long process. In the West the second step was long delayed by the collapse of the old order under repeated barbarian invasions, but by the beginning of the eleventh century, the Church's legal tradition revived and three of its most prominent and influential new collections of canons appeared. Two were by bishops and were prompted by pastoral concerns and an attempt at renewing and reforming the Church; the third grew out of a new interest in law as such. The collection of Burchard, bishop of Worms, which appeared about 1015, had about seventeen hundred different canons arranged topically in twenty books—the earlier, chronological arrangements were becoming increasingly unwieldy—and was compiled for the education of the clergy of Worms, though its wide diffusion points to a far more general need. The *Decretum* or collection of canons by Ivo, bishop of Chartres (d. 1115), followed by a broader based *Panormia* were likewise prompted by pastoral concerns, although they were also more sophisticated. There was now more commentary, more concern with reconciling contradictory canons: whether a canon was irrevocable or not and whether dispensations should be granted under certain circumstances.

Gratian

Between the *Decretum* of Ivo of Chartres and the 1140 collection of the jurist Gratian, also called the *Decretum*, the pope had made a highly consequential declaration. In 1075 Gregory VII proclaimed that in all matters the bishop of Rome was the supreme legal authority in the Church, and that not only the laity but all bishops and priests were subject to his jurisdiction and his authority. Gratian's collection of canons, whose full title is *The Concordance of Discordant Canons*, thus became in effect the law of the entire Western Church. The *Decretum* was hardly the work of a bishop whose concerns were chiefly pastoral or administrative; Gratian was a master jurist, trained in and influenced by the new school of Roman law at Bologna.

The *Decretum* has two main parts. The first is arranged in 101 divisions (*distinctiones*), beginning with twenty authoritative pronouncements on the nature of the law—natural law (see II/5), human law, Church law, the law of princes, enacted law, and customary law are all passed in review—as well as the sources of the Church's law. These are followed by twenty further distinctiones on the functions of the Church's various offices. The second part is made up of thirty-six hypothetical "cases" (*causae*) that raised specific difficulties. Each case was followed by a presentation of texts from the Fathers, councils, and popes that might resolve it, or not. The second part also includes what appear to be two free-standing tracts on the complex subject of penance (see II/5) and the consecration of sacred things, what the Mishnah calls *qaddushim*. A whole system of sacramental jurisprudence developed out of the latter; baptism and marriage, for example, were now viewed primarily as contracts, with the rights and obligations of each side set forth in detail.

In the post-Gratian era in Western Christianity, the Church's law almost entirely supplanted Scripture as the primary basis for moral judgments. In 1234 Pope Gregory IX formally completed Gratian's work with the *Five Books of Decretals*, in which all previous papal pronouncements were collected and edited by Raymond of Peñaforte. Additions by Boniface VIII (1298), Clement V (1317), John XXII (1325), and a miscellany called *Communes* (to 1471) followed. From 1491 on, these were printed as a single collection of canon law accompanied by the standard commentary (glossa ordinaria) on both Gratian's *Decretum* and Gregory's complementary *Decretals*. Gratian's work nonetheless continued for centuries to be the basic study text for canon lawyers.

Canon law in a sense defined the Latin Church as an organization since it governed almost every aspect of its life from its most general beliefs to the smallest and most prosaic details of human activity. Even after the Reformation, the new confessional churches that emerged from the medieval Great Church (see I/6), whether Lutheran, Calvinist, or Anglican, quickly had to develop their own codes of Christian conduct and their own ways of instructing the faithful in them.

Catechesis and Catechism

From the New Testament onward, various forms of the Greek verb *katechein* are used to describe an elementary form of Christian instruction (so Gal. 6:6), and soon afterward the noun *katechesis* emerged as a technical term for the initiatory instruction given to candidates for admission into the Church. Catechesis was normally given by the local bishop during Lent, and then the catechumens, or "those under instruction," were admitted to baptism on the Holy Saturday preceding Easter. The word "catechesis" never lost its wider meaning, however, of instruction in the rudiments of the faith.

In the Western Church the Latin *catechismus*, or "catechism," served as the normal translation of *katechesis*, "instruction in the faith," but in the fourteenth century "catechesis" and "catechism" began to be differentiated. The former continued to mean "instruction" but in the increasingly book-oriented society, "catechism" was used more and more to describe the textbook or manual by which this instruction was imparted. The book was to be used by the instructor, to be sure, since those being catechized were still only rarely literate. With the invention of movable type, the catechism became quickly and firmly rooted in the printed book tradition. These printed catechisms or "brief compendia," as they were sometimes called, were invariably presented in four parts: the creed, the sacraments, the Ten Commandments, and prayer.

The catechetical genre took on a new life in 1520 when Martin Luther, who was already breaking with the Roman Church, published in German his *Brief Form of the Ten Commandments, of the Creed, and of the Lord's Prayer*. The scriptural commandments were pointedly moved in front of the statement of the Church's own theological beliefs, while the sacraments, though not entirely omitted, were reduced to "Supplements," at least with regard to Baptism and the Eucharist. In 1529 Luther took the principles enunciated in his *Brief Form* and reproduced them in a German booklet titled the *Small Catechism*—it was later followed by a more diffuse *Large Catechism*—which almost immediately became what has been called "the most typical and influential statement of the Protestant faith."

Luther's enormously successful *Catechism* provoked two notable responses. The first was by the Swiss Reformer John Calvin, whose *Catechism* appeared in Geneva in 1541. He rearranged the order somewhat—the creed once again came first—and adopted a far more didactic and prescriptive tone. This new way of life was still being formulated and Calvin did not hesitate to lead rather than urge the believer to it. As he himself put it in a letter to the English government in 1548, "There ought to be a common formula of instruction for little children and ignorant people that serves to make them familiar with sound doctrine. . . . The Church of God will never be preserved without catechesis."

The bishops who gathered at Trent in 1545 recognized, as had Luther before them, that ignorance was an enormous problem among Christians and that Luther had been far more successful than the Church in addressing it with his *Catechism* directed at a popular and largely unlettered audience. There had been earlier replies to Luther's highly effective works, chief among them the catechism composed for German Catholics by the Jesuit Peter Canisius (d. 1597) in one version for college students, another for adolescents, and a third for mere beginners. But the Council of Trent wanted something more definitive. It talked about an official catechism off and on through its long sessions, but not until 1566, two years after the official closure of the council, did the *Catechism for Parish Priests by the Decree of the Most Holy Council of Trent and published by Command of Pius V, Supreme Pontiff* actually appear. It was published the next year in Germany, with Canisius's supervision, under the title *Roman Catechism*, by which it was thenceforward more generally known. In most respects the *Roman Catechism* followed the traditional form: its four parts covered the articles of the creed, the sacraments, the Ten Commandments, and the Lord's Prayer, though now, thanks to the Reformers, with a distinct effort to locate all its teachings in Scripture.

An Islamic Catechism: The Pillars of Islam

The Quran is part kerygma or preaching—this is particularly true in the Meccan suras, where the point is conversion—and part instruction, where the Book lays out, sometimes generally, sometimes specifically, what it is to be a *muslim*, one who has submitted to God. The picture of what makes up a Muslim life grew far more detailed at Medina, where Muhammad was the head and authoritative guide of a Muslim community in being, an umma now free to practice its beliefs in public. We have already seen some of the general circumstances surrounding their institution (see I/3). The Quran provides some specifics regarding prayer, almsgiving, and fasting for the believers, who had, in addition, the practical example of the Prophet himself to guide them. Later generations filled out the picture, based on the preserved recollections of the Prophet's sunna (see II/3). From this emerged the Pillars of Islam, a summary statement of what constituted, in very broad terms, the obligations of the Muslim:

1. The profession of faith (shahada): "There is no god but The God, and Muhammad is his envoy" (*la ilaha ill'allah wa Muhammad rasul Allah*). The first part is a straightforward affirmation of monotheism; the second, of the validity of Muhammad's mission and message.

2. Prayer (salat), that is, formal prayer with prescribed words (mostly quranic) and gestures recited at five prescribed times daily in any decent place and facing Mecca. The noon prayer on Friday is to be said in common, hence the need of a prayer place or mosque (see II/6).

3. Alms-tithe (zakat), the annual payment of a percentage of the value of one's property—the percentage varies according to the type of property—for the support and succor of the umma's poor and needy.

4. Fasting (sawm) during the twenty-eight days of the lunar month of Ramadan, a time rendered sacred by the sending down of the Quran. The fast is understood as a complete abstention from food, drink, and sexual activity beginning at first light and continuing until sunset.

5. Pilgrimage or hajj, the performance at Mecca and environs of certain prescribed ritual acts on the eighth, nineth, and tenth of the lunar month of the hajj (Dhu al-Hijja) (see II/6).

Women's performance of religious duties are limited by two general considerations. Domestic duties (e.g., the raising of small children) are typically regarded as exempting women from ritual obligations. Monthly impurities also prevent women from participating in ritual acts. Women may not attend the mosque or even fast during Ramadan while menstruating. They are not, in any event, often seen at public prayer, and if present, are in a restricted or remote area of the mosque.

Although the Pillars of Islam became the point of departure of a vast body of prescription regulating Islamic behavior, they reflect neither the tone nor the urgency of Muhammad's message, particularly of the earliest revelations. The Meccan suras of the Quran have a dramatic eschatological emphasis, expressed now in commercial terms and now in the vivid images of Jewish and Christian apocalyptic. God who created the world will also be its judge. When the Day of Judgment comes, accompanied by chaos and confusion, the Lord of the World will open the accounts of all humankind and reckon each at his or her worth. For those who have gravely sinned or hoarded their goods out of meanness of spirit, there awaits a fiery Gehenna of extreme suffering. But the magnanimous person who has submitted his will to God and committed her goods to the needy and downtrodden will be rewarded in a garden paradise of luxurious ease and splendor. Indeed, this is why the Prophet was sent, to "warn" humankind that the reckoning was close at hand.

Sharia, the Muslim Way

To pass from Justinian to Muhammad, who was born only a few years after the death of that emperor, is to move from the well-lit domain of a millennial tradition of Roman law codes and all the apparatus of a sophisticated legal scholasticism to the shadowy domains of unwritten tribal custom and a society in slow and uncertain transition from the nomadic to the sedentary life. The Quran battles against the customs of the era of ignorance (*al-jahiliyya*), and its Medina suras in particular are filled with prescriptive enactments in an attempt to give form and shape to a new, specifically Muslim way of life. To the non-Muslim scholar, the enactments in the Quran might appear to be Muhammad's taqqanoth, the creation of new institutions to improve the conditions of social, economic, and religious life. But they were, in the eyes of the Prophet who delivered them and of his fellow Muslims who received them, nothing less than the words of God and hence genuine mitzvoth, absolute scriptural injunctions.

Implicit in all Muhammad did and preached was the notion that there was an Islamic "way" (*sharia*), which resembled the Jewish and the Christian way in that it came from God, and which stood in sharp opposition to both the religious paganism and degenerate tribal custom of the contemporary Arabs. But the Islamic way was no more explicit and formal than the random precepts of the Quran that defined it, and at Muhammad's death, God's revelation was ended and the Quran had become forever a closed Book. At that very moment, however, the Muslim community, endowed with only the most rudimentary religious and secular institutions, was poised at the beginning of an immense military and political expansion that would carry it within a short space of time from Spain to the Indus.

The Islamic law or sharia constituted the prescribed pattern of Muslim behavior, and originated in only one ground, God's will. Sharia is made available to its intended beneficiaries either through his formal revelation in the Quran or mediated through the instruction or example, in short, the customary behavior of his chosen Prophet, Muhammad. But neither the Quran nor the Prophetic sunna are themselves sharia; the divine commands and prohibitions must be lifted or extracted from either or both. Law that is simply lifted from either of those two venues is formulated from the precepts lying, without ambiguity or contradiction, on the face of the text. All else must be extracted from beneath the received words.

Not all of the Quran is given over to legal matters. By one count, only 350 verses, or somewhat less than 3 percent of the received quranic text, is legal in content. These verses have been further broken down, with some disagreement on details, into 140 on dogmatic and devotional matters like prayer, fasting, pilgrimage, and the like, 70 on questions of personal status (marriage, divorce, inheritance, etc.), 70 more on commercial transactions (sales, loans, usury), 30 on crimes and punishments, another 30 on justice, and a final 10 on economic matters. This is merely a material description. Not all these verses are in the form of explicit commands or prohibitions, and there are overlaps and even contradictions among them, the latter of which have to be resolved either by exegetical harmonizing, that is, by showing that the contradictions are only apparent, or else by invoking the principle of abrogation, whereby a later command cancels an earlier (contradictory) one (see II/1).

There is no explicit statement in the Quran that the Prophet's sunna has the normative value of the Book itself, but there are strong hints that this is so, as in Quran 4:80: "He who obeys the Prophet obeys God." (Compare also the somewhat more oblique 53:3 and 59:7.) Islam's lawyers eventually came to agree that the Prophetic sunna too constituted ground for sharia. But in the extensive body of legal hadith, too, some directives were explicit, some required extraction, and a considerable number of conflicting or contradictory hadith likewise needed resolution.

The analytical study of Islamic law is, then, a critical enterprise requiring both skill and finesse, and it has trained and exercised the minds of most Muslim intellectuals from the ninth to the nineteenth century. The discipline is called *fiqh*, jurisprudence—its practitioner is a *faqih*; plural *fuqaha*—and it is devoted to two chief tasks. The first is the inspection and validation of the grounds of sharia, not merely the Quran and the authenticated and consensually validated sunna of the Prophet but the more problematic area called "personal effort" (*ijtihad*) where the experts cease to be text-tied exegetes and take wing into the empyrean of interpretation supported only by analogy and logic. Second, Islamic jurisprudence undertakes to work out the application of the law in its various "branches." It is here that fiqh also calculates the specific moral gravity of human acts (see II/5).

From Prophetic Tradition to Law

We possess only the vaguest idea of how the Muslims conducted their legal affairs in the first century after Muhammad's death. The recognized head of the umma, the caliph (see I/8), was also regarded as the community's chief judge (*qadi*), as Muhammad had been, and he delegated this judicial power to others in the provinces of the new Islamic empire (see below). But how the qadis rendered their judgments to other Muslims—Muslim justice applied only to Muslims; Jews and Christians continued under their own juridical traditions—was probably on the basis of local custom, caliphal instruction, their own understanding of the Quran, and perhaps an embryonic sense of an Islamic tradition (see II/3).

Some found such pragmatic and even secular arrangements in God's own community unsettling, and out of that dissatisfaction, which was reinforced by political, financial, and tribal disenchantment with the current dynasty of Muslim rulers, there arose in certain traditionist circles—the notorious "partisans of hadith"—the first debates over what it meant to be a Muslim and to pursue an Islamic way in all its ethical and legal implications. The results are sketchy, but to validate their conclusions the early pioneers in Muslim jurisprudence appealed not only to the Quran, as might be expected in a revealed religion, but increasingly to the sunna of the Prophet. The latter was by no means the only or even the chief method used to fashion the norms of Muslim conduct at that point; legal scholars could still resort, in certain cases, to local custom or the exercise of their own legal discretion.

One jurist would not have it so. The Egyptian lawyer Shafii (d. 820) argued for the absolute priority in Islam of the custom of the Prophet over that of Muhammad's contemporaries and followers, no matter how well intentioned or pious the latter might have been. Further, he maintained, with great consequence, that the Prophet's sunna was authentically contained in the great body of reports transmitted by those who had lived and worked with him (see II/3). And what of the Quran, God's own Word? Shafii had already faced the issue: the Quran never contradicts the traditions, but the traditions from the Prophet explain the Quran. No sunna ever contradicts the Quran; it merely specifies its meaning.

In the traditional Islamic view, then, the Quran was Scripture, whereas the sunna of the Prophet and, by extension, the consensus of the umma that was presumably reflected in the same sunna, was tradition—but not in the sense of customary law nor in the charismatic sense understood in the Christian paradosis. The Prophetic sunna too was tradition, but somewhat in the manner of the Mishnah. The Mishnah possesses some very imperfect chains of authorities (isnads), few of which go back before Hillel, none before the Maccabees. For the earlier period one must always be content with "Moses received the Torah [always glossed to include the unwritten Torah] from Sinai and handed it on to Joshua, Joshua to the Elders, the Elders to the Prophets, and the Prophets handed it on to the men of the Great Assembly" (Mishnah Aboth 1:1). Eusebius is more detailed in drawing up in his *Church History* the lines of the apostolic succession in the various sees of the Great Church, but bishops were not much given to reciting isnads of their predecessors back to the Companions of Jesus before pronouncing on faith and morals. Episcopal consecration sealed what was an internalized tradition; Islamic tradition, in contrast, was reported, often copied down by the recipient, and certified by the tradent in the manner of a contract.

The earliest fuqaha or legal theorists in Islam were aware that they were filling in large empty spaces between the Quran's rather limited injunctions. They had grounded the case for their own view of the law on a consensus (*ijma*) of scholars in their "school." Shafii was uneasy with the notion of a local consensus. Where the Quran was silent and there was no explicit hadith on a given subject, he preferred to appeal to the consensus of the entire Muslim community, its acceptance of a practice such as circumcision or of an institution such as the caliphate, for instance. To bolster his own wavering confidence in the legal applicability of consensus, Shafii not unnaturally cited a hadith to the effect that the umma would never agree in error (see I/5, II/5).

The Administration of Justice in Islam

The Quran was sent down to restore justice to the world: to induce humans to recognize the "claims of God" (*huquq Allah*) as Creator and Lord, and, consequently, to restore justice to humans' dealings with one another. The society to which this message was brought was not without its own version of justice. Mecca was in the process of urbanization, but the prevailing mode of justice there was still largely based on the Bedouin notion of a customary tribal law (sunna) administered, where necessary—the tribes frequently took justice into their own hands—by an arbitrator (*hakam*) chosen for his sagacity or, on occasion, his charismatic qualities.

The substitution of quranic norms of justice for Bedouin ones was neither a short nor an easy process. The hakam, for example, continued to function side by side with fully developed Muslim institutions of justice for many centuries, though there were restrictions on the cases that could be submitted to such arbitration. The effort was made, somewhat haltingly at first, but eventually with great success, to convert Arab custom into Muslim law. The first sign of the intent to do so was perhaps a significant change in nomenclature. Judges appointed under Islamic authority were not called hakams, or arbitrators, but qadis, decision makers, a deliberate echo of *qada*, the verb used in the Quran to describe God's own divine power.

The Qadi

The Muslim tradition, which, like its monotheistic counterparts, attempts to legitimate its institutions by tracing them back to the origins of the community, credits the earliest caliphs—the Quran knows of no such official, or of any other, for that matter—with the appointment of the first qadis. Such may not be the case, and Umar's oft-cited instructions to his qadis are certainly spurious. Rather, the Umayyad caliphs (r. 661–750), or their governors, appointed the first qadis, who were, consistent with Umayyad practice, the delegates of the governor of the province, in whom full administrative and judicial powers resided, though without much distinction of function between the two powers. The provincial amir was himself, of course, delegating for the caliph in both those jurisdictions.

The practice of these early Islamic judges was of a very mixed quality: quranic injunction, local custom, their pre-Islamic predecessors' methods and norms, and their own discretionary powers all played a part in the judgments rendered by the Umayyad qadis. Though there was as yet no fully formed body of Islamic law at that point, the sharia was in the process of elaboration in various circles in late Umayyad times, not, however, in support of current local practices, but often in opposition to them.

To the Abbasids (r. 750–1258) belongs the credit of linking this still nascent sharia with the justice being meted out by the qadi. This was in effect what the philosopher and belletrist Ibn al-Muqaffa had suggested to the caliph al-Mansur (r. 754–775), but the Abbasids did not follow the rest of the prescription and attempt to exercise some control over the law itself. Harun's (r. 786–809) chief qadi Abu Yusuf did codify and systematize some of the legislation regulating taxes on the subject peoples, but neither caliph nor sultan exercised any legislative functions until Ottoman times (see below), and the rulers' absolute power to appoint and dismiss judges never quite compensated for their lack of control over the law itself.

By the time the Abbasids replaced the Umayyads in the mid–eighth century, the qadis were no longer "legal secretaries" of the governor or simple government employees; they were now specialists in what was rapidly developing into a mature legal system of sharia. The qadi was increasingly bound to that law, not, as previously, to the will and policy of the governor. The result was the growth of an independent judiciary, but only in the sense that the qadi was bound to a higher religious authority. He continued to be appointed—and dismissed—by the government and, as a price for his independence, he progressively lost control of criminal law—Islamic religious law recognized no prosecutory powers—which the state judiciously reserved for its own police power (*shurta*). The qadi in the end heard only those cases presented to him: in Islamic law no action was possible without a plaintiff.

The Qadi's Justice

In principle, the qadis justice was the only justice for Muslims—and only for Muslims: the dhimmis of the Abode of Islam rendered justice in their own communities according to their own laws—and no person or class was exempt from it. No one is above the law in Islam. The qadi's judicial power was absolute within his own geographical jurisdiction, but as the caliphs and their sultanic reflections in the successor states began to centralize the administration of justice, hierarchical arrangements appeared. In the early days there was a qadi only for each provincial center, followed, under Harun al-Rashid, by the creation of the post of grand qadi (*qadi al-qudat*), who at first was simply the official qadi of the capital of Baghdad, but who soon assumed the role of the chief justice of the entire Abode of Islam. The Fatimid Shiites soon adopted the same practice to assert their sovereignty, and the process came full term in 1264 when the Mamluk sultan Baybars appointed a grand qadi for each of the four legal "schools" followed by Muslim jurists (see below).

Qadis of whatever rank—there were eventually considerable distinctions of costume to denote rank—were government appointees and served by reason of delegation of the ruler's *sultan* or power. The justice they administered was based on legal norms beyond government control, but the qadis themselves were by no means free of government pressure or the temptations of peculation or bribery, particularly since the question of fees apparently remained open. Here too, as elsewhere in Islam, the dynastic principle was soon in evidence: families of qadis reached over many generations, and they were invariably drawn from a narrow base of municipal notables.

Muslim historians and biographers have left a wealth of information on qadis and the operation of their courts. Sessions were frequently though not invariably held in the mosque. Judgments were only rendered when suit was brought—there was no prosecutorial office and the qadi could not refuse to hear a case brought before him. The action was initiated by a complaint lodged by a plaintiff against a defendant. The qadi was the sole adjudicating authority. Essentially, he—women could serve as qadis but only in rather extraordinary circumstances—reached his decision principally on the basis of oral testimony. Documentation and physical evidence have never loomed large in the judicial process, and though the qadi could depose experts on the matter at hand, his verdict rested primarily on the reliability of witnesses and their oral testimony, which constituted the almost unique form of evidence. There was no appeal. In certain cases there was a prescribed quranic penalty (*hadd*) for specific crimes; in other instances the penalty was left to the qadi's own discretion. These included a kind of house arrest, fines, and imprisonment. Actual executions appear to have been quite rare. Some penalties were exacted by the "civil arm;" others fell to the qadi to administer through his agents.

The qadi's powers did not end with rendering judgment on cases brought before him. He also possessed a kind of extraordinary jurisdiction that extended into such religious matters as superintending public prayer and mosques, the charge of orphans, widows, and the divorced, and even such secular matters as finances and administration.

The qadi's once broad jurisdiction has shrunk over the centuries. Even under nominally Islamic regimes there grew a body of secular or civil law, often disguised as one form or other of executive decree (see below), that progressively narrowed the qadi's field to personal law, matters touching on divorce settlements and inheritances, for example. The process was hastened in the early twentieth century when many Middle Eastern regimes adopted a constitutional base with a full body of explicitly secular law and a secular judiciary. In the newer, professedly Islamic states like the kingdom of Saudi Arabia and the Islamic Republic of Iran the sharia has been restored to some semblance of the law of the land and the qadi reestablished as a primary judicial authority.

Responsa and Fatwas: The Mufti

Among both Jews and Muslims, where the teaching authority was a matter of education or certification rather than the charismatic magisterium of the Christian bishop, there arose lawyers, who by their position in the great yeshivas or simply by community assent, were looked on as capable of rendering an informed opinion on legal matters. These opinions, which were generally nonbinding and enjoyed only as much authority as the person issuing them, were called responsa among the Jews—in Hebrew, literally "queries and answers"—and fatwas among Muslims. The person capable of rendering such was, and is, known as a mufti.

The rabbinic responsum as a distinct legal and literary form arose out of the renown of the Babylonian Talmud, which had quickly become a standard guide to Jewish Torah behavior. The Talmud itself was "closed," but at its completion many issues of law and conduct remained open—or were freshly opened by circumstances. To solve them, interested Jews addressed their concerns in writing to the gaons or heads of the Babylonian yeshivas at Iraqi Sura and Pumbeditha, or later, in their reincarnation at Baghdad at the heart of the caliphate. The responsum was the gaonic answer to the query posed. According to one source, which may have been interested in giving weight and authority to the responsa, the questions were posed to full rabbinic assemblies at their biannual meetings in those places and the gaon reflected on that discussion in composing his response.

A subtle but distinct change in the rabbinic responsa occurred in the eleventh century with the decline in importance of the Iraqi yeshivas and the subsequent attempts to make Talmud law more accessible, as we have seen, through its codification in Maimonides' *Mishneh Torah* and Joseph Karo's *Shulkhan Aruk*. Thereafter the queries, and their answers, grew more concrete, more detailed, and more minute since most of the more general and principled issues had already been addressed in the earlier literature. Second, as the authority of the gaons declined, that of regional rabbis throughout the Middle East and Europe grew accordingly, and questions were now addressed to, and responses received from, authorities much closer to home and more attuned to local conditions and local problems.

The practice of posing and answering questions is already apparent in the Quran, where many of the revelations represent responsa to queries, hostile to be sure, put to the Prophet. But though the questioner was mortal, an unnamed Meccan or Medinese, it was not Muhammad who responded in the Quran, but rather God. We may be assured that Muhammad responded as well, both to hostile queries and then, increasingly, to the questions of his own followers seeking enlightenment or understanding on ritual and others matters concerning the new faith. Some of his answers are embedded in the massive body of hadith. But with the Prophet's passing, who was to answer such inevitable questions posed by a still incomplete understanding and rapidly changing circumstances? We do not know, nor do we have any certainty on what basis such questions would have been answered since there was not yet in place any fixed body of teaching that might be called "the Islamic law."

The sharia emerges into our line of vision early in the ninth century, and with it a defined class of experts, the ulama (sing. *alim*), who produced and glossed it. Their glosses were, in the main, scholastic and theoretical, new building blocks in the edifice of the sharia, but ordinary Muslims had other, more concrete concerns. In matters of contest, they had perforce to go to the qadi for a binding judgment, but in matters of conscience, on whether this or that act was licit or not, they turned, as we might expect, to one of the ulama for guidance. The response given by a qualified alim constituted a fatwa. It was the application of the sharia, as understood by the jurisprudent in question, to a practical matter of conduct, and those who rendered fatwas have been called, with justice, "the creative mediators of the ideal and the real of the sharia."

The Qadi and the Mufti

The qadi was, then, functionally a judge in that he rendered a judgment in a case brought before him by two contesting parties: he decided between them. The mufti, in contrast, rendered a nonbinding opinion in response to an individual's query. There were other important differences as well. The qadi was an official of the state, appointed and paid by the government—in the context both "state" and "government" are expressed by the single Arabic term *dawla* —and his judgments were enforced by the appropriate police powers of the government. His qualifications were few: he had to be a male, free, sound of sight and hearing, and as a political appointee, the qadi was dependent on and answerable to the state. The mufti, however, was a scholar, a member of the ulama whose support, both in his training and in his present position, derived from the pious foundations called *waqf* (see below): he was beholden to no one.

There is no case law in Islam and so the judgments of qadis in no way constituted a precedent for future decisions nor did they extend the purview of the sharia. A fatwa, however, though nonbinding and unenforceable in the context in which it was originally delivered, had a more profound effect on the sharia. Fatwas were recorded and collected, and some—those that expressed a new interpretation of a point of law rather than a mere recitation of the appropriate scriptural and hadith texts—have constituted, no less than the conclusions reached by the academic ulama, an extension of the sharia. Indeed, the mufti has been described as holding a position on the Islamic legal spectrum somewhere between the practice-normative qadi and the faqih or academic jurisprudent exercising his "personal initiative" or "interpretation" (ijtihad) within the walls of the madrasa.

The Schools

The early evolution of Islamic law took place in widely scattered centers across the Abode of Islam, and not even Shafii's attempts at imposing a kind of order on its development eradicated or even inhibited the continued growth of different schools of legal interpretation, each recognized as orthodox and legitimate by the others. Thus the Shafiite, Malikite, Hanafite, and Hanbalite "schools," which were founded by and named after early masters of Islamic jurisprudence, flourished, and continued to flourish, among Muslims. They differ on specific points of theory and practice, but their differences are not very substantial, nor do their practices much differ from the positive precepts of Shiite law, though this latter has a considerably divergent view of what lawyers call "the roots of jurisprudence." The four major Sunni schools recognized, with varying degrees of enthusiasm, the Quran, the sunna of the Prophet (as expressed in the hadith), the consensus of the community, and a measure of ijtihad as the basis of Islamic law. The Shiites relied heavily on the infallible teachings of the Imams and rejected out of hand community consensus, which had in fact betrayed them and, in their view, ignored both God's will and Muhammad's explicit intentions with regard to the Imamate (see I/8).

Shiite Law

Shiite law is based on a foundation quite different from that of the Sunnis. As we have seen, early Sunni lawyers like Shafii argued that Muslim law should be extended beyond the Quran's explicit prescriptions to include the Prophet's own utterances. Shiites would have no problem with this in principle, but the hadith had been transmitted on the authority of the Companions of the Prophet, that same early generation of Muslims who had chosen Abu Bakr, Umar, and then Uthman in place of Ali to head the Muslim community. Hence the Companions' testimony is rendered suspect in this as in all other matters.

Shiites extend the law beyond the Quran—but on the authority of the traditions reported from the divinely appointed and infallibly guided Imams. The latter passed down traditions regarding the Prophet, it is true, but they could also pronounce on their own authority, something denied to later generations in Sunni Islam. Thus the Imams, down to their Great Concealment among the Twelver Shia in 941, represented the same kind of ongoing revelation on matters of faith and morals as claimed by Christian bishops and in particular, after the erosion of their powers and the growth of his, by the pope, the bishop of Rome.

Shiite Imam traditions multiplied as rapidly as had the Sunni Companion hadith and were eventually subjected to the same kind of critical scrutiny as their Sunni counterparts. And just as in Sunni Islam, there issued from this scrutiny what came to be regarded as canonical collections of "sound" traditions, that is, those whose chain of transmitters had stood up to the investigation of biographers and historians. The four principal such collections are, as we have seen, those of al-Kulayni, Ibn Babuya, and two by al-Tusi (see II/3).

There are no great divergencies between Sunni and Shiite law in practice, but two examples deserve notice. Unlike the Sunnis, the Shiites permit the practice of temporary marriage (*muta*), a sexual union for a limited period of time, even hours, in exchange for a fixed sum of money. The Sunnis regard this as mere prostitution; the Shiites claim, perhaps correctly, that the Prophet himself allowed it and that it was only outlawed by the caliph Umar. Since the Shiites do not accept the authority, political or legal, of any of the first three caliphs, muta stands. *Taqiyya*, or dissembling, is a characteristic Shiite teaching born as a reaction to living as an often persecuted minority under Sunni sovereignty. Indeed, Muhammad himself had lived under such circumstances, and according to the Shiite understanding of Quran 16:106, which promises the wrath of God will descend on those who disbelieve "except for those who are compelled but whose hearts are firm in faith," it is permissible to dissemble one's beliefs, specifically one's Shiite beliefs, when there is danger of losing life or property. Though generally associated with Shiites, taqiyya was also permitted to the Sunni Muslims of Spain, for example, when they were threatened with death if they did not convert to Christianity (see I/8).

Ijtihad

Since the lawyers of Islam were essentially rabbis and not bishops speaking comfortably *ex cathedra*, they had early begun to employ various forms of legal reasoning that have been the staples of lawyers always and everywhere. The earliest generations of Muslim jurisprudents had often simply rendered an "opinion" (*ray*) on a matter of practice in the still ill defined field of Islamic law, and more often than not this was sufficient to settle the matter. By the generation of Shafii, however, things had become considerably more complex, and the Egyptian lawyer was clearly attempting to rationalize legal thinking when he insisted that "opinion," which was nothing more or less than the lawyer's using his own interpretative powers on a disputed or uncertain point of law, should become more rigorous by being based solely on a text of the Quran or a hadith—as opposed, say, to some local custom—and that it follow a recognized procedure. That procedure was generally some form of analogy (*qiyas*): the present case shares the same principle as an explicit commandment or prohibition in the Quran or the hadith and so it too may properly be judged as commanded or prohibited.

Analogy was acceptable to Shafii, as it was to most subsequent jurists, but only if it was used to erect "hedges for the Law," to use the talmudic phrase, and not to extend exceptions into general rules; that it start from the literal and not the allegorical understanding of the text; and that, finally, it be regarded as the fourth and weakest of the "roots of the Law" after the Quran, the custom of the Prophet, and the consensus of the umma. Where personal initiative became considerably more problematic—one lawyer ungraciously described it as "carrion, to be eaten only when no other food was available"—was when it was extended to pronounce something licit or forbidden in the name of equity (*istihsan*) or public interest (*istislah*) of the umma, areas where, as we have seen, the rabbis had no fear of entering with their taqqanoth.

One law school, the Zahiris—so called because they wished to base their legal conclusions only on the literal or apparent (*zahir*) meaning of the Quran— rejected all personal reasoning out of hand, and though the Zahiris eventually disappeared from the legal landscape in Islam, their misgivings about ijtihad continued to trouble many others. "Personal effort" was still human intelligence interpreting God's infallible word, and insofar as it was human, it was capable of error, a dangerous possibility when it concerned matters of salvation. Its results were somewhat easier to accept, however, if all the schools agreed on a particular application, and it may in fact have been this underlying notion of consensus (*ijma*), in this case of the schools, that saved ijtihad as a legitimate source of sharia.

The Closing of the Gate

After Shafii and as a result of the debate over the validity of independent reasoning, the freedom granted to earlier jurists to elicit legal conclusions from even the most traditional material was severely circumscribed, and by about 900 a new consensus was developing that the "gate of ijtihad" had "closed." Lawyers might dispute matters common to the schools, but the Quran and the hadith were henceforward off the table. Interpretative ijtihad was replaced by *taqlid*, "imitation" or "adherence," whereby the jurist was now bound to follow the teachings of the jurists of the classical schools of the classical era. The "closure of the gate of ijtihad" has an ominous ring to it, but should be understood in a sense not very different from the closure of the Talmud, as a herald for the advent of scholasticism. Scholars had to couch their legal speculations in the form of commentary and explication on an established body of masters, in this case the developed doctrine of the canonical schools.

The analogy with the Talmud should not be pressed too closely, however. In a sense, Islamic law was fundamentally in place by the beginning of the tenth century, just as the Mishnah was complete in the third, and the two Talmuds in the sixth. But all these latter were formal texts, whereas the sharia continued to exist, even after the tenth century, in the form of a somewhat inchoate, if consensually agreed on, mass of propositions whose exact formulation had only as much authority as the jurisprudent from whose pen they came.

One lawyer who attempted to pry open the gate of ijtihad—successfully, in the eyes of some increasingly influential modern Muslims—was Ibn Taymiyya (d. 1328). This Syrian jurist belonged to the Hanbali school, the most conservative of the Islamic legal traditions. The Hanbalis resisted "innovation" on all fronts, and yet they were uneasy with the notion of the closure of the gate of ijtihad. It was not so much because they favored the sometimes dangerous personal effort but rather because they doubted the possibility of any real consensus of scholars. Consensus was, as we have seen, the validating principle of ijtihad but many Hanbalis thought of consensus as a literal majority of all the ulama, which was unlikely in the best of circumstances. Thus, the door of ijtihad still remained theoretically ajar for Ibn Taymiyya, the most prestigious of the Hanbali jurists.

Note: Today the gate of ijtihad seems agape rather than merely ajar. Early in the nineteenth century, some of Islam's progressive intellectuals used the Hanbali arguments about the impossibility of a consensus to assert their own right to practice ijtihad to modernize Islamic practice. The argument and its conclusion also proved useful to modern Muslim states that required, or at least desired, some Islamic underpinning for their reforming legislation. Thus, in 1957 Tunisia passed a Law of Personal Status that argued that the Quran permitted polygamy only if all the wives could be treated with absolute impartiality and that this should be regarded as a precondition of a polygamous union—a position never previously held by the ulama. Since that was practically impossible, polygamy was declared illegal.

More recently, fundamentalist Muslims have likewise asserted the right to ijtihad, though for very different ends from those envisioned by the modernists.

The Hierarchization of the Ulama

The question of who had the right to pronounce a finding in a matter of law—in short, who was a mufti—generally solved itself in Sunni Islam. Various members of the ulama created their own preeminence by their community-recognized learning and the probity of their judgments, and at their head stood the rare *mujtahid mutlaq*, the "absolute interpreter" whose authority, like that of his rabbinic counterpart, transcended his own place and his own time. But the ulama were also subject to hierarchization, whether the government arranged them so, as it did in the Ottoman Empire, or because they sorted themselves out on their own, as happened in Imami Shiism.

The relationship of the Ottoman sovereigns and the ulama of the lands of their empire was one of mutual dependence, though the locus and gravity of that dependence shifted over time. The Ottomans, who were at base Turkish tribespeople with a variety of suspect religious alliances in their past, needed the ulama, the guardians of Sunni tradition and conservatism, as guarantors of their own orthodoxy, and indeed of their own legitimacy as rulers in the Abode of Islam. The ulama responded with instruction and approval. From gratitude and to seal the bargain, the Ottomans extended to the ulama their considerable patronage and access to a power the ulama had never previously enjoyed in Islam.

The first official to feel the warming breath of Ottoman patronage was the chief military qadi (*qadi asker*), a kind of judge advocate general. Under Mehmed II (r. 1444–1481) the office was doubled and there was a qadi asker for Anatolia (the East) and another for Rumelia (the Balkans). Then, under

Sulayman (r. 1520–1566) there was a change in emphasis. The qadis were, as we have seen, judicial officials and had always been a charge of the government. Sulayman placed over them a mufti, a jurisconsult rather than a judge: he elevated the mufti of Istanbul to the position of chief religious officer of the empire under the title of *Shaykh al-Islam*.

Sulayman may have had more than legitimation of his sultanate in mind. He has gone down in Ottoman annals as *al-Qanuni*, the "Lawgiver," a bold and novel assertion in an Islamic context where God is the Sole Legislator (see below). Few questioned the sultan's right to make executive law at that point of empire, but it was a delicate matter in the doing and the qanun had to be seen to be in conformity with the sharia, or at least not to contradict it. Sulayman's own collection of qanun introduces itself as "The imperial *Book of Qanun*, whose agreement with the Holy *Sharia* has been established," and that establishment was in large part provided by having a mufti as the chief religious official of the empire.

Beneath the Shaykh al-Islam and then the two judge advocates general were a whole series of qadis, all of whom enjoyed the title of mullah: the chief justice of Istanbul and its three principal suburbs, those of the earlier Ottoman capitals of Bursa and Adrianople, of Damascus and Cairo, of Jerusalem, Smyrna, Aleppo, Salonika, and Yenisehir. Associated with them were the imperial household chaplains, the sultan's religious tutor, the two imams who conducted the Friday services wherever he happened to be, and finally two members of the ulama, one of whom served as the sultan's chief physician and the other as court astrologer responsible for choosing the auspicious moments for various official events.

All of these grand mullahs were officers of the state and enjoyed its generous emoluments and awards, whether in titles, cash, costume, or the potentially lucrative right to appoint or dismiss a veritable army of underlings. Beneath their competencies were a vast array of minor religious figures and functionaries down through provincial and local levels. Appointments in those serried ranks came from above and ambition rose from below.

Just as the Ottomans arranged their judiciary in rigid hierarchical ranks descending from the judge advocates general, so in a second order the muftis of the realm were similarly arranged under the Shaykh al-Islam. It was he who appointed the chief mufti in each of the principle cities of the empire. But whereas the government in effect made a qadi, the Shaykh al-Islam simply appointed a mufti. These latter served no terms but held their offices for life, and though the Shaykh al-Islam could silence or interdict a mufti, he could not deprive him of his office, which rested on his qualifications, not his appointment.

In 1826 the reforming sultan Mahmud II (r. 1808–1839) cut the economic and institutional props from beneath this lavish arrangement. The chief mufti or Shaykh al-Islam became a minister of state, with his own offices—previously he had run the empire's religious affairs from his own palatial residence in Istanbul—and the sultan at the same time created a ministry of waqf. Thus not only was the religious establishment, which had previously enjoyed government support, now brought under political control but so too was the chief source of its income, the empire's extensive system of pious endowments. Later the educational system was likewise taken out of ulama hands and placed under a ministry of education, the judicial system under a ministry of justice, and the drafting of fatwas committed to a commission of legal experts.

Ijtihad Unchained

Note has already been taken of the intervention of the Iranian ulama—or mullahs, as they are more often called in Iran—in the affairs of the state (see I/8). Both the power and the inclination to do so resulted from a sea change in the powers of the Shiite ulama that occurred in the eighteenth century.

The jurisprudential side of Shiite law lagged somewhat behind what was occurring in Sunni legal circles, but when Shiite thinkers began to reflect on the roots of jurisprudence, the dominant view came to be the highly conservative one: that only the Quran and the Prophetic hadith—"reports," as the Sunnis called them, but *akhbar*, or "accounts," in Shiite legal jargon—constitute the sole basis of a Muslim behavioral code. The Akhbaris, as they came to be called, ruled out, like their Sunni counterparts among the ahl al-hadith, any resort to speculation or ijtihad. Others were more liberal: a trained and sober interpreter might indeed use rational techniques to extend the religious foundations (*usul*) of the law. So argued the so-called Usulis, though to no great effect; from the late tenth to the eighteenth century the Akhbaris controlled the centers of Shiite religious learning in Iraq and Iran. They were, on principle, mere tradents, passing down, mechanically and without speculative enlargement, the accounts transmitted from the mouths of Muhammad and the Imams.

In the second half of the eighteenth century, after, and perhaps because of, an attempt by the Türkmen ruler of Iran, Nadir Shah (d. 1747), to return Iran to Sunnism, the Usuli ulama, who had been rendered all but speechless by Akhbari theory, rose up and, in a kind of religious coup d'état, drove the Akhbaris from the Shiite centers of learning and piety at Najaf and Karbala in Iraq. Thereafter the Usulis controlled the legal-theological system of Imami Shiism, and since interpretation of the law was now ranked higher than mere transmission, the Usuli ulama enjoyed new and extensive powers in the shaping of religious sensibilities among the Shiat Ali.

The Usulis quickly began to institutionalize their new powers. The mujtahid, the legal scholar qualified to practice ijtihad and so interpret the law, became a revered figure in Shiite Islam. On the then prevailing view, all Muslims had to be either a mujtahid, an authoritative interpreter, or a "follower" (*muqallid* < *taqlid*: obedience to authority qua authority). But whereas in Sunni Islam ijtihad was the result of training and skill in jurisprudence, in Shiism the mujtahid's authority was eventually linked to the infallible authority of the Imam, from whom the mujtahid enjoyed his power of "general representation." That is, he might serve as a spokesperson to the community of the Imam's will; the community, for its part, had to follow without question. Thus the Shiite mujtahid became an "exemplar for emulation" (*marja al-taqlid*).

There was always more than one of these authoritative teachers in Shiite Islam, but as their numbers crept slowly upward—there were only three or four at the beginning of the nineteenth century—a degree of hierarchization inevitably set in. The chief mujtahids began to be designated as *hujjat al-islam*, or "proof of islam." The creation of the title, rather than checking the inflation of "exemplars," seems instead to have enhanced it, and by the beginning of this century there were enough "proofs" in the community that some began to be designated by the now familiar Ayatollah (*ayat Allah*, "divine sign"). Where the process appears to be heading is to a type of "Romanization," to the acknowledgment of a single mujtahid mutlaq, a kind of *prima mulla assoluta* with infallible and unquestioned authority.

Customary Law and Governance in Islam

In the Islamic lands the sharia had no competition until the mid–nineteenth century. The Ottoman sultans, among others, did attempt quietly to create a kind of secular statute law by decree, what might be called in modern terms an "executive order," though they never dared called them sharia. Instead they were known as qanuns (Gk. < *Kanon*). Then, in the nineteenth and twentieth centuries, many of the new nation-states that emerged out of the former Abode of Islam adopted secular, Western-style constitutions and as a result the sharia jurisdiction, although never completely abandoned, was increasingly restricted to areas of personal status.

The sharia was never an entirely closed system in either theory or practice. Though we cannot always document their practices with precision, it seems persuasively clear that the earliest Islamic judges thought they possessed, and actually used, a wide discretionary power they exercised by consulting and even incorporating local customary law into their administration of justice. As the theoretical structure of the sharia grew more scholastically rigid, however, the jurisprudents became increasingly loathe to admit the notion of customary law or local practice (*urf, ada*) as a legitimate "root" of the divinely decreed and timeless sharia. But if customary law was a repugnant notion to the fuqaha, the largely undefined but no less real powers of the ruler had within them a general category called policy or governance (*siyasa*), which had, if not more profound effects on Muslim life than the traditional roots of the sharia, then at least more openly acknowledged ones.

Siyasa was based on the ruler's need to govern the commonwealth of Muslims in an appropriate Islamic way. Just as the qadi was called on to administer individual justice in accordance with God's decree, so the ruler, whether caliph or Imam in succession to the Prophet or simply a sultan, the possessor of political power (see I/8), had to see to it that administrative justice was done. So much the jurisprudents would concede, but the sharia put in the rulers', hands few instruments to achieve it and little latitude to devise it themselves. The "market inspector" (*muhtasib*) was a recognized agent of administrative justice, but he functioned on a local scale and so was of little help in reckoning with the larger issues of siyasa.

Qanun: The Sultan's Law

Muslim rulers ended by devising their own siyasa, with or without the sanction of the jurisprudents. The boldest and most successful instance is undoubtedly that of the Ottomans. Like other Turkic nomads, they came from a strong customary law tradition in Central Asia. Some nomads, like the Mongols, were accused by the legal establishment of never leaving off their observance of the customary law of the steppe even after they became Muslims, but the Ottoman Turks had a sound reputation as defenders of Sunni orthodoxy against the Shiites of Iran and tireless holy warriors (*ghazis, mujahidun*) on the frontiers of Islam before their ascent to the pinnacle of power in the Abode of Islam.

At first the Ottomans seem to have cared little for the niceties of the Sharia— their use of the devshirme and forced conversion of dhimmis (see I/8) is but one example of this nonchalance. Yet between 1453, when Mehmed II captured imperial Constantinople (later Istanbul) and thus brought Ottomans onto the international stage, and 1516–1538, when the Arab (and Islamic) heartlands of Syria, Egypt, Arabia, and Iraq were added to their dominions, the Ottomans turned sharply and notably toward Sunni orthodoxy. The Hanafite school of law was embraced with enthusiasm, the Holy Places of Islam were generously endowed, and the Ottomans began to fashion an Islamic state, or better, an empire, with the assistance of qanuns, their carefully crafted version of statute law.

Qanuns were not invented by the Ottomans, but they perfected the instrument, perhaps by reason of their closer contact with the Roman legal tradition still alive in Constantinople. The emperor's will was one of the "roots" of Roman law—the primary one in its latest stages of development—and the Ottoman sultans from Mehmed II onward did not hesitate to make such enactments, not, as they understood it, in contradiction of the sharia, but as its implementation. More, these were published in codified form, and, since they represented the pleasure of the current ruler, had to be reconfirmed by each one of his successors. Mehmed's first "code" (*qanun-name*) was of criminal law and was published in 1453–1456 to regulate the conduct of "the flock" (*reaya*), that is, the Ottomans' subjects, though they were never called that until the nineteenth century. In 1477–1478 this was followed by a code defining the hierarchical structure of the empire, and, toward the end of Mehmed's reign, by an economic code.

Sulayman I, the Ottoman sultan known to the West as "the Magnificent," was called al-Qanuni, "the Lawgiver," by his own historians. The title does not do him justice. Sulayman did in fact publish a wide-ranging set of qanuns that regulated the behavior of his subjects in minute detail. But he was also responsible for a major codification of the sharia: under his direction, Ibrahim ibn Muhammad, the leading faqih of Aleppo, prepared a book titled, in the rhetorical style of the times, *The Confluence of the Seas*, which is a full-scale codification of the sharia in its Hanafite understanding.

These enactments remained in force in the lands under Ottoman sovereignty from Algeria to Iraq to the Balkans down to the mid–nineteenth century when modifications of the sharia, or rather, the limitation of its purview to ever narrower areas of social behavior, were openly called "reform," and when the sources of these modifications were first identified with the legal ideals of the European secular tradition.

Jewish Rabbis and Islamic Ulama

Between Constantine and the beginning of the Reformation, Christianity, like temple Judaism, operated within a system of dual authority symbolized by the Gospel image of the "two swords" (Luke 22:38). Those two swords represented the temporal power of the emperor (which was neither entirely secular, since from Constantine's day he was understood to rule over some sort of idealized Christian commonwealth, nor entirely spiritual, since both the emperor's feet were firmly planted in the Roman imperial tradition) and that of the head(s) of the Church, in the East the patriarch of Constantinople and in West the pope in Rome. At its highest level that duality often appears like hand-to-hand combat between powerful individuals, but in the ranks below, Christendom's elite was unmistakably its clerics, who controlled its sacramental system and, through their possession of the teaching authority (see II/5), shaped the behavior and beliefs of all Christians.

The ministry of the principal sacraments and the magisterium were both spiritual powers possessed by the Christian clergy not by training habit, or experience but through the conferred gift of the Holy Spirit. Neither Judaism nor Sunni Islam had a clergy in anything like the same sense, and in both those cultures lawyers were and remain the leaders of the religious community.

Rabbis were the uncontested elite of Jews living in both Christian and Muslim societies, where they had no genuine secular competition and very few religious rivals—the holy man or zaddik was one, and the later "pietist" movements such as Hasidism also challenged mere legal learning. The rabbi's prestige arose from his mastery of the law, which could be certified by the masters or yeshiva he had attended or simply by the community's recognition.

It is tempting to see in the Muslim ulama the rabbis of Islam. In a sense the comparison is just. Both groups constituted a relatively well defined class that enjoyed the power and prestige of a religious elite by reason of their mastery of religious law, and both received a standardized education in jurisprudence in an institutionalized setting. Neither were legislators in the strict sense, but both rabbis and ulama were at the same time the conservative guardians and the cautiously innovative exegetes of a long and complex legal tradition.

But there were important differences. Jews were granted a degree of community autonomy, first in the Roman and Sasanian Empires, and then in the dhimmi and later the millet system under which they lived for long centuries in the Abode of Islam. That freedom was a concession dictated from above, and within it the rabbis served, by delegation and with the acceptance of their coreligionists, as the administrators of that restricted autonomy. They not only maintained a legal tradition; they also administered it, as judges and surrogates of a higher judicial authority, that of the patriarch, the exilarch, or the geonim (see I/6).

The Muslim ulama, in contrast, at least the Sunni variety, were only one element among the classes and elites contesting for power in the Abode of Islam. Before Ottoman times they neither possessed nor delegated any political authority, and they eschewed the administration of the sharia, a task that fell to the government-appointed and -supported qadi. Their power lay elsewhere, in the prestige they enjoyed as the custodians of the obviously Islamic component in what was professedly an Islamic society; in their independence of the state, which they could castigate or applaud as circumstances dictated; and in the network of marriages by which they could forge ties with other powerful classes like the large landowners and the wholesale merchants. Unlike their episcopal counterparts, the ulama did not hold the keys of the kingdom in their hands; they could neither bind nor loose nor force a caliph to his knees or out of the Church. But power they possessed, a genuine political power. Like their Jesuit contemporaries in Europe, they educated an Islamic intelligentsia in their school system. After the eleventh century higher education across the face of Islam was uniquely ulama-inspired and directed in madrasas, where Islamic consciences and indeed Islam itself were shaped through the instrument of the sharia.

Until relatively recent times, the law school, or yeshiva, was the exclusive form of Jewish higher education, and the same is almost as true of Islam. But whereas the yeshiva was a financially marginal institution in Christian and

Muslim societies where Jews themselves were politically marginalized, in Islam, where religion and empire were two sides of the same community, the madrasa, its faculty, and students generally enjoyed adequate to lavish financial support. This came, however, not from the state but from private individuals through the institution of waqf. Almost every Muslim intellectual from the eleventh to the nineteenth century received his higher (and increasingly standardized) education in the Quran, hadith, and jurisprudence in the all-male classrooms and courtyards of the madrasa.

> **Note:** As an institution waqf or endowment falls under the general heading of charity (*sadaqa*), in this instance a voluntary one, in contrast to the alms-tithe (*zakat*) obligation of all Muslims. The Muslim jurist al-Kasani (d. 1189) defined it as "a continuous or closed charity for the sake of God and his religion." From the legal point of view, waqf was a complex contractual institution. By his public and witnessed declaration the owner of a property or of an object with value surrendered his right to proprietorship of that same property or object: he deeded its ownership and, more important, its income, to God. But before the transaction was completed, the donor exercised his right to specify the disposition of its continued income, after expenses, which included the upkeep or continued operation of the property and the fees of the waqf executors.
>
> At this juncture, the disposition of the income of the waqf-ed property, an important distinction occurred. The waqf donor could immediately name a specific charity, the construction and/or support of a religious institution, for example, a mosque or a madrasa, in which case the income from the property went to that institution in perpetuity. This was known as a "charitable endowment." But it was clearly within the donor's rights to name members of his own family, or even himself, as the primary beneficiaries; hence, to create a "family endowment." But there were limits to his beneficence. Since every waqf was by its nature perpetual, once the named beneficiaries of a family waqf were all gone, the income reverted to a charity that had also to be named in the waqf charter. Thus, every family waqf eventually turned into a pious endowment. Disputes about family waqfs were not generally handled in the qadi's court but by the state as belonging to the realm of the "claims of God" or, to put it somewhat differently, the common good.

The difference between the rabbis and the Sunni ulama rests finally in the latter's conviction that they are the interpreters of the sharia, whereas the rabbis regard themselves as the custodians of a Torah that is "no longer in heaven" but rests instead in the hands of the rabbinate. As a result the rabbis have through the centuries practiced ijtihad with far less hesitation and far fewer qualms than their Muslim counterparts. Although both groups think themselves competent to render responsa on specific questions of law, the rabbis' ready issuance of both gezeroth to protect the law and taqqanoth to advance the common good has few parallels among the Sunni ulama.

5

God's Commandments and Human Morality

THE BEHAVIORAL CODES of the three monotheistic communities were thought to rest on God's Will, as expressed in the commandments and teachings he laid down in Scripture. The matter, as it turned out, was far more complex.

Values and Value Systems

Here we are concerned with the systems of values attached to human acts. By "systems" is meant that such values have been ordered into some kind of coherent whole. Without one version excluding the other, such systems fall into two main classes. One derives its values from a principle or principles immanent (internal) to the act or its agent, and the second from a transcendent (external and higher) principle or principles. Though both terms are used broadly and often loosely, we here follow the lead of historical usage and call the first an ethical system and the second a moral system. In the present context, the pertinent ethical systems are those of Greco-Roman antiquity and its legacy; the moral systems are those elaborated within the three religious communities of Jews, Christians, and Muslims.

Not only are the principles of ethical systems immanent to the field of human action; they are also, in consequence, naturalistic and are discovered and expressed in the public discourse we call politics, as happened among the Greeks and Romans, and eventually in philosophy. Second—and this is true of moral systems as well—the primary emphasis is on "normative" behavior, what ought or is expected to be done by the moral agent, not what was actually done by one or more or even most professed adherents of the system. But both ethical and moral systems, to the extent they become institutionalized in a culture, rapidly develop techniques to guarantee that the normative will also become the actual behavior.

A society's normative ideals are expressed in law. Civil laws define and punish crimes, offenses against the society or individuals as members of the civil society. Religious law is directed toward defining and punishing sins, offenses against God or God-prohibited actions against other individuals in the religious community. Thus, murder is both a crime and a sin because the state has forbidden what God had already forbidden: homicide. But Greek Stoic philosophers thought they detected a broader gauge of behavior. In their view, laws were not merely products of human legislators. Rather, they reflected a behavioral ideal planted by a Universal Reason in the nature of all things. Reflection, then, should permit humans to detect the good for any nature by an inspection of that nature. What is good for humankind is what is in accordance with human nature. This is the tradition of natural law, and it found easy entry into religious systems that read the good in the will of a transcendent God: what God willed for humans was embedded in their natures and revealed by reason of a special dispensation. The Stoics discovered law by inspecting human nature; Moses, by listening to the voice of God on Sinai. It was, however, the same law because it proceeded from the same source. God was both Creator and Revealer, Moses both prophet and lawgiver.

Natural law made its official appearance in the Christian legal system, the one called canon law, in the *Decretum* of the jurist Gratian, composed sometime about 1140 (see II/4). Gratian was a trained lawyer who had studied Roman law and so was capable of positioning the Church's emerging statute law in the broad range of behavioral patterns represented not only by the natural law of the philosophers but the imperial law of the Roman Empire and the customary law still in practice in Western Christendom. According to Gratian, law existed in God's Will. It was then revealed by God and could be discerned in all created nature, specifically in human reason and conscience. Human legislation is mere "statute" or "enacted" law (*lex*) and should be consonant with the higher system of justice (*jus*) represented by natural law. The same is true even of the Church's law. "Enactments," Gratian wrote, "whether ecclesiastical or secular, if they are proved to be contrary to natural law, must be totally excluded." Human judgment can fail; God's creative and providential Will cannot.

That is the high ground. What the Greco-Roman ethical tradition principally contributed to the monotheists' moral systems was the fruit of a long, richly detailed, and highly intuitive scrutiny of human character. Plato, Aristotle, and the Stoics lay bare the wellsprings of human action and devised a typology of human personality. Sin, the concrete reprehensible act—*hamartia*, "missing the mark," the Greeks called it—interested them far less than vice, the habituated and habitual character trait that produced such an act. The formation and content of monotheistic morality had a strongly personal cast: sin is an offense against God or, more specifically, against something God willed. The motivation for such acts was somewhat problematic. An "evil impulse" or Satan was sometimes fingered as the immediate culprit, whereas for the Christians Original Sin provided a more general explanation.

Once the Jews, Christians, and eventually the Muslims came in contact with Greek ethical theory, these explanations of why humans acted despite God's express will became somewhat less than satisfactory. The monotheists did not need the Greeks and Romans to tell them that "the good that I would do, I do not" (Rom. 7:19), that your head (or Scripture) tells you one thing and your heart (or some other part of the anatomy) tells you quite another. What the Hellenic ethical tradition did do was explain to the Scripturalists, who were very good at keeping score, the rules of the game. But first the monotheists had to explain to themselves why there was a game to begin with.

Whence Evil?

For most people, evil is a given of both the human and the cosmic condition: it happens, to me as well as to timberlands and flood plains, sometimes with discernible causes and sometimes without. In monotheism, however, and among the elites charged with explaining such things, the occurrence of evil, whether humanmade or at the hands of nature, represented a problem of enormous magnitude in a world created and governed by an all-good God. Their explanations run off in numerous different directions, into the theory of Original Sin, for example, or the notions of free will and predestination (see below), but one very popular answer to the question "Whence evil?" tapped into a primitive layer of the biblical past that underlay the monotheistic core.

Monotheism never quite succeeded in banishing all the gods the One True God replaced. Formal and public worship of the rivals of Yahweh and Allah was banned, of course, but private rites of other deities survived, powers sometimes concealed under other names, sometimes transformed into angels or saints. The most successful survivors were the demons, those omnipresent, somewhat dangerous, and sometimes malevolent figures—they could be friendly and even entertaining at times—who show up on almost all spiritual landscapes. Whatever they were called, the demons were mysterious, unpredictable beings who possessed powers beyond our own and were generally held responsible for what might be called the lowercase inexplicable.

Jesus and his followers lived in a Jewish world whose views of the moral universe were cast in unmistakably dualistic terms. Evil was not something that lingered like a bad odor in the corners of the cosmos but was a dynamic, personalized force that opposed the Will of the Creator God. In the mildest form of explanation, evil was simply a malevolent impulse that prompted humans to immoral or unnatural acts; in its most extreme, and unorthodox, expression, evil was the work of a powerful rival deity locked in mortal combat—a popular image in some Jewish and most Christian writing—with the good God for the souls of humankind. This latter, clear-cut dualism with its sharp dichotomy between good and evil, the forces of light and darkness, and the warfare between them, was a widely held belief in the religion of Iran, in Manichaeism, and in the extreme forms of Gnosticism, but it is also visible, in somewhat mitigated form, in Jewish post-Exilic apocalypses, in the writings produced at Qumran, and in many of the early Christian writers. For all the latter, it was no god, of course, who promoted evil—these were all professed monotheists—but a being who, for all his power and malicious intent, was a creature of, and subservient to, the One True God. His name was Satan.

The Diabolic, the Demonic

Demons haunt the margins of the Bible but none rose to the prominence of the one who was not a demon at all initially. In the earliest passages where the word occurs, *satan* is merely a common noun, an "adversary," someone who opposes. But in later passages like Zechariah 3:1–2, Job 2:1, and 1 Chronicles 21:1, the adversary's function has sharpened into that of an accuser, even an instigator of evil, and the personification has deepened: the adversary has become Satan. The New Testament follows the Septuagint and translates "satan" as *diabolos*, "slanderer," though at times the word is kept in its Greco-Hebrew form as *satanas*. This Satan is a more active agent. He tempts Jesus to a variety of sins (Matt. 4:1–11). He "enters" Judas to lead him to betray Jesus (Luke 22:3). He has others in his charge (Matt. 25:41), who are called "angels," including Baalzebub (Matt. 10:25), the Bible's notorious "Lord of the Flies" (2 Kings 1:2–6). In the end, however, Satan, "who seduces the world," together with his hosts, the enemies of God, will be defeated (Rev. 12:7–9).

In the Gospels Satan is both universal and familiar, not merely "the adversary" but a seducer, tempter, and possessor. Paul's view is more sweeping. Somewhere in the background of his thinking lies a cosmic battlefield. A moral war is going on there, to be sure, but also a more personal combat between Satan and Christ, between the "prince (*archon*) of this world" and the ruler of God's kingdom. "This world," "the present age," is our world of human history, and Satan, whose grip has been weakened by the first coming of Christ, will nonetheless rule it until the Second Coming. Paul's perspective proved useful in the early Church when Satan's activity could be discerned in the dissidence that threatened the early communities of believers. Heresy was not, as the word *hairesis* implied, simply a matter of making a wrong choice; it was the work of Satan.

The worldview that lies not too deeply within the writings of Paul and many of the early Christian Fathers, that there is a basic moral and perhaps even metaphysical conflict between this world into which Christ descended and some other moral and spiritual realm where God rules absolutely, seems close to what a slightly later generation of Christians identified as Gnosticism (see I/5, II/9). The chief and most fundamental difference between them turned on whether this world was the creation of the good God—the Gnostics, at least some Gnostics, said "no"; Paul and the others said "yes"—and whether the prince of this world was God's subordinate or equal.

Although it may have been implicit in the Bible, by New Testament times it is unmistakable that Jesus and his Jewish followers had identified Satan and his cohorts as angels, in this case, as angels gone very bad, the result of what was thought to be a fall from God's favor. We cannot trace all the strands of the story of this fall, a staple in the later Christian and Muslim traditions on the subject, but one is a visionary parable in Isaiah (14:12–14). An early form takes its point of departure from an enigmatic reference in Genesis 6:1–4 to the "sons of gods" having intercourse with the "daughters of men" and begetting a race of giants. We do not know when the sons of the gods became transformed into angels, but the story appears under full sail in the first book of Enoch, where the lustful angels are called "Watchers" and are cast out of heaven for their fornication. Jude (4–5) knows all about the story and how God has reserved eternal darkness for them.

Over the centuries between Irenaeus in the second to Augustine in the fifth, a coherent picture of Satan, his origin, role, and destiny, was fashioned in Christian theological circles. Satan was a created angel, hence his extraordinary powers. But at some point—whether before or after the creation of humankind is not clear—he and a number of his fellow angels were moved by inordinate pride to disobey God (the story of the fornicating Watchers was discarded) and were cast out of heaven, their natural home, into the lower planetary world. Thus Satan was not intrinsically evil, as the Manichaeans and Gnostics would have it, but he freely chose to sin, just as Adam did. The Fourth Lateran Council of 1215 stated it in dogmatic terms: "The devil and the other demons were indeed created by God good by nature, but they became bad through themselves; man, however, sinned at the suggestion of the devil." Moreover, Satan's always evil intentions, again like Adam's sometime inclinations, are the consequence of that angelic "original sin." His "kingdom" has no reality: it is an association, a fraternity, a tong. Satan is no prince; he is the dean of a college.

Humans may repent their sins and hope for salvation, but Satan and his followers have no such hope. For some unknown reason, God has withheld from them the grace he grants humans. In the end, Satan and his followers will be damned (see II/10), but in the meantime they roam the created universe, he as the devil, they as demons, and maliciously seek to bring humankind low. Satan had wished this from the beginning, when he took the form of a serpent and seduced Adam and Eve into sin (Gen. 3:1–7). He tried again unsuccessfully with Jesus. And the work goes on. The deluded pagans worshiped his demons as gods, and they still manifest their remarkable powers under the cover of magic. They can possess humans, just as they did in Jesus' time (Luke 11:15–25) and must be exorcised by a special ritual. But above all, Satan is the tempter: he cannot cause humans to sin—there are no causes when it comes to free will—but he can seduce by his wiles and considerable intelligence.

The Jinn, Shaytan, and Iblis

The world of pre-Islamic Arabia is unmistakably demonic, and not even the Quran's determined monotheism could obliterate the traces of an energetic, and personified, animism. The principal gods worshiped by the Arabs in the era of ignorance were, as far as we can make out, heavenly beings, at least in their origins, but the landscape was also filled with lesser, more familiar creatures called jinn. The jinn were "spirituals"—they were composed of fire rather than our clay, according to the Quran (15:27)—and were the near relatives of the Greeks' *daimones* and the Romans' *genii* but with a special wilderness cast that made them dwell in remote and slightly sinister places. The jinn were themselves somewhat sinister. They smelled of rather thin evil but possessed preternatural powers that they occasionally put at humans' disposal, sometimes for good, sometimes for ill, reflecting the later Western distinction between black and white magic. They aided Solomon in his projects (Quran 27:17, 39–42) for example, and, somewhat less beneficially, they inspired poets—who were termed *majnun*, "jinn possessed"—something Muhammad had constantly to deny about himself (Quran 36:69; 79:4).

In the Quran, the jinn share human traits and destiny. They too were made to serve God (51:56), though they may fail and end in hell (6:128). Some seem to have overheard Muhammad and converted to Islam (72:1–19). They can "beguile" humans (41:29), but no more apparently than we can each other. The problem was that, at least at Mecca, they were progressively divinized. The Meccans claimed the jinn were God's kin (38:158) or companions (6:100). It is not surprising, then, to discover that sacrifices were offered them (6:128) and their assistance sought (72:6).

The jinn generally offered no moral competition to Allah, but one of their number did. This was a shaytan, for the Meccans a rebellious jinn—or jinns; the name is also used in the plural, *shayatin*—capable of great evil. The shaytan of the Quran is somewhat of an anomaly, now a highly malicious jinn from a demonic and folk strand of the Arabs' belief system, now a personified fallen angel descended, as his name makes clear, in a direct line from the biblical Satan. But in one important respect, Shaytan is not Satan. The fall of the angels, which is treated more than once in the Quran, centers around not the quranic Shaytan but another familiar New Testament figure, Iblis, whose name is undoubtedly some truncated form of *diabolos*. After the creation of Adam, God orders the angels to bow down before his mortal creation (15:30–33; 17:61). Iblis, in 18:50 "one of the jinn," alone refuses and God casts him forth from heaven with the words "You are accursed. You are cursed till the Day of Doom" (15:33–34). As with the fallen angels of the Christian tradition, the sentence will not be executed on Iblis until the Last Judgment. Until then, whether he is an angel or a jinn—a question on which the Muslim tradition is most uncertain—Iblis has the power to attempt to lead astray humans, though not true believers (15:39–42). His first conquest is Adam and Eve (2:34–36; 20:116–121).

Sin and Atonement in Israel

Almost from the beginning, humankind falls short of the Creator's expectations: Adam and Eve sin at the very outset of the Bible story. That was before the Covenant, however. Sins committed after God's pact with Abraham and his heirs are violations of a sacred contract. The Torah has a great many names for such offenses, though they are chiefly represented there as *het* ("missing the mark")—and later, by the rabbis, as *averah* ("crossing the line"). The expressions might seem to imply mere inadvertence, and indeed the Bible does recognize, in Numbers 15, the difference between unconscious or inadvertent sin and the "presumptuous" sin that has "brought the word of the Lord into contempt and violated His command" (30–31). The rabbis later added another distinction, that between grave and light offenses, which became the mortal and venial sins of the Christian moral theologians.

The mortal sins of the Israelites, which were read as acts of rebellion against God, were accompanied, like their counterparts in the Quran, by specific and severe penalties. One penalty was *karet*, the "cutting off" already alluded to (see I/5). Karet is prescribed in the Torah for a number of offenses against God and his commandments. The contexts in which the word occurs leave little doubt that being "cut off" includes, preeminently, being cut off from life, the ultimate penalty that God himself may exact—"death at the hands of heaven," the rabbis called it—a reckoning that at times occurs immediately (Lev. 20:17), at times later, or perhaps even among one's descendants. But the community too could exact this price (Exod. 31:14–15), and we are given a striking example of its actual occurrence in the case of an Israelite who is discerned gathering wood, and so working, on the Sabbath and is killed for his offense (Num. 15:32–33).

We cannot be certain how many Israelites were actually put to death for committing the capital crimes in the Bible's considerable list. Whatever their number, and the evidence suggests it was small, the power to carry out such executions was severely limited by the Jews' progressive loss of their political sovereignty to others. The handing over of Jesus to the "secular tribunal," in this case to a Roman inquisition, because the Jews lacked the power to execute him (or anyone) (John 18:31), was very likely true. The jurisdiction of Jewish religious courts became as circumscribed as those of the Christians and Muslims later were under progressively more secular states.

Acquittal

Apart from these acts of profound rebelliousness against God, sin was not regarded as an irreversible or irremediable state. God takes no pleasure in the "death of the wicked." He would prefer "that the wicked mend their ways and live" (Ezek. 33:11). The prophets addressed the issue of repentance and reformation, but the Torah's chief emphasis is the formal restoration of the relationship between God and humans that the sinner broke by transgression. Sin requires expiation. That begins with restitution or recompense if the aggrieved party is another mortal (so Exod. 21:30); only after that has been effected can the sinner proceed to sacrifice in propitiation to God (Lev. 5:14–6:7). If God alone has been offended, the sinner is bound to sacrifice, and the Bible describes the highly prescriptive sin sacrifices to be offered through the Aaronite priesthood in the temple (Lev. 4:1–5:13).

> **Note:** A considerable and often baffling terminological thicket surrounds the Bible's discussion of what are called in English "sin," "guilt," "atonement," and "expiation." Some of the offenses that require a "sin offering" are moral faults, like failing to come forward as a witness (Lev. 5:1), whereas others, like a mother's condition after childbirth (Lev. 12:6), are, in the biblical scheme, merely natural "disorders" that require righting. Josephus tried to sort some of this out in his *Antiquities* (3. 230–232) by classifying sin offerings as required for inadvertent transgressions. The guilt offerings of Leviticus, in contrast, had to do with conscious violations of the Law, in short, what we would regard as sin.

With the destruction of the temple in 70 and the disappearance of even the possibility of expiation through sacrifice, the prophets again provided later Judaism its alternatives to ritual expiation for sin: repentance, prayer, and good works. The rabbis insisted that all these must be accompanied by confession, in private or in a liturgical setting, as on the tenth of the month of Tishri, Yom Kippur, or the Day of Atonement (Lev. 16:1–34; 23:26–32). This self-accusation was not, in any event, made to any intermediary agent but directly to God.

The Yom Kippur expiation ritual described in Leviticus includes the liturgy of the scapegoat. The high priest, who officiates throughout, casts lots over two unblemished male goats. The one on whom the lot falls is "for the Lord" and is subsequently sacrificed. The other is "for Azazel," presumably a wilderness-dwelling demon that had to be exorcised. Later in the liturgy, the high priest lays both hands on this goat and "confesses over it all the iniquities of the Israelites and all their acts of rebellion, that is, all their sins" (16:21). The goat is then released to a special warden who will take it into the desert: "The goat will carry all their iniquities upon itself into some barren waste" (16:22).

Note: Leviticus 16:29 prescribes a strict fast on what it calls "the tenth day of the seventh month" and the Muslim tradition has Muhammad (and the pagans of Mecca) observing a fast on Ashura or "the tenth," presumably the atonement fast of Yom Kippur. Muhammad changed his practice, however, at Medina when he found the Jews obstinate to his claims. Muslims were bade to fast at a different time, the lunar month of Ramadan, but the Ashura appears to have survived, now transferred to the tenth day of the first month of the Muslim year, Muharram (see II/6).

Generally speaking, atonement is not an important feature in Islamic moral thinking. Indeed, it enters almost obliquely through the identification of the hajj's animal sacrifice, which was almost certainly a pre-Islamic feature of that ritual, with Abraham's sacrifice of his son (Quran 37:102–107). God relented, the account continues, and allowed Abraham to substitute an animal for the son the Lord had first demanded. The subsequent sacrifice was regarded as one of atonement. But for what? The immediate context suggests it was for the idolatry of Abraham's family, most notably of his father. Its expiatory resonance carried no further in Muslim thinking, however.

Jesus' Moral Teaching

Christian morality is based, not surprisingly, on Jesus' own teachings, as reported verbatim in the four canonical Gospels and then glossed, or rather, explained and enlarged, in the other writings that constitute the New Testament. Jesus' moral instruction fits comfortably, if not perfectly, into the framework of contemporary Jewish morality, though perhaps—one is not always sure what the contemporary Jewish moral emphases were—with somewhat greater stress on social justice. The so-called beatitudes, particularly in their Lucan version (6: 20–26), point strongly in this direction, as do many of the parables, the oblique miniature narratives characteristic of Jesus' teaching style.

If Jesus' observance of the Torah commands can be qualified as "ordinary," in the sense that it reflected what we surmise was common practice, his moral concerns in the area of social responsibility brought him into rather tense conflict with the Pharisees, whose program emphasized punctilious individual observance. The Pharisaic "brotherhoods," circles of those with shared purity concerns, were necessarily closed and exclusive, particularly when it came to sharing food, whereas Jesus describes his own preferred audience (and table companions) as the despised "publicans and sinners" who failed to maintain Pharisaic standards of purity (Mark 2:15–17).

In one respect, however, Jesus' teachings unfold in a moral context quite different from the Torah's own. In Jesus' time Jewish belief in an Afterlife was both widespread and detailed (see II/10). God's punishment of the sinner was effected in Gehenna and his rewards were bestowed in the garden (paradise) of humankind's utopian origins. There are still strains of the older biblical morality in the Gospels, that the wages of sin were visited on the next generation, for example—"Who sinned, this man (born blind) or his parents?" (John 9:2)— but the moral background of the Gospels is an unmistakable eschatological landscape that passed quickly and easily into Christian theodicy.

There is eschatology in the foreground as well. Jesus' moral teachings are intimately tied to his principal message, namely, that "the Kingdom of God is at hand" (Mark 1:15) and his closely related messianic claims. He came, he said, "not to abolish the Law but to complete it" (Matt. 5:17). Did that completion consist in what could be read as his sharpening the moral sensibilities beyond observance? Or were his instructions guidelines, perhaps even temporary guidelines, until the coming of the End? Or was the Torah to be superseded by a new messianic dispensation?

Pauline Morality

There are grounds in the Gospels for all three positions on Jesus' teaching, yet it is not at all clear which Jesus' earliest followers adopted once they were on their own. Though Paul and his correspondents in the 50s assumed that the End was nigh, Paul did not think that the Torah was superseded, at least not for the Jews who followed Jesus, despite the fact that there was at present no need for the Gentile converts to place themselves under it. Yet Paul's own reading of what constituted Christian morality, although unmistakably Christ-centered, relied remarkably little on Jesus' specific instructions. Nor does it obviously appear like a series of stop-gap measures before the End. His impatient counsels on marriage (1 Cor. 7:8, 25–26) and his advice to maintain the social status quo (1 Cor. 7:17) might suggest such, but, by and large, Pauline morality seems to be fashioned for the long term.

The Gospels' teaching on morality seems profoundly conditioned by a rural Palestinian environment. Social justice is a persistent theme and, indeed, some modern interpreters see Jesus as primarily a social reformer, not in the fiery manner of a first-century Savonarola, perhaps, but more akin to contemporary Cynic philosophers who taught by the example of their lives or by gently oblique tales like Jesus' parables. With Paul, the moral landscape changes, and there is no mistaking the fiery citizen of Tarsus for a peasant sage. The moral setting is Greco-Roman and decidedly urban, and the Gospels' penchant for social justice yields in Paul to a more intense and more personal aversion to the sins of the flesh.

Paul was a Jewish, now a Christian, moralist with a Greek's ethical understanding of virtue and vice. He shared Plato's conviction that we are in the middle of a rather unequal struggle between the flesh and the spirit, but he substituted for Plato's mythic explanation of why that should be so his own Christian *mythos* of Adam's sin as the cause of the flesh's domination of the spirit. He shared the Aristotelian and Stoic view of the vices as extravagances, repeated immoderate acts allowed to harden into habitual traits of character. But there is no cool analysis here; the heat rises off the page (Rom. 1:26–31). Even the frequent lists of virtues and vices (Gal. 5:19–23; Rom. 1:29–31, etc.) that Paul offers his nascent Christian communities for guidance, although not very different from those found in contemporary Stoic moralists, have about them a moral urgency not usually found in such catalogs.

One trait Paul and the Gospels share on the matter of morality: their instruction is occasional rather than systematic. Both Jesus and Paul were addressing pressing or prominent questions, often ones quite explicitly put to them by their interlocutors, who were, in Jesus' case, often hostile. Paul's advice, like his social context, was more far-ranging—urban rather than rural, with no urgent political issues of the type Jesus had to respond to when pressed.

Original Sin

Jesus' ethical teaching added little to the Bible's repertory of specific commandments. But Paul's view of the displacement and perhaps annulment of Torah sins, together with his understanding that Jesus' redemptive death had expiated human sin (see I/2), not only past offenses stemming from Adam's original sin, but all subsequent sin as well, effectively separated Christian moral thinking from its Jewish antecedents.

Jewish moral thinking recognized the operation of an "evil impulse" (*yetzer ha-ra*) that promoted sin, an "impulse of a man's heart, which is evil from his youth" (Gen. 6:5; 8:21). The rabbis later balanced this notion by positing a force in the other direction, a "good impulse" (*yetzer ha-tov*) that comes into play when an individual becomes a "man of the Law" (*bar mitzvah*) and accepts the Torah. Though the existence of the yetzer ha-ra was not explicitly connected with Adam and Eve's sin in Eden, Paul, like the account in Genesis 3, linked Adam's sin with death: through this act of disobedience by the primal man, death had entered human experience. Paul went beyond the Bible, however, linking death with not only the original sin but also humans' consequent sinfulness. That all were sinners might be stated as a matter of fact—all are known to sin (so Gen. 6:5, 8:21; Job 4:17, 14:4, 15:14, etc.)—but if there was any aboriginal cause, it was far more likely Eve. As the postbiblical Ben Sira put it: "Sin began with a woman and because of her we all die" (25:24). Paul too joined the ideas of sin and death but placed the blame firmly with Adam, so that "through the disobedience of that one man [Adam], the many were made sinners" (Rom. 5:19).

The notion of hereditary sin reappeared in a vigorous fashion in Augustine's writings as a fully articulated theory of Original Sin, which, after some initial opposition, became a linchpin of Christian moral theology. In this view, as a direct result of Adam's sin (the "originating sin"), all humans—except Mary, whom a much later generation of Christians came to think was the beneficiary of an immaculate conception—were born with an almost irresistible inclination to sin. Precisely how irresistible tormented innumerable Christian thinkers after Augustine.

This perverted skewering of human nature, which Augustine defined as concupiscence, the yearning for self-gratification, and which forever disrupted the divine order of things, could be cured only by "grace." This was God's free gift of love, and it provided the moral strength necessary for the individual Christian to resist sin. But once sin did occur, it required a more institutional remedy, the sacrament traditionally called Penance, to erase it and its consequences (see below).

Manichaeism

Augustine, the fifth-century bishop of Hippo in North Africa—his see, once a thriving Christian center, is now a village in Algeria—was and remains the Church's most considerable, and most influential, moral thinker. His thoughts on Adam's original sin formed part of his profound reflections on sin, evil, and the human condition that were prompted by his own experience and his prolonged polemic against the views of his contemporary Pelagius (see below).

One important part of Augustine's experience was his early association with what is called Manichaeism. Mani was an Iranian prophet who in 241 c.e. received a call to propagate a new message that would in effect complete the earlier revelations given to humankind. He composed his own *Great Gospel*, which he preached as far as India and then back to the western borders of the Iranian Empire. After initially enjoying the shahs' favor, he eventually fell afoul of the powerful Iranian priesthood, the Magi, and was crucified and then beheaded in 277.

Mani's teachings were carried by his disciples into the Roman Empire, where they found numerous converts, and as we have seen, resurfaced in twelfth-century Christian Europe as Catharism (see I/5). Like Christianity, Manichaeism had a fully organized church with a hierarchy of authorities and a strong missionary dynamic. Its message was embodied in a complex myth that ends in the struggle of two great principles, the Father of Greatness, the principle of good, and Ahriman, the principle of evil. To combat the Evil One, the Father of Greatness creates the Mother of Life and her son, the Primal Man. This is followed by a further complex of acts in the cosmic drama of the struggle between good and evil, conceived, in the Iranian manner, as light and darkness. The light of goodness is scattered across material creation, which is Ahriman's preserve. What is left of the light in this evil world is chiefly embodied in Adam and Eve, and thus the final act of salvation will be the redemption of this primal pair. A series of messengers was sent by God to help extricate Adam from the material world in which he is enmeshed—Jesus, Buddha, and Zoroaster are all among them—and finally there was Mani, the "seal of the prophets," the same title later given to Muhammad in the Quran.

The soteriological kernel of Mani's message was a gnosis, a wisdom that saves (see II/9). Its history was spelled out in the great cosmic myth outlined above, which explains how humans first became immersed in matter and how our true destiny is to return to the realm of the light. Manichaeism offered a practical means of salvation founded on this gnosis. It rested on the most severe asceticism, especially for the Elect, the privileged adepts who constituted the central core of the Manichaean Church and served as exemplars to the other, less stringently bound believers called the Hearers. This characteristic asceticism had as its objective a veneration for the spark of Light that is life and an uncompromising refusal to cooperate with the further propagation or dispersal of matter. Vegetarianism was the Manichaeans' form of life affirmation, their refusal to marry and propagate children a pointed example of their negation of matter.

Manichaeism was an economical solution to the existence of evil in this world, a conundrum that never ceased to bedevil monotheists who affirmed the existence of a single, all-good creator God yet saw the good suffer and the evil inexplicably prosper. Mani cut the knot by simply positing the existence of two gods or, to use a favorite Manichaean figure, two principles of light and darkness: one, the author of good; the other, the source of evil. According to the Manichaeans, life was an ongoing war between the good and the evil God that took place here in the material world where the Prince of Darkness ruled. For Mani and his followers, there was no question, as there was in Judaism, Christianity, and Islam, of explaining how the good God could even have permitted evil—he surely could not have created it. Many in the ancient world were attracted to this clean-cut explanation for the existence of evil. Among them was Augustine, who was a member of the Manichaean Church between 373 and 382. Although he eventually repudiated Manichaeism and became a Christian, something of their disdain of the flesh and their view of it as the source of evil never left him.

Augustine as Moralist

Augustine's view of morality was shaped not merely by his own personal experience but by his understanding of how humans know, choose, and act. That understanding was at base Platonic. For Augustine, as for Plato, man is essentially spirit, a soul (which he calls, variously, *anima*, *animus*, and *spiritus*) that uses a body. As a knower, that soul is called mind; as the storehouse of recollection, it is known as memory; and as the motive force of action, will. By this latter faculty, the soul can choose to turn its attention to the body, which is an act of perversion, or on itself, which reveals its own glory but also its own lack of some higher good. For Augustine, that higher good is understood, and thus human happiness achieved, when the will turns the soul toward God. God is the *summum bonum*, the supreme good of which Augustine speaks in his most sustained presentation of his ethical philosophy, the eighth book of his *City of God*. The supreme good is defined there as "the good we seek for itself and not because of something else and, once it is attained, we seek nothing further to make us happy." God both illumines and instructs the soul turned toward him, through an intuition of moral ideals (*rationes aeternae*), for example. These are intuitive perceptions of the eternal law, which is nothing but "the reason and will of God." It is not, however, understanding but love that drives the human quest for happiness: what is done must be done for the love of God, not from fear of the consequences. "Love and do whatever you wish," Augustine famously said. Love God, that is, and virtue will follow almost of necessity.

This brightly lit Hellenic style rationalism has another, darker side that flows from Augustine's Manichaean preoccupation with sin. Following what he regarded as the teaching of Paul and the universal Church, Augustine proclaimed that Adam's original sin was also ours. It had traumatized humankind; it had distorted the natural order that once existed between God and humans; and it introduced a fatal flaw in human beings. We do not even understand how serious the consequences of that primal act were. The human race is now a "condemned mob" (*massa damnata*), and the only way to salvation, as Augustine himself could attest, was with God's gratuitously bestowed divine favor or grace (*gratia*). For years before his conversion, Augustine had known the truth of God's law and been incapable of acting on it. Only through the supernatural assistance called grace did he finally turn to God.

Augustine's invocation of grace goes back to Paul. In Paul's letters "grace" (Gk. *charis*) is used both generally to designate God's goodwill as well as in the narrower sense adopted by Augustine, as God's saving will manifested in Jesus. This grace for Paul justifies us all, "through His act of liberation in the person of Christ Jesus. . . . For our argument is that a man is justified by faith quite apart from success in keeping the law" (Rom. 3:24, 28). And again, "It is through his [Jesus Christ's] favor that you have been saved through faith" (Eph. 2:8). In other places in Paul, grace is contrasted with "works," religious acts—in Paul's Jewish context, observance of the Torah—that do not have the power to save (Rom. 11:5–6; cf. Gal. 2:21; 5:4).

Augustine and Pelagius

Brooding pessimism about his own unaided powers of doing what he knew to be morally right brought Augustine into collision with Pelagius. The latter was an ascetic reformer coming to prominence at Rome with his program of sturdy Christian observance of God's law: humans had the power to change their lives. This required unrelenting work and effort, but was well within human capabilities and, moreover, was demanded by God. What God required was no longer, of course, the "good works" referred to by Paul—namely, the performance of the Torah mitzvot—but rather the observance of a Christian morality. In effect, Pelagius was denying the long-term consequences of Original Sin that Augustine had strenuously argued and graphically depicted. For Pelagius, Augustine's views undermined the human need or desire for moral effort. Augustine was creating Christians who thought either that sin was unavoidable or that God's grace would overcome it. In either case, there seemed to be little incentive to make the effort required to lead a moral life. Augustine replied in his *Nature and Grace* by citing one of his favorite Gospel parables, that of the Good Samaritan. Like the man set upon by thieves on the road to Jerusalem, humankind has been left half-dead from Original Sin. God wishes not the impossible but that humans do what they can and otherwise ask for the healing medicine of divine grace.

So the issue was joined. In 418 Augustine assembled in Carthage a synod of two-hundred African bishops who dutifully proclaimed the centrality of grace in helping us understand God's commandments and his giving us the power to love so we may fulfill them, "since each is God's gift, to know what we ought to do and to love in order to do it." This was Augustine's synod, but in 431, at the ecumenical council of Ephesus, the Great Church also condemned what it understood as Pelagius's position. It was not the end of Pelagianism, however. Western monasticism was based on Pelagius's principle that, whatever the role of divine grace, only human striving effectively achieved salvation. At a council held at Orange in 529, the bishops devised a somewhat conciliatory formula, which later received papal approval and so became Church teaching. According to it, after the Christian has received the grace of baptism, "all the baptized, with the help and cooperation of Christ, are able and obliged to fulfill what pertains to the soul's salvation, if they are willing to work at it faithfully. . . . In every good work we do not begin it and are then helped by God's mercy, but He first inspires us with faith and love of Him, . . . so that we can with His help fulfill those things which are pleasing to Him." All baptized Christians, then, are capable of achieving salvation, not, as Augustine seems to suggest, only those who are preordained by grace. If grace does come first, it assists us in performing the good works by which we may achieve salvation.

Penance and the Sacramental System

No one had read Paul as issuing a license for Christians to sin with impunity; he, and certainly his readers, understood "atonement" not as license but as the expression of the Christian's participation in the merits of Jesus' death. This was generally effected through what eventually developed as the sacramental system. This was constituted of certain acts whose performance brought the Christian the "blessing" or "favor" (Gk. *charis, charisma*; Lat. *gratia*) of God, generally known as grace. By the twelfth century the number of sacramental acts had stabilized at seven: Baptism, Confirmation, Penance, participation in the Eucharist, Marriage, the reception of Holy Orders, and the Final Anointing before death. Baptism initiated the believer into the community and five of the others brought favor and spiritual strength to the Christian in good standing. Penance dealt directly with the issue of sin, toward which all humankind was inclined as the result of Adam's fall.

Penance has four basic elements: first, repentance; then, confession of the sin in some public or ecclesiastical forum, which later came to be understood as confession to a priest. The priest provided the next element, the imposition of a penalty or "penance" in the narrower sense of the word, and it was he who, as the Church's agent in the mediation of the merits of Jesus' death, finally granted absolution.

In the early Church, Penance was initially a public act that could occur only once in a lifetime (and consequently was often postponed till the approach of death), but it was gradually replaced by a different form used in the Celtic Church in England and Ireland. In monastic circles there, Penance was a private matter between sinner and confessor and occurred as frequently as circumstances dictated. This usage spread to the Latin Church in the sixth century and eventually became the norm throughout the Latin West—Eastern Christianity has remained closer to the original practice. Sacramental penance was given new and extraordinary prominence in the Latin West by the Fourth Lateran Council of 1215, whose twenty-first canon required of every adult Christian annual confession to a priest, absolution, and reception of the Eucharist. The statute brought the faithful under the control of the Church since it meant at least some consultation with the clergy—the penalty for failure to fulfill the annual obligation was excommunication—who could use the occasion to question, instruct, and direct the lay Christian in a manner not previously available. The Christian now truly belonged to the Church, held by a bond both sacramental and canonical. Finally, as the canon of Lateran IV made explicit, the secrecy of the confession and so the privacy of the penitent was protected in an absolute manner.

Priests assisted in their new duty by various books and manuals that instructed how the sinner should be guided in examining his or her conscience so that all sins be confessed and what types and degrees of penances should be imposed. The Celtic Church was a pioneer in the matter of expiatory acts imposed on the sinner in requital for sin. These were generally calibrated in accordance with the gravity of the sin, ranging from a pilgrimage to Jerusalem (for a homicide), through a series of graduated fasts and abstentions, to the saying of prescribed prayers. But the gravity of a sin depended on a number of very variable circumstances, and to guide the confessor through this complex landscape of sins and their punishments, the Celtic Church published penitentials, confessors' guides to the imposition of a penance appropriate to each sin. The penances were generally light, however—one or another of a number of prayers to be repeated. "It is better to give a light penance so that the sinner will perform it and go to purgatory," one such guide said, "than to give a hard and burdensome penance which the sinner will not perform and go to hell."

After the Council of Orange, the controversy over God's favor versus human efforts in the light of Original Sin seems to have died down. Augustine was regarded as a pillar of early Church orthodoxy, while monasticism, with its often strenuous practice of asceticism, continued to be widely practiced in an effort to storm the gates of heaven with good works (see II/8). Christian theology, meanwhile, had quietly moved away from Augustine and his Platonizing view of the soul onto an alternate set of philosophical principles that produced, a theology with very different emphases.

Those new philosophical principles derived from Aristotle, who was now available to the Church's new university-trained theologians in complete and accurate translations (see II/7). Aristotle's psychology was more naturalistic than Plato's—humans are a natural and organic union of soul and body—and so moral theology too moved its foundations in the same direction. For Thomas Aquinas, for example, human connection to the flesh was no longer either an unnatural distortion or a prison sentence: grace came to the natural individual. If grace elevates human nature, it is also firmly constructed on it. Grace does not replace a depraved nature; it builds on it.

Thomas was a Dominican monk, a member of one of the monastic orders that practiced lifelong asceticism. The pursuit of Christian asceticism by the Dominicans and others raised no accusations of Pelagianism. But the Church was also increasingly attaching grace to the practice of good works, in the form of indulgences a practice that succeeded in drawing attention back to the issue of what precisely salvation consisted of.

Purgatory and Indulgences

The penitential system as understood by the medieval Church had several consequences, two of which are particularly interesting. The absolution granted by the Church in the name of Christ—the operative text is Matt. 16:19, "I will give you the keys of the kingdom"—might indeed return a sinner to a "state of grace," but it was not generally thought that the penance exacted, however onerous, actually quit the sinner of his or her debt to God. Heaven and hell were places of eternal and absolute reward and punishment; what seemed to be required was an intermediate state where souls who had indeed merited heaven by having ended their lives in a state of grace might requite the spiritual punishment still due for unconfessed venial sins—this during the period between the individual's death and the increasingly remote General Judgment at the end of the world. Thus there emerged in Western Christianity—fully visible by the decades between 1150 and 1200—the notion of purgatory, a "middle place" of pain and torment like hell, but temporary in its nature, where the repentant sinner made appropriate atonement and was then released to heaven.

> **Note:** One of the most striking and original portraits of purgatory as an imagined *place* is the middle section of the *Divine Comedy*, the prodigious religious and political epic of Dante Alighieri (d. 1321). His Purgatory is an enormous walled mountain midway between heaven and hell; it lies exactly opposite Jerusalem in the southern antipodes or world counter to our own. On the mountain there are seven concentric terrace circles reserved for those being purified of their indulgence in one or another of the seven deadly sins of pride, envy, anger, sloth, greed, gluttony, and lust. In Purgatory Dante leaves Virgil, his guide to the Inferno, and encounters Beatrice Portinari, his dead lover, who is, like much else in the *Purgatorio*, a redemptive bridge leading from hell to heaven.

If logic carried forward the idea of making room for some quittance from or alternative to the irreversibly eternal pains of hell, the same logic surfaced in other monotheist circles, though it led to a somewhat different solution. As we shall see (II/10), both Jews and Muslims thought there was a physical atonement for sin immediately after death, not in some other, adventitious place, but in the tomb-grave itself. The "torments of the tomb" suffered by the newly deceased at the hands of God's agents were a graphic feature of speculation and legendary embroidery on the immediate sequel to death by both the rabbis and the ulama.

Purgatory eventually became Christian dogma—one of a number denied by sixteenth-century Protestant reformers on the grounds that they had no basis in Scripture. But its mere appearance and acceptance by most Christians carried another notion in its wake: that living Christians, sometimes called the "Church Militant," could reduce the sufferings of their dead loved ones, the "Church Suffering," by their own good works, or indeed could "bank" those same good works for their own future use. The Church not only earmarked such good works—visits to shrines, particularly those in the Holy Land, were especially favored, and the Crusades were garlanded with merits—but also laid out in detail the exact degree of "forgiveness" (*indulgentia*) attached to each. These "indulgences" ranged from a plenary or full forgiveness of the atonement due to sins—indulgences did not absolve from sin; the sins in question had already to be confessed and absolved—to specified years, months, or days that would be subtracted from a stay in purgatory. When money began to change hands in exchange for indulgences—cash contributions toward the construction of St. Peter's in Rome were one glaring example—many were outraged, not least among them Martin Luther.

> **Note:** The popularity of both purgatory and indulgences received a powerful boost on 22 February 1300 when Pope Boniface VIII published the bull *Antiquorum fida relatio*, proclaiming that year a "jubilee year" and promising "great remissions and indulgences for sins" to be gotten by "visiting the city of Rome and the venerable basilica of the Prince of the Apostles." Boniface may have intended to continue a somewhat vague custom of a century before, but the basic notion of a jubilee year goes back to Leviticus 25:10, where God decrees every fiftieth year a jubilee, with "remission to all the inhabitants of the land." In Church practice, the time of jubilee years, with the accompanying plenary or full indulgence of the penalty for all confessed sins, has fluctuated from twenty-five to thirty-three to fifty years. Still observed by the Roman Catholic Church, the jubilee interval appears to have stabilized at twenty-five years. The most recent jubilee year was 2000 C.E.

Purgatory is a tradition with strong resonances in both Judaism and Islam. Neither the rabbis nor the ulama were entirely convinced that Gehenna/ Jahannam was a place of eternal punishment. Heaven would last forever, but there were profound doubts on the eternity of hell. The Quran itself (10:107, 78:23) seemed to suggest that Jahannam too would be destroyed at the end of the world. Christians alone were fully convinced of hell's eternity. Hell and its torments had, then, a recognized distinct purgatorial effect for Jews and Muslims (see II/10). What separates Christianity from the other two, besides making purgatory a quite distinct place, is the issue of intercession. Jews and Muslims pray for the dead, but without a great deal of theological support. Christians, in contrast, believe—and set in place a mechanism to effect it— that the living can shorten the purgative punishment of the dead and hasten their way to paradise.

Who Will Be Saved?

The notion that God, who knows all, has chosen or "elected" to save certain of humankind runs deeply back into Christianity, and perhaps into Judaism as well. Judaism entertained the idea of a "Book of Life," (Exodus 32:32 at one end of the Bible, Malachi 3:16–17 at the other), which recorded the good deeds of the worthy. " 'They will be mine,' says the Lord of Hosts, 'My own possession against the day I appoint.' " The Gospels make no mention of such a book, but Jesus is quite explicit that places of honor have been reserved "for those to whom it has already been assigned by my Father" (Matt. 20:23; cf. John 10:29). With Paul, all doubts on the matter disappear. The Letter to the Romans says clearly, "For those whom God knew before ever they were, He also ordained to share the likeness of His Son . . . and those whom He fore-ordained, He also called, and those whom He called, He also justified" (8:29–30). In Ephesians, the presentation is even more detailed: "Before the foundation of the world, He chose us in Christ to be His people . . . and He predestined us to be adopted as His children through Jesus Christ. This was His will and pleasure in order that the glory of His gracious gift, so graciously conferred on us in His beloved, might redound to His praise. . . . In Christ indeed we have been given our share in the heritage, as was decreed in His design whose purpose is everywhere at work" (1:4–11).

Predestination reentered the mainstream of Christian speculative thought when the notion of God's infinite knowledge and power was brought into contact with the doctrine of Original Sin, namely that the sin of Adam and Eve created a permanent and congenital weakness in human nature. So Augustine held and in rigorous enough fashion that he thought it impossible that humankind should be saved in this lapsed state except by a special intervention of God's favor. That all were not saved is clear from Scripture, and Augustine did not hesitate to draw the painful conclusion: humanity was by its fallen nature damned—a massa damnata—all except those whom God freely, and gratuitously, elected to save. The rest would go their inevitable way to perdition.

In the millennium between Augustine and the Reformation, the Christian Church found few ways to meaningfully accommodate the patently conflicting notion that virtue was dependent on moral choice, as the Greek ethical tradition unanimously affirmed and as Scripture itself seemed to imply at every turn. For most, the human freedom to make that choice, free will, as it was called, was simply axiomatic, a primary given of experience. So, Duns Scotus counseled early in the fourteenth century, "one should not seek reasons for things for which no reason can be given." This freedom was thought to reside preeminently in the will.

The Absolute Will of God

This emphasis on the will—generally termed voluntarism—also came to be applied to the theologians' understanding of how God worked in his mysterious ways. Since human freedom continued to be regarded as an incontrovertible given of experience, the answer to the problem of determinism or, in religious terms, of predestination was sought in God's Will. Voluntarism is not so much a doctrine as a matter of emphasis. Aquinas, who is not thought of as a voluntarist, already distinguished between God's absolute power, whereby he can do things other than those he has foreknown and preordained, and his ordinate power, by which he does only what he has foreknown and preordained. "For God does things because He so wills; yet He is able to do them not because He wills but because He is such in His nature" (*Summa theologiae* 1.1.25).

In later discussions of the topic, this same distinction was applied to God's Will itself. Besides the distinction between an absolute Will, whereby God can do anything he chooses, and an ordained Will, which is effectively determined by his own choice—that is, the state of things as they are—the divine Will suffered other fault-line distinctions as theologians probed for a conceptual space large enough to accommodate both divine omnipotence, which can and does determine all, and human freedom to choose between good and evil. Thus, William of Ockham's (d. 1349) powerful insistence on the difference between God's absolute power, which knows no limitation, where black can be white and good, evil—a sentiment later echoed, almost exactly, by Calvin—and his ordained power represented by our moral world, where God has ordained that the good will be rewarded by salvation and evil punished by damnation, allowed a later theologian like Gabriel Biel (d. 1495) to locate both human freedom and the merit of good works in God's ordained moral system, where he has bound himself, so to speak, by his own decision.

Luther had read Ockham and he had read Biel. In the former's depiction of God's *potentia absoluta*, he found a powerful gloss on Augustine's insistence that all rested in God's hands, most especially salvation, which was God's free and arbitrary gift to a portion of humankind. Luther could not follow Ockham, and particularly not Biel, into what appeared to be the comforting Pelagian landscape of meritorious good works that the fourteenth- and fifteenth-century theologians had found within God's *potentia ordinata*. God's sovereignty is not mitigated in the slightest since what he has determined is not that humans should be free, or obliged, to win their own salvation. Only God's good pleasure will save.

Ockham had used the interplay of God's absolute freedom on one hand and his ordination on the other to explain God's arbitrary establishment—as arbitrary, say, as the setting out of the dietary laws—of the "special" causality of the Church's sacramental system and the formal means of transferring his grace to humanity. Not so for Luther, who saw the individual standing alone before God, left to hope for his own salvation in fear and trembling, without the assistance of clergy or sacraments. Only faith could save, faith mediated through God's Word, as read in the Scripture or preached to the faithful.

The Disputed Question of Nature and Grace

The issue of grace and salvation, of God's free gift or human efforts, was thus in the forefront of theological discussion in the opening decades of the sixteenth century. Luther's views on the subject were shaped not only by what he had read in William of Ockham and in Gabriel Biel, but by what he saw occurring in the churches of Germany and what he felt in his own heart. Sometime between 1512 and 1515 he had his "tower experience," a sudden revelation that convinced him that the heart of the Gospel lay in the fact that faith alone justifies and saves. Then, in 1517 the papal legate Johannes Tetzel came to Germany to promote the rich indulgences granted by Pope Leo X for contributions to the construction of the new basilica of St. Peter's in Rome. An angry Luther, then an Augustinian monk and professor of theology at Wittenberg, posted on the door of the cathedral there ninety-five theses, some of them denying the validity of indulgences applied to the souls in purgatory and attacking much of the moral theology that lay behind them.

For Aquinas, grace had to come to one before any possibility of virtuous action, but once God's grace was infused in the human soul, it was the recipient's responsibility to cooperate, to do the best possible and, if successful, then salvation would come to him as his due. For Thomas's immediate successors, this did not leave nearly enough room for human freedom and, consequently, they made a major revision in Thomas's theory of grace and salvation. Nature and grace were still among the theologians' *quaestiones disputatae*, subjects of debate on which numerous (though not all) opinions might legitimately be discussed. For Ockham and Biel, grace was not infused gratuitously but as a reward for already having done one's best in the circumstances of nature: the exercise of natural virtue brought the gift of grace, and it was at that point, in cooperating with this newly infused grace, that salvation came as one's just due.

Though it may not have been intended as such, this late scholastic explanation offered by Gabriel Biel among others was read by Luther as an unhappy combination of Pelagius's position (moral activity wins God's grace) with Augustine's (moral acts in cooperation with God's grace win salvation), and he labeled it "the new Pelagianism." But he also saw somewhat deeper into the system. The evil genius behind this kind of thinking, Luther concluded, was Aristotle and his theory of virtue. Aristotle's *Ethics* and its theory that virtue was a habit acquired only through the repeated performance of moral acts had brought on the Pelagianism that Luther associated with the whole of medieval scholastic theology (see II/7).

Justification

Paul had spoken of Christian destiny in terms of salvation and redemption, both of which imply being brought back from some perilous or threatening state. Augustine had already defined that perilous state as the corruption of humanity due to Original Sin. Humankind no longer stood condemned because of some actual evil they themselves had committed, which would have rendered the question of justice simple, but because of a natural and inherited condition. After Augustine individuals had to be redeemed from the consequences not of their own but of another's sin, Adam's, which made sinners of us all. Luther saw with increasing clarity that that redemption was achieved by God's gratuitously given favor or grace. The term of art by Luther's day was "justification." The individual was rendered justified in the eyes of God by God's sharing a degree of his own righteousness. It is a gift; we do not earn it.

If grace is a favor on God's part, the human reciprocal is faith, or, as Luther put it, "Justification is *by* grace *through* faith. "We are justified by faith alone," Luther maintained. But faith for Luther was not so much believing *that* as belief *in*—or, as it appeared to him and the Reformers who followed him, *trust* in God. To use one of his own figures, *faith that* believes that the boat exists; *faith in* enables us to step aboard and *entrust* ourselves to it.

By 1520 Luther was no longer merely disputing a difficult question with his fellow Catholic theologians; he had in effect broken with the Church of Rome. That year, he published three tracts in which he denied many of the Church's practices and institutions, and in the last of them, *On the Freedom of the Christian*, he announced the Christian's liberation through faith, a liberation from the obligation to perform good works. This lay well beyond the understood limits of the debate *de gratia*, and on 15 June 1520, the pope replied with the bull *Exsurge Domine* in which forty-one of Luther's 1517 theses were condemned as heretical. His writings were ordered destroyed and he himself was formally called on to recant. Luther replied by burning the papal bull and a number of Catholic books. Finally, on 3 January 1521, the Vatican issued the bull *Decet romanum pontificem* excommunicating him.

Doubly Saved and Doubly Damned

The medieval approach to the question of election and salvation was to remain within the lines sketched out by Paul, that some are chosen or elected for salvation, and Augustine's emphasis that, as a result of the Fall, all humanity is marked for damnation, except those God has freely elected to save. The medieval theologians chose, however, to move their emphasis in the direction of God's overarching love of humankind and so of his predisposition to save all, an emphasis that shifted the responsibility for damnation back to human acts. That was not Luther's idea, nor Augustine's, of how salvation occurred, and Luther's pessimism about the human condition and his remarkable faith that only God's good pleasure saves, refocused attention on the Pauline election texts and on Augustine's massa damnata characterization of humanity.

Augustine thought that all humanity was damned by reason of its fallen nature and that after Adam's sin God elects to save some portion of his creation and abandon the rest to their fate. But toward the end of his life, Augustine also put forward what had come to be called a "double predestination" theory whereby some were elected for salvation and the rest equally "elected" for damnation: God damned as determinedly as he saved. Luther inclined toward this latter view, but the doctrine of double predestination is most closely linked with John Calvin (d. 1564), the French Reformer of Geneva who regarded himself—and in many ways was—a faithful follower of Augustine.

Calvin's *Institutes*, his masterpiece (which cites Augustine far more than any other authority), went through numerous editions. With each revision, the issue of predestination, which was laid out quite briefly in the work's earliest version, was treated (and argued) in more detail, chiefly, it would appear, because the subject had aroused the most interest, and opposition, among the Reformer's followers, rivals, and enemies. It was indeed a hard teaching. For Calvin, if only occasionally for the later Augustine, the saved and the damned were both subjects of God's quite arbitrary election. "All are not created in equal condition; rather, eternal life is foreordained for some, eternal damnation for others" (*Institutes* 3.21.5). Neither group deserved their fate. And there was a disturbing corollary, which Calvin seems to have accepted, though without much enthusiasm: Christ had died to redeem not all of humankind but only the elect. Why? the answer is the same as Calvin gave on predestination itself: because it pleased God to do so.

The Council of Trent on Justification

The Council of Trent was convened in 1545, a year before Luther's death. It was Rome's response to the Reform, a traditional assembling of the bishops of Christendom to address the issues raised by Luther, Calvin, and the other, now numerous Reformers across Europe. The assembly took up the matter of salvation and justification in its sixth session in 1547. Luther had begun by asserting, in the spirit of Augustine, that the sinner *became* righteous; later in his career he came to believe that by grace the sinner was *declared* righteous. The bishops at Trent returned to Augustine's view that justification was a process of regeneration and renewal that took place within human nature. Grace worked with nature to elevate it; it was not something that simply covered over or masked a nature that was fatally afflicted. The Council condemned the doctrine of justification through faith alone.

Augustine had argued in his Platonic way that just as the soul, which is superior to the body, gives life to the body, so God's grace, which is "something above men," enables humans to perform moral acts (*City of God* 19.26). Grace is not then according to nature but rather a supernature. This quality of grace became the chief focus of Catholic discussions of moral theology in the days after Trent. Aquinas had accepted Augustine's analogy between grace and the soul, but in his naturalistic Aristotelian psychology, the soul was the "form" of the body, its natural perfection, and so for Thomas supernatural grace became

> **Note:** As a matter of fact, the Reformers had distinguished justification from sanctification: justification began through faith, but sanctification followed through good works. In July 1998 the Vatican and the Lutheran Church issued a "Joint Declaration on the Doctrine of Justification" that stated: "Together we confess: By grace alone, in faith in Christ's saving work and not because of any merit on our part, we are accepted by God and receive the Holy Spirit, who renews our hearts while equipping and calling us to good works."

in a sense "naturalized." It enabled the Christian to share in the life of God and at the same time live a perfectly natural, and perfectly Christian, moral life. Thus Thomas and all who followed him down this path restored to integrity the fatally flawed fragments of human nature on which Augustine had so ruefully gazed.

The Magisterium Restored

Many who embraced the Reform did so not only because of what they regarded as the Church's reprehensible practices but also because they had became disillusioned by the increasing "Aristotelizing" of the Church's theologians in the thirteenth century and the skepticism that seemed to grip so many in the fourteenth. In the end, the papacy agreed with the Reformers, at least to the extent of wresting the magisterium away from the theologians (see I/5). But while the Reformers were uncertain where such an authority should rest in the world of sola Scriptura and the "priesthood of all the believers," the Roman See asserted it of itself. Rome was *mater et magistra of* all the churches. Luther wished to restrict the Roman See's right to pronounce on matters of salvation to what was found in Scripture and, carefully, in the witness of the earlier, and still pristine, Church. Rome's riposte, at Trent and with increasing emphasis in the decades that followed, was to invoke the magisterium, the right to teach in an authoritative manner.

The Roman claim had been put forward well before the Reformation, as Luther himself recognized. In 1519, arguing against the papal representative Johann Eck, he had stated that "It is certainly not within the power of the Church or the pope to lay down articles of faith or even laws of mores, that is, of good works, on the ground that all these are handed down in Sacred Scripture. All that is in their power to do is to declare articles [that is, of faith, found in Scripture], and secondly, for the external beauty of the Church of God, to regulate ceremonies." This the Council of Trent explicitly rejected, laying down in what has been called its "foundation decree" its adherence not only to Scripture but also to "those traditions relating both to faith and to mores"—here probably religious practices—as either verbally from Christ or dictated by the Holy Spirit, and "preserved in continuous succession in the Catholic Church."

Trent's argument was here made on behalf of the Church, the Roman Church, to be sure, but the defenders of the papal magisterium as such found their principal champion in Robert Bellarmine (d. 1621), a Jesuit theologian of Louvain and the Roman College, the latter one of the Church's own "universities." The pope or a general council can err, Bellarmine conceded, on matters of fact, which rely on information and human testimony, or when functioning as private teachers of faith or morals. But neither the pope nor a general council can make a mistake when it is a question of setting forth definitions of faith or general precepts of morals. In this declaration of Bellarmine, a theologian working for the papacy, and which the papacy took for its own, it is clear that the post-Reformation Roman Church had effectively wrested the magisterium from the hands of the professional theologians, of which Bellarmine was one, and placed it firmly in the hands of the hierarchy, with the pope as the final arbitrator in all matters, magisterial as well as jurisdictional.

A Conference on "Aids"

The university faculties were not soon or easily silenced, however. In the sixteenth century, the intellectual heart of Catholic Europe beat most strongly and loudly in the universities of the Iberian Peninsula, this time not on the subject of justification but on the operation of its instrument. If grace had now been worked into a naturalistic understanding of human nature in Catholic circles, its coming upon the individual had still to be reconciled with God's foreknowledge of all things. Theologians in the sixteenth century fought bitterly over the question of God's "assistance," some, namely the Dominicans, insisting that God promotes or propels humans to moral action with grace, while others, chiefly Jesuits, thought this explanation sacrificed too much of human free will and argued instead that God knew beforehand what an individual would choose, and if that action was—or was going to be—virtuous, God provided the grace necessary to perform it.

Thus erupted the highly contentious, often highly personal, and still unresolved controversy called, in theological shorthand, *de auxiliis*, "On Aids," the "aids" or "helps" in question being the graces bestowed by God to enable us to avoid sin and do good. It attempted to answer the question of how God, who makes all things be so, could know what we are going to do without making it so. How could God save us (as only he could) while appearing to only *help* save us? To perform this extremely difficult and delicate task required extraordinary conceptual ingenuity and linguistic agility, but neither was lacking in the theology faculties of the late sixteenth century. Jesuits and Dominicans each offered their own highly varied menu of God's graces—sanctifying, efficient, sufficient, antecedent, congruent, and actual—to explain how God could know and yet not know, will save and yet not save.

Finally, Pope Clement VIII, who had asked for written opinions on the subject, and then appointed a commission to study the matter, in 1602 ordered the principals to appear before him to thrash out the issue in person. Between 1602 and 1605 there were sixty-eight sessions on what came to be known as the Conference on Aids (Congregatio de Auxiliis). Clement VIII died in 1605 and the task was taken up anew by Paul V. There were seventeen more sessions between 1605 and 1607. In the end the pope decreed on 5 September 1607 that each side might continue to hold its position on the matter, though without condemning or reviling the other, and further, no book might be published on the subject of God's "efficacious grace" until the pope should grant permission. This was, needless to say, a very long time in coming.

The Crisis in Catholic Morality

In his defense of the papal power to teach authoritatively on matters of faith and morals, Bellarmine also addressed the issue of conscience that had troubled the Reformers. In cases of moral doubt, "so that it not act against its conscience, it [the Church in its members] is obliged to believe that good which he [the pope] orders and that bad which he prohibits." The same lesson was found, keyed down to more popular consumption, in one of the chief instruments of the Catholic Counter-Reformation, the *Spiritual Exercises* of Ignatius of Loyola, founder of the Jesuits, with its eighteen rules for "thinking with the Church."

But even in the Catholic world, neither the pope nor the general councils had pronounced on all moral matters, and Bellarmine's "cases of moral doubt" must have seemed considerably more numerous and more complex in the rapidly expanding and increasingly secularized world of the sixteenth and seventeenth centuries than they had in the twelfth or thirteenth. And although the discussion of moral problems and their resolution was still the preserve of university theologians—now those of the new Catholic universities of the Counter-Reformation; twenty were founded by Pope Gregory XIII (r. 1572–1585)—the questions often came from below. Trent had decreed an emphasis on the education of the clergy as well as on the catechesis of the laity (see II/4), and the university theologians had to provide a workable moral theology for parish priests and rural vicars. Where once handbooks of penances had served, now the resolution of matters of conscience was required.

That guidance came in the first instance from the experts, the theologians at the older but still Catholic universities like Paris and at the newer ones like Valladolid and Salamanca in Spain and Coimbra in Portugal. Trent had set its seal of approval on the Aristotle-based theological system of Thomas Aquinas, and it was in the context of Thomistic scholasticism that the theologians of the sixteenth and seventeenth centuries attacked the moral problems arising from a world undergoing extraordinary social, economic, and political transformation in a climate of religious upheaval.

To one Spanish professor, Bartolomeo de Medina, falls the distinction of having defined one of the era's most problematic concepts. "If an opinion is probable," he wrote, "it is permitted to adopt it, even if the opposite (opinion) is more probable." A probable opinion, he continued, is one "stated by wise men and confirmed by very good arguments." Thus the troubled topic of "probabilism" was added to the agenda of theologians and lawyers alike. Medina was writing Latin, not English, and so when he spoke of a moral choice that was "probable," he was not referring to a position that was "likely," as the English word suggests, but one that was *probabilis*, that is, subject to proof by weighty opinions or substantial arguments or, as appears from the definition, even one that is "merely probable" as opposed to another position that might in fact be more provable, probable (*probabilior*), or persuasive. The view that the person confronted with such a choice was obliged to choose the latter "more probable" course of action soon came to be called "probabiliorism." Quickly too other possibilities of moral choice appeared, or better, were discovered by the ingenious moralists: a more conservative one that maintained that the choice of a probable alternative was available only when the two choices were equally probable (the position called "aequiprobabilism") or, even more rigorously, that in important matters one had always to choose the "safer" moral option, that is, the choice more conducive to saving one's soul, no matter how "probable" the other possibilities might be.

This spectrum of moral choices, aptly described as an "elaborate moral shorthand," is nothing more than an attempt to address the problem of moral choice, an attempt undertaken by academics, it is clear, not by pastors charged with the care of souls. Medina had laid out what he regarded as a reasonable basis for making such a choice, that it should have behind it both the external weight of competent authority, the "wise men" of the definition, and the intrinsic force of "very good arguments." What followed, however, was the degeneration of the probabilist position into one more properly labeled "laxist," that is, in doubtful cases, a moral choice is rendered "probable" or "provable," and so permissible, by the invocation of *any* orthodox authority or by putting forward almost *any* argument to justify it.

The degradation of what appeared to be a reasonable standard into a broad permissiveness came about in the academic laboratories of the moral theologians, that is, in the moral case studies (*casus conscientiae*). This case study approach, called casuistry, which was designed to provide guidance for confessors in giving spiritual counsel, not for shoppers at the boutiques of moral choice, has acquired a bad name. As happened in its rabbinic parallel, *pilpul*, which was also based on careful reasoning and often oversubtle distinctions, the casuists' ingenuity often overwhelmed their moral sensibilities. Every possible moral choice was soon accompanied by a line of reasoning calculated to render it *probabilis*. Indeed, one practitioner was so skillful in constructing *probabilitas* that he came to be known, not exactly admiringly, as the "Lamb of God" because he had taken away so many of the sins of the world.

Jansenism

One of the matters at issue in the moral thinking of Christian theologians of the thirteenth and following centuries, indeed in theological thinking generally, was supernaturalism. The entire Platonic worldview was based on a fundamental disjunction between the imperfect and contingent order of the material world and the eternal and unchanging world of the *eide*, those true beings that serve as prototypes of our attenuated version of what we mistakenly think is "reality." For a Jewish Platonist like Philo or a Christian Platonist like Augustine, the eide were simply and sensibly the ideas of God, the unique Lord of that higher realm. But God was also the Creator, and so our material world, created willfully and in his own image, was a deliberate reflection, in some manner, of his own.

None of this is far from what later Platonists held and taught; Christianity added its own radical turn in the intrusion of God's reality into our own contingent universe, in God's very creation of the universe, not by an internal and eternal necessity, as the Platonists had it, but by a free and voluntary act; by God's self-revelation through Scripture; overwhelmingly by the Incarnation, the taking-on of flesh by God's Son and his redemptive death on the cross; and finally, in God's moral sustinence of his creatures through his favor. We are saved, according to Augustine, only by this condescension from on high into this invincibly sinful world—the price of Original Sin—that exists below. "It is not something that comes from man but something above man that makes his life blessed."

Thomas Aquinas eased back from this position by stressing, in quite Aristotelian fashion, the cooperation of grace with human nature: grace was supernatural, above nature but somehow connected to it. By availing oneself of this supernatural power offered by God, the human agent could achieve effects that went beyond unaided nature. Supernatural grace was no longer a "magic bullet" to cure us of sin but a powerful additive that led to the creation of "infused" moral virtues far superior to their natural counterparts. The Council of Trent embraced this Thomistic teaching on "natural" supernaturalism as the perfect retort to the Reformers' reading of Augustine, but Augustine was still a Father of the Church, and there were Catholic Augustinians who were unwilling to surrender Augustine to the Protestants. One was Michel de

Bay or Baius (d. 1589), a professor of theology at the Catholic university of Louvain and one of the delegates at Trent, whose detailed study of Augustine led him not unreasonably to conclude no more than thirty years after Trent that Original Sin had robbed us of our natural end. Grace, immortality, and freedom from concupiscence had all been natural to us. After Thomas, at least some of his interpreters were moved to suggest that God's grace was totally extrinsic to human nature, and even though without grace we can achieve our natural human end, we cannot attain our supernatural end of salvation unless God bestows it on us. Baius may have been reacting to that stance in the name of Augustine, but his writings were nonetheless condemned in 1567; among other things he maintained that it was actually Pelagius, not Augustine, who said "God does not command things which are impossible." The main attempt to replace Thomistic moral theology with Augustine's came later, from someone who had read Augustine with his teacher Baius. This was Cornelius Jansen (d. 1638), bishop of Ypres, whose *Augustinus* was published two years after his death.

The battle over what came to be called Jansenism was not entirely over the *Augustinus*. The rabid struggle between Dominicans and Jesuits over the operation of "assisting" grace had not dissipated despite the papal order for silence on the subject. It had simply moved to the new arena of practical morality and the jousting match over "probable" moral opinion in which the Jesuits generally took what they regarded as the more humane and compassionate position in matters of morality, the same condemned by their opponents as unacceptably laxist. It was in reaction to this, the Thomist sweep in the field of moral theory and the Jesuits' perceived laxism in casuistry, that Baius and Jansen reread Augustine and then made a case once again for humans' natural (postlapsarian) depravity. Grace did not build on nature, as Thomas had it; grace replaced the ruined foundations of human nature and God built on it what nature could not.

This latest war of the moral theologians broke out at the university of Louvain, the seat of the entrenched Augustinians. The Jesuits tried to block the publication of the *Augustinus*, while the Jansenists accused the Jesuits of Pelagianism, the standard Christian recrimination against anyone seen leaning too heavily on good works as the means of salvation. The Jesuits in turn condemned the Jansenists as "Calvinists," the standard Catholic charge against those who seemed to suggest "God's good pleasure" alone saved. In this instance, the pope sided with the Jesuits, and papal bulls issued in 1653, 1656, and 1705 condemned the Jansenist theses on salvation. The long battle between Plato and Aristotle, between Augustine and Aquinas, between the Jansenists and the Jesuits was resolved, for the moment in favor of Aristotle, the "cool and rational, even humanist optimism" of Thomas Aquinas, and the Society of Jesus.

From Pascal to Alfonso di Ligouri

The Jesuits suffered near fatal wounds in their encounter with Jansenism. They had won the theological battle—Rome after all was on their side—but they may have lost the moral war. The Jansenists, with their severe, even ascetic morality, had enormous influence in France, where the Church had fallen into a post-Reform ruin that Trent had never succeeded in clearing away. Jansen's disciples' preaching of a pristine moral purity and vigor appealed to the élan and fervor of many French intellectuals, the *parti dévot*, aristocrats, and even the clergy, who resented Rome's, and the Jesuits', often high-handed ways. One wellspring of the Jansenist moral revival was the community of Cistercian nuns and their admirers at the convent of Port Royal in the fields outside Paris. It was from Port Royal that one convert to the movement, the mathematician Blaise Pascal, launched his elegant and deadly broadside against "Jesuit morality" in his famous *Provincial Letters* published in 1656. The *Letters* were an ironically mocking indictment of the Jesuits' moral teaching on the grounds that they could produce the most sophistical reasons so as to render almost any opinion "probable," and thus, by their moral cleverness, condone even the most reprehensible behavior. The Jesuits had, according to Pascal, "put a pillow under the elbow of the sinner." Rome was not as amused at Pascal's exercise as the French intelligentsia, and the *Provincial Letters* were straightaway placed on the *Index of Prohibited Books*. It should have been the last word, but a wound had been inflicted on both the Jesuits and the Church's moral stature.

Both extremes, the by-grace-alone Augustinianism and radical morality of the Jansenists—they reminded Voltaire of Scotch Presbyterians, which he did not intend as a compliment—as well as the laxist positions of the hypercasuists, were condemned by the magisterium and the Catholic consensus. The Jesuits spent most of the second half of the seventeenth century attempting to put their own house in order, though still wavering between probabilism and the narrower standard of probabiliorism, that in moral matters one must always follow the more probable position.

It was neither a Jesuit nor a Dominican who gave its heading to a Church badly adrift in a moral quandary. Rather, it was the Italian theologian Alfonso di Ligouri (d. 1787), whose personal sanctity led to his own canonization in 1839, and whose writings stabilized Catholic teaching on morality. His *Theologia moralis*, first published in 1748, with nine editions during his own lifetime, adopted a common-sensical approach to morality—if it seems wrong, it probably is wrong—though with enough stiffening in the standards to rule out any degree of laxism. The only truly doubtful questions, Ligouri advised, are where opinions are truly and equally divided pro and con. In that case, and in that case only, it is permissible to follow any "provable" opinion. In all other instances of doubt, the weight of the consensus, the "more probable opinion," determines what should be done. All this, it should be noted, has to do only with doubtful cases. In the overwhelming number of moral choices, Ligouri pointed out, the teaching of the Church is traditionally consistent and unmistakably clear.

Muhammad as Moral Exemplar

Like his monotheistic coreligionists, the Muslim derives from the revealed Word of God his general precepts of morality as well as both counsels and detailed prescriptions on behavior. The Quran is addressed to all humankind, calling them to goodness (*al-khayr*, "the better"), to justice, equity, and especially righteousness (*birr*), which is explicitly defined in Quran 2:177. The message of the Meccan suras in particular was intended for all who are willing to listen, but as the message and the mission proceeded, the Quran's instruction was increasingly directed, without any formal change in address, to the Muslims who make up the community or umma. Hence, the Quran is both the "Guidance"—a frequent self-characterization—for all humanity and, more precisely, a manual of behavior for the Muslim believer.

Jesus' primary role in the Christian faith was that of redeemer, the messianic son of God whose sacrificial death on the cross redeemed humankind from sin. But the Son of God was also "Son of Man," which, though the Christians thought of it preeminently as a messianic title, still possessed its literal Aramaic resonance of *bar adam*, a human, "in all things like us," as the author of Hebrews put it, "sin alone excepted" (4:15). It was perfectly natural, then, that Jesus should become the exemplary model for all Christians. It did not turn out exactly so, however. The two primary images of Jesus were, in the Eastern Church, *christos pantokrator*, Christ regnant, lord of the world enthroned in majesty, and in the Latin West, Jesus crucified, the vilified servant hanging ignominiously on the cross. The first elicited awe, the second loving gratitude; neither suggested emulation. The Church found its models elsewhere: in the early martyrs who bore witness to their faith with their blood, and later in the "confessors," those who showed forth their faith not by their deaths but by their lives—lives that were of course blameless but also marked by extraordinary self-denial and self-abnegation (see II/8).

Muhammad was more genuinely "in all things like us"—there was no mirror-image Godhead to either outshine or overmaster Muhammad's humanity—though Muslim piety attempted, quite successfully, to add its own disclaimer of "sin alone excepted" (see I/3). Furthermore, the canonical portrait of Muhammad suffered none of the narrative thinness of the Gospels' account of Jesus' three scant years of reported ministry. The Gospel narrative is concerned with things other than showing forth, in the manner of one of Plutarch's biographies, for example, Jesus' character exemplified in action. Its purpose was rather to show how he had fulfilled the messianic prophecies of the Bible, how he demonstrated his messianic powers through cures and exorcisms, and how, even in the unlikely circumstances of an arrest, a trial, and a very public execution, Jesus was still the Messiah and triumphed from beyond the grave. There are also in the Gospels Jesus' moral teachings, most of them well within the Jewish moral tradition of the time, and, finally, the more idiosyncratic and still somewhat problematic moral instructions embedded in Jesus' characteristic parables. Of Jesus' own exemplary moral conduct, we are given relatively little.

Muhammad lies well concealed behind the Quran, which was delivered through him yet is only occasionally about him. But outside the Quran, there is no such reticence. There was, moreover, in early circulation an enormous body of reports that professed to give the Prophet's own moral instruction on almost every conceivable subject and provided, moreover, vivid vignettes of Muhammad at prayer and at meals, on campaign and en famille, as husband, father, judge, statesman, and military strategist. Both the private Muhammad and the public Prophet are on full display in the hadith (see II/3).

> **Note:** Although there are some personal details in the classical biographical tradition that properly begins with the *Life* composed by Ibn Ishaq (d. 768), the works that applied vivid flesh and lively blood to the portrait belong to a somewhat different genre. Called either "The Proofs of Prophecy" or "The Good Qualities (of the Prophet)," these are essentially collections of anecdotes, and as such they stand much closer to hagiography than to biography. Like the apocryphal Gospels of the Christian tradition, they present the life of their subject after a fashion, but their chief interest is in his personality, character, appearance, and miracles. The earliest example of the type is "The Good Qualities" of al-Tirmidhi (d. 892), which was endlessly glossed and expanded and formed the basis of the most influential of these personal and character studies of the Prophet, the "Authentic Definition of the Truths of the Chosen One" by the severe Spanish jurist and chief justice of Granada known as Qadi Iyad (d. 1149). All later such works merely expand and elaborate the earlier glowing portraits of the traits, human and more than human, of the Prophet of Islam.

Tradition provides, then, a fully fleshed-out if at times self-contradictory portrait of the Prophet, and it has served from the time of its construction in the eighth century down to the present as the template and measure of the ideal Muslim life. And not merely in matters of moral choice: the hadith offer a broad and varied menu of preferred social behavior, of etiquette rather than morality. The latter notion of etiquette (*adab*) was later integrated into Islamic moral thinking generally.

Islamic Morality

As a manual of morality the Quran is obviously incomplete, at least in the sense that its general principles of behavior have not been drawn out into every one, or indeed many, of the forms that such behavior might take. A great deal more detailed instruction was provided by the body of traditions handed down about the Prophet's own behavior, but there still remained the considerable task of explaining, ordering, and adducing into their particulars the general moral principles provided by revelation. This fell to the science of jurisprudence (*fiqh*), which Ghazali defined as "the science of scriptural rules established for the regulation of the acts of those who are obliged," that is, the Muslims. Dialectical theology (*kalam*) (see II/7), in contrast, took up the investigation, explanation, and defense of the principles themselves, among them the not inconsiderable task of reconciling God's all-determining Will and humans' responsibility for their own acts (see below).

General jurisprudence had as its subject the "roots of the law," whereas particular jurisprudence, the "science of the branches," was devoted to placing a moral template atop the range of conscious human activity to provide guidance for the Muslim. Accordingly, at one end of the spectrum of human acts are those, like prayer, that are judged "mandatory" or "obliged" (*fard*) and so are morally incumbent on the believer. At the other end are practices that are simply forbidden, like usury (Quran 3:130).

Note: The categorization of foods stands somewhat obliquely on that of human acts. Some foods are indeed forbidden (*haram*) to Muslims by reason of their substance, like pork (Quran 2:167) or wine (5:92), or, in the case of meats, by the manner of their preparation, if they are scavenged, for example, or not properly slaughtered. Foods that meet these latter criteria are termed *halal*, "kosher," and so permitted. Here, as elsewhere in Islamic law, circumstances condition the obligation: where ritual slaughter is impossible, Muslims may use Jewish butchers, and where no other nourishment of any type is available, they may eat nonhalal foods.

Between the absolutely required and the absolutely forbidden stand three intermediary moral categories. In the middle is the morally neutral (*mubah*) act that lies entirely in the discretion of the agent. Toward the side of virtue lies a field of acts that are "recommended" (*mandub*). Verging toward vice are the "cautioned" or "discouraged" (*makruh*) acts. In all cases, however, the internal state, the agent's intention (*niyya*), is crucial in determining the morality of a given action.

The lawyers divided prescribed actions into those directed toward God as his due, the "acts of worship" (*ibadat*) that constituted Islam's ritual code, and the "moral acts" (*muamalat*) that described and evaluated transactions between individual Muslims, where consensus played a powerful role. The ritual acts that constitute one category of the Muslim's obligations are based on God's right and humans' consequent obligations. The moral acts, however, are acquired obligations. They had their pre-Islamic origins in transactions, chiefly having to do with land use, and they never quite lost that original sense even as they broadened into a moral category. For Ghazali, for example, the muamalat, which form the heart of Muslim ethics, consist either of exchanges like trading, selling, lending, debt, and the like or of contracts and their dissolution, hence matters of marriage, divorce, slavery, emancipation, and so forth.

This is a rather notable narrowing of the field of moral activity—the matter submitted to the muftis for their opinion (see II/4) was, of course much broader. Otherwise notable was the role played by the very typical Arab notion of adab, a kind of social etiquette that included both a "style" and a body of information. Adab was what was expected in a polite society; what actually occurred was *adat*, the community's customs or manners. Thus, throughout Islamic history, consideration of the morality of the muamalat has had a powerful sociological constituent, one that took account of both adab and adat in determining how a Muslim should act in given circumstances. It was powerful enough, in any event, for an observer like Ibn Khaldun (d. 1406) to make the science of moral acts one of the rational sciences rather than a "revealed science"—to regard it as an ethical rather than a moral concern, as those two terms have been used here. The distinction continues to resonate in the modern Muslim tendency to regard the "ritual duties" as unchanging and unchangeable, while the construction of the moral acts is in part determined by the givens of society.

Ibn Khaldun had a great deal of evidence to suggest to him that the regulation of behavior was more properly rational than revelational, even though revelation was filled with moral counsels and directives. Muslim intellectuals had long been aware that there was an extensive theoretical literature in

> **Note:** The Arabic translators of Greek ethical studies, whether individual, like Aristotle's *Nicomachean Ethics*, or sociopolitical, like Plato's *Laws*, worked under a considerable handicap since they had little or no grasp of the Hellenic adab—what the Greeks called *paideia*—that informed those works. Aristotle's *Politics* was, in fact, the only work of the philosopher that the translators passed over.

Greek on practical and humane ethics, what the Arabs came to call *akhlaq*, perhaps the "ethics of character."

Islam also had available a broad range of descriptive works on ethics and popular morality, as represented, for example, by the various "Mirrors for Princes" that Islam had inherited from its pre-Islamic Persian past or in the Greek aphoristic works plentifully available in Arabic translation. This material had quickly worked its way into a large body of original works in Arabic ranging from belletristic essays to manuals for the scribes and sometime courtiers who peopled the chanceries of Islam and were intended to introduce them to the refinements of adab, which invariably included a healthy dose of the wit and wisdom of the Greeks.

> **Note:** The integrity of the original (borrowed) sources is probably best preserved in the Arabic works professedly devoted to akhlaq. Aristotle's *Ethics* together with Porphyry's commentary was a major component in them, as was the physician Galen's eclectic *On Ethics*. The connection between medicine and philosophy was pervasive among both Muslims and Jews, more so than among the Greeks, from whom they learned both sciences, or among the Latin Christians, who learned from them in turn. The blending of these authorities, Peripatetic, Neoplatonic, and late Pythagorean, comes together in Ibn Miskawayh (d. 1030), whose *Ethics* was the most influential of the Muslim effort to fashion a philosophical ethic. He had successors, most notably Nasir al-Din Tusi (d. 1274), who broadened the field to include Ibn Sina's psychology, and al-Dawwani (d. 1501), who added a Shiite sensibility to the by now familiar Greek mélange.

Free Will and Predestination in Islam

The issue of free will and predestination that Christianity eventually rendered moot, or perhaps, in the Roman case, mute, Muslims had inevitably to take up afresh. The God revealed in the Quran possesses, no less than his counterparts worshiped by the Jews and Christians, unlimited knowledge and an absolute capacity to do whatever he wills. But since the Quran more often asserts the principle of God's omnipotence than it shows it in operation, as the Bible does, Muslims were left to their own devices when it came to working out the details of the operation of God's all-powerful Will. The need to do just that arose early in Islam. It was among the first of the theological issues to confront the community—promoted, it has been maintained, by Christian polemicists—which had to resolve its apories without the Prophet's assistance and in a very different political and intellectual climate from that in which the Quran had first been revealed.

There was no mistaking the Quran's message: God, who possessed an absolute power that is manifested first in his creation and then in his providential sustenance of the world, is also the world's judge. Punishment follows upon sin, sometimes in this life, as the Bible insisted, and certainly in the next, as the Gospels declared. The Quran's emphases in this matter are closer to the Gospels': humans will be judged by God at the End Time (see II/10), and they will be recompensed exactly for their belief (or disbelief) and their deeds. The virtuous will find their reward in paradise and the wicked will burn eternally in hell. Here on earth we can only hope for God's mercy; at the Judgment we will experience God's perfect justice, mitigated only by the possibility of the Prophet's intercession.

The vivid message in the Quran's reflections on paradise and Gehenna are wellknown; equally forceful are the Quran's assertions of God's predestinating power over all things, including, in quite explicit fashion, all human actions. Humans act only, and to the extent that God empowers them to do so, by his decree. Later Muslims found grounds in the Quran for distinguishing in this matter of God's Will between his absolute and eternal decree (*qada*, literally, "judgment"), as represented in Quran 2:117; 3:47; 39: 35 and 40:48, and the divine decree (*qadar*, literally, "measure") that spells out limits in time, in the terms imposed on a given human life, for example, or the goods God allots to this individual or that. Qadar is, in short, the measure of being.

Having established this distinction, Muslim theology chose to understand qada, which differs little from William of Ockham's potentia absoluta, as an essential attribute of God and so, in Islamic ontology, eternal and free of all contingency and change. Contingency enters the picture with qadar, "the relationship of the essential Will with things in their particular realization." Qadar is God's Will as it works out in human life, and it presented no notional problems in its "measuring" aspect, as in alloting a short life or a long one, health or illness, good fortune or bad, where it functioned without let. The problem arose, naturally, with those acts for which humans are held responsible by God as if they, not he, had created them. Traditional Muslim thinkers turned away from this possibility, which seemed, inescapably, to ascribe an act of creation to mortals. They much preferred to live with Scripture's own paradox of an omnipotent Creator who judged humanity for what appeared to be the Creator's own actions.

A Rationalist Solution

The paradox of an all-powerful and yet just God confronting morally responsible human agents who possessed the freedom of choice that such responsibility inescapably implied, and for God to curb his freedom by sharing that sovereign quality with his own creation, made as little apparent sense in a Muslim context as it did in a Jewish or Christian one. As remarked, many

Muslims, like most Jews and Christians, simply embraced the paradox and attempted to live within it. But the need to explain thrust Christian theologians into the heart of the problem, and, under the same rationalist impulse, from the same Greek philosophical sources, some Muslims were provoked into a similar enterprise. Islam's first and enduring rationalists were the Mutazilites (see II/7). They prided themselves on being, among other things, defenders of God's justice. Though many, indeed most, Muslims would maintain that they were undermining rather than defending that principle, the Mutazilites certainly concerned themselves with moral issues, though in a profoundly theological rather than a practical sense. Indeed, the summa of the Mutazilite thinker Abd al-Jabbar (d. 1025) has been called "the most extensive discussion of ethics preserved in Islamic literature."

To preserve God's justice, the Mutazilites felt themselves constrained to resolve the tension between God's absolute Will and humans' freedom of choice in favor of the latter. The decision was prompted not so much by humanistic considerations as by the demands of reason. If God was just and if humans were punished and rewarded for their actions, both quranic givens, then humans must have freely chosen them: in effect, they created their own moral acts. if this was so, then God's Will, or at least some aspect of it, his qadar, is conditioned by human choice and hence contingent, subject to an external condition.

In traditionalist eyes, God's absolute Will could be nothing but arbitrary. Things were good or evil simply because God said they were, because that was "God's good pleasure," as the Quran had it. The Mutazilites found that an unacceptable notion and preferred the other, apparently more just option, even though it meant that God had to conform to some external necessity. God decreed the good because it was already good, good by nature. God is no less bound with respect to his creation. Having created humankind with the merciful intent of saving it, God is constrained to provide the means of salvation. Though the Quran suggests at many turns that God abandons some individuals, that he "allows them to wander," in this case, to perdition, the Mutazilites would not have it so: God must offer the "Guidance." Humans are free to accept or reject it—his Will is unfettered—but God's favor or grace (*lutf*) is given necessarily.

Acquiring Responsibility

The Mutazilites' bold assertion, in the face of unmistakable quranic evidence to the contrary, that to preserve God's justice humans had to deserve their final end, and in order to do that they had to be free to choose, to "create" moral good and evil, did not win much support among Islam's traditionalist thinkers, whether lawyers or theologians. If the lawyers were largely content to accept that God's predetermining omnipotence and human punishment or reward could coexist within God's justice, "without asking how" (see II/7), some theologians did attempt to supply the "how." According to the solution proposed by the school of al-Ashari (d. 935), and thereafter generally accepted as Islamic orthodoxy, what connected humans to their divinely predestined and divinely executed actions—God predetermines all and God actually does all—was their "acquisition" (*kasb, iktisab*) by the human (apparent) agent. This "acquisition" is, no less than the capacity to act, a divine creation, to be sure, but while eschewing genuine secondary causality by created beings, it established an ontological link between the "agent" (actually the subject) and the act that followed and for which the human had now "acquired" responsibility.

How, then, is a Muslim to behave in a universe dominated by God's absolute and quite arbitrary Will? According to al-Ghazali, who was an Asharite in his theology, the answer is best supplied by Islam's mystics, the Sufis. Their constant striving for an obliteration of self made the best of them acutely aware that there is nothing besides God. From this insight arises humans' sole hope, *tawakkul*, the total resignation of the created will to God's Will. If humans could but extinguish their own desires, Ghazali counsels, "your hope, confidence, and trust would be placed in Him, since He is the unique and exclusive Agent."

This system of moral theology, where all depends on God's Will and where humans are morally determined in act and end by nothing other than "God's good pleasure" has been justly called "ethical voluntarism." In its ontological aspects, it is what has been known in the West as "Occasionalism" (see II/7).

Consensus on Matters Moral

Consensus (*ijma*) is the often unacknowledged key to the sharia. It arose of necessity from a system based on a revelation that was closed by a single definitive event, the Prophet's death, rather than by consensus, as happened in the case of the Jews and Christians who themselves signaled the end of the incremental growth of their Scriptures by some form of gradual but nonetheless effective community agreement. The sudden closure of the Quran occurred as the umma was beginning its astonishing growth into a community linked by little else than their monotheistic faith, their possession of the Arabic document that had proclaimed it, and certain ethnocultural ties. The absence of detailed behavioral and institutional norms was in part met by the equally astonishing growth of hadith purporting to supply moral guidance from the Prophet's own example (see II/3). As a legal instrument, the hadith soon collapsed under their own weight. For ninth-century Muslims there were too many to be convincing, just as for the modern non-Muslim, they are too good to be true. The attempt to reground the certitude of the proliferation of

Prophetic reports led to the canonical collections of sound or healthy hadith. Muslim scholars then had in hand a reliable closed body of reliable and authoritative data from which to fashion a workable code of Muslim behavior.

Quran-based reasoning on moral matters has always been selective in the sense that all the verses of the Revelation, like its counterpart in Judaism and Christianity, are of equal truth, and so the citation of any one of them is in theory definitive. The fastidiously trained jurist might recognize the contradictions between one quranic verse and another and seek to justify them by applying the principle of abrogation (see II/1), but for most the quranic *ipse dixit* was enough. The same attitude seems to have prevailed in the matter of the hadith. Such an attitude, that "all's fair in Quran and hadith," leads to moral probabilism, namely, that a defensible position is a permissible one; however attractive a notion that might be to radical or amateur moralists, it never was such to Muslim jurists. How, then, in the absence of a determining moral authority, was the Muslim to decide among the varying probable positions founded on Quran or hadith or, more disconcertingly, on the "opinions" of jurists who attempted to work out solutions to moral questions on the basis of their own "personal effort" (*ijtihad*; see II/4)? The answer turned out to lie in consensus.

The agreement of the community of Muslims had its own seeds of anxiety, in the suggestion, for example, that moral truth was what most Muslims thought it was rather than what God said it was. A solution was quickly forthcoming. The authority of consensus rested with God, as explained in an already noted Prophetic saying that inevitably appeared in all discussions of the subject: "My community will never agree in error" (see II/4). Another aspect of the problem was addressed in a second hadith: "You are better judges than I in temporal matters," the Prophet is reported to have said of himself, in addressing future generations, "and I am a better judge than you in what concerns your religion." In matters of faith, then, the Quran and the hadith rule alone; in matters of morality, community consensus may also provide a reliable guide.

The operation of consensus is apparent in the matter of circumcision. The pre-Islamic Arab practice had no warrant in the Quran itself, and yet there are sound hadith that seem to prescribe it for both men and women. The Muslim consensus decided early on that male circumcision was indeed an obligation, whereas there was no general agreement on the matter of female circumcision, which is, consequently, practiced by some Muslims, ignored by others, and decried by still others.

Consensus, it is clear, is mutable, though such changes occur slowly and only with difficulty. The arguments for change take the traditional form of a debate over the "true" and hence "only" interpretation of quranic passages that are often opaque and occasionally contradicted (or "cancelled") by others, or of summoning up hadith that appear to resist the current consensus. What has changed is not the evidence but moral sensibilities, they drive the attempt to change the consensus, just as another set of moral sensibilities shaped it in the first place. Whereas an earlier generation of Muslims preferred to veil its women and make divorce solely a male prerogative, some more recent Muslims prefer women to be unveiled and to make divorce initiation a right of both members to the marriage contract. Both groups resort to quranic exegesis and hadith citation to support their preferences; what distinguishes the more modern arguments is the often unacknowledged presumption of historical conditioning.

6

Divine Worship

IN ITS MOST GENERAL TERMS, worship is the human acknowledgment, in some formal way, of God's existence and power. That acknowledgment may occur in a number of registers (e.g., praise, thanksgiving, petition), and its chief forms, often combined, are prayer, or direct address of God, and ritual, the performance of certain acts thought to be acceptable or pleasing to God. The word "liturgy" or "liturgical" adds to both prayer and ritual the notion that either or both are formal, public, and generally, social. There are, of course, private and individual prayers and private rituals, but they are generally not the subject of discourse in the three monotheistic religious communities.

Shekinah / Sakina

The Torah, which has remarkably little to say about prayer, is highly detailed in its prescriptions on how God wishes to be worshiped. This is to be done principally through the ritual of sacrifice (offerings of animals, grains, and wine) to be performed at specific times, in specific places, by specific personnel. The place was sanctified by God's presence—sometimes in the Bible his "glory" (*kabod*); later his "presence" (*shekinah*)—which, the Israelites were instructed, was especially present, though not depicted, between the wings of the mythic cherubim who rested atop the cover of the chest called the Ark of the Covenant (2 Kings 19:15).

Shekinah is a biblical term (Exod. 25:8; Lev. 16:16) referring to God's presence or "indwelling" among the Israelites. The word has had a long history. *Shekinah* for the Kabbalists was one of God's ten *sefiroth*, or emanations (see II/9), and later rabbinic and Hasidic authors understood the term chiefly in the sense of God's immanent presence in the good or in pious individuals. The early Israelites, however, seem to have understood it more literally and more communally as God's dwelling, in an almost physical sense, among his people, even in the form of a cloud, illumined by night (Exod. 40:36–38). That presence presumably rested in Jerusalem even after the disappearance of the Ark, where the earlier tradition had localized it. Only after the temple and city itself were destroyed by the Romans in 70 c.e. did the persistence of God's shekinah begin to concern the rabbis. Numerous rabbinic sources of the fifth and following centuries assert that the shekinah still rested "behind the western wall." If at first that expression referred to the city's western wall, which the Romans had left standing, it was by the seventh or eighth century transferred to the western wall of Herod's surviving temple platform, more precisely to the still visible section running northward from the southwest corner.

Islam has a similar notion enfolded in the quranic term *sakina*, and in Quran 2:248 there is a rather precise biblical reference to the sakina of God in the Ark of the Covenant along with "relics" of Moses and Aaron. Elsewhere (48:18), God sent his sakina down on the Muslims on the eve of battle to strengthen them, and the term occasionally occurs (9:40; 48:4, 26), in the same sense of a confirming and strengthening presence within the believer. Later, however, it moved into the rabbinic direction and began to signify God's indwelling in the pious, most notably Muhammad, and eventually the sense favored later by Kabbalists: the sakina is a form of spiritual illumination enjoyed by the mystic.

Sacrifice

As the Torah makes clear, sacrifice is the chief form of worship prescribed for the Israelites, whether to honor God or give thanks, for purification, atonement, or feasting. The four legal books of the Pentateuch lay out its modalities in detail, but they do not always agree with each other, or with our other, later, Second Temple witnesses, Philo and Josephus, or our posttemple source, the Mishnah. Sacrifices (*qodashim*, "holy things") were offered either by and for the community or for individuals—but always in the temple, and always in a purified state. Priest, offerer (there were ablution pools at the temple entry), and even the sacrifice had to be free of defilement and imperfection, whether in their offering, sacrificing, or consuming of the sacrificial objects. The latter were herd animals (oxen, cattle, sheep, goats), fowl, meal, oil, or wine.

Commonly the daily community sacrifices (*tamid*) were offered, morning and evening, to open and close the temple services, and they were paid for from the temple tithe of a half-shekel. Each offering was a male lamb, slaughtered by the priest, then completely burned (a "holocaust," from a Greek word meaning "entirely burnt up") with a mixture of flour and oil. Some of the blood was sprinkled on the altar and the rest poured on its base. More substantial animal offerings were sacrificed for the community at each new moon, for all major festivals, and on Yom Kippur. Individuals also offered holocausts, an ox, a lamb, or a kid (which the offerer killed by slitting its throat, although the priests butchered and burned them), simply to honor or glorify God, as Philo points out. Individuals also presented animals as sin and guilt offerings (see II/5), the meat of which belonged to the priests, who later cooked and ate it while still in the temple. Finally, there was the category of "shared offerings," quadrupeds sacrificed to give thanks, fulfill a vow, or simply as a freewill offering. These animals were partially consumed on the altar—this was God's share: the Bible speaks plainly of the offerings being God's "food" (Lev. 6:8; Num. 28:2) —while some parts (the right thigh and breast) were given to the priest and the rest back to the offerer. Neither group had to consume the flesh of this sacrifice in the temple; it might be taken home and shared with the family.

The intervals of sacrifice were marked off by measures of sacred times: the appearance of each new moon—the Israelites followed, and the Jews still do follow, for liturgical purposes, an adjusted ("intercalated") lunar calendar—as well as the High Holy Days. The latter stretched from Rosh Hashanah (New Year's Day) across ten days to Yom Kippur (Day of Atonement) at the beginning of each lunar year (September–October); Muhammad too is said to have marked this festival as Ashura before his falling-out with the Jews of Medina. Finally, there were the three great pilgrimage (*hag*) festivals celebrated at the spring sowing (Pesach, Passover), the spring harvest seven weeks later (Shabuoth, Weeks or Pentecost) and the fall harvest (Sukkoth, Tabernacles).

One odd feature of these liturgies, many of them described in the Bible in great detail, is that they are unaccompanied in our sources by any type of prayer—dedicatory, imprecatory, apotropaic, or other. Israelite sacrifices were, to all appearances, rituals without words, however difficult that is to imagine. But the Quran too provides rituals without prayers—the hajj for example. In this case a prayer liturgy either grew around the ritual or was there, unreported, from the outset.

Was it the apparent lack of prayer, and so of focused intentionality, that prompted the prophets of Israel to sometimes speak critically of the regime of temple sacrifice (Isa. 1:11–14; Amos 5:21–23; Jer. 7:21–22)? They did not denounce the sacrifices as such but decried their unintended effect of converting morality into mere ritualism. Mercy is preferable to sacrifice, Hosea proclaimed (6:6), and later Jesus, who disdained what he regarded as the Pharisees' moral ritualism, quoted him with approval (Matt. 9:13; 12:7).

The Jesus Sacrifice

Jesus lived in late Second Temple times, and though he stressed the moral content of the Law, he had no substantial quarrel with temple sacrifices, even the voluntary ones (Matt. 5:23–24). It is difficult to say, however, whether he had the temple ritual in mind at his own Last Supper (see below), when he said his own blood was "of the New Covenant, poured out for many" (Mark 14:24). Elsewhere in the Gospels, Jesus is identified with the "lamb of

God" (John 1:29; 19:14, 36), and the obvious sacrificial associations of his death on Passover are made explicit in Paul: "Christ, our Passover lamb, has been sacrificed" (1 Cor. 5:7); and again, "Christ loved you and gave himself up on your behalf, and offering and sacrifice whose fragrance was pleasing to God" (Eph. 5:2).

If Christ is the Passover sacrifice for Paul and others of the first generation, he became both the sacrifice and the sacrificing high priest for the author of Hebrews (9:23–29). In this same influential New Testament text, Jesus is explicitly compared to the sin, or better, purification offerings made by the Israelites (Lev. 16:27 = Heb. 13:11–12). This image of Jesus as both the voluntary sacrificial victim and the priest of sacrifice endured in Christianity. So too the reenactment of the Eucharist was universally construed, at least down to the Reformation, as a sacrifice—the "sacrifice of the Mass" in Latin Christianity—with the Church's sacerdotal minister standing in for Jesus and the elements of bread and wine on the altar transformed into the sacrificed body and blood (see below).

> **Note:** Animal sacrifice was a feature of pre-Islamic ritual at Mecca. Although the ritual was given by God, the Quran, which describes sacrifice, expresses certain reservations regarding it (22:32–36; cf. 5:106). Even so, the practice is imposed on Muslims (sura 108), principally in the performance of the hajj (see below). The "festival of the sacrifice" (*id al-adha* or *id al-qurban*) occurs at Mina on the tenth day of the Hajj month. The offering must be a herd animal—the expenses of offering a large animal may be shared—whose head is turned toward the Kaaba and whose throat is slit, much in the manner and intent of Jewish temple sacrifice, so that the blood drains out on the ground. Although eating the flesh afterward is permissible (Quran 22:33), giving it as food for the poor is regarded as meritorious. While this festival is taking place at Mina, other Muslims around the world join in the celebration of the id al-adha by making, if they wish, their own animal sacrifice, sharing the food with neighbors and the needy.

The Jewish Priesthood

According to the Torah given on Sinai, God also established a special hereditary caste of males descended from Aaron who alone would be authorized to conduct the sacrificial rituals (Exod. 28:1; cf. Lev. 8–10). These priests (*kohen*; pl. *kohenim*) took up their posts in the taboo inner court of the temple, received the offerings from other Israelites, and then prepared and sacrificed those offerings. As already noted, these offerings were in some instances totally consumed, while in others the unconsumed part of the sacrifice was reserved for the priests' use. It could hardly have been otherwise since everything offered to or in the temple was thereby rendered taboo (*qorban*) and removed from common use (see Mark 7:9–13). The priests themselves as well as their families had to observe a stricter ritual purity than the rest of the Israelites. Priests continued to serve in the temple and in general to act as the community's religious guides until the temple's final destruction, when their leadership role—although not their liturgical functions—passed to the rabbis.

The Synagogue

We are not entirely sure how the Jews worshiped during the two or three generations of their forced exile in Babylonia, whether they built themselves a temple there, as some other Jews in the Diaspora seem to have done, or simply began substituting prayers for sacrifices, perhaps in the community assembly centers called synagogues (Heb. *bet ha-knesset*), which some have speculated came into existence during that experience. There were, at any rate, synagogues in Eretz Israel after the Jerusalem temple was rebuilt with no suggestion that they were surrogates for the temple. With the destruction of Herod's temple in 70 c.e. and the cessation of sacrifice, however, Jews began substituting prayers for sacrifices and using the already existing synagogues as their chief place of public worship. With what difficulty and opposition we do not know. Neither was prayer limited to the synagogue. A significant element of Jewish worship takes place in the home—Sabbath celebrations, for example—and the presence of a domestic liturgy for such is a distinctive trait of post–70 c.e. Judaism.

The public synagogue service took place on the Sabbath, a weekly day of rejoicing and restraint from work, and on other holy days of celebration, atonement, or recollection. The service began with recitations from the Scriptures, first with serial passages from the Torah distributed across either a three-year cycle current in Palestine from the second to the fifth century c.e. or a single-year cycle that was in use in Babylonia at about the same time and that eventually came to prevail in most Jewish communities. The recitation of the weekly Torah passage, which was accompanied verse by verse by the Aramaic translation (targum; see II/2), was followed by an appropriately chosen passage of about ten verses drawn from the Prophets and again accompanied by a targum. After the chanting of a psalm, the preacher began the homiletic part of the liturgy. He first cited an "opening verse" of his own selection from the Prophets or the Writings, and then proceeded to weave this into the Torah and prophetic passages to form a coherent exegetical and ethical whole. Jesus is depicted in the Gospels as giving just such a homily, albeit a very abbreviated one (Luke 4:16–21).

> **Note:** The Jews laid down the foundation of what has come to be called
> the "weekend," but full development of the notion is a modern phe-
> nomenon since it embraces what the Jews and the Christians regarded as
> the last day of the week, *shabbat* or Sabbath, and the first, "Sunday." The
> first day of the week was an ordinary working day for Jews and the ear-
> liest Christians, but for the latter it soon became "the Lord's day" (Rev.
> 1:10) since Jesus rose on that day (Mark 16:2). As such it began to take
> on a privileged status and, as the Christians grew apart from the Jews
> (see I/5), they dropped their earlier observance of the Sabbath and moved
> some of its solemnity, and consequence, to Sunday, the "day of the In-
> vincible Sun." The Invincible Sun (*Sol Invictus*) was the closest the Romans
> had to an established or state religion at the time of Constantine's con-
> version, but a divinized sun obviously had no future in the Christian Ro-
> man Empire. Although the name "Sunday" lingered on into English—in
> the Western Church it was officially *dies dominica*, the "Lord's Day"—it
> was legislated into a holy day by the state and celebrated by Christians
> as a commemoration of Jesus' resurrection and, somewhat in the Jewish
> manner, observed as a day of rest. The Jewish and Christian notions of
> what constituted "rest," however, varied widely. The Christians often
> parsed it merely as cessation from commercial and entertainment activities.
>
> The Muslim Friday, the "day of assembly" (*yawm al-juma*), likewise
> began its career as a reaction—Muhammad's own reaction, it appears—
> to the Jewish Sabbath, once again in the sense of deliberately choosing a
> day for common prayer that would distinguish the Muslims of Medina
> from the Jews. On that day the community prayer is celebrated (see be-
> low), and though it is not formally a day of rest in the sense that normal
> activities, usually commercial, had to be suspended, it is becoming assim-
> ilated by Muslims worldwide into an expanding notion of the "weekend"
> as nonworking days.

The synagogue rituals were understood by the rabbis as an explicit replacement of the liturgies of the destroyed Jerusalem temple. There are no early
examples, but the essential form of synagogue worship can be reconstructed
from early preserved homiletic commentaries on Scripture that follow a standard format and presumably reflect synagogue practice. Private prayer, normally three times daily, and the domestic liturgy of Judaism, which has no real
parallel in either Christianity or Islam, have left far fewer traces of their evolution. Even though they are largely composed of scriptural passages, and some,
like the Shema and the "Eighteen Benedictions" (Shemoneh Esreh) of the
Amida, the central prayer of the Jewish liturgy, were already being recited—
standing, while facing Jerusalem—in some form during the mishnaic period
and perhaps even earlier, the formalization of the Jewish liturgy—even allowing

for regional and sectarian differences—was the work of medieval scholars in Europe and the Abode of Islam.

The Jewish sacrificial cult ended with the destruction of the temple, and thereafter its place was taken by services that offered prayers of praise and expiation rather than live sacrifices for those same ends. But Judaism was far more than the offering of prayers or even a certain type of ethical behavior. What Moses had been given on Sinai, the written Law of the Torah and the oral tradition finally embodied in the Mishnah and Talmud, were not simply the terms of a covenant to be observed by every Jew but the stuff of a special liturgical vocation. The *bet ha-midrash*, the "house of study," where the Talmud was pondered with such loving care, was as much a place of worship as the synagogal *bet ha-tefillah*, the "house of prayer," and the study of Torah and Talmud was a moral imperative as efficacious as prayer.

The Eucharist

Jesus and his followers, we can be certain, participated in the temple liturgies in Jerusalem, and, as we have seen, "as he regularly did" (Luke 4:16) in synagogue services in Galilee. But Jesus left his lasting liturgical legacy in the so-called Last Supper, the meal he celebrated with his circle of Twelve the night before his death. It had many aspects of a Passover meal (but many disparities too), and that was how Christians soon chose to see it. The earliest Christian communities may have celebrated both a community meal (see below) and a Eucharist (from the Gk. *eucharizein*, "to render thanks"), but the latter quickly became the chief form of Christian liturgical worship.

The eucharistic scene is remembered in Mark, Matthew, and Luke as well as by Paul in similar, though by no means identical, detail. It took place on Thursday evening, after the sunset that began Passover (John, who makes no mention of the Eucharist but does note a meal shared by Jesus and the Twelve, puts it on the night *before* Passover). Jesus and the Twelve were in an "upper room" somewhere in Jerusalem. They were at table when Jesus took bread—if this was indeed Passover, it would have been unleavened bread or matzoh—blessed it, broke it into pieces, and distributed them to the Twelve, saying, "Take this; this is my body." Then he took a cup of wine, likewise blessed it and gave them to drink, with the words "This is my blood of the New Covenant, which has been poured out for many." Paul, the earliest witness to the event, added the command "Do this in memory of me."

The entire act is strikingly un-Jewish, at least in the earliest Christians' quite literal understanding of it. Jesus pronounced the bread and wine his own body and blood and then bid his followers to eat and drink it, an act in which he himself apparently did not take part. Each piece of this ritual raises a Jewish echo perhaps—the Bible resounds with echoes—but as a single event, which is the way our sources present it and the Christians understood it, the Eucharist has no Jewish parallel. If Jesus was a priest, which the texts themselves do not suggest, and the Passover seder was moreover a domestic, not a priestly, event, his offering of himself not in his own person but in the form of his disembodied "body" and "blood" makes little sense in a Second Temple Jewish context. Flesh was indeed offered on the altar in the temple—and if the Last Supper was a seder, there was flesh on that table as well though Jesus chose not to identify *that* with his body. In temple sacrifices the flesh was never the priests' own. Blood was dashed on the altar but never drunk; indeed, blood, or at least bloodletting, was a notorious source of impurity in Jewish eyes.

Jewish liturgy is symbolic and historical. It remembers events; it commemorates promises received and weeps for disappointed hopes. Like the Bible itself, it is both a record and a celebration. Christian liturgy is cosmic and yet professedly literal. "This is my body" seeks at the same time to draw God down from heaven and exalt matter to a supernatural plane in a manner alien to Muslim and Jew alike. Both of the latter know how to be literal—all prayer is literal—but do not endeavor either to ground God or to sanctify matter. God will intervene in history when and where he will, but he will not dwell among us.

As the Christians became increasingly self-aware and began to develop their own particular liturgy, it is natural to think they behaved like the Jews they were, and they built on Jewish liturgical practices familiar to all of them. Such appears to have been the case, in fact, and the earliest Christians had a prayer meeting (*synaxis*) constructed on the model of a synagogue service and a separate eucharistic celebration that may have had associations with Passover. Eventually the two became fused in the eucharistic liturgy, whose original parts are still fairly evident. The first is the Mass of the Catechumens, that is, the liturgy open to those under instruction (*katechesis*) for baptism (see II/4), and here the synagogue antecedents are obvious: there were readings from Scripture (Bible/Paul/Gospels, often reflecting one on the other) and a homily, all standard acts of a synagogue service. When this was completed (and those not yet baptized were dismissed), there followed the Eucharist proper, with the offering of bread and wine, their consecration, using the same formula Jesus did at the Last Supper, and their transformation—"transubstantiation" (one-substance-into-another) is the later technical term—into the body and blood of Christ, which was then distributed and consumed the ("communion") by the faithful in attendance.

Liturgies Eastern and Western

The Eucharist and other sacramental and nonsacramental forms of Christian liturgy became more elaborate and more standardized over time. At first they were conducted, like some contemporary synagogue services, in private homes, which also served as a "church" (*ekklesia*) for the community. With the end of the persecutions, Christians, like the Jews, constructed a special prayer hall that took over a common type of Roman building with no religious connotations, the royal audience chamber/courthouse or basilica, and modified it for Christian liturgical purposes.

The exact manner in which the Eucharist was celebrated varied from place to place. Most of the available material for the reconstruction of the early Christian eucharistic liturgy, like the Didache of the late first or early second century and the Apostolic Constitution of about 380, refer to a type of service used in the urban centers of Syria to about 400. Another, different form was current in Egypt about the same time. Both of these were in Greek, but the Eucharist was early celebrated in Christian Aramaic—the dialect called Syriac—at Edessa, and it is still used in Eastern churches today as the Liturgy of Mari and Addai. In Rome and the empire's African provinces, services were in Latin, and again, the form of the Roman "Mass," as the eucharistic liturgy was called, differed in details from contemporary Eastern versions of the same service.

What followed in the East testifies, as certainly as the evolution of the hierarchical structure, to the growing centralization of the Great Church and the consequent standardization of its practices. A "liturgy of St. James," which may have had its beginnings in Jerusalem, and a parallel service in Egypt attributed to St. Mark began to drive out all the local liturgies in the patriarchal sees of Antioch and Alexandria, respectively. With Constantinople's growth in political power and prestige, the capitals' own liturgical practice, the so-called St. Basil, not only dominated in the churches of Anatolia but, as nationalism and separatism grew in Syria and Egypt, gained an official cachet as *the* liturgy of the Eastern Orthodox Church.

Within these Eastern types there were, of course, all manner of variations, but certain elements remained constant. The division into two parts has already been mentioned. The first, the synaxis, was preceded by the "little entrance" of the celebrants into the sanctuary area, and was composed of readings from the Bible, Paul, and the Gospels, interspersed with psalms, and concluded by the dismissal of the catechumens. At this point the Eucharist proper began. After the "great entrance" were various prayers of greeting and commemoration, the recitation of a creed (*symbolon*), and the kiss of peace. The diptychs, lists of the living and the dead in communion with a particular church, were read and a number of offertory prayers recited. The priestly celebrant then began the most sacred part of the liturgy, the Anaphora or "Bearing Aloft," which he initiated by exhorting the faithful to lift up their minds to God. A hymn to the angels followed, then a remembrance (*anamnesis*) of Jesus' passion, and an invocation (*epiklesis*) directed to the Holy Spirit to descend on the bread and wine that had been placed on the altar. There was a final blessing, and the Anaphora ended with the Lord's Prayer. What remained was the breaking of the bread, now transformed into the body of Christ, and the sharing of the wine/blood with the faithful.

A certain evolution can be traced in the rites just sketched in their fully developed form. The earliest examples, the liturgy embedded in the Apostolic Constitution, for example, were more obviously oriented toward prayer than toward ceremonial. With the liturgies called James and Mark, a new dramatic element appeared. The altar became a stage for the sacrifice of the Christ before a cosmic audience: angels, priests, people. Finally, with the liturgy attributed to St. Basil, the ecstatic quality became subdued and the imagery and expression more restrained. The language is precise, almost juridical, rejecting the more abstract terminology derived from Greek philosophy that was beginning to make inroads into the theological discourse of the period.

Eucharistic Issues: Who, When, and How?

The transformation of bread and wine into the body and blood of Christ, if that is indeed what occurs in the Christian eucharistic liturgy, is quite obviously an extraordinary event. Its manner was often discussed in Christian circles and, in the end, its explanation sundered Christianity into East and West and then was part of a second, no less grave fissure in the Western Church. The first issue was how and when the transformation of the bread and wine took place, and the second was over what exactly occurred at that moment.

The earliest Christians knew how and by whom the Eucharist was celebrated, but we do not. At first the Eucharist seems inexplicably tied to, and yet distinct from the agape or love feast (1 Cor. 11:17–34), which was a community meal of some sort. When was the Last Supper reenacted and who stood in for Jesus? Our sources do not tell us.

At some point the Eucharist was presided over or "celebrated" by a priest (see I/6), or a bishop in his function as a priest, since the two powers, the magisterium and the sacerdotium, were distinct, even though they might be held by the same person. He pronounced the words of Jesus: "This is my body. . . . This is my blood." The Western Church thought, or assumed, that the words pronounced by the priest first over the bread and then over the wine effected their becoming the body and blood of Christ. But the Eastern eucharistic liturgies, that is, the "scripts" for the reenactment of the Last Supper used in the Eastern Church, had it otherwise. In those versions, the Holy Spirit was bid "to come upon these offerings and make them holy," and at that point of epiklesis the miraculous transformation took place. In the West, the priest pronounced and consecrated; in the East, the priest pronounced and the Spirit consecrated.

What precisely happened at the moment of consecration, whether effected by the words of the priest or through the agency of the Holy Spirit, was no less troublesome an issue. Christian theologians of the Middle Ages, who borrowed the Aristotelian theory of substance (the underlying substratum of a being) and accidents (the perceptible but superficial modifications of that substratum), used the art term "transubstantiation" to explain. The substance of the bread and wine were entirely transformed, it was said, into the substance of the body and blood of Christ, though the accidents (color, taste, texture, etc.) of the bread and wine remained. This was affirmed as Church dogma by the Fourth Lateran Council in 1215.

The Reform Liturgy

For the Protestant Reformers the Eucharist, now referred to by the more scriptural expression "the Lord's Supper" (1 Cor. 11:20), was still reckoned, along with Baptism, as one of the authentic New Testament sacraments (see II/5), but with a somewhat different understanding. For the Catholics' transubstantiation, Luther substituted consubstantiation, whereby after the consecration *both* sets of substances, bread/wine and Christ's body/blood, coexisted in the eucharistic elements. It was a diminished miracle perhaps, but still a miracle. Ulrich Zwingli (d. 1531), the Swiss Reformer, would not have it so. He regarded the Lord's Supper as a memorial rather than a sacrifice and maintained that neither transubstantiation nor consubstantiation took place. The bread and wine remained; only their association was changed. The miracle had disappeared. Calvin's position was somewhere in between. He denied the fact of transubstantiation but continued to affirm that in receiving the elements, the Christian in fact received the power or virtue of Christ's body and blood. *Virtus* has been substituted for *substantia*; the once physical miracle has been "spiritualized."

By way of response to the Reformers' contentions, the Council of Trent in 1551 reaffirmed the doctrine of transubstantiation, though perhaps somewhat more guardedly than heretofore: "By the consecration of the bread and the wine a change is brought about of the whole substance of the bread into the body of Christ and of the whole substance of the wine into the blood of Christ. This change the holy catholic church properly and appropriately calls transubstantiation."

Christmas

While Sunday and Easter have, at least in English—which may suggest where the mischief arose—rather peculiar pagan names for Christian holy days, Christmas announces itself somewhat more straightforwardly: Christ's Mass. Its pagan antecedents lie hidden, however, in the date, 25 December. Though the death date of a famous person was sometimes marked, no one paid much attention to birth dates in the ancient world since there was nothing notable about infants or children. No one quite knew, then, the date, much less the day, of Jesus' birth, any more than they did that of Muhammad. We can guess from a number of clues that Jesus was born in 4 B.C.E., the last year of Herod's reign, but there is nothing in the Gospel texts to render the date more precise, nor even to indicate that Christians concerned themselves about it.

We do know when Jesus' purported birthday was introduced and why. In 274 C.E. the emperor Aurelian decreed that the cult of the Invincible Sun constituted the official *religio* of the empire. It was not a momentous move and testifies more to the popularity of Mithraism, in which the Sun cult was central, and the emperor's astuteness in trying to make political capital of that fact than to some sea change in the religious sensibilities of millions of people. The Sun was particularly celebrated on its "birthday," the winter solstice (21 December) and the days following. When Constantine embraced Christianity at the beginning of the next century, he began the process of Christianizing the cult practices of the millennium-old empire over which he ruled. State funds were channeled into Christian building projects, like the massive enshrinement of Jerusalem and Palestine; Roman law was rewritten to condemn practices inimical or acceptable to Christianity and entitle the Christian clergy; and, in the realm of cult, Easter was separated from the Jewish Passover (see I/6). It was then that the Sun's Day was converted to a Christian holy day (see I/5), and the last day of the celebration of the Sun's birthday, 25 December appropriated, as the day of Jesus' own nativity, the *dies natalis Domini*.

Muslim Prayer

The Quran shows no interest in the earlier Jewish temple cult, though there is good evidence that Muhammad himself originally prayed facing Jerusalem. The Quran's one possible reference to the Eucharist (5:117–118) suggests that it was thought of as some kind of meal sent down from heaven to sustain the believers. Islamic liturgy lay not in those directions, however; it was more akin to that of rabbinic Judaism in that it was grounded in prayers. The pagans at Mecca had prayed, after a fashion, a practice the Quran characterizes as "whistling and clapping of hands" (8:35). Muhammad substituted, on God's command, formal liturgical prayers (*salat*). These daily prayers are largely unspecified as to their content, frequency, and times in the Quran, but the details were quickly supplied from the Prophet's sunna. Muslim prayers are made up principally from God's own words in the Quran. They are preceded by a ritual ablution and accompanied by appropriate gestures and prostrations; they are the heart of the Islamic liturgy and the chief worship obligation of every Muslim.

Muslim liturgical prayer is composed of units called "bowings" (*rakas*). The first in any series always begins with the phrase "God is great" (*Allahu akbar*), recited with the hands placed, palms outward, at each side of the face. This is followed by the recitation of "The Opening" (*al-Fatiha*), the initial sura of the Quran, and one or more other passages from that Book. Next is a bowing from the hips, after which the worshiper returns to an erect position. The worshiper then kneels and touches forehead to the ground, then sits back on the haunches. This is followed by a second bowing like the first. Though the practice is still somewhat fluid in the Quran, prayer soon became standardized at five times a day—Jews are required to pray three times a day—when the faithful are summoned by a "caller" (*muadhdhin*; Eng. "muezzin") at the appropriate times. These were at daybreak (*subh* or *fajr*), noon (*zuhr*), midafternoon (*asr*), after sunset (*maghrib*), and finally, the early part of the night (*isha*). At first, the prayers were said facing Jerusalem, as the Jews did—Christians faced toward the East—but later the direction of prayer, the qibla, was changed toward the Kaaba at Mecca.

Friday Prayer and the Mosque

The Muslim's daily prayers might be said in private in any decent and dignified setting, but the noon prayer on Friday had special liturgical significance in that it was a prescribed congregational prayer. Friday came to be called the "day of assembly" (*yawm al-juma*) and the place of that congregation, the "assembly" (*jami*). This latter is what we call a mosque, though the English word goes back to another Arabic word describing another function of the same place: *masjid*, a place of prostration or worship.

The first mosque in Islam was the courtyard of Muhammad's own house in Medina (see I/3). Its successors in the Islamic diaspora served much the same purpose as the original building; a simple structure used indifferently for political assembly and liturgy. There were few architectural requirements: flowing water for ablution before prayer in an open court and a tower or minaret from which the muezzin might summon the faithful to prayer; within, a niche (*mihrab*) to note the qibla or prayer direction (toward Mecca), and a raised throne (*minbar*)—as opposed to the Christian pulpit, a kind of raised podium—which originally served as a sort of political rostrum but developed, with the progressive restriction of the mosque to liturgical functions, into a pulpit for the Friday sermon.

The Hajj

Daily prayer is one of the Pillars of Islam, obligations incumbent on all Muslims (see II/4). Another is the hajj, the pilgrimage to the holy places of Mecca and its environs, which every Muslim must make at least once during his or her lifetime, if circumstances permit. This complex ritual, much of which is both time- and place-tied, unfolds between the eighth and thirteenth days of the lunar pilgrimage month (Dhu al-Hijja).

The hajj was a long-standing pre-Islamic ritual in the environs of Mecca; how long we cannot say, although its rites seem redolent of primitive Semitic practices. They antedated Muhammad's lifetime, at any rate, as did the umra, the more local Meccan festival celebrated by the townspeople in and around the Kaaba. Though Muslims are loathe to imagine the Prophet in any connection with paganism, we have no real reason to think that Muhammad did not participate in the hajj before his call to prophecy in 610, nor indeed even after that date, at least until his departure for Medina. He participated in the umra at Mecca in 629 and 630, and there were Muslims on the hajj of 631, though not Muhammad himself. His first and last Muslim hajj occurred in 632, the so-called Farewell Pilgrimage. On that occasion, by word and example (his sunna) he made whatever modifications were deemed necessary to purify this ritual that in Muslim eyes had originally been instituted by Abraham himself (Quran 22:27).

How much did Muhammad change? We are ill informed on the pre-Islamic hajj, but some judgments are possible. First, the commercial fairs associated with the earlier pilgrimage were either abolished or disappeared soon after Islam. Second, some of the more manifest trappings of paganism were removed. Prayers, arrivals, and departures that fell at sunrise or sunset and so suggested sun or planetary worship, for example, were moved slightly off those points in an effort to break the earlier associations. Animal sacrifices that had been commonplace in and around Mecca were abolished; only the one at Mina somewhat inexplicably survived. But for all that, remarkably little seems to have been changed in what was, to all appearances, a very old and very primitive series of rituals.

The hajj was not, at any time we can observe it, a single, unified ritual act in the manner of a drama but a concatenation of barely connected activities spread over a number of days. Or so it appears to us since whatever etiological myths the Arabs once possessed to explain these now baffling rituals are entirely lost. Perhaps they had already disappeared by Muhammad's own day. The Quran provided the believers with their own properly Muslim explanations. The hajj rituals were now understood in reference to Abraham and his sojourn in Mecca. Here at Arafat Abraham stood and prayed before God. Here at Mina he was bidden to sacrifice his son and then given an animal in substitution. Here too Abraham was tempted by Satan, and so the three "Satans" in the form of pillars are stoned. And so on.

Besides the Haram or sanctuary area in the middle of town, Mecca is surrounded by a larger taboo area that is marked by points or "stations" along the main roads leading into the Holy City (see I/1). At or before he or she reaches one of those points, the pilgrim must enter a taboo state, *ihram* or "haramization," by undergoing a complete ablution, donning a special garment made of two simple white sheets, one tied around the waist and reaching the knees and the other draped over the left shoulder and tied somewhere beneath the right arm. Head and insteps must remain uncovered. This is for the men; no particular dress is prescribed for the women, though most are fully covered, head to toe, in white. This garment and this alone is worn throughout the pilgrimage, and no further washing or grooming is permitted. Nor are sexual relations allowed: any indulgence in the latter renders the hajj void.

On entering Mecca, the pilgrim should proceed as soon as possible to the performance of the *tawaf*, the sevenfold, counterclockwise circumambulation of the Kaaba, the first three at a somewhat quickened pace. Pilgrims attempt to kiss or touch the Black Stone embedded in the eastern corner of the Kaaba as they pass it, though the pilgrimage throng often makes this impossible. The tawaf completed, the pilgrim goes to the place called Safa, beyond the southeast side of the Haram, and completes seven "runnings" between that and another place, called Marwa, a distance altogether of somewhat less than two miles. Though once at the two ends of a public thoroughfare, both places, and the way between, are today enclosed in an air-conditioned colonnade. The tawaf originally formed part of the umra, but the running between Safa and Marwa was connected to it by Muhammad himself, as we can still read in Quran 2:153.

There is a certain flexibility in the performance of those Meccan rituals—some prefer to do them very late at night when the weather is cooler and the crowds thinner—but precisely on the eighth of Dhu al-Hijja the hajj proper begins. The pilgrims proceed to Mina, a village five miles east of Mecca, where some pass the night, while the rest proceed directly to the plain of Arafat, eleven miles from the Haram, where they spend the night in what becomes, for that solitary evening, one of the largest cities in the Middle East. The next day, the ninth, is the heart of the hajj. The pilgrims, now many hundreds of thousands, assemble and stand around the tiny hill of Arafat. At times sermons have been delivered during this interval, but they have nothing to do with the ritual, the point of which is precisely the standing before God, from noon to sunset. Just before sunset occurs the "dispersal," a sometimes pell-mell rush to Muzdalifa, a village halfway back toward Mina. The night is spent here: the next morning, the tenth, there is another dispersal as the pilgrims hasten to Mina, where the ritual Stoning of Satan, the casting of seven pebbles at a stone pillar; occurs.

With the Stoning of Satan, the hajj has reached its official term, but a number of rites that are part of the pilgrims' desacralization remain. As already noted, the pilgrim must sacrifice an animal—this is the id al-adha celebrated by the entire Muslim world—though some Muslim legal experts permit, on the basis of Quran 2:196, ten days of fasting (three on the hajj, seven later) as an acceptable substitute for this blood sacrifice. The men's heads are then shaved, the women's locks lightly clipped, to signal the end of the ihram state—the sexual prohibitions remain a short while longer. The pilgrims return to Mecca, perform another tawaf, are sprinkled with water from the well of Zamzam, and then bathe. The next three days, the eleventh, twelfth, and thirteenth of the month, complete the desacralization. The pilgrims return to Mina, now entirely freed of all taboos. On each of the three days the pilgrims again stone the great pillar there, as well as two smaller ones. The hajj is then complete, and though it is in no sense part of the ritual, many pilgrims proceed to Medina to pay their respects at the Prophet's tomb before returning home.

> **Note:** The complexity of the hajj is augmented by the fact that most pilgrims perform it only once in their lifetime. Part of the complexity is attributable to the Quran's permitting the performance in tandem with what had once been two distinct rituals (with the trace of a third, the "running" between Safa and Marwa): the umra and the hajj. Lawyers later decided these could be combined in several different ways and worked out the modalities. Muslims on hajj do not have to overly concern themselves, however: Mecca has had from the beginning a guild of professional guides who shepherd the pilgrims through everything from lodging to liturgy to leaving.

Intercalation Prohibited

The hajj of 632 completed, Muhammad turned to other connected matters. It was probably soon after the Farewell Pilgrimage that he announced the revelation banning the practice of intercalation (Quran 9:36–37). In modern societies the establishment of an accurate and useful calendar seems like a purely civil act controlled by scientists at best and politicians at worst. This is not so in religious societies where the calendar controls most of the community's ritual activities.

One of the issues at stake for both the accuracy and the usefulness of timekeeping is the practice known as intercalation, the insertion at fixed intervals of a day or days into the year to keep the counted year in synchronicity with the sun, and so with the agricultural seasons. The earth quite unreasonably takes 365 and a quarter revolutions on its axis to get around the sun and so those following a solar calendar have a quadrennial "leap year" with 366 days to make up the difference: an additional day is intercalated in February every fourth year. For those on a lunar calendar—that is, those who keep track of annual time by the moon's twenty-eight-day revolutions around the earth—the problem of keeping up with the solar-dictated agricultural seasons is more severe since twelve of these lunar revolutions will leave the lunar "year" eleven days short of its solar counterpart with every cycle of the earth around the sun.

The Christians, under Roman influence, followed a solar calendar as soon as they moved away from their Jewish roots, but the Jews continued to use, at least for religious purposes, their traditional lunar calendar, which the Bible itself had enshrined by making the appearance of the new moon a festival celebration. The pre-Islamic Arabs too followed a lunar calendar and, like the Jews, practiced intercalation. For the Jews the agricultural festivals of Sukkoth and Passover continued to mark the fall harvest and the spring sowing respectively, whereas for the Arabs the umra remained a spring feast and the hajj continued to be observed in the fall.

But no longer, the Quran ruled. God had abolished intercalation, and so what were originally seasonal festivals and holy days, the hajj, umra, and the month of Ramadan, now moved freely across the solar year, each cycle falling eleven days earlier in the solar year than in the preceding one. Indeed, the umra grew so detached from its original seasonal celebration that Muslims often simply attached it to the beginning of the hajj and celebrated both together. We can only speculate what was behind this ban. Most likely it was intended to disconnect Muslim religious practices from all their pre-Islamic associations, pagan or Jewish, since those earlier holy days were all seasonal.

The Enshrinement of Jerusalem

Holy cities like Mecca have always invited the politically minded to gain advantage by making public and visible investment in the place, particularly its holy locales. As we have seen, David, Solomon, and Herod all engaged in such enterprises in Jerusalem, with varying results, as did various Muslim rulers in Mecca and Medina as well as Jerusalem. But the two who achieved the most lasting effects, if not to their reputation, then to the city of Jerusalem, were David and Constantine. Each took a settlement that was not particularly regarded by their subjects and converted it into something very different. David's achievement had both political and religious results that last to this day. By moving there himself and by bringing the Ark of the Covenant into the town and making arrangements for its permanent housing there, the king of Israel made the Jebusite settlement of Jerusalem into the political and religious capital of the Israelites. It has always remained such for the Jews, even absent both sovereignty and shrine from that place.

David was only the second king of Israel, but Constantine rested on even less certain terrain: he was the first Christian emperor of a political enterprise, the imperium romanum, that stretched, in one form or another, a millennium into the past, a thousand pagan years by Christian reckoning. He grasped the reins of rule firmly, even fiercely, in the face of his political rivals, and he acted no less decisively in the Church, though here without the slightest precedent. In the wake of his bold initiative of summoning and presiding over the Council of Nicaea, he directed the bishop of Jerusalem to identify sites connected with Jesus' life and death in Palestine and to enshrine them in appropriate, imperial fashion—a project to which the province's governor was pointedly told to render every assistance. Thus began Jerusalem's religious rehabilitation.

There was a Christian community in Jerusalem from Jesus' day onward, first Jewish Christians, and then, after 135, a Gentile Christian community with Greek bishops. They would likely have remembered some of the sites connected with Jesus' life, even after Hadrian's extensive remodeling of the city. According to the local Christians, the site of both Jesus' execution and his burial lay beneath the temple of Jupiter Capitolinus, the city's tutelary deity, which Hadrian had built on the northern side of the city's new forum.

At Constantine's command, the site, which had been outside Herod's wall on that side of the city but now lay well within Hadrian's city, was excavated and cleared. Not only was the site found, but in the excavation were discovered three crosses, one of which was miraculously demonstrated to be Jesus' own. Both the rock-hewn tomb and Golgotha, the mound on which Jesus was crucified, were laid bare. Over the tomb was built a circular domed edifice, which opened on its eastern side to an uncovered courtyard where Golgotha stood, now surmounted by Jesus' cross. On the eastern side of this porticoed court lay Constantine's enormous basilica, with its monumental entry opening onto the *cardo*, the main colonnaded street that ran north-south through Jerusalem. A similar building was constructed over the grotto identified as Jesus' birth site in Bethlehem, another at the place where Jesus stood on the Mount of Olives. Finally, a shrine was built around Abraham's oak near Hebron.

Christian Pilgrimage

Two general types of activities fall under the notion of "pilgrimage." The first refers to certain acts of worship that can be performed only at certain times or places. These time- and place-tied rituals are exemplified in the Jews' obligation to celebrate the three great annual *hag* festivals of Pesach, Shabuoth, and Sukkoth in Jerusalem at the appropriate seasons and the Muslims' once-in-a-life-time obligation to perform the hajj on the appointed days in and around Mecca. Properly speaking, these may be better thought of as liturgies. Pilgrimage is also used of voluntary journeys in the three religious communities and is properly a pious visit—what the Muslims call a *ziyara*, in opposition to the liturgical hajj—a voyage from here to somewhere else, as the Latin name *peregrinatio* signals. That "somewhere else" is a holy place of a number of different types. It might be a locale where salvation history has unfolded—Sinai, for example, or the site of the crucifixion in Jerusalem—where the pilgrim might relive and, indeed, liturgically reenact that event. It might be the dwelling of a holy man or woman, where one might attend and gaze on one of those friends of

God thought to embody perfect virtue (see below). Finally, and most generally, it might be one of the sites sanctified first by the earthly presence and
now by the sacred remains of the martyrs and confessors of the faith.

Jerusalem is the archetypical goal of the pilgrim. The sacred history of the
three monotheistic religions unfolded there, and within its walls lies Jesus'
tomb, its presence testifying to his earthly life, its emptiness bearing witness
to the miracle of his resurrection. There may have been an occasional curious
visitor to Jerusalem before Constantine's enshrinement project, but once this
work was begun—and continued by members of the imperial family and other
wealthy and pious Christians—pilgrims began to arrive to participate in what
developed as a stational liturgy: a series of rituals performed at Easter time
commemorating the events connected with Jesus' final days in Jerusalem at
the very places where they occurred. Many of the pilgrims wrote of their experiences, which served as a further incentive to pilgrimage. More and more
sites in Jerusalem and its vicinity were identified as having to do with Jesus,
Mary, the Apostles, and other members of the first generation of Christians.

There is no sign that Christian pilgrimage to Jerusalem, now sustained by
a network of hostels and other facilities, in any way abated when the Muslims
accepted the city's peaceful surrender in 635. Jerusalem's new sovereigns devoted their attention chiefly to the ruined temple mount. They cleared Herod's
monumental platform and built on it first a mosque, al-Aqsa, at its southern
end and then, in 692, the shrine of the Dome of the Rock in its middle.

The chief Christian holy place, the Church of the Anastasis or Resurrection—
Holy Sepulcher is a later and Western name—the Muslim rulers of Jerusalem
mostly ignored, though not out of any sense of respect. According to Quran
4:157 and its standard Muslim exegesis, Jesus' death on the cross was only apparent. The Jews *thought* they crucified him; in fact, he ascended alive into
heaven, whence he will return to signal the end of days (see II/10). In this view,
it is not entirely unexpected that the Muslims, who venerate Jesus as a great
prophet, should have little regard for the Anastasis, the site, according to the
Christians, of Jesus' execution, burial, and resurrection from the dead. The
Muslims call it by a rude name, and the Egyptian sultan al-Hakim found the site
so offensive that in 1009 he ordered it demolished. It was soon rebuilt, however, though on a much reduced scale, and Salah al-Din, when he retook
Jerusalem from the Latin crusaders in 1187, was likewise counseled to destroy
the offensive place. But Salah al-Din understood better than his counselors
the nature of holy places. "The Christians would still be making pilgrimages
here," he said, "even if the earth itself were dug up and thrown into the sky."

Al-Hakim's deed was horrific, of course, and when news of the destruction
of Christendom's primary holy place reached Europe, it added to the developing groundswell of resentment that eventually led to the Crusade some ninety
years later. Al-Hakim's act was followed by another event pregnant with consequence. As noted, the Byzantine emperor had been allowed to underwrite

the reconstruction of the Holy Sepulcher in the 1030s; then a few years later, when the walls of Jerusalem had fallen into disrepair, his successor agreed to supply money and labor for their rebuilding. But there was a stipulation: the Christians alone would be allowed to live in the newly walled quarter of the city—the northwest quadrant—and their affairs would rest solely in the hands of the Christian patriarch of Jerusalem. Thus, in the 1060s, three decades before the European Crusade, there was a walled Christian quarter in Jerusalem, an enclave more or less free of Muslim control and dependent, to some extent, not on the city's Muslim rulers but on the Christian emperor in Constantinople. The principle of an external protectorate over the Christian population, often invoked by the European powers from the sixteenth century onward, had been established in Jerusalem and still exists, in a mitigated form, even today.

The Western Wall

The principal Jewish holy place in Jerusalem in late medieval and early modern times was the western wall of the temple, and it provides a not untypical example of how a Jerusalem holy place began with the presence of God and ended up in the hands of lawyers. As we have seen, at the destruction of the first temple by the Babylonians in the sixth century B.C.E., many Israelites were convinced that God's enhoused presence, his shekinah, had gone elsewhere. It would return, Ezekiel promised (44:1–4), and presumably it did, to the second temple of Zerubbabel and Herod. But what occurred in 70 C.E.? In 135? Where was God's sacred presence that gave sanctity to the precinct? We have seen that Jews defied the Roman ban and returned to the temple mount after the destruction, yet it was not to sacrifice, nor perhaps even to pray, but to lament the misfortune that had fallen on the place. The midrashim of the seventh century C.E. maintained that God's presence had never left the Western Wall, but they were almost certainly referring to the western wall of the city, not, as understood in the sixteenth century, the western face of Herod's platform. This is not to suggest that Jews ceased to revere the temple site; they simply were not permitted to enter it. The Jews assembled for Sukkoth on the Mount of Olives, and it was there, some suggested, that the shekinah had come to rest.

It is not easy to trace the tradition's subsequent growth, but by the sixteenth century Jerusalem Jews had found a new place to pray—with the appropriate adjustment of the earlier rabbinic exegesis—in the narrow open space between the towering western face of Herod's platform and the house of the nearby Muslim mosque and Moroccan quarter. Squatters' rights had in effect been established. But in the nineteenth century, after a progressive liberalization of Jerusalem's municipal administration and the Jerusalem Jews' growing support by some of their European coreligionists, the tiny piece of ground called the Western Wall—1,290 square feet to be exact—became a major source of contention between the Jews and the Ottoman authorities. Under other circumstances the two sides might have taken up arms, but this was a Muslim time in a Muslim land and so the issue ended up in court—a Muslim court, which found against the Jews. In the wake of World War I Jerusalem was no longer Muslim, however, but British, at least in a mandatory sense. The British had their own courts, but they preferred, as we might today, an international commission, whose findings, which continued to restrict Jewish access and usage, were incorporated into Palestinian law by an Order in Council in 1931.

The Israeli conquest of the Old City was cataclysmic; not only were the tables turned, but the entire city. Quickly, the Moroccan quarter was bulldozed away and the space before the wall broadened out. The Muslims appealed to the 1931 Order in Council, but that was a dead letter. Vigorously alive, however, was the argument among Jews about whether the site was holy or historical. It was both, obviously; the real question was who had jurisdiction—the Ministry of Religious Affairs, who wanted to convert it into a synagogue, the Department of Parks, who wanted to preserve it as a landmark, or the archaeologists. To pray or to dig at the foundations of Herod's temple? The answer was—as UNESCO sputtered ineffectively in the background—the usual pragmatic Israeli one: a little of both, with a strict, though imaginary, line of demarcation between the sacred Torah stands and the profane bulldozers.

Popular Devotions in Christianity

The Jews' centuries-long position of monitored submission to the political and religious authorities of Christendom and the Abode of Islam guaranteed that most forms of Jewish piety would remain chiefly, and safely, within either the home or the synagogue and so necessarily local. When pious behavior did take more public forms, as in the movement called Hasidism (see II/8), it passed from cell to cell, from community to community, without taking to the streets or rising to the threshold of popular attention. The same was true of the Christian dhimmis under Islam and the Muslim Mudejares who lived in Christian Spain (see I/8), but elsewhere Christians and Muslims were free to express their piety however they chose.

Christianity took on a public persona with Constantine's conversion. Christians were thereafter free to worship as they pleased, often with government support. Churches and shrines grew monumental in size and lavish in decoration with the help of both public and private patronage. But the buildings were Church property and what went on in them—the liturgy—was conducted, and managed, by the Church's episcopal ministers and, more generally, by the decrees of episcopal synods and councils. The liturgy became increasingly standardized and essentially static. Locally there were cults of martyrs of the faith whose grave sites or remains—their *relicta*, or "relics"—attracted a certain degree of attention (see below). In Jerusalem, the grave site of Jesus, the Holy Sepulcher, received particular attention and generated both a special liturgy—that of the stations, mentioned above—which the cult of the martyrs did not, and a pilgrimage practice that was genuinely international.

Christian devotions remained church-centered and chiefly liturgical until the Middle Ages when the piety of Latin Christendom began to express itself in new ways. The contemplative piety of monastic Christianity, whether Western or Eastern, was and remained essentially private, personal, and likewise static. In medieval Christianity, there was, however, a sharp increase in public, dynamic lay devotionalism. In art, literature, and practice, a new degree of religious self-expression manifested itself across Latin Europe. The walls, choirs, altars, and chapels of churches came alive with manifold scenes from the lives of Christ, his mother, and the saints. Multiple panels served to turn these into genuine narratives. Lives of saints, like Jacob of Voragine's *Golden Legend* (ca. 1270), began to proliferate even before the introduction of printing. Moral advice, exhortation, and explanation found a new voice in the Middle Ages, when the *Imitation of Christ* of Thomas à Kempis (d. 1421) became an international best-seller. Sermons became a popular art form, particularly in the vernacular, and even an event, if the preacher was celebrated. Both the Dominicans, the Order of Preachers, and the Franciscans took preaching seriously and they took it to the streets in the thirteenth century (see II/8).

The Cult of Mary

Devotions were often directed toward persons and things, to the passion of Christ or his birth, the saints and their relics, the Eucharist. Christian devotion to the passion turned the crucifix (the representation of Jesus on the cross) into an international symbol of Latin Christianity—Eastern Christianity preferred Christ regnant, *christos pantokrator*—and made scenes of his passion and crucifixion the most common subject of European art, followed closely by the Madonna (Mary and the infant Jesus). Feast days in honor of Mary were publicly celebrated as both popular festivals and formal additions to the Church's ever swelling liturgical calendar: her birth, her presentation in the temple, the angel's announcement of her pregnancy (the "Annunciation") her purification after the birth of Jesus and the taking up (the "Assumption") of her mortal remains into heaven. Prayers like the Ave Maria ("Hail Mary" from Luke 1:28 plus 1:42) became enormously popular. The practice of repeating led rapidly to the "rosary," the repetition of this prayer in series, strung out along scenes from the life of Mary, and counted on knotted or beaded cords.

Mary had no great shrine in medieval Europe, but "Jesus sites" proliferated by the simple expedient of transferring to European soil—particularly when the failure of the Crusades made travel to Palestine difficult and dangerous—the "stations" connected with Jesus' last days in Jerusalem. The move was effected two ways: by transferring to European locales, the churches of Rome, for example, the blessings—technically indulgences (see II/5)—attached to visits to the original locations in Palestine, or by constructing replicas of those places, with greater or lesser degrees of realism, in churches or outdoors at sites like Mount Verna near Varallo in northern Italy. In 1486 the Franciscan Bernardino Caimi, former superior of the Franciscans in Palestine, constructed there realistic life-size tableaux of scenes from Jesus' life, each located in its own chapel along the sides of the mountain. As the pilgrim struggled along the steep path, he or she was in effect making the Stations of the Cross like a participant in the events. Versions of this same ritual became a popular devotion along roadsides and inside churches throughout Western Christendom.

From Piety to Dogma: An Immaculate Conception and Prophetic Impeccability

Though Mary figures rather prominently in the stories of Jesus' birth recorded by Matthew and Luke, she does not play an important role in his public life as depicted in the Gospels nor, indeed, in the New Testament as a whole. Her virginity (also affirmed in Quran 9:21) was an element in Jesus' messianic claim since it fulfilled the prophecy of Isaiah 7:14, as Matthew points out (1:22–23). In the apocryphal Gospel of James, Mary's virginity is extended to include the periods during and after Jesus' birth. This would necessarily imply the demotion of what the Gospels call Jesus' "brother and sisters" (Mark 6:3) to the status of cousins. This was precisely the issue between Jerome (d. 420) and his contemporary Helvetius. In arguing against Mary's virginity, Helvetius may have been concerned that her lifelong celibacy not only undermined the reality of her marriage to Joseph but downgraded Christian marriage generally. Jerome's view, however, upholding Mary's "perpetual virginity," prevailed in the Church.

There was a theological explosion early in the fifth century around using the word "God-bearer" (*theotokos*) in reference to Mary, but the usage was confirmed at the Council of Ephesus in 431—even though the issue of Jesus' divinity and humanity, which lay behind the argument about Mary as theotokos, was not resolved until the Council of Chalcedon (see II/7). In the Western Church, meanwhile, interest in Mary grew very gradually. Augustine, who died the year before Ephesus, stayed close to his scriptural base and so did not seem to regard Mary as a subject of theological contemplation, though his view of her perpetual virginity was similar to Jerome's.

Cult was another matter. Although in the early Church there was no celebration of Marian holy days, by the sixth century there is evidence that her Assumption was being celebrated, without controversy, among both Latin and Eastern Christians, even though it was not finally defined as dogma by the Roman Catholic Church until 1950. The doctrine of the Immaculate Conception—the view that Mary was conceived, alone among humankind, without Original Sin—made its first appearance in the works of Paschasius Radbertus (d. 865), but was strongly resisted in many quarters. Bernard of Clairvaux (d. 1153), one of Mary's earliest and most fervent medieval champions, opposed it, as did the next century's most eminent Franciscan thinker, Bonaventure (d. 1274), and most eminent Dominican theologian, Thomas Aquinas (d. 1274). They thought the Immaculate Conception undermined the redemptive mission of Jesus, who had died for *all*. The solution was discovered by Duns Scotus (d. 1308), who simply redefined the problem. Jesus saved humankind in two ways: by redeeming those who had already sinned and by preserving his own mother from sin *tout simple*. The bishops at the Council of Trent were sufficiently convinced by Scotus's argument to exclude Mary from its affirmation of the reality and universality of Original Sin.

Behind the theologians was an extraordinary growth in popular devotion to Mary, ritual celebration of her life, prayers addressed directly to her, commemoration of her life and virtues in legend, art, and literature. Mary receives extensive coverage, for example, in the *Golden Legend*, a collection of saints' lives written circa 1270, extant in more than nine hundred manuscripts, and then one of the most reproduced texts of the early age of printing. To the Reformers, this outpouring of veneration, with little or no basis in Scripture, seemed like superstition run riot, and the cult of Mary, together with that of the Church's saints of the post-Patristic age, was disparaged, discouraged, and eventually all but disappeared. This was not so in Roman Catholicism. Counter-Reformation Marian piety lost none of the medieval fervor and the Church encouraged its spread. The climax of this growth was the proclamation of the Immaculate Conception as Church dogma by Pius IX in 1854, "by our own authority," as his decree read.

The definition of the Immaculate Conception was the end point of a process driven by a combination of popular piety, which was often ahead of the theologians, and the application of a kind of logic to the development of doctrine. Jesus' extraordinary status either demanded as a theological necessity or required, because it was appropriate, a parallel elevation in the status of the one who bore him. A similar combination can be observed at work in the development of doctrine regarding Muhammad, particularly in the matter of his impeccability (*isma*). There is no suggestion in either the Quran or the hadith that Muhammad was without flaw; indeed, one verse of the Quran (93:7) has God saying of his Prophet, "Did We not find you in error and guide you?" The implication of this verse, and the assumption of the earliest Muslims, was that before he received his call in 610, Muhammad too participated in the rituals of pagan Mecca. This assumption would likewise explain the event called the Opening of Muhammad's Breast. Sura 94:1 has God say to Muhammad, "Did We not open your breast?," an enigmatic statement explained in the biographical tradition as a physical act that becomes, in its performance, a spiritual cleansing of the Prophet's heart. It takes place, according to one account, just before his Night Journey and Ascension (see I/3), when he was shown the contents of revelation. In this reading, Muhammad seems to be sanctified not in utero, as Christians held with respect to Mary, but *nel mezzo del cammin di vita*.

A countervailing view was soon in circulation. As one quranic commentator explained, it is perfectly proper to say that before his call, Muhammad learned gradually like all humans, but to suggest that he shared his contemporaries' paganism, "God forbid!" Even the story of the "satanic verses," which is likely an old one, fell by the wayside (see I/3). Where Muhammad is portrayed in the hadith as praying—"I confess my sins. Forgive me all my sins, for there is none that forgives sins save You"—was meant to be taken not as autobiographical evidence but as a calculated example set for the believers.

The "impeccability" of the Prophet—indeed, of all prophets (Quran 4:151)—was discussed among theologians as early as the end of the eighth century. The Mutazilites, for example (see II/7), held as an article of faith that Muhammad was immune to unbelief (*kufr*) and major sins both before and after his call to prophecy. Soon even minor sins were ruled out, though the door was not quite closed to "inadvertences." As a Muslim "creed" of the mid–tenth century put it, "Muhammad . . . did not serve idols, nor was he at any time a polytheist, even for a single moment. And he never committed a grave or light sin."

There were always those, however, who shied away from such rationalizing logic and attempted to stay somewhat closer to what seemed to be the quranic evidence that before his call Muhammad was no different from other humans. Muslims unanimously held that Muhammad constituted a flawless model of human behavior during his Prophetic career. He was not only proclaiming Islam; he was living it with the absolute perfection that rendered him the "beautiful model" (Quran 33:21).

The Veneration of the Saints

Jesus' resurrection was a triumph over death, a triumph shared with all his followers. Although this was true for all Christians, a special posthumous regard developed for the martyrs who died for their faith in the Roman persecutions, much as a later generation of Jews thought the Maccabees had done. There is evidence of a memorial cult connected with the remains of the martyr Polycarp in the second century, and by the third there were memorial buildings over martyrs' graves outside the cities of the empire, while the anniversary of their martyrdom was celebrated in both liturgical and literary form. In the new religious climate established by Constantine's conversion, simple tombs were expanded, after the transfer of the saint's remains from suburban grave-yards to an honored place in the city's center, into magnificent churches where the saint's feast day could be celebrated before large crowds with litur-gical pomp. As we have seen, Constantine also constructed notable churches over the sites associated with Jesus' life and death.

Christianity early institutionalized the veneration of its holy men and women. The martyrs were the first to be so honored, but with the end of the persecutions and the execution of Christians, the same veneration was soon extended to the "confessors," those holy men and women whose lifelong pursuit of virtue pro-claimed their sanctity as eloquently as the blood of the martyrs did theirs. They too might be venerated, though never adored, and it was permissible to request their intercession with God—Islam is particularly firm in its denial of interces-sory powers to any human, excluding Muhammad (see II/10)—but the line between veneration and adoration is thin indeed. Augustine had warned about crossing that line, and the Ecumenical Council held in Nicaea in 787 made a careful distinction between the worship (*latreia*) and adoration owed to God alone and the respect and veneration (*douleia*) that might be paid to the saints. However complex the matter might be, there was a small attached rider: Mary, the Mother of Jesus, might be paid a kind of superveneration (*hyperdouleia*).

Canonization

However it was defined or whatever it was called, the private and public ven-eration of the sainted dead worked its way deep into the liturgical and devo-tional life of the Church, Eastern and Western. As the number of venerated dead increased, so did their apparitions and the miracles attributed to them. The Roman Church sought, as in all else, to control the process. "Canoniza-tion" means that someone has pronounced dogmatically on a given saint's authenticity. The first papal attestation of such was issued by John XV in 993. As papal power increased, so did the papacy's control of the cult of saints, and in 1234 an earlier decretal by Alexander III that no one could be so venerated without the official approval of Rome became part of canon law. It appears not to have slowed the growth of the cult of saints and their relics, however. By the time of the Reformation both were regarded by many as abusive, and Luther struck out vigorously at the veneration of saints as pagan practice in Christian guise. He argued that saints' lives were now so overgrown with leg-end it was impossible to know much for certain about many of them; that grace was a gratuitous gift of God, not a function of the good works of the alleged saint; and finally, that salvation was a matter between God and the individual, without either priests or saints as intermediaries.

Popular and local devotional cults generally preceded formal canonization, and institutionalization inevitably followed as commemoration of the new saint was added to the appropriate day of the liturgical calendar, where he or she might have to compete with a number of others or even with a celebration of Jesus or Mary: it did not do to be martyred on 25 December! Increasingly Christians began to use saints' names for their newborns, though only the Middle Eastern and Hispanic Christians in direct contact with Muslims, who overwhelmingly called their male children Muhammad, chose Jesus as a name for their sons.

In 1563 the Counter-Reformation Council of Trent reaffirmed both the veneration of saints and the blessings inherent in their relics, while advising a cautious assessment of the authenticity of the latter. A series of papal instructions gradually institutionalized the process of canonization, beginning with those issued by Pope Benedict XIV between 1734 and 1738, which formalized past practice and prescribed a new, more skeptical emphasis on the candidate's "heroic virtue." Canonization has become increasingly stringent with the passage of time, at least until the pontificate of John Paul II (r. 1978–present), and many of the "popular" saints of an earlier, less skeptical age have been quietly abandoned by the official cultus.

The saints of the Eastern Christian Churches differ little from those venerated in the West save that there is no centralized authority in the East to control the cult or regularize the process whereby one becomes, in effect, *hagios*. Tradition, consensus, and popular piety are still the Eastern benchmarks of the cult of the saints.

Eucharistic Devotions

Devotion to the Eucharist was another medieval manifestation of popular piety. As we have seen, the primary Christian liturgy was from the beginning a celebration or reenactment of the Last Supper. What was new in the Middle Ages was a particular attention to the Host or consecrated bread. Sometime about 1200, the Host began to be held aloft after the moment of consecration and then, sometime after that, bells were rung to focus the attention of the faithful on the elevation of the Body of Christ. Soon the Host was displayed outside the eucharistic liturgy in special shrinelike receptacles called "monstrances," some of them of extraordinary richness and remarkable craftsmanship.

The climax of eucharistic devotion was the institution of a special feast day to celebrate the Body of Christ, Corpus Christi. At the request of a visionary nun of Liège, the feast was inaugurated there in 1246. In 1264 Urban IV made it a Church-wide holy day, to be celebrated with a special liturgy on the Thursday following the celebration of Trinity Sunday, the first Sunday after

Pentecost. Popular piety made its own arrangements, however. The Host began to be carried in public processions on that day and for several days afterward. The celebrations were emotional, sometimes riotous, and with secular trimmings like games and amusements. Thomas Aquinas composed two special Latin hymns for the liturgy. One began "Tantum ergo," the other, "O salutaris hostia," and both remained on the lips of the faithful until the Second Vatican Council (1962–1965) decided that God was not best hymned in Latin.

Popular Devotions in Islam

There is nothing remotely like these Christian devotions in Sunni Islam. Its liturgy, principally the five-times-daily salat, is as fixed in performance as its Christian counterpart, the Eucharist, and far less dramatic since the Eucharist is essentially a reenactment. Islam has neither stational liturgies like the Christians' annual ritual celebration, between Thursday and Sunday of Easter week, of the events of Jesus' last days in Jerusalem nor commemorative liturgies like the celebration of the basic eucharistic liturgy in honor of some saint, no mass for the dead or marriage mass. Sunni Islam's only "seasonal" liturgy—as already noted, Muhammad's ban on intercalation rendered true seasonal celebrations impossible—is the time- and place-tied hajj. Despite occasional attempts, however, the ritual has not as a whole been successfully "translated" to other places save the sacrifice made at Mina on the tenth day of the hajj month, which, as we have seen, is replicated elsewhere in the Muslim world, though more as a custom hardened into precept than as a commandment.

Sunni Islam's sole commemorative holy day is Mawlid al-Nabi, the Prophet's birthday, the twelfth day of the lunar month called First Rabi. The first mention of its formal celebration among Sunnis is not until the beginning of the thirteenth century, as a court celebration, but soon the common people and most notably the Sufis had taken up the celebration. In 1910 the Ottoman sultan declared it a national holiday in his empire. The liturgical heart of the feast day is the recitation of a lengthy poetical panegyric, likewise called a *mawlid*, recounting the creation of the preexistent Muhammad, the "Muhammad Light" (*nur muhammadi*), the genealogy of the Prophet, the "annunciation" to his mother, Amina, that she will bear the Prophet, and a description of his actual birth. The day and its celebration are, however, still regarded in some circles as something of an "innovation" (*bida*), a somewhat more opprobrious term in Arabic than in English. The underlying cause may be its widespread adoption in Sufi circles, a move that rarely enhanced the orthodoxy of anything in Islam. The Muslim cult of the saints, the friends of God (see below), many with their own mawlid, is likewise not highly regarded in more fastidious Islamic circles.

Not only does the Muslim salat suffer no liturgical expansion; the avenues for the spread of local piety are missing in Muslim religious culture. Blessings (*barakat*) abound in Islam, but they are diffused over a wide variety of persons and objects. There is no sacramental system to channel and regulate their dispensation, no clergy to propagate them, no Church to institutionalize them, no authority or faculty to validate their orthodoxy. The spread of a great variety of devotions across Christian Europe both before and after the Reformation (which had attempted to curb such) was largely the work of the religious orders, international organizations under a centralized leadership that have no parallel in Islam, nor in Eastern Christianity, where monasticism was far more decentralized, contemplative, and self-absorbed than its Western counterpart (see II/8).

Pious devotions in Sunni Islam were nourished by neither popular literature nor popular art but the picture is dramatically altered when one turns to Shiite practice. As we shall see, there is a central narrative among the Shiites, the martyrdom of Husayn at Karbala in Iraq in 680, that has been dramatized and rendered into a liturgy recitative, the "Garden Recital," and celebrated by Shiite Muslims the world over during the "ten days" (*ashura*) at the beginning of the month of Muharram. More, the primary Shiite "saints," the Imams descended from Ali to his seventh or twelfth successor (see I/8), were far more than mere holy men or even simply God's friends; rather, they were God's chosen, earthly reflections of a higher reality, infallible heads of the umma. The births and deaths of all of them are celebrated in the Shiite calendar—many as national holidays in Iran—as well as the anniversaries of Ali's wife Fatima and their daughter Zaynab. These "Fourteen Pure Ones" (Muhammad, the Twelve Imams, and Fatima) are celebrated at their tombs, Muhammad, Fatima, and Hasan in somewhat muted fashion under the watchful eyes of the Sunni Saudis in Medina, the others in Iraq and Iran with great popular enthusiasm.

These reenactments and celebration of the Imams underscore how Shiite Islam differs from its Sunni counterpart in the matter of devotions. For the Shiites, there are genuine and uncontested saints in the Fourteen Pure Ones and particularly the "Holy Family" of Ali, Fatima (sometimes referred to as "The Virgin," *al-batul*), Hasan, Husayn, and their sister Zaynab, who have been the subject of endless eulogy. Their lives have been taken as paradigms of the perfect Muslim man and woman and scenes from them have even been used, despite the prohibition on iconic depiction, for arousing and guiding popular devotion. Moreover, there exists a Shiite "Church" in something close to the Christian sense in that there is a hierarchicized clergy of mullahs whose authority is greater and concerns more pastoral than those of the Sunni ulama (see II/4). The Shiite mullahs have both encouraged and ratified the popular practices surrounding the Imams that lie at the heart of Shiite devotionalism.

The Friends of God

The cult of saints, living or dead, was not an entirely natural development in Islam, which placed an almost infinite gulf between a transcendent Allah and his creation here below. It occurred nonetheless, and with some speed. Note has already been taken of the opposition to the Mawlid al-Nabi. Muhammad, who never claimed to be anything other than mortal (Quran 18:110), and stoutly refused to produce supernatural signs to verify his claims as a prophet, was soon after his death credited with marvelous powers, and those gifts and graces (*karamat*) bestowed by God on his Prophet were quickly extended to God's "friends" (*wali;* pl. *awliya*), male and female. The cults of these friends of God, whether the founder of a Sufi order (see II/8), a local holy man, or the Prophet himself, were popularly patronized, and the devout were richly rewarded with generous blessings—ranging from medical cures or fertility to luck in marriage—that were attached to visitations to the tomb shrines of saints, generally called *qubba*s by reason of the distinctive small domed building over the site. Women in particular, who were not encouraged to participate in public prayers and generally did not find the mosque to be a welcoming place, often made pilgrimages to local tomb shrines with petitions for favors or intercession. All of this combined to make such places and their rituals a center and focus of Muslim spiritual life, particularly in the countryside.

Islam possesses one prototypical martyr, Husayn, the son of the fourth caliph, Ali, and Muhammad's grandson. After an adventuresome voyage eastward across the steppe from Medina, he and his companions were slaughtered in an Umayyad ambush at the town of Karbala in Iraq on the tenth day of Muharram in 680. Both the day and the place have taken on extraordinary significance for Muslims, particularly the Shiites. Not only has Karbala become a richly endowed shrine and pilgrimage city, but the celebration of the tenth of Muharram has generated a rich liturgical and dramatic reenactment (*taziyeh*) of Husayn's martyrdom (see below). Husayn's body is interred in a magnificent tomb in Karbala, but his head is said to be preserved—the vagaries of relics are well known—in the Husayn mosque in Cairo, a genuine Muslim relic.

These cults did not pass unremarked. The school of jurisprudence founded by Ahmad ibn Hanbal (d. 856) was particularly outspoken in its criticism of the cult of saints, particularly at their tombs. The greatest Hanbalite eminence of the Middle Ages, Ibn Taymiyya (d. 1328), issued fatwas and wrote broadsides against them. Even though he was not in a position to do much about this extremely common practice, many of his opinions found an echo in the preaching of Muhammad ibn Abd al-Wahhab (d. 1791), the conservative ideologue behind the rise of the House of Saud in Arabia. In 1813 the Wahhabis emerged from central Arabia to destroy Husayn's tomb shrine—since rebuilt on a far more sumptuous scale—and when they took Mecca and Medina early in the nineteenth century and again, more permanently, in 1926, the zealous Wahhabi "brethren" destroyed the tombs of many of Islam's earliest and most venerated heroes. They did not, however, touch the largest tomb shrine of all, that of the Prophet Muhammad at Medina. Indeed, the Saudis, as we have seen, enlarged and elaborated it.

Three Dramatic Narratives: Passover, Passion, and the Death of Husayn

Each of the three monotheistic communities has master narratives embodying the events crucial to its existence and identity. In a sense, each of the Scriptures plays that role, and the retelling of that text is an important part of the community's religious and even social life. But within those sacred books are even more central stories that must be told and retold for Jews, Christians, and Muslims to preserve their identities. One such for the Jews is clearly their release from bondage in Egypt and their passage to the promised land. Early on the story was connected with the holy day(s) of Passover (Pesach), which may have begun as a spring agricultural festival—the Feast of the Unleavened Bread (matzoh)—but ended as a celebration of the "Exodus" that took place after the Lord's angel slaughtered the Egyptians' firstborn and "passed over" those of the Israelites.

Exodus 12:1–36 explains Passover and how it was to be celebrated. After the construction of the Jerusalem temple, Passover became one of the three pilgrimage festivals all Israelites had to celebrate annually in Jerusalem, but with the temple's destruction in 70 c.e., many Jewish rituals were displaced to the synagogue or home. Passover continues to be marked in the synagogue with special prayers, but it has become the central focus of Jewish domestic ritual. It is the subject of a special Passover liturgy (seder) that reenacts the Israelites' hasty meal before departing Egypt (Exod. 12:8–11). Equally important is the accompanying narrative, the haggadah or "telling," which fulfills the biblical injunction that the story of how God led his Chosen People out of Egypt should be retold by future generations (13:8).

The piety and ritual of Western Christianity primarily emphasized the historical Jesus, whereas the Easterners pursued their particular vision of the Triumphant Christ (Gk. *pantokrator*, "all-ruling"). It is not surprising to discover that the liturgy—whose central act, the Eucharist, was already a reenactment ("Do this in commemoration of me," Jesus is reported [1 Cor. 11:25] to have said) of what may have been a Jewish Passover reenactment—began to be performed in increasingly dramatic form throughout Europe. Hymns were expanded to include dialogue and then dramatic action. Performances moved from the interior of the church outdoors to its courtyard, and finally to the market square; the vernacular replaced Latin in what were increasingly lay performances since a papal decree of 1210 forbade the clergy to participate in such spectacles. The matter was spiritual, however, and the Gospels provided the text, as did the Old Testament and even the lives of saints. Eventually the entire Christian dispensation, from Creation to the Second Coming, which was already being rehearsed in stone, fresco, and mosaic on the facades and walls of Europe's cathedrals, also became the subject of miracle and morality plays presented on festival and holy days in medieval Europe's cities and towns.

The tradition of performing dramas faded at the time of the Reformation—they had in many instances become degraded through contact with carnival plays—but the passion play, undoubtedly the most popular form of medieval religious drama, has survived into modern times. The passion play dramatized the Gospels' (harmonized) narratives of Jesus' last days, from his Last Supper to his crucifixion and resurrection. The form enjoyed continued popularity in Catholic Germany, and in 1634 the residents of the Bavarian alpine town of Oberammergau—present population 5,000—put on a passion play in fulfillment of a vow of gratitude at the town's being spared a terrible plague the previous year. The play was performed every tenth year—since 1680 on the decimal year—and persists down to the present, with the townspeople playing the traditional roles.

> **Note:** The Oberammergau passion play has undoubtedly become more famous than it was in the past as the sole surviving example of a colorful medieval Christian practice. Early in the twentieth century it began to generate imitators elsewhere, notably in the United States. But it has also become notorious as the very public expression of the anti-Semitic sentiments in the Gospels, which unmistakably make the Jewish priesthood responsible for Jesus' death; Hitler attended the three hundredth anniversary performance in 1935. The three hundred and fiftieth anniversary performance in 1985 was altered in response to Jewish protests.

Drama was not among the arts that found a distinct place in traditional Islamic culture, though in more recent times all the popular forms, from grand opera to soap opera, are performed in Muslim societies. Traditional Islam had its dramatic narratives, to be sure, the encomia of the Prophet on his birthday, for example, and the laments recited or chanted on the tenth of Muharram in memory of Husayn's martyrdom. These "garden recitals"—they derived mainly from a Shiite work titled "The Garden of the Martyrs"—were generally stationary and delivered by a professional reciter, but they were processional liturgies as well. There is evidence for public processionals in honor of Husayn in Baghdad from as far back as the tenth century, when mourners with tattered clothes, streaming hair, and blackened faces circled the city walls on the tenth of Muharram, beating their breasts and chanting their dirges. This took place when there was an Alid-leaning dynasty ruling in the capital, but when an out-and-out Shiite regime was established in Iran in the sixteenth century (see I/8), the processions became full-scale pageants with many of the participants dressed as characters in the Husayn-related events being portrayed.

In the mid–eighteenth century the Husayn pageants and garden recitals fused and produced in Iran, and in Persian, a genuinely dramatic performance in a fixed place before a stationary audience, the taziyeh, or "consolation." At first these dramas were performed at street intersections or open areas in the town, but eventually, in the nineteenth century, special arenas were constructed, either permanently or temporarily, for their performance.

Though the liturgical event may have begun merely to commemorate Husayn's slaughter, soon other themes and other figures from Shiite history were introduced. In the end, the taziyeh proved to be a more open-ended performance than its Christian passion play counterpart. The latter remained closely tied to the Gospel texts and to a faithful presentation of events that were not only historical but sacramental. Taziyeh, in contrast, knew no such textual or theological restraints. Like the Passover haggadahs, which are readily altered by Reform Jews to reflect changing perceptions, conditions, and needs—the Orthodox hew faithfully to a text whose central core goes back to the ninth century—the taziyehs vary greatly in their textual and dramatic presentation.

Idols and Images

Among the laws given to Moses on Sinai, one expresses a concern about the Israelites' use of "images." "You shall not make for yourself a sculpted image, or any likeness of what is in the heavens above, or on the earth below, or in the waters under the earth," God says (Exod. 20:4–5) in what has come to be known as the Second Commandment. Later—Deuteronomy is certainly a later version of the laws laid down in Exodus—the reason for the prohibition is spelled out. The Israelites are commanded to destroy all the sacred sites in the land that will one day be theirs. "Tear down their altars, smash their pillars, put their sacred posts to the fire, and cut down the images of their gods, obliterating their name from that site" (Deut. 12:1–3). It was not, then, art— which would still be understood as "craft" for many centuries after this text was written—that bothered the Lord, but what the artisans made, the images, effigies, and representations of the other claimants to the title of "god."

The defiantly aniconic God of the Israelites had good reason for his concern. Throughout most of their history down to the Exile, the Israelites were plagued by their penchant for idols and idol worship. The Bible makes no effort to dissemble their attraction, from the golden bull set up during Moses' absence with the Lord on Sinai (Exod. 32:1–10) to Jeroboam (1 Kings 12:28–31) and his successors as kings of Israel making a similar cult the official policy of the state. How seriously the problem was taken by some of God's spokesmen emerges clearly from this witheringly sarcastic attack on idols by the prophet Isaiah: "The makers of idols all work to no purpose; and the things they treasure can do no good, as they themselves can testify. They neither look nor think, and so shall they be shamed" (44:9–10). Indeed, the Quran attributes many of the same sentiments to Abraham (21:51–67), the first to turn away from idols to the One True God. He upbraids his idol-worshiping father and the rest of his family with the taunt "Do you worship, besides God, these things that can do you neither good nor harm?" (21:66; 26:73).

After the Exile and with the Jews' exposure to another, Greek form of paganism, the problem appears to have shifted its focus from idols of mythical or imagined deities to the cult of images of the ruler, living or dead. From Alexander onward, the Greeks and then the Romans had taken to "deifying" their great men, not, to be sure, in the monotheists' sense of a deity who created and sustained the cosmos, but in the more homely fashion of recognizing the *theios aner*, the man whose preternatural qualities were manifested by his power, wealth, or deeds. This recognition of charisma was a natural gesture; the Romans occasionally required veneration of deified rulers as an act of political and cultural solidarity. The Jews and Christians understood it as no such thing, of course, and the mishnaic tract devoted to idolatry, Abodah Zarah, or "Alien Cult," went even further in describing what constituted "idols" in the second century C.E. Some rabbis forbade all images on the grounds that they were liturgical objects, but a more general ruling restricted the prohibition only to images of humans that "bear in hand a staff or a bird or a sphere." On the face of it, this rabbinic ruling appears to be directed against emperor worship, since, as the Palestinian gemara on this passage explains, primarily regalia from the imperial iconography is being referred to: "A staff because he ruled the world with it, a bird, as it is written, 'My hand has found like a nest the wealth of the peoples', a sphere because the world is made in the shape of a sphere." The Babylonian comment on the Mishnah passage is more terse and far more direct: "It refers to the statues of kings."

Whatever the rabbis were talking about, the synagogue builders appear not to have been listening. Floor mosaics from fifth-century Palestinian synagogues depict not only biblical scenes like the binding of Isaac (see I/1), but even the Greek sun god Helios riding in his chariot in the center of a zodiacal circle or standing in majesty with a globe and a whip in his hand. This more relaxed attitude has left its echo in the Palestinian Talmud, which even offers a brief sketch of its history: "In the days of Rabbi Yohanan [third-century C.E.], they [the Jews] began to paint on walls, and he did not prevent them. . . . In the days of Rabbi Abun [fourth-century C.E.], they began to make designs on mosaics, and he did not prevent them."

The Jews of late antiquity, when both the synagogues and the texts in question originated, were obviously capable of distinguishing an act from its intent and, more importantly, idolatry from mere decoration. Leviticus, for example, had said quite straightforwardly, "You shall not make idols for yourselves, or set up for yourselves carved images or pillars or place figured stones in your land to worship upon" (26:1). When the much later Targum Jonathan paraphrased that passage, he helpfully rendered it as: "You shall not set up a figured stone in your land, to bow down to it, but a mosaic pavement of designs and forms you may set in the floor of your places of worship, so long as you do not do obeisance [*or* prostrate yourselves] to it."

One of the motives for this relative, and by no means universal, leniency was that the Jews were at ease on the issue of idolatry. Image-worship was no longer a major problem or concern. Already in the second century B.C.E. the book called Judith was suggesting that "There is not one of our tribes or clans, districts or towns, that worships manmade gods today. This did happen in days gone by, and that was why our ancestors were abandoned to their enemies to be slaughtered and pillaged, and great was their downfall. But we acknowledge no God but the Lord" (8:18–19).

Emperor Portrayal, Christian Style

It must have taken the Christians some time to adjust their attitudes toward images with some religious content that might fairly be thought of as either idolatrous or at the very least unseemly. One such image was an imperial portrait. Christians had once been executed for refusing to worship such, and already the New Testament Apocalypse (Rev. 20:4) refers to the fact. But when a Christian emperor was the subject of the portraiture, there appear to have been few misgivings about the depiction. Far from being scandalized, the church historian and Constantine's biographer Eusebius (d. 340) took theological comfort in this particular type of image. Constantine's portrait on the coins that circulated everywhere in the empire had him looking heavenward "as if praying to God." His statues above the imperial cities' gates represented him "standing upright, gazing up to heaven, and stretching out his arms in the manner of a man praying," a source of edification, to Eusebius's way of thinking, for all who entered there.

Eusebius himself understood there were limits, however. What of portraits of Jesus, he was asked by the emperor's sister Constantia. There is no way the "form of divinity"—Eusebius is not even certain that is the right term—can be captured by an artist, and there is, besides, the danger of lapsing into a kind of idolatry. But Jesus was after all a man, subject to portraiture, and was being portrayed in Eusebius's day, as both Eusebius and Constantia knew. In the end Eusebius was constrained to resort to the biblical argument and, interestingly, to appeal to what seems to have once been the common Christian practice of avoiding images. "Can it be," he warns Constantia, "that you have forgotten that passage in which God lays down the law that no likeness can be made either of what is in heaven or what is in the earth beneath? Have you ever heard anything of the kind either yourself in church or from another person? Are not such things banished and excluded from churches all over the world, and is it not common knowledge that such practices are not permitted to us alone?"

Christian Images

That early churches once had few or no images in them but that in the fourth century Christian pictorial representations were beginning to appear is confirmed by a letter of the bishop Epiphanius (d. 403) to the emperor Theodosius: "Which of the ancient Fathers ever painted an image of Christ and deposited it in a church or a private house? Which ancient bishop ever dishonored Christ by painting him on door curtains? Which one of them ever made a spectacle of Abraham, Isaac, Jacob, Moses, and the other prophets and patriarchs, of Peter, Andrew, James, John, Paul, and the other Apostles by painting them on curtains or walls?" Epiphanius was not edified by what he saw, and he had further problems with the arbitrary portrayal of the saints, now as elderly, now as youths. The cure, he suggested to the emperor, was to collect and remove the images from the churches and to cover the walls with whitewash, leaving only the sign of the cross. Theodosius did not follow the bishop's advice, and Christians continued to adorn their churches with images of Jesus and the saints, despite taunts from pagans, whose spiritual view of the deity had already made them remote from the idolatry of their ancestors, and particularly from the Jews, whose own position, though fluid, could hardly countenance the Christians' practice.

Eventually there were no more pagans, but the argument with the Jews went on. It was taken up by the Christian theologian Leontius early in the seventh century, not long before the arrival of the first Muslims. Earlier in his tract "Against the Jews," Leontius had pointed out that the Bible itself shows that the Jews had little reluctance to surround themselves with images, and in the most sacred of places: in the Tent of the Presence—witness the golden cherubim—and in the temple in Jerusalem. He then takes another course. "You do obeisance to the book of the Law," he addresses his imaginary Jewish interlocutor, "but you do not make obeisance to the parchments and ink but to the words contained in them. And it is thus that I do obeisance to the icon of God, for when I hold the lifeless representation of Christ in my hands, through it I seem to hold and do obeisance to the Christ. . . . As I have often said, in every greeting and obeisance it is the purpose of the action which is in question." It is not worship but veneration that the Christian is offering to images. And, Leontius concludes in triumph, "You call us idolaters when it was Christian saints and martyrs who destroyed the temples of the idolaters."

Christian Iconoclasm

In 787 an ecumenical council was convened at Nicaea, the site of the first general council of the Church, to settle the matter of image worship, which had been troubling the Eastern Church for more than half a century. As part of their deliberations the bishops requested a report from a certain John, a Jerusalem presbyter, who described for them the events earlier in that century that had led to the outbreak of image-smashing in the Byzantine Empire. This story appears, in one version or another, in most Byzantine accounts of the initial reaction to the veneration of images in the Christian Roman Empire. According to it, Byzantine iconoclasm, the "smashing of images," was a Jewish-inspired plot that took wing because of a credulous Muslim caliph who banned images and image worship in his realm. If such had occurred, whether at Jewish prompting or not, it probably happened in 721, and not long afterward the "infection" spread next door into Byzantine Anatolia, the land the Muslims called "Rum." A number of bishops apparently succumbed, and they in turn caught the ear of the emperor Leo III (r. 717–741), himself a native of the Syrian frontier region and, as one Byzantine historian had it, a notorious "Saracen sympathizer." Several imperial edicts against images were issued beginning in 726, and the effects are described in the life of a contemporary holy man, Stephen: "sacred things (were) trodden upon, (liturgical) vessels turned to other use, churches scraped down and smeared with ashes because they contained holy images. And wherever there were venerable images of Christ or the Mother of God or the saints, these were consigned to the flames or were gouged out or smeared over."

The destruction continued under Leo's son and successor Constantine V (r. 741–775), who in 754 convened a council to make prohibition of images part of the Church's official teaching. As the creed issued by that council put it, echoing Eusebius four centuries earlier, "This man [the painter] makes an image and calls it Christ. Now the name 'Christ' means both God and man. Hence he has either included, according to his vain fancy, the uncircumscribable Godhead in the circumscription of created flesh, or he has confused that unconfusable union . . . and in so doing has applied two blasphemies to the Godhead, namely through the circumscription and the confusion. So also, he who reveres images is guilty of the same blasphemies." The council concluded, "Anyone who presumes from now on to manufacture an icon, or to worship it, or to set it up in a church or a private house, or to hide it, if he is a bishop or a presbyter or deacon, he shall be deposed; if he is a monk or a layman, he shall be anathematized and deemed guilty under imperial law as a foe of God's commands and an enemy of the doctrines of the Fathers."

Among those who rallied to the defense of the veneration of images was John of Damascus (d. 749), scion of a Christian family that had long served in the Muslim civil service in Damascus. John followed another course, however; he retired to a monastery near Jerusalem where he wrote tirelessly in defense of Christian orthodoxy. For him, that included the veneration of images of Jesus, his mother, and the saints. He wrote a special treatise *On the Holy Images* defending *ikonodouleia*, the Christian veneration of icons, as sacred images were called in the East, and he returned to the argument in his theological summa, *On the Orthodox Faith* (4.16). God has made humans in his own image, John argued: that is the foundation of our reverence for each other, because the other is the image of God and "reverence for the image passes over to the protoype."

As for the argument that the Christian veneration of images smacks of pagan idolatry, John points out that they are quite different in kind, just as Jewish sacrifice, which God permitted—indeed, commanded—was different from pagan sacrifice, which God condemned. True, God forbade the use of images to the Jews, and rightly since "who can make an imitation of the invisible, incorporeal, uncircumscribed, and formless God?" But what has changed from the biblical circumstances is the enfleshing of God in the person of Jesus Christ, who became in truth a man, one who might be touched and felt and seen.

The empress Irene suspended the iconoclast decrees in 780, and the issue of image worship was apparently settled forever by the Seventh Ecumenical Council, that held in Nicaea in 787. It rejected the policy of Leo III and the theology of Constantine V. "We keep unchanged all the ecclesiastical traditions handed down to us, written or unwritten," the council decreed, "and of these one is the making of pictorial representations. . . . We therefore . . . define with all certitude and accuracy, that just as the figure of the precious and life-giving cross, so also the venerable and holy images, as well in painting and mosaic, as of other fit materials, should be set forth in the holy churches of God. . . . And to these should be given due salutation and honorable reverence (*proskynesis*), not indeed the true worship (*latreia*) which pertains to the divine nature alone."

This sweeping declaration was by no means the end of the controversy over images, neither in the Western Church, where it resurfaced during the Reformation (see below), nor in the Eastern, where it first arose and would arise again shortly after this council. In 815 the emperor Leo V, called the Armenian, reinstituted the ban on images and their veneration. This time the ban lasted until 843 when the empress Theodora, widow of the iconoclast emperor Theophilus, had the final word over her dead husband by summoning a council that met in 843 and issued the lengthy *Syndikon of Orthodoxy*—the text is still read in Eastern churches on the first Sunday in Lent, a day annually celebrated as the Feast of Orthodoxy. It boldly proclaimed: "Let us declare, let us assert, let us preach in like manner Christ our true God and honor his saints in words, in writing, in thoughts, in deeds, in churches, in Holy Icons, worshiping him as God and Lord and honoring them as his true servants."

At this remove, the controversy over images seems unnecessarily long and inexplicably violent: much of the rich artistic heritage of the Eastern Church was destroyed during the two iconoclast interludes (726–780, 815–843). The icons represented something more than art, however. The icons of the East were not mere representations; they were physical objects, most often richly framed and ornamented paintings frequently believed to possess miraculous powers. For the Eastern Church they were sacramental, a sacralization of the material world, a second and lesser, though still wonderful, incarnation of the spirit. For the theologically sophisticated, they represented superstition and primitivism; for the ordinary believer, they too were the Word made flesh.

Stripping the Altars: Images and the Reform

Widely accepted in the East and the West, the question of the veneration of representations of Jesus, his mother, and the saints made a sudden, and perhaps unexpected, appearance at the very beginning of the Reform movement in Western Christianity. Some in the Church may have been alarmed, even shocked, by the ever growing externalization of religion in the form of rituals, devotions, and the cult of images, but Luther's thrust back toward Scripture as the unique basis of Christian belief and practice put the veneration of images once again on the ecclesiastical agenda. They were firmly nailed there not by Luther himself but by one of his colleagues at Wittenberg, Andras Bodenstein von Karlstadt (d. 1541). Inspired by Luther, Karlstadt began in 1521 to put his own reading of Scripture into practice, which included, boldly and defiantly, the destruction of all sacred images, first in his own Augustinian monastery and then in city parishes. Karlstadt published what became the seminal Reformation tract on the subject, *On the Abolition of Images*, in which he argued that the Bible was clear on this point: image veneration was a form of idolatry.

Luther was appalled. Karlstadt, who also attacked the idea of Jesus' real presence in the Eucharist, was simply denying sacramentalism, the efficacy of material to work in and on the spirit. The reckless destruction of images in churches and convents was, moreover, one more manifestation of the social disorder that Luther had feared and was already breaking out all over northern Europe in the wake of the more radical Reformers. By 1524 Luther was at war with Karlstadt, with images one of the prominent issues. Karlstadt seemed to yield a bit on the subject, while Luther and his followers were prepared to permit a restrained use of the sacred image, notably the crucifix (a cross with an effigy of Jesus on it), since, as Basil wrote long before and the Church thereafter ceaselessly affirmed, the honor offered to the image passes to its prototype. But Karlstadt found willing ears elsewhere. Zwingli in Zurich and Calvin in Geneva both embraced iconoclasm, and statues and holy pictures were smashed, defaced, and burned in the churches of the "puritan" Reform, while the organ and all forms of instrumental music were banned from the worship service.

Islam and the Graven Image

From the outset, the Prophet made no secret of his intentions regarding the omnipresent idols of the Arabs. Tribes that embraced Islam during his lifetime were required to destroy their idols or, if they were incapable of bringing themselves to perform such an act, the Prophet dispatched some more convinced Muslims to do the demolition work for them. When Muhammad finally entered Mecca in triumph in 630, he put his intentions into action in his native town. The scene is described in the traditional biography:

> The Messenger entered Mecca on the day of the conquest and it contained 360 idols which Iblis (or Satan) had strengthened with lead. The Messenger was standing by them with a stick in his hand saying, "The truth has come and falsehood has passed away" (Quran 17:81). Then he pointed at them with his stick and they collapsed on their backs one after another. . . . When the Messenger had prayed the noon prayer on the day of the conquest (of Mecca) he ordered that all the idols which were around the Kaaba should be collected and burned with fire and broken up. . . . The Quraysh had put pictures in the Kaaba including two of Jesus son of Mary and Mary herself, on both of whom be peace. . . . The Messenger ordered that the pictures be erased, except those of Jesus and Mary.

We know little of what to make of that last curious event; the Kaaba was later rebuilt and there is no further trace of the pictures (icons?) of Jesus and Mary. We can say, on the basis of the Quran, that for all Muhammad's opposition to idolatry, there is no sign in the Book of any preoccupation, no open approval or disapproval even, of pictures or images. But conditions must soon have changed, since by the time we come to read the collections of Prophetic traditions, they are filled with condemnations of images and image-making: "Abu Talha reported the Prophet as saying, 'The angels do not enter a house which contains dogs or pictures.'" Or again, "Aisha told that she had screened a store room of hers with a curtain on which there were figures and the Prophet tore it down. So she made two cushions out of it and had them in the house for sitting on." And, much more circumstantially,

> Said ibn Abi Hasan said: "When I was with Ibn Abbas a man came to him and said, 'Ibn Abbas, I am a man whose livelihood comes only from

the work of my hands, and I make these representations of things.' Ibn
Abbas replied that he would tell him only what he had heard from God's
Messenger. He had heard him say, 'If anyone makes a representation of
anything, God will punish him until he blows a spirit into it, and he will
never be able to do that.' Then when the man gasped and became pale,
he said to him, 'Out upon you! If you must do so, make representations
of these trees or of anything which does not possess a soul.' "

We do not know when those traditions were put into circulation. If they are
authentic, we are faced with the same kind of dilemma that the figuratively
decorated synagogues of Palestine posed to a supposedly aniconic Jewish tradition. Muslim coinage bore representations of the caliph down to the reign of
Abd al-Malik (r. 685–705). Even after that date Muslim sovereigns continued
to build Syrian steppe villas decorated in a style that was not merely figurative
but even aggressively and suggestively secular. It is perhaps safer to conclude
that Islam came to its iconophobia gradually, and that the Prophetic traditions
reflect a later and not a primary stage in that evolution.

The later official Islamic sentiment on images is clear enough, however. This
is how it is expressed in one of the standard Islamic law books, a commentary
on the hadith collection of Muslim written by the Syrian jurist al-Nawawi
(d. 1377). All fear of idolatry is gone, and the reasons for the prohibition are
overtly theological:

> The learned authorities of our (Shafiite) school and others hold that
> painting a picture of any living thing is strictly forbidden, because it is
> threatened with grievous punishment as mentioned in the Prophetic
> traditions, whether it is intended for common domestic use or not. So
> the making of it is forbidden under every circumstance, because it im-
> plies a likeness to the creative activity of God. . . . On the other hand,
> the painting of a tree or of camel saddles and other things that have no
> life is not forbidden. Such is the decision on the actual making of a pic-
> ture. . . . In all this there is no difference between what casts a shadow
> and what does not cast a shadow. This is the decision of our school on
> the question, and the majority of the Companions of the Prophet and
> their immediate followers and the learned of succeeding generations
> accepted it. (*Guide to an Understanding of Muslim* 8.398)

The Word as Decoration

Jews and Muslims have a particular attachment to the Word as expressed in
terms of language. Hebrew and Arabic are both sacred languages, and both
are in a sense the language of God himself. But there is an important difference. The Jews lost their Hebrew as a living language while the Bible was still

in the process of formation. As a result, some of the last sections of the Book of Daniel are not in Hebrew but in Aramaic, the related Semitic language that had become by post-Exilic times the lingua franca of the Jews and many others in the Middle East. Ezra had the Scriptures translated, presumably into Aramaic, at the ceremony renewing the Covenant at the return from Exile (Neh. 8:7–8), and by the second century B.C.E. its seems that many Jews were getting their Scripture from either the Greek Septuagint (like the Greek-speaking Philo and Paul as well as the authors of the Gospels) or else the Aramaic targums (like the Aramaic-speaker Jesus), without a great deal of notice. There were some complaints, of course, but not about the fact of translation—merely, in the case of the Septuagint, of its lack of accuracy.

Although the Jews turned to the vernacular, the Muslims did not. Their Scripture frequently boasted that it was "an Arabic Quran," and while Muslim piety might regard the Book's style, diction, and syntax as paradigms of perfection, Muslim theologians soon converted them into miracles. Muhammad had been instructed to respond to his critics by challenging them to "bring a sura like it" (Quran 1:13; 10:38; 28:49). They could not, of course, and thus was born the notion of the Quran's inimitability, most specifically of its language and style, which was, at base, the validating miracle of Islam, the theological counterpart of Jesus' resurrection from the dead.

Veneration of text and language thus went hand in hand in Islam, and the emphasis on both was strengthened by their already noted aversion to figurative arts. As we have just seen, Muslims took God's prohibition against idols as seriously as the Jews, and, like the Jews, they extended it, though not at all times or in all places, to figurative and pictorial art generally. Muslim decoration frequently took the form of repetitive geometric or vegetal patterns, the so-called arabesque. This type of decoration did not originate with Islam; it can be observed on many of the Roman monuments of the Middle East, in Syria, for example, which antedate Islam by many centuries.

The other Muslim alternative to figurative art seems to have been Islam's own special creation, or at least emphasis. Large, elegantly inscribed writing appears unmistakably as decoration, not merely as information, on Greek and Roman buildings and in miniature form on coins. Muslims too put inscriptions on their coins—from which figures were eventually removed—and early on in their buildings, like the Dome of the Rock (692), which has mosaic inscriptions in the interior. But as time passed, the writing on buildings in particular, though it still conveyed information, had taken on a life of its own as it was transformed from writing to calligraphy. Extraordinarily ornate writing runs around the portals, across the facades, or up and down panels on the walls of most great Islamic monuments of the Middle Ages. Its design is often stunningly intricate and complex, almost unreadable in fact, in the manner of modern graffiti. In most cases the literate viewer probably needed little help understanding the content since texts were usually familiar quranic ones.

It was purely and simply the Word that was being magnified by artistic enhancement.

There is little parallel among the equally aniconic Jews. From the tenth century onward Jews produced artistically illuminated manuscripts in Muslim Egypt, though without figurative representations. Two centuries later, when Jewish manuscript illumination began in Christian Europe, representations of sacred or ceremonial objects were portrayed, and later, in the seventeenth and eighteenth centuries, figures of rabbis and others began to appear. But there is no exaltation of Hebrew into the monumental public calligraphy of Arabic. It is not difficult to understand why. Islam was official: it controlled the public life of the Middle East and what was permissible in it. Jews lived under the dhimma which would have made the public display of Hebrew not only unlikely but dangerous.

7

Thinking about God

HELLENISM WAS DISTINGUISHED by its confidence in the human intellect's ability to discern the nature of the universe and humankind's purpose in it. The upper end of the Greeks' ambitious intellectual program, the study of the principles of being or philosophy, led to an ultimate principle of being, namely, God. The branch of philosophy devoted to the programmatic study of God—his existence, nature, and attributes—was called theology. According to one common version of the theology circulating in the ancient Mediterranean world, God was a primary spiritual principle, eternal, all-knowing, and all-good, from whose goodness and intelligence there flowed, as light from the sun, the descending order of beings in the universe, from the pure spirits on high, through the heavenly bodies, and, on earth, the highest vital form, intelligent humanity, to the lowest, the lifeless beings of the mineral kingdom. All this could be demonstrated, it was thought, by the most rigorous scientific proofs.

Mythos and Logos

Theology, discourse about God according to the principles of reason, was the invention of a people without benefit of revelation. It is unnecessary here to discuss the origins of Greek religious thinking except to note that by the time they began to produce a literary record, the Greeks were already expressing at least some of their religious sentiments in the form of myth, complex narratives about a whole family of anthropomorphized but immortal gods and goddesses with characteristics ranging from the majestic to the ridiculous.

That is what the Greek myths were about. As narrative, *mythos* is a special form of discourse divorced from time and only circumstantially connected with place. Like art, it simply offers itself without explaining its presence or arguing its own validity. For all its aesthetic splendors, a later generation of Greeks grew unhappy with the mythological account of the gods. Both the mythical form of discourse and the value system inherent in the myths themselves were challenged in an evolving Greek society by new ethical attitudes and particularly by a different kind of human understanding that found its external and formal expression in a new form of discourse called *logos*.

Logos is essentially an approach to understanding that pursues causes and is, at the same time, a mode of discourse that can give an account of that pursuit; that argues and demonstrates rather than simply narrating; and that is subject to verification by criteria external to itself. The categories of truth and falsehood, which are totally irrelevant to myth, are part of that verification apparatus. Logos is, in short, what we call science and what the Greeks more broadly termed philosophy.

By Socrates and Plato's generation, philosophers were applying logos discourse to every corner of the known universe as well as to the domain of human activity. In the next generation, Aristotle formalized the method of logos in a series of works on logic (the science of logos), and then went on to distinguish and organize the already vast body of knowledge that had been won by philosophy. It was not Plato and Aristotle who introduced God or the gods, once only the subject of myth and the object of ceremonial worship, to the scrutiny of logos; nor, once introduced, did the supernatural surrender its more traditional hold on the minds and hearts of the Greeks. But Plato and Aristotle joined God and reason in a manner that profoundly influenced Western thinking about God, and that both stimulated and disturbed the chosen guardians of the divine Self-portrait, the Jews, Christians, and Muslims.

Greek philosophy, or rather its branch called "logos about the divine" (*theologia*), did not begin by presuming God's existence, even though every Greek accepted the fact of that existence. Its task was instead to demonstrate— to prove scientifically—the existence and nature of the divine. Few had any doubts this could be done, and the Greek theologians laid out with their usual elegant ease the various arguments, later so familiar, from the design and order of the universe, the consensus of humankind, and the necessity of a first cause in the great chain of being as it descends and of a final cause to which it returns.

All these arguments simply attempted to demonstrate, in more or less rigorous form, what the Greeks, Romans, and others already knew. Where the new science departed more radically from commonly held opinions was in the portrait of that being or beings whom the Greeks called "the Immortals." The method of logos soon stripped from the divine two of its most obvious and universally recognized attributes: plurality and anthropomorphism. Theology, with its hierarchical view of reality, struck at the heart of ancient polytheism—there was but one, supreme God—and denied that this God could be anything but pure spirit, beyond flesh and bones, surely; beyond human affects such as love and hate; beyond thought, perhaps; and even, some maintained, beyond being itself.

The theologians' vision of God as a single, transcendent, and spiritual cause was not yet monotheism. Although it removed the Supreme Being from direct contact with the material universe, it posited a great many intermediary beings below God's remote transcendence. Some were intelligences without matter; others dwelled in the planets. These beings too were divine, God's own eternal emanations, which descended by degrees to the intelligences shared by humankind.

The theologians were not unmindful of the shambles they had made of popular religious attitudes and beliefs. Some professed not to care, but others such as the Stoics attempted to salvage the traditional myths by allegorizing them. Homer was a theologian, it was argued, but his manner of describing the nature of the gods was determined by the quality of his audience, whereas the speculative theologians could present the same truths in the unvarnished scientific language of philosophy. Even the mystery religions with their transparently primitive rituals could be explained in rationalistic terms for the newly sophisticated Mediterranean intelligentsia.

Revelation in the Judeo-Islamic style of a deity communicating through human agents the truths necessary for salvation was an alien notion to the Greeks. If the gods spoke to humans, as they assuredly did in dreams and through oracles, it was to warn or counsel some fairly circumscribed act, not to proffer covenants or salvation. If salvation was to occur, it would be through human beings' use of their own intellectual faculties to discover what the good life was and the skillful and prudent way to achieve it.

The Theology of Philo of Alexandria

Theology was one of the manifestations of Hellenism that came to the Near East in the wake of Alexander the Great's conquests in the fourth century B.C.E. It took root in the schools of higher learning that grew up in newly founded cities like Alexandria and Antioch, and in more popular form spread among the Hellenic and Hellenized intelligentsia that was a by-product of Greco-Roman urbanism in the eastern Mediterranean. Note has already been taken of the encounter of Hellenism and Judaism in both Palestine and the Diaspora. Greek ethical ideals, for example, are present and visible in third-century Jewish writings like the biblical Qohelet (Ecclesiastes in the Septuagint) and in the second-century Wisdom of Jesus ben Sira.

Such works may be categorized as semipopular presentations intended for a general, literate audience. For evidence of more formal philosophical and theological speculation among Second Temple Jews, one must turn from Palestine to the Diaspora community in Egypt. The first Jew we know professed interest in Greek theology was a certain Aristobulus, who was from a high-priestly family and worked in Alexandria in the second century B.C.E. The scattered fragments of his works, which were written in Greek, show a typical theologian at work, albeit for the first time on Jewish scriptural material.

At once we are counseled against being trapped into a literal interpretation of the Torah, which in Aristobulus's own day had been translated into Greek. A literal approach to the text, favored by the traditionalists, shows up nothing particularly unusual about the Torah, but an allegorical understanding reveals Moses as a true prophet who shared the philosophers' gift of wisdom, though Moses' account is, for all its metaphorical expression, superior to the Greek version of wisdom by reason of its obvious antiquity.

The themes touched on by Aristobulus—the identity of Greek and Jewish wisdom, for example, which is revealed by the prudent application of allegorical exegesis—were not only taken up by his fellow Alexandrian Philo (ca. 50 C.E.) but generously enlarged. Philo's language was Greek; he too read the Bible in the Septuagint version, and he too attempted to effect a reconciliation between Scripture—which is essentially a narrative discourse (*mythos*)—and the Hellenic scientific logos. The literary form he chose was an extended commentary on the opening books of the Bible, and although Philo's exegetical method is Stoic and many of his philosophical assumptions are Platonic, his subject throughout is the Jewish Scripture.

For Philo, God is absolutely transcendent. He is, at the same time, the One and beyond the One. But he is also, in the best Platonic and scriptural tradition, the Creator. From God's mind, as water from a spring or light from a torch, come forth the eternal Forms (Gk. *eide*, transcribed in Latin as *ideae*, which has led to the highly misleading English translation as "Ideas"), the Platonic prototypes of all being. Indeed, Philo is the first we know to conceive of Plato's eide as noetic and to identify them as God's thoughts. They descend in a great chain into the created world, becoming progressively more material in their descent. Chief among these Forms, which Philo calls *logoi* after the Stoic fashion, is the supreme Logos, which Philo boldly describes as the "first-begotten of the Father" and the "second God." The Logos descends into the material world par excellence where it is embodied in human reason: it dwelt in Moses and is immanent in all humans as intelligence.

Greek theologians had for some time been experimenting with the notion of a Logos or Word or Reason—the Greek term is extraordinarily polymorphous—as the first emanation of God—the Platonic view of the cosmos invariably rested on the metaphor of God as the sun or a spring and the universe as his "overflow"—as well as the instrument of creation. The Hellenic influence is perhaps visible in earlier Jewish authors' treatment of Wisdom as a personified entity somehow distinct from God and even as an agent in Creation (see I/1). If Philo's language on the Logos appears somewhat bold, it was certainly not construed as a retreat from monotheism. On the contrary, it seems designed to protect God's transcendence and at the same time establish a link between this now philosophically remote Creator and his distant and somewhat degenerate creation.

Earlier theologians had to take into account the fact that poets and others had had their say on the subject of God, and they had attempted to reconcile "poetical" and "speculative" theology by allegorical exegesis. Philo's task was somewhat different. He accepted the reality of a historical revelation to Moses on Sinai without hesitation or reserve, just as he accepted the truths contained in that revelation. He also accepted the truth of philosophy, and saw no contradiction between the two, at least in principle. There were, in fact, differences—the Greeks generally believed, for example, in a universe that was created but eternal and in a providence that was general but did not descend to particulars. Some of the apparent differences between Scripture and philosophy could be resolved by applying rationalizing exegesis to the former, but where Philo deemed reconciliation impossible, he resolutely followed Moses, not Plato.

Philo's language was Greek and so he read his Bible in translation: Scripture came to him clothed in Greek raiment, with its own set of connotations, some of them already philosophical. But he took the decisive step in converting scriptural notions into philosophical ones by means of allegorical exegesis, thereby opening the Septuagint to a type of discussion denied to the legal exegetes. The enterprise has been going on ever since—much the same way Philo had conceived it. Philosophical thinking about God was carried forward not only among the Jews—Saadya Gaon and Maimonides are two outstanding examples; see below—but in Christian and Muslim circles after their own encounters with rational Hellenism. Third- and fourth-century Christians received their (Hellenic) education in the Gentile universities; Muslim thinkers, after the translation movement had carried the critical works of Aristotle and Plato into Arabic. What remained to Philo's successors among the Jews, Christians, and Muslims was to explore and bridge the full extent of the distance that separated the new philosophical currency from the older and more familiar scriptural discourse, a necessary and perhaps necessarily impossible task.

Philo's work was greeted with no visible enthusiasm by the Jews of Palestine. To the Pharisees and other non-Hellenized Jews there, it was probably inaccessible in any event, and although the voice of the Palestinian "Hellenists" of the day can be heard on political questions, it is inaudible on religious matters. Philo's work must have been read in the Diaspora—Paul for one appears to have been aware of it—and it found its most appreciative audience among the Hellenized converts to Christianity, first from among the Jews and then the Gentiles. The Logos at the opening of John's Gospel probably owes nothing to Philo, but it was obviously capable of a Philo-like interpretation, which was freely applied at Philo's own city of Alexandria less than two centuries later by Christian Hellenists like Clement and Origen.

Athens and Jerusalem

Theology did not come into Christianity through Philo alone. In Paul and the Gospel of John there are theological notions, that is, ideas expressed in the abstract conceptual terminology typical of theological rather than scriptural discourse. Paul and John were no doubt exposed to theological ideas that they accepted and used. There was already an abundance of such in the Jewish noncanonical literature, which, as has been noted, portrayed the divine Wisdom and the Messiah as spiritual realities that existed from the moment of Creation. Paul took up and combined both notions in his description of Jesus as the preexistent Logos.

Though neither Paul nor John argued theologically—they simply asserted by virtue of their own authority as Apostles—logical demonstration and proof were the hallmarks of the philosophical method, as every Jewish and Christian thinker who came into contact with philosophy at this time was aware. Apostolic authority might impress new Jewish Christians, but it did not much appeal to the Gentile *intelligentsia* as an alternative to proof, and so something the Gentiles could and did understand was eventually substituted. Some of the early Gentile Christians inevitably turned to philosophy in their attempt to explain the new faith, but those who did recognized the attractive dangers of speculative theology. Although some, like Philo and Justin, the Christian philosopher martyred about 165 c.e., thought that "the wisdom of the Greeks" and "the wisdom of God" could be reconciled, Paul set the two at odds as natural antagonists (1 Cor. 1:20–24).

In a sense Paul was right. The monotheists had a guaranteed source of truth about God and humans in Scripture, and so whenever there was an obvious conflict between the givens of Scripture and the findings of philosophy and theology, the conflict had to be resolved in favor of Scripture. Theology held, for example, that since God cannot undergo change or modulation, cannot pass from inaction to action, from potency to act, in the jargon of the schools, the universe had necessarily to be an eternal emanation of God. Moreover, God's transcendence barred him from management of creatures below him: he created beings and then turned them loose to function according to their own programming or natures. The scriptural view of both Creation and Providence was quite different from the reasoning of the theologians, and the latter had to yield to the former. Theology might ask the questions, but Scripture provided the secure answers.

In sacred theology (as opposed to the rational theology of the Greeks), then, reason played servant to revelation. But the actual relationship was much less serene. If unaided human reason could reach an adequate knowledge of God and the end of humankind, what need was there for revelation? Why was the prophet superior to the philosopher? Because, Philo attempted to answer, the prophet converted God's truths into behavioral codes: someone like Moses was not only a prophet but a lawgiver.

The firmest statement of the early Christians' opposition to the wisdom of the Greeks was expressed by a Latin lawyer, Tertullian (d. after 220), who rhetorically exclaimed, "What has Athens to do with Jerusalem? What agreement between the Academy and the Church?" Tertullian had witnessed the effects of Gnosticism, and had, like others, traced its errors to Greek philosophy. The connection confirmed his conviction that faith alone was sufficient for the Christian, since the entire truth had been revealed. Tertullian was willing not merely to accept but even to boast of the differences: the Christian believes in the paradoxes of Christianity precisely because they are absurd.

Tertullian, who had considerably greater confidence in human reason when it manifested itself in the form of Roman law rather than Greek philosophy, may reflect a basic cultural difference between the Latin and Greek forms of Christianity. Clement of Alexandria (d. ca. 215 c.e.), who came from a very different environment, showed none of Tertullian's disdain for philosophy, and he uttered no apostrophes against "wretched Aristotle." For Clement the works of human reason served the same purpose for the Gentiles as the Law did for the Jews: they were an "evangelical preparation," as Eusebius later called it. Greek wisdom was true wisdom in that it was the product of an intelligence that humans share with God or of a special kind of natural revelation that the Logos gave the Gentiles. Clement, who knew Philo's work exceedingly well, was aware of Philo's arguments justifying recourse to philosophy— that the Greek thinkers had read the Scriptures and expropriated many of its doctrines—and he did not hesitate to invoke it for his own case. The Christians were now merely returning the favor, much as the Israelites helped themselves to the Egyptians' valuables as they took leave of Egypt, the better to build a temple to the Lord (Exod. 11:2–3). This gleeful example of "pilfering from the Egyptians" is from Origen (d. ca. 254 c.e.), a distinguished alumnus of the Platonic school in Alexandria and the author of *On First Principles*, Christianity's pioneer attempt at presenting the truths of Scripture in the form and language of systematic theology. In speaking of the Father, Jesus the Logos, and the Holy Spirit, Origen described each as a separate "essence" or "substance" (*ousia*) and an "individual" (*hypostasis, hypokeimenon*), and then characterized the divine trinity of individuals in one God as "consubstantial" (*homoousios*).

Theology and Creeds: Nicaea to Chalcedon

Christianity had perhaps little choice but to embrace the Hellenic theology: its early intellectuals had all been educated in that system. Thus, if they were going to explain Christian doctrine to themselves and others, they had first to convert scriptural mythos (as the Hellenized Paul had already begun to do) into the currency of Hellenic-style logos. Son of God, for example, was the Gospels' biological metaphor to explain Jesus' relationship to Yahweh, for which the philosopher-theologians of the fourth century substituted the terms of current scientific discourse: generation and substance, modality, subordination, eternity. An attempt to think of Jesus in the latter terms led the

Alexandrian cleric Arius (d. 336) to propose that Jesus, as "Son," had necessarily to be subordinate to his "Father," who was, by definition eternal and un-
begotten, while for Jesus, "there was a time when he was not." Logically this
made sense, perhaps, but when this teaching became widespread, the bishops
convened in council at Nicaea in 325 (see I/6) declared it heretical and issued
their own dogma affirming that Jesus was "begotten, not made" of the Father,
and was consubstantial with him. The latter was a term of art in logos but
exceedingly remote from Scripture. Furthermore, the Greek definition of the
Trinity as "three individuals (*hypostases*) in one being (*ousia*)" became in Latin
"three persons in one substance," the very translation causing an additional
problem. The bishops continued to support their positions by citing Scripture, but invariably dogma was set forth (see I/5) in the language of theology.
Not surprisingly, even though there were important canon lawyers (see II/4),
the theologians among the clergy (a double filter) constituted Christianity's
elite for much of its history.

At Nicaea the bishops pronounced dogmatically on the relationship of the
Father and the Son, but the work of translating scriptural ways of talking and
thinking into the scientific (i.e., theological) idiom of the times had scarcely
begun. The issue of Jesus himself remained. Christology was a matter of
decoding titles in the New Testament, but in the decades that followed
Nicaea, Christian intellectuals attempted to understand the Jewish Messiah in
theologically coherent terms. Scripture might simply assert that he was both
man and Son of God, but fourth- and fifth-century theologians had to reconcile those assertions in terms of contemporary philosophical discourse: how
could Jesus' single personality encompass both a human and a divine nature?

Culture, tradition, and theological ingenuity supplied varied answers. Some
emphasized Jesus' humanity: he was a man God had glorified to divine status.
This view may have developed out of an original Jewish-Christian position
that saw Jesus' messiahship as acquired or bestowed, likely at his resurrection.
Others, under a demonstrably more Hellenic influence, regarded Jesus as
eternally and dominantly divine, the Godhead clothed in flesh, so to speak.
The first position came to be known as Nestorianism, and perhaps reflected an
older, Jewish way of looking at Jesus; the second was termed Monophysitism,
and was clearly more congenial to some of the Hellenically minded theologians. The ecumenical council convened at Chalcedon in 451 condemned
both and asserted against all logic—but unmistakably *with* Scripture—that
Jesus was "complete in Godhead and complete in manhood, truly God and
truly man," and that each nature, the human and the divine, could use the faculties of the other, or, as we might now put it, each operating system could use
the applications of the other. As the thesis of redemption had already implied,
God had to have died on the cross; by its dogmatic definition, the Council of
Chalcedon affirmed that this had indeed occurred. Hellenic philosophy had
as one of its objectives "to save the *phainomena*," or, "to explain the evidence"

by putting forward a reasonable hypothesis. Sacred theology's intent, as demonstrated clearly at Chalcedon, was, however, "to save the *theologoumena*," the beliefs of the faith.

The Council of Chalcedon had enormous political consequences in the Middle East. The Western Churches accepted the formula—it had in fact been proposed by the pope—as did the Greek-speaking "imperial" or Melkite Churches under the control of Constantinople. But the "national" and "vernacular" Churches in Egypt, Abyssinia, Syria, Armenia, and Iraq did not; they preferred their own Monophysite or Nestorian views of Jesus' divinity and humanity. Theological difference was not necessarily a heresy in the fifth century, but unwillingness to affirm the creed of an ecumenical council was, and as the fifth century turned into the sixth, the theological argument had become political. On the eve of the Muslim expansion into their territories, the Eastern Churches were in a state of considerable theological turmoil and political disarray.

The Muslims Encounter Aristotle

The revealed monotheistic religions came in contact with the scientific mode of inquiry—investigation or explanation of phenomena on rationally and dialectically defensible principles—on several different occasions, but nowhere so painfully or productively as in their contact with Hellenism. In some instances the monotheists learned Greek, as Jews did in the Diaspora in the second and first centuries B.C.E. and the Christians two or three centuries later, and so became Hellenes in the narrower linguistic sense. Elsewhere, however, Hellenism's cultural goods had to be translated, into Syriac, for example, for the benefit of the only fitfully Hellenized Christians of inner Syria and Mesopotamia; into Arabic for Muslims and Jews of the ninth-eleventh-century Abode of Islam; and finally, into Latin for Christians of eleventh- and twelfth-century Europe who had all but forgotten their Hellenic heritage. Of chief concern in the present comparative context are the latter two instances: the passage of Greek scientific-philosophical works into Arabic and their effect on the religious culture of Islam and Judaism, and then the translation of many of those same works from Arabic into Latin and their effect on medieval European Christianity.

Muslims probably first came into contact with theology not in its Greek form but in its Christian adaptation, which has already been characterized as sacred theology—that is, Hellenic rationalism in the sometimes awkward service of scriptural faith. This likely occurred when Muslims moved into what were still overwhelmingly Christian milieus in the Middle East. Free will and predestination seem to have been high on the list of debate topics (see II/5), as well as the Trinity, which the Quran itself had questioned. The polemic must have been rather one-sided, at least until the Muslims began to equip themselves with the dialectical weapons of their religious adversaries. Sometime late in the eighth century, Muslim intellectuals, principally in the new cosmopolitan capital of Baghdad, had put at their disposal the foundation works of intellectual Hellenism: summaries and adaptations of Plato's dialogues and full translations of practically all of Aristotle's works (together with assorted later Greek commentaries on them), as well as the geometry of Euclid, the astronomical geography and alchemy of Ptolemy of Alexandria, and the medical works of Galen, among others. This was technology transfer on a massive scale, this passage of the intellectual goods of one culture into the quite different idiom of another. The bridge-builders of this transfer were the highly cultured Syrian Christians of Iraq, most of whom had left the ecumenical fold in the wake of the Council of Chalcedon and consequently had little esteem for the "imperial" (Melkite) Church of Byzantium. Their language, Syriac Aramaic, served as the intermediary stage between Aristotle's Greek and the Muslims' Arabic.

The translation movement from Greek into Arabic lasted no more than two-hundred years—it was all but over by 1000—and its effects, along with a parallel absorption of Indian and Persian material via Iran, were profound. It gave new and highly creative energy to Muslims' interest in medicine, pharmacology, mathematics, physics, optics, astronomy, astrology, and alchemy. The latter two sciences were exact and highly esteemed in antiquity and the medieval era, though viewed with disapproval by the religious authorities, astrology because it was too fatalistic, alchemy because it was too *creative*. But this Hellenic inheritance also confronted and challenged the very principles of Islam, as it had those of Judaism and Christianity, and there its effects were considerably more problematic.

Falsafa

Greek mathematics, astronomy, and medicine all had illustrious and creative sequels in their new Islamic environment. Some Muslims also attempted to construct on this inherited Greek foundation a kind of Muslim rationalist philosophy by proposing a view of God, the universe, and humans that was consonant with both the new science and the tenets of Islam. The experiment was dubbed *falsafa*, and its practitioner a *faylasuf*, straight out of the Greek *philosophia*. Its rationalistic intent and interests were as clear as the origin of its name.

The very first master of falsafa, al-Kindi (d. ca. 870), set out a series of disturbing positions. Most ominously, he posited the existence of a human rational wisdom that ran parallel to the sacred wisdom of revelation. In Kindi, human wisdom, to which the lawyers had granted some small autonomy under the rubric *ijtihad* (see II/4), was given direct access to God: what the Prophet had gained without toil by God's gift, the philosopher could also attain by laborious intellectual effort. It was a generous if somewhat grudging concession to philosophy. The physician and philosopher al-Razi (d. 925) not only granted the philosopher access to a knowledge of God; he denied it to the prophets of revelation. Philosophy was the *only* wisdom. This was apostasy and disbelief (*kufr*) pure and simple, and though not many other philosophers were willing to go as far as al-Razi, the dangers of the rationalist position were manifest. Falsafa did not have a brilliant career in Islam, despite the efforts of such men as al-Farabi and Ibn Sina to reconcile faith and reason in a more sophisticated manner than Kindi, and with greater Islamic sensibilities than those displayed by Razi.

Unlike Kindi, al-Farabi (d. 950) was unwilling to write off prophetic revelation as a separate and independent means of attaining enlightenment. He approached the question from the distinctive angle of political philosophy, distinctive not with regard to his mentor Plato, of course, but in the light of the history of later Greek philosophy, which betrayed no interest whatsoever in political philosophy. Farabi's ideal state was to be ruled by someone who combined both intellectual and practical enlightenment, the qualities of the philosopher and the prophet. The true prophet, according to Farabi, could take the truths shared with the philosopher by reason of surpassing intellect and convert them, through the imaginative faculty, into the figured truths of a revelation like the Quran or the concrete realities of a law like the sharia. But what Farabi said of the "prophet" was true of all prophets, and there was no apparent attempt to defend the unique quality of the Islamic revelation.

Ibn Sina, whom the Latin West called Avicenna (d. 1038), could explain no less than Farabi both the need and process of prophecy revelation and wrote a special treatise, *On the Proof of Prophecy*. The process could be devised easily enough within the capacious categories of Greek cognitive theories, with which Ibn Sina and Farabi were well acquainted, but the need for revelation, if the same truths were available to unaided human reason, was quite another matter. Here philosophers fell back on familiar Platonic and Gnostic ground. Not everyone was capable of reflective reasoning, and it was for the great mass of the unphilosophical that God—the God of the ignorant and the learned alike—chose to reveal his truths through a prophet.

The argument is not unlike that found among Sufis and other mystics in pursuit of private revelation. The Law is not for them; it is for the masses. Ibn Sina could savor that line of reasoning, since he was not much removed from the mystical stance in his own later philosophy. Many of the Greeks in the Platonic tradition had argued that discursive reasoning had its limits, and that final knowledge of God was the result of illumination, an intuitive leap to God, of "the alone to the Alone," as Plotinus famously put it. That moment took on great importance for Ibn Sina. Illumination (*ishraq*) or gnosis (*marifa*) does not loom large in Ibn Sina's philosophical encyclopedias like the *Book of Healing* or his *Book of Scientific Knowledge*, but his later mystical treatises make it clear that this intuitive union with the divine was central to what he was beginning to conceive of as a kind of esoteric philosophy.

The lonely band of Muslim philosophers, most of whom continued to affirm and practice Islam and made some attempt at reconciling their new Greek-style learning with their Islamic beliefs, remained, for all that, marginalized and suspect for most Muslims. They were not insignificant—Islam's chief medieval theologian, Ghazali (d. 1111), had to take up intellectual arms against them. But philosophy was not a terribly attractive calling for Muslim or Jew, chiefly by reason of its views on Creation, its exaltation of secondary causality at the expense of the Scripturalists' sense of God's continuous creation, its denial of divine providence, and, finally, its problems with the resurrection of the body, all of which ran counter, directly or indirectly, to the teachings of the Bible or the Quran.

Talking about God: The Muslim Beginnings

By the eleventh century there was among Muslims a distinctive theology called *kalam*, literally "speech." In its subject matter—the investigation from a scriptural, that is, quranic, base of the nature and attributes of god and his role in the universe—was not terribly different from the contemporary Christian enterprise called theology. Its method was systematic and broadly Aristotelian, again like its Christian counterpart; but unlike the Christian discipline, kalam did not occupy the center of the intellectual and religious spectrum among Muslims. Although visible, theology was neither vigorous nor highly regarded in Islamic circles.

From the twelfth century onward full-fledged kalam works by Muslim authors are available, but if we proceed backward up the theological stream, kalam's course becomes less and less certain, its traces less evident, and its origins all but unknown. If, however, we understand theology broadly as an interest in the fundamental religious issues raised by Muhammad's message, its origin was even earlier, and its point of departure, it appears, political.

Early in the troubled caliphate of Ali (r. 656–661), a group called the Kharijites had raised the question, as we have seen (I/5), of who was a Muslim and who should rule the Muslim community. On the first point they took a rigorist position. The practicing Muslim was the only true Muslim; any other was a sinner and, indeed, an apostate. On the imamate or leadership issue, the Kharijites took a radically egalitarian stand: any (practicing) Muslim might lead the community. Neither view prevailed in the broader Muslim community, but the principled connection of morality and leadership they had mooted did not disappear. When the caliphate passed into the hands of the Umayyad family in 661, the question became even more pointed since the Umayyad caliphs neither were nor pretended to be model Muslims. Nor did they appear to many to be ruling the rapidly expanding Abode of Islam by what could reasonably be considered—few of the politico-moral guidelines of a Muslim polity had in fact yet been established—Islamic principles.

Some thought the Umayyads should be turned out, by force if necessary, on grounds of their irreligious conduct, but the caliphs found other, profoundly theological sentiments that were more to their liking, namely, that all was in the hands of God, who possessed all power. In politics as in life, what would be would be, including the Umayyad caliphate. This was theology wearing the mask of politics, and beneath it was the same issue of free will and predestination that had occupied religious thinkers among the Jews and Christians (see II/5). Now for the first time it began to engage Muslims, not because they inherited the problem from contemporary Christians but because the issue was moved by circumstances in their own, particularly Islamic context. The caliph Abd al-Malik (r. 685–705), the same ruler who built the extraordinary Jerusalem shrine known as the Dome of the Rock, solicited an opinion on the subject of free will and God's predestining power from a leading religious figure of the time, Hasan al-Basri (d. 728). Hasan was a pietist rather than a theologian, and his preserved response to the caliph is a theological meditation on God's will and human freedom. It is not yet theology in the formal sense, however, since the case for free will and responsibility is not argued but simply asserted through skillful citation of the Quran and the Prophetic traditions.

The use of dialectical argument rather than scriptural citations in addressing theological questions became more common shortly after this exchange between the caliph and the holy man. The question of God's omnipotent predetermination and human free will and responsibility, the latter still parsed in the political context of removing the head of the community, continued to exercise religious thinkers. At some point, however, perhaps by the end of the eighth century, the problem began to be addressed in dialectical terms, that is, using logical arguments to buttress and advance scriptural ones. At first this argumentation was built on pointers or "signs," in Arabic *dalil*, where smoke points to fire, for example. The technique is highly reminiscent of Stoic logic, and these earliest practitioners of dialectic likely picked up the method reading translations of Greek medical works—there was a lively Hellenically inspired medical tradition in Christian Iraq—which were deeply concerned with methodology in general and logic in particular. The master at whose feet the Muslims learned to sit was Aristotle.

Learning to Speak Dialectically

As we have already seen, much more than Aristotle was translated from Greek into Arabic, but Aristotle's works were the linchpin of the entire Hellenic heritage in the Abode of Islam since they provided instruction in the critical scientific method that may have been the attraction of that learning in the first place. We cannot be certain what prompted Muslims to translate, or to have translated (Syrian Christians seem to have done most of the work), Aristotle and the others, or what moved Muslim rulers like the caliph al-Mamun (r. 813–833) to underwrite that activity. The Muslims did not inherit a thriving Hellenic school system with Greek philosophy, history, and letters intact within it. The philosophy faculty at Alexandria may have survived into Islamic times in attenuated form—the old philosophy was a sometimes dangerous enterprise in the Christian era—but what the incoming Muslims did find in newly conquered Egypt, Syria, and even Iraq was a thriving Christian theological enterprise that had absorbed a great deal of both Plato and Aristotle in various forms and knew how to brandish the Aristotelian dialectical weapons to their polemical advantage.

It may have been a Christian Aristotle then that first attracted Muslim attention, perhaps an Aristotle used by one Christian sect or another even before Muslims were drawn into the fray. But eventually they were: once they had experienced the effects of Aristotelian dialectic on their own, often still inchoate beliefs, Muslims were moved to attempt to expropriate their opponents' weapons. The Syrian Christians for their part understood the travails of traveling too far in Aristotle's company. They had translated Aristotle's logic and dialectic, most of the small treatises known collectively as the *Organon*, but stopped short of entering the dangerous waters of the substantive treatises like the *Physics, Metaphysics, Ethics*, and *On the Soul*. The Muslims' translators, most of them Syrian Christians bi- or trilingual in Greek, Syriac, and Arabic, ignored the warnings and plunged headlong into the full body of Aristotle's work. The adventuresome and the faylasufs went further and began to speculate along the same lines as their Greek predecessors, an enterprise that quickly attracted the attention of traditional Islamic scholars, hadith collectors, and early Islamic lawyers, and was almost as quickly rejected as both profane and dangerous.

But the traditionalists as well as the collectors of hadith were not immune to the new learning since in cosmopolitan ninth- and tenth-century Baghdad it often came wrapped not so much as science as Christian polemic. By then, however, there were at hand Arabic versions of the same intellectual weapons the Christians possessed, and soon not only traces of Hellenic-style dialectic but the very counters and concepts of the new logic began to appear in the works of Muslim authors. It was called "dialectic," or more literally—and with an obvious nod toward the Greek *logos*—"speech" (*kalam*) and its practitioners "speakers" (*mutakallimun*). The same locution appears in Thomas Aquinas when he refers to his Muslim authorities and adversaries as *loquentes in lege Maurorum*, "speakers of the Moorish religion," or, as has been more recently suggested, as "the Chattering Classes" by their opponents.

An Islamic Inquisition

As reasoning, kalam was not terribly rigorous (though neither was Aristotle himself when using his own method), but in some quarters its deeper implications began to manifest themselves rather quickly. If God is indeed one and unique, then all else, it was reasoned, must be other than he, and so part of his creation. Most Muslims would intuitively agree—what else is Islam if not the most stringent monotheism?—though not perhaps when the consequences were spelled out: the Quran too must be created. By the time this proposition was being advanced in the late eighth century, Muslim piety had already promoted the Quran, with substantial hints from the Book itself, to a position of sanctity not unlike the Torah's among Jews. The Quran, the unique basis of Muslim belief, was eternal, inimitable, and uncreated. "Impossible" was the rejoinder of Islam's new rationalists: if the Quran were uncreated, it too would be God, just as the Christians claimed of *their* Divine Word, Jesus.

Those who followed logic and began to argue for the "rational" position on the Quran's createdness were known in Muslim religious history as Mutazilites. In this and their other characteristic positions—they also wished to strip God of his "eternal" attributes on much the same logical grounds—they represent the earliest attempt at systematically assimilating notions of Greek philosophical logic into Islamic religious thinking. Their patron was al-Mamun, the same caliph who sponsored many of the Aristotelian translations at Baghdad and who had undisguised sympathy for Shiites (see I/8). Earlier caliphs had taken occasional summary steps against men who had seemed dangerous, whether to the faith or to the regime, but al-Mamun, whose policies of governance emphasized centralization and control, took a long stride down that path in initiating the *mihna*, or "scrutiny"—a less kind translation would be the evocative "inquisition," though the later Christian phenomenon was far more complex, widespread, and long-lasting (see I/5).

Unlike his caliphal predecessors, who may have punished deviance but never undertook to define orthodoxy, al-Mamun decreed that Islamic "orthodoxy" consisted of belief in the Quran's createdness. This was the subject of the scrutiny, and those who failed it were subject to flogging or imprisonment. The theological point may strike someone not listening to religious discourse in early-ninth-century Baghdad as a rather arcane issue on which to construct a theological loyalty oath, but beneath it was an enormous iceberg of philosophical argument that derived in turn from Aristotelian notions of matter, space, time, and, indeed, God himself.

As often seems to happen, al-Mamun caught one very large martyr in his net. Ahmad ibn Hanbal (d. 856), the leader of Baghdad's traditionalists, preferred jail to a created Quran, and the forces of conservatism and, on a larger plan, of decentralized religious authority had their rallying point. He was soon released, however, and the whole affair was made to seem a fiasco. Ibn Hanbal became a kind of living witness to the traditional faith, a Galileo in reverse, so to speak: *e pur' **non** si muove*. The mihna lingered on a few more years until in 848 the caliph Mutawakkil abandoned the dogma of the created Quran. But the damage had been done. What earlier caliphs of the House of Abbas had envisioned as an open society had become polarized, the rationalists confronted the traditionalists and, by way of corollary, the philosophical theologians took on the lawyers. In the end the latter triumphed. Aristotelian dialectic and parts of the philosophers' problematic found some modest foothold in dialectical theology, and were allowed an untenured place on the edges of the legal curriculum, the only one that counted in Islamic higher education. But the fear of rationalism was not easily dispelled, and there was a caliphal ban on selling books dealing with kalam or falsafa in 892, which was repeated again in 897.

The upheavals of the last decades of the ninth century were connected to the rise of Ismailism (see I/8), a political and ideological movement esoteric philosophical underpinnings are unfolded in the preserved *Tractates of the Brethren of Purity*. The contents of the *Tractates* turn out to be not so esoteric; they are a familiar blend of Neoplatonic occultism crossed with Aristotelianism and spiced in this instance with a goodly dose of Neopythagorean numerology. The *Tractates* give off the strong odor of later Greek philosophy from beginning to end, albeit in a thin Islamic disguise. The disguise was soon seen through by the Sunni intelligentsia; one critique, by the philosopher Abu Sulayman al-Sijistani (d. after 1001), is particularly telling for our purposes. The Ismailis have attempted the impossible, he says, to combine Islamic law and falsafa. But it cannot be done: falsafa is merely the findings of human reason, but "Islamic law is derived from God by means of an envoy between Him and humankind and by way of revelation."

Kalam Matured

Ibn Hanbal and his followers wanted nothing to do with the newfound skill in argument that, when applied to what they regarded as the foundations of the faith, led to "innovation," which was, at best, mischief, and, at worst, heresy. Most Muslims probably agreed, and once official caliphal support for the Mutazilites was withdrawn, the Hanbalites, as they came to be called, hesitated no less in taking their anger to the streets of Baghdad and voicing their opposition to innovators and rationalists than did the fifth-century Christian monks of Alexandria, Antioch, or Constantinople. But even as they did, forces of reconciliation were at work. Tradition credits the first step to al-Ashari (d. 935), who was neither a philosopher nor, in the end, a mutakallim. A promising Mutazilite scholar, Ashari decided, for various alleged reasons, to adapt the Mutazilites' avowedly rationalist positions to what had become, without benefit of clerical definition or sanction, a form of popular orthodoxy. By the tenth century, Muslim beliefs had approached a kind of consensus, one that read the Quran somewhat literally and took as its guideline for understanding the Quran and living a Muslim life, the "sunna of the Prophet", the body of sound traditions reported from Muhammad. This was Ashari's base line of a genuine Islam, and he proposed what Philo had pioneered for Jews and Origen for Christians: to combine, in some fashion, what then constituted Islamic belief with the Mutazilites' rational approach to belief—in short, to construct what would be called in Christian terms a sacred theology. Thus came into existence kalam, or dialectical theology.

Ashari's pioneer version of kalam was notoriously heavier on hadith than on dialectic, as kalam would always be, but it nonetheless represents the Muslim mainstream's effort to assimilate Aristotelianism, at many removes, into Islamic religious culture. Its effects from Ashari onward were unremarkable, and its most considerable practitioner, al-Ghazali, a professor of jurisprudence in the chief Baghdad madrasa, found kalam sadly inferior to mysticism as a path to God. The most Ghazali would concede was that kalam was a useful defensive weapon, "like a protective troop along the pilgrim road." Ibn Khaldun later tried to phrase it more systematically: "Kalam is a science that argues from logical proofs in defense of the articles of faith and to refute innovators who deviate in their dogmas from the early Muslims and Muslim orthodoxy."

Ashari did not entirely convince the Hanbalis, but the strict hadith-minded could not prevent a version of Asharite kalam from winning a modest place in the spectrum of Islamic orthodoxy as a legitimate instrument for explaining and defending revelation and the Prophetic traditions. The opportunity for showing kalam's usefulness as a dialectical weapon was most apparent in the resistance to Ismaili Shiism, which rested its convictions on the infallible teaching (*talim*) of an Imam, but was in fact suffused with the models and methods of Greek philosophy. Sunnism's defense against the new learning being brandished against the traditional ways of thinking and talking about God was taken up by Ghazali, who sought to discredit not only the Ismailis but also the philosophers who were their inspiration. He did so not by falling back on hadith arguments, which would have been rejected out of hand by his opponents, but by infusing kalam with sufficient rigor to meet the opposition on their own ground. The philosophers, chiefly Farabi and Ibn Sina, were taken on in *The Incoherence of the Philosophers*, and the Ismailis in a whole series of polemical treatises directed explicitly against them.

Ghazali was by no means a theological reactionary. He expropriated into his version of kalam far more of Ibn Sina than Ashari could conceivably have dreamed, and he accepted and glorified a form of Sufism whose intellectual foundations ran deep into Neoplatonism. Ibn Sina and Ghazali are central figures in later Islamic theology. Ghazali's critique of Ibn Sina's cosmology and of the Greek cosmology that lay behind it made it forever suspect among Islam's dialectical theologians. But in following Ibn Sina onto the path of illuminationism, Ghazali opened to his successors the royal road to theosophy (see below). Traditional kalam is not a distinguished discipline after Ghazali and Fakhr al-Din al-Razi (d. 1209). Indeed, conservatives like the Spaniard Ibn Hazm (d. 1064) and the Syrian Ibn Taymiyya (d. 1328) show a great deal more intellectual vigor in attacking the rationalist tradition than the mutakallimun in defending it.

> **Note:** For all their learning, the Ismailis were political radicals who did not hesitate to use terrorist methods to achieve their ends. Assassination was one such tactic, and the Ismaili assassination in 1049 of the caliph's prime minister, Nizam al-Mulk, who had appointed Ghazali to his teaching position, made the theologian fearful of his own life. Ghazali left his post in Baghdad in 1095 and spent years incognito, first in Damascus and then in a tiny Sufi convent above the Golden Gate in Jerusalem, before returning to Baghdad and resuming his teaching. It was during this period that he wrote his most famous work, *The Revivification of the Sciences of Religion*.

The reasons sacred theology had so mild an effect on Islamic religious culture are fairly evident. The only institutionalized form of higher education in Islam was the madrasa, which was, from its beginning to the present, unabashedly a school of Islamic law. The overwhelming majority of Islam's intelligentsia passed through that system and so, whether they practiced or not, were ulama trained in hadith-oriented jurisprudence. Asharite kalam, found only a modest handhold in the madrasa curriculum, as a kind of innocuous minor pursuit. Thus kalam was undersubscribed, undersupported, and undervalued; in the end it found it had little to say. Only at the extremes of the enterprise were there signs of vitality, at the outer margins of the Greek tradition and at the outer limits of the Muslim community.

Muslim Creeds

Not even the Muslim traditionists (see below) were entirely immune to the new rationalism of the type first practiced by the Mutazilites and resumed in a far more mitigated sense in the kalam. We cannot always measure the traditionists' response to kalam-type arguments since the traditionists defended their position more often with polemic than with dogmatic statements. Christianity, as we have seen, defined and redefined itself in a series of credal statements, and in the positive dogma and negative anathemas issued by the councils.

Islam had no comparable conciliar structure, and its closest approximation to a creed in the sense of a baptismal formula is the simple shahada: "There is no god but The God and Muhammad is his envoy." By the mid–eighth century, longer statements in the form of a creed (*aqida*) began to appear anonymously in legal circles. Contrary to what one might expect, they have nothing to do with the two basic elements of the shahada, which are the affirmations required of the individual Muslim, but rather address themselves to the issues in current religio-political disputes. Thus the ten articles of the Fiqh Akbar I take their stand against Kharijites, Shiites, and the partisans of free will, and so probably date from around 750, when these issues were current.

A century and a half later, the twenty-seven articles of the Testament of Abu Hanifa reflect the Mutazilite controversy about the createdness of the Quran, taking a strongly Hanbalite and traditionist stance in opposition, and markedly more adventuresome than its predecessor in attempting to define faith and adjudicate between the relative importance of faith and good works. Technical kalam vocabulary also makes its first appearance. A third document, the Fiqh Akbar II completes the evolution. This late tenth-century creed shows clearly the penetration of kalam into traditionist thought. Like its predecessors, it is not a declaration of what one must believe to be a Muslim but is less than a systematic Asharite statement of position on the theological arguments of its day: the corporeality of God, the allegorical understanding of Scripture, and the reality of the divine attributes.

All these so-called creeds were manifestly not documents to live by but somewhat sectarian statements on problems troubling the early lawyers and mutakallimun. Many of the points were still in contention at the time of composition, but if one moves forward to Ghazali's era and beyond, when a consensus of sorts had developed in Sunni Islam, the Muslim creeds resemble a Christian catechism. They are highly stylized, albeit abbreviated and simplified treatises of scholastic theology, like the catechism inserted by Ghazali himself in his *Revivification of the Sciences of Religion*; the *Articles of Belief* of Najm al-Din al-Nasafi (d. 1141); and, at the very dawn on modernism in the Middle East, the *Creed* of al-Fudali (d. 1821).

The creeds are the closest the community of Muslims ever came to defining orthodoxy. Like their Christian counterparts, they arose in the context of dispute, as a response to other views about God, humans, and the universe that the community, or at least its religious leaders, judged at variance with the Quran, the sunna or simply Muslim sensibilities. In place of these deviant beliefs, the creeds express propositionally and affirmatively what seems fair to call a Sunni Muslim consensus. It may be summed up as follows.

Regarding God, his Nature, and Attributes:

God is one, unique, without associates or offspring; He is eternal and unchanging; His existence can be proven from the contingency of the world; God is other than humankind; incorporeal, hence the quranic descriptions of Him should be accepted "without asking how" (*bila kayf*) [see below]. And yet God will be "seen," *bila kayf*, by the faithful in the world to come. God enjoys preeminently the quranically attested attributes of omnipotence, omniscience, life, will, hearing, seeing, and speaking, as well as all those others that constitute His "most beautiful names" (see I/1). The Quran is the uncreated speech of God.

Then, God's Will:

God's will is sovereign in the world and is always and everywhere effective; indeed, as many hold, God predestines events beforehand (see II/5). All human acts, like all events, are created by God but they are attributed to humans or, as some say, "acquired" (*iktisab*) by them, since they proceed from an internal power created in humans at the moment they act.

The Last Things:

The signs of the End Time are all genuine and real, including the questioning by Munkar and Nakir and the torments of the tomb (see II/10), and when the End does arrive, God will judge all humankind. Some few people, Muhammad chief among them, will be permitted to intercede for sinners among the Muslims at the Judgment; prayers and alms offered by the living will also avail the dead; Paradise and Gehenna exist now and will forever.

Revelation:

God has sent both apostles and prophets to humankind. Muhammad is the "seal" or last of them, and he and the other prophets have been preserved from sin (though perhaps only grave ones). Against the Shiites, it must be held that after Muhammad the first four caliphs were the best of men; only good must be spoken of the Companions of the Prophet (see II/3).

Belief:

Faith is knowing in the heart, confessing by the tongue, and, according to most, performing good works. Faith is due solely to God's guidance and unbelief to abandonment by Him.

Reason and Revelation in Islam

The debate over the competing claims of reason and revelation was long and loud in Islam, where the piety-minded proved far less willing to succumb to the blandishments of a Hellenic-style rationalism than their earlier or later counterparts in Christianity, for example. "Reason" and "revelation" were not the framing terms of the debate among Muslims, however. The discourse generally centered around the use of rational-type arguments in the face of what may be called traditionalism.

The Muslim version of this perennial debate was in fact three-sided, or rather, there were two debates among three parties. The first, which is the best known in the West since it involved some familiar figures in medieval philosophy, was that between the faylasufs and the dialectical theologians (mutakallimun), famously the already noted debate between Ghazali and his philosophical adversaries, most particularly Ibn Sina, with the rejoinder of Ibn Rushd (see below). The other, far more widespread and much more consequential for Islam, was that between the same kalam theologians and a broad strain of Muslim thinkers who may be called "traditionalists."

> **Note:** "Tradition" (*hadith*) is, as we have seen, an art term in Islam and serves as a kind of shorthand—"Prophetic tradition" is fuller and more explicit—referring to the report of a saying or deed of Muhammad (see II/3). Those who transmitted, collected, or studied such reports were called "traditionists" (*muhaddith*; pl. *muhaddithun*). "Traditionalist" and "traditionalism" are broader (and modern Western) terms and are used here of all those who regard the Quran, the hadith—collectively, the sunna, or custom, of the Prophet—and consensus as the primary basis of Muslim belief and practice. All traditionists were also traditionalists in that sense, but the latter group also included people who might more properly be thought of as theologians.

There were few if any rationalists in Islam, if that term is understood to mean an absolute dependence on human reason for the derivation of norms of belief and behavior. Nor is it clear that there were many, even among the faylasufs, who regarded reason as a primary, though not the unique, instrument for deriving those norms. The philosophers were apparently suggesting reason's independent and equal status in acquiring truth—that the truths vouchsafed by revelation could also be arrived at by properly using human reason. This claim was understood to threaten Islam and weapons, including that of rational argument, were raised against it by scandalized believers.

The other debate was more subtle and had to do with matters of degree. Just as there was hardly a Muslim, no matter how Hellenized a rationalist, who put reason before revelation, there was scarcely a pietist who did not avail himself, however clumsily, of rational arguments in explaining or defending his position. In that sense, Muslim thinkers were rational, though only rarely rationalists. Even Ibn Taymiyya, the prince of Muslim traditionalists, medieval and modern, thought there were two kinds of "indications" in the Quran; one class he called "revelational," the other "rational," because "its truth is known through the intellect." And he held as fervently as his theological counterpart Ghazali that there was no contradiction between them.

But if all sides could agree that there was *some* place in Muslim religious discourse for rational argument, there was equally general broad disagreement on where that place was and how broadly it extended. For traditionalists, the foundations of Islam lay squarely and exclusively in the Quran, the sunna of the Prophet, and what the Quran (4:115) calls "the way of the believers," technically referred to as "consensus" (*ijma*) and already explored in Muslim moral teaching (see II/5). Consensus is a somewhat ambiguous term, but its most conservative understanding—and the one held by most traditionalists—is that it embraces matters held in common by Muhammad's Companions (*sahaba*), that is, his contemporaries, those who stand in the eyewitness position in the hadith transmission chains (see II/3), as well as the first generation or two of their followers—in short, "the Fathers" (*al-salaf*) (see II/2). More liberal Muslims might broaden "consensus" to the agreement of the entire Muslim community in whatever era, but one of the characteristics of the traditionalist wing of Islam is that it closely monitors "consensus" as a determinative element in Islam and limits it to the Fathers and those who transmitted and protected the Fathers' legacy, namely, the traditionists.

Moreover, the traditionalists opposed all "innovation" (*bida*) or departures from the received revelation and its understanding by the Fathers, which is precisely where the argument arose between the traditionalists and their more rational-minded theological brethren. The mutakallimun revisited the Fathers' conclusions on matters like the conflict between free will and predestination (see II/5) or the question of the existential nature of the divine attributes. Disagreement and often contentious dispute ensued, which was, the traditionalists argued, the enemy of the faith since it had to do not with matters of behavior, where the Fathers themselves had disagreed, but with matters of principle, where they had not.

God Supreme: Islamic Occasionalism

Muslims' denial of any necessary link between the human agent and the acts he or she appears to bring about simply extends in moral terms a profound denial of all secondary causality, that is, of any ontological or necessary connection between cause and effect (see II/5). Ghazali put it with absolute clarity in his *Incoherence of the Philosophers*, whose intended target was not the long-dead Greek thinkers, where such "incoherence" arose, but their Muslim heirs like Farabi and Ibn Sina. "According to us," al-Ghazali states in the name of the mutakallimun, "the connection between what is usually declared to be a cause and what is believed to be an effect is not a necessary connection. Each of the two things has its own individuality and is not the other. Their connection is based on a decree of God to create them in a successive order." According to Ghazali, our own past experience and constant (though still not necessary) repetition brings about the natural expectation that we call an "effect." To Ghazali's mind we cannot demonstrate causality. We simply observe the coincidence of fire and burning; we assume, though we cannot demonstrate, that one follows necessarily from the other.

What the kalam position looked like to Islam's theological rationalists can be read out vividly from two attacks on it, one by the Jewish lawyer, physician, and philosopher Maimonides (d. 1204) in his *Guide for the Perplexed*, and the other by the Spanish Muslim Aristotelian Ibn Rushd (d. 1198) in his *Incoherence of the Incoherence*, written as a direct refutation of Ghazali. As Maimonides put it, kalam recognized no stable natures in things but only a succession of accidents that, absent a subsistent base, had to be created and recreated in every successive moment of time. The Creator was, of course, God, the only truly subsistent being in the universe. God likewise created the *habit* of one accident following another so as to create the impression of a necessary connection, between fire and burning, for example. "According to them," Maimonides writes, referring to the mutakallimun, "there is no body endowed with the power of action. . . . The ultimate agent is God." What we call a cause is nothing but the *occasion* of God's next action, which we transform into an effect by the habit or concurrence he has also created. The habit gives consistency, predictability, and even hope to human life. We know God will not interrupt the habitual sequence of events and produce unhabitual consequences, as he does in the case of a miracle, for example, except for our own good. There is a further escape clause, at least for Ghazali. If God does alter a habitual sequence, he can also remove the habit: "the knowledge of the habitual is at the time of the interruption removed . . . and He no longer creates it."

Ibn Rushd

Kalam was not much respected by the faylasufs, who recognized that this theology argued dialectically in the manner of Aristotle's *Rhetoric* and *Topics* rather than by scientific demonstration as described in his *Analytics*. That may have been, but kalam's value was that it did not lead, as falsafa did, to propositions that were either overtly or implicitly *kufr*, or disbelief. Ghazali was Islam's premier traditionalist—*Revivification of the Sciences of Religion* is arguably the most influential book written by a Muslim—but he was also skilled in the techniques of falsafa. He took on the rationalists in his *Incoherence of the Philosophers*, where he proposed to demonstrate, with falsafa's own methods, that the propositions contrary to the Muslim faith were also contrary to reason. Ghazali made particular reference to the faylasufs' insistence on the world's eternity (in the light of God's immutability) and their denial of God's provident care of individuals (in the light of God's transcendence). Ghazali's arguments prevailed in traditionalist circles, but the Hellenic view of the universe and how it functions, with which their philosophical doctrines were inseparably connected, penetrated deep into Islam's intellectual circles, Sunni and Shiite, scientific, theological, and mystical.

Ibn Rushd, also known as Averroes, was a familiar figure to medieval Latin Christendom: he appears, exotic and unmistakable, in the left foreground of the School of Athens, Raphael's famous pictorial representation of the hall of fame of Western philosophy. Ibn Rushd was beyond any doubt Islam's most cogent and learned Aristotelian, and he wrote his *Incoherence of the Incoherence* to refute Asharite kalam in general and Ghazali's sophisticated defense of it in particular. Nor did he spare Ibn Sina in the process. With his unparalleled knowledge of Aristotle, Ibn Rushd was capable of identifying and dismantling the Platonic-Aristotelian hybrid that typifies and shapes the philosophy of Ibn Sina and almost all the faylasufs.

Ibn Rushd alone among the Muslims saw Aristotle whole, and so he could distinguish the Greek's authentic thought in the complex philosophical mélange that had been concocted in late antiquity and had passed into the unknowing possession of the faylasufs. Thus, the universe was not the product of a divine emanation, as Farabi and Ibn Sina thought because earlier philosophers had misunderstood Aristotle; nor was it composed of atoms linked only by God's will, as the kalam maintained in a misguided effort to defend God's omnipotence. As Aristotle had demonstrated, efficient and final causality reigned everywhere, from God, the First Cause, to humans, the moral agents.

In another, briefer work, *The Decisive Treatise*, Ibn Rushd turned from the mutakallimun to a defense of philosophy against what was in twelfth-century Spain a far more powerful body of antagonists, the lawyers. Ghazali's works had been burned in public when they arrived in Spain for the first time; even relatively mild versions of Asharite kalam aroused the Spanish jurisprudents, who were fiercely attached to Maliki traditionism. But by the beginning of the twelfth century there were new religious and political stirrings among the North African Berbers. In 1121, one of them, Ibn Tumart, was proclaimed Mahdi, or the Rightly Guided One, who would unite all human beings in observing Islamic law and so prepare them for the End Time. His Berber followers, who were called "Unitarians" (*al-muwahhidun*; in English, Almohads), eventually ruled over all of North Africa from Tunis to Morocco and the southern half of Spain, and created a new religious and intellectual climate that permitted the work of Ibn Tufayl (d. 1185), a highly imaginative faylasuf, and Ibn Rushd, while forcing the theologian Maimonides into exile.

The paradox of the divergent fates of Ibn Rushd and Maimonides simply repeats a greater one in the Mahdism of Ibn Tumart. A Sunni of the Sunnis, Ibn Tumart borrowed the Shiite ideology of the infallible Imam to complement his role as Mahdi. He and his followers followed the strictest principles of Islamic law, forced conversion on Jews and Christians, and at the same time took up theological positions associated with Mutazilite and Asharite kalam, and, in the case of Ibn Rushd, encouraged a reconciliation between sharia and falsafa; or to state it in Ibn Rushd's more modest fashion in *The Decisive Treatise*, is the study of philosophy permitted or even obligated by the Islamic law?

The answer was, of course, yes: as Ibn Rushd explained it, the Quran commands a study of God's purpose in the universe, and that is the goal of philosophy. The principal objection to this smoothly argued conclusion is raised immediately. Philosophy, which lays its own independent claims to truth, has often been at odds with the truths of revelation. The differences, according to Ibn Rushd, are only apparent, and arise from two different modes of expression: the figurative, metaphorical language of Scripture and the scientific language of philosophy. Thus the solution lies where it had always lain from Philo onward, in the allegorical exegesis of Scripture. Ibn Rushd even pressed the point: philosophers, not mutakallimun or lawyers, are uniquely qualified to interpret Scripture, since they alone possess a true understanding of its "real," philosophical meaning.

The Voice of Conservative Islamic Orthodoxy

Many Muslims were staunchly conservative, hadith-minded, and quite unwilling to have any traffic with theology, dialectical or rational. Their objective was not to define or understand God, but simply to describe him, "as He described Himself in His Book and as the Prophet has described Him in the sunna." These words, which are as good a description of Islamic orthodoxy as any, are those of Ibn Taymiyya who has already been noted in the context of the war against heresy (see I/5). He belonged to the conservative school of jurisprudence founded by Ahmad ibn Hanbal and knew firmly and decisively what a Muslim was and how a Muslim should believe and act. Ibn Taymiyya argued strongly against the rationalists' approach to God, those who would "strip" God of his quranically attested attributes—the Mutazilites would retort they were not "stripping" but "distancing" any notion of createdness from God's essence—in the name of a more spiritually exalted deity. At the other end of the spectrum, Ibn Taymiyya found equally unacceptable the blatant anthropomorphism of some of his more literalist conservatives. And finally, he rejected the mystics' freewheeling figurative and allegorical approach to the sacred text.

Ibn Taymiyya preferred the characteristic teaching of the Hanbali school. It is called tafwid, and means granting God a kind of "power of attorney" on matters of faith, leaving belief in his hands, or, as it was famously formulated, believing in God "without asking how" (*bila kayf*).

Jewish Kalam

Lawyers like Ibn Taymiyya remained, not surprisingly, unconvinced by Ibn Rushd's *Decisive Treatise*, and after Ibn Rushd no Muslim spoke so broadly and boldly for the rights of the philosopher vis-à-vis the lawyer on one hand and the mutakallim on the other. Ibn Rushd's voice continued to echo in Christian Europe but not in the Abode of Islam. There were, however, other voices, speaking in somewhat different accents, that continued to raise the issue of reason and revelation in the Arabic-speaking world. Chief among them, as we have seen, was that of the Jewish physician, philosopher, and talmudic scholar Moses Maimonides (d. 1204), whom Almohad persecution had driven from Spain to North Africa and eventually to a long and successful career in Egypt.

Maimonides came in the midst of a long tradition of Jewish theology in the Middle Ages. The practice of speculative theology begun by Philo and so suddenly abandoned was taken up once again under Islam by the *gaon* Saadya ibn Yusuf (d. 942). Learned in both the Scripture and the mystical tradition, Saadya was the first Jew to follow his Muslim Mutazilite contemporaries into the kalam. The result was the earliest systematic treatise on Jewish theology, the Arabic *Book of Beliefs and Opinions*. There is no mistaking who Saadya was nor what he was about. In his preliminary discourse he assured his readers that his task was primarily to confirm the truths of revelation and clear up doubts, not to establish new truths. Truth, he explained, arises generally out of the senses, reason, and intuition, to which he, as a member of "the community of monotheists," added a fourth: authentic tradition or revelation. An entire treatise of the work is devoted to defending the validity of prophecy in general and of the Torah in particular, and another to the redemption of Israel.

Saadya was clearly not a philosopher on the Greek model but a theologian of the type developing within all three of the monotheistic religions of revelation. All hastened to acknowledge that revelation was the primary source of truth. But even though revelation was originally verified by miracle, it could be shaken by both internal doubts and external attacks, and so stood in need of the support of rational arguments. All the Muslim mutakallimun would agree on those propositions, and though they might differ on the necessity of rational understanding, they all cast philosophy to play Hagar to Scripture's Sarah.

Even in Saadya's lifetime, other Jews were discovering the attractions of falsafa as an autonomous discipline without the manacles of a bond servant. But it was primarily in the vigorous new Jewish centers in Spain that scholars began to seriously pursue philosophy. The century between Ibn Gabirol (d. 1050 or 1070) and Ibn Ezra (d. 1164) witnessed a remarkable development of Jewish Neoplatonism. It even found its own Ghazali in Judah Halevi (d. 1141), whose *Book of the Khazar*, though cast in the form of a debate among a philosopher, a Muslim, a Christian, and a Jew in the presence of the king of the Khazars, had much the same intention as Ghazali's *Incoherence of the Philosophers*: to give the lie to the philosophers' claims to arrive at the truths that only revelation, here specifically a Jewish, biblical revelation, could provide.

A Guide for the Perplexed

The response from philosophy ignored Judah Halevi, though not the problem he presented. Maimonides' *Guide for the Perplexed* is an apologia for philosophy and the role of reason in religious discourse, but it is much more besides. Ibn Rushd and Maimonides shared a common conviction that Aristotelianism was a more rigorous and truthful account of God and the universe than that offered by the prevailing Neoplatonism. They also had a common "political" concern about the fate of the uninstructed believer caught among the unenlightened traditionism of the lawyers, the half-learned arguments of the mutakallimun, and the hard truths of philosophy. Ibn Rushd was less restrained in his expression but more prudent in his proposals; allegorical exegesis, for example, ought not be broadcast among the ordinary believers. Maimonides was more cautious in the involuted *Guide*, but more willing to provide guidance for the ordinary Jew in other contexts. In both the introduction to his *Mishneh Torah* (see II/4) and his *Commentary on the Mishnah* (Sanhedrin 10.1), Maimonides set down the thirteen fundamental propositions of Jewish belief in the dogmatic form of orthodoxy rather than in the more traditional halakic mode of orthopraxy (see I/5). "Blind observance" was no more satisfactory for Maimonides than "blind faith" had been for Clement or Origen.

Maimonides' *Guide* was at least partially intended to help the Jewish believer move from simple talmudic piety to an affirmation of the deeper principles of the faith by patiently explaining the allegorical exegesis of Scripture, particularly those passages that might suggest God is corporeal. But it was also designed to guide the more sophisticated student around the perplexities raised by the kalam. The dialectical theologians were dangerous because they pretended to explain. They were, in fact, dialecticians rather than philosophers, and their arguments are riddled with errors, as Farabi had pointed out two centuries earlier. And yet Maimonides would not blindly follow the philosophers. In a revealing passage he shows no hesitation in setting aside Aristotle's demonstration for the eternity of the universe as unproved; and since it is an open question, Maimonides prefers to follow, without benefit of formal proof, the teaching of Scripture "which explains things to which it is not in the power of speculation to accede."

Maimonides had confidence in the power of prophecy and its promulgation in a revealed Scripture, and devoted a long section of the *Guide* (2.32–48) to explaining and defending it. But unlike his mentor Farabi, whose arguments he followed here, Maimonides was willing to make a case, as Saadya had done, for a special Jewish revelation and to set Moses apart from the other prophets. Thus Maimonides was committed to defending the rational and philosophical basis of the Torah, a task to which Farabi never had to address himself with respect to the sharia. The philosophy of the Scriptures is, of course, concealed; its natural science lies within the "Work of the Beginning" and its divine science in the "Work of the Chariot." Explaining these two themes, which were favorite points of departure for Jewish mystics and the subject of frequent cautionary remarks by the rabbis (see II/9), is the alleged program of the entire *Guide*. Having indicated by these programmatic remarks that Scripture contains both a physics and a metaphysics, Maimonides could proceed to disengage these two sciences from the errors of the mutakallimun and reconstitute them on the basis of his own Aristotelian convictions.

Falsafa and Kalam

Ghazali and Maimonides, one arguing for kalam and one against, had much the same effect on their successors. A purely rationalist philosophy, whether from Aristotle or from al-Razi, remained unacceptable to the adherents of a revealed religion, and even the falsafa accommodations of a Farabi, an Ibn Sina, or an Ibn Rushd could not conceal the fact that they prized philosophical over religious wisdom, Athens over Mecca, and could make no case for the unique status of the latter. Maimonides, in contrast, could and did make such a case for Jerusalem and so "rationalized" the Law by skillfully applying a political philosophy, which the Muslim philosophers could not. Islamic law was rationalized nonetheless, not by the faylasuf Farabi, but by the mutakallim Ghazali.

Ghazali and Maimonides both argued that the conclusions of human reason did not have the final word in the process of understanding; many of them were faulty even in their own terms. Nor could human reason be ignored. After Ghazali kalam, Jewish, Christian, or Muslim, could no longer afford the luxury of being dialectical rather than totally demonstrative; if it was going to be the handmaiden of Scripture, it must at least be an honest woman.

Received Wisdom

The Western experience of Aristotle was different from Islam's from the outset. Some Greek philosophical works, including Aristotle's *Organon*, were translated from Arabic into Latin in late antiquity, notably by Boethius (d. 525), a Roman senator in Gothic Italy. Thus literate Latin churchmen in the early Middle Ages had at their disposal fairly substantial summaries of Greek philosophy—generally of the Stoic variety but highly veined with Plato and Pythagoras—from the hands of Cicero among others. And there was, finally, the already imposing structure of a Christian theology, a Latin synthesis of scriptural witness with philosophical thinking erected on a Platonic base by Augustine. It is little wonder, then, that Christian theology, from the age of the Fathers down to the mid–eleventh century, was in the main Plato's, with his attractive emphasis on enduring spiritual realities and the immortality of the human soul. Not until the eleventh century did the Platonic view of the world that underlay Augustine's towering theological edifice begin to be questioned—and questioned at its Platonic heart: whether there were in actual fact universal realities like the "good" or "justice" to which our mental concepts corresponded. Christian reality was philosophically grounded on those Platonic absolutes, and when they began to be contested by influential thinkers like Abelard (d. 1142), the Church's intellectual foundations could be heard by some to tremble.

The most serious challenge to Plato's own view of an unchanging world of universal and eternal Forms had been mounted by his own student, Aristotle, many of whose writings took the form of an extended commentary and critique of Plato's positions. Aristotle the scientist was also Aristotle the realist, and for him reality consisted first of concrete individuals. These may belong to identical species—their essences or forms, for example, humanity, are identical—but they are rendered individual by the material component in their composition. The human intellect is subsequently capable of abstracting that essence, of mentally separating it from its material component, and so of grasping the "universal" that lies behind it or, as Plato would have it, above the individual. The intellect does not create those essences or forms; it extracts them from the matter that individuates them.

The Christian theologians in the West were made newly aware of this assault on the Platonic universe in the early twelfth century when, in Muslim Spain and Sicily, and to a lesser extent in Provence, Greek scientific and philosophical works, including Aristotle's, were translated from Arabic into Latin. Science and philosophy traveled together in the Middle Ages, as they had in antiquity. Aristotle's reputation first as a natural scientist—occasionally even as a magician: science and magic also traveled together—and then as a logician carried Western churchmen into the bosom of his metaphysics, thus into a world quite different from Plato's and, more consequentially, from Augustine's.

Spain and Provence chiefly interest us here since that is where the philosophical translations were done. As with the earlier versions from Greek into Arabic, an intermediary version was employed, in this case a Hebrew one. There was also political patronage, notably the Castilian kings Alfonso VII (r. 1126–1157) and Alfonso X (r. 1252–1284) and the reigning archbishops of

Toledo. And just as the Arabs had originally translated not merely the works of Aristotle but also those of his late antique commentators, which had substantially shaped their own understanding of that philosopher, so too the Latin translations of Aristotle were accompanied by translations of Muslim faylasufs like al-Farabi and Ibn Sina—both of whom had accepted the late antique synthesizing of Plato and Aristotle—and, most importantly, the Cordovan Ibn Rushd. Though this latter philosopher, like the other faylasufs, knew no Greek, he had studied the Arabic Aristotle (and his ancient commentators) closely and was, moreover, a thinker of some originality in his own right. Consequently Ibn Rushd's views influenced, and bedeviled, Western theology for at least a century after his arrival in Latin translation.

Where Ibn Rushd arrived was where the Aristotelian corpus itself had come to rest, in the faculties of the Western universities that in the mid-twelfth century were emerging from the cathedral schools of France and the municipal schools of Italy. The new universities were centers of study, corporate bodies of masters and students where teaching was offered according to a fixed curriculum, standard tests administered, and universally recognized degrees granted. Salerno was a pioneer, where translations of Muslim medical authorities ignited new studies in that field, followed by Bologna, which was in the van of a renewed interest in Roman law. In theology, the universities in Paris and Oxford led the way. Both had begun as clerical schools, but by the beginning of the thirteenth century they had, besides the expected theology faculty, a faculty of arts, whose course of study included, in the approved ancient fashion, instruction in grammar, logic, and rhetoric.

The hallmark of the Western universities—these "special guilds for the manufacture of learned men," as one historian has described them—was its broad view of learning. Its faculty was prepared to offer instruction in several different disciplines in both the humanities and theology, not merely, like the madrasa and yeshiva, training in religious law. The school texts were read—this was the *lectio* of the medieval curriculum—and commented on by licensed masters, much as in the madrasa. The difference was that the master texts in the madrasa exclusively consisted of the hadith of the Prophet; those in the university included, among others, the works of Aristotle.

Sacred Theology, Western Style

The Western Arabic-Latin translation project of the twelfth century, like the earlier passage of some of the same material from Greek into Arabic within the Abode of Islam, introduced highly sophisticated secular learning, both method and matter, into religious cultures, though under very different circumstances and with very different results. Aristotle and the other Greek thinkers were imported, across a deep divide of cultural discontinuity, into an

Arab society that had no experience of such learning and possessed nothing that could in a formal sense be called theology, reasoned discourse about God. Exposure to such learning produced a few genuine Muslim philosophers— none of them were "churchmen" as Muslims might understand that term, and Hellenic discourse was otherwise assimilated into the Muslim worldview in only the most rudimentary terms. The Muslim view of God as an all-powerful Will that predetermined all and then determined even the slightest events— the already noted outlook called Occasionalism—left little space for the Greeks' essentially intellectualistic, nondetermining God who instilled "natures," principles of action, into the world system and then allowed them to operate "naturally" and humans to puzzle out their workings on the available evidence.

When European Christians encountered the Aristotelian corpus freshly translated from Arabic in the twelfth century, they were encountering an old, though perhaps neglected, friend. The medieval Western world had never lost contact with its Latin antecedents and, through them, with their more remote Greek past. Moreover, medieval Christianity possessed an early and highly persuasive theological synthesis from the hand of Augustine, which, even though Augustine himself knew no Greek, had its roots in earlier Christian theologians in Antioch and Alexandria. Both the Western and Eastern Churches had already debated the complex theological issue of the Trinity, and the Western Church had acquired a large, flexible, and sophisticated Latin theological vocabulary by the fourth and fifth centuries. It also had Aristotle's *Organon* and knew how to use that powerful heuristic tool.

The introduction of the "new" Aristotle via the Arabic versions in the twelfth century was actually exposure to a richer and fuller Aristotle, one that now included not only the logic but the full range of the physical and metaphysical treatises, his work on the soul and on ethics. It was followed by a third wave of Hellenism in the thirteenth century when Western scholars began to translate Aristotle once again, this time directly from the Greek. The effect of this full encounter with Aristotelianism was itself twofold: the first wave of translations, the Greco-Arabic Aristotle, enabled Western churchmen and intellectuals to grasp the full range of the Aristotelian worldview.

Thomas Aquinas

This new understanding of Aristotle did not create a theology, as it did in Islam, but it provided an approach to the world and its workings that differed from the prevailing Christian Platonism. This new perspective threatened Christianity's intellectual foundations, until Thomas Aquinas (d. 1274) successfully created a Christian Aristotelianism out of this new learning. Thomas provided an explanation of the cosmos, in Aristotelian terms, that was both coherent and intellectually persuasive, that did justice to the scriptural givens of Christianity, and at the same time that did not appear to overturn the Augustine edifice within which the Western Church had grounded its theology. The Thomistic synthesis, laid out in all its dialectical splendor in his *Summa theologiae*, did in fact dislodge the reigning Platonism, at least for a time, and put in its place a new theology inspired by Aristotle's epistemological and metaphysical realism and undergirded by his arguments and methods.

Aquinas was the willing heir not just to Aristotle but to the whole Aristotelian legacy, the mixed bag of Greeks and Muslims who had become attached to the Aristotelian canon. If Aquinas felt free to appropriate where suitable for his own use, to adapt, discard, or refute the work of the *loquentes in lege Maurorum*, he was also aware that Islam presented both a challenge and a lively threat to Christendom. A product of that awareness was his *Summa contra gentiles*, by whom he meant the Muslims. Jews and heretics might be convinced by appeals to Scripture, but the Muslim "Gentiles," who did not accept the Bible—the situation, we have seen, is somewhat more complex— could be appealed to by reason alone. The *Contra gentiles*—a project suggested to Aquinas sometime after 1265 by his fellow Dominican Raymond of Peñaforte (d. 1275), the point-man of the Church's program to convert the Jews and Muslims—set out to do precisely that. It proposed to rationally demonstrate Christianity's essential truths and to at least show that reason did not preclude beliefs such as the Trinity, for example, in matters of faith.

Scholasticism

The methodology apparent in Aquinas's work and that in fact characterizes Latin Christian theology and canon law—to a certain extent, its Islamic counterparts as well—is known as scholasticism. The phenomenon presupposes that there is an absolutely authoritative text (or texts) and that the most praiseworthy and productive intellectual enterprise that might be undertaken is explication of the text(s) in question. This preoccupation with text and its meaning leads in diverse directions, including determining which texts are authoritative and so creating a canon (see II/3). Of principal concerns here, however, is the second element in the notion of scholasticism, the treatment of that authoritative text.

Ancient scholasticism is on fully display in literary circles in Hellenistic Alexandria where the works of the "classical" age—its practitioners' conviction that they are successors to a more magisterial era is one of the telltale signs of scholasticism—were weighed; canonical lists of tragedians, historians, orators, and so forth drawn up; editions of their works prepared; and the works themselves submitted to analysis and interpretation. In the philosophical academies of the same era, a similar process was under way. As it progressed, Aristotle began to emerge, probably on the basis of his logic, as the authority par excellence, and his works became the subjects of school commentary, presented orally by the master (often from notes) and recorded by a student. Commentaries followed the text paragraph by paragraph, each enlarged and explained in turn, or else the whole was summarized and explicated. In other instances, Aristotle's own method of aporia and lysis, the exposition of a problem followed by its resolution, was often employed.

Among Jews and Christians the authoritative text was, of course, Scripture. The Jews eventually added the Mishnah and its own commentaries, the two Talmuds (see II/3); the Christians, the group of early Church writers later known collectively as the Fathers (see II/2), who served as authorities for all parties well into the Reformation and beyond. Early Christian scholasticism— the Bible was the authoritative text and its interpretation the primary intellectual concern—flowed naturally out of its Jewish antecedents, and like the Jews, Christian exegetes were influenced by the methods of literary criticism developed by Greek scholars in Alexandria, where allegorical exegesis, for example, was applied as a matter of course to Homer and other poets.

In the early Middle Ages, Christian biblical scholasticism encountered another strain of scholastic activity common in antiquity, the method of dialectical analysis described in Aristotle's *Organon*, which became the prevailing approach to texts in the philosophical schools. As work in the scribal schools of the Carolingian era accelerated, collections began to be assembled of excerpts from the Fathers on one hand and from classical authors on the other. At the same time monks developed the art of the "gloss," a marginal comment, and then eventually the interlinear notation as well, intended to clarify the text. The collected patristic excerpts served this end admirably well, and all through the Middle Ages the Christians' biblical text was accompanied by the glossa ordinaria, a standardized introductory commentary that guided the reader through the interpretation of the sacred text, much the way Jewish Fathers like Rashi (d. 1105), whose remarks were likewise displayed surrounding the Hebrew text, guided the Jewish reader to an understanding of the Torah (see II/2).

If the Bible was a text around which commentary grew by accretion, the *Sentences*, another medieval hallmark, was a manufactured authority. It was itself a collection of biblical, patristic, and contemporary Christian authorities arranged not along the text of the Bible but topically and so, by its selection and arrangement, with a theological agenda of its own. The most famous *Sentences* were those compiled in 1155–1158 by Peter Lombard, bishop of Paris, and arranged in four books dealing with the Trinity; Creation and Sin; the Incarnation and the Virtues; and the Sacraments and the Last Things. The work met some opposition at first for its approach to the Trinity and Christology, but it was vindicated at the Lateran Council of 1215, and thereafter became the standard theological textbook of the Middle Ages. Almost every major theologian down to Thomas Aquinas produced a formal commentary on Lombard's *Sentences*.

Latin Averroism

Thomas had before him not only the mid-twelfth-century translations of Aristotle by way of the Arabic but eventually new versions done directly from the Greek—most of them by a Flemish Dominican polymath William of Moerbeke (d. 1286) later the Latin bishop of Corinth—and so could proceed somewhat differently from his immediate predecessors. It was not possible to separate Aristotle from his Arab paraphrases and commentaries, to see the Greek directly rather than through the eyes of Farabi, Ibn Sina, and Ibn Rushd. Western thinkers could not distinguish something they called "Averroism." It was easier to coin the word than to define the reality, however. Ibn Rushd had indeed had a great deal to say about Aristotle. Some of it constituted perceptive insights into the meaning of Aristotle's thought—both Aquinas and Dante considered him *the* commentator on Aristotle—and these became part of Latin Aristotelianism without note or remark. Elsewhere, however—for example, in his remarks on the workings of the "agent intellect," the crucial and always operating illuminative function in human intellection that Aristotle had cryptically remarked came "from outside"—Ibn Rushd offered his own explanation. He located the agent intellect, that he regarded as a single, universal faculty for all humankind, in the lowest of the celestial spheres (see II/9). Given the premises, this is a plausible and coherent position, but not in a Christian context. The intellect is the talisman of the soul's immortality, and a universal intellect of any kind would render impossible the basic Christian belief in individual immortality. Thomas, among others, would have none of it.

The Two Faces of Truth

Ibn Rushd's speculations on the agent intellect were an attempt to explain an obscure though critical issue of Aristotelian epistemology. Elsewhere, however, the Muslim faylasuf went deeper and closer to the philosophical bone. As we have seen, earlier Muslim philosophers had been criticized within traditionalist circles, most notably by al-Ghazali in his *Incoherence of the Philosophers*, for embracing or, perhaps more accurately, being driven to positions that were contrary to the teaching of the Quran and the Muslim faith. Ibn Rushd answered Ghazali in due course with his *Incoherence of the Incoherence*, which attempted to show that the famous jurist-theologian comprehended neither falsafa nor Islam. But the piece was counterpolemic purely and simply; Ibn Rushd understood with perfect clarity that God's revealed word and reason's inquiry did not lead down the same congruent path. Rather than choose one or the other, however, renounce either Islam or philosophy, Ibn Rushd proposed a theory of double truth, one of revealed religion and the other of philosophy, both equally valid, albeit in open contradiction, which we are incapable of resolving.

This so-called double truth theory was by no means new. It had been proposed before in all three religious cultures by both exegetes and mystics, among others, though in a more polite and acceptable form, namely, that there were different levels of understanding God's truth and that they were not open to all. The ordinary read the Quran (or the Gospels or the Torah) and that was enough; the philosopher, the mystic, and the adept penetrated more deeply into the infinite depths of God's Word and found in those unlit places something more profound and perhaps, though few dared utter it, more true. One truth with many paths levels of understanding was an acceptable if not always comfortable notion in Judaism, Christianity, and Islam. But Ibn Rushd's dichotomous double truth was not.

No one much heeded the notion of a double truth in Muslim circles because when Ibn Rushd died, Islamic falsafa died with him. But when the notion resurfaced in the thirteenth century in the faculty of arts at the university of Paris, where Ibn Rushd *was* read, it attracted a great deal of attention. The university and its right to grant its graduates licenses to teach were under the supervision of the bishop of Paris, and in 1271, and again in 1277, that bishop, Stephen Tempier, by virtue of his jurisdictional powers in matters of faith and morals (see II/5), issued a decree condemning not Ibn Rushd's explanations but what was perceived to be the cause of the problem: various Aristotelian teachings (see I/5).

Though provocative, the Paris condemnation was a brief incident, and the Thomistic Aristotelians at Paris and elsewhere managed to make clear to the authorities that there was only one truth. Although it was undoubtedly taught in Scripture, it was universal and so accessible to—and understood by—Aristotle and other ancients. Many remained unconvinced, however. Some still thought Ibn Rushd had a point, that science or philosophy could not be reconciled with Scripture, or, as the more radical would have it, with the teachings of the Church; that faith and understanding were two different chairs that one could attempt to straddle but that could never be stacked. Others, like the Franciscan theologians Bonaventure (d. 1274) at Paris and later Duns Scotus (d. 1308) at Oxford, were not Thomists and hence not Aristotelians, and chose to remain faithful to Augustine's Platonic synthesis.

Note: By the end of the fourteenth century, Ibn Rushd had disappeared from the history of philosophy, European and Islamic. He was restored to the West as a creative thinker in 1852, when the French intellectual Ernest Renan, who is far better known for his historicist *Life of Jesus*, published *Averroes and Averroism*. Ibn Rushd was "rediscovered" by the Arab world when part of Renan's work was translated into Arabic by the Syrian Christian Farah Antun at the end of the nineteenth century.

The Reformation and Christian Systematic Theology

In 1509–1510, Martin Luther, a monk of the Hermits of St. Augustine, performed the traditional scholarly exercise of writing a commentary on Peter Lombard's *Sentences*. Luther was then still very much a scholastic theologian in his methods, terms of reference, and framing of problems, but he was inquisitive and restive. Soon Luther was reading Aristotle's *Physics*, *Metaphysics*, and *Ethics*, as well as Augustine, and, perhaps most significantly since it put him in direct contact with Scripture, he was lecturing on Paul's Letters to the Galatians and Romans. Many of these concerns were swept aside in 1517 when Luther posted his famous theses against the Church's practice of granting indulgences and so became embroiled in the larger controversy on grace and salvation (see II/5). But just before then, he published his *Disputation against Scholastic Theology*. In it the question of grace is present, but it is linked to the broader question of how Christian theology should be done.

Luther's adversaries in this matter are not so much Thomas and the earlier scholastics as figures both closer and more remote from his own time. At the head of the file stood Aristotle, whose rationalism had infected all of theology. "The whole of Aristotle is to theology as darkness is to light," Luther all but shouted in the fiftieth of his Wittenberg theses of 1517. Philosophy, declared the father of the Reformation, dealt with, dialectical truth, and when it came to faith, "dialectical truth is rather outside, under, above, below, around, and beyond it." In this sense, Luther, who was a doctor of theology and a professor at the university of Wittenberg, was following close on the heels of Ockham himself, though the Englishman had separated theology from faith on epistemological grounds, whereas Luther's movement away from theology seems to have been prompted by somewhat more private convictions. His dissatisfaction with the current theology may have sprung directly from his closer engagement with Scripture in 1515–1516, when his duties required him to lecture on the Psalms and Paul. If so, Luther had allies. Humanists too, like Erasmus of Rotterdam, were criticizing the Church for its dry and lifeless theological treatment of what remained living texts. Scripture would be his text, Luther wrote to his own bishop in 1518, after the storm had broken; "It is shameful for a theologian to speak without a text." His text was thus not Aristotle, as it was for the theologians, but the New Testament and, it should be added, canon law and the writings of the Fathers, where all true demonstration rested. Luther was arguing in effect for exegesis to replace dialectic, for a biblical theology in place of the dialectical theology taught in the Church's school to the Church's clergy.

Luther, when he wrote, was chiefly engaged in polemic. Calvin, in contrast had not so much to resist as to build. He was a pedagogue from the first, perhaps, and the earliest version of his Latin *Institutes of the Christian Religion*—which he himself translated into French as the project went on—was intended to instruct beginners in the "new faith," which, in Calvin's view, was not new at all but the pristine and original Christian belief. Calvin's revision of the *Institutes* continued for twenty-three years, but the last Latin edition, completed in 1559, envisioned the somewhat more sophisticated audience of "church leaders" who needed guidance in their reading and interpretation of Scripture.

The *Institutes* is systematic but it is not a work of systematic theology. The matter—book 1 on God as Creator, book 2 on God as Redeemer, book 3 on Grace, and book 4 on the External Means of Grace—are arranged in a clear and logical fashion, but the doctrine is derived directly from Scripture (with confirmatory evidence from the early Fathers, particularly Augustine). Calvin, like Luther, regards theology as the child and handmaiden of scriptural exegesis, and the *Institutes*, for all its orderliness and systematic clarity, is essentially a work of exegesis enlisting Scripture in the erection of a new edifice of faith. Unlike Thomas's *Summa theologiae*, written in and for a thirteenth-century university environment, the mid-sixteenth-century *Institutes*, which was directed to a broader (though by no means popular) audience, lacks most of the dialectical and scholastic apparatus of a *summa*. The adversarial positions are generally treated polemically; it is derived from hermeneutical principles rather than from speculative ones.

But scholasticism was far from dead in Reform circles. The rules of intellectual engagement had not changed, and soon after Calvin's death Reform theologians began to return to the Aristotelianism so often attacked by Luther and his contemporaries. In Geneva itself Theodore Beza (d. 1605), professor of theology at the Geneva Academy from 1559 to 1599 and the foremost Calvinist theologian of his generation, published between 1570 and 1582 the three volumes of his *Tractationes theologicae*. In them he proposed to give a rationally coherent explanation, that is, one consonant with Aristotelian logic, of Calvin's theology. The *Tractationes* lacked the influence of the *Institutes*—it is hardly a training manual—but it attempted to argue far more philosophically and rigorously the points simply propounded by Calvin, some of which, like the theses on atonement and predestination, had become the subject of strenuous dispute with both Lutherans and Catholics.

The Wisdom of Illumination

Later Hellenism, the Greek legacy to which Islam fell heir, was by no means purely Aristotle, nor even pure Aristotle nor pure philosophy, for that matter. Late antiquity had rather insouciantly commingled the Platonic and Aristotelian traditions and added a considerable and generally unacknowledged dollop of Stoicism. Another potent strain in this mélange was a broad current of occultism that ranged from a resurrected Pythagorean number mysticism to

Hellenistic magical practices. This was theosophy pure and simple, the belief that there was a wisdom (*sophia*) beyond what the human intellect could achieve. It had passed through deep channels from remote antiquity, through the agency of mythic sages like Hermes Thrice Great (Gk. Trismegistos), who possessed—and brokered—the wisdom of the Greeks, Egyptians, and Babylonians. Adepts still had access to this hidden wisdom in the transitional age that caught up an expiring paganism on one end and an emerging Christian intellectual tradition on the other. In Christianity, it was called *gnosis*; in Judaism, *hokma*; and in Islam, *hikma* (see II/9). In all three versions, Greek science, philosophy, and theology were subordinated to an overarching belief that through this "learning" not merely understanding but personal salvation could be achieved.

The notion of salvational wisdom entered Islam with the rest of the Hellenic legacy and penetrated Muslim religious thinking through not kalam but other, less obvious channels. We can note it only when it surfaces in a more distinct literary form. It is apparent, for example, in a somewhat sanitized form, among the Ismaili Shiites (see I/8), whose *Tracts of the Brethren of Purity* survives and contains a good deal of half-digested Platonic-Pythagorean wisdom put to the service of an Islamic instructional program. More vital and consequential is another strain of ancient theosophy that seems to have passed from Ibn Sina who knew his Plato and Aristotle but announced on several occasions his preference for an "illuminative wisdom" (*al-hikma al-mashriqiyya*) or, as some would render it, an "oriental wisdom."

One who rejected Ibn Sina's claim was the Persian philosopher-theologian Shihab al-Din Suhrawardi (d. 1191). He had studied with somewhat undistinguished masters in Iran—many of them logicians—before going west in 1183 to Aleppo, where was appointed tutor to al-Malik al-Zahir, then governor of the city and heir apparent to the Muslim hero of Crusades, the Ayyubid sultan Salah al-Din. The circumstances are murky, but through some combination of court intrigue and suspicion of (Shiite?) heterodoxy, Suhrawardi was executed in Aleppo at his student's order and with the encouragement of his student's famously enlightened father. The formal charge was *zandaqa*, by then the preferred term among Muslims for incurable heresy (see I/5).

During his time in Aleppo Suhrawardi composed his major works, including his *Wisdom of Illumination*, the Arabic tract—he was the first of the Islamic faylasufs to write extensively in Persian as well—that was the climax and term of his construction a philosophy in a new key. The clef of that key was "illumination" (*ishraq*), a nondiscursive and intuitive manner of knowing that stands in explicit contrast to the demonstrative science of the "Peripatetics" (*mashaiyyun*), the term that henceforward stands for the Aristotelian tradition in falsafa and was represented, for Suhrawardi and all who came after, by the work of Ibn Sina. Despite his claims, Ibn Sina had no share in the true illuminative wisdom, as was explained by no less an authority than Aristotle himself, who appeared to Suhrawardi in a dream.

In Suhrawardi's new schema, metaphysics (*ilahiyyat* the "things of God") was divided into two distinct sciences, one general and one special. The first had to do with the philosophically familiar (Aristotelian) world of secondary causality: its subjects were existence, substance, accidents, time, and motion. The second, special metaphysics, was distinguished not so much by its subject, which we can supply as "spiritual beings," as by its epistemology: whatever we know about this other domain, what Suhrawardi called the "imagined" or "figured world" (*alam al-khayal*), we know by nondiscursive means, by "veridical dreams" and "visionary experiences."

At the outset of his work, Suhrawardi remarked "I did not attain (the wisdom of illumination) by discursive thought but through something else, and only afterward did I seek proofs for it." The "something else" was an intuitive grasp of "the realities" of the type achieved by Islam's classic mystics, the "intoxicated" Persian Sufi-Bistami (d. 876) and the executed Iraqi al-Hallaj (d. 922) (see II/9). The similarity was not fortuitous. When Suhrawardi explains how one can achieve this illumination, he charts a path very similar to the one that leads to a Sufi initiation. A long retreat and an ascetic regime of self-cleansing purification enables one to access the supernatural "light" that is within us all—there is a marked strain of self-knowledge or self-revelation in Suhrawardi. This is followed, eventually and only for some, by an actual illumination of the philosopher's intellect by one of the divine lights that circle through Suhrawardi's philosophy like celestial spheres. The wisdom of illumination is finally achieved under the guidance of the "Light of Lights," the self-emanating Being whose essence and attributes are identical, and who is, to be sure, God.

The School of Isfahan

The main impact of Suhrawardi's thought was felt in Iran, although his *Wisdom of Illumination* was apparently not translated into Persian until about 1600 by the Indian Sufi al-Harawi. There was, beginning with Shahrazuri in 1288, a steady stream of Arabic commentary on Suhrawardi's work, but Illuminationism's growth into a fully elaborated and systematized "school" had to wait until Iran's conversion to Shiite Islam in the early sixteenth century and the subsequent appearance in the new Safavid capital of Isfahan of the celebrated philosopher-theologian Mir Damad (d. 1631) and his even more famous student, Mulla Sadra al-Shirazi (d. 1640). Both men illustrate the continuing powerful hold of Ibn Sina and his Peripateticism on the later falsafa tradition in Islam. His encyclopedic *Book of Healing* remains a primary text and the Aristotelianism it represents, the "discursive" (*bahthi*) method, as Mir Damad calls it, is never quite displaced by the "intuitive" (*dhawqi*) approach that Suhrawardi made the methodological center of Illuminationism.

The School of Isfahan, as it is now called, identified with Mir Damad, Mulla Sadra, and their followers, were integrationists who attempted to combine the legacy of Ibn Sina's meditated Aristotelianism—the "originals" still being read in Baghdad in the tenth century had long since disappeared into the synthesizer that was Islamic falsafa—with what they had learned from Suhrawardi. Out of such disparate spirits as the faylasuf Ibn Sina, the lawyer-theologian Ghazali, the daring intellectualistic mystic Ibn Arabi (see II/9), and the anonymous esotericists who fashioned Shiite cosmology, Mir Damad and Mulla Sadra created a unified discourse. What came to be called transcendent theosophy (*al-hikma al-mutaaliyya*) was possessed of enough integrity and vigor to survive to the present day as a viable form of philosophy for many Muslim intellectuals.

In their own day, however, the School of Isfahan represented neither the official ideology of Iran's Shiite sovereigns—who, like the overwhelming majority of Islam's rulers, much preferred lawyers to philosophers of any stripe— nor a popular or even widely accetped movement, even in Iran. The school was actually one sage, often isolated, passing on his learning and insights to another, without benefit of academic or institutional underpinning or any form of patronage. Nor did the school find much support among the traditional theologians, the Shiite mutakallimun. "If God thought the people had enough intelligence (to do philosophy)," one of them remarked, "He would not have sent them Messengers and Prophets." It was the accusation perennial, the hit direct, on the underlying assumption of falsafa in Islam.

8

From Desert Saints to Muslim Sufis

The Way of the World

All three monotheistic movements grew out of a perceived distinction between God, "who alone is holy," and the present circumstances in which humankind finds itself. These circumstances are often referred to as "the world" or "this world." Though God had looked on this world, which was, after all, his creation, and pronounced it "good" (Gen. 1:4, etc.), his devotees often took a somewhat more pessimistic view of their circumstances, as did God himself on occasion, since there were elements in that creation, some humanmade but others quite natural, that he wished to keep distant from his presence.

How and why the world that seemed so pristine in Genesis became so dangerous and even so evil a place was variously explained. Genesis offered its own reasons, humankind's moral delinquency chief among them, a theme elaborately glossed by the Christians into the doctrine of Original Sin (see II/5). Others, like the Gnostics, went even further and declared that the good God could not possibly have made the vile world in which we now live: its creation was necessarily the work of a malign Anti-God (see I/5). This last exceeded the bounds of monotheistic orthodoxy, but the more tempered view that this world was morally dangerous settled deep into the religious sensibilities of Christians, Muslims, and, to a somewhat lesser extent, Jews. Christians and Muslims could contrast the toils and dangers of this world with the rewards and punishments of the next world; for the Israelites generally, and for many Jews thereafter, the perfect justice of the Afterlife was simply not available (see II/10).

Just how perilous this world could be for Israelite and Jew is amply illustrated in the Torah, which charts every moral and physical pitfall found in creation. It was, Paul complained, like a road map of sin (Rom. 7:7), in which all the dangerous curves were clearly marked. Yahweh instructed his worshipers exactly what parts of his creation, acts and objects, should be avoided (and kept away from him). The Christian and Muslim Scriptures naturally follow suit, and all three sacred texts set out codes of behavior for the believer (see II/4).

The Issue of Jewish Asceticism

> The divine law imposes no asceticism on us. It rather desires that we should keep the equilibrium and grant to every mental and physical faculty its due, as much as it can bear, without overburdening one faculty at the expense of another. . . . Nor is diminution of wealth an act of piety, if it is gained in a lawful way, and if its acquisition does not interfere with study and good works, especially for him who has a household and children. He may spend part of it in almsgiving, which would not be displeasing to God; but to increase it would be better for himself.

These are the words of Judah Halevi, the sometime Spanish poet and philosopher—he eventually repudiated both enterprises—written between 1130 and 1140 and addressed in a fictionalized dialogue to the king of the Khazars, a tribe near the Black Sea, who was conducting an inquiry into the claims of different religions. When Judah wrote the lines, putting them into the mouth of his own alter ego, he had before him the long history of an ascetical tradition that flourished among Christians and Muslims alike, a tradition from which he was explicitly separating contemporary Judaism.

Christians practiced what they called *askesis* and the Muslims after them *zuhd*; both words are normally translated as "asceticism." Before it got swept into a religious context the Greek word meant a regimen or way of life, the "basic training" of the soldier or the athlete. As practiced by the early Christians, askesis still looked like its pagan prototype. It meant, first of all, supererogatory practices and devotions, that is, over and above those prescribed; it required some form of self-denial; and it usually involved a degree of separation from society. Where the askesis of the Christian differed from that of the athlete or the soldier was in its intent. Christians adopted this often harsh regimen for religious motives, to curb the will, for example, to control the passions, or, finally, to make a statement of disapproval of the world.

God's scriptural charts are the matter of law, not of asceticism, although often the former points the way to the latter. On some level, asceticism operates on the principle that if the law prescribes a degree of abstention from something, then even more abstention is better. The ascetic is often bent on pushing the "fences of the law" to the far horizons, though without benefit of the authority of God's writ. Pharisaic severity is not asceticism since it is, in their view, mandated by Torah, written or oral. The ascetic makes his case, if the need arises, by attempting to discern what is behind a legal prohibition and then voluntarily extending that prohibition into new but related areas: the logic of analogy frequently drives ascetic practice. Finally, there is a kind of circumstantial asceticism or, perhaps better, an eschatological asceticism in which the approaching End Time dictates a special lifestyle. The Essenes in their camp at Qumran illustrate the type, but the classic example is John the Baptist, clothed in the skins of animals, eating only locusts and honey, and proclaiming the coming of the Kingdom (Matt. 3:1–4).

Repentance (*metanoia*), literally "changing the mind," the Orthodox Jew's *teshubah* or "return," or what the New Age moralist might call "attitude adjustment," was what John was preaching at the Jordan, and it is not entirely clear whether he was offering his own way of life as a model for others' behavior. One of those others was Jesus of Nazareth, who shared none of John's preferences in food and clothing, although the two men were preaching much the same message. Indeed, one of the most profound uncertainties of Jesus' own preaching is whether his moral intention was an eschatological asceticism, a "lifeboat ethics," or, as the Christian community had perforce to think with the End Time receding into the far horizon of the future, morality for the long haul. The teaching itself appears, on the face of it, to embody a long-term morality rather than a short-term ascetic, and Jesus' own manner of life has none of the sheer urgency that characterized John's brief moment.

Although some small case might be made for an inclination toward the pleasures of the table (Luke 7:34), the Jesus of the Gospels appears to be not so much denying himself as uninterested in the pleasures and pursuits of the world. He was more focused on the faith in God that made such a lack of interest and concern possible than on the dangers of indulging in them. A craftsman in Nazareth, Jesus gave up his profession to become an itinerant preacher, or perhaps even something of a scholar, in his native Galilee, supported, it appears, by friends and followers, many of them women (Luke 8:3). He was unmarried, we assume and the Christian tradition dogmatically asserts, though at least one of his followers, Peter, is so casually revealed to have had a wife (Mark 1:30) that we must wonder about all of them. Celibacy, at any rate, does not appear to have been an issue with Jesus and his followers. He associated easily with women, some of whom were devoted followers— Mary and Martha in Bethany (John 11:1–2) and Mary of Magdala (Luke 8:2), for example. Women first bore witness to his resurrection, or at least to the empty tomb (Mark 16:1; Matt. 28:9; John 20:11 ff.).

There is no doubt that membership in the Jesus movement required a degree of self-denial. "If any man would come after me," Jesus taught, "let him deny himself and take up his cross and follow me" (Mark 8:34). Numerous dismissive remarks are made in the Gospels about the vanity of wealth and the wealthy (Matt. 19:13–24; Luke 6:24; 8:14). They have the appearance of commonplaces, however, and Muhammad says many of the same things, albeit in very different social and economic circumstances. One of Jesus' teachings on the subject was of great consequence, however. When asked by someone what he must do to gain eternal life, Jesus told him to keep the commandments, that is, to observe the Torah. But the young man persisted: he was observant. Jesus then responded, "If you would be perfect, go, sell all you have, give to the poor, . . . then come follow me" (Matt. 19:10–21). The later Christian tradition read that as Jesus' invitation to a higher calling, the opening of a broad vista down a high road—"if you would be perfect"—to the Kingdom of God. It was, as it turned out, the charter phase of voluntary Christian asceticism.

The Desert a City

In late antiquity, the most common form of the pagan holy man was a hieratic figure cherished by urban elites but remote from society and eventually repudiated by it (see II/6). His Christian replacement began in an exactly contrary fashion, by deliberately withdrawing from the world into the wilderness. And the notion that drove him from city into desert was asceticism.

Asceticism as a distinctive movement first appeared within Christianity after the expectation of the End Time had been relaxed and in the midst of a still pagan Mediterranean world. It manifested itself in the urge to withdraw from the world and, in the best-known example, from a sinfully pagan city, Alexandria, to the wildernesses that stretch almost endlessly on either side of the Nile. But if the city was the epicenter of a sinful world, the desert was the dwelling place of the demonic and the impure. The Israelites who had wandered for forty years in such a place recognized it in the ritual of the scapegoat driven out into the wilderness to appease the demon Azazel (see II/5), which is perhaps echoed in the New Testament (Luke 8:24). Jesus himself was led into the wilderness for forty days to be tempted by Satan (Mark 1:12–13).

The Christian tradition identifies Antony (d. 356 C.E.) as the first to practice for religious motives the type of "retreat" (*anachoresis*) known in Egypt as far back as when the first pharaoh conceived the idea of building a pyramid and the first prescient Egyptian thought he might be better off in the wilderness than in the toils of a royal corvée. Antony was likely not the first Christian to flee the world in that literal sense, but his well-publicized desert career—Athanasius (d. 373), the bishop of Alexandria and the hero of the war against Arianism (see II/7), was his biographer—provided the incentive and model of anchorite life for future generations of like-minded Christians. Antony made his home in the wasteland under the relentless Egyptian sun and practiced the kind of ferocious self-denial that almost immediately became the hallmark of Christian asceticism and turned Antony himself into a celebrity.

Charisma, holiness, *baraka*, or "blessing," as the Muslims had it, when embodied in the Christian saint (*hagios*), the Jewish zaddik, or the Muslim friend of God (*wali Allah*) (see II/6), has almost always and everywhere attracted public attention—to see, to hear, to touch the holy person is somehow to share in his or her gift—and, inevitably, provoked emulation in the strong of heart. Soon the area around Antony's poor hut was crowded with others who had come to look on and maybe even stay and imitate the famous holy man who had defeated the world. Then his admirers had their own admirers and disciples. In a short time "the desert" had become, in a famous phrase, "a city." Men and women flocked to the badlands of Egypt and soon began to live a common life in community (*koinobion*). Christian asceticism passed into its second phase, from the eremitic (Gk. *eremos*, "empty," "alone") to the cenobitic. Neither ever entirely replaced the other, but the cenobitic or community form of Christian monasticism was more easily institutionalized—and more easily controlled—and had the longer, more profound effect on Christendom as a whole.

Obedience of the Spirit

Community life has its obvious economies of scale, if it is permitted to speak in that fashion of lives lived at close to a subsistence level. More importantly, it provided the psychological support of mutual example for a like-minded community embarked on an enterprise of daunting difficulty. Finally, community life provided the ultimate corrective to an aspect of the human appetite that had been previously uncovered by that same moral exemplarism. The first "solitaries" (Gk. *monachoi* > monks) quickly discovered that they had carried the world with them into the desert. It was located not in distant Alexandria but in their own unruly limbs and heads, and they practiced the most astonishingly fierce forms of asceticism in their efforts to annihilate it. Self-denial gave way to self-mortification and, some would say, to masochism pure and simple in their lengthy vigils, punishing fasts, and flagellations of the flesh that became desert commonplaces in the fourth and fifth Christian centuries. This was not only in Egypt. Richly detailed accounts of the "fathers of the desert" circulated throughout Christendom, and soon there were ascetics bent on the same relentless pursuit of self-denial in Palestine, Syria, and Anatolia, though the rigors of the climate made the pursuit of desert-style asceticism somewhat problematic in the more northerly regions.

The practitioners of this rigorous and often violent form of self-abnegation were called "athletes of God." The title was just—the professional athletes of Greece and Rome had practiced askesis—but the striving of those desert athletes turned out to be highly competitive as well. If Aba Shenoute could fast for a fortnight, then the Blessed Macarius a little farther down the same wadi could hold out for a month, or more, if really challenged. One-upmanship had come to the desert, followed by the blazing insight that here lay a truly cardinal vice: the will was being gratified even as the flesh was groaning *no más*. And just as quickly, those clinicians of the soul found its cure, obedience of the spirit.

Obedience was the final piece in the great triptych of monastic virtues. Poverty meant owning nothing and craving even less. Celibacy meant renouncing even those sexual activities permitted the Christian, foreswearing, in effect, marriage. But the desire for goods and carnal pleasures, for all their mischievously sublimated forms, are relatively easy to detect compared to the needs and demands of what a much later generation would call the ego. The Christian ascetics devised an institutional cure, however. Monks living in community would be governed by a rule, an impersonal superego to which their own wills would be subjected and, to fill in the interstices of the rule, a human superior whose (generally innocuous) commands would represent the will of God writ small, so to speak. The monastic superior, another monk, any monk, neither the brightest nor the best nor the most blessed—all those traits would render obedience reasonable and so easy—was the last and most potent of the instruments of self-abnegation designed for the monastic life, and obedience, of the letter and of the spirit, its most difficult demand.

The Saints in the City

The fourth century was the incubation period of Christian sanctity; by the fifth and sixth it was mature enough to return to society and attempt to transform it. The monks of the East, where asceticism had proceeded most vigorously from the hermit's cave to large communities in Egypt, Palestine, and Syria, frequently swarmed from the countryside into the streets of Alexandria, Antioch, and even Constantinople to demonstrate support for one side or the other in the Christological disputes that shook those two centuries (see II/7). Others stayed in place and drew crowds from the cities and even from the inner steppe by their reputation for sanctity, verified by public miracles. Simeon (d. 458), for example, the eccentric holy man of the spaces north of Aleppo who fled the world vertically rather than horizontally, sat on his lofty pillar for thirty-odd years and dispensed both advice and blessings on both the town dwellers who had come out to see him and the Bedouin who assembled around his column's base at the end of their seasonal treks from the desert into the sown. On other occasions, the holy man became the spokesperson of the empire's oppressed, standing before magnate and prince to make their case.

Whence this extraordinary power? Charisma is perhaps its own adequate explanation, but circumstantial elements contributed as well. By the fifth century the ancient oracles had fallen silent and the pagan priesthoods were in ruins. Out of this religious disintegration at the end of the ancient world stepped the Christian holy man. He had triumphed over both the world and his own desires and so spoke from a great moral height. This "ruthless professional," as he has been called, was listened to. He counseled, he mediated, he intervened, all on an individual basis: *this* man, in this time and this place, was thought to embody the supernatural.

The Rule of St. Basil

Basil, the wealthy nobleman who was himself a monk and later the bishop of Caesarea in Cappadocia, had considerable knowledge of monasticism in most of its Near Eastern varieties. He had visited monastic communities in Egypt, Palestine, and Syria about 358, and his own earlier experience of the disorganized and even anarchical monastic tradition in his native Cappadocia led him to draw up rules for the governance of monastic life, one of the first and most influential sets of regulations, from the sublime to the banal, that became the very stuff of Christian monasticism. Basil's rules are extant in a longer and a shorter version, and they outline in great detail not only the ideals but the practices of the monk's life from standards of admission to the monastery to the manner of dress there.

For Basil, community life was far preferable to the eremitic because of its greater social good. It was, in fact, Basil who established the social goals— with their economic and intellectual consequences—so evident in monastic life in the West, where Benedict took over much of Basil's thinking for his own *Rule* at Monte Cassino (see below). Basil believed in work, physical and intellectual, and the life of the monk was to be one of regulated work and prayer. Daily morning and evening prayers were not uncommon in some of the larger Christian churches, but Basil set a standard of monastic prayer eight times a day, beginning at dawn and proceeding at three-hour intervals through the day and night. This daily community recitation or cantillation of prescribed prayers—the Divine Office, it came to be called—at fixed hours of the day and night became one of the most characteristic traits of Christian monasticism, and may even have left some mark on Muhammad, who endorsed night prayers early in his career (Quran 73:23).

Basil put the monastery under the firm control of the superior (*hegoumenos*) or abbot, as he was called in the West, a monastic officer who later enjoyed the same powers and privileges as a bishop. The Great Church went even further in its own enactments. Monastic communities, it turned out, could be as troublesome to Church order as occasional individual monks, and the theological disputes of the fifth and sixth centuries were often accompanied by monastic riots. The Council of Chalcedon reacted in 451 by placing monastic communities under the jurisdiction of bishops, and succeeding councils attempted, not always successfully, to strengthen the hierarchy's grip on the so-called athletes of God. In the sixth century, when the imperial government began to intervene more directly in affairs of canon law, the emperor also took up the cause of monastic regulation and reform.

Eastern monasticism developed generally in conformity with the Basilian model and ideal, as did its slightly later Western counterpart. But there were profound differences between the two. As we shall see (II/9), the Eastern monks followed a path that led, quite consciously, to mysticism, while the monastic communities of the Latin West became increasingly engaged with the world, first in social missions and then in intellectual pursuits that by the thirteenth century made members of the mendicant orders the era's chief intellectuals. In the East, the Chalcedon decree placing monasteries under the firm control of local bishops effectively prevented the Eastern monastic enterprise from developing into the kind of "international" bodies that in the West were responsible (and responsive) to the pope alone. Although individual monks exercised great and continuous influence in the East, there were no Benedictines, mendicant friars, or Jesuits to enlarge and shape that Church.

Benedict and the Benedictines

The beginnings of formal monasticism in the Western Church occurred in the mid–sixth century when Benedict (d. ca. 550), first a hermit and later the head of a small community of monks at Monte Cassino in Italy, set down rather simply the guidelines for a monk's life as he understood them. This *Rule of St. Benedict*, which drew on Basil's earlier work as well as the desert fathers' example and Augustine's thinking, became the touchstone of communities of ascetics down to the turn into the thirteenth century when new problems produced new forms of the religious life.

In Benedict's *Rule*, community governance is designed to be paternal: the head of the house or abbot (< Gk. and Aramaic *abba*, "father") was to rule over its members precisely like a father over a family, combining compassion with justice. The brethren, whether priests or not—Benedict was not himself a priest and the priesthood does not loom large in most forms of medieval monasticism—owed the superior complete and perfect obedience. The abbot's orders had to be followed, no matter how difficult or apparently unreasonable, since he was speaking in the name of Christ. The abbot's permission was required for many things, great and small. For his part, the abbot was expected to need his brethren's counsel in major decisions affecting the community; he was also required to delegate authority to some of the community's more pious and intelligent members. Whereas the abbot's assistants and delegates were appointed, the abbot himself was elected by all the community members; where this proved impractical, a smaller group would do so. If an idle or corrupt community chose an abbot like itself, the local bishop or another abbot—later religious orders were generally exempt from such episcopal oversight—could overturn the election and appoint another in his place.

Candidates for membership in the community had be warned of the rigors of the life ahead of them and carefully screened for evidence of piety and humility. Each candidate then proceeded through a probation period, the novitiate, during which he restudied the rules and examined his own intentions. If, at the end of this probation, both the candidate and the members of the house were agreeable to his admission, he was permitted to make vows of poverty, celibacy, and obedience to the superior and promised to uphold and observe the *Rule*. He exchanged his worldly clothing for the simple garb of the monk, a rough black tunic, hooded cloak, and shoes made of whatever material was cheap and available.

His vows completed, the Benedictine monk embarked on the regimen that would mark the rest of his life: prayer, reading, and work. He was counseled to practice patience and humility in his own heart, charity and compassion toward his brethren, and obedience to those placed over him. He was to sleep with the others in one room, fully clothed, and rise to chant the prescribed prayers in common. There were to be two cooked meals a day, afternoon and evening. Wednesday and Friday were fast days during Lent, as were other large stretches across the year. All meals were to be taken in silence, while one of the brethren read from Scripture or some other edifying text.

Benedict regarded prayer as the central and crucial activity in the monk's life—he called it the work of God—and specified when and how it was to be performed. Prayer throughout the day and night was a very old tradition in Christianity, and the monks of the Egyptian desert were already meeting at fixed times for communal prayers, usually recitations from the Psalms, all of them in the course of a single year. Bernard fixed the prayer schedule in detail for the monks of the Western Church. The Divine Office consisted of eight distinct moments called Lauds (in the earliest morning), Prime (at the "first hour" or about 6 A.M.), Terce, Sext, and None (at the third, sixth, and ninth hours of the day), Vespers (early in the evening, before dark), Compline (before retiring), and Matins (sometimes said at midnight, though Benedict prescribed it for 2 A.M.).

Note: All the Psalms, hymns, and prayers used in the recitation of the Divine Office—now called the Liturgy of the Hours in some circles— were originally found in different books, but from the eleventh century onward, particularly as the mendicant orders became more mobile, they began to be collected in a single book called the *Breviary*. This compendium has been revised on many different occasions, the last in 1971. The full range of the "hours" described above was performed within monasteries but also for the general public in cathedrals by the canons or clergy attached to the cathedral (see below). In the Roman Catholic Church all clerics are obliged to read the daily prescribed passages in the *Roman Breviary*, the monastic orders to recite it in common, all other clerics to say it in private.

The monastic day was generally filled with activities. The chanting of the Divine Office took up large intervals, and these were alternated with physical work, either in the fields or within the house, copying manuscripts in the scriptorium or simply cleaning, mending, building. The point was to avoid idleness, reputed by all the authorities to be one of the principal enemies of the monastic life.

The Benedictine rule was adopted in ever increasing numbers—and in varying styles—by new religious communities springing up across Europe, and it received a powerful political impulse when Charlemagne ordered it be the standard in all the monasteries of his empire. One such was the Benedictine house founded in 909 at Cluny near Macon in Burgundy. Through the efforts of a series of effective, energetic, and diplomatic abbots like Peter the Venerable (d. 1156) who governed there, Cluny became the model Benedictine monastery, just as Benedict's rule had become the standard of the monastic life. Other "Cluniac" houses followed in its tracks, and soon there was a network across Europe, each attempting to emulate Cluny's increasingly elaborate celebration of the Divine Office (with a consequent lessening of physical labor in the monks' day), careful management, and scrupulous observance. By the mid–twelfth century there were more than a thousand such foundations, but thereafter the powerful French monastery's influence began to wane in the face of new monastic impulses, like those of the more flexible and active friars known as Franciscans and Dominicans.

Benedictine Experiments: Carthusians and Cistercians

The power and affluence of the well-organized Cluniac monasteries had successfully institutionalized, almost corporatized, the Benedictine way of life, but at the price, perhaps, of its initial ascetic impulse. Yet there were "Benedictines" who explored other paths to perfection. One was Bruno (d. 1101), a German-born, French-raised Benedictine monk who attempted to return to a tradition even earlier than Benedict, to the hermitic life of the earliest fathers of the desert. In 1084 he founded a house at La Chartreuse, in the French Alps east of Grenoble, in which he attempted to combine the Benedictine rule with the solitude of the early hermits. The monks at this and subsequent "charterhouses," as they came to be called, lived in individual "cells"—tiny suites with a workroom, living room, and small enclosed garden—where they labored in silence, prayed, ate their meager bread and vegetables—two or three times a week only bread and water—and slept in solitude. But this Carthusian life was also a communal one. The monks assembled in the church to sing at least part of the Office together, ate together in a common refectory on certain feast days, shared a community library, and took weekly walks together. There were at the beginning but thirteen monks in the solitude of the "upper house," while in a nearby "lower house" lived the twenty-odd "lay brothers" whose work helped support the contemplative monks in their solitude.

At first there were no Carthusian rules as such, but eventually a desire for papal approval prevailed and so a combination of Benedict's *Rule* and the "Customs" that had grown up at La Chartreuse since Bruno's day were submitted to Rome and approved by Innocent II in 1133. Its provisions were simple: the Carthusian monks spent the day (and part of the night) praying in solitude, meditating, reading, performing manual labor, and, above all, chanting or reciting the Office.

If the Carthusians represent a bold attempt at redrawing the Benedictine prototype of the monastic life, the other twelfth-century approach to that life was more directly a reform—more precisely, a reform of the Cluniac version of it. In 1098 twenty-one monks and their abbot, Robert, left the Benedictine house at Molesmes in Burgundy and founded a new monastic establishment at Cîteaux near Dijon with the express purpose of following Benedict's *Rule* to the letter. They would live and dress simply, in unbleached white instead of the traditional Benedictine black, and theirs would be simple worship—much cut down from the elaborate Cluniac version, in plain buildings free of any image or ornament, all quite different from the corporate Cluny style.

Whereas Cluny had provided a model other houses in other places imitated, the monks of Cîteaux (Lat. *Cistercium*), or Cistercians, founded their own "colonies." As the enterprise prospered, particularly after Bernard of Clairvaux (d. 1153), the leading churchman of the early twelfth century, joined the abbey in 1120 and put his prodigiously gifted pen at its disposal, monks were dispatched from Cîteaux to create new houses, not as independent units but as carefully regulated and supervised "daughterhouses" of the "motherhouse." Cluny had created a network, but Cîteaux, an empire and, in effect, the first religious "order." Control was maintained through annual visits of the abbot or his delegate from the motherhouse to its "offspring" as well as by an annual general chapter or assembly of all the abbots. It was an effective system for maintaining a high level of observance as well for charting and implementing policy, and the model of the Cistercian empire was used by the Franciscans and Dominicans in their own organization and indeed in most of the European religious orders that came after.

Canons Regular and Other

In the Western Church the form of monastic life associated with Benedict of Norcia began to spread in the eleventh century into more public venues. One way was through the adaptations of the Benedictine life undertaken by the monks at Cluny and then those embodied in the Cistercian and Carthusian variants. Another was set in motion by the ecclesiastical reforms of Pope Gregory VII (v. 1073–1085) and his successors, themselves inspired by Cluny. The reforming popes assumed the Christian monks were leading lives akin to those of Jesus' Apostles, an assumption fraught with consequence in the thirteenth century (see below). But in the eleventh it meant only that the ordinary Christian clergy, now understood to be latter-day Apostles of the Lord, should do the same. In many parishes this was impossible, but for the clergy attached to the city cathedrals it was not. In the mid–eleventh century, under the influence of the Benedictine houses, they began to organize into quasi-monastic communities.

These clerics were called canons. They adopted the monastic rule attributed to Augustine of Hippo—it was likely by one of his disciples—and were recognized by the papacy as formal religious communities under the rubric Canons Regular or Augustinian Canons. They led a community life, eating, sleeping, and chanting the Divine Office together like their monastic counterparts. But they were also clerics, ordained to the Church's ministry, and served various priestly roles in the city's parishes. The Canons Regular of St. Augustine manned the Church of the Holy Sepulcher during the Crusades, for example, and were wardens of the church into which the crusaders had converted the Muslim Dome of the Rock. These latter canons lived in quarters erected on the northern edge of the platform on which the Dome still sits.

The Mendicant Friars: Franciscans and Dominicans

Benedictine-style monasticism yielded in the thirteenth century to a more flexible type of religious community living. First Francis of Assisi and then Dominic de Guzman founded religious orders of men who took as their mandate the wider propagation and defense of the Word of God and the care of souls. Like the earlier monks, these two orders of friars (< Lat. *fratres,* "brethren"), the Franciscans (Order of Friars Minor) and the Dominicans (Order of Preachers), chanted the Office in common in monasteries, but their chief spiritual tasks lay outside, in catechesis (see II/4) and in the explanation and defense of Christian teaching. The friars could be moved hither and thither across Christendom as need or opportunity presented itself, as it did in the battle against heresy or in the propagation of the faith. Finally, the new friars were "mendicants" or beggars, the Franciscans quite literally so. Both orders were vowed, though with somewhat different nuances, to corporate as well as individual poverty: the order itself was to own nothing and support itself solely by freewill offerings. Other monastic groups followed their lead, and later in the century the Carmelites and the Augustinian Hermits both became mendicant orders of friars.

Franciscans and Dominicans had quite different points of departure. Francis (d. 1226) was an Italian merchant moved by a personal vision of what the Christian life should be in its highest and most ideal form; Dominic (d. 1221) was a Spanish cleric with a sense of mission joined to an idea of how the Church might meet the challenge of the Cathar heresy (see I/5). Francis was the son of a well-to-do Italian businessman of Assisi and led a rather religiously careless life until 1205, when he experienced a series of visions that inspired him to take up a life of what he understood to be evangelical poverty. Like Jesus, he owned nothing and existed entirely on the charitable alms of others. He preached to others, rather loudly but with great effect.

Within five years Francis had attracted sufficient attention and enough imitators that what he inspired and then led can be called a movement. In 1209 or 1210, he submitted what must have been a somewhat sketchy "rule"—it has not been preserved—to Pope Innocent III (r. 1198–1216), who in an equally sketchy fashion approved it. In 1212 a woman named Clare requested permission from Francis that she and a number of other women be permitted to follow the same rule in community. The permission was given and thus came into existence the Second Order of St. Francis or Poor Clares, which eventually received its own papal approbation in 1253. There was also a Third Order for those who wished to live in the Franciscan spirit but were unable, by reason of marriage or other commitments, to assume the full burden of the Franciscan life (see I/5). The Third Order of St. Francis was approved in 1289.

Francis was devoted to preaching the message of the Gospels, and his followers fanned out throughout Europe and even into the crusader war zones of the Middle East. Francis's own personal goal was to preach the Gospel to the Muslims, and in 1219 he got his wish. He accompanied a crusader army in an attack on Egypt and got himself across the lines into the camp of the sultan

Note: With the failure of the First Crusade and Salah al-Din's recapture of Jerusalem in 1187, all the Latin clergy were expelled from the churches expropriated or built by the crusaders, and the "native" clergy, chiefly Greek and Syrian, reoccupied them. But the Latins were not gone for long. Sometime about 1244 Latin clerics, specifically the Franciscans, were allowed by the city's Muslim rulers to return to Jerusalem and even to find a place in the Church of the Holy Sepulcher. The Friars had their position confirmed by papal bull in 1342, whenceforward they exercised a virtual monopoly—recognized by the Muslim authorities—over whatever ecclesiastical footholds Western Christians managed to acquire in the Holy Land and over whatever Christian pilgrims arrived there from Europe, whom they housed, fed, and guided around the holy places. To this day a Franciscan enjoys the title "Custodian of the Holy Land" (*Custos Sanctae Terrae*).

al-Kamil, who gave him a courteous hearing but declined to become either a Franciscan or even a Christian.

Francis had little time for regrets. He had to return to Europe to solve serious problems in his own communities. Francis had guided the movement by personal instruction and example, but as its numbers and houses increased, control began to slip from his not always terribly interested hands. The pope required a new and formal rule to guide the various communities that professed to be following Francis's example. Francis provided one version in 1221 based on his own severe idea of poverty. He tried again two years later; and this version was approved by the pope that same year. Thus came into existence the Fratres Minores, or Friars Minor, more popularly the Franciscans. Francis died in 1226, not entirely happy with the movement he had created, which was passing inevitably into other less idealistic, if more practical, hands. He was canonized with remarkable speed in 1228.

Dominic de Guzman was a different man with a different idea: he shared neither the visions nor the radical ideals of Francis. He was an ordained priest, had attended a university, and was the prior or head of the Canons Regular of the Osma cathedral in Spain. He accompanied his bishop who had been commissioned to investigate the spread of Catharism in Languedoc on the other side of the Pyrenees. Dominic soon came to understand that the Cathars, a puritanical movement with a largely popular following, had to be met on its own, ground by preaching in the public squares by a clergy living simple and exemplary lives. If Francis was chiefly motivated by Jesus' teaching and example of poverty, Dominic's inspiration was Jesus' sending forth his disciples to preach his message to the entire world.

Dominic's activities received the preliminary approval of Innocent III in 1205, and he and some of his companions began to use a monastery at Prouille near Toulouse as their center. Innocent had given permission to adopt a monastic rule and Dominic chose the *Rule* of St. Augustine, the same that governed most Canons Regular, to which he added a series of "Customs" tailored to the goals of these new highly mobile and very public monks. Dominic's combination of old and new received formal papal approbation in 1216 as the Order of Preachers, or Dominicans. Honorius III added his own expectations of Dominic and his followers: "We approve your Order with the full expectation that the brethren will be champions of the faith and true lights to the world."

Dominic's companions fanned out from Prouille and established Dominican houses across France, Italy, and Spain. In 1220 the first general "chapter"—an assembly of the order's superiors—was held in Bologna and drew up a full set of "Constitutions" to support and codify the earlier "Customs" and in particular embraced the notion of poverty as a way of life. The Dominicans, like the Franciscans, became mendicants. They could own no property; they would exist on whatever alms were given them by the faithful.

The subsequent history of these two totally new departures in Christian spirituality and ecclesiastical organization reflect both the personality and the purpose of their two founders. Francis of Assisi, the visionary and mystic, was moved by the ideal of personal holiness, which he thought was best achieved by emulating Jesus' life and particularly Jesus' poverty; his order attempted to follow in his steps. The earliest Franciscans were much like Francis himself. They were laymen, not ordained clerics, most of them barely educated. They were fired, however, by the ideal of personal sanctification through evangelical poverty and they endeavored to carry that same message throughout the Church by their impassioned preaching. Dominic, in contrast, was moved by a tactic and a mission. His program was crafted to effect a very specific end, the preaching of the genuine Christian message to combat heresy—the Latin *Dominicani* was neatly punned into *Domini canes*, "the Lord's attack dogs"— and to save souls lost to the Church. Dominic was both a cleric and university educated, and the Dominicans tended to be the same. Although Dominic was principally a preacher, teaching soon enjoyed parity with preaching among his followers. Dominicans became prominent in the medieval Church's intellectual life through their work in the new universities founded in Europe at about the same time the orders were. The Franciscans eventually followed Dominic's offspring into the university faculties, but thirteenth-century thought is dominated by the imposing Dominican Thomas Aquinas.

Is Perfection Possible? The Franciscan Controversy

Almost all the religious communities that appeared in the Western Church began with one individual's vision of perfection—albeit a vision conditioned by a long history of asceticism—that attracted others to the achievement of that same ideal. The Church oversaw such movements and so the vision was soon "regularized" or routinized. In short, the epigones became a religious order. Such orders proved attractive to increasing numbers of the faithful and at the same time useful to the Church. To make them even more attractive and more useful, the popes granted the new orders various privileges that in many cases eased the rigorous idealism of the founder. Idealism was sacrificed to practicality: the orders became more accessible and more effective.

In time, often a short time, a reaction set in. Some of the religious discovered, or remembered, that the ideal of the founder and the first members differed from the community's current life. Reforms were attempted. Some failed and their proponents disappeared back into the community or out into the world. Others ended in one or another form of schism or in the creation of another legitimate and legitimated branch of the order, the "observants," or even, in certain extreme cases, the creation of a variant condemned by the Church. Two notable exceptions to that nearly universal process were the

Carthusians and the Jesuits (see below). The Carthusians, whose boast was "never reformed because never deformed," were designed not to "succeed": the austerity of their life was such that few could sustain it, and their eremitic and severely cloistered way of life made them unlikely agents of any Church project short of the members' own salvation. The Jesuits, in contrast, were programmed for success. Their way of life was from the start flexible enough to permit almost any adaptation. They were intended from the outset to assist the papacy and so their use in assorted Church activities led to no deformation: the Jesuits bent and twisted but never broke.

The most notorious example of radical schism within a religious order oc-curred among the Franciscans. Francis of Assisi's vision of evangelical poverty burned purely and brightly and at the same time was highly persuasive to kindred spirits. But once those kindred spirits began to live in common and pursue community goals, the vision's purity had perhaps necessarily to yield to practicality. Francis's ideal was that friars should survive—and not much more than that—by either begging or performing the meanest sort of labor; that they should live like the poorest of the poor. His ban on money was absolute: the friars might not even handle it. But even during his lifetime, particularly during his absence in the Middle East in the early 1220s, some of his follow-ers under the leadership of the practical-minded Brother Elias were already adapting his original rule to bring Franciscan communities more in line with traditional monastic houses. In 1230, to settle what was already becoming an issue among some of the friars, Gregory IX issued a papal bull, *Quo elongati*, drawing a distinction between the ownership of property, which was forbidden by the Franciscan rule, and its use (and, as it soon turned out, its administration), which, by Gregory's understanding, was not.

Francis himself appears to have known and understood what was happening, and though he approved of the modified *Rule* of 1223, his final words, as recorded in his *Testament*, included a plea for fidelity to the evangelical ideal of poverty that had moved him in the first place. Franciscan houses began to divide, the bull of 1230 notwithstanding, between those who wished to adhere to Francis' dramatic vision, whatever the cost, and those who wished to yoke it to the service of the Church, though at some cost, it was clear, to the ideal. The case for the pragmatists seemed self-evident, and perhaps self-imposed as well. To train religious preachers and to enter the swelling intellectual life of the thirteenth-century Church required planning, organization, and resources far beyond anything Francis could have imagined. The rigorists' argument drew on the example of Francis himself and of the earliest friars, but soon the con-troversy deserted history and descended into deeper theological waters, notably the nature and extent of Jesus' own poverty, the evangelical model that consti-tuted the foundation of Francis's—and the Franciscans'—practice of that virtue.

The controversy between the parties broke out, as noted, in Francis's own lifetime and lingered on for two centuries, often with tragic consequences.

Finally, in 1619, a papal bull recognized as a legitimate form of Franciscan life a group called the Capuchins, who were devoted to the literal observance of Francis's *Rule* "down to the slightest detail," as the bull put it, and without recourse to "the declarations concerning it [the *Rule*] promulgated by the Roman Pontiffs." There were later divisions of the principal Franciscan parties, but the recognition of the Capuchins (so called from the pointed hood they wore in imitation of Francis) established that, women (the Poor Clares) and laymen (the Third Order of St. Francis) aside, there were three heirs to Francis of Assisi within the Church: the Conventuals, the Observants, and the Capuchins.

Francis's ideal of a life of evangelical poverty lay at the root of all three of these communities. The Conventuals were in effect Francis's immediate followers, whose observance of the original *Rule*—which Francis in his final *Testament* said should never be tampered with—was in fact modified by a series of papal bulls from *Quo elongati* onward. The papal decrees' intent was generally to mitigate Francis's *Rule* by granting various easements. The papacy, for example, would actually own the order's resources, a non-Franciscan would administer them, and the Friars would merely have their use without proprietorship. Many Franciscans felt they could live with this arrangement without compromising their consciences; notable among them was Bonaventure, minister general of the Friars between 1257 and 1274 and, after Francis, the most famous and influential Franciscan of the thirteenth century. Bonaventure recreated the Franciscans by redrawing the order's constitutions and then refashioning the life of Francis himself. To this end he composed the *Legend of Francis*, a biography that a general chapter ordered should be the only official one, just as another chapter had mandated that Bonaventure's constitution should replace all earlier versions of the Franciscan rule.

The increasingly fierce struggle among Francis's heirs, each with its own properties, personnel, and constitutions—the Observants' was drawn up by Juan de Capistrano (d. 1456)—raged on until Pope Leo X convened a Franciscan "summit" in Rome in 1514. The pope subsequently issued a bull, *Ite vos*, that formally separated the Conventuals and the Observants into two distinct Franciscan orders. For some this was still not enough, and the severe ideal of Francis of Assisi's poverty continued to beckon. It was finally assuaged in 1619 with papal recognition that the "superobservant" Capuchins constituted a third, autonomous member of the Franciscan family.

Military Orders, Christian and Muslim

The so-called military orders, religious under arms, are closely associated with medieval Latin Christianity, though there were analogous institutions in Islamic society (see below) from which the Christian version may have drawn inspiration. In the Western Church the military order combined newly evolving forms of monasticism with the emerging ideal of a knightly code of honor, in a word, of chivalry. The new figure was not so much a monk who had turned to arms as a knight, a member of Europe's nobility, who embraced the ideals of Christian monasticism, particularly those of the new canons regular—monks who were under vows and Church discipline but who nonetheless lived and worked in the world.

The military orders were born during the twelfth-century Crusades, in Palestine, the newly conquered Holy Land that had been in Muslim hands since the seventh century. The coming together of monk and knight first took place in the Hospital of St. John, a pious foundation near the Holy Sepulcher that antedated the Crusades. It was run by Benedictine monks who were joined, after the Latin conquest of Jerusalem in 1099, by the knight Raymond du Puy. As early as 1113 the brethren there who cared for the sick had been recognized by the papacy as a distinct monastic Order of the Hospital of St. John. When in 1120 Raymond became the master, he extended their mission from treating the infirm to protecting pilgrims and visitors to the Holy Land from Muslim attacks.

Though this latter military activity long remained secondary for the Hospitallers, the notion of monks in arms quickly spread among the knights of the Latin kingdom. In 1118 the Frankish nobleman Hugh of Payens had collected eight other knights to devote themselves to the protection of pilgrims on the dangerous road from Jaffa to Jerusalem. In 1127 he argued his vision of an association of knightly monks to Bernard of Clairvaux, the influential Cistercian who breathed new vitality into Christian monasticism in the twelfth century. Bernard was won over and wrote a pamphlet titled "In Praise of the New Knighthood" to encourage recruits. In 1129, thanks in large part to Bernard's enthusiastic support, a council at Troyes recognized the new order, the Poor Knights of Christ. Baldwin II, the Latin king of Jerusalem, installed them in the Aqsa mosque, known to the crusaders as the Templum Solomonis since they believed it to be the site of Solomon's palace (the actual temple, which they called the Templum Domini, was identified with the Dome of the Rock). Hence the later, more popular name, the Knights of the Temple of Solomon, or simply the Templars.

A series of papal bulls in the 1130s and 1140s shaped the life, style, and fortunes of the new military order and, by implication, those of most of their successors and imitators. The way of life was based on Bernard's Cistercian ideal, but these knights—who were expected to provide their own mounts and equipment—were, like their sergeants and squires, monks, not clerics. Sacerdotal functions were performed exclusively by chaplains, who were members of the order but did not bear arms. As in the traditional monastic orders, the individual Templar took a vow of poverty, but the order itself acquired enormous properties, castles, and their surrounding lands throughout the Latin kingdom and, when the value of this truly professional standing army was recognized, in Europe as well. The Templars, the Hospitallers as they became increasingly militarized, and the somewhat later Teutonic Knights—another military order that grew out of the German-run Hospital of St. Mary in Jerusalem—became the military backbone of the crusader enterprise in the Middle East. That back was broken by Salah al-Din on the field of Hattin in 1187, and when Acre, the final Latin enclave, fell to the Muslims in 1291, the Hospitallers withdrew first to Cyprus and then to the island of Rhodes, which they purchased in 1307. The Hospitallers held out on Rhodes against repeated Muslim attempts, by the Mamluks of Egypt and then by the Ottomans, to dislodge them by force. Sulayman the Magnificent finally succeeded in 1522, and the surviving knights were permitted to withdraw to Malta, where they resisted new Ottoman assaults until the Ottoman naval threat disappeared from the Mediterranean. The Hospitallers subsequently evolved into the Knights of Malta, a still surviving association of philanthropic Catholic laymen.

The Templars had a much briefer and less heroic history. With the fall of Acre they seem to have lost their direction. In 1307 they became the object of deep suspicion to Philip the Fair of France, whether for heresy, as he claimed, or for the king's need of money, as others have thought. In 1312, after a series of trials and public hearings, the pope, Clement V, allowed himself to be persuaded that the order should be suppressed (see I/6). Its properties were formally transferred to the Hospitallers, although informally they fell into Philip's pocket. The Teutonic Knights moved in 1291 to Venice, then in 1309 to Marienburg in Prussia, where they became in effect lords of the land. They expanded their holding rapidly but eventually came into conflict with the ambitions of Poland and Lithuania, who together defeated the Teutonic Knights at Tannenberg in 1410, effectively undermining the order's power and prestige.

Both the Templars and the Hospitallers had properties in Spain as well as elsewhere in Europe, and the Christian princes soon attempted to use them in the war against the Muslim states in the Iberian Peninsula, most notably Alfonso I of Aragon, who in 1131 named both orders among the heirs to his kingdom. The military orders were not easily persuaded to open a second front against Islam in Spain. They might use the Spanish kingdoms to recruit knights and raise money, but their primary objective still lay in defending Jerusalem and the Holy Land. But by 1143 the Templars had taken up arms in Spain and a few years later the Hospitallers followed suit for "the defense of the western church which is in Spain, for the defeat, overcoming and expulsion of the race of the Moors, and the exaltation of the holy Christian faith and religion," as one princely decree put it.

The example of the Templars and Hospitallers soon bred local Iberian versions of military orders. The Order of Calatrava was founded in Castile in 1158, that of Santiago, or St. James, in León in 1170, and a bit later perhaps, the Order of Alcóntara, also in León. All shared the explicit purpose of the knights of Santiago, "that they might stand like a wall of fidelity against the frenzy of the infidel." Support for the local Spanish orders was strong among the princes since the international Templars and Hospitallers were too powerful to be controlled and at the same time only fitfully committed to the Spanish enterprise.

As already remarked, the members of the military orders led a life based on that of the older monastic communities. They wore distinguishing habits, a tunic, often white, over their armor, and emblazoned with a distinctive cross or some other symbol. The members lived together, performed the daily office, though many of the knights, who were illiterate, simply attended rather than participated in the collection of prayers said or chanted in common by the chaplain or clerical members of the order. Provisions were made for the knights' absences from their houses on military affairs, and those of the Order of Santiago were even permitted to be married, though they were expected to abstain from sexual relations with their wives during the prescribed periods of fasting. The knights were forbidden to indulge in the "worldly pleasures" of hunting or taking part in knightly tournaments.

Although the Christian military orders shaped themselves on traditional monastic lines, the combination of military and religious service in a conventual setting had occurred even earlier in Islam. We are poorly informed about their origins and development, but from an early era there were fortified "monasteries" called *ribat*s along Islam's frontiers, particularly its seacoasts. They were manned not by the regular soldiery of Islam but by Sufis, as that term is understood in its most elastic sense (see below). These Islamic "monks of war" were neither as tightly organized nor as tightly controlled as their later Christian counterparts, but they did spawn, out of a ribat on the south Saharan frontier of Islam, a movement of "Ribat Men" (*al-murabitun* > Almoravids) who spread their reforming arms and ideology across North Africa and into Spain.

The Rise and Fall of the Society of Jesus

In 1521 the Basque courtier-soldier Iñigo of the town of Loyola took a ball in the leg during the French siege of Pamplona. During his painful convalescence he underwent a conversion, not through a supernatural visitation— those would come later—but by reading the not terribly exceptional *Life of Christ* by Ludolph of Saxony and the collection of saints' lives called *The Golden Legend*. It was the conversion of a hidalgo, a late-blooming cavalier like Don Quixote whose chivalrous instincts now summoned him not to courtly exploits but to valiant deeds on behalf of his Savior. A year later Ignatius, as he ultimately chose to call himself, was in retreat at Manresa and the nearby monastery of Montserrat casting his new insights into a spiritual formulation that would sustain not only his own convictions for a lifetime but those of his followers for another five hundred years (see II/9).

Ignatius's initial impulse was to make a pilgrimage and perhaps stay and work in the Holy Land, but when that proved impossible he decided instead, with great zeal but still without a great deal of focus, "to study." Everywhere he settled, whether as a somewhat irregular student at Alcalá and Salamanca or later as a formal matriculant from 1528 to 1535 at the university of Paris, he attracted others, sometimes for his guidance—women found him particularly admirable—and sometimes to emulate him. The latter he called, in his military way, the "Company of Jesus." The title proved too modest. This company rapidly expanded from platoon to brigade to army strength and as the Society of Jesus, it became one of the major weapons in the Roman Church's counterattack on the Reformation. Recognized by Rome as a religious order in 1540, the Jesuits, as they were quickly tagged, represented a revolutionary development in Western monasticism. Bound by the monastic vows of poverty, celibacy, and obedience, these plainclothes monks—they dressed as ordinary clerics—were also freed of the obligations of the choir and the chanting of the Divine Office, though they were bound by a special fourth vow of obedience to the pope to go wherever and do whatever he and the Church requested.

Ignatius, who died in Rome in 1556, may have envisioned those charges as ministering to the poor and catechizing in the streets, but it turned out quite otherwise. The Dominicans, the "attack dogs of the Lord," and the Franciscans as well, were potent resources in the Church's struggle with heresy in the twelfth century; then in the thirteenth they took their place in the vanguard of Europe's new university intelligentsia. The Jesuits were quickly caught up in another war, this one against the sixteenth-century Reformers. They may have fought in the forward trenches throughout southern Germany and engaged in undercover work in Elizabethan England, but their main work was restoring the spiritual and intellectual arsenal of the Roman Church. In 1548 Ignatius responded to a request by the Spanish viceroy and sent ten Jesuits to open a school in Messina. Neither he nor the Jesuits who stood in those lecture halls could possibly have understood that the Society of Jesus had taken its first, almost unwitting step toward becoming the schoolmasters of Catholic Europe. After Trent, the Roman Church reconstructed itself, and the chief architects and master builders of that project were the Jesuits.

The growth of the Jesuits was rapid and prodigious, in numbers, the extent of their operations—Jesuits were in the vanguard of Christian missions from Paraguay to Japan—and influence. Jesuits had friends in very high places and, inevitably, enemies there as well. Their increased power and influence with both popes, with whom they had forged a close alliance from the start, and with the aristocracy whose educators they had been for generations, was matched by a parallel rise in European popularism, secularism, and anticlericalism that would come to a head in the French Revolution. But before revolution shook the thrones of Europe, it shook the Jesuits from their lofty perch. Their end began, somewhat implausibly, in Portugal, where in 1750 the new prime minister was the Marquis de Pombal, who had earlier served as ambassador to England. Pombal combined an admiration for how the English dealt—imperiously—with their Church with a strong-willed desire that the state, not the Society of Jesus, should control the "reductions," the large reservation-like estates in Paraguay where the Jesuits sheltered their Indian converts from the moral and mercantile iniquity of the white man. In Jesuit lore the *reducciones* were Christian utopias; Pombal, who had gotten control of the territory by treaty with Spain in 1750, was convinced that gold-mining was going on behind the hymns and rosaries. He ordered the reductions seized, the Indians turned out, and the Jesuits banished from the Portuguese New World.

The war had just begun. Pombal carried it to Rome, claiming that the Jesuits had "exercised illicit, public, and scandalous conduct" in Portugal and its colonies. It was an uncertain time in Rome and the charges slid through. In 1759 the Jesuits were civilly banned—a kind of corporate dissolution—in Portugal. Similar charges were brought in France. The Jesuits of Martinique were also running plantations, poorly, as it turned out, and there was a public bankruptcy and an even more public scandal. The case came before parliament, where the Jesuits' many enemies, the Jansenists chief among them (see II/5), had their long day in court. The parliament found against the Jesuits and in 1764 Louis XIV signed the decree dissolving the order and giving its members the choice of either renouncing their vows or leaving the country.

The Jesuit pogrom now had a momentum of its own. Attacks followed in Spain, Naples, and Parma, where the charges—that the Jesuits were antimonarchical and condoned regicide—were overtly political. In 1767 the Society of Jesus was dissolved in Spain and its two dependencies of Naples and Parma. These were all principally civil dissolutions, initiated and executed by the state. Lacking was ecclesiastical suppression—the pope's, and so the Church's, renunciation of the Society of Jesus. In February 1769 there was a new pope, Clement XIV, and an offensive was immediately mounted against the Jesuits by the monarchs of France and Spain through their so-called crown cardinals. It was clear from the outset that the pope would have to yield, whatever his misgivings. On 16 August 1773 he signed the document suppressing the Society of Jesus. It was not by a bull, however, addressed to and immediately effective in the entire Church, but by an executive order that took effect only when and where it was officially promulgated. In some places, most notably Catherine the Great's Russia, it was never published, and so a narrow string of Jesuits continued the line until the storm blew over. It did by 1814 and the Society of Jesus was reconstituted in the Roman Church, not terribly chastened but never quite the same shining creature it had been before the Marquis de Pombal bethought himself of certain fabulous ranches in Paraguay.

The Holy Mountain

The monastic center of Eastern Orthodoxy has long been the complex of monasteries and hermitages in what is called the Holy Mountain. Mount Athos is in fact the easternmost rocky finger of the Chalcidice Peninsula that hangs from the Greek mainland into the Aegean Sea east of Salonika. Christian hermits lived there from an early date and their number gradually swelled with the arrival of fugitives from one or another of the theological quarrels that occasionally disturbed the Eastern Church. But Athos's real beginning as a monastic center dates from the arrival of the celebrated monk Athanasius of Trebizond sometime about 960. He introduced the cenobitic life to the mountain by founding, with considerable imperial help, a large monastery, and thereafter cenobites and hermits lived side by side, though not always easily, on those craggy wooded slopes. Others followed Athanasius's lead, and as the number of monasteries proliferated—there were sometimes more than thirty and the total number of monks at times reached ten thousand—a form of republican government eventually evolved. The monks within the monasteries lived acording to the rule of St. Basil, but common affairs on the Holy Mountain were managed by a council of abbots—in the Eastern Church the monastic superior was called *hegoumenos*—under the leadership of one of them, the *protos*, or "first."

> **Note:** The Eastern Church developed its own modified form of cenobiticism, which is also visible in the Carthusian lifestyle of the Latin Church. Eastern monks often lived in a *laura* (or *lavra*), a monastic compound that included both a monastery proper, with chapel, choir, and refectory, where the monks could come together for common liturgical and social exercises, as well as individual cells (*kellia*), where the monks actually lived and spent most of their time in solitary prayer and contemplation.

The Byzantine emperors generally looked favorably on this jewel in the crown of Eastern monasticism. At the end of the eleventh century Alexis Comnenus (r. 1081–1118) removed the monasteries of Athos from the control of all lay and ecclesiastical authorities except that of the emperor himself. Andronicus II (r. 1282–1328) took the final step and placed jurisdiction over Athos, which he called "this second Paradise, this starry heaven, this refuge of all the virtues," under the sole control of the patriarch of Constantinople. Andronicus may have derived his picture of Athos from the life and career of its most famous citizen, his contemporary Gregory Palamas (d. 1359), longtime monk of the Great Laura of Athos, sometime hermit and archbishop of Salonika, and full-time defender of the form of Athonite spirituality called Hesychasm (see II/9).

The fall of Constantinople and most of the rest of the Eastern empire to the Ottoman Turks left the Holy Mountain intact but increasingly impoverished. The Muslim Turks did not generally interfere with the monks, yet they exacted their customary tribute, and the monasteries, which had lived mostly on patronage and alms, were hard-pressed to pay it. At this point the monastic life experienced another adaptation: the introduction of the "idiorhythmic" style. In an effort to make the monasteries self-supporting, monks were permitted to own private property and allocated their own time between prayer and some form of sustaining work. The idiorhythmic monks began to group themselves into "families," tiny communes or cooperatives that were somewhat more viable than the individual worker-monk.

Salvation, at least in the fiscal sense, came to the Holy Mountain with Slavic monks and Slavic, chiefly Russian, patronage, which buoyed up Athos's declining numbers and perilous finances. The entire complex suffered terrible physical damage to its priceless icons and manuscripts at the hands of the retreating Turks in 1822, but since that time it has survived through a combination of an adamantine tradition, a willingness to adapt to tourism—throughout most of its history, no female of any species could set foot, hoof, or claw on Mount Athos—and a renewed interest of the Eastern intelligentsia in this most demanding of all spiritual vocations.

The Personal Life of Muhammad

Muhammad lived in circumstances quite different from Jesus'. Mecca was a commercial center as well as a religious one; given the importance of its shrine, religion was quite clearly the principal business, and as some modern interpreters would contend, business may have become the religion of Mecca as well. Muhammad had a modest but discernible role in at least the town's business: he married a local entrepreneur, Khadija (see I/3), and tradition puts him in charge of her commercial caravan interests. The Quran, at any rate, is filled with mercantile terms about humankind's accounts, God's reckonings, and painful audits at the End Time.

Note has already been made of Jesus' sometimes disparaging remarks about wealth and the wealthy. The Quran is less interested in wealth than in the attitude it engenders. Its earliest preaching to the Meccans is aimed directly at the arrogance and niggardliness of the wealthy who think that property is their due and who do not share their gains with the poor and the needy. Circumstances were quite different at Medina, however. Muhammad and his community of believers came rather quickly to share the prosperity that was so dangerous to the Meccans, though it was now the Prophet's responsibility to say how it should be used (Quran 59:6–10). At Medina the Quran encourages the Muslim raiders with the promise of "rich spoils" (48:19), and tradition tells of the immense fortunes in loot acquired by some of the early Muslims. But those same raiders are warned not to be overly concerned with booty since God too has "spoils" in store for the faithful (4:94).

As we have already seen (II/5), Muhammad was the exemplar of all human virtue for the Muslim, and although we are treated to a broad portrait of the man in the hadith that make up the custom of the Prophet (see II/3), we do not always know what to make of the details. Many of the Prophetic reports seem to be fighting a later war, some praising asceticism, others deploring it; some making the Prophet parsimonious, others lavish. The Quran granted the Prophet a large share of the spoils of his increasingly successful raids (59:6), and it permitted him as many wives as he chose to have—a "privilege granted to no other believer" (33:50–52). But for all that, Muhammad does not appear either self-aggrandizing or particularly concerned with personal wealth, either at Medina, when he possessed it, or at Mecca, when he did not. The Prophet's wives—their exact number appears somewhat uncertain, perhaps as many as thirteen—represent a different issue, one dear to later Christian polemicists who found ample material in the hadith to paint the Prophet of Islam as a sensualist with an eye and a taste for women. As one famous hadith put it, "When it comes to this world (*al-dunya*), women and perfume have become dear to me," to which is quickly added, "but my heart's delight is in prayer."

Whatever the precise truth of all these reports, Muhammad was clearly no ascetic. He was neither excessive nor abstemious in his conduct, a rather remarkable trait in a man who knew both poverty in his early years and extraordinary worldly success in his middle life. "I am but a mortal like you," he is made to say in the Quran (18:110), and both the Quran and the sunna confirm that assertion. Nor did Muhammad preach to others any discernible degree of voluntary self-restraint or self-denial with respect to the legitimate pleasures of life.

This World and the Next

If the Prophet of Islam was a "moderately sensual man" in person, his religious priorities were more radically defined, at least as they issue from the Quran. The Quran has a strong sense of the distinction between "this world" (*al-dunya*) and the "next world" (*al-akhira*). "Know," the Quran says (57:20), "that the life of this world is only a frolic and a mummery, an ornamentation, boasting and bragging among yourselves, and lust for multiplying wealth and children. It is like rain so pleasing to the cultivator for his vegetation which sprouts and swells, and then begins to wither, and you see it turn to yellow and reduced to chaff. There is severe punishment in the Hereafter, but also forgiveness from God and acceptance. As for the life of this world, it is no more than the merchandise of vanity." More, our desires are often displaced: "You want the frail goods of this world, but the will of God is for the other world"

(8:67). There is no necessary contradiction between the realms; it is simply that the next world is where judgment will be passed on our use of the goods of this world—there that those who have used them well will find their place of reward, and those who have used them ill, their punishment (see II/10).

The Quran's teachings differ little in this regard from the Gospels', even though the exemplars in the two instances may be sending somewhat different messages by their personal conduct. And though both men had the same concern for ritual purity—the Jew Jesus arguably somewhat less than the more "Jewish" Muhammad—neither redrew the strict lines between the sacred and the profane that are found in the Torah. If the Torah looked on this life as a dangerous place, it was not by reason of its attractions but because its clustered but clearly marked land mines of impurity threatened (apparently) both God and humans. The Jew, properly cautious of where the dangers lay, was free to enjoy the rest of the terrestrial landscape. The Christian and the Muslim were under a different kind of restraint, as we shall see.

Although the distinction between this world and the next is drawn in the Quran, each with its own set of values, it is not fully fleshed out. The sins of this world seem to be chiefly of the spirit: lack of trust in God, lack of generosity toward the poor and needy. Intoxicating wine is prohibited (2:219)—though it is served in Paradise (47:15)—and this is new; likewise forbidden are certain foods, most notably pork (5:3), and this is not. Judaism had gone there before, though the Muslim food menu is far less restrictive than the Jewish one. In addition, the Muslim had the example of the Prophet, which was, as already noted, not entirely unambiguous when it came to the licit things of the world.

The Beginnings of Muslim Asceticism

What prompted the first Muslims to separate themselves from their fellows by practicing asceticism (*zuhd*), that is, a lifestyle with a notable degree of self-denial, appears to be a sense of contradiction between the increasingly successful and extravagant ways of many Muslims and the general simplicity and otherworldliness of the quranic message. That disparity did not seem to bother Muhammad himself, who suffered neither pangs nor nostalgia over his Meccan poverty, though the prosperity enjoyed by him and his companions at Medina was merely a thin shadow of what followed in the first century of Islam. There appear, in any event, here and there among the persons known to us in that first century, some few individuals who "withdrew" from contemporary society, not in the manner of the Christians' headlong flight into the wastes of Egypt but more cautiously and circumstantially. A number of them bore the title of Sufi.

The word "Sufi," with its derivation from *suf*, "wool," or "woolen cloak," has loosed a broad wave of speculation about the possible Christian origins of the Muslim phenomenon. A distinctive woolen cloak, though such may also have been worn by the poor and prisoners in Muslim society, converts rather neatly into the rough monastic habits worn by Eastern Christian monks with whom both Muhammad and his followers were well acquainted: pre-Islamic Arab poetry knew about wandering male and female monks. The Quran, or perhaps just its language, is ambivalent on the subject of Christian monks and monasticism (*rahbaniyya*). A famous verse has God remarking that after sending earlier prophets, he sent Jesus "and gave him the Gospel, and in the hearts of those who followed him, We placed compassion and kindness. And monasticism, they created it, which had not been prescribed for them by Us except for seeking the pleasure of God; yet they did not observe it as it should have been rightly observed" (57:27).

The meaning, and so the translation, of the bit of the verse beginning "And monasticism . . ." remains uncertain. Is "monasticism" in parallel with "compassion and kindness," a virtuous practice begun by the Christians of their own volition, or is "monasticism" contrasted with what immediately precedes, as a blameworthy human innovation? In Arabic the verse yields both meanings, and its inherent ambiguity is reflected in early Muslim comments on it. We cannot say which is the more probable interpretation, but most commentators ended by reading the verse in a pejorative sense, namely that monasticism was a Christian innovation, unrequired—perhaps even undesired—by God. It is no surprise then that there soon began to circulate a tradition on the subject attributed to Muhammad himself. "No monasticism in Islam," the Prophet is reported to have said.

Christian-inspired or not, there was, as it turned out, a monasticism of sorts in Islam. The early individuals identified as Sufis voluntarily repudiated or withdrew from the life lived by most ordinary Muslims by sharply reducing their material possessions and by adopting practices of self-denial, fasting, for example, in ways that far exceeded those prescribed in the Quran.

Certain devotional practices characterized the early Muslim pietists (see below), but their asceticism chiefly concerns us here. The virtue that was their principal goal is best resumed in the Arabic word *tawakkul*, or "trust in God." It meant placing oneself completely in the hands of God, "like a corpse in the hands of its washer," a phrase and a notion not very different from Ignatius of Loyola's advice to his companions to be "much like a corpse" when it came to the will of God, to have in short no desires of one's own. A Sufi who had achieved this was in fact a "mendicant" (*faqir*), literally "a poor man," or a "child of the moment" (*ibn al-waqt*), according to another dramatic phrase. The early Sufis strove to be indifferent not in the manner of Stoic *apatheia*, a state of being immune to affect that required an active regimen; rather, they were careless of them, as careless as "the birds of the air" or the "lilies of the field," Jesus' own exemplars of God's providing the wherewithal for his creation.

We know little besides some biographical details about the earliest Muslim Sufis, but we can observe almost immediately the differences and similarities between them and their Christian monastic contemporaries, of whom they must generally have been well aware. There was no Muslim flight to the wilderness; their ancestors had just recently come in from the wildernesses of Arabia. The cities of the new Islamic empire were filled not with pagans and paganism but with Jews, Christians, and Muslims of their own faith. Sufis by and large remained in the cities: their "flight" was personal and interior. Nor did their practices of self-denial have the fiery ascetic edge so notable in the Christian holy men and women of the Middle East. Muslim Sufis practiced asceticism, to be sure, occasionally of a severe type, but it was always more occasional, more temporary, and more self-forgiving than its Christian counterpart. One reason may be that it passed far more quickly from an end to a means. Sufi asceticism found its mystic vocation far more quickly than did the Christian version of self-denial.

Sufi Convents: Khanqah, Ribat, Zawiya

There are numerous scholastic tracts in Arabic on the theory and practice of Sufism (*tasawwuf*), on Muslim ascetical and mystical theology, as they might be called in Christianity, but for most Muslims the reality of Islam was the *tariqa*, or brotherhood, into which Sufis began to assemble themselves. As in Christianity, the earlier eccentric "hermit" saints of Islam came to Sufism as a social enterprise, with the various community houses that were the counterparts of the Christian monastery.

In Christianity, as we have seen, the cenobitic life may have been more sustainable in the depths of the wastelands than the eremitic, but the *koinobion* soon developed its own moral character with obedience to a superior, and later to a rule, as its most highly prized virtue. In Islam, Sufis seem originally to have come together under one roof by reason of the attraction of a single master, with the master and his circle often moving from place to place. In the end, these circles became more stationary, with a fixed abode variously called a *khanqah*, *ribat*, or *zawiya*, a *tekke* among the Turks, and a *dargah* in the Persianized Sufi circles of India.

The khanqah, the Sufi convent or lodge, first appeared in an Islamic religious context in the tenth century. It had its origins on the eastern edges of Iran—the word itself is Persian—where it may have owed something to residences for the Manichaean elect. The word, and perhaps the institution, was borrowed by Islamic sectaries. By the early eleventh century, however, the

Sufi Abu Said (d. 1048) was already drawing up rules for Sufis living in a khan-qah, and in short order the khanqah was a recognized institutional ingredient in what was emerging as normative Sunni Islam. The khanqah was introduced into Egypt in 1174 by Salah al-Din as part of his program to reappropriate that land from Ismaili Shiism.

The charter documents for the founding of khanqahs indicate that they were intended as places where Sufis could live, pray, and pursue their vision of a mystical vocation in common, under a rule that stipulated their behavior and a sheikh who guided their spiritual progress. As it evolved, the khanqah be-came a more public institution, with the characteristics of a Friday mosque—a minaret and a pulpit for Friday sermons—so that what began simply as a Sufi residence with an oratory or prayer hall eventually became a mosque with boarding facilities for Sufis. As the "normalization" of Sufism proceeded in Sunni Islam, these became madrasas as well: by the mid–fourteenth century, khanqahs had spaces where sharia was taught.

> **Note:** There is ample evidence that there were khanqahs for both men and women in medieval times. The females may have been older women, many of them widows and poorer than their male counterparts. Though socially somewhat different, the women practiced the same *dhikr* exercises (see below) as the men, had a religious guide of their own, a sheikha, and even had their own prayer leaders and preachers.

The ribat had its own transformational history. At one point it was a forti-fied structure built for defensive purposes along the coasts of the Abode of Islam. This military side of the ribat is strikingly in evidence in North Africa, where just such places were matrices for the movements of the fanatical Almoravids (see below). In the Middle East, however, the ribat became a hostel for poor and needy men and women and even, in time, for the professional poor, the Sufi faqirs.

The zawiya, the Perso-Indian dargah, was an altogether more personal place. It was generally built for a specific Sufi holy man and his followers. The zawiya became a sort of "religious house," the home residence of a single tariqa, often with the saintly founder entombed, more or less grandly, on the premises.

The Sufi Orders

The point of Sufi associations, like their counterparts in Christianity and Judaism, was essentially the imitation of and instruction by a recognized holy man. In the tenth century communal Sufism was a vocation for the few and the elite. There was no question at first of rules or a formal way of life. Tasawwuf was everywhere different, everywhere centered on a recognized master whose task was to show forth the Sufi's intimate union with God rather than to explain or define it. As Ghazali was later to remark, the Sufi life "cannot be learned but only achieved by direct experience, ecstasy, and inward transformation."

By the thirteenth century, the system had become transformed and the movement's elitist aspects yielded to a more general membership. It was then that the greatest and most prolific Sufi "orders" came into existence, each with many spiritual offspring of its own: the Qadiriyya, founded by Abd al-Qadir al-Jilani (d. 1166); the Mevlevis, founded by Jalal al-Din Rumi (d. 1273) and the Shadhiliyya, which takes its name from Abu al-Hasan al-Shadhili (d. 1258). The teaching had become institutionalized into a doctrine and method, and the life of those living in the community was governed by a rule, as the influence of the Muslim legal tradition began to manifest itself. Tariqas now had formal identifications validated by a chain of masters going back to the holy man who was its "founder," or better, its anchor, since it is transparently clear that none of the early friends of God intended to "found" anything. Finally, in the fifteenth century, under the Ottomans, tasawwuf became a fully articulated system of distinct and characteristic "religious orders," both popular and corporate in character, with an emphasis on both "membership" and the now full-blown cult of the saintly founder.

As we have seen in the case of Christianity, the rule governing the community of ascetics can be either constructed, as it was in the case of a Basil or a Benedict, or else, as in the case of the Franciscans, inspired directly by the living example of the founder. Sufi orders almost universally attempted to follow the second paradigm. The sainted man who stood at the head of the file of Sufis was not so much a founder, as has been said, as a paragon or paradigm around whom followers collected in the original khanqahs in the hope of sharing, by association and imitation, his baraka, the blessing or grace he possessed. The rule evolved from an attempt to recollect and emulate at least his behavior. But two things must be noted. The rule did not come from the saint, as it did in Christianity, and it required no one's formal approval or approbation. In Christianity, there was no "order" until it was approved, and, in the West, approved by the highest authority, the bishop of Rome.

If the founder of a Christian religious order possessed a baraka, as they were generally thought to since the Church later formally canonized almost all of them as saints, the best that could be hoped was that it might be shared through the agency of the rule. But the charisma disappeared with the saint: Francis of Assisi was followed by Brother Elias among the Franciscans, Ignatius of Loyola by Father Diego Lainez as the head of the Jesuits. In Islam it was quite otherwise. The saint's baraka was a spiritual gift that could be transferred, like episcopal powers in Christianity and those of the Shiite Imam in Islam (which may in fact have influenced the evolution of this Sufi belief), to a designated successor. Thus the baraka of the founding father passed down to his order, preeminently to his successor as sheikh or master who served as its mediator, but also in a lesser yet no less real degree to all the tariqa's members. Its passage was marked by a series of rituals and guaranteed by the *silsila*, or spiritual chain, that passed, like the isnad of the hadith, unbroken from the founder to the newest recruit.

Both the baraka of the founder and the rule that attempted to capture it in practice were institutionalized within the convent, particularly in the order's mother house. It was in that zawiya, as it was most often called, that the sainted founder was ordinarily buried, his tomb was venerated, and his spiritual descendants carried on the ascetical and mystical practices he had begun. This and the other Sufi convents were built and supported, like Islam's mosques and madrasas, by the type of pious foundation called *waqf* (see II/4), and the externals at least of the life prescribed for the Sufis who dwelled there were set down in the charter document.

The Sufi initiate took an oath of allegiance (*baya*, the same word used for the pre-Islamic allegiance oath to the tribal sheikh and then to the earliest caliphs) to the founder of the order and to his present-day earthly successor and deputy, the current link in the spiritual chain that led uninterrupted back to the saintly founder. The initiate in a Christian religious order made three permanently binding vows to God: one of personal poverty, one of celibacy, and one of obedience to the rule, as expressed in the will of the superior. The difference between the Christian monk and the Sufi becomes clearest precisely in this matter of the oath/vow. The Sufi swore allegiance to an individual, the monk to a rule, or an ideal. Even more telling, perhaps, was the fact that the Sufi initiate received, again at the baya, the *wird*, or prayer formulary proper to his order. Part of the wird was like the monks' office and would be recited in common and in public at the dhikr of the tariqa (see II/9). But part too was personal and secret. The secret formulary was imparted to the Sufi initiate, expanded by degrees, and would become complete on the occasion of his final oath of allegiance. Members of a zawiya met regularly for a "session" (*majlis*), where besides the prescibed liturgical prayers (*salat*), the dhikr and the wird were performed, the latter often with the help of a Muslim "rosary," a beaded cord called a *subha* (see I/1). Sometimes there was a common meal eaten either in silence or while listening to spiritual reading.

Sufi tariqas had immense popular appeal in Islam, not least because they were a social and spiritual reaction to the increasingly clerical and legal character of what had come to be official Islam, which was dominated by a rabbinate with powerful economic, social, and political connections. Functionally, the Sufi orders filled many of the same roles as the Christian clergy generally in the medieval West. Like the diocesan or local clergy of the Western Church, the Sufi "brethren" (*ikhwan*) were drawn from and remained close to the local community and its people, and they offered, like their Western clerical counterparts, diverse spiritual and corporeal services to their fellow Muslims.

Their dhikrs in town and countryside provided an ongoing liturgy with an emotive, dramatic, and mystical content not present in the daily salat, which was, in essence, a private devotion. Finally, the tombs of holy Sufis became, as we have already seen (II/6), a rich source of blessings (*barakat*) and graces (*karamat*). What the dead saint delivered from beyond the tomb, so too could the living sheikh of the tariqa as the recipient of the founder's own charismatic karamat. Both were channels through which blessings, favors, and protections against ills and tragedy might flood to the ordinary Muslim. The Christian Church directed those blessings through the highly institutionalized and de-personalized sacramental system; Sufism accomplished the same end through its personalized and decentralized rituals celebrating the friends of God, both living and dead.

Sufis in the Service of Islam: Chishtis and Bektashis

The Sufi tariqa known as the Chishtiyya had its remote origins in the migration of a holy man named Ibn Ishaq from his native Syria to the town of Chisht near Herat in Afghanistan. Ibn Ishaq was linked back to the Prophet by a typical silsila, and he in turn grounded a new Sufi tradition in eastern Islam. Among his disciples, the first to establish himself was the Chishti eminence Muin al-Din, the seventh in a line from Ibn Ishaq, who took up residence at Ajmer sometime around 1200. By his death in 1236 his reputation for piety was immense, and his tomb at Ajmer became the magnetic center from which the Chishti tariqa spread.

The early Indian Chishtis kept their distance from the rulers of the Delhi sultanate (1192–1398), the first Muslim polity in India, but they were closely and centrally controlled by their own sheikhs. The sultan Muhammad ibn Tughluq (r. 1324–1351) had other views on the popular and influential tariqa, however, and he mandated the spread of the Chishti hierarchy across the breadth of his lands. Under this new regime, the central authority of the order broke down and each local "house" went its own way. At Delhi meanwhile, Ibn Tughluq and his successors extended to the Chishtis their affluent patronage, which meant, as it usually did, considerable royal investment in the order's shrine tombs (*dargah*), particularly those of Muin al-Din and the next great Chishti eminence, Nizam al-Din (d. 1325), with the expected consequence of increased pilgrimage to those newly adorned and magnified sites.

If some Chishti sheikhs were used to undergird the sultanate in Delhi, others served to legitimize regimes that had declared their independence of Delhi in the Deccan, Bengal, and Gujarat. And the Mughuls who succeeded them were, for all their religious eclecticism (see I/5), little different in their observance of the rituals of popular piety that flowed from the profound and influential Sufi presence in the Muslim lands of India. Akbar (r. 1556–1605), the greatest of the Mughul princes, made fourteen pilgrimages to Muin al Din's shrine at Ajmer.

What distinguished the Chishtis from their fellow Sufis and made them so reluctant to take and hold the royal hand was their poverty: they completely rejected property ownership and lived entirely on alms. "Trust in God" was their byword, a trust that permitted them to accept initiates even before the latter converted to Islam: formal conversion should follow spiritual conversion, they felt. Their accommodating attitude made the Chishtiyya enormously popular in India's pluralistic religious environment. Both their mystical theology, with its natural inclination toward an Ibn Arabi–type pantheism (see II/9), and their relaxed posture—what many would call carelessness—toward the niceties of Islamic observance fashioned the Chishti tariqa into a kind of osmotic surface through which local Hindu practices and beliefs passed into popular Islam and, of course, eased the way for Hindus themselves to become Muslims.

Another Sufi accommodation with similar results took place in the Ottoman Balkans. Sufism ran through the Ottoman domains in as many varieties as Christianity, but the dominant tariqa in the Balkans, and in Turkish Anatolia, during the fourteenth to the eighteenth century, was that of the Bektashis. Though the officially sanctioned version of Sunni Islam favored by the Ottomans was taught in the madrasas supported by the sultans, these essentially urban institutions were far outnumbered by the tekke, as the Turkish Sufis called their khanqahs. These popular folk lodges gave little formal attention to either theology or the mysticism that characterized earlier Sufism; the Bektashis never encountered a belief or a practice they didn't like. In the more rural and provincial areas of the Abode of Islam, of which the Balkans were a prime example, their tekkes became the equivalent of the parish church, and its leader, the *baba*, the local clergyman.

The Bektashis had a curious history. Their origins seem unmistakably Shiite, in their adulation of Ali and his family for instance, and associated in some manner with the Qizilbash, the "Redheads" who eventually emerged as the rulers of Shiite Iran, the Ottomans' most intransigent enemy. The Bektashis nonetheless declared themselves Sunnis, at least in the officially Sunni Ottoman Empire, and the Ottomans, pragmatists as usual, accepted them as such. The Ottomans may have been being politically prudent as well. The Bektashi dervishes had forged a close association with the Janissaries, the Ottomans' elite military selected out of the devshirme levies (see I/8), and when the Janissaries came to their bloody end in 1826, the Bektashis disappeared with them. By then, of course, the Balkan peoples were already attempting to separate themselves from the Ottoman Empire, but for the previous four centuries, the eclectic and accommodating Bektashis, organized in their rural lodges under the direction of their often highly charismatic babas, were the single most potent force for the propagation of Islam in the Christian Balkans.

Although the Bektashi influence was paramount in propagating Islam in Bulgaria and Albania, it was less so in Bosnia, at least on the evidence available from the urban landscape. Bosnian Islam was more traditional and more orthodox (as Islam understood that word) than that being spread by the Bektashis elsewhere—a Turkish visitor in the mid–seventeenth century described the Bosnian Muslims as "God-fearing people, of pure, upright, and untroubled faith"—and we see why. The first tekke in Sarajevo, built before 1463, belonged to the Mevlana order made famous by Jalal al-Din Rumi, and another built in 1500 was to house members of the Naqshabandi order. The Turkish traveler referred to above counted forty-seven tekkes—along with more than a hundred mosques—in Sarajevo alone when he passed through in 1660. More were scattered through the countryside, but apparently very few were founded or manned by compliant Bektashi dervishes.

The Chinese Rites

The Chishtis in India and the Bektashis in Anatolia and the Balkans readily adapted, as we have seen, to local, non-Muslim religious circumstances, and this supple willingness to accommodate undoubtedly made them successful agents in eventually effecting the conversion of much of the local population to Islam. Similar success seemed to be beckoning the Jesuit missions in China in the seventeenth century. Unlike the Muslim Sufis, however, the Jesuits appealed not to the masses but to the elites. Under the leadership of Matteo Ricci (d. 1610), who entered China with great difficulty, the few Jesuits there attempted to master the intricacies of Chinese language and learning; to become, in effect, mandarins. The Chinese were modestly flattered, but what won their abiding interest was the revelation of European science. Maps were the key that first unlocked China to the Christian mission, particularly a map that convincingly demonstrated to the Chinese that, contrary to their firm belief, there were other, and great, powers on the face of the earth. The Jesuits' maps, and their considerable scientific learning, won the foreign Christians a hearing.

Although the Jesuits' own assimilation to Chinese secular culture posed no problems, the Confucian cast to many Chinese beliefs and practices did raise ideological questions for the missionaries. Did Chinese and the Christians worship the same God, their "Lord of Heaven" or "Sovereign Lord"? Was the veneration of Confucius and their own ancestors a compromise of Christian religious precepts or merely the acquiescence in traditional cultural practices? The Jesuits thought the latter and allowed their converts to call on God with the traditional names and continue their time-honored practice of venerating Confucius and their ancestors. The Jesuits had Christian rivals, however, in the Dominicans and Franciscans who entered China after them and were also proselytizing among the Chinese. The Friars protested the Jesuit accommodations, and the case went to Rome.

The issue was placed before the papal ministry called the Congregation for the Propagation of the Faith, which heard the Dominican case and condemned the Chinese rites in 1645, only to reverse itself in 1656. The Jesuits continued their work and converts became more numerous. The emperor Kangxi seemed more than favorably inclined, and in 1692 he issue a decree noting that "the Europeans are very quiet . . . do not commit crimes and their doctrine has nothing in common with that of the other sects of the empire nor has it the tendency to excite sedition." Consequently, the Christian missionaries and their converts were not to be opposed or prevented from performing their devotions. Rome was still not convinced, however: it seemed to many that Confucianism was not a philosophy, as the Jesuits maintained, but a religion. Pope Clement XI thought so. In decrees he issued in 1704, followed by a formal bull in 1715, he condemned the prayers and rituals sanctioned by the Jesuits in China and forbade anyone claiming to be a Christian to perform them, either in public temples or at their own domestic shrines.

The papacy had made a decision, and the Jesuits and the other religious orders, who had come around to the Jesuit way of thinking on the issue, had to submit, even though the bull was a fatal blow to the Christian missions in China. News of the papal decision eventually reached court circles in China and Kangxi reacted. "I have never seen a document so full of nonsense," he announced in 1721. "To judge from this [papal] proclamation, their religion is no different from other small, bigoted sects of Buddhism or Taoism. . . . From now on, to avoid further trouble, Westerners should not be permitted to preach in China."

Christian and Muslim Religious Orders

A Sufi tariqa was essentially a collection of local chapters bound together by their common devotion to a single saintly founder, from whom they derived both their legitimacy and their spiritual privileges. The Western religious orders, monks, friars, and clerks regular, all formed societies closely regulated within the Church they served, and many of them were, no less than the Church itself, international in scope. The Western Christian orders were legitimized by formal papal approval of their rule and organization and they were regulated by the norms of canon law; they were controlled from Rome through a superior general who resided there and internally through visitations and general chapters. Islam had no supreme spiritual authority like the pope, nor did the tariqas have elected officials. The sheikh's authority was charismatic and permanent, not attributed and temporary, like that which prevailed in Christian monastic communities, and his jurisdiction was local.

Muslim rulers, like the Ottoman sultans, who also claimed the title of caliph, attempted to control the tariqas by appointing a "sheikh of sheikhs" to serve as a liaison between them and the orders, but the office was never successful. The sheikhs and their followers in the tariqas were essentially a local phenomenon grounded in popular support, and though the government might squeeze the waqf endowments that supported them, it had no way to limit or undermine the tariqas' authority.

The Western Church could dispose its religious orders when and where it pleased, to proselytize the nonbelievers in newly opened lands, for example—as the Franciscans did in the New World and the Jesuits in the Far East—or to combat the Church's enemies at home—as the Dominicans did the Albigensians in the south of France and relapsed Jewish and Muslim converts in Spain (see I/5) and as the Jesuits did Protestants in southern Germany. Indeed, the Jesuits, who took a particular fourth vow of obedience specifically to the pope, were founded precisely to provide the Holy See with a rapid response force. The Sufi orders, though they generally recognized the political authorities under whom they lived, did not serve them, and their relations with Islam's other spiritual elite, the ulama, were often antagonistic. The ulama never explicitly condemned the Sufis' striving for a closer, more personal relationship with God—the Sufis' links with the Prophet were perhaps too strongly forged. But the more conservative among them were often outspoken in their condemnation of Sufi practices, the dhikrs that included music and dance, for example (see II/9), and the Sufis' often extravagant veneration of the sainted dead (see II/6).

Suppression

The religious orders of both Christendom and the Abode of Islam were prestigious organizations, often wealthy, and always powerful—in Islam by reason of their popular support and their independent spiritual authority; in Christianity because of their sophisticated, flexible organization and their freedom from local control. In the West that wealth and power was sometimes seen as a threat by local bishops who had little or no control over these international bodies, and by local princes and magistrates who were often disturbed by the orders' papal allegiance. In Islam, by the nineteenth century the tariqas constituted a broadly based popular movement whose ideals were in fundamental disagreement with those of the emerging secular regimes in the Middle East. In both venues fear led to suppression. We have already seen, for example, the pressures brought to bear by Philip IV of France to effect the suppression of the Order of the Knights Templar in 1312; and how the Jesuits, who were regarded as equally powerful in their heyday, suffered dissolution at the hands of the state in Portugal, France, and Spain until 1773, when Pope Clement XIV was prevailed on to suppress them worldwide.

Almost from their first appearance in Islam, the tariqas were under attack by both the political authorities, who eventually came to guarded terms with most of them, and the ulama, who never did. By the nineteenth and early twentieth centuries the latter's opposition had grown so strong that many of the Sufis' most public practices and rituals—which were denounced as "innovation" (*bida*) (see I/5)—were banned. Sufism was itself suppressed by the new Turkish Republic in 1925, and elsewhere both traditionalists and modernists grew increasingly critical of Sufism. The tariqas seemed ill suited to the progressive and increasingly secular notions emerging in the colonial regimes and their independent successors in the new nation-states of the former Dar al-Islam. Neither did Islamic Fundamentalism, which above all seeks authenticity, find room for Sufism in its imagined vision of an authentic Islamic state.

Jewish Brotherhoods in Galilee

Their association with Islam seems to have drawn some Jews closer to Sufi ideals of communion with God, particularly to the kind of asceticism Judah Halevi thought was foreign to Judaism. This is one conclusion, at any rate, that may be drawn from Bahya ibn Paquda's *Duties of the Heart*, an eleventh-century Jewish ethical treatise (written in Arabic) with a marked interest in asceticism. But there were similar currents visible elsewhere among the Jews that had nothing to do with Islam. In the twelfth and thirteenth centuries, for example, Jewish pietist groups in Germany were also advocating ascetic practices alien or unknown to earlier Jews.

None of this seems particularly institutionalized. Where ascetic practices, mystical goals, and some degree of community organization more visibly came together was Safad, the center of Jewish Kabbala in the sixteenth and seventeenth centuries (see II/9). Despite its economic prosperity as a textile center, Safad was never more than a small town—there were no more than ten thousand Jews in all of Palestine in the mid–sixteenth century—and yet the Jews there divided themselves into numerous different congregations: Sephardis from Spain, Ashkenazis from Europe, and Mustarabim, "wanna-be Arabs" in the Arabized Hebrew of the day, that is, Arabic-speaking Jews from Palestine and the vicinity. It was in this closed but sectarian environment that adepts of Safad's chief cottage industry, Kabbala, began to organize themselves into *haburoth*, or "brotherhoods." Unlike synagogue communities, however, which were constituted along ethnic lines, the haburoth collected around recognized spiritual leaders, masters of the Kabbala, much as contemporary Sufi tariqas did around their sheikhs.

Apart from reverence for their master and shared mystical goals, the members of a Safad haburah were linked by a loose set of "rules of piety" (*hanhaqoth*), which, although not nearly so formalized as the rules of either a Christian religious order or a Sufi tariqa—the members of the haburah did not, after all, live under the same roof—provided discipline and spiritual guidance for the members. Great self-restraint was recommended in matters of food— "Your table will serve as an actual altar upon which you slaughter your evil inclinations"—as well as sexual restraint by practicing the same "modesty of the eyes" that Ignatius of Loyola was prescribing for his contemporary Jesuits: "Acquire the habit of always keeping your eyes cast down so that you do not chance to gaze upon a woman forbidden to you." Members were told to fast on Thursdays and to refrain from meat and wine on Sundays, the Christians' holy day; to speak Hebrew with the "associates"; and to confess their transgressions of the "rule" publicly in what appears to be a general chapter of the brethren.

Saints without Rules: The Hasidim

Kabbalah was a Jewish alternative to the lawyerly pursuit of God through the dense pages of the Torah and Talmud (see II/9), an alternative the rabbis permitted some of their own but denied the ordinary Jew. To these latter, the Kabbalists' arcane and convoluted understanding of the "reality" behind plain texts and the material world would appear hopelessly difficult, as it was probably intended to be from the outset. But deep within Kabbalah lay the mystic's urge to approach God in a paradoxically more direct way, an urge too powerful to remain concealed within the folds of esotericism. In Islam mysticism became popularized in the Sufi orders; in Christianity by such post-Tridentine clerics as Ignatius of Loyola and Francis de Sales, who in the late sixteenth century brought an easily assimilated and tightly controlled version of the monks' spiritual exercises to the secular clergy and the laity alike. In Judaism, it was the Hasidic movement that in the eighteenth century divested Kabbalism of some of its more esoteric and inaccessible features to render it a kind of popular revelation.

The movement called Hasidism—the *hasid* in Hebrew is the pious man— that appeared in Eastern Europe at the beginning of the eighteenth century was an unmistakable reaction to a series of ills that had befallen the Jewish community and the cure that had been prescribed by the rabbis. There were Jews in Eastern Europe from the early eighth century, but the scattered settlements from the Crimea north to the Baltic were greatly swelled by the Jewish emigrations from Western Europe ignited by crusader zealotry in Germany and France in the eleventh and twelfth centuries, and then by the devastating plague called the Black Death that ravaged Europe in 1348–1349.

Casimir, king of Poland (r. 1333–1370), invited the Ashkenazi or European Jews to settle in his lands, which they did in large numbers. The Jewish settlements east of Germany, in Poland, Galicia, and the Ukraine prospered; they largely governed themselves in a benign political climate.

That period of settlement and growth was followed in the mid–seventeenth century by misfortunes improbable in size and scope. In 1648 Cossack troops plowed with impunity through the helpless Jewish settlements in Poland and the Ukraine. By one estimate, nearly half the Jewish population was wiped out. In the wake of that devastation government support and protection almost entirely disappeared, and the Jewish communities were subjected to the extortionate demands of the state, the Church, and whatever bandits happened to be in the vicinity. Then the Jews were suspected of colluding with the Swedish invaders of Poland in the midcentury and more havoc followed. That was the setting of hopelessness and despair in which the messianic message of Sabbatai Zvi (d. 1676) went abroad from the Middle East into the Jewish settlements in Eastern Europe (see I/2). In the eighteenth century another messiah arose in Poland itself when Jacob Frank (d. 1791) claimed to be Sabbatai's successor and heir. The results were the same: raised expectations of relief from on high, dashed hopes, and, finally, apostasy, Sabbatai Zvi's to Islam, Jacob Frank's more dangerously to Christianity, where he found a ready audience for his tales of the perfidious Jews.

The rabbinic response to these travails from within and without was to circle the wagons even closer. There was salvation only in Torah and Talmud, through a minute legal analysis of texts or a plunge into their esoteric depths in the company of Kabbalah. Those who would not or could not follow those high but narrow roads were condemned to whatever the largely uneducated world of the Jewish peasantry could contrive to solace or save itself, a rich mix of demons and incantation, or magic and miracles.

The adepts and manipulators of these latter arts were generally known as "masters of the name," but one such eighteenth-century holy man was somewhat different. Rabbi ben Eliezer (d. 1760) came to be called, in studied contrast to the contemporary small-bore magicians and miracle mongers, Baal Shem Tov, "Master of the Divine Name," or, in the manner of the time, by the Hebrew acronym Besht. He began his career not very differently from other masters of the name: born of poor parents in a tiny village near the Ukrainian-Polish border; poorly instructed in Torah and, perilously for himself and others, self-taught in Kabbalah; an herbal healer, part-time laborer, and part-time preacher. But in 1736 he began to mine a richer vein. It is difficult to distinguish his thoughts from those of his later, more learned followers, but this is where the nucleus of what eventually came to be called Hasidism or "Pietism" emerged. It was, in brief, a path cut somewhere between learned talmudic legalism and the Kabbalists' sometimes impenetrable esotericism. It rejected both extremes and at the same time devised an acceptable—to its devotees, at any rate—version of each. Like similar movements in Christian Europe on the eve of the Reformation, Hasidism preferred simple devotion over punctilious and erudite observance. Like the Kabbalists, the new pietists saw God everywhere, but now in the simplest of objects and actions. The Besht preached, in that blasted place, a religion of joy: simple, joyous worship, straightforward joyous observance—quite simply, a joyous life.

The Apostolic Succession in Eastern Europe

Many consider the learned Rabbi Dov Baer, called the Maggid or Preacher, the real founder of Hasidism. A disciple of the Baal Shem Tov, Dov Baer played a scholarly and organized Bonaventure to the Besht's Francis of Assisi. His learning was real and serious, profound and genuine enough to attract the attention of other influential rabbis, not all of it benign, to the teachings of the Besht. But at Dov Baer's death in 1773, the various Hasidic communities in Eastern Europe began to go their own ways, each under the guidance and inspiration of its own zaddik, and the history of Hasidism from the nineteenth century to the present has been the story of distinct Jewish communities with a shared ethos, as marked by strict orthodoxy as by their Beshtian inheritance of joyfully finding God in every act and object, but each with a distinct identity of its own. They preserved the integrity of that identity in the first instance by adhering with absolute fidelity to an apostolic succession of *rebbes* in a kinship descent from the founding father: Nahman (d. 1810) of Breslau in the Ukraine; Shneur Zalman (d. 1813) and the Schneersohn family in Lubavitch in Byelorussia; Sholom Roqeah (d. 1855) in Belz in eastern Galicia and Shelomah Halberstam (d. 1886) in Bobova in the western part of that same region; Yitshaq Meir Rothenberg Alter (d. 1866) in Gora Kolwara (Ger) near Warsaw; and Michael Teitelbaum (d. 1841) at Satu-Mare (Satmar) in what was then Hungary and is now Romania, to name only some of the zaddikim revered as founders of Hasidic fraternities.

The spiritual affiliation of each Hasidic community with its sainted founder through the "chain" of his equally blessed successors has been strengthened over time by shared ideals and objectives (often expressed in the literary legacy of the founder), by what became typical ritual practices, as well as by a close (and closed) community life that supported a distinctive lifestyle. That lifestyle is most visibly manifested in a manner of dress. Some elements of Hasidic dress, like dark clothes, head coverings, uncut hair, and prayer shawls with fringes, are simply a matter of following legal prescription. But in other particulars—for example, the size and shape of the head covering, the cut of the clothes, the styling of the hair—males of each Hasidic community effect, like members of Christian religious orders, some version of the style current in the time and place of the founder, fur hat, knickers, and all.

The Habad

One of the most brilliant young scholars attracted to Hasidism at its beginnings was Rabbi Shneur Zalman, who studied in Poland with Dov Baer and
was so learned in both Kabbalah and Talmud—he wrote a highly esteemed
commentary on the *Shulkhan Aruk* (see II/4) at the age of twenty-five—that
he was appointed by Dov Baer to return and confront the growing opposition
to Hasidism that was particularly strong in the yeshivas of Lithuania. From
1772 on, those opponents (*mitnaggedim*) showered excommunications on the
Hasidim. The result was a standoff, though Zalman was imprisoned by the
czar's police after he was denounced to them by the local mitnaggedim.

Zalman's advantage as a polemicist was his erudition, but his ability to think
and write clearly and systematically, most evident in the treatise called *Tanya*,
when seen through the prism of his charismatic gifts, made his particular
brand of Hasidism potent and long-lived. It was called Habad, a Hebrew
acronym for wisdom (*hokmah*), understanding (*binah*), and knowledge (*daat*),
and it rested firmly on the teaching set forth in the *Tanya*, with its stress on the
typical Hasidic themes of God's immanence—"There is no place that is
empty of Him"—which so disturbed the rabbis' traditional understanding of
God's supreme transcendence, and what is called in Hebrew *hitlahavut*, intense feeling about God. District from other Hasidic movements, however,
was the Habad's strong insistence on the power of the intellect in approaching God. In Zalman's unique vision, humankind's divine quality is intellectual
and resides in the brain, which must by our efforts control the animal soul,
which finds its seat in the heart—an insight directly opposite that proposed
by Gregory Palamas and embraced by the mystics of Eastern Orthodoxy
(see II/9).

Though he was inevitably regarded as a zaddik, Shneur Zalman, does not
always appear comfortable in that role, particularly where it seemed to imply
something more than human gifts, as it did in many cases. He preferred the
title rebbe and firmly denied that he possessed the power to work miracles.
His twentieth-century successor, as we shall see (II/10), permitted himself,
with what degree of uneasiness we cannot tell, a far more dramatic, almost
apocalyptic role.

Shneur Zalman's son, who succeeded him, moved Habad's center from
Lithuania to Lubavitch in Byelorussia, where it remained until 1915. From
1915 onward, the Habad headquarters moved from town to town in Russia
and Poland. In 1940 the Habad hierarchy fled the impending war in Europe,
and since then the movement has been based in Brooklyn, where in 1950
Rabbi Menachem Mendel Schneerson (d. 1994) succeeded his father-in-law
as master. Like his predecessor, this rebbe was intent on drawing God's presence into every sphere of human activity, and thus "to sanctify the mundane."

While other Orthodox groups turned protectively inward toward their own salvation, the Habad turned boldly outward to face and convert the world, a world constituted in the first instance of all their fellow Jews, to draw the observant toward the Habad, and to lead the "secular Jew" back to Torah. In their reading of Scripture, the Habad remained resolutely fundamentalist and literalist; yet, with equal resolution, they grasped all the tools of modernity, particularly science.

Like other Hasidic groups, Habad's solidarity was built on an intimate personal connection of each member, and, by implication, of every Jew, with the charismatic person of the rebbe. At the heart of this ostensibly sectarian movement lies a profound universalism: the rebbe is the master of all; the Habad is the authentic Judaism to which all Jews by nature belong. To achieve this, they have constructed, as the Benedictines once did within Christian monasticism, formidable tools to reach outside the cloister of their tightly knit community into the larger world of Jews: schools, publications, and public religious celebrations to which all Jews are invited. Nor should the Gentiles be ignored or neglected; they should be exhorted to abide by the Noahide Commandments (Gen. 9:1–17), which God revealed for their special guidance.

9

Leaping from the Dark into
the Light: Mysticism

MYSTICISM IS here simply understood as the pursuit and achievement of an immediate experience of God. It thus differs both from theology, which tries to understand God through discursive intellectual means, and from the various forms of orthopraxy, which attempt to approach God, to become more godlike, through observant behavior with regard to his Law.

Face to Face with God

The contemplation of God, or to put it in simpler and more startlingly anthropomorphic terms, seeing God face to face, would seem to be an unavailing prospect in religious traditions that held so firmly to God's utter transcendence. But this was not beyond all hope or expectation. From Abraham to Jacob, Moses and thence to Isaiah, certain chosen individuals had had a direct experience of Yahweh. Apart from Abraham, who still had some of the insouciance of Adam and Eve chatting with God, it was an extraordinary and scarifying moment for them all. God was, as a later generation of Christians had it, *totaliter aliter*, "utterly otherly," and the dangers of stepping across the line that separates God's domain from humans' lesser abode is graphically represented in Yahweh's warnings to the Israelites not to approach the mount of Sinai where a theophany was about to occur and in the purity rules that God dictated to preserve the integrity of his holy house (see I/6). Yet Moses went up that mountain, and survived, as did other gifted or daring luminaries throughout biblical history.

More often than not these privileged individuals were prophets elected by God to bear his message, and the experience of God was the reward, or price, of that election. In later times, however, fear of the encounter appears to have subsided somewhat. The experience became less one of confrontation than of transport. The subject, whether Ezekiel or Daniel or Enoch, was carried out of himself, fell into a dream or a reverie or a trance, and then not a single encounter with God but a protracted visionary experience occurred. But whereas Ezekiel was borne aloft by the Spirit of God, the first mortal to have been so blessed, and even stood before the throne of God, Enoch was carried off on a well-charted heavenly journey, at the end of which he stood in God's presence: "Behold, in the vision clouds upheld me . . . and the winds in the vision caused me to fly and lifted me upwards and bore me into heaven. . . . And I looked therein and saw a lofty throne" (1 Enoch 14:8, 18, 20). Enoch lived long before Ezekiel and Daniel, of course, but his extraordinary life experience (Gen. 5:24), which the Jews later understood to mean that he had not died but that God had taken him up alive into heaven, made him an attractive vehicle on which later post-Exilic authors could project their own apocalyptic visions. Many of these accounts of heavenly journeys ended in a witnessing of the End Time (see II/10), but the heavenly travelers from Ezekiel to Enoch to the apocryphal "Esdras" (Ezra) inevitably found themselves before God's throne.

Celestial voyages became a common trope in accounts of a mystical experience—Paul was "caught up to the third heaven" (2 Cor. 12:2) and Muhammad to the seventh—and the terrain the travelers crossed became somewhat stereotyped in a manner that strongly suggests that here, as in the case of the similar "tours of hell," we are more often in the presence of literature than of personal experience. Although several of the Greek counterparts to these heavenly voyages into the realm of the divine, most famously the one described by Plato in his *Phaedrus*, move over the same mythic rather than personal landscapes, a more personal aspect was embedded in the Greeks' reflections on the contemplation of God as well. They believed, some of them undoubtedly on the basis of their own experience, that a human could achieve a vision of the Absolute.

The Beginnings

The monotheists' mysticism did not begin, however, in the halls of academies. For Jews, Christians, and Muslims alike, it started in Scripture, with Moses on Sinai, or the transport of Ezekiel, or in the Gospel account of Jesus' transfigured revelation of his divinity to Peter, James, and John on Mount Tabor (Matt. 17:1–8), or in the Quran's celebrated description of God's shining forth "like a lamp in a niche" (24:35), or perhaps in Muhammad's own miraculous ascension (see I/3). These were only points of departure, however, hints that direct experience of God might be possible. None of the examples suggested that the encounter was the doing of the mortals who achieved it. From beginning to end, the Christian and Muslim traditions held—the Jews' somewhat less certainly—that God bestowed the experience of himself, not the efforts of his creatures, no matter how holy they might be.

The Adepts of Qumran

Even though Christianity presents us with the first concrete evidence of a system that can be identified as Gnostic, that may not be the absolute source of the phenomenon. Traces of that way of regarding the cosmos and humans' role in it appear in an even earlier religious context—the same, in fact, that produced Christianity itself, namely, the largely anonymous apocalyptic and wisdom circles influential in post-Exilic Judaism (see I/1). Some of the evidence for such thinking is fossilized, like the testimony of the Mandaeans, a curiously hybrid sect that still exists, tenuously and uncertainly, in southern Iraq and whose traditional literature shows signs of being still another, in this case Gnostic, outgrowth of the divergent strains of first-century Judaism. Some have professed to see the alleged Jewish roots of Gnosticism in such biblical Apocrypha as the Book of Enoch. Most of the Jewish Apocrypha are, however, so carefully concealed within false names and fictive contexts that we have little idea of historical context for such thinking. Nor do we know much about the actual individuals or circles who were meditating on those ideas of a heavenly wisdom or a heavenly journey.

At Qumran we have just such a historical context, however. On the evidence, the Essenes who lived there show no signs of being mystics, and the community at Qumran may not have been a Gnostic association at all. But its preserved literature, which includes several of the biblical Apocrypha, shows that the members entertained apocalyptic expectations, and that such expect-ations deeply colored their highly privileged reading of both the canonical Jewish Scriptures and the Apocrypha (see II/2). They were, moreover, the likely bearers of that apocalyptic tradition into the nascent Christian community. Qumran, Christianity, and Gnosticism all come together in another interesting context. Patristic sources attribute the origins of Gnosticism to Simon Magus, the Samaritan wonder-worker who was a contemporary of the Apostle Peter (Acts 8:9–24). Simon's own teacher was Dositheus, who was connected with John the Baptist, an eschatological preacher who may himself have been raised an Essene.

The Celestial Chariot

If this path, however ill defined, leads from apocalyptic Judaism to Christian Gnosticism, the connection between the mystical element implicit in apocalypticism and the observance-focused Pharisaic and rabbinic strain in Judaism is almost totally invisible. But there is reason to think that the Pharisees—

Josephus is the best example—deliberately underplayed this apocalyptic side of Judaism, particularly for the benefit of the Romans. We cannot, at any rate, get at the precise beginnings of Jewish mysticism since what pass as the earliest mystical texts date from the ninth century. There is good reason, however, to think that what those texts were talking about took place much earlier. We have, for example, an account of Yohanan ben Zakkai (d. ca. 80 C.E.), a crucial figure in the passage from Pharisaic to rabbinic Judaism (see I/2), engaged in a matter-of-fact discussion of common mystical and apocalyptic themes. This and other clues point to the rabbis of the post-70s era as the starting point of express speculation about the possibility of more intimate contact with God. The divine enthronement on a mythical chariot (*merkabah*) described in the first chapter of Ezekiel was the point of departure for such thoughts, and the various heavenly journeys through the palace-temples (*heykaloth*) described in the apocryphal literature of Second Temple Judaism led the way. Merkabah and heykaloth are the twin poles around which early Jewish mysticism unfolds, all of it in otherwise highly legalistic and observant rabbinic circles, from the second to the tenth century in the Middle East, when they were supplanted by the system known as Kabbalah then emerging in France and Germany (see below).

"Four Who Attempted to Enter Paradise"

To face God's majesty was an always dangerous and sometimes reckless enterprise, as many incidents in the Bible attest, but so too was talking about it. The rabbis counseled care in discussing the "Mysteries of the Chariot," as they called that Ezekiel-inspired vision of God, with the young, the unlettered, or anyone unlikely to understand. It is by no means certain that speculation about Ezekiel's mysterious celestial chariot led to experiential mysticism. There is a good deal of surmise in the preserved merkabah accounts, and there are many descriptions of what happened to the rabbis engaged in that speculation, but there is no sign that any of those rabbis ever attempted to mount the chariot or did anything other than engage in very bold exegesis of the notorious passage in Ezekiel (1:4–28). What *is* certain is that the treatment was esoteric; the Mishnah (Hagigah 2:1; cf. BT Hagigah 14b) strongly recommended that such talk be restricted to the spiritually sophisticated, to circles of mature scholars and adepts who would not misunderstand the radical new way of approaching God. The rabbis were getting somewhat closer to the Burning Bush of God's presence than was comfortable, or safe, and they warned one another to be careful.

At some point, however, the clues begin to point toward Akiba, the rabbi associated with the insurrection against Rome in 132–135 C.E. led by Bar Kokhba. Akiba's myth, which is enshrined in the Mishnah supplement called Tosefta, recounts in parable form the story of the four rabbis who "attempted to enter *pardis*," a term that means "park" or "orchard" and may refer either to the celestial paradise or to a royal enclosure generally. Three of the four failed, with grave consequences; but the fourth, Rabbi Akiba, succeeded: "he entered in peace and came out in peace." The parable is obscure, but it seems to describe an experience rather than exegesis and so may mark Jewish spirituality's passage into a true experimental mysticism.

God's Love, God's Body

Rabbi Akiba is enmeshed in another mystical thread: the rise to exegetical prominence of the biblical Song of Songs, Solomon's canticle to erotic love that celebrates in explicit terms the physical qualities of the beloved. The Song of Songs is a rather graphic description of an erotic encounter between a man and a woman, a bridegroom and a bride, but its inclusion in the Bible suggests that the Jews early on were reading it in a figurative or allegorical fashion, just as the Christians later did. The "bride" stands nicely for either Israel or the Church, and "her" various, and considerable, physical attributes have offered a juicily seductive invitation to generations of exegetes to exercise their imaginations. But the Song is mostly about foreplay, it appears, with the actual act of union postponed like an unresolved Wagnerian chord. The Song was perfectly suited, then, to mystical exegesis, and the fact that it was transparently a heterosexual union was merely an additional challenge to the male mystics/exegetes who were attempting to "mate" with an unmistakable male in the person of Jesus Christ. The sounds of gender bending—but not breaking—are unmistakably present throughout the long exegetical tradition of the Song of Songs.

A related phenomenon is the appearance of the curious work called *Shiur qomah*, "The Measurement of the Height," that is, of God's body. Again, its point of departure was the Song of Songs. As just noted, this flavorful erotic poem was a favorite subject of both Jewish and Christian commentary, but the anonymous author of the *Shiur qomah* bypasses both the poetry and the eroticism and offers instead a list of God's members, their often unintelligible names, and their gigantic dimensions. Obviously the grossest form of anthropomorphism is here being stood on its head to reveal something new and profound about the reality of God. It may also have been an experienced reality since the journey to God's throne-chariot began to come together with the "description" of God in the "Measurement" in the phenomenon known as heykaloth or palaces mysticism.

The Palaces

The heykaloth of the stories that have come down to us are understood as the temple-palaces of the planetary spheres through which the mystic must ascend—each one represents a "trial" of knowledge for the adept—in order to reach God's dwelling in the seventh heaven. The journey is described in two preserved works of the period, the *Lesser Heykaloth*, attributed to Rabbi Akiba, and the *Greater Heykaloth*, credited to his disciple Rabbi Ishmael.

As already remarked, the heavenly journey was a commonplace theme in the Jewish apocalyptic literature of Second Temple times, but as it developed, so too did the schematics of the new version. Each planetary palace now had a gate, at which stood an archangel guardian. The adept carried with him various "seals," probably esoteric versions of the name of God, and these enabled him to enter each succeeding palace. We are confronted here with a patently magical scenario for getting results—once within the palace, the voyager got a wish fulfilled—by uttering the correct formula, and this may indeed be the main point, and interest, of these works. The focus shifted, in any event, from an experience of God to the journey thither: the means became the end. In fact, the most complete example of the genre, the *Book of Heykaloth*, which purports to describe the heavenly ascent of the patriarch Enoch, seems to be little more than an anthology of such descriptive set-pieces. If there ever was an experiential mysticism behind these heykaloth texts, it was in the end submerged beneath purely literary concerns and the not inconsiderable charm of the esoteric.

The Book of Creation

Standing uncertainly between the early heykaloth on one side and the thirteenth-century Kabbalah on the other is the work of speculative theosophy called the *Sefer yetzirah*, or *Book of Creation*. It made an early appearance, in the fourth Christian century perhaps, and the work is filled with the kind of half-mythic, half-scientific speculation that characterized much of later Greek philosophy. Its subject is the other "restricted" topic of the rabbis, the Work of Creation. If the merkaba mystics drew their inspiration from Ezekiel, the anonymous author of the *Book of Creation* got his from Genesis. The tract explains the origins of the universe through thirty-two "paths of wisdom" comprising the twenty-two letters of the Hebrew alphabet and the ten basic numbers, the decad. The latter are called *sefiroth* in the text, a name and concept that would have a long history in Jewish mystical circles. The book's views are not entirely surprising. For the Pythagoreans, a Greek philosophical school that had a renewed vogue in late antiquity, numbers were the basic building blocks of the universe. Moreover, the Jews, like many others, expressed both letters and numbers by the same symbols; *aleph*, for example, expressed both the first letter of the alphabet and the first of the ordinal numbers.

Views on the primacy of both language and numbers were already being discussed in other Jewish venues: the Mishnah had said that the world was created by "ten divine utterances" and that the letters of the Hebrew alphabet were the instruments of creation. But the *Sefer yetzirah* took these ideas and

> **Note:** *Gematria* (Gk. *geometria* > Heb. *gimatriyyah*) is the practice of converting Hebrew words into the numerical equivalent of their letters and using the result to elicit an allegorical meaning from the text. This is different from straightforward speculation on the significance of numbers in Scripture, like Philo's or Augustine's meditations on the meaning of the six, or seven, days of creation. Gematria rather excavates the meaning hidden in the name by turning over a text, in a sense, and reading the bar code on its back. The method became a favorite among the Kabbalists as well as Muslim theosophists. The *Book of Creation*, however, never resorts to gematria as such.

expanded them into a systematic presentation whereby the sefiroth were associated with limits (the compass directions, up and down, beginning and end, good and evil), while each letter governed a specific element in each of the three realms of the heavens, time, and the human body. Embedded in the grammar of language, the author maintained, were the laws of nature themselves, the same kind of "natural" religion that induced Abraham to worship the One True God without the benefit of revelation. The *Book of Creation* is about cosmogony, the origin of the universe, and cosmology, its order and arrangement, and very little about God, Israel, or the Covenant. The book is not mystical in any experimental sense of the word, but it gave subsequent generations of mystics the blueprint of an esoteric system of the universe that lay beneath the exoteric biblical account and what amounted to an open invitation to penetrate even deeper into that mystery.

From Christian Asceticism to Mysticism

The Christian quest for direct experience of God differed from its Jewish and Muslim counterparts in that it was, from the beginning, Christ-centered: union with God for the Christian invariably means union with Jesus. The theme of union with Christ was already boldly struck in Paul, whose own personal experience of Jesus on the road to Damascus (Acts 9:3–6) grounded his authority as an Apostle. Paul's letters are filled with expressions depicting the Christian's life, death, and resurrection as occurring "in Christ" and "with Christ." Furthermore, there is Paul's powerful figure of the Christians' constituting the body of Christ (1 Cor. 12:27–28), even being the "members" of a body (1 Cor. 6:15), of which Christ is the head (Eph. 4:15–16). Finally, in sharing in the Eucharist, in partaking of the bread and wine, the Christian is sharing in the body and blood of Christ (1 Cor. 10:16).

The reception of the Eucharist provided matter for spiritual meditation for countless generations of Christians and provoked profound affects in many,

but it was not necessarily a mystical experience in the sense that term is being
used here. The mystic's union with God was both intuitive and sensual and, by
its nature, a rare and unique occurrence. But for all its intuitive and personal
qualities, it was also describable and even explicable; a large body of writing
from the pens of Christians and Muslims professes to describe the experience
of God and direct it into institutional channels that might enable the faithful,
or at least the more spiritually sensitive among them, to achieve it for themselves. That achievement was undergirded by a theory of how union with God
was possible in the first place and then, somewhat more pragmatically, what
the methods by which it might be obtained were. The theory came, not surprisingly, from the Greeks.

The Greek philosophers never believed that askesis in the take-no-prisoners
Christian manner led directly to *theoria*, or contemplation. Rather, self-
restraint, whose perfect state the Stoics called *apatheia*, or the immobilization
of the passions, was the chief aid in pursuing a philosophical life, which the
later Hellenes regarded much in the manner of a religious calling. For Greek
intellectuals the route to contemplation lay not so much through mortifica-
tion of the flesh as through a rigorous intellectual program. The climax of this
ascent from the "low" sciences like physics to the "high" like mathematics—the
degrees of abstraction from matter charted the upward trajectory—reached its
climax in theology, which brought the seeker to a knowledge (*episteme*) of God
(see II/7). Beyond the achievement of episteme, however, remained a gap between the knower and the known that could be crossed only by an intuitive
leap, the "flight of the alone to the Alone," as the philosopher Plotinus (d. 270)
described it. This grasp of the divine was not so much an achievement as a
gift: God reached down and lifted rather than the seeker climbing up into the
presence of the divine.

This was the legacy that lay before the Greek Christian intelligentsia who
sought the high road to God. Even before Antony withdrew to the desert and
set in motion the ascetic currents that eventually flowed into monasticism (see
II/8). Eastern theologians such as Origen (d. ca. 254), who studied Platonism
with the same teacher as Plotinus had at Alexandria, were fashioning a new
ideal for the ascetic Christian, that of the contemplative life.

Whereas the earliest Christian ascetics stressed a simple scriptural meditation,
the imitation of Christ, and the training of the will, such fourth-century
Christian masters of the spiritual life as Evagrius in the East and John Cassian
in the West changed their regard from the will to the intellect and its illumination. At the upper end of the ascetic's "spiritual ladder," whose lower rungs
still consisted of practical asceticism, stood the new ideal of unity with God,
theoria or *theologia*, as it was called in the new Hellenic-inspired vocabulary.
The "purgative way" of the ascetic now led to the "unitive way" of closeness to
God, and finally to the mystics' goal, the "illuminative way" and the reception
of the divine light.

Evagrius (d. 399) of Pontus in northwestern Anatolia was ordained a minor cleric by Basil the Great in Cappadocia and then served under another eminent theologian, Gregory of Nazianzum, in Constantinople. Though it was soon obvious that Evagrius was himself an accomplished theologian, he was neither a model cleric nor even a model Christian—not, at any rate, until he underwent a personal conversion and became a monk in Jerusalem in 383. Next he traveled to the heart of Christian monasticism in the Egyptian wilderness, where he became a disciple of the celebrated ascetic Macarius and wrote most of the works on which his later renown rests. Many of them were theoretical (and occasionally of dubious orthodoxy), but by far the most influential was his *Chapters on Prayer*, which became a handbook of monastic spirituality in Eastern Christendom.

After Origen, who profoundly and, as some said, dangerously influenced him, Evagrius was among the first early ascetics to deliberately connect the practices of Christian monasticism with the chiefly Neoplatonic doctrines being propagated in the academies of late antiquity, an intellectual milieu increasingly familiar to Christians. In Evagrius's Platonic anthropology, humans were souls imprisoned in bodies. The body was useless for the Christian, and the monk's goal was to free the spiritual soul from its toils. According to Evagrius, this was achieved by ceaseless prayer, one of the master motifs of Eastern spirituality. "Prayer," wrote Evagrius, "is a continual intercourse of the mind with God. . . . It is a habitual state of imperturbable calm. It carries to the heights of intelligible reality the mind which loves wisdom."

The language is unmistakably Platonic. The intellect was the divine element in humankind, and only through prayer, inward and highly intellectualistic prayer, did the soul raise itself to God. Evagrius had little need of either Scripture or Jesus in his spirituality. What the monk was striving for, according to Evagrius, was *theologike*. It was preceded by *praktike*, or asceticism, and *physike*, contemplation of the natural world, and was nothing less than the vision of God, described as "light without form, beyond human expression and representation." The Beatific Vision was the achievement of this last stage of the mystic's quest and it brought solemn quietude (*hesychia*) to the adept's soul. Apophatic (ineffable) theology was thus introduced into the mystical discourse and practice of the Church.

Approaching the Unknowable

If the Christian desire for direct experience of God found encouragement in the Gospel story of Jesus' Transfiguration, it rooted its theory of how this was possible in the Genesis account of Creation. It was stated there that God had created Adam "in His own image and likeness" (1:26), a claim not made for the rest of creation, and that he made Adam from the dust of the earth and then breathed into him his own spirit (2:7). Since, according to Paul, we all participate in the life of the "new Adam" who is Christ (1 Cor. 15:45–49), we must all share in God's image, likeness, and life, a conviction powerfully underlined by the theandric nature of Jesus Christ, "true God and true man," as the Council of Chalcedon defined him. This is the conceptual foundation of all Christian mysticism, this analogy of being that bridges the yawning gap between the earthbound this and the ineffable Other.

It was likely God's very ineffability that encouraged humans to approach him. The theologians, whose confidence in knowing anything about God was based on that same analogy of being, understood the Godhead in two basic ways. One was through the approach of supereminence: God was simply human virtue writ large, writ Very Large. Or conversely, God could be understood by the absence of limitation. God was not only Very Good; he was beyond goodness, indeed, beyond being itself. This latter route was the celebrated *via negativa*, the path into nothingness popularized in Christian circles by the anonymous early sixth-century Greek theologian concealed under the name Dionysius the Areopagite, a rather unremarkable gentleman mentioned in passing in Acts 17:34. "God is in no way like the things that have being," Dionysius wrote. "We have no knowledge at all of His incomprehensible and ineffable existence." Many Christian mystics, who had a much more affective view of God than their Muslim counterparts (owing chiefly to the Jesus factor, but with some basis in the scriptural portraits of God as well), found the prospect of the dark atop Sinai, the "cloud of unknowing," as one English mystic later put it, far more inviting than the blinding light of the Transfiguration.

Dionysius offered the Christian not only a convincing notion of what God was (or was not) but an explanation of how to arrive at that understanding. He may have called his work "theology," but that term included for him, as it did for the Eastern Christians generally, both discursive thought and an intuitive grasp of God, in short, what is here being called mysticism. We achieve it, Dionysius says, by leaving behind our concepts of God, by ending what we call thought. Thus, we must go beyond reason, thought, and knowledge. "Beyond the outermost boundaries of the world, the soul is brought into union with God Himself."

The Jesus Prayer

For Christians, asceticism—often a lifetime of asceticism—was the royal road to mysticism, but the way to experience of God could be eased, even hastened, by somewhat more practical steps. Christians and Muslims alike often employed techniques in their mystical quest. Jewish mystical techniques were often pronouncedly formulaic and focused on approaching God, whereas Christians and Muslims employed emotive and physical means to experience God.

Western Christendom's highly institutionalized and more closely monitored spiritual environment did not much favor such techniques, but Eastern Christians were considerably more experimental. Western monastic prayer, for example, the recitation of the Divine Office, was a public and tightly structured community exercise (see II/8); the more idiosyncratic spirituality of the East favored more personal forms of worship, chief of which was the so-called Jesus Prayer.

The Jesus Prayer is a direct address to Christ, generally in the form of "Lord Jesus Christ, Son of God, have mercy on me," though there are both shorter and longer variants. The prayer itself goes far back into Christianity, as might be expected from its simplicity, but its developed use as a Christian mantra did not emerge until the sixth and seventh centuries among the monks of Egypt and Sinai. It is first fully described in the *Three Methods of Prayer* of Simeon, called "The New Theologian" (d. 1022). As a mystical technique, the Jesus Prayer required repeated and rhythmical repetition. Its repetition was guided by a kind of knotted "prayer rope" (*komboskoinion*) obviously related to the telling devices of East Asian spiritual practice, and to the Muslims' subha and the Latin Christians' rosary, which served the same purpose (see I/1). Its regularity was emphasized and enhanced by a consciously rhythmical breathing, another inheritance from the East, which by the thirteenth century had developed a liturgy of its own in Eastern Christendom. The adept was to be seated, head and shoulders bowed, eyes turned down and inward, the gaze directed into the heart or the navel. The breathing was to be regular and rhythmical, brought into coordination with the words of the prayer or, later, the beating of the heart. Finally, the attention, like the gaze, was to be focused inward with the intent of ending thinking, as Dionysius had counseled, and replacing it with the emotive action of the heart.

Hesychasm

One of Evagrius's most prominent disciples was John Climacus (d. 605), a monk of Sinai whose *Ladder of Divine Ascent* stands a world apart from Basil's community-oriented and highly regulated version of the monastic ideal. John's monk strives, in the best Evagrian tradition, for the tranquillity (*hesychia*) of body and mind that invites the divine grace to fill the soul with light from on high. Neither tranquillity nor divine illumination were novel ideas in the fifth century, but they were becoming the centerpieces of monasticism in the East—in Simeon the New Theologian's writings, for example. They erupted into controversy on Mount Athos, a veritable society of monasteries in northern Greece (see II/8), where by the fourteenth century the achievement of hesychia was conditioned by an elaborate set of physical exercises that had less to do with traditional Christian asceticism than with a type of Byzantine yoga: contemplation of the navel, regulated breathing, and the repetitious intoning of the Jesus Prayer. The climax of this regimen was an infusion of the divine light, the same seen by Jesus' disciples on Mount Tabor (Mark 9:2–8; Matt. 17:1–8), and a union with the divine essence—in short, a kind of deification (*theiosis*).

Both the Hesychasts' prayers and their desired experience of God had roots that ran deep back into the Christian tradition. What attracted attention to this particular complex of method and experience were the terms in which that latter experience was expressed and the inexorable bond forged between means and end. The Eastern monks, particularly the hermits of Mount Athos, who were practicing the Jesus Prayer to its fullest extent, claimed that such prayer led to a vision of, and participation in, the uncreated divine light of Tabor streaming from heaven directly into their own navels. Like most attempts at describing a personal experience of the supernatural, this one is probably freighted with too much literalism, and its opponents had great sport characterizing the Hesychasts as *omphalopsychikoi*, or "men with their souls in their belly buttons."

But the issues put before the Christian world by this eye-catching practice of some Eastern monks were complex. In sophisticated theological circles it was easy enough to parody and mock the hermits gazing at their navels in their cells on Mount Athos, but the larger questions they presented to believers were, first, what precisely was the role of prayer in salvation, and, second, how was it possible, if at all, for a limited being to come into direct contact with God's Ineffable Being? It was the latter metaphysical question the opponents of Hesychasm took on and its practitioners chose to defend. The protagonist in this instance was a Greek monk of Calabria, Barlaam, who had come to Constantinople and gained prominence as one of the leading intellectual lights of the patriarchate. He was a staunch defender of Eastern Orthodoxy and wrote numerous works attacking the Western position on the *Filioque*, the phrase the Latins had added to the Nicene Creed suggesting that the Holy Spirit proceeded from the Father *and the Son*. But he conducted the polemic in what was to Eastern theologians a new and very unfamiliar fashion. Barlaam was well schooled in the methods of Western scholasticism and used them effectively against their Latin practitioners. His newfangled approach attracted the unfavorable attention of one of the longtime hermits of Mount Athos, Gregory Palamas (d. 1359), who offered his own views on the matter. Barlaam was not much taken by them and began now more closely to inspect the Athonite practices that were already common knowledge in Eastern circles, namely the practice labeled Hesychasm. He was appalled by what was going on and what was being claimed, and he attacked both practice and theory in writing. At the urging of the patriarch, who had himself been a monk of Athos and a disciple of Palamas, the saintly hermit of Athos responded and the issue was joined.

God's Energies and God's Essence

The Hesychast position leaned heavily, like the Neoplatonic metaphysics that lay behind it, on the venerable analogy of God and the sun. Creation was, in effect, an emanation, an outpouring of God's unlimited goodness, which, like the shining forth of the sun's rays, in no way diminished, it was thought, the source from which they proceeded. The same figure served the Hesychasts. The light they saw was not God himself but his "rays" or, to put it more philosophically, his "energies" (*energeiai*) rather than his essence. This was the heart of the issue: whether it was possible to distinguish between God's essential being and his energies, the playing out or manifestation of his powers or, more generally in this type of discourse, his attributes, and whether one might predicate some degree of reality of these latter. In Christianity, the Platonizing Hesychasts said "yes"; their Aristotelizing opponents said "no." Among the Muslims, who had taken up the same question in a somewhat different guise (see II/7), the Mutazilites, like the Christian Aristotelians, from whom they may have learned this particular lesson, likewise said "No, there is no reality to these so-called attributes of God." The Hanbalis, and after them the majority of Muslims, said "Yes, there is." God's attributes, though distinct from his essence, were, like the light of Tabor that transfigured the Hesychast monks, both eternal and uncreated. This view became Muslim orthodoxy and, in a council held in Hagia Sophia in 1351, Hesychasm was also declared to constitute orthodoxy in Eastern Christendom.

The Hesychast debate, which attracted many others besides Barlaam and Gregory Palamas, also raised the question of the nature and purpose of prayer. According to the general Western understanding, prayer had necessarily to be a prayer of petition, an attempt to bring our will to conform with that of God. In its highest form prayer leads to contemplation, the elevation of the intellect to God. Prayer for Aquinas, as for Barlaam after him, was a habit and, once acquired, it transfigured human actions so that one could be said to pray unceasingly, as the Fathers had taught. Palamas and the Hesychasts thought otherwise. For Palamas, unceasing prayer meant being in constant communion with God, a gift primarily achieved by the ascetic monk since he could pursue the goal of reaching up to God by his unremitting asceticism and have God reach down by his love: the human being transcended and God condescended, as it has been aptly put. At its climax, this prayer achieved actual union with the Creator; the Divine Light from on high literally diffused the human's soul, and the mystic experienced here below the same divine revelation that the saints did in the Afterlife.

Spirituality, Eastern and Western

In a broader perspective, Hesychasm and the opposition it engendered was another phase in the conflict between Eastern and Western Christian spirituality and ecclesiology. Affective and quietist mysticism of the Hesychast type was not unknown in the West: it is present in the spirituality of the Franciscans, the Carmelites, and even in lay movements like that of the "Illuminists," the Alumbrados of sixteenth-century Spain, and even the radical Reformers like the Quakers. Generally speaking, however, this approach to prayer and its effects was either controlled or marginalized. Western mysticism preferred, both officially and unofficially, the more humanistic ideal of intellectual contemplation and to elide professed mystical experience of the divine into personal and hence inimitable phenomena. Those like Barlaam who opposed Hesychasm in the Eastern Church were, many of them, informed by the same humanistic and intellectualistic ideals that were guiding Western Europe into the Renaissance; many of those who most profoundly disagreed with Palamas supported the union of the Churches (see I/6). To affirm Hesychasm as orthodoxy and to identify Eastern Orthodoxy with Hesychasm, as the Eastern Church did in councils in 1341, 1347, and 1351, was to sever another strand of Eastern Christian contact with the West as effectively as if an anathema had been pronounced against humanism. It also marked the monks' triumph over the theologians in the Eastern Church. Increasingly the hierarchy of the Eastern Churches—Bulgarian, Serbian, and Russian as well as Greek—were made up of Athonites and their disciples, men whose training and perspectives had been shaped within sequestered monasteries, not inside universities or the churches of the great cities of the empire.

The Spiritual Exercises

The exercises pursued by the monks of Mount Athos or Monte Cassino, no less than those of the Muslims who chose to follow the Sufi way, were private ventures conducted under the tutelage of an experienced older mentor in what amounted to an often protracted spiritual apprenticeship. Early on in the age of printing, it occurred to an invalided soldier that the same effect could be achieved somewhat more quickly and efficiently. At the very start of his new, dedicated life as a Christian, Ignatius of Loyola, the Basque courtier turned saint (see II/8), conceived of the idea of setting down in writing his own experiences, not as autobiography, but in a schematized form that might be followed by others who could thus be led to a similar change of mind and heart. This was the origin, sometime about 1522–1523, of the *Spiritual Exercises*, a remarkable document in Christian spirituality. It was nothing less than a program for changing a life, or rather, for changing one's own life since the *Exercises* are notoriously nonprescriptive: direct and laconically understated, they are devoid of both mystery and spiritual sentimentality. The *Spiritual Exercises* cover four "weeks" and were actually intended for a month of guided prayer and meditation on both the mysteries of Christianity and the state of one's own soul. After a largely introspective first "week," the second is devoted to the life of Christ, the third to his passion and death, and the last to his resurrection appearances. The *Exercises'* director and his subject were also provided with various rules and guidelines, for the "Discernment of Spirits," for example, as a guide for observing and evaluating spiritual states, for "Thinking with the Church," and on "Three Methods of Prayer," one of which seems remarkably reminiscent of the Jesus Prayer.

There is nothing radical or even new in the *Spiritual Exercises*. Its spirituality is standard—Thomas à Kempis's *Imitation of Christ* was Ignatius's favored reading—and the tone is gentle: guidance rather than command is the mode. But the work is shrewd in its psychology and, most importantly, pragmatic. It is, if not mysticism, than at least a potent spirituality for everyone, the conversion of high Christian seriousness into a form that can be internalized and then used by any Christian. All can follow in Ignatius's footsteps: every layman can become a monk, every Christian a saint.

The subsequent career of the *Spiritual Exercises* branched off into two different but parallel directions. The first was the "retreat" whereby the Christian, or a group of Christians, withdrew temporarily from society and their everyday pursuits to follow a specially tailored and conveniently shortened version of the *Exercises*. The Jesuits themselves, the members of the religious order Ignatius had founded, might be expected to make the full *Exercises* at the beginning and end of their long training, but for the ordinary Christian, three days might suffice or, at best, a week. This new spiritual activity was to be performed under the direction of a skilled spiritual guide who had an additional Jesuit manual, the *Directory* (1599), to help him apply the *Exercises* in this somewhat modified setting. Second, the *Spiritual Exercises* sent the Jesuits and, in their steps, the Catholic Church, on the path toward the spiritual guidance of the laity (see I/6). Where once the clergy had chiefly administered the sacraments, the new spirituality of the post-Trent (and post-Jesuit) era required them to provide spiritual counsel and guidance, not merely in the confessional, where clergy and laity had their most frequent and privileged encounters, but in the broader range of social contacts that the Jesuits and others encouraged in the sodalities, confraternities, and pious associations that became increasingly common in the era of Catholic reconstruction that followed the Council of Trent.

Muhammad Cleansed, and Rapt

Muslim ascetical pursuits, which tended to be somewhat more occasional and less wilderness-oriented than they were in Christianity, soon took on their own mystical aspirations, with a yearning for union with a God whom most Muslims properly regarded as absolutely transcendent. Sufism, like all forms of mysticism, has as its acknowledged object an immediate experience of God, an experience usually expressed in terms of union (*tawhid*) or identity (*ittihad*).

The Christian mystics who passed from a careful cultivation of self-denial to a desire to stand before the divine throne, or even to look on the face of God, had ample precedents in their still meditated-on Jewish and Hellenic pasts. The early Sufis knew of no such transports to other realms. They had instead the example of their own master. After an initiatory ritual, the prophet Muhammad himself had once ascended to the highest heaven and communed with God. These two events, called respectively, the Opening of Muhammad's Breast and the Ascension, are rich in subsequent Islamic associations but are only touched on, in a typically oblique fashion, in the Quran. "Did We not open your breast, and take from you your burden which was breaking your back?" asks Quran 94:1–3. The biographical and exegetical tradition wove a story of an angel physically opening Muhammad's breast, either early in life or immediately before his vocation as a prophet, removing whatever imperfection existed there and pouring into its place plenteous faith and wisdom.

This cathartic initiatory procedure is followed immediately in the mystics' imaginings by Muhammad's being carried in his sleep—he is described as taking his rest in the sacred space near the Kaaba—first to Jerusalem—the famous Night Journey of Quran 17:1 (see I/3)—and thence, from the temple site in the Holy City, to the highest heaven. This is the Prophet's Ascension (*miraj*), which is never quite described in the Quran but is often celebrated in literature and art. Some of its details seem extrapolated from what were almost certainly traces of the Prophet's actual visions, like the ones described almost in passing in Quran 53:1–18. The Quran's own annotation of these visions is minimal in the extreme, but the Sufi tradition, including the Prophetic reports (*hadith*) that purported to go back to Muhammad himself, placed the Ascension firmly and forever in the context of Muhammad's heavenly journey. The Prophet is borne aloft by a sacred steed through the seven heavens of the ancient and medieval cosmologies (see II/10) to stand in God's presence.

As in the Jewish "chariot" and "palaces" literature of celestial ascent, each heaven of Muhammad's journey is entered only after a challenge and a response given to its prophetic guardian—Adam in the first heaven, then Jesus, Joseph, Idris (Enoch), Aaron, Moses, and finally, in the seventh heaven, Abraham. Beyond this patriarch is God himself, who, according to Muhammad's own account reported in the hadith, "inspired in me what He inspired." There then follows another altogether typical "bargaining" sequence (cf. Abraham's on behalf of the doomed Sodom in Gen. 18:20–32) in which God initially assigns fifty daily prayers to the Muslim community, which Muhammad gradually bargains down to the canonical five.

This prophetic paradigm proved infinitely fruitful for the Sufi mystics. They too had their own "ascensions" over the same terrain, though often embellished with new details, to end in the same awesome place before the throne of God. Now in the sacred company of the prophets assembled there was Muhammad himself to greet his mystical fellow traveler.

Did Muhammad See God?

Although Muslims generally agreed that the faithful would see God in the Afterlife (see II/10), there was a notorious dispute over whether the "vision of God" might ever be achieved in this life. One strand of that debate went off in the direction of the mystics, whose experiences of the divine were generally cast in the opaque language of metaphor and symbol with an overcoat of highly charged poetry. Occasionally, however, the cloud of allegory lifted and the traditional Muslim was confronted with the statements of someone like al-Hallaj, who identified himself with God, or an Ibn Arabi, who left little doubt that he had seen God (see below). The Muslim consensus was not very sympathetic to such claims, but another instance provoked a more attentive and cautious attitude, that of Muhammad himself.

The Quran is well aware of the case of Abraham, whose contact with God was direct, though its mode was unspecified, and more particularly of Moses, who begged God, "Show me Yourself that I may gaze upon you" (7:143). Muhammad's revelations, no less than Moses', came from God, but the Quran gives little or no testimony on how they occurred. The Quran does have Muhammad admit, in order to quiet skeptics who thought he had "wandered," that he had had two supernatural visions (53:1–18)—he saw one "mighty in power, possessed of wisdom"—though without specifying who precisely it was that he saw. To open and expand these texts the exegetes had available a large number of Prophetic sayings, some of which addressed the matter of the vision of God rather directly. The statement "You shall not see God until you die" appears explicitly to deny the possibility of such a thing during life while implicitly affirming it after death. But the declaration is directed to the believers, and most commentators could easily adduce an exception for prophets in general and for Muhammad in particular.

Another widespread hadith the jurists judged authentic had Muhammad say, quite baldly, "I saw my Lord." Exegetes approached the text from several directions. One connected it directly to the visions described in the opening lines of sura 53 and interpreted it quite literally. Others understood it as referring to a quite different occasion and then had to choose whether the sight was "with the eyes of the body," that is, literally, or with "the eyes of the heart," which could refer to a dream vision. The latter would validate the authenticity of the experience—the dreams of all the prophets were veridical—while softening its "corporeality" (*tajsim*). The debate then moved into the question of how God appeared. Some held, with a nod to Islam's mystics, that God appeared in a "figured manifestation," that is, he adopted a quasi-material appearance appropriate to the occasion. Sura 53, meanwhile, began to develop its own exegetical history. If some of the earliest commentators thought the lines meant that Muhammad had twice seen God, some of the later hadith showed a marked preference for Gabriel, not God, as its object, just as the later suras of the Quran begin to identify that angel as the agent in God's revelation to Muhammad (see II/10).

There is, indeed, one hadith that sums up the dispute about Muhammad's vision of God in a nutshell. It is related on the authority of Muhammad's wife Aisha, who reported that the Prophet told her there were three terrible lies about God. The very first was the claim being made by some that Muhammad had seen God. The reporter to whom Aisha was telling the story was taken aback. What about the Quran's references to his visions (53:13; 81:23)? "Yes," Aisha responded, "I was the first to ask him about that." And Muhammad replied: "It was only Gabriel. I did not see him in the actual state in which he had been created other than those two times." This suggests, of course, that the quranic revelations were all purely auditory.

The Sufi as Mystic

For the earliest Sufis, the friend of God was the individual who observed the sharia with well-intentioned scrupulosity and spoke to God in prayer. This person possessed no special gifts, nor could he or she, in the minds of most, press any claim to a particular knowledge of God save that God gave his friends at the Judgment. There were, however, countervailing notions. Developing concepts of a Gnostic wisdom, private revelation, and divine illumination separated the mystic, the individual who had experienced God, from the simple ascetic by assigning the former a state, as either goal or achievement, different from that of other Muslims.

The meditations of the early Sufi Rabia (d. 801) on the lover's longing for the beloved, with its focus on a personal and essentially private relationship between the creature and her God, may have contributed to the same end. She wished, she said, for the veil to be removed so that she might look upon the Beloved. For some, however, looking was not enough. Abu Yazid (d. 876) of Bistam in Iran, who was separated by but one generation from the Zoroastrianism of his grandfather, was initiated into the mystical tradition of a certain

Abu Ali, the "Indian" (al-Sindi), who was apparently himself a recent arrival in Islam, since at the time of his coming to Bistam he knew not even enough Arabic to negotiate the Quran. Al-Bistami, as Abu Yazid is more often called, taught him Arabic and the sharia and received from Abu Ali in return instruction on the "Realities" and the "extinction of self in the unity of God."

There is no more of Abu Ali; thereafter only the voice of Bistami is heard, captured solely in what he called "paradoxical utterances," vivid and excited exclamations in his native Persian. Through their subjective fervor shines a fundamental shift in the mystic's approach to God. Earlier Sufis' visionary meditations had striven to render present the distant perspectives of the Judgment. Bistami could not wait for the eschaton; he cast himself headlong into the ecstatic position already granted to the Prophet. For many years, Bistami confessed, he had cultivated nothing but his own self. Then, with the suddenness of an illumination, he saw all of creation in a new light. It became corpselike in his eyes, and once he put off his own self, "like a serpent stripping himself of his skin," Bistami began his personal experience of the "heavenly ascent." Carried before God, he begged to be invested with God's Unity, Selfhood, and Oneness. It was granted. As Bistami himself described it, he was clothed in the divine attributes—"I became a bird whose body was Oneness and whose wings were Eternity." There followed, if our understanding of the sequence of Bistami's "utterances" is correct, the final experience of "extinction in the unity of God." He arrived at the point of nonbeing, and after resting there for ten years, Bistami passed "from the Not to the Not by way of the Not." Stripped of his own personality, the mystic stood before God's Essence, and from his lips came the most startling of his paradoxes: "Glory be to Me! How great is My Majesty!" Then he added: "Enough of myself! Enough!"

The Growth of Sufi Theory

Reports of Bistami and his experiments with extinction and the mystical union traveled rapidly to Baghdad, where the reigning Sufi authority was Abu al-Qasim al-Junayd. Junayd (d. 910) read the "Glory be to Me" in a prudential sense that acquitted Bistami of blasphemy, but he clearly accepted the possibility of what Bistami had described, a mystical union with God. According to Junayd's own formula, this state of union (*tawhid*) was achieved "by separating the Eternal from what has been created in time."

Perhaps this is already a degree of abstract conceptualization alien to Bistami, but Junayd also had a theory of why and how humans may aspire to this extraordinary possibility of union with God. It arose from Junayd's meditation on the Quran passage (7:172) where God summons before him the still-uncreated sons of Adam and has them bear witness that Allah is their Lord. Others read this famous "covenant" (*mithaq*) as a precreation revelation; Junayd, however, saw it as a clear testimony to a special kind of existence possessed by souls before their creation in time and a pledge to those souls of the possibility of later, in their earthly lives, reestablishing such a spiritual existence "in Him."

Before the mystic could advance (or regress) to this state of primordial spiritual existence, he or she had first to labor for that "self-extinction" (*fana*) already explored by Bistami. Junayd's version of fana is well within the quranic usage of that term, namely, a divesting of the worldly self, but when he came to its complement, *baqa*, or continued subsistence-in-God, he was invoking his own somewhat philosophical understanding of humans' preexistence, which was suggested and confirmed by his exegesis of the covenant passage, as a thought in the mind of God. The goal proposed to the mystic by Junayd was, then, no more than a return to humans' original spiritual roots. The enormity of reclining on the bosom of God must have been substantially diminished by the realization that before temporal existence began, humans were created in that very same posture.

Subsistence-in-God was by no means the end of the process. Junayd knew that the mystic had inevitably to return to a quotidian state and reassume his or her individual personality. The mystic underwent a change, both internally and externally. The mystic who had experienced the glories of divine unity now saw the world in a new light, with the clarity of sobriety, according to Junayd, and "his actions in the world become a pattern for his fellow men." Bistami had emerged from his transports in a state of high intoxication; Junayd's mystic in a cold and even sad sobriety, condemned to live in the world with the remembrance of a briefly restored state of pristine, indeed preexisting, innocence.

The preexistence of souls, though a familiar feature in Platonic thought, was hardly a staple in early Islam. In ninth-century Baghdad, Junayd had ample opportunity to instruct himself on Hellenic thought, but we have no direct evidence that he had done so. Our suspicions are somewhat stronger in the case of one of Junayd's contemporaries. Al-Tirmidhi, surnamed al-Hakim, "the Sage," was born in Tirmidh in Iran, was "converted" to Sufism from the traditional sciences at the age of twenty-eight, and took up residence at Neyshabur when his orthodoxy became suspect in his native town.

Tirmidhi is represented by an impressive number of works, but the most influential was his *Seal of the Saints*, a somewhat disjointed assemblage composed of more than 150 disputed questions in the Sufi tradition. The *Seal of the Saints* is a dense tract, but its ideological base is clearly exposed. The Muslim faith tradition is grounded in an understanding of prophecy, whose ultimate exemplar, the "Seal of the Prophets," was Muhammad. Tirmidhi set down next to prophecy another grade of spirituality, that of "sainthood." In its widest acceptance, sainthood (*walaya*) characterized the entire Muslim community by reason of its shared profession of faith. There is, however, a more particular and elite class of "saints," namely, those individuals who share an illuminative understanding given by God and who stand higher in the spiritual ranks than the prophets. Thus, in the same way that Muhammad was the "Seal of the Prophets," so Jesus was the "Seal of the Saints."

Tirmidhi's exaltation of the saint over the prophet seems remarkable on the face of it, but it had its antecedents among Sufi writers; there is even a hadith to that effect that was accepted by traditionists. Tirmidhi's position was based on ideology, however, not tradition. The prophet as lawgiver—and Tirmidhi understood that not all prophets were such—was by that very qualification constituted a "commoner," a notion that ran counter to Tirmidhi's elitist spirituality whereby higher truths were communicated by inspiration or, to use his own figure, by the diffusion of spiritual "lights," another notion with a long and fruitful history in Muslim mystical circles.

Sufism and Gnosticism

There is patently a metaphysics at work in Tirmidhi, if not in the more experimental Bistami. Sufism had progressed from its early exclusive concern with what the Christian tradition called the purgative way—in Muslim terms, "renunciation"—to an immediate experience of God, and now, finally, to a worldview that verified and explained that experience. Earlier Sufis had pondered their own and others' experiences along the purgative way and had elicited from them both the notion of self as the focus of humans' selfish drives for gratification and that of understanding, a God-given faculty for distinguishing between good and evil. Both notions belonged to ethics and were useful psychological insights for doing good and avoiding of evil. Yet by Tirmidhi's day, soul, understanding, and spirit were all parts of an elaborate metaphysical structure that far exceeded the bounds of ethics. In the late eighth century the thought of certain Sufis was invaded by a metaphysics of light that colored their cosmology, their anthropology, and their view of the spiritual lives of both God and humans. Put in its simplest form, the new metaphysics affirmed, contrary to the Islamic tradition, consubstantiality of God and the spiritual element in humans: the Light that is God's essence has descended through a series of emanations, the last of which is the human spirit.

Thus stated, the thesis is no different from what was commonly understood by later Platonism or from the version of the theory propagated by the Muslim representatives of the Platonic tradition. There were, however, somewhat different versions of that metaphysics, including the Sufis' own, which point toward sources other than purely philosophical ones. The mystical Sufis did not subscribe, for example, to the belief that the divine light in humans was entirely a natural disposition on the basis of which any individual might aspire to union with its metaphysical source. The Sufi version was elitist in its conviction that the substantial radiation from God was a gift limited to the "privileged" and that the knowledge founded on it was not merely an exalted form of natural intellection (Gk. *episteme*; Ar. *ilm*) but a special wisdom (Gk. *gnosis*; Ar. *marifa* or *hikma*) granted to the "saints."

The Muslim mystic was, in the finished version, a Gnostic. How he or she came to these beliefs is not immediately apparent. The mystic was in a sense surrounded by possibilities: translations of Greek works like the "Theology of Aristotle" or some piece of Hermetica; contacts with one or another of the marginal groups with Gnostic attitudes within the Abode of Islam, like the Manichaeans or the mysterious theosophist-scientists of Haran called Sabians; or encounters with some Islamic sect that itself had already accepted a Gnostic view of reality, the Ismaili Shiites, for example (see I/8). The latter is, perhaps, the most attractive possibility. The Neoplatonist Plotinus was not, after all, a genuine Gnostic, whereas others, like the Sabians, were wrapped in a complex cosmic mythology unacceptable to Muslims, sharing a worldly pessimism that had no counterpart among the Sufis of the tenth and eleventh centuries.

Sufis and Shiites

A primary characteristic of the Sufis' view was their belief in the ongoing nature of revelation, their bringing into partnership, much to the advantage of the latter, the prophet and the saint as dual repositories of the divine truths. Thus in its earliest form, that put forward by Bistami, for example, the Sufi merely claimed a share in the extraordinary experience given to Muhammad. In its later versions, Muhammad and the Sufi became existential equals in the class of the "privileged," with the difference that Muhammad typified the class of prophets whose union with God was "frozen" in the public revelation that followed, whereas the Sufi was the beneficiary of an ongoing revelation.

This is somewhat similar to what was being asserted by Shiites of the circle of the Imam Jafar al-Sadiq (d. 765); the Shiite Imams were just such repositories of ongoing revelation by reason of their special connection with its divine source. To the extent that the experience of the "Realities" was limited in each generation to a single designated individual descended from the family of Muhammad, Fatima, and Ali, the Sufi would presumably quarrel with the Shiite view. The Shiites were arguing for a spiritual elite of the very narrowest dimensions and one based on a dynastic and thus a political consideration; the Sufi mystic opened the experience of God to an entire class of spiritual aristocrats, the friends of God.

As long as Shiism was a political and social movement and Sufism essentially an association of ascetics, there were Shiites who bore the title of Sufi. But when both Sufis and Shiites turned to ideology, a Gnostic ideology, the separation of the two groups became apparent. The traditionalists may have considered the mystic al-Hallaj a Qarmatian (see below), but only because the Qarmatians had transcended, as the Sufis themselves had, the lingering Shiite connection with history in the person of an Alid Imam. Sufis and Shiites were competitors, not allies, from the mid-eighth to the twelfth century, when Sufism had its next enlarging encounter with Gnosticism.

Part of the complex of ideas shared by Sufism and Shiism even at this early stage was the concept of Muhammad's preexistence. Plotinus had criticized the Gnostics of his own day for multiplying the spiritual emanations produced by the First Cause, and the cosmos of pre-Islamic Gnosticism does indeed appear to be filled with a bewildering array of transcendent Intellects that inhabit the upper World of Light. Among these hypostases was one called simply "Man." According to one Hermetic account, God produced a Primordial Man who was incorporeal, immaterial, and impeccable. There was already a hint of this idea in Plotinus, and the anonymous genius or mischief-maker who converted selected passages in the *Enneads* into the "Theology of Aristotle" altered that hint into an unmistakably Gnostic version of the First Man. Even earlier, Philo too had postulated the creation of a spiritual archetype of man possessed of exactly these same qualities and identified with Adam.

The closure of all of these themes, the Primal Man of Gnosticism, the Intelligible Man of Philo, the preexistent Jesus of Hellenic Christianity, and even, perhaps, the Gayomart of Iran, in the Muslim theory of a Muhammad of Light is an immensely complex historical problem. Its full implications did not unfold until both Sufism and Shiism had become far more theosophical than they were in the tenth century. Al-Tirmidhi had already grasped the essentials, however.

Al-Hallaj

Tirmidhi was by no means the only metaphysician of his generation of mystics. Sahl al-Tustari (d. 896), though not represented by the same kind of literary evidence, interested himself in the same psychological problems and Gnostic solutions as Tirmidhi. He too argued for an elite "community of saints" who, by sharing in the primordial light, were privy to the mysteries of the Godhead. This may have been part of the saint's inheritance from all eternity, somewhat in the manner that Junayd understood the precreation covenant between God and the children of Adam.

Sahl's most famous pupil was, by all accounts, Husayn ibn Mansur al-Hallaj, who at the very beginning of his own career studied with Sahl and followed him into exile at Basra in 874. An Iranian by birth and, like Bistami, but one generation removed from Zoroastrianism, Hallaj soon deserted his mentor for the Baghdad Sufis, among them al-Junayd. Al-Hallaj stayed there for somewhat more than twenty years, living a life of austere retirement. It was, however, only a prelude. Hallaj broke with his Baghdad masters over what had become a cardinal tenet of Sufism; that the Realities were the esoteric property of a spiritual elite.

As a result of his disagreement, Hallaj left Baghdad and took up a life of public preaching in Khorasan and Fars, though now no longer dressed as a Sufi. This first public ministry lasted for five years, after which Hallaj returned briefly to Baghdad and then resumed his travels in an even wider eastern arc that took him through Turkestan and parts of India. In the course of his journeys, Hallaj made perhaps fatal contacts with the revolutionary Qarmatians (see I/8) and the notorious heretic philosopher-physician Muhammad ibn Zakariya al-Razi (d. 925).

On his return to Baghdad in 910, Hallaj began to experience some of the political and theological repercussions of what he had done and said. He held, as others had, cautiously, before him, that the canonical obligations of Muslim law could be replaced by more spiritual activities. More generally, and more provocatively, he rendered mysticism part of the public domain by displaying his own miraculous powers and by asserting for all to hear that the union of the saint's soul with God's spirit was a reality achieved by love and not a metaphor. "I am the Truth," Hallaj openly avowed, appropriating for himself one of God's names. True union between the two—the mortal human and his or her transcendent God—could be achieved only by identifying the two substances. Although this notion was anathema to Islam, it had, the outraged theologians noted, ample precedents in Manichaeism, where the human soul was a fallen spark of the Divine Light.

Hallaj was formally accused of *zandaqa*, or heresy (see I/5), on the basis of a judgment rendered against him by the lawyer Ibn Dawud. There was an attempt to arrest him in 913. He escaped, was pursued and captured. A trial was held in 915 before the grand vizier at which the political charge of being a Qarmatian propagandist was added to that of zandaqa. Hallaj was convicted and jailed for eight years. The issue was not settled, however. He was tried again, convicted once again, and in March 922 Hallaj was scourged, mutilated, suspended on a gibbet, and finally decapitated. His body was burned and the ashes thrown in the Tigris.

There is little in Hallaj without parallel in Bistami, Tirmidhi, Tustari, and Junayd, the first three of whom suffered exile for their teachings. Al-Hallaj was not profoundly respectful of the letter of the sharia, an attitude that had unfortunate political resonances in a Baghdad terrified by the Qarmatian threat of anarchy. Also, Hallaj was more outspoken than his predecessors on the theme of the infusion of divinity into the mortal soul as the basis of a mystical union. Tirmidhi and Tustari tempered their thoughts with a quasi-Gnostic intellectualism; al-Hallaj cast his in the more dangerous language of love.

Hallaj's execution did not solve the problem of Sufism in Islam. It may have sharpened the issue, however, and in so doing provided the ground for an eventual resolution. Sufism was strengthened by its first martyr, but it had received a sober warning as well. The language of intoxication with God was not the currency of the Dar al-Islam, and few after Hallaj were imprudent enough to think so. The joys of the mystical union were concealed in the metaphors of poetry, the convolutions of quranic exegesis, or the dense pages of speculative theory. And here too lay the means of détente with orthodoxy.

The Sufi Way

In the tenth century Sufism found its literary voice. At first its tones were chiefly hagiographical, collections of anecdotes and the sayings of those men and women who had won a reputation for piety in Islam. Eventually these branched out into systematic collections of Sufi biographies, like the *Classes of Sufis* of al-Sulami (d. 1021), the monumental *Embellishment of the Saints* of Abu Nuaym al-Isfahani (d. 1038), and what ultimately became the classic statement of Sufi theory, the *Epistle* of Abu al-Qasim al-Qushayri (d. 1072). All these works differ among themselves in scope and emphasis, but they share a common understanding of the purpose and methods of Sufism: to experience the unity of God at the term of a series of highly articulated stages of personal striving, marked at its more advanced levels by the dispensation of certain equally well defined graces from God. From these authors one can elicit some generalized notions about the structure of the Sufi way (*tariqa*). Their treatment is rarely theoretical, however, since the works in question generally illustrate their points rather than argue or explain them.

The path to perfection began, of course, with a "conversion," a turning through repentance from the ways of the world toward a consciousness of God. This was, by common consent, the first of the "stations" (*maqamat*), and was followed by a series of similar stages: scrupulosity of conscience with regard to moral action, self-restraint from even legitimate pleasures, voluntary poverty, patience, abandonment to God, and, finally, the most perfect station, that of divine complaisance, where the striver was in perfect conformity with God's will.

These stations were the fruits of the mystic's own exertions and akin to the steps along the Christians' *via purgativa*. But once achieved, the Sufi's further spiritual progress depended not so much on personal effort as on the benevolent and gracious mercy of God, who bestowed the various "states" (*ahwal*) on the soul. Here too the way was carefully mapped. The Sufi theoreticians distinguished between the "states" of love, fear, hope, longing, intimacy, tranquillity, contemplation, and certainty. These were by their very nature transitory, as was the culmination of the Sufi's striving and the terminus of the way: unification with God.

The boundary line between the stations and the states marked a great turning in the history of morality. The "stations" echoed, with many mutations and refinements, the traditional Greek view of virtue. For Plato, Aristotle, and the Stoics, virtue was a habit of the soul; it was acquired by an askesis of one type or another and depended on continuous human efforts. By the first and second Christian centuries that notion had been joined by another, quite different one—that virtue was a gift of God, a "grace," as the Muslim would put it. In the Sufi works of the tenth century these two very different sets of virtues were arranged in a continuous series, separated only by the passage from station to state.

The same conjunction had already been accomplished by the Christian mystics of the seventh century. Christianity too knew a tradition of virtue as an acquired habit. This method of "action" (*praxis*), as it was called, owed nothing to Hellenic ethics. Rather, the Christian view of virtue as praxis grew, like its Muslim counterpart in the stations, from a meditation on the teachings of Scripture and the example of the founder. But because early Christian asceticism manifested itself in the monastic life, the "practical virtues" of the Christian holy man or woman found their principal statement in the monastic "rules" that appeared in the Near East from the fourth century onward. Islam, which prized asceticism but did not valorize it in monasticism, knew no such rules until the appearance of the first Sufi "orders" in the thirteenth century.

Practical Sufism

The Sufi's transport was a transient state, a brief exaltation into the presence of God. For some it was a unique and almost random event, but it is clear that in Islam many pious souls aspired to this state and they took well-defined and even scholastic steps to attain it. The convert to Sufism was regarded as a mere novice and was placed under the direction of a sheikh already accomplished in the spiritual life. At first that elder may simply have been a skilled and experienced director of souls, but eventually that ideal was replaced, as it was in Eastern Christianity, by the notion of a charismatic guide, a "spiritual father" who possessed the gift of divine grace (*baraka*). For the Muslim no less than the Christian, progress through the stations began as a jihad, a struggle against one's worldly inclinations that reflected the ascetic tradition of the earliest Sufism. The sheikh led him through the stations by means of exercises like the examination of conscience, meditation, and the constant repetition of God's name. Obedience was expected to be prompt and total.

The spiritual terrain that led from asceticism to the very presence of God was as carefully mapped by Sufi theoreticians as it was by Christian mystical theologians. As already noted, the Muslim masters formalized the Sufi path to the Absolute into a series of "stations," or stages of ascetical practice and self-control that were followed in the more experienced and advanced Sufi by the "states" through which God's grace rather than the Sufi's exertions guided the now purified soul upward toward union with himself. This well-charted landscape seems brightly lit and schematic, and it is far more suggestive of theory rather than practice. The preserved Sufi biographies show spiritual paths that are far more erratic, however, and the Muslim attestations of actual mystical experiences are of a darker, more painful, and at the same time more ecstatic quality than the handbooks would lead us to expect.

The closest we come to the sense of an actual experience of God is in the great body of Sufi poetry, much of it in Persian, which has charmed, edified, and inspired many Muslims, and perhaps has startled and even shocked almost as many more. To experience God is to experience the ultimate Other. In Christianity, the person of Jesus builds a human bridge between the finite and the Absolute, but there is no such inviting passage in either Judaism or Islam. Jewish mystics by and large turned prudently aside at that final moment, but Muslim mystics have been far more daring in facing the experience and attempting to describe, if not explain, the ineffable.

The spiritual master introduced the novice into two of the most common practices of Sufism, what were called "recollection" (*dhikr*) and the "hearing" (*sama*) (see II/8). The term *dhikr* has its spiritual, internal sense of recollecting God's name (Quran 18:24; 33:41) and his blessings, but its more visible form in Sufism is the ritual repetition of set formulas, notably the Muslim profession of faith or of the ninety-nine "beautiful names" of God (see I/1). The dhikr was generally a community exercise, though it could be performed privately, and it was preceded by the tariqa's distinctive litany or *wird*, the poetical prayers composed by the founder. The recollection was pronounced in rhythmical unison by the brethren and it was often accompanied by controlled breathing, as was the Jesus Prayer used to the same end in Eastern Christianity. A succession of postures was recommended, again similar to Hesychast practice: "Begin the recital from the left side of the chest, which is, as it were, the 'niche containing the lamp' of the heart, the focus of spiritual light." Another expert recommended beginning with the head lowered over the navel. Then as the first syllable of "Allah" was pronounced, "raise the head from the navel to the level of the brain, then pronounce the remainder of the word on the secret navel."

The objective of the dhikr was praise and worship of God, but there was a practical end as well, the achievement of the ecstatic state of annihilation (*fana*), which was for the Sufi a natural antecedent of union with the Divine. There was also often an elaborate ritual of singing and dancing with which the dhikr might be commingled. This sama was a virtual "spiritual concert," and though it was highly characteristic of certain Sufi associations such as the celebrated whirling dervishes who followed the teachings of the Persian mystic Jalal al-Din Rumi (d. 1273) at Konya in Turkey, the practice was not everywhere approved or accepted. There were extravagances, to be sure, in these rituals, and more than a few traditional and conservative Muslims were scandalized at what had become, on the eve of modern times, performances rather than spiritual exercises.

Spiritual Hierarchies

At some point in their respective evolutions, the Gnostic current in Islamic Sufism encountered its parallel strain in Shiism. Though this union was officially consummated in the creation of the Safavid state in Iran in the sixteenth century, the liaison was being prepared much earlier. It is not certain when the affinities between Shiism and Sufism first developed, but the foundations were already present, as we have seen, when Shiism elaborated its theory of the Imam as a charismatic figure who possessed an authoritative spiritual knowledge and imparted it exclusively to Shiite adepts.

One of the characteristics of the Gnostic worldview is its belief in a series of supernatural beings; they appear in series because they are commonly regarded as the descending emanations from the single primordial principle. In their Greek version, they are often called "Aeons" and they antedate the creation of our world. It was the descent, often unwilling, of one of them that set off the drama of redemption that would be achieved through gnosis.

It appears that from early on in the development of Shiism, their ideologues, whether the Imams themselves or other, unidentifiable thinkers, had been exposed to a potent form of Gnostic esotericism. Already in the canonical Shiite Imam traditions collected by al-Kulayni, Ibn Babuya, and others in the tenth century (see II/3), both Muhammad and the Imams were brought into being before the creation of the world. According to this Shiite foundation myth, in the beginning there was only a world of shadows; God created the Prophet and the Imams in the form of divine lights to illuminate that preexistent place. They first recognized the essential Oneness (*tawhid*) of God and attempted to teach it to the other as yet unenlightened spiritual beings. This primordial light possessed by the cosmic Muhammad and the cosmic Imams passed into Adam at the moment of earthly creation, and here on earth the same drama of light and shadow-darkness is played out in human history: Adam and the other prophets are bearers of the light in both its exoteric or "open" (*zahir*) form, what we call "revelation," as well as its esoteric or "closed" (*batin*) form available only through a properly allegorical reading of Scripture and privileged teaching, and in each prophetic cycle they attempted to spread it among their fellow humans. The cycle of Speaker-Prophets, each followed by a series of Interpreter-Imams, continued until it reached its destined term and perfection, Muhammad and the line of Imams descended from Ali ibn Abi Talib (see I/8).

The Apotheosis of Ali: The Alawis

Early on, the presence of some of these notions, most notably an exaggerated reverence for the Imams, led to the characterization of certain strands of Shiism as *ghulat*, or "extremists" (see I/5). The main body of the Shiat Ali eventually found its own comfortable level of "orthodoxy" on these matters, but some "extremist" strands managed to survive. One such are the Nusayris, now more commonly called the Alawis, who are centered in the northwest of Syria and make up perhaps 10 percent of that country's population, though they presently dominate its political structure.

According to tradition, the eponymous founder of the sect, Ibn Nusayr, was a supporter of the tenth Imam, Ali al-Hadi (d. 868), and the favorite disciple of the eleventh, Hasan al-Askari (d. 874). His doctrine, or at least the teaching of the community that now claims his name, starts with the ghulat premise that Ali is, quite simply, God, or more accurately, God's manifestation. According to their version of the Gnostic myth (see I/5), the Alawis were divine lights cast from heaven for denying Ali's divinity. They were immersed in matter and condemned to another ghulat staple, continuous reincarnation or metempsychosis (*tanasukh*). The Alawi is redeemed only by recognizing the divinity in one of the seven cycles of God's historical self-manifestation.

In each of these manifestations, God, who is referred to, in the best Gnostic fashion, as the Essence (*al-mana*), is accompanied by two lesser beings, one called the Name or the Veil and the other, the Gate. Thus, God took flesh in the successive forms of Abel, Seth, Joseph, Joshua, Asaf (the legendary vizier of Solomon), Peter, and Ali ibn Abi Talib, whence he passed into the eleven earthly Imams of the Shiite succession. But God was not recognized in his divinity because of the concealing presence of each respective Veil, namely, Adam, Noah, Jacob, Moses, Solomon, Jesus, and Muhammad, each of whom deflected attention away from the Essence. The function of the respective Gates was to propagate the true message. Thus, Salman al-Farisi, a semilegendary Persian follower of Muhammad, was the Gate in the generation when Ali was the Essence and Muhammad his Veil, and Ibn Nusayr himself served as the Gate for the eleventh Imam. Recognition of the true identity of the Essence means release from the cycle of human reincarnation and return to a contemplation of God as eternal light.

The promotion of the Imams above the prophets, most notably of Ali above Muhammad, is a temptation Shiites resist only with great difficulty. The Alawis succumbed. Not only was the Imam Ali superior to the prophet Muhammad; he was God incarnate.

The Fathers of Islamic Theosophy: Ibn Sina and Suhrawardi

The profusion of cosmic presences participating in both the spiritual and the historical dimensions inevitably blurred the distinction not only between Imams and prophets but between those two and the saints. The Shiites glorified their Imams under the cover of this ideology of a celestial hierarchy, but

Sunni spiritualists were soon drinking from the same sources and used them to nourish their increasing interest in the "saint," and particularly the archetypal saint, the "axis" or "pole" (*qutb*) around whom the saints of each generation revolved. From the twelfth century onward, the distance among Imam, prophet, and saint grew even smaller with the evolution of what some call theosophical Sufism and others Sophiology or Illuminationism. *Hikma* (wisdom) is, quite simply, *gnosis* in Muslim garb.

The chief agent of the turning of both Islamic philosophy and mysticism in the direction of theosophy was the philosopher Ibn Sina (d. 1038). His contribution to the development and refinement of Islamic philosophy in its then current blend of Plato and Aristotle was enormous (see II/7). Yet there are suggestions throughout his work that Ibn Sina had, behind and beyond his public and scholastic treatments of philosophical themes, a more esoteric "illuminationist wisdom" (*hikma mashriqiyya*) whose contents could only be hinted at. The obliqueness of Ibn Sina's own allusions make its identification somewhat problematic, but a great many Muslims who came after him understood Ibn Sina's esoteric philosophy as some form of mysticism, and unhesitatingly identified its author as a Sufi.

Whether or not he was a Sufi in any formal sense, Ibn Sina heavily emphasized some form of divine illumination (*ishraq*) as the means whereby the philosopher and the prophet received their knowledge. But the point at issue was neither prophet nor philosopher but how we know. In the Peripatetic model for Ibn Sina's theory of knowledge, sense knowledge and intellection were intimately connected. The intelligible forms of things existed prior to our knowing them, that is, prior to their becoming intelligized. They subsisted in material things, whence they came, via sensation, into the human intellectual faculty. Here they were converted under the action of what Aristotle

> **Note:** Both Plato and Aristotle shared the conviction that the heavenly bodies were alive and so ensouled. Plato thought their souls were within the spheres, but Aristotle preferred to move them from without by an accompanying (but external) intellect that is the object of each celestial body's love. Aristotle needed fifty-six of these intellects to move the fifty-six bodies required to explain the observed motion of the seven planets and the crystalline sphere in which the "fixed" stars were embedded (see II/10).
>
> Ibn Sina drastically reduced the number of intellectual movers to ten by placing the mover-souls back inside those same eight spheres, plus one for the "first heaven" beyond the fixed stars and another to move the souls of humans. Each sphere still had its accompanying disembodied intellect, which is recognized by the celestial soul as its good and around which it revolves. The tenth and lowest of these separated intellects served as the "Giver of Forms" to humankind and the cause of human intellection.

had called the agent intellect into actually intelligized forms. Ibn Sina all but swept away that realist, sensist base of intellectual knowledge. In his view, the intelligible forms are given to the human intellect by that same agent intellect, the tenth and lowest of the divine celestial intellects and the human intelligence merely reflects them, "as in a mirror."

In Ibn Sina's worldview, and for many after him, the descending series of disembodied celestial intellects are identified with the cherubim of the Judeo-Christian tradition, and the tenth of them, the agent intellect or Holy Spirit, with Gabriel, the archangel who was God's instrument for revealing the Quran to Muhammad. The celestial souls animating the heavenly bodies are likewise angels, though of a lesser perfection since they are embodied in the heavenly spheres. Both grades, the cherubim-intellects and the secondary celestial souls, are gifted with intelligence and will, to a more perfect degree than humans.

It was not, at any rate, passive reception of a gift that occupied Ibn Sina but individual effort and individual achievement in the pursuit of union with God. There is nothing in him of the passage of a spiritual baraka from master to novice, no charismatic "chain" on which to mount effortlessly on high.

One of Ibn Sina's most influential interpreters read him somewhat differently, however. Suhrawardi (d. 1191) took up and completed the Avicennan "visionary recitals" and interpreted the philosopher's illuminationist philosophy as a genuine renaissance of Persian wisdom. For those ancient sages of Iran, the First Being was Xvarneh, "the light of glory" of Zoroastrianism, and that opened for Suhrawardi the opportunity of converting what had been for Ibn Sina and al-Ghazali an epistemological metaphor into a true metaphysic. Existence and light are identical; the Necessary Being is Absolute Light. The "light" is Iranian, perhaps, but the notion of an "absolute" derived directly from the Greek tradition that underlay the thought of so many Muslim thinkers.

Though the Sunni lawyer and theologian was probably a less congenial figure to him than the Shiite philosopher, Suhrawardi learned as much from Ghazali as he did from Ibn Sina. Ghazali (d. 1111) had already anticipated, as we shall see, a new task for philosophy, and Suhrawardi developed it with enthusiasm. Speculative knowledge, the wisdom that comes from research and investigation, was simply a preparation for the "wisdom that savors," the experimental knowledge of God. Philosophy thus received its justification and at the same time was assigned an appropriate place as preparation for the final stages of the search for the Absolute. Suhrawardi likewise followed Ghazali in elaborating the rich possibilities of allegorical exegesis in the service of mysticism.

A modern distinction has been drawn between the "mysticism of infinity" and the "mysticism of personality," with the accompanying argument that later Sufism is unmistakably in the former category, which acknowledges God as the Ultimate and Unique Reality, whereas this material world of ours possesses only the "limited reality" of a distant emanation from the One Being. In this latter view, all Reality is in fact One, a position not very congenial to

Muslim revelation, which stresses the gulf between the Creator and his creation, and which preached, even in its mystical mode, an approach to God through moral activity, not identity with him. Union or identity (*ittihad*) with God was already a troublesome Sufi concept for the traditionalists, but even more scandalous was the message broadcast by the influential Spanish philosopher and poet Ibn Arabi (d. 1240): that of the "unity of Being," which was for most Muslims an elision of God and his creation, not a single, pantheistic description of being (see below).

> **Note:** The Sufis were by no means the only proponents of Gnosticism in the Abode of Islam. There are Gnostic premises at the base of most of the occult sciences that flourished in the ancient and medieval world—alchemy, for one. The ease with which so many of them passed from one to the other of the very different religious climates of ancient Greco-Roman paganism, Near Eastern Islam, and both Eastern and Western Christianity and Judaism underscores both the appeal and adaptability of Gnosticism. And in Islam, Gnosticism demonstrated that it could adapt itself as readily to political as to scientific ends.

Suhrawardi's work, with its assertion of Persia's place in the history of Wisdom, its attractive metaphysic of light, its developed theory of allegorical exegesis, and its valorization of experience over theoretical knowledge, provided a program for Iran's philosophers and mystics, and a convenient bridge on which they might thereafter meet. That the meetings were frequent and rewarding is attested by the twin traditions of mystical poetry in Persian and the ill-charted but impressive course of theosophical and philosophical speculation during the reign of the Safavids in Iran.

Defender of the Faith

The Ismailis, as we have seen (I/8), were a subdivision of the Shiites who, unlike the main body of the Shiat Ali in the Middle Ages, had a political program for overthrowing the Sunni caliph and replacing him with a revolutionary Mahdi-Imam (see II/10). They were not successful in their political aims, but they had access to and put to effective use the entire Gnostic apparatus of cosmic history, in which the Shiite Imams became the Gnostic Aeons; a secret revelation of the Realities that lay hidden in the concealed (*batin*) rather than the evident sense of Scripture; an Imam-Guide who possessed an infallible and authoritative magisterium (*talim*); and an initiated elite that formed, in the Ismaili case, the core of an elaborate political underground. At their headquarters in Cairo, a city that the Ismaili Fatimids founded in 969, agents were instructed in the Ismaili gnosis and program, and were sent forth with the "call" (*dawa*) of the Mahdi-Imam to cells and cadres that had been set up in the caliphal lands in Iraq and Iran.

The intellectual defense of Sunnism against the claims of the Ismailis and of the extravagances of Shiites and Sufis alike was undertaken in Baghdad by the lawyer and theologian Ghazali in a series of tracts that attacked what he called "the Esotericists." But the issue that engaged Ghazali appears in all its complexity in a more personal statement, his *Deliverer from Error*, which describes his own investigation of the competing claims on the faith of the Muslim. Faith tied to simple acceptance on the authority of others (*taqlid*) was insufficient for Ghazali; it could be shaken by the conflicting claims put forward by different parties and sects within Islam and by the equally strong adherence to their own faith by the Christians and Jews. Unless he was prepared to lapse into agnostic skepticism, as Ghazali was not, there had to be some other way to personal certitude for the seeker after truth. Four possibilities presented themselves: the way of speculative or dialectical theology—*kalam*—which professed to support its religious beliefs with rational argument; the way of the philosophers, who laid claim to true scientific demonstration; the Ismaili way, which promised religious certitude by relying on the teaching of an infallible Imam; and finally, the way of the Sufis or mystics, which offered intuitive understanding and a certitude born of standing in God's presence.

To some caught in the dilemmas of faith, there was an undeniable attraction to an infallible talim such as the Shiites, and more particularly the Ismailis, were offering. Ghazali could reply that if such were the answer, then it was far preferable to accept the infallible teaching of the Prophet than that of a derivative Imam, whose teachings turned out to be some debased form of Greek philosophy in any event. But neither can really cure the malady: part of the human condition is to doubt and disagree, and on the rational level the only solution to such ambiguity was not to throw oneself on the authority of another but to work out an answer with patience and intelligence, an answer based equally on the Quran and the principles of right reason. The solution was, in short, Ghazali's own rigorous version of kalam.

In his pursuit of certitude, Ghazali finally turned to mysticism. It was, as remarked earlier, a way (*tariqa*) that could be entered either from its scholastic, intellectualized side or more personally by approaching it through experience. Ghazali, with deep intellectual commitments and training—"knowledge was easier for me than activity"—entered by the first path: he read the classical theoretical treatises and the lives of the Sufi saints. It was a mistake, as he soon learned. It is better, he concluded, to experience intoxication than to know how to define drunkenness. Ghazali nonetheless began straightaway to define *tasawwuf*. The Sufi way began with the *via purgativa* of asceticism and led to an annihilation of self (*fana*). Ever higher states followed, visions of the angels and the spirits of the prophets. Finally, the desired experience of God was achieved by some, whether called "infusion," "connection," or "identity." There Ghazali broke off and retreated. It was all wrong. Apprehension of God was incommunicable, and one could learn more from associating with Sufis than from explanations of their activities.

Making Sufism Safe for Islam

Ghazali's spiritual autobiography might appear to be a series of radical turnings, of entrances and hasty withdrawals. The withdrawals are more apparent than real, however. He accepted and never surrendered the case for an intellectually strengthened theology. Ghazali admitted the philosophers' claims to possessing in the logical method an instrument for gaining certitude. He conceded that for most Muslims a simple acceptance on faith was an inevitable and not entirely unworthy course. And he argued strenuously yet carefully that there was a legitimate and important place in Islamic life for the experimental knowledge of God claimed by the mystics. All these themes are woven together in his great Muslim summa, the *Revivification of the Sciences of Religion*.

The *Revivification* had its desired effect. Muslim theology did become more rigorous by prudently expropriating the methodology of the philosophers, without accepting all their conclusions. Mystical union with God and the Sufi way that led to it won a degree of cautious acceptance. Ghazali's language on mysticism in the *Revivification* is a carefully moderated version of "sober intoxication." When speaking more personally, he could and did go further, however. His *Niche for Lights* is a meditation on the famous "Light Verse" in the Quran (24:35), which served for Muslim mystics the same provocative function as the opening chapter in Ezekiel and the Gospels' Transfiguration episode did for Jews and Christians.

The doctors of Islam embraced the *Revivification*. The mystics meditated on the *Niche for Lights* and found there all the themes converging in the Sufi consensus: the identification of God's essence with a Light whose ontological radiance was creation and whose cognitive function was to illumine the intellects of the saints and prophets; the distinction between the "plain" (*zahir*) and "concealed" (*batin*) sense of Scripture, and the need of allegorical exegesis to elicit the latter; the elitism that distinguished the mystic from all others in Islam and the esotericism that makes revelation of the Realities to the noninitiated—we can hear the rabbis' similar warnings—a dangerous and highly inadvisable enterprise. Suhrawardi and Ibn Arabi are already present in embryo in the *Niche for Lights*.

Spiritual Resurrection

Ghazali made Sufism safe for Islam, but he did not disarm the Ismailis, whose ideological and military assault on Baghdad continued for well more than two centuries, though not always with the same methods. In the twelfth century, the Ismaili apparatus in Iraq and Iran broke loose from Egyptian political control and pursued its own revolutionary course. It decentralized the insurrection by seizing isolated strong points and took up the demoralizing weapon of assassination against Sunni political and religious figures. Sunni opposition hardened against these so-called Esotericists, and the Ismailis were forced to play their final trump, the announcement of the End Time, the Spiritual Resurrection (*qiyama*).

The Ismaili qiyama was not a variant of the Jewish or Christian apocalypse. It was the glorious termination of the cosmic cycle of history. The millennia-long series of Prophets and Imams, of public revelations and private understandings was at an end: the Age of Perfection had dawned. There is something faintly Pauline in the Ismaili declaration of the end of Islam and the abrogation of the Islamic law. But whereas Paul could substitute a New Covenant for the Old and hail the New Law of Jesus indwelling in the members of the Church community, the Ismaili theology of the Resurrection did not give its adherents a reenergized sense of mission, but represented an admission that Sunni Islam was beyond its reach. Paul might surrender his expectations for the Jews to his hopes for the Gentiles, but for the Ismailis there was no gentile mission; paradise was limited to the narrow confines of their mountain fortresses, where the Mongols found and destroyed them (see I/8).

On the Edge: Ibn Arabi

Muhyi al-Din Muhammad ibn al-Arabi, or simply Ibn Arabi, was born of an old and distinguished Arab family at Murcia in Spain in 1165. His father served as a high official in the new administration of the reformist Almohads in Seville (see II/10), and the son trained in both the polite and the "serious" sciences that would have taken him in the same direction. But Ibn Arabi underwent a profound religious experience, likely when he was still in his early teens, and eventually chose to follow the Sufi life. To embrace this manner of life was a social step down, but Ibn Arabi remained a Sufi to his death, and in the end he enjoyed far greater fame and influence than he would ever have had as a statesman or courtier in al-Andalus.

A Sufi education was acquired by apprenticeship and was often peripatetic. Ibn Arabi, who was, on his own testimony, already the beneficiary of a divine illumination, went nonetheless from teacher to teacher in Spain—where he trained with some notable women Sufis—and in North Africa, learning from the current masters of spirituality and theosophy and practicing the prayers, vigils, and fasts of a dedicated ascetic. Ibn Arabi was also a lifelong and remarkably productive writer. No one is sure of the size of the "books" that stand behind the medieval lists, but some seven hundred titles are credited to him, and nearly two hundred works are still extant under his name. There were visions as well, dramatic encounters with the divine in Marrakech, Fez, and Tunis. One such commanded him to make the hajj, and in 1201, Ibn Arabi was on the road to Egypt and the Holy Cities.

It was a creative turning point. During his two years in Mecca Ibn Arabi wrote his collection of love poems called *The Guide to Desires*, inspired by the daughter of his Meccan mentor, and which he later had to explain was really about God: "When I refer to 'full-bosomed and shapely women who appear like suns'," he pleaded, "one should consider all this to be but the divine mysteries and the heavenly lights." He also began the *Meccan Revelations*, a monumental undertaking that he worked on all of his life. Later on, in his passage through Sufi centers in Turkey, Iraq, and Syria, where he began to attract influential disciples, Ibn Arabi composed his meditations on the prophets called *Settings of Wisdom*. He finally settled in Damascus, where he lived from 1226 until his death in 1240, the acknowledged genius, *al-shaykh al-akbar*, the *Doctor Maximus*, of Islamic mysticism.

The "Greatest Master" was somewhat more than that. Among his prodigious output, the *Revelations* is a gigantic, sprawling work—it runs to thirty-seven volumes in its most recent Arabic edition—and is dauntingly disorganized. Little wonder: like all his creations, the *Revelations* was written in fits of inspiration and deliberately without plan. "In what I have written I have never had a set purpose," Ibn Arabi boasted. "Flashes of divine inspiration used to come upon me and almost overwhelm me so that I could put them out of my mind only by committing to writing what had been revealed to me. Some works I wrote by the command of God, sent to me in sleep or through mystical revelation." The *Settings of Wisdom* is one of Ibn Arabi's most accessible works since it is brief and possesses an organizing structure, namely, the spirituality, which Ibn Arabi calls the "setting" or "bezel" of wisdom, of each of twenty-seven prophets from Adam through Moses and Jesus to Muhammad. It was revealed to him in a single dream; indeed, he affirmed that the Prophet himself had dictated it to him in Damascus toward the end of the month of Muharram in 1230. Many of his Muslim readers thought that Ibn Arabi's works came from someone other than God, however; they found his ideas aberrant, misleading, and extremely dangerous.

Ibn Arabi's mystical experiences are described in an engagingly straightforward and often startlingly detail—he unabashedly tells of his conversations with God, Muhammad, and various Sufi saints, dead and alive—and yet they are embedded in an extraordinarily complex metaphysic and epistemology that constitutes his "system." Of "system" of course there is none save that within Ibn Arabi's own head, which is revealed piecemeal and randomly across the enormous body of his written work. Modern readers of Ibn Arabi are more likely to be baffled than offended by the vast acres of writing before them, some of which look familiar in their sentiments, others impenetrable. The familiar flows from the combination of Neoplatonist metaphysics and Gnostic theosophy that appeared early in the Islamic mystical tradition, is readily discernible in Ibn Sina and Suhrawardi, and pervades much learned and esoteric mysticism in Islam. Ibn Arabi used both the concepts and the terms of that worldview. What is impenetrable is his manipulation of those concepts within his own unsystematic system, combined with his fondness for paradox, his loving embrace of contradiction, and, at base, the originality of his spiritual vision.

Ibn Arabi himself offered a quite different explanation of his inspiration to his readers: he was an extravagantly privileged author, and his works were matter for a privileged, and restricted, audience. There are in Ibn Arabi the usual warnings about sharing such readily misunderstood mysteries with the common man, a standard trope among the esotericists, but the Greatest Master was somewhat more explicit. Mysticism was like sex, he explained: "Knowledge of the mystical states can only be had by actual experience. The mind of man cannot define it nor arrive at any understanding of it by deduction."

The Seal of the Saints

Ibn Arabi's privilege as an author (and authority) is put equally bluntly. Spanish soil is rich in the quality that nourishes mystics. In the sixteenth century alone, Teresa of Avila, John of the Cross, and Ignatius of Loyola all left indelible marks on Christian spirituality. But none of them had anything close to what this Muslim mystic of al-Andalus attested that God had bestowed on him. He was, Ibn Arabi claimed, among the most spiritually gifted of God's creatures, a saint and more than a saint. Muslims, following al-Tirmidhi, usually distinguished between two types of religious gifts given to humans: that bestowed on the prophet and that possessed by the saint or friend of God (see II/6). In Ibn Arabi's view, both were recipients of divine revelation, the first to disseminate it formally as law among humankind, the latter for his own instruction and to confirm the authenticity of the prophet's message. This would have been startling news for most Muslims, had it been shared with them, but there was more. In some cases, truly exceptional individuals—Ibn Arabi called them prophet-saints and put himself among their number—were authorized to authenticate hadith that the jurists rejected and to reject others that the tradition declared sound, in short, not merely to reinterpret but to rewrite Islamic law.

For Ibn Arabi, saints were intimately tied to the prophets, the line that began with Adam and ended with Muhammad, the seal of the prophets. In like manner, there would also be a seal or climax to the saintly line derived from the "Muhammadan" legacy. There is no doubt about the identity of the "Seal of Muhammadan Sainthood" *(walaya muhammadaniyya)*, the "sainthood that pertains specifically to the community that is Muhammad's in the mode of appearance." It was Ibn Arabi himself: "I am the Seal of the Saints, just as it was attested that Muhammad was the Seal of the Prophets." In the end, he continued, all the prophets will be placed under the authority of Muhyi al-Din Muhammad ibn al-Arabi, not excluding Jesus himself: "Although Jesus is a Seal, he himself will be sealed by the Muhammad Seal."

The Teaching and Its Opponents

Ibn Arabi appears to have excited more admiration than opposition during his own lifetime. His more extravagant mystical claims were likely limited to the small circles of Sufi adepts and sympathizers in which he traveled, and his own personal behavior was both edifying and meticulous—meticulous enough, at any rate, not to arouse either doubt or suspicion in more traditional Islamic circles. The opposition came afterward, with the more general circulation of Ibn Arabi's own teachings.

Ibn Arabi's "teachings," or the spiritual foundations of his spirituality coherently arranged, are the product of a slightly later generation, notably of his most famous disciple, Sadr al-Din al-Qunawi (d. 1274). Al-Qunawi was a Persian Sufi who shared Ibn Arabi's company at Konya and wrote the first and most influential commentary on the *Settings of Wisdom*, the most accessible of the master's writings. Al-Qunawi, who was also chiefly responsible for Ibn Arabi's later and continuing vogue in Persian and Shiite mystical circles, "systematized" Ibn Arabi, and it was in that manner, a later generation's reading the Settings of Wisdom through the eyes of al-Qunawi, that Muslims came to know the teachings of Islam's premier mystic.

Ibn Arabi's approach to the mystic's quest for God plunges directly into the heart of two of the great, cross-cutting issues of monotheism: God's similarity or dissimilarity to us, his creation, and God's simultaneous Oneness and patently multiple manifestations. The first paradox begins with the monotheists' conviction that in some sense we all have our being "in the image of God," and yet between him and us yawns an enormous chasm of "otherness" *(ghaybiyya)*. Christians contrived to cross that chasm in the person of Jesus Christ, who stood athwart it, while Muslim theologians in the main stood on the hither shore and warned against the dangers of *tashbih*, "pointing to similitudes." Their preferred posture was *tanzih*, "stripping impurities" from the portrait of God. Some Christian mystics passed down that same via negativa en route to an experience of God, but Muslim theologians used it for safer projects, to defend the deity against the anthropomorphisms to which his creatures seemed so prone. Ibn Arabi embraced both. The mystic should be "the one with two eyes," someone who acknowledges God's transcendence and at the same time can savor, and take advantage of, God's "withness" (*maiyya*) with respect to ourselves.

In Ibn Arabi's version of creation, God unfolds himself in time and space out of a primordial longing to contemplate himself in the mirror of the cosmos: *tajalli*, "self-disclosure" and *kashf*, "unveiling" are two of the most pervasive concepts in Ibn Arabi's understanding of God. This is accomplished, in good Platonic fashion, on the basis of eternal spiritual archetypes (*ayan thabita*), which serve as the model of creation. This divine self-disclosure occurs in two "moments," the first in an "imaginal world," an ontological realm distinct from the purely spiritual world above it and the corporeal world below it, though partaking in some of the perfections and limitations of both. It is the world of imagination (*khayal*)—though not our human imagination, which is mere fantasy; the "imaginal world" is real in a profound sense. It is what Ibn Arabi often calls a *barzakh*, an isthmus or bridge that both separates and links. Below this is our material world, where God's image, already reflected in the imaginal world, grows progressively dimmer, though it can still be found by many within the human heart and soul and by a very few, the friends of God, in the imaginal world, to which they can, on occasion, mount.

Thus for Ibn Arabi our world is nothing other than a self-manifestation or reflection of God; it is the same as God, differing only in its degree of perfection, by its admixture of nonbeing. It seemed to follow, then, if anything can be said to "follow" in Ibn Arabi's mystical dialectic, that God and the world, the Creator and his creation, are one. This is the basis of the notorious doctrine dubbed the "Oneness of Being" (*wahdat al-wujud*)—an expression that Ibn Arabi himself does not seem to have used—an adherence to an ontological monism—"There is only One Being"—that became the chief focus of later attacks on Ibn Arabi.

Among the earliest Muslims to find fault with Ibn Arabi's vision of God and the world was the redoubtable Syrian jurist Ibn Taymiyya (d. 1328). He confessed that what he had first heard inclined him favorably toward the Spanish mystic, but that on reading the *Settings of Wisdom*, he recognized not only Ibn Arabi's implicit denial of many of Islam's fundamental tenets but the broader danger to the community in the disrepute he had cast on Sufism. For Ibn Taymiyya, Sufism was a behavioral science, one that led its sincere practitioner to a more perfect observance of the sharia, not, as Ibn Arabi seemed to claim, to a more intimate understanding—Ibn Arabi would doubtless have preferred "discovery"—of God's ineffable essence.

A scholar with a pronounced appetite for controversy, Ibn Taymiyya took on Ibn Arabi in four separate tracts in which he first identified and then attacked what he regarded as Ibn Arabi's unorthodox positions. First and foremost, of course, was the by now programmatic "Oneness of Being," where, according to Ibn Taymiyya, the Sufi failed to separate God's Being from the being of his creatures; indeed, God seemed to share existence with everything, "even jinns, devils, sinners, dogs, and swine." It was the price Ibn Arabi paid for professing, as almost all mystics have, though in his case more explicitly, more enigmatically, and more provocatively, the "similitude" that prevails between God and his creation as the *imago Dei*. Of Ibn Arabi's equal insistence on "distancing" (*tanzih*) God from all else, Ibn Taymiyya takes little note.

There was far more in the *Settings* to disturb a traditional sharia-minded jurist, and Ibn Taymiyya exposed it all. Among others innovations, there was the disturbing notion of those "eternal beings" (*ayan thabita*) that in more innocuous Platonic settings were God's ideas and served as models for creation but to which Ibn Arabi had granted both subsistence and even a determining role in the creation of the universe. Ibn Taymiyya unerringly identified them as purely noetic identities and denied them any extranoetic reality—thinking so does not make it so—and reclaimed for God the sole power of creation, which God effected, as the Quran clearly stated, out of nothing. As for Ibn Arabi's claim to a degree of sainthood that made him the peer of the prophets, Ibn Taymiyya, who was suspicious of the cult of the saints generally (see II/6), had nothing but scorn. The notion arose, he concluded, as did most of the errors in Ibn Arabi's teaching, from the privileged exegesis of the Quran and the hadith that all the esotericists claimed for themselves and was in fact perversely wrongheaded and malevolent.

Ibn Taymiyya may have been right about the metaphysics but wrong about the message: a lawyerly prosateur critiquing a mystical poet; a logician trying to make sense of a spiritual conjurer. But he may also have been right in a more profound sense in judging that this meta-Islamic thinker was, by that very fact, un-Islamic. In the sequel, in any event, Ibn Taymiyya's attack, the first of many from traditional Muslim thinkers, came to represent a widely held view of Ibn Arabi in the Arabic-speaking Sunni world: his works were at best dangerous and at worst blasphemous. The judgment was rendered quite explicit by another jurist more famous as a historian. While serving as chief justice in Egypt, Ibn Khaldun (d. 1406) issued a judicial decree (*fatwa*) against certain "would-be Sufis," including by name Ibn Arabi. Their works, he ruled, "reek of downright unbelief and reprehensible innovation." Indeed, they made the inquirer "wonder whether these people can be treated at all as members of the (Muslim) community and counted among followers of the sharia." As for their works, which included, again by name, the *Settings of Wisdom* and the *Meccan Revelations*, "when found they must be destroyed by fire or washed off with water until all traces of writing disappear."

The Beginnings of Kabbalah

The development of an esoteric and mystical form of Judaism, which evolved simultaneously, if far less publicly, with the legal work of the rabbis, eventually came to be called Kabbalah, literally "that which is handed down." The Mishnah too had once been "handed down," but the distinction between Mishnah and Kabbalah is the same as that which can be observed between Greek philosophy and Hellenism's occult sciences; between Christian theology and Gnosticism; between the teachings of the Islamic lawyers and those of the Sufis. One kind of knowledge is public, literal, and discursive; the other is esoteric, allegorical, and mystical. It is, finally, the difference between theology and theosophy; between law and allegory; between intellect and intuition.

Kabbalah represents a tradition of Jewish mysticism that can be identified, not always neatly nor always convincingly, by the presence of certain themes and symbols within it. The elements of the system made their first appearance in the *Sefer ha-bahir*, the *Book of Brilliance*, from northern Spain or southern France at the end of the twelfth century, and Kabbalah reached its first climactic moment in the *Sefer ha-zohar*, the *Book of Splendors* by Moses de León (d. 1305), which remained the classic statement. Between them, Provence and the remnants of al-Andalus, or to use its Hebrew name, ha-Sefarad, where both these works were produced, remained the matrix of Jewish mystical speculation for almost two more centuries. In 1492, however, with the expulsion of the Jews from Spain, the adepts of this esoteric wisdom were scattered across the Mediterranean. Thereafter Kabbalah was both the possession and the product of the Sephardic diaspora, in Salonika, Istanbul, and then, after 1517, when the Ottomans became the masters of the Arab lands, in Safad in Galilee, which became a thriving Jewish settlement and increasingly the magnet for rabbinic adepts of Kabbalah, who fashioned a new version of the tradition, a kind of "Kabbalah for everyone" (see II/8).

From the beginnings of Jewish speculation on esoteric matters, the rabbis had attempted to limit its exercise to restricted groups of mature scholars. By and large they were successful, and the tradition of an exclusive and elitist gnosis was maintained throughout the long and obscure history of early Kabbalah. But at Safad, particularly with the work of Isaac Luria (see below), the program changed: the search for enlightenment was no longer to be the preserve of the privileged, educated few but matter for the masses. The effects of popularizing such speculation were diffuse and explosive. Popular Kabbalism, a notion that would have frozen the blood of earlier rabbis, produced, in one degree or another, the messianic convulsions of Sabbatai Zvi in the seventeenth century (see I/2) and the no less powerful impulse called Hasidism in the eighteenth (see II/8).

The Zohar

That the kabbalistic tradition was deeply esoteric is manifest at every turn, nowhere more patently than in the classic already referred to, the *Zohar*, written—or better, composed—in Spain between 1270 and 1300 by Moses de León, a native of Guadalajara. According to the report soon circulating together with the book, the actual author was Shimon bar Yohai, a Mishnah-cited authority who lived in Galilee in the second century of the common era. How the work got from second-century Palestine, where no one had ever heard of it, to thirteenth-century Catalonia was exceedingly mysterious—it was, quite simply, "handed down," which is what Kabbalah, after all, is about. The transmission of the *Zohar* is so mysterious that modern scholars are inclined to credit it to the modest Moses de León himself (who went to the trouble of composing it in Aramaic, though trailing incriminating Spanish syntax behind it) rather than to Shimon. The entire medieval tradition thought it was Shimon's, however, and his cult as the father of mystical Judaism is still very much in evidence in Galilee today.

The *Zohar*, with all its credentialed antiquity from the heartland of rabbinic Judaism, opened a spacious new window onto Judaism's sacred texts. The bulk of the immense, sprawling work is given over to an esoteric exegesis of the five books of the Torah, divided, in the classic fashion of the rabbinic midrashim, according to the liturgical recitation cycle of the Law (see II/6). But unlike the scholarly or exhortatory commentaries that constituted the heart of the Jewish exegetical tradition, the *Zohar* swung loosely about the text, wrapping it in a tissue of stories and tales, which led, in their oblique fashion, deep into the pool of esoterica that constituted the common Mediterranean inheritance of Jews, Christians, and Muslims alike.

Moses de León did not invent Kabbalah. The *Brilliance* had gone before and, much earlier, the *Book of Creation*. Indeed, the famous Provençal rabbi Nahmanides (d. 1270) wrote a commentary on the Pentateuch that also glossed the text by adducing esoteric explanations. But the earlier treatises had been anonymous (and highly recondite), while Nahmanides, for all his esoteric learning, still treated the text in the integral manner of his more traditional predecessors. Nahmanides pointed this way and that to the strange passing scenery along the side of the road; the *Zohar* left the road, and then took the reader on a ride that was at the same time poetic, illuminating, and entertaining. With some justice, it has been called "a mystical novel based on the Torah."

The World of the Sefiroth

Beneath this superficially accessible world of stories, parables, and images lies the same basic system that informs all of Kabbalah. We are still in world of the sefiroth, the ten divine emanations that make their appearance in the *Book of Creation*. Though the *Zohar* eschews the didacticism of many of the treatises built around the sefiroth, they are present and fundamental, and they remain so in all Kabbalah. They are a familiar by-product of ancient Gnosticism. Though the names are somewhat different, the ten sefiroth—The Crown, Understanding, Wisdom, Power, Love, Beauty, Majesty, Endurance, Foundation, Presence—are another version of the Gnostic Aeons, eternal, hypostatized emanations from the First Principle, which the Kabbalists called En Sof, "The Limitless." Indeed, the Gnostic myth of disorder in the pleroma, the spiritual world above our own, is repeated in the kabbalistic versions of that same cosmic drama.

According to the kabbalistic retelling of the Gnostic myth, the lowest of the sefiroth, the one called Shekinah or "Presence" (see II/6) and identified as a female element or principle, is "shattered"—the "breaking of the vessels" is a standard of the kabbalistic dynamic—and scattered amidst the lower, material world, the Gnostics' *kenoma*. In the Christian version of what follows, one of the other Aeons, Christos, descends in fleshly guise into the kenoma to effect the salvation of the scattered shards of the fallen Sophia, but the Jewish version is remarkably different. Integrity is restored—the process is called precisely that, *tikkun* or "restoration"—to the world of the sefiroth by the acts of individual Jews. Prayer, devotion, observance of the commandments, and rigorous asceticism will all restore the Shekinah to her rightful place. The Christian Gnostics had in effect mythologized Jesus Christ, but the Kabbalists did the reverse and converted myth into history, a history no longer controlled by God but by his creatures.

The Kabbalists expended an extraordinary degree of energy and ingenuity on spinning out the permutations of the sefiroth, which turn out, on close inspection, to be not emanations from God, as in the Neoplatonic Greek model, but a range of activities within God. "They are God and God is they," as one formulation had it. The En Sof advertised its own ineffability: it was not only infinite; it was also indescribable. What the Kabbalists were doing, however, was charting, like nuclear physicists, the activities of the subatomic components of what we had been led to believe was the irreducible principle of being. The En Sof, like the atom itself, had, after all, a highly active interior life.

But if the En Sof proved not to be so ineffable after all, it still remained un-approachable. None of those skilled "nuclear scientists" thought to penetrate the En Sof or themselves enter the world of the sefiroth. What is termed "Jewish mysticism," though it had its affective side and counseled the cultivation of devotional practices in its "rules of piety" (*hanhaqoth*; see II/8), at least some of which were intended for popular consumption, was far more speculative than experiential. Almost from the beginning, Jewish mystics were searching for knowledge of God rather than experience of him, how to get from here to There rather than the Being There so prominent in the accounts of Christian and Muslim mystics.

There is no doubt that many of the Safad adepts had what might be generally considered mystical experiences. But it is noteworthy that these were invariably cast in the form of an encounter not with God (or the En Sof) but with an intermediary, in the case of Joseph Karo (see II/4), a *maggid* or angelic messenger or, as his disciples thought of Isaac Luria, with no less than the prophet Elijah. In each instance, what occurred was the transmission of privileged knowledge, in short, additional Kabbalah. And the experience could be induced. Isaac Luria recommended something he called *yihud*, "unity" or "unification," and although in other systems this might be thought to suggest union with the divine, for the Lurianic adept it meant stretching out on the grave of an earlier zaddik and concentrating on the prospect of arousing the soul of the dead saint. If successful, the yihud or union could be used to channel the esoteric learning of the dead zaddik into that of the living adept.

Isaac Luria

This arcane and convoluted understanding of the "reality" behind plain texts and the material world now appears hopelessly difficult, as it was probably intended to be from the outset. But deep within it lay the mystic's urge to approach God in a paradoxically more direct way, an urge too powerful to remain concealed within the folds of esotericism. In Islam mysticism became popularized in the Sufi orders; in Christianity by such clerics as Ignatius of Loyola and Francis de Sales, who in the late sixteenth century brought an easily assimilated and tightly controlled version of the monks' spiritual exercises to the secular clergy and the laity alike; and in Judaism by the Hasidic movement, which in the eighteenth century divested Safad Kabbalism of some of its more esoteric and inaccessible features to render it a kind of popular revelation (see II/8).

The man most responsible for this was the greatest and most influential of the Safad Kabbalists, the already mentioned Isaac Luria (d. 1572). He was born in Jerusalem of recently arrived Ashkenazi—that is, European—parents and received his early training in rabbinics in Egypt, where he also discovered, apparently on his own, the attractions of Kabbalah. Shortly before 1570 he went to Safad and studied briefly with the most famous Kabbalist of the time, Moses Cordovero (d. 1570), himself the student of the redoubtable rabbinic lawyer Joseph Karo. Cordovero's strength was systematic thinking: his meditations, in the form of an immense commentary on the *Zohar*, on the complex world of the sefiroth was as coherent as it was imaginative. Cordovero died shortly after Luria's arrival in Safad, and thereafter the younger man passed quickly from being a student to being a teacher, or more accurately, a zaddik with his own circle of disciples, many of whom became the leading Kabbalists of the next generation—and Luria's reporters. Luria wrote little; most of what is known of his approach to Kabbala comes from his students' notes.

Central to Luria's thinking was the already noted theory of tikkun, the "restoration" of the Shekinah to its antelapsarian state by spiritual exertions, now not of a single adept, but of the entire community. Thus Luria included the whole body of Jews, at least the spiritually aware Jews, in his bold project of redeeming God. Behind this powerful Lurianic notion was an equally powerful experience: that of the new exile of the Jewish people and the grief it provoked. The exile in this instance was from ha-Sefarad, the beloved al-Andalus or Muslim Spain, and the "mourning for Zion" was felt most poignantly in Zion itself, in Eretz Israel, before it passed out into Jewish hinterlands of Europe where it saddened, and exalted, new generations of Jews and kindled their own zeal for tikkun.

Kabbalah for Everyone: Hasidism

From what we can see of Baal Shem Tov through the dense clouds of legend that came to surround his life, he does not seem to have been intent on founding a movement, but by his death in 1760, there was one in existence (see II/8). Among its earliest achievements was the formalization of its own charismatic leadership cadres. The leaders of the Hasidim were effectively zaddikim, literally "just men" but perhaps better, "justified men." These were the spiritual leaders in each generation, and later in each branch of Hasidism, a lifeline to the divine, so to speak, through whom the ordinary Hasid maintained connection to God. The zaddikim, or *rebbes*, as they were also commonly called, were, like the *pirs* of Sufism and the Imams of Shiite Islam, not merely guides but conduits of divine favor and blessings.

These "saints" opened up an attractive possibility familiar from the Kabbalah and now taken up with enthusiasm by the Hasidim, that of *tikkun olam* or "repair of the world." The phrase had a long history. Early on it referred to the rabbis' ability to "order aright" the life of the community by their decrees. It was also used in an eschatological sense of God's perfecting the world in the End Time. In the Kabbalah that eschatological reading of *tikkun olam* was applied to the "repair" of the fractured state of the Plenitude (*pleroma*), whose pristine perfection had been shattered in the great cosmic drama (see I/5).

The notion of the zaddik, the charismatic "axis," as the Muslims referred to their sanctified Sufi masters, of God's blessings, when joined with Baal Shem Tov's stress on joyous piety, sent waves of enthusiasm coursing through the Jewish communities of eastern Poland, northward into Lithuania, and southward into the Ukraine and Hungary. There were shortly pietists all along those eastern marches of Europe, in the seam between Latin and Eastern Christianity and Ottoman Turkish Islam, singing and dancing before the Lord with an abandonment that doubtless brought relief to their harried souls but caused other Jews, particularly those schooled in strict rabbinic observance, to look askance at these devotees of a simple and very unfettered piety. The naysayers or mitnaggedim, were to be found in the principal yeshivas of the day, many of which were located in what is now Lithuania.

What most disturbed those opponents of the Hasidic movement was the substitution of somewhat remarkable personal piety for learning. The easy going, even freewheeling devotions of the Hasidim, who seemed to pray when and where they wished and who favored, moreover, the Sephardic to the now standard Ashkenazi ritual, rites sometimes fueled with alcohol, it was said, stood in sharp contrast to the punctilious and learned style of the traditional rabbinic communities. The mitnaggedim had even more profound concerns, about Hasidic ignorance and laxity, their apparent pantheism, and their dabbling in Kabbalah, which was always regarded with a certain anxiety by the rabbis. The Hasidim preferred to experience God rather than to serve him by seriously studying and punctiliously observing his commandments.

The conflict between the Hasidim and the traditionalists ended with each side, if not capitulating to the other—the two strains still remain distinct—then with each assimilating many of the other's virtues. The Hasidic rebbes became more learned in Torah and their communities more observant, while the *rosh yeshivah*, the rabbinic schoolmaster, gradually took on some of the spiritual aura of the zaddik. The two approaches to a Jewish life elided into one "orthodox" type in the face of an even more distinct challenge to tradition, the movement of Jewish Reform (see I/5).

10

The Last Things

IN GREEK *ESCHATON* MEANS "END," and from the perspective of the three monotheistic communities, that "end" is understood in two related, and sometimes conflicting, senses. It refers in the first instance to the end of the individual: what, if anything, occurs to a person immediately after death. It is a starkly personal and individual concern. But the three faiths are also, and perhaps even more thoughtfully and fretfully, concerned with the End Time, the absolute finale to God's plan for the cosmos, and what might lie beyond. There was, as it turned out, a great deal beyond. The End will mark only the end of history; beyond "The Day" and "The Hour" stretches eternity, not the mere prolongation of time but an entirely new dimension of being. Eternity is a state or condition, and while theology undertook to explain in what it consisted, "eternity" simply pronounces of itself that it has no beginning or end: humans will enter it in progress.

End Time Scenarios

The End Time was and remains a complex affair for Jews, Christians, and Muslims, with an elaborate and articulated scenario for the series of acts that will constitute it. Its formal production design began with the visionary apocalypses of post-Exilic Judaism when privileged individuals were permitted to espy the future. The subsequent reports of these journeys into the Beyond, Jewish, Christian, and Muslim, were filled with circumstantial details of events and their sequences, of topography, of personalities, and even of dialogue. It was left to later and more generally sober theologians and jurists to put some order into these visionary recitals, to filter out elements that proved useless or unacceptable, and to try to incorporate other and older details that had somehow been overlooked. By their own Middle Ages, all three monotheistic communities had a relatively coherent idea of what would occur at the End Time, a schema or scenario for the more sober-minded, a vivid picture for those who took their instruction from preachers, poets, or the walls of churches.

In what seems to be the earliest, preapocalyptic vision of the End, Jews were already connecting the "Day of the Lord" with Jerusalem, a tie that persists among Jews, Christians, and Muslims to the present day. "In the days to come," Isaiah prophesies, "the mountain of Yahweh's house" will tower above all else, and the nations of the world will say, "Let us go up to the mountain of Yahweh that He may instruct us in His ways" (2:2–3). If that is still vindication without judgment, the judgment soon followed. In Isaiah and his fellow prophets, Israel will be judged and purged before it can be made whole again (2:12–22), and in Zephaniah that judgment is extended to all the nations of the earth. In Ezekiel the notion of a collective judgment on nations, which he shares, is supplemented by a powerful new idea. Individuals too will be called to judgment: Israelites will be saved or condemned on their merits (11:17–21).

The most consequential biblical text on the End Time is undoubtedly the book of the prophet Joel. "Alas, the day is near, the day of the Lord, it comes, a mighty destruction from the Almighty," he intones (1:13). Joel's point of departure is a plague of locusts, but he soon broadens it into an apocalyptic vision of the Day of the Lord. History has passed into eschatology, and it carries with it into the End Time the tone of harsh moralism and images of doom and destruction that earlier prophets like Amos had used to describe impending political disaster. On the Day of the Lord Israel's enemies will attack Yahweh (2:1–17). There will be signs and portents—"the sun shall be turned into darkness and the moon into blood" (2:31). There will be few survivors, "in Jerusalem, a remnant whom the Lord will call" (2:32). God will sit in judgment. He will "gather all the nations together and lead them down to the Valley of the Lord's Judgment" (3:1–2). Then Israel will be vindicated, when "the Lord roars from Zion and thunders from Jerusalem" (3:16). God will lavishly reward Israel with all the pleasures of a parched people: "All the streams of Judah shall be full with water, and a fountain shall spring from the Lord's house" (3:18).

Many of elements of the End are present, then, in the prophets, as they describe an imminent political or natural disaster that is transferred into a distant, eschatological doom. But there is no evidence in those texts of when such an event might take place, whether in history or beyond: it is simply in the future. What located it more precisely was the connection of God's judgment, which is powerfully present in the Bible, to a more novel concept, the resurrection of the dead (see below). This was thought of as a collective national resurrection and, by implication, an End Time event. This opening up of the Beyond becomes apparent in post-Exilic times, though we cannot say what—the experience of exile itself, exposure to Zoroastrian notions of a Judgment and an End, or the spread of the Greek idea of the soul as spiritual and immortal—induced the new thinking.

This uneasy sense of the imminence of the End and the rapid alternation of political despair and supernatural hope produced the apocalypses of Second Temple Judaism. Texts like those attributed to Enoch and Ezra the rabbis kept out of the biblical canon as "extraneous books" (*seferim hitzonim*), but these nevertheless left their indelible imprint on Jewish sensibilities—and Christian and Muslim as well—regarding the End of Days.

The End, Judgment, and Punishment/Reward are the three main acts of all eschatological scenarios, each enlarged with illustrative, instructive, or even entertaining detail. The End is extended backward to embrace a prelude that might be called Signs: how do we know when the End will come? "No man knows the day or the hour," of course, but a great many believers have spent a great deal of time calculating it nonetheless. There will be perturbations of nature and perturbations of the spirit, and to the latter belong the false messiahs, false Christs, and the Muslims' "Deceiver." Loose ends are to be tied up: Enoch and Elijah must return to suffer death, to whom the Muslims would add Jesus (see I/3). For the Christians, Israel must be converted, in history, before Act 2 can begin. The climax comes with the defeat of God's enemies—here the Messiah and Mahdi figures are in evidence—followed by the destruction of the world, the great conflagration in which the material cosmos perishes.

Before the Judgment proper can begin, the resurrection of the dead must occur, a prodigious and prodigiously troubling event. Then the wicked and the good, the sheep and the goats, will be solemnly summoned to God's tribunal, their virtues and vices spelled out—angels have been recording these in books—and judgment rendered. It is in fact no different from what was decreed for each individual at the moment of death (see below); now, however, God's justice is vindicated to all. The judgment itself is swelled by the desire to make certain that no heroes and particularly no enemies of God go unnoted. This is a time for settling some very human scores since the enemies of God, as Dante showed, often live up the street or in the house next door.

Acts 1 and 2 of the eschatological drama are broad canvases for painters and poets; Act 3, "Punishments and Rewards," has ample graphic space as well, but it became more precisely the scratch pad for the theologians and jurists who there, in the midst of the cool running waters of paradise and raging flames of hell, had to explain how any of this could happen.

After Death, What?

Before the judgment comes death, the death of the believer and the infidel, of saint and sinner alike. From the outset, the Bible seems to have very little idea about, or interest in, what follows death. Total annihilation is a difficult and indeed sophisticated notion, and the ancient Israelites rather preferred lifelessness, an existence, but precisely a lifeless one, in a shadowy place called Sheol. Though descriptions and location are vague, and its conceptualization has not been thoroughly thought out, Sheol is generally a dark, silent underground place—its other names are "the grave" or "the abyss"—and, where they are specified, its principal inhabitants seem to be those who died violently or were not treated to appropriate burial, or, on another reckoning, all the dead. "There the wicked cease from troubling," Job says of Sheol. "There rest those whose strength is spent. Prisoners are wholly at ease; they do not hear the taskmaster's voice. Small and great alike are there, and the slave is free of his master" (J3:18–19).

The thought that the troubled in particular were consigned to Sheol may have led to, or perhaps simply made it useful for, another idea—that of retribution. Israel was thought to be punished for its sins in this life, but some of the prophets began to add another dimension to their moralizing, namely that Israel's enemies would be punished for their iniquities in the gradually more distinct landscape of Sheol. The idea is put forward by both Isaiah (14:15) and Ezekiel (32:18), who consign Egypt and Assyria to Sheol for their crimes against Israel. There is no suggestion that Ramses and Ashurbanipal will meet any Israelite in those dour precincts, but moral thinking about Israel too was changing in the great upheaval surrounding the fall of the first temple. There was a new idea of justice abroad—divine justice (see I/1)—and it was signaled as such when Jeremiah announced, "No longer will people say, 'Parents have eaten sour grapes and the children's teeth are set on edge.' But everyone shall die for his own sins: whoever eats sour grapes, his own teeth will be set on edge" (31:29–30). Ezekiel echoes Jeremiah when he has God himself proclaim, "The person who sins, only he will die" (18:14). Ezekiel then goes on to his own precise denial of collective responsibility: "A child shall not share in his parent's guilt, nor shall a parent share in a child's guilt" (18:20).

Death and Judgment

Though their language might seem to suggest it, neither Jeremiah nor Ezekiel was proposing that God's justice is meted out to the individual in an afterlife: it is during mortal existence that the individual will be made to settle accounts with God. The Israelites of that age had as yet no strong conviction of personal survival after death. But their post-Exilic successors did, and beneath the scenarios of the early Second Temple Jewish apocalypses lies the unquestioned assumption not only that there is life after death but that individuals will somehow survive the grave to participate in God's final act of judgment and to be judged on their own merits as well. Only in post-Exilic times, in Maccabees, for example (2 Macc. 12:43–45), where Judah "took due account of the resurrection," as well as in other Jewish Apocrypha, did there emerge the notion that this life's sins and virtuous acts would be punished or rewarded in particular places after death. The first is identified as Gehenna, the smoldering garbage pit of Jerusalem, and the latter as the Garden of Eden, the primordial place of Adam and Eve's utopian bliss. This was Jesus' afterlife landscape as well, and the belief that there was some form of life after death, and that the Lord's justice was served there on the Day of Judgment (*yom ha-din*) universally prevailed in rabbinic Judaism, as it did in Christianity and Islam.

The Particular Judgment

In the Gospels there is evidence of Christian belief in both a cosmic End Time that includes a Last Judgment as well as in a more particular judgment rendered on the individual immediately after his or her death. The general judgment was an important part of Jesus' messianic message, as it would be of Muhammad's, whereas the particular judgment is mentioned merely in passing. It appears most clearly as the premise of a parable (Luke 16:19–23), which is actually about the reversal of fortune. A poor man named Lazarus dies and "is carried away by angels to be in the bosom of Abraham." An anonymous rich man also dies, but after his burial he is found "in Hades, where he is in torment." The same notion of an immediate judgment is present when Jesus turns to one of the men being crucified with him and assures him that "today you will be with me in Paradise" (Luke 23:43).

This is not an urgent motif in Jesus' preaching—more likely it was simply current Jewish belief—but in the sequel it was accepted teaching in Christian circles, even though the primary New Testament emphasis is unmistakably on the Last Judgment (see below). The Church Fathers seemed content to receive the particular judgment as doctrine on the basis of the scanty Gospel references—Augustine cites the Lazarus–rich man story in his defense of a judgment immediately after death. The fact of such a judgment gave little pause; far more troublesome was the meting out of either punishment or reward in its wake. We cannot say what Jesus' own idea of individual survival was, but soon his followers, now chiefly converted Gentiles, thought of the soul as an immortal spiritual entity that at death separates from, and survives, the body. How it was possible to punish that disembodied soul with the notoriously physical pains of hell, "where the devouring worm never dies and the fire is not quenched" (Mark 9:48), was, on the face of it, problematic.

The Resurrection of the Body

When the Andalusian Muslim faylasuf Ibn Rushd (d. 1198) took up the difficult problem of bodily resurrection in his *Incoherence of the Incoherence*, he noted that "resurrection has been mentioned in different religions for at least a thousand years. . . . The first to mention bodily resurrection were the prophets of Israel after Moses, as is evident from the Psalms and many books attributed to the Israelites. Bodily resurrection is also affirmed in the New

Testament and attributed by tradition to Jesus." The matter was not so simple, however, as we have just seen. The resurrection of the body and its reunification with the soul, how this was achieved and when, raised substantial problems in all three religious communities.

There may be earlier mentions of postmortem survival in the Bible, but the first unmistakable reference to a bodily resurrection appears in Ezekiel's celebrated vision (37:1–8) of a field of "dry bones" into which the Lord breathes life. "The breath entered them, and they came to life and stood up on their feet, a vast multitude." "Those bones," the same text continues, "are the whole House of Israel." And there is more. This is prophesy and the Lord is speaking of the future: "I will lift you out of your graves, O My people, and bring you to the Land of Israel" (37:10, 13).

This is clearly a national resurrection, an eschatological restoration of the Benei Israel to Eretz Israel, but in Daniel's later vision resurrection grows somewhat more precise and is connected with the notions of punishment and reward: "Many of those who sleep in the dust of the earth will awake, some to eternal life, others to reproaches, to everlasting abhorrence" (12:2). Thereafter the resurrection of the dead became a standard feature of visions of the Afterlife and a crucial element in the workings of God's justice. In later Second Temple times it in fact became a divisive point between the Pharisees and the Sadducees. The Pharisees held, according to Josephus, that "souls have an immortal vigor in them (and the) power to move and live again" (*Antiquities* 18.1.4)—a view shared by the earliest Christians (e.g., Mark 12:23–26) and certainly by Paul, who cited it as a sign of his own (Pharisaic) orthodoxy when summoned before the Sanhedrin (Acts 23:6–10).

Paul was a Pharisee, or at least educated as one (Acts 22:3), and so it is not remarkable that he should follow the Pharisaic position on resurrection. But what of his master, Jesus? In Mark 12:18 Jesus is approached by some Sadducees, who, as the Gospel remarks, "say that there is no resurrection." They pose him a legal conundrum: a woman has married seven different husbands in series, all of whom predecease her. To which of them will she be married at the resurrection, "when they all come back to life"? The intent was probably to demolish belief in the Afterlife by a legal reduction to the absurd, but Jesus takes the question seriously and gives a serious answer. There is no marriage after the resurrection: the risen are like "angels in heaven," and so, one supposes, in some sense immaterial. "Have you never read in the Book of Moses," Jesus continues, "in the story of the burning bush, how God spoke to him and said, 'I am the God of Abraham, the God of Isaac and the God of Jacob' (Exod. 3:6)? God is not the God of the dead, but the God of the living" (12:26–27).

Thus Jesus' answer too is in perfect agreement with the teaching of the Pharisees, and his attempt to establish it out of the Torah is the polemical tack taken by the later rabbis when they debated the resurrection question in the Talmud's Sanhedrin tractate. "Debate" is perhaps not the word. The Sadducees, who had resisted the Pharisaic view in the name of a more Torah-derived position, were no longer a force in Jewish life after 70 c.e., and so the Pharisaic teaching on the Afterlife as a place of punishment and rewards became, in fact, Jewish orthodoxy. Witness, for example, the second of the Eighteen Blessings introduced into standard synagogue worship in this era: "You, O Lord, are mighty forever, You quicken the dead, are mighty to save. You sustain the living with loving kindness, quicken the dead with great mercy . . . and keep Your faith with those who sleep in the dust. Who is like You, Lord of mighty deeds, and who resembles You, O King, who kills and quickens and causes salvation to spring forth."

The rabbis were in general agreement on the subject of the resurrection of the body and its reunion with the soul; in dispute was who would be resurrected—all of Israel, as the Ezekiel passage seemed to indicate, or only the just of Israel? Since there was also consensus that the resurrection would occur in Eretz Israel, what of those who died in the Diaspora? This latter anxiety led to the widespread custom of reburying Diaspora Jews in Jerusalem, and particular in the Valley of Jehoshaphat or Kidron, where it was widely believed the Final Judgment would take place. Christians and Muslims shared that belief, and the Kidron Valley became a favored burial place for Jews, Christians, and Muslims alike down to the present day.

The Seed, the Statue, and the Conjunction of Materia and Forma

From the New Testament onward a belief in the resurrection of the body remained an essential tenet of Christianity. Yet Christians, as always, felt impelled to explain it to themselves, much as Jesus had or the ex-Pharisee Paul to the skeptics of his day, and so provided a template for their beliefs: "You may ask," Paul begins, "how are the dead raised? In what kind of a body? How foolish! The seed you sow does not come to life unless it has first died, and what you sow is not the body that shall be, but a naked grain; and God clothes it with the body of His choice, each seed with its own particular body. . . . What is sown in the earth as a perishable thing is raised imperishable. Sown in humiliation, it is raised in glory; sown in weakness, it is raised in power; sown as an animal body, it is raised as a spiritual body" (1 Cor. 15:35–44).

The metaphor of the germinated seed was attractive, but the notion of a spiritual body posed considerable problems that generations of Christians struggled to resolve, especially the Platonically inclined intelligentsia who had thought of the body as merely the tomb or prison of the soul. They much preferred to rise as angels. And the body, as everyone recognized, was in a constant state of flux, down to its final dissolution in the tomb. Was it reassembled, resuscitated, or renewed? "Regermination" was one popular answer to the problem: after death, our seed germinates again; it is the same person—with the identical DNA, we might say, grown, or cloned, anew. The explanation was not popular with Augustine, however, since it involved process, which for him meant corruption. If the resurrected body was to be incorrupt, as it must, it must also be remote from all change. Augustine thought the body would be reassembled, no parts lost, in its most beautiful state—in one place he guessed that might be somewhere near the age of thirty, perhaps because it was Jesus' age at his resurrection—without change (hunger and eating, wasting and growing are all banished) and without defect, though it might be argued that the martyrs would bear the glorious scars of their suffering for Christ. Indeed, the growing cult of the relics of the martyrs (see II/6) may have contributed to the attractiveness of the reassemblage model of resurrection.

Thus the resurrection question passed into the debate menu of medieval Latin Christianity, where Augustine, as usual, provided the lead. But there was soon a new voice in the debate, that of Aristotle. With the thirteenth-century rediscovery of Aristotle by the Latin West, whose consequences are most visible in Thomas Aquinas (see II/7), the discussion took a different direction. As the Aristotelian model of being replaced the earlier Platonic one, the concept of a human being as a natural and organic union of matter and form began to steer the discussion of human survival and resurrection. The form of the human being—form now understood in the Aristotelian sense of the active and organizing principle of a being—was the rational soul, which was thus the surviving personality of the individual. But the human formal principle, the soul, is ordered toward its material principle, corporeality, and, in the case of any given individual, toward this particular matter, what we call our body. Individual survival is then principally a question of survival of its immortal spiritual soul, but a soul that is incomplete without the material body toward which it is naturally ordered.

Thomas remained bothered by the details raised by age, genitals (of what use are they in the Afterlife?) and hence gender, by cannibalism, mutilation, and all the changes the flesh is heir to. Each had to be dealt with in turn, but the Aristototelian body-as-matter/soul-as-form paradigm—the hypothesis is called hylemorphism—provided a stable philosophical model for an anthropology and, with a little shoehorning here and there, for the resurrection of the flesh.

In the Meantime . . .

At about the same time Thomas and his fellow Aristotelians were rewriting the Christian history of the soul, the Church confronted the lingering issue of what happened to a person immediately after death. Christians had long since agreed that the soul and the body would be reunited at the Last Judgment, and under those circumstances, the physical pains of hell and fulfillment of paradise made sense. But in the meantime, as long as the body rests (or rots) in the grave, some argued, the soul must be in a kind of slumber or hibernation. That was a minor strain of belief at best, and most Christians preferred to believe that the punishments of the wicked and, especially, the rewards of the just immediately followed death, "without asking how." The early and widespread cult of first the martyrs and then more generally of the saints testifies to the strength of the conviction that Christianity's heroes went, like Lazarus, immediately to their reward (see II/6).

But questions remained unanswered, and in 1274 the Second Council of Lyons pronounced that souls free of sin went directly to heaven, though some continued to maintain—Pope John XXII (r. 1316–1334) among them (see below)—that they did not enjoy the full presence of God, the so-called Beatific Vision, until they were reunited with the body at the cosmic finale. John's successor, Benedict XII, addressed the issue of the Beatific Vision in 1336, but in 1439, at the Council of Florence, the matter was settled more programmatically for the Western Church—and presumably for the Eastern as well, since these were the dogmatic terms of the reunion of the Churches (see I/6). The council's statement of faith declared that upon death, sinless souls would immediately enjoy the Beatific Vision whereas sinners would be consigned directly to hell. There was as well—the real point of the declaration, directed at the Eastern Church—an intermediate state called purgatory, reserved for those who still required atonement for their previously confessed sins (see II/5).

The Cosmology of the Other World

Tradition placed the site of the Last Judgment in the Valley of Jehoshaphat, on the eastern side of Jerusalem. The localization of the rest of the eschatological drama was somewhat more problematic and depended on how the dramatists viewed the world and its parts. The ancients shared two views of the universe. On a popular level, the earth was a circular but flat surface, surrounded at its rim by a body of water the Greeks called Ocean, and covered with a vault containing the planets and the stars. Mythical lands and places, like the Garden of Eden, the Happy Isles, or the Elysian Fields, could be placed at its remote and imperfectly known outer edges, much the way, for example, that Muslims located Eden in Sri Lanka. Places of punishment, the various "hells" often connected with fire, were located beneath the earth.

Eventually all versions of this popular imaging of the earth had to compete with the scientific model associated with Aristotle and Ptolemy. In this view, the earth rests stationary at the center of the planetary system. Around it revolve seven crystalline spheres in each of which is embedded one of the seven heavenly bodies (outward from earth: Moon, Mercury, Venus, the Sun, Mars, Jupiter, and Saturn). Beyond them is the revolving sphere of the "fixed" stars, and beyond that is the pure crystalline, and hence completely invisible, sphere whose motion is imitated by all the others. Beyond that is the Empyrean, the "Fiery," which exists outside all time, space, and motion. This is the monotheists "heaven," the "Abode of God and all the blessed."

In this scientific view of the universe, which came to prevail among the educated in all three monotheistic communities and which that Dante recapitulated and fleshed out in his *Divine Comedy*, hell remained firmly under the earth, though its point of entry, which the Greeks and Romans located in various caves and caverns around the Mediterranean—Virgil's *Aeneid* popularized the region around Lake Avernus in southern Italy—became fixed in the Valley of Hinnom (Heb. *Ge Hinnom* > Gehenna), the place south of Jerusalem that had once served as the city's smoldering and malodorous garbage dump. The site of the place of reward was a more complex question, however. There were two competing, sometimes conflicting, and sometimes harmonized versions of where the virtuous would find their final rest, paradise or heaven.

The older, more physical notion was that this would take place in the pristine utopia of Eden, the untroubled Garden of Adam and Eve. If the Original Sin committed there led to paradise lost—*paradis* is the familiar Persian loanword for "park"—the blameless could hope to find rest in that same paradise regained. So many Jews and early Christians believed, and so too all Muslims still believe since that image of the Garden (*janna*), together with many of its physical details, is deeply embedded in the Quran and Muslims' consciousness shaped by the Quran.

There was no place for a terrestrial Eden in the scientific view of the universe to which the monotheists were all eventually introduced. God dwelled in the timeless space beyond the seventh heaven, and the notion of bliss for the believers was slowly transformed into a desire to dwell with God, and, as we have seen, even to anticipate this fortune by gazing on God in this life. Second Temple Jews began to lay out the geography of such a mortal journey through the spheres to the Throne of God, and it became a staple of meditation, and expectation, among Jewish, Christian, and Muslim mystics alike (see II/9). The return to God and the enjoyment of his presence was an increasingly attractive prospect for the virtuous. It was reinforced by the notion that the soul—the immortal spiritual soul that emerged from contact with Greek philosophical theories—had originated in the heavens and at birth had descended through the spheres, acquiring in its descent the various astral influences. This premise made astrology, which attempted to read those influences, endlessly fascinating to ancient and medieval men and women of all faiths. The dead, then, did not merely "go to heaven"; they were returning to their original home.

Mapping Paradise and Hell

The simple vision of the Afterlife entertained by the early Israelites became increasingly complex, and increasingly incoherent, as new ideas, some self-generated, some learned from others, had to be worked into the mix. When Sheol, for example, reappears in the apocalyptic texts of late Second Temple Judaism, it has different chambers within it, some for the righteous and some for the wicked who are awaiting a final judgment. In 1 Enoch, the Jerusalem landmark of Gehenna makes its first appearance as the place where the wicked will be punished. Paradise too appears for the first time, God's original "Garden," along with the quite different concept of "heaven," where the blessed will shine like stars—some very unbiblical notions are at work here—and will be blessed "like the angels of Heaven." Finally, the World to Come (*olam ha-ba*) makes its debut. This is still only a somewhat mysterious open door, however; it must await the rabbis to turn it into a portal. As for paradise, the book called 2 Enoch makes the picture far more explicit. In what is now a full-scale tour of heaven, we are introduced to the notion of an "earthly paradise," which the traveler spies from the third of the seven heavens.

The elaboration of paradise, like the slightly later elaboration of hell, is part imaginative speculation and part response to an enlarged moral sensibility. Christians, Jews, and Muslims alike became convinced that there were grades or levels of felicity in the Afterlife, just as there were levels of punishment there: the more righteous the believer or the more perfect his or her love of God, the more perfect the vision of God in heaven. At first, this expressed itself by locating the more righteous higher in heaven and the more malignant deeper in hell, or by greater joy for the former and more severe pain for the latter. Hell represented fewer problems in this regard, and Gehenna turned out to be a very physical place indeed. The writers of late antiquity and the Middle Ages had little trouble imagining painful torments and, in the end, torments perfectly suited, on the Tantalus model, to the evils committed during life, like starvation for the gluttonous or lacerated lips and a torn tongue for the liar.

The presentation of paradise proved problematic, however, since all the blessed had perforce to be happy—"Everywhere in Heaven is Paradise," as Dante put it—and all invidious comparisons ruled out. All will enjoy the same pleasures and all will somehow be in the presence of God. And yet the same passage of the *Divine Comedy* continues, "though the grace of the Supreme Good does not rain there in equal measure" (*Paradiso* 3:88–90). All were not equal in heaven. The solution, generally speaking, lay in proximity. All the blessed were in the presence of God, but some were closer to the Throne than others; all gazed on the Face, but some saw it more clearly than others. The dominant metaphor in all faiths is light, which has the virtue of partaking of both the material and the physical. All see the light, but the truly blessed are so close that they are blinded by it.

A Heavenly Journey

As already noted, the multistoried versions heaven and hell made their formal appearance in monotheism in the Jewish apocalypses of the post-Exilic era, but what began as a frame tale more often reappeared, particularly in the haggadic midrashim, as simple exposition. The anonymous rabbinic narrator simply described the Garden and Gehenna in ever increasing detail. Dante represents the continuation of the journey tradition in Christianity, but the true sequel to the heavenly journeys of Enoch and others, and perhaps the source, as some have suggested, from which Dante derived his model and many of his details, is the trope of the celestial journeys that first appeared in the Quran and had a luxuriant afterlife in Islam.

A heavenly journey stands at the very heart of Muslim spirituality. The prototype is Muhammad's own ascension (*miraj*) Into heaven during the famous Night Journey that carried him from Mecca to Jerusalem, thence to the highest heaven and back to his native city, all in the course of one night (see I/3). The Quran does no more than allude to it, but the journey, and particularly the Prophet's transit through the heavens, quickly became the stuff of Muslim legend. It soon showed up in enlarged form in the biographies of the Prophet. Eventually there were freestanding treatises devoted entirely to the Ascension of the Prophet—it would have been the translation of one such into Italian that possibly fell into Dante's hands—and Muslim artists, despite the prohibition against images, found the Ascension a rich ground for illustration.

In its quranic setting the story was perhaps intended to explain the divine origins of Muhammad's revelations, and so it continued to do. But as the story became enlarged, it began to include a glimpse into hell and its inhabitants, either on the way to Jerusalem or from the vantage point of the third heaven. In later versions, the seven heavens of the standard cosmology no longer housed Muhammad's prophetic predecessors as they had in the earliest accounts but were populated by a great variety of angelic spirits. The Muslim exploration of heaven had begun.

The Quran introduces two forms or levels of paradise. Sura 55 says that "for those who fear to stand before God, there are two Gardens" (v. 46), and shortly after (v. 62) adds, "on this side [*or* above] these are two more Gardens." By one reckoning, then, there are four "gardens for the blessed," and the Muslim commentators were quick to work out the details. The *Book of the States of the Resurrection*, an anonymous medieval manual for the Afterlife, numbers seven in all, probably to render them symmetrical to the seven heavens of the traditional Ascension. The sixth is called Firdaws, "Paradise," and the seventh and highest, the "Garden of Eden." "This is the capital of the Garden," it adds, "and is higher than all the other Gardens."

This is no mere celestial topography, although there is a great deal of that in these imaginative reconstructions. Like the double "Garden" of the rabbis and Kabbalists and Dante's many circles of paradise, the Muslim enlargement of heaven is due in part to an attempt to accommodate God's justice, to give the blessed their just desserts. One bold imitation of the Prophet's own journey was to justify a personal revelation. In his *Meccan Revelations*, the Spanish Sufi Ibn Arabi (d. 1240) describes an ascent into the upper world, in this case of a philosopher and a "theologian," though the latter is clearly Ibn Arabi himself. The philosopher receives instruction, at once philosophical and mystical, at each of the seven planetary spheres, but then, like Virgil in the *Divine Comedy*, he is left behind at the edge of the seventh sphere and the theologian proceeds alone into the Beyond. He passes through familiar terrain with its quranic landmarks until he reaches the Throne of God, where the divine mysteries are finally revealed to him. This is no eschatological journey, however; the theologian returns to earth with the philosopher, who now converts to Islam.

Dante's paradise is a complex place, as are his hell and purgatory. In part this is demanded by the enormous cast of characters, mythic and historical, ancient and contemporary, that the poet has to sort out around the Afterlife. But the complexity also reflects two religious traditions, the Jewish and the Christian, and perhaps a third, the Muslim, that had given much thought to the subject of the Afterlife and particularly its geography. It is a long way indeed from Sheol and "the bosom of Abraham" to Dante Alighieri.

Living High: The Angels

Heaven's "aborigines," so to speak, are the spiritual beings called angels or, more literally, "messengers" (Gk. *angelos*), even though delivering messages was only one of the things they did. Angels are famously present in all three monotheistic belief systems, from the most sophisticated to the most popular levels. They were, in their fully conceptualized form, a grade of beings somewhere between God and humankind. They were immaterial and immortal like God, though limited in their powers and confined by the mode of their existence to a place—medieval Christians were fond of debating how one could localize, "on the head of a pin," for example, beings that had no extension. Angels resembled humans in that they were creatures, though superior in their possession of an intellect unhampered by any connection to matter.

This is high medieval logic about angels, an angelology, but the species had somewhat more modest beginnings. In the Bible this sort of angel (*malak*) was probably a late (post-Exilic?) addition to the worldview of the Israelites. When the angels do appear, they serve as messengers (Gen. 16:7; 32:1), attendants at God's throne (Dan. 7:10; Tobias 12:15; cf. Rev. 8:2–5), which forever established their dwelling in heaven, and even agents of God's will (2 Sam. 24:16–17; 2 Chron. 21:15–20; Dan. 10:9–13; cf. John 5:1–4). In the post-Exilic Apocrypha, most notably the Book of Enoch, the angels are promoted to new duties, like promulgating God's law (cf. Acts 12:23). Another strand in the history of angels runs through some biblical passages (e.g., Gen. 16:7–11) and emerges in Jesus' own words (Matt. 18:10), namely, that each soul has a guardian angel.

Some of these biblical angels have names and shapes that reveal older and more mythic origins for the later, purely spiritual beings. Michael is the patron and defender of Israel (Dan. 10:13, 21; 12:1). Gabriel (Dan. 9:21–27) has an expanded role both in the Gospels, where he announces the births of John the Baptist (Luke 1:11, unnamed) and Jesus (Luke 1:26), and in the Quran, again as the bearer of the news of her conception to Mary (19:19, unnamed) and of the Quran itself to Muhammad (2:97). He is also a helper to believers (2:97–98, with Michael). And finally, there is Raphael (Tob. 3:25 ff.). The angels also appear as what can be called "types," like the cherubim in Ezekiel (1:4–14) and elsewhere—their effigies stood in the inner shrine of the Jerusalem temple and sat atop the Ark of the Covenant—where they are depicted as winged, human-headed lions or oxen. Winged seraphim are mentioned in Isaiah's vision (6:6), though without much detail. Even at their most spiritual, long after their animal bodies had disappeared, wings remained a permanent part of the iconography of angels.

The Gospels inhabited the same Jewish world where angels, now more obviously anthropomorphized, were active messengers and agents of God's will. Paul takes us to a somewhat different place, however. His is a spiritual cosmos dominated by certain spiritual powers he calls "principalities, powers, and dominions" (Eph. 1:21), and elsewhere (Col. 1:16) he adds "thrones." But the same beings are also called malevolent and malicious (Eph. 6:12), perhaps because they were angels worshiped as gods, a practice apparently widespread in Paul's day in the eastern Mediterranean, as it later was at Muhammad's Mecca (see below). Much of this demonic-angelic landscape was swept away, or at least aside, by the spread of Christianity, though the Neoplatonically inspired and Gnostic-enlarged emanation systems provided more than enough space for a world of intermediary spiritual beings—whether called Aeons, Imams, or Sefirot—that are distributed hierarchically between the unique First Principal and the unruly multitude that constitutes our material world.

Angels in Arabia

In a rare historical aside, the Quran celebrates the Muslims' victory over their enemies at Badr Wells (see I/3). First, a somewhat enigmatic reference (3:13) implies, there seemed to be twice as many in the Muslim host as there actually were. The allusion is not entirely clear to us, nor may it have been to Muhammad's listeners, as the Quran's own gloss on itself reveals later in the same sura. God speaks to Muhammad: "Remember when you said to the Believers: 'Is it not enough for you that your Lord helped you with three thousand angels sent down (at Badr)?' Yes, and if you remain firm and aright, even if the enemy should come against you here in hot haste, your Lord would help you with five thousand angels on the attack" (3:123–125).

The angels that miraculously appeared to swell the Muslims' numbers at Badr were familiar creatures not only to the Muslims but to the pagan Meccans as well. Besides the named Semitic deities like Uzza, Manat, and al-Lat who were worshiped in Muhammad's Mecca, other supernatural beings formed part of the religious landscape. But Muhammad and his compatriots occasionally parted company on the subject of angels. Indeed, there may have been some confusion between the so-called daughters of Allah and angels (cf. 21:26) since the argument about the implausibility of God's having only daughters is common to both (37:149–150). Elsewhere, the pagan Meccans are quite explicitly accused of worshiping angels, and these in the form of women: "And they make into female angels (beings) who themselves are servants of al-Rahman. Did *they* witness their creation?" (43:19).

The Quran has its own developed "angelology," much of it similar to Jewish and Christian beliefs about such beings. Though they do not appear in the very earliest revelations, angels, or supernatural creatures we assume to be angels, turn up in various roles in the Meccan and Medinese suras— Gabriel and Michael are identified by name (2:97–98). They are witnesses of both the Creation (2:30–34) and the Judgment (25:25), singers of God's praises around his heavenly throne (40:7; 42:5), and "watchers" who record the deeds of humans. Angels are unmistakably God's creatures who serve as both his winged messengers (15:8; 35:1), to Abraham (11:69–73, etc.), for example, and to Mary, mother of Jesus (19:19). Finally, they are the individual guardians of human beings (13:11; 82:10–12).

After leaving Mecca, Muhammad had done with the angel-gods of the Quraysh, and after the battle of Badr, angels are no longer said to appear in human form: in the quranic accounts of the angels after Badr, their presence is unseen and humans are no longer aware of their operations, signaling not only a new sense of angels' role but of the relationship between God, angels, and humans. Before Badr the angels served God chiefly in celestial or eschatological functions; later, they are used to serve God's purposes with humankind, primarily to assist the latter in their struggles. They even come to the aid of the Prophet himself in an otherwise unspecified family quarrel (61:3–4).

The Vision of God

The expectation of seeing God is doubtless biblical in its origins. The intimate, even familiar portrait of God in Genesis surely enhanced such a hope, and even the awesome encounters of Moses with his Lord in Exodus, while underlining the privilege, and dangers, of such occasions, reinforced rather than ruled out the possibility. To experience God in such a direct fashion is a theme that exalted and troubled a narrow circle of mystics and their critics, but its occurrence in the Afterlife was the hope of all believers.

The notion of seeing God, even in the Afterlife, was problematic on several scores. It reeked, to be sure, of what the Muslims called corporeality (*tajsim*), the grossest form of anthropomorphism. Even if the expression "face of God" or "seeing God" was softened into something more acceptable like "being" or "living" in the "presence of God," the troublesome issue of "similitude" (*tashbih*) did not disappear. But whereas the traditionalists fought the notion of a vision of God for the living—the enemy here were the Hesychasts and Sufis like Ibn Arabi (see II/9)—they simply acceded when it came to the reward of the blessed. Both Scripture and tradition were too strong and clear for any Christian or Muslim to resist the conclusion that in eternity the righteous will "be with God," however that might be explained. According to Aquinas, who devoted an entire question of his *Summa theologiae* to how we can possibly know God, we know him in the Afterlife even though we cannot comprehend him (1.12.7). God is infinitely intelligible—just not to us.

Note has already been taken of the belief that it must be the *person*, not the soul, that enjoys the God's presence, which led some to conclude the reward of the Beatific Vision, as the Christians called it, must necessarily be postponed until after the resurrection and the Last Judgment. The "some," as already mentioned included, Pope John XXII, who late in 1335 delivered a sermon in which he attempted to follow Scripture on the matter. The pope "opined," as some maintain, or "defined," as others say, that the righteous who died before Jesus' own redemptive death rested in the "Abraham's bosom" mentioned in Luke 16, and that afterward, they and all the others who die in God's grace before the End Time will rest "under the altar." This enigmatic place is described in Revelations (6:9–11) as a sanctuary for martyrs and others, who are counseled there to "rest a little while longer," that is, till the Last Judgment.

John XXII died soon after his public pronouncement, and his successor, Benedict XII, hastened in 1336 to issue a papal decree, "which is to remain in force forever," on the controverted subject of the Beatific Vision. All the blessed, it announced, "even before they take up their bodies again," will "see the Divine Essence, and even face to face, without the mediation of any creature . . . ; rather the Divine Essence manifests itself to them plainly, clearly and openly, and in this way they enjoy the Divine Essence."

The early suras of the Quran provide abundant details on the rewards and punishments that will follow the Reckoning. There the rewards of the blessed are chiefly couched in terms of the pleasures of the Garden of Eden, or simply, the Delight. The Meccan chapters of the Quran spell them out in detail: the blessed will recline on couches, dine on fruits, and imbibe the otherwise forbidden wine, served by the much discussed (chiefly by Christian polemicists) virginal houris (the "dark-eyed ones") of paradise (43:70–73; 44:54; 55:46–78; 56:11–39, etc.). Later, in the Medina revelations, there is a noticeable shift in emphasis toward the enjoyment of God's "approval" (*ridwan*) as the ultimate reward of the believers (9:72). In one key verse, however, there appears to be an allusion to an actual vision of God in the Afterlife: "On that Day the faces of some will shine, looking toward their Lord" (75:22–23). Another (83:15) states, "that Day shall they (the transgressors) be veiled." Numerous hadith fill in the details, many of them in highly literalistic terms. The blessed will "visit" God every Friday, escorted into the Presence, the men by Muhammad and the women by his daughter Fatima, passing on their way the various pieces of cosmic furniture the tradition located there, the heavenly Kaaba (52:4), for example, and the "Guarded Tablet" (85:22), the prototype of the Quran. Finally, "the veil is lifted" and God appears to the faithful, shining "like the full moon."

The blatant anthropomorphism of these scenes caused uneasiness in some quarters, as might be imagined. The Mutazilites, Islam's early rationalists (see II/7), simply read the "looking toward their Lord" verse in another way to eliminate the spatial implications of "turning" and the physical one of "seeing." There was further relief to those anxieties in a hadith where Muhammad reports God as saying, "I have prepared for My servants what no eye has ever seen nor ear heard nor human heart ever felt." This provided a welcome rejection of all similitude and enabled the majority of Muslims to embrace the reward of a "vision of God" (*ruyat Allah*), even though, like Aquinas, they could not explain it. It was in this form that the Beatific Vision took its place in various Muslim creeds: "The faithful will see Him in Paradise, with their bodily eyes, but without making comparisons (between Him and us) (*tashbih*) and without explaining (*kayfiyya*, "howness")."

With a Little Help from the Creator

Whereas the Muslims generally eschewed "howness" on mysterious matters like this, Christians often ran out and embraced it. Once again Augustine charted a path to the daunting subject of seeing God. It is the human intellect that "sees" God, not the eyes of the body—later in his life he returned to the literal truth of "sees"—and it does so only because it has been given the means by God himself. That means is the special favor (*gratia*) bestowed on the blessed. And that is love (*caritas*): it is God's love transfigured into the love of God that raises the earth-bound human intellect to the exalted point where it can "see" God.

Medieval Christian theologians approached the problem somewhat more technically. They had been instructed by their Greek predecessors that sight takes place through a medium, namely, light. But the Beatific Vision seemed to preclude that: God had to be seen without mediation, in himself. Or so thought the Western scholars. The Easterners had other ideas almost from the outset. Schooled in the ineffability of God, who is best approached through the via negativa, the Eastern Fathers, and then the mystics who came after, were prompted to explore a medium through which God might be known or intuited. God could be known, of course, from his "signs" (*ayat*), as the Muslims called them, the Creator's fingerprints on his creation. But that was to know *about* God. There is a far more direct way to know God, as direct as is possible to our defective state, that is, by experiencing him in his "energies" (*energeiai*) as God chooses to manifest them to us. This same venerable medium, now transposed into a divine light, served the Hesychasts as the means of connecting the monk with God, as well as Muslim mystics like Ibn Arabi, who preferred to call them "manifestations" (*tajalli*) (see II/9).

Westerners were somewhat more convinced that they could stare directly into the face of God. The secret, Aquinas explained, much as Augustine had earlier, is that in our present state we cannot possibly know God—our intellects are not programmed to apprehend such an object—unless God transforms us. And that is precisely what happens to the blessed in the Afterlife: they are transformed by what Augustine called grace but which Thomas prefers to name the "light of glory," a term that has the additional merit of staying within the accepted scientific theories of vision.

Paradise Lost: Maimonides (and Others) on the World to Come

Thomas was by no means the only medieval thinker to have rediscovered Greek philosophy. Two generations earlier, the Jewish philosopher-jurist Moses Maimonides (d. 1204), working in the falsafa milieu of Muslim Spain (see II/7), knew of these other more philosophical models for the human being and its survival. One of the influential rabbinic texts on the Afterlife occurs in the mishnaic tractate Sanhedrin (10:1), beginning, "All Israelites have a share in the world to come (*olam ha-ba*)." The most systematic medieval treatment of this passage occurs in Maimonides' celebrated *Commentary on the Mishnah*. Maimonides was far from a mainstream rabbi, of course, and his attempt at ordering and clarifying the sometimes discordant and often legendary accounts of the Afterlife circulating among Jews bears the telltale marks of a professional explainer and convinced rationalist. Most interesting about his treatment, however, is that it lays out, albeit somewhat schematically, current— that is, medieval—Jewish thinking on the Afterlife.

According to Maimonides, the Jews' expectations of the End Time include a number of basic ingredients that are held singly or in combination. Some, drawing heavily on the imaginative homiletic midrashim (see II/2), stress the luxury and pleasures of the terrestrial paradise awaiting the just and the pains and fiery suffering of Gehenna. Others look rather to the End as the Days of the Messiah, whose coming will mark the vindication of Israel and the casting down of her enemies. Some look forward to the resurrection of the dead, the reuniting of families, and the resumption of a normal and untroubled social life, while still others believe that the End will fulfill all their personal desires: good health, good fortune, and a long and prosperous life with many children.

Maimonides was not terribly sympathetic with such literal and materialistic views of the World to Come derived in large part from midrashim, which, like their Muslim and Christian counterparts (to which the Christians added a great deal of extremely graphic visual art), stoked the popular imagination on the Afterlife. For Maimonides, steeped in the philosophical heritage of Hellenism, the final good could be no other than the intellectual contemplation of God. Maimonides had his own text, in this case a talmudic one, on the true joys of the Afterlife. Berakhoth 17a reads: "In the world to come, there is no eating, drinking, washing, sexual intercourse; the righteous sit with their crowns upon their heads and enjoy the radiance of the Divine Presence (*shekinah*)" (see II/6). For Maimonides it was an easy exegetical step from "crowns upon their heads" to intellectual contemplation. Quietly, the matter of a physical resurrection is put aside: the intellect will survive the death of the body and through the intellect the just of Israel will realize the final good, the contemplation of God.

Islam's rationalists faced much the same problem with the rewards of the Afterlife, except that the texts they had to explain were not merely of the popular, midrashic type, of which there were many in Islam, but were found in the Quran itself. The Quran's first Meccan audience had problems accepting its teaching on resurrection (13:5; 19:66, etc.)—though not, apparently, on the pleasures of paradise—and Islam's own later rationalists, from the faylasufs through the Mutazilites to Asharite theologians, and even some not terribly rationalistic masters of the Sufi way, also found incongruities in the Quran's graphically physical description of the rewards of the Garden (see below).

Muslim orthodoxy generally stayed close to that quranic baseline, however, even though some less traditional believers, while asserting the truth of the Quran's account, developed a kind of "secondary" exegesis that converted those physical pleasures into spiritual ones. The chief of these latter was, particularly for Sufis, nothing less than the vision of God. A few went even further. Ibn Sina, for example, unmistakably regarded the spiritual sense of the Quran's eschatology as primary: a return to the body is a punishment, not a reward; the just will find their true reward as intellects separated from the body. The ordinary Muslim cannot rise to this height but will have to remain content with the experience of those apparently sensual pleasures in a more earthbound faculty, the imagination. Sufis followed the path of their choice, to partially allegorize the physical pleasures of paradise or simply to allegorize them away in favor of the unveiling of the "Divine Face"—the expression is quranic (2:110, etc.)—a state many of them claimed to have achieved already in this life.

Salvation

All monotheists share the notion of salvation, which both Jews and Christians parse as redemption, being saved from a parlous state. Muslims think of it in terms of an individual's saving himself in a morally neutral universe: God will judge, and those who have chosen wickedness will be punished, whereas those who have chosen the good will be rewarded, though always and everywhere hovers the question of predestination (see II/5). But for the Christians and Jews, redemption is quite a different matter. For Jews it is primarily Israel that will be redeemed: God's people will be freed at last of the subjugation imposed on them by the hostile Gentile world. For Christians, the emphasis rests heavily on individual redemption. The individual has fallen under the subjugation of sin—a legacy of Original Sin (see II/5)—and at the End Time will share at last in the full redemptive act begun with Jesus' death on the cross. In Judaism and Islam, God simply grants salvation; in Christianity, Jesus became the Redeemer by his sacrificial death. What was called in the Bible the Day of Yahweh becomes in the New Testament the Day of the Lord, that is, of Jesus Christ, who, according to Paul, had already anticipated its results in his own suffering, death, and resurrection.

The Quran does not cast the future hope of humankind in terms of either redemption or salvation. What is promised is rather "prosperity" (*falah*), a term that occurs often in the Quran and refers to success in both this world and the next. Say your prayers, the Quran advises, and "perhaps you will prosper" (62:10). Muhammad and his followers are counseled to "strive"—the root is the same as that of *jihad*—"with their possessions and themselves, for them await good things: they are the prosperous ones" (9:88).

This form of salvation is not for Muslims alone. According to the Quran (30:30), all humans are born with a sense of God's "original religion" (*fitra*), as it has been called. *Fitra* is a difficult quranic word, but it appears clarified in a Prophetic tradition: "Every infant is born according to the fitra, then his parents make him a Jew or a Christian or a Zoroastrian." Many thought this meant that everyone comes into the world a *muslim*, at least in the sense that Abraham was, and then are "perverted" by parents into other beliefs. If not gifted with revelation, such a one has but to look at the signs (*ayat*) that God in his mercy has strewn across the universe to understand his uniqueness and generosity (30:20–25). But for Muslims there is a special guidance: the Quran (2:185), with its own clear *ayat*—a word that soon came to refer to the Quran's individual verses. The Book also characterizes itself as a *furqan*, a "criterion." This too is a difficult word, but its contexts suggest that the entire range of its values is germane here: criterion, revelation, salvation. The Quran is then, in its own words, both a guide and the instrument of salvation, since, as we have just seen, the end for humans is the generous endowment of prosperity, the successful reaping of rewards in this life, and an entry into the Garden that is God's reward to the just in the Afterlife.

Religious Zionism: Hurrying the End

Jewish biblical Apocrypha of the third and following centuries B.C.E. give a vivid view—an "unveiling" or apocalypse, as it was called—of God's final judgment on the world and his vindication of Israel. As already noted, there were variously imagined scenarios to what many felt, perhaps as a desperate reaction to Israel's worsening political and economic condition under the shadow of the Greeks and Romans, was a rapidly approaching End Time. As a sign of the last days, the political and social order would fall into ruin; natural disasters would occur on an unparalleled scale; false prophets would emerge and mislead many. But eventually God's justice would prevail, signaled by a final battle between the forces of good and those of evil in which some foresaw the emergence of a divine agent, the "anointed one" (Heb. *mashiah*; Gk. *christos*), a Davidic king, perhaps, or a priest, who would preside over Israel's final triumph over her enemies and her acknowledgment by the Gentiles. The world as we know it will end and God's rule will then prevail, unto eternity.

Some measure has already been taken of the course of that messianic idea across Jewish history (see I/1, I/2). The unfortunate consequences that flowed from the messianic claims of Jesus of Nazareth, Bar Kokhba, and later Sabbatai Zvi neither reinvigorated nor quenched Jewish expectations that one day Israel would be redeemed and that an anointed one would play some role in that act. By all accounts, that redemption would be eschatological and decisive, but even though eschatology comes to term in some other dimension, it *begins* in history. There are manifest signs that the End Time is drawing nigh in every era of human history, and many Jews principally concerned themselves with the human role in initiating that last act in the cosmic drama

of redemption. Would the "breaking in" of the End Time be sudden or gradual? Will it come at God's pleasure or will it depend on Jewish repentance?
Will Israel's salvation be political—with the Jewish people finally delivered
from their earthly oppressors—or will it be solely a vindication in glory? Will
there be a new political order or a fresh new world?

These were the questions that exercised the rabbis, both the lawyers and the
mystics among them, throughout the early Middle Ages. One of the defining
moments in the discussion is recorded in the Talmud. There we are told that
the Israelites had shared in three oaths. One was "not to ascend the wall."
God, for his part, "adjured Israel not to rebel against the nations of the world"
and "adjured the idolaters not to oppress Israel over much" (BT Kettuboth
111a). The first reference is to an extrabiblical story of how the tribe of
Ephraim, Joseph's children in Egypt, mistakenly tried to "ascend the wall" of
exile and leave that country before God so willed. They were punished by
death, and as a result, Israel has sworn not to "hurry the end" like the impatient Ephraimites and to bear oppression rather than rebel against it.

The oath was taken seriously in rabbinic circles, though it was always
regarded as haggadic and hortatory rather than halakic and prescriptive in
the one area where it might be thought critical—that is, in the matter of *aliya*,
the "going up" or returning to Zion. Migration to Eretz Israel was a live if not
burning issue for at least some Jews from the time of the Muslims' conquest
of Palestine and their lifting of the five-hundred-year Roman ban against
Jewish settlement in Judaea. Some Jews, notably the Karaites who lived there
and feared for their own sectarian survival, urged immigration, while others
were not so certain that resettlement in Zion contributed anything to holiness.
No great numbers were involved, in any event, though from the Crusades
onward, when life in Europe became more perilous for Jews, the pace of
migration quickened somewhat, and a number of famous Jews, like the Spanish poet Judah Halevi (d. 1141) and the French scholar Nahmanides (d. 1270),
took up residence in Zion. Rabbis still argued pro and con, however, on its
advisability.

Political Zionism and Eretz Israel

Though a longing for Zion and the prayer for the hasty rebuilding of
Jerusalem echoes throughout Jewish history, the founding fathers of modern
political Zionism who met at Basel in 1893 were staunchly secularist: "Zionism has nothing to do with religion," one of them proclaimed, and the movement's early history was largely to bear him out. But though they disclaimed
religious motives, the Zionists' language calling for a return to Israel echoed

messianism's promise of an "ingathering of the exiles." Thenceforward this dream of a secular state of Israel, and its propaganda, confronted the normative Orthodox rabbinate with a choice: whether to condemn the dream, embrace it, or accommodate it. What, after all, had the "State of Israel" (*Medinat Israel*) to do with the "Land for Israel" (*Eretz Israel*) or the "citizens" of a Jewish nation-state with the biblically enjoined "kingdom of priests"?

The answer of many was "nothing," and that was the stance taken by the Lubavitcher and Hungarian Hasidim among others, since the Zionists were by their acts committing the Ephraimite sin of forcing or hurrying the End. In the 1920s and 1930s the more extreme among them bitterly denounced even the Agudat Israel, the association that encouraged Orthodox migration to Palestine—and who were, as a matter of fact, opposed to Zionism—as unwitting dupes of the Zionists. The Land of Israel, the Holy Land, was, moreover, too religiously charged for Jews to live there. Others viewed it differently. Some among the European Orthodox, like the members of the Mizrachi movement, could keep messianic expectations separate from the Zionist program for a Jewish state and judge the latter on purely historical grounds. Finally, there were those for whom political Zionism opened new perspectives on both messianism and eschatology.

Today the choices for the Orthodox seem to have narrowed to the two extremes. On one side the ideological followers of Rabbi Abraham Isaac Kook (d. 1935) and the Gush Emunim, the "Block of the Faithful," have sacralized the State of Israel and look on its foundation, preservation, and prosperity as a clear messianic portent. In their eyes, the 1967 victory over the Arab states and the Jews' recovery of the Old City of Jerusalem was a sign of divine favor, and the surrender by the government of even the smallest sliver of Eretz Israel is a betrayal of God's will. On the other side, the Edah Haredit, (haredim; see I/5) the organization of Jerusalem's Ultra-Orthodox community, the Satmar group among the Hasidim, and the Neturei Karta, the "Watchmen of the City," the most entrenched opponents of Zionism, all consider the State of Israel a purely secular creation and worse, a perversion, since Jews have substituted humanmade laws for the Torah in a land that can be governed by no other. Some even read the Holocaust as God's divine judgment on Israel's sins, the chief of which may have been Zionism's violation of the three oaths. The "redemptionists," who followed the lead first of Rabbi Abraham Isaac Kook and then of his son, Zvi Yehudah Kook (d. 1982), regard Zionism as "the movement for concrete redemption in our time." Zionism is not a matter of "forcing the End" but of God forcing humankind through the instrumentality of the secular Zionists to recreate Israel. For these Orthodox there is no personal messiah but rather a messianic idea, Zionism, and a messianic event, Israel.

The Birth Pangs of the Messiah

As already noted, the Lubavitcher or Habad Hasidim of Byelorussia were at the outset strongly opposed to Zionism and the foundation of the State of Israel. In 1904 Rabbi Shalom Dov Schneersohn, the fifth master of Habad, proclaimed that the Zionists would "never prevail against the will of God." They did prevail, with or without God, and the Habad, unlike the Hungarian Satmar, adapted to the new reality of a State of Israel by founding a base there, Kafr Habad. Since then they have expanded their activities into almost every aspect of Israeli life. Still maintaining their theoretical opposition to a secular Jewish state, the Habad have participated in state activities and have sought to influence both Israel's foreign policy and domestic legislation.

The Lubavitcher Habad is a manifestation of Hasidism that began, like all the others, in Eastern Europe but has shown remarkable vigor after its translation to the United States (see II/8). Like the early Christian monastic orders, Habad has set Hasidism on a new path with its bold turn toward the world. But besides its activist program in pursuit of religious goals, the most striking characteristic of contemporary Habadism is its embrace, not of a messianic ideal, which is now built deeply into Judaism's foundations, but of a messianic reality. At its beginnings, the Habad too was a quietist movement with respect to social and political issues, and it concentrated instead on the inner development of the individual. Collective redemption was not the Habad style. As we have seen, the appearance of Zionism in the last quarter of the nineteenth century provoked a great deal of self-examination in Orthodox circles, Hasidim and mitnaggedim alike. The Habad response was negative. Zionists were regarded as forcing the End, and Habad members were warned that cooperation in any form was contrary to all their religious teachings. With the Holocaust and the events leading up to it, the rebbe's attitude, in this instance Joseph Isaac Schneersohn (d. 1950), underwent a dramatic change. As in the past, a catastrophic event summoned forth the expectation of immediate redemption: from the pogroms at the beginning of the twentieth century to the Holocaust at its midpoint, the Jews were witnessing, in the rebbe's view, no less than "the birth pangs of the Messiah." "Polish up the buttons on the royal garment," Rabbi Joseph Isaac joyfully proclaimed.

The sense of the messianic end's immediacy grew even more acute under his successor, Rabbi Menachem Mendel Schneerson (d. 1994)—the family name was slightly altered from the more European "Schneersohn"—for the very opposite reason. All apocalyptic scenarios plotted a time of troubles, followed by an almost utopian era of the rule of the Messiah. If the first half of the century triggered the response that the End Time was upon us, the latter part of the second half, with its prosperity (particularly in America), the collapse of the Soviet Union, the end of the Cold War, and the disappearance of the threat of nuclear destruction, seemed utopian indeed. The rebbe began to assure his followers that the Messiah was already in the world and called for increased spiritual intensity to hasten eschatological action. The Habad community responded and public advertisements began to appear announcing the Messiah's coming. In 1991 the rebbe said openly and unambiguously that this was the year in which "King Messiah comes."

Although Rabbi Schneerson, exercising the same kind of reticence perhaps that Jesus had, never made the claim on his own behalf, some of his followers not unnaturally regarded the rebbe himself as the Messiah and began to circulate petitions in the Jewish community at large asking people to join them in begging the rebbe at last to openly declare himself. The project was greeted with horror in some circles. Most Jews had long since given up any expectation of the immediate appearance of a messiah, and for those with longer memories, what the Habad was proposing appeared like a replay of the tragic events surrounding the messianism of Sabbatai Zvi in the seventeenth century (see I/2), save that in this instance there were no violations of Jewish law, no assertion that the Torah had been transcended. Rabbi Schneerson died in 1994 without making the longed-for declaration and before any decisive eschatological act could be undertaken.

Realized and Futurist Eschatology in Christianity

Paul, eventhough he never knew Jesus in the flesh, was well aware that Jesus had died and been raised from the dead and in that sense the work of redemption was complete. But his letters also reveal that in the mid-50s, twenty-five years after Jesus' death, Christians were convinced that Jesus, who had been taken up into heaven as his followers watched (Acts 1:9), would come again (1 Thess. 2:19), if for nothing else than to gather up those who had died (4:13–16). And this would happen soon, since "those who are still alive shall join them, caught up in the clouds to meet the Lord in the air" (4:17). There is no cataclysmic scenario implicit in these remarks, which occur after all in a letter addressing certain concerns, but in 2 Thessalonians we are transported right to the heart of Jewish apocalyptic and to the trials and tribulations that must necessarily come before the Lord returns (2:1–12).

The Gospels' own unveiling of the End Time occurs in Mark 13, with parallels in the other Synoptics. This is a condensed and selective version of Jewish apocalypses from Daniel to Baruch, tailored, to be sure, to the new Christian conviction that the messianic figure who appears in some of them was in fact Jesus of Nazareth. In the Gospel account, which is put in Jesus' own mouth, he tells his followers that "they will see the Son of Man coming in the clouds with great power and glory" (Mark 13:26). Moreover, the event will come soon—this is written more than fifteen years after Paul had already assured Christians it would: "Truly I tell you: the present generation will live to see it all" (Luke 13:30). In another context, Matthew and Luke pass on from their "sayings source," now known as "Q" (see I/2), Jesus' statement that "the Kingdom of God has already come upon you" (Matt. 12:28; Luke 11:20).

These early appreciations of Jesus' purpose and role illustrate a tension that runs through the earliest Christian writings between fulfilled eschatology—the conviction that the Kingdom is now, whether understood to have begun when Jesus took on flesh, or at the opening of his public ministry, or even at his resurrection—and futurist eschatology—the belief that the Kingdom will be soon, that is, it will find its fulfillment with the Second Coming of Christ. For Paul, as we have seen, one of the chief motives of the Parousia was to effect the resurrection of the dead, which he understood to be one of the principal effects of Jesus' own resurrection. Beneath that issue there may have been, however, a deeper concern by those steeped in Jewish apocalypticism that the well-rehearsed signs of the eschaton had not in fact occurred, a reality that prevented many Jews from assenting to Jesus' messiahship and a theme that continued to be sounded in Jewish polemic against Christians.

At some point, the Christians must have realized that the Parousia was not about to take place in the near future and set about harmonizing messianic acts that had occurred and were still to occur. We do not know when the process began, but it is already visible, though incomplete, in both Paul and the Gospels. Paul, for example, preaches as the primary work of Jesus not the inauguration of the End Time but the redemptive act of his sacrificial death on the cross, an act whose benefits Christians can continue to share by participating in Paul's bold metaphor, in the "body of Christ" (1 Cor. 12:27, etc.), that is, his community. The meditation runs in a somewhat different direction in the Lucan Gospel and Acts. The emphasis there is on Jesus' teaching, which becomes his principal legacy and is extended after his ascension through the Church, its authorities, and institutions.

A Christian Apocalypse

Realized eschatology triumphed over futurist eschatology in the Christian tradition, and the Pauline and Lucan strands were braided into a single conviction about the messianic work of Jesus Christ and its continuation in the Church. But the Jewish apocalyptic legacy never disappeared, and a belief in the eventual Parousia or Second Coming is incorporated into the Christians' creed, which affirms that "he [Jesus] will come again to judge the living and the dead."

The most striking testimony to Christian futurist eschatology—and in a sense the most Jewish of the texts incorporated into the New Testament—is the last book in the collection, known simply as the Apocalypse or Revelation. It purports to be a letter by a certain John (1:1)—which Church tradition eventually identified, together with the similarly named author of the fourth Gospel and the letters in the New Testament, as John, the "beloved disciple" of Jesus—and it is directed to the seven principal Christian churches of the Roman province of Asia, what is today western Turkey. The author was on the island of Patmos and claimed he had received the text to be sent to those churches from Jesus himself (1:9–19).

The first three chapters bear the messages to the seven churches: they are filled with prophecy, admonition, and rebuke. Chapter 4 begins the apocalypse proper, and it stands fully in the tradition of the broad literary stream that flows from Daniel to 2 Esdras. It is a visionary recital, as John is ordered by a voice from heaven to "come up here and I will show you what must take place hereafter" (4:1). The latter unfolds in a series of visions, all cast in the highly poetical and parabolic language of apocalypse. It begins before the fantastic throne of God, who is holding a scroll with seven seals. These will be opened by "the Lamb with the marks of sacrifice on him" (5:6). The seals are broken and disasters spill forth, among them four horsemen, of whom the fourth, "pale horse, pale rider," is death (chaps. 6–7). Then seven trumpets are blown (chaps. 8–11) and eventually seven bowls are poured out (chaps. 16–17). In between (chaps. 12–13) we are shown the adversary of God and the Lamb, namely the dragon (Satan) with his angels and the beast. The latter is likely Rome and the author attempts to be helpful: "This calls for skill; let anyone who has intelligence work out the number of the beast, for the number represents a man's name and the numerical value of the letters is 666" (13:18).

Opposite the beast and his bestial ally—possibly the Antichrist of 1 John 2:18, 22, and others—stand the Lamb and 144,000 "who have his name and the name of the Father written on their foreheads" (14:1). In the end, the beast's city, Babylon (Rome), is destroyed and Jesus triumphs (16:19–19:10). The beast and the Antichrist are thrown into a sulphurous lake and Satan is bound in chains for a thousand years (20:1–3), the millennium (see below; and, on Satan, II/5), after which he must be released "for a little while" when the final cosmic battle is fought and the final victory of God celebrated (20:7–15). The book closes with the vision of a new Jerusalem descending from heaven, built of gold and precious stones, save it has no temple, "for its temple was the sovereign Lord and the Lamb" (21:22).

Millennialism / Chilianism

The last book of the New Testament was crucial in shaping Christian ideas and images of the coming messianic era. All notions of Jesus' earthly return or of Israel's historical restoration, which are still fitfully visible in the Gospels, were by now discarded. The setting of the Parousia is cosmic in the style of the Jewish apocalypses, with liberal borrowings from the visions of Daniel and Ezekiel. History is not entirely left behind, however. The Christian ekklesia was even then in the anteroom of the Parousia. This is the age of suffering and the reign of the Antichrist, the former experienced in the death of the Christian martyrs at the hands of their persecutors, the latter identifiable in the person of no less than the Roman emperor. It is probably Domitian (r. 81–96 C.E.), the Christian persecutor, who lies not too deeply concealed behind Revelation's traditionally oblique and referential style.

But this was still only the prelude: the cosmic climax lay ahead. The Second Coming of Jesus the Messiah will mark the beginning of the thousand-year (Lat. *millennium*) reign of God's justice (Rev. 20:4), when, as Daniel said, "his saints possess the kingdom" (7:22), and at whose completion the world itself would come to an end. At first it was thought the millennium of Christ's reign would begin only with the Second Coming itself, and thus, in a sense, the countdown to eternity had not yet begun. From the third century, however, the view began to prevail that Christ's Incarnation was the beginning of the messianic millennium, which meant that the clock was indeed running.

The Church early on took note of such a speculative theological calculus, dubbed "chilianism" (Gk. *chilias*, "one thousand" = Lat. *millennium*) by the Greek theologians of the Christian East. They preferred to read sacred history as internal and spiritual rather than as political, and an overtly political chilianism was forcefully condemned at the Council of Ephesus in 431. It did not put an end, however, to the fascinatingly attractive notion of being able to figure out God's plan. By a very simple calculation, the year 1000 C.E. might very well mark the end of the world. Many Christians believed that such would indeed be the case, and the end of the first millennium of the Christian era was marked by extraordinary manifestations of both piety and panic, from pious depression to outright hysteria, from passive resignation to frantic means to secure salvation at what was thought to be, quite literally, the eleventh hour of the world.

The Reign of the Spirit: Joachim de Fiore

The Book of Daniel's division of the span of history into four world empires, the Assyrian-Babylonian, Persian, Greek, and Roman (2:36–45; 7:2–27), remained decisive for many, but the Christians' view—already put forward by Paul—that the New Dispensation superseded the Old provided another perspective. Here the great divide appeared not at the eschaton, when temporal history yielded place to its triumphant cosmic conclusion, but at Jesus' Incarnation (or Death, or Resurrection, it could be, and was, argued), when the New Covenant, Christ's Kingdom, replaced the Old. Augustine, as we have seen (I/7), identified Christ's Kingdom with the Church, and contrasted it, now understood as the City of God, with the parallel but ephemeral City of Man. It was not Augustine's only approach to history, however. He too embraced the Pauline-inspired theological schema and divided human history into an era before the Law (the era of the patriarchs), under the Law (Israel) and after the Law (the Christian era).

Augustine was not much concerned with the end of the latter era, but the question exercised others, none more controversially than Joachim de Fiore (d. 1202), a Cistercian monk of Calabria who dangerously combined personal sanctity, prophetic vision, and theological imagination. An earlier mystical theologian, Dionysius the Areopagite (see II/9), had divided world history not into stages but states, which in his view corresponded to the Old Testament, the New Testament, and a third, new state that will be achieved in heaven with God. Joachim, whose works were submitted for and received the pope's approval, thought otherwise. He laid the template of the Trinity on history. The Old Testament was the era of the Father and that begun at the Incarnation was the era of the Son. The New Testament frequently refers to a Paraclete, the Holy Spirit that will come upon Christ's faithful. If most thought the Holy Spirit was present in the Church after Pentecost, Joachim projected that state into the future, not to a cosmic era in heaven but to a historical one here on earth. With the coming of the "Eternal Gospel," the Church and its institutions would be dissolved, Greeks and Latins united in fellowship, the Jews converted, and all humankind would live under the Eternal Gospel referred to in Revelation 14:6. Joachim made some calculations, based on the hints given in Revelation: the catastrophic end of the present era and the beginning of the reign of the Eternal Gospel would take place in 1260.

Joachim was safely dead by 1260, but many had read and heeded his words. Among the Franciscans, a circle of Joachimites arose and eventually found an institutional home in the "Spiritual" Franciscans, a radical branch of this religious order that became highly critical of the Church as the far too earthly vehicle of the Eternal Gospel. The Spirituals attempted to be somewhat more particular about the approaching End. The emperor Frederick II was identified as the Antichrist, and even his death in 1250 failed to dampen their conviction that the end was nigh. Word began to circulate in Joachimite circles that the Spirit had started to desert the Old and New Testaments sometime about 1200, and an "Introduction to the Eternal Gospel" by a certain Fra Gerhardo proposed that Joachim's own writings were in fact the Eternal Gospel that would replace them. The work was examined and condemned by a papal commission in 1256, which included some of Joachim's own teachings in the anathema. Meanwhile 1260 came and went in quite ordinary fashion and the Joachimite movement began quietly to disappear. It was still potent enough, however, that later that same decade Aquinas devoted an article of his *Summa theologiae* to refuting Joachim in the form of the proposition that "The New Law will not last to the end of the world" (1.2.106.4).

The utopian longings for a perfect Christianity that were born of chilianism or the thousand-year reign of Christ lingered on into the Reform era, particularly among the Bohemian followers of Jan Hus. The radical Hussite wing known as the Taborites attempted to emulate the communal fellowship of the first Christians described in the Acts of the Apostles (2:42–47). This was an isolated curiosity; far more consequential was the turn to activism, the Christian revolutionary fervor that led to the German peasants' revolt in 1525. It was opposed by the main body of Reformers—the chief Protestant credal statement, the Augsburg Confession drawn up by Philip Melanchthon in 1530, explicitly condemns chilianism, which it identifies as a "Jewish doctrine"—and suppressed it with great violence. But official disapproval did not end attempts by certain Reformers to establish Christ's kingdom here and now, by force if necessary. The Anabaptists and Bohemian Brethren on the continent and the Puritans in England were among that number, and they shared many of the same messianic longings that soon after manifested themselves among the Jewish followers of the messiah Sabbatai Zvi (see I/2).

Abraham the Intercessor

If there is punishment beyond the grave and if, as Jews, Christians, and Muslims affirm, it is, at least for some, transient in nature, the possibility of alleviating or modifying God's judgment arises. Putting that hope into practice is called intercession. The prototype of such action is Abraham, who early in the Bible attempts to sway God's justice with regard to the sinful people of Sodom. Even though there is protracted "bargaining" by Abraham with God (Gen. 18:23–33), he is in the end only partially successful: thanks to Abraham's intercession, Lot and his family alone are spared in the wholesale destruction of the Cities of the Plain (19:29). The Quran is aware of the event, its outcome and its implications, though it spells out the latter somewhat differently. God says to Abraham after his plea for mercy for the "people of Lot," "Do not look for this. The decree of your Lord has gone forth and a punishment that is not to be averted has come upon them" (11:77).

The Quran is aware, then, of the perhaps irresolvable conflict between God's mercy, which wills forgiveness for humankind—"In the name of God, the Compassionate, the Merciful" echoes like a litany in the Quran—and God's justice, which issued the decree against Sodom. The Jewish midrashic enlargements of the story had earlier shown the same ambiguity. "If you want the world to endure," the rabbis have a very rabbinic-sounding Abraham say to God, "You cannot have strict justice, but if You want strict justice, the world cannot endure. . . . You want both the world and strict justice, but unless you give way a little, the world cannot endure" (Genesis Rabbah 49:9). Elsewhere the Quran seems to come down on the side of God's justice. Abraham also attempted to intercede on behalf of his own father, who was a pagan, though not with any great hope of success (19:48). In the end, we are told, Abraham declined to intervene: "I have no authority for you from God in any way," he said (60:4), and "he separated himself" from his father (9:114).

The Quran opens the question of intercession into larger vistas, but its emphasis is not where the Abraham story puts it—namely, in changing God's decree in the here and now—but on the larger issue of whether there is any intercession at the Judgment for those who need it (see below). These are the sinners who have, like the people of Lot, provoked God's anger and are about to answer to God's justice at the End Time reckoning that confronts every mortal. Here too there were ample Jewish and Christian antecedents. Both the possibility and the practice of intercession on behalf of the dead make their famous first appearance in Maccabees, where the question is, however, of interceding not for sinners but for Israel's dead heroes. Judah the Maccabee makes propitiation—and since this is pre-70 Israel, it is by sacrifice—on behalf of the dead, "that they might be released from their sins." And he did it, we are told, in the full expectation that they would be raised to glory by his act (2 Macc. 12:44–45). The story shows that there was, among at least some Jews, a new view of the Afterlife, or the World to Come, where sinners would be punished and virtuous dead would be "resurrected" and, finally, where intercession was possible.

Abraham's reputation as a friend of God and so an intercessor spilled over into this new eschatological domain as well. Note has already been taken of Jesus' moral story of a poor man named Lazarus who died and went off to dwell "in the bosom of Abraham," while a rich man who died soon after went "to Hades, where he was in torment." In despair the rich man calls out, "Abraham, my father, . . . take pity on me! . . . I am in agony in this fire." Abraham replies: "There is a great chasm fixed between us; no one from our side who wants to reach you can cross it, and none may pass from your side to us" (Luke 16:22–26). In Christianity, the one who could pass was, of course, Jesus Christ, and in John's Revelation, Jesus says explicitly that he has "the keys of death and Hades" (1:18). Christ, then, is the intercessor par excellence for Christians; indeed, he "pleads our cause" at God's right hand, according to Paul (Rom. 8:34).

The Muslim Dead

The rituals surrounding death are simple ones in Islam. The body of the deceased is ritually washed and wrapped in a shroud, some brief funeral prayers (*janaza*) are said in a mosque immediately after the canonical salat, and the interment—cremation, traditionally forbidden in Judaism and Christianity, is also not countenanced in Islam—takes place as quickly as possible, sometimes on the very day of death. The Quran says nothing of this; its attention is directed almost exclusively to the larger stage of the *yawm al-din*, the "Day of Judgment," as it is called in both Arabic and Hebrew.

In the face of this quranic silence on what happens between death and the Judgment, the events that follow an individual Muslim's death unfold in a somewhat confused fashion in the literature on the subject. This is due in part to the freedom of the popular imagination to cast details into that silent vacuum and in part to the difficulty of reconciling what are called in Christianity the "general" and the "particular" Judgment. All Muslim accounts do agree that the hour of death, what immediately precedes and follows an individual's passing, is a painful and troubled time, rendered even more difficult by the widespread belief that Satan makes a particular effort to persuade the believer to desert the faith just before dying.

At death, the spirit (*ruh*) or soul (*nafs*)—to the chagrin of the philosophers, the two words are often used together or interchangeably in these accounts—leaves the body. At once a moral distinction is discernible. The believer's soul slips easily from the body and is escorted by white-clad angels through the seven heavens, pausing, much in the manner of the Jewish "palaces" accounts (see II/9), to deliver the appropriate password to the guardian of each sphere, until it reaches the Throne of God, though not God's own presence. According to some accounts, the souls of the sinner and the unbeliever attempt to make the same ascent but they are turned back. Yet at some point, the souls of the believer and sinner alike must be returned to the cadaver to undergo the punishment of the tomb.

> **Note:** The Muslim notion of a grave ordeal may have had rabbinic origins. Early on the rabbis held that the bodies of the newly dead experienced pain, chiefly, it appears, for purgatorial purposes (see II/5), namely to atone for sins committed during life (BT Sanhedrin 47b). Thereafter pains of the grave became synonymous with judgment of the grave. And the judgment is "public": an angel causes the dead souls to assume bodily forms so that they may be recognized by the other dead. The punishments are exacted by angels, either the single Angel of Death or a group of five such, and they exactly fit the sins being punished, whether of the lips, the eyes, the ears, or the limbs.

There are suggestions but no clear warrant for this ordeal in the Quran. The hadith, however, describe in graphic terms the violent scrutiny, indeed a test of faith, given the newly dead, who are ordered to "sit up," by two mysterious angels, Munkar and Nakir. The torment of the grave is affirmed as dogma in various Muslim creeds, chiefly because it was challenged by Islam's early rationalists, the Mutazilites (see II/7), who choked on the notion of punishments being visited on a dead body. The traditionalists had reluctantly to concede, relying on a puzzling quranic remark—"Thereof We created you and thereto We return you, and thence we bring you forth a second time" (20:55)—that God had to reunite the soul once more with the body for the verse to make sense. Finally, the newly deceased is confronted by two other figures, one attractive and fragrant, the other repellent and malorodous, who represent the good and evil done during life. At the end of the ordeal, the appropriate chastisements are meted out to those who deserve them—a kind of purgatorial process for those who in the end will not deserve hell—and, for the faithful, the fitting rewards, a foretaste in the tomb itself of the pains of Gehenna and the pleasures of paradise. Then, according to most accounts, a sleep comes upon the dead until the Final Hour, the Resurrection, and the Judgment.

The Quranic Eschaton

The Quran preaches the Final Judgment in as vivid terms as the New Testament and the Jewish Apocrypha, though there is no clear evidence that it was believed to be imminent, or that Muhammad was in any sense its herald, as Jesus was thought to be. Like its Christian and Jewish counterparts, the Muslim eschaton unfolded in a series of acts, connected at the near end to each individual's death and judgment and at the far end to a universal Day of Judgment (*yawm al-din*) or Day of Resurrection (*yawm al-qiyama*). At "the hour," a trumpet will sound and the world will be rolled up like a scroll. At the trumpet's second call, the dead will issue forth from their graves and be reunited with their bodies. The great judgment, the Reckoning (*al-hisab*), will follow: each mortal's book of deeds will be read and assessed, the deeds weighed. The just will be granted Jannat Adan, the Garden of Eden; the wicked, Jahannam, or Gehenna. The Quran averts to this judgment scene often in the early suras, and though the pictures of the End are vivid and detailed, they are impressionistic rather than schematic. Jahannam is only one of seven different names for hell in the Quran, for example. The later exegetical tradition often enhanced the details in an imaginative fashion, while the jurists and theologians, as we have seen, who also had a considerable body of hadith on the subject to account for, attempted to reduce the Quran's eschatological snapshots to a systematic account. What exactly went on at the End, and in what order, was never precisely settled, but jurists devoted considerable attention to the events, particularly those with political implication, that preceded the End, and to the question of intercession—whether it was possible for the human living, or perhaps just the dead saints, to intervene on behalf of the sinner at the Judgment.

Intercession in Islam

The Quran warns strongly against counting on any assistance before God's tribunal: "If you ask forgiveness for them seventy times, God will not forgive them because they have rejected God and His apostle" (9:50). And again, of the

Day of Judgment, "the wrongdoers will have no friend or intercessor to make things easier" (40:19). Indeed, the general principle is stated with great clarity: "Beware of the day when no soul can give satisfaction for another, and no compensation taken for it, and they will not be helpful" (2:45; cf. 2:123). These verses seem to be directed toward unbelievers, that they should not count on last-minute assistance to save them from damnation. Another set of verses takes on another expectation. The gods worshiped by the pagan Meccans have no power, either in life or in death: "No intercessor will they (the dead sinners) have from among those they have associated with God" (30:13). "Shall I take gods besides Him?" the pagan is made to say. "If the Merciful One intends some adversity, their intercession will profit me nothing" (36:23).

Those points are made with respect to the unbelievers; it does not mean that the faithful should lose hope. There is, at it turns out, the strong possibility of intercession (*shafaa*) at the Day of Judgment on behalf of those who have submitted but have nonetheless sinned. The Quran repeats again and again that such intercession occurs when and if God allows it (20:109; 34:22). It does not say who enjoys the privilege—the angels perhaps—but the Muslim tradition was quick to extend it to the prophet Muhammad, who on God's orders was granted special favors (17:79; 93:5), including, it was thought, the power of intercession. The hadith fleshed out the modalities. Muhammad is portrayed as praying for the dead, and the custom remained normative among Muslims. Another tradition has all the earlier prophets ceding their powers of intercession to Muhammad, and he, in turn, exercises them on behalf of the members of the Muslim community. What followed was simply a jurists' debate on how far those intercessory powers extended. For serious as well as light sins? On behalf only of those who repented (the Christian position on intercession) or for all sinners? In the end, the traditionalists supplied what became the normative answers: Muhammad will intercede for all sinners and for all sins.

A Savior Returns

As the jurists and theologians read the evidence for the approach of the End Time, the Muslim community will be riven with schism and sectarianism. God will send relief, however, in the form of the Mahdi, the Guided One who will be a man of Muhammad's house—he too will be named Muhammad ibn Abdullah—and he will unite Islam. The notion is not quranic: Muhammad could hardly have foreseen the breadth of his community, much less that it would suffer from schisms, and the mortal and dead Prophet could scarcely serve as his own Messiah. Rather, the belief seems to have arisen in the schismatic civil wars of the first Islamic century and to have had its origin in the same circle that eventually matured into Shiism (see I/5). According to the Shiites, the Mahdi would indeed be someone from Muhammad's house: a descendant of the Imam Ali. If the Mahdi was a Shiite notion, it was soon embraced by Sunnis, not as a certification of the Alids in this life but as an expectation of help from the Prophetic House in the next. What precisely that help would be depended, as it did in Judaism, on what form of the eschatological scenario one was reading. Enough Muslims read it in political terms to make the Mahdi an even more potent symbol of insurrection or apocalyptic revolution than the Messiah was for Jews (see I/1).

The next act in the eschatological drama will begin with the coming of the Antichrist, the Deceiver (*al-Dajjal*), who will introduce another reign of terror that will last until the appearance of Jesus, who, according to the Quran was taken up into heaven alive and must return to earth to suffer death. On his return, he will slay the Antichrist, and then the Final Judgment depicted in the Quran will take place.

The swirl of messianic expectation in mid-eighth-century Islam was as real perhaps as that which roiled Palestinian Judaism in the first century. Umayyad extravagance, joined to growing doubts about the legitimacy of the new dynasty and its pretensions, provoked the Islamic reaction, Greek and Roman oppression the Jewish one, to which were added doubts about the Hasmonaean kings, the Herodians who succeeded them, and even, in some quarters, the high priesthood of the temple. Palestinian political and religious unrest ended in two ill-fated insurrections against Rome, the second of which had a distinct messianic aura surrounding its leader, Bar Kokhba. Muslim dissatisfaction came to term in the Abbasid Revolution of 750, although this turned out to be no more than the replacement of one caliphal dynasty by another that rode to power in the wake, or on the promise, of Alid messianism, which had become focused on one of Ali's sons.

Early on in Shiism, supporters of Ali's family pinned their hopes for a restoration on either of two branches of his descendants. One was the line of Muhammad ibn al-Hanifiyya ("son of the Hanifite woman"), the offspring of Ali and one of his tribal wives, and the other was either Hasan or Husayn, the sons of Ali's union with Muhammad's daughter Fatima. The claims of the first were advanced, as we have seen (I/8) by al-Mukhtar, and even though they did not achieve their original end of putting an Alid on the caliphal throne, the title that allegedly passed from Ibn al-Hanifiyya's son Muhammad to the first of the Abbasids bolstered the latter's claims to legitimacy. For all that, it was the scions of the Ali-Fatima line who triumphed, not in the sense that they ruled but insofar as they controlled and shaped Shiism in both its Ismaili and its Imami varieties.

But the shadowy Ibn al-Hanifiyya was more than a pretender to political power: he appears to have been among the earliest in Islam to be regarded as the Mahdi. Behind him stood perhaps the prototype of Ali himself, whom many of his followers believed would one day return to guide the community.

Indeed, some of Ali's followers denied that he had died at all. Whatever the metaphysics that stood behind this belief—early on the notion current in Shiite extremist groups was that Ali was in some manner divine (see II/9)—the conviction that the Imam, eventually, the *last* Imam, would return to his community spread among Shiites of all shades of belief.

Whether he had died or disappeared, the Shiite Imam's reappearance was a return from another dimension of someone who had once been alive. The sentiment is parallel to the post-Exilic Jewish (and eventually Islamic) beliefs about Elijah or Enoch. The growth of the Shiites' conviction that the last Imam, whether the seventh or the twelfth, had gone into concealment and would one day return is the plausible result of two factors: a denial of the death of a revered leader, which was apparently squelched in the case of Muhammad but persisted in the case of Ali; and what can be called in a general fashion messianic expectation. Messiahs are born of despair, in particular a despair that political processes, or even, more generally, historical processes, can never achieve the desired end. In the Muslim case, it was likely engendered by the Abbasid Revolution's failure to restore one of the People of the House, always understood as uniquely the Alid branch of the Prophet's house, to the Imamate. The Abbasids, having unseated the Umayyads, declined to yield the Imamate to an Alid, and the Shiites took their disappointed hopes to another place. The Hidden Imam had gone, concealed in another dimension and so safe from the Abbasid authorities. But he will one day return as Messiah to restore the true Islamic dispensation.

The expected return of Jesus, who underwent his own concealment when he was taken up, glorified but unmistakably in a physical condition, from the slopes of Olivet to his Father in heaven (Acts 1:6–14; Quran 4:158), was postponed within one generation of Christians from the immediate future to the indefinite future. This transformation of expectation may have occurred even more quickly among the Shiites. Present hope had gone in Shiite circles of the ninth and tenth centuries. The believers settled in for the long haul toward the eschaton, and those who were impatient enough to start counting down the days and years to the End Time, and so the return of the Imam, were warned to refrain from such dangerous exercises.

> **Note:** Impatience sometimes triumphed. Though concealed, the Hidden Imam, or Imam of the Ages, as he was also called, provides ongoing direction to the Shiite community, as we have already seen (I/8). More than counsel, his somewhat more direct intervention has been spectacularly invoked—and was believed to have occurred—at two moments in modern Shiite history. The first was in the Iranian Constitutional Revolution of 1906–1911 when the Shiite ulama announced that opposition to the new constitution was tantamount to taking up arms against the

> *(continued)*
> Hidden Imam. The same recourse was taken in 1979 in the Iranian Revolution. This time there was a more particular focus. The Ayatollah Khomeini (d. 1989) was universally recognized as a spokesman of the Imam, and by enthusiasts even as the Imam himself, returned at last to "fill the world with justice and righteousness," or, if not the world, at least the new Islamic Republic of Iran.

The Mahdi

From somewhere in that same terrain of hopes and disappointment the Sunnis found their own explanation of an End Time savior. He is called *al-mahdi*, or the Divinely Guided One. *Mahdi* did not begin its career as an eschatological epithet; indeed, any number of prominent figures in early Islam were so characterized for their saintliness or upright conduct, and one Abbasid caliph—the Umayyads went by their ordinary names but the Abbasids much preferred throne titles to mere names—assumed al-Mahdi as his throne name, and another al-Hadi, the Divinely Guiding One, without any notable eschatological implication. The first association of that characterization with the End Time was apparently connected with Jesus, whom the Muslims expected to return not merely to succumb to the mortal necessity of death (see I/3)—his tomb is prepared next to Muhammad's at Medina—but, much as the Christians believed, to initiate the final stage in the history of the cosmos. In the Muslim version of that scenario, the Mahdi was simply a characterization of the Jesus of the Parousia. But Jesus was a mythic personality and, as noted, pious and disappointed Muslims of the mid–eighth century required more concrete and more immediate relief. A Mahdi-prince was projected into the immediate present, a historical rather than an eschatological messiah, to right present wrongs and to inaugurate a more authentic Islam.

Sunnis, like the Shiites, placed their hopes in the Abbasids, the first for relief, the second for fulfillment. Both were disappointed, and while the Shiites had their own candidates standing in the wings in the person of the Alid Imams, the Sunnis had none. There was no need, then, for either a concealment or a return: the Sunni Mahdi was simply postponed to the indefinite eschaton, not as Jesus—though some continue to maintain that Jesus and the Mahdi are one and the same—but next to Jesus, and subsequent Muslim scenarios of the End Time preferred to assign separate roles to the Mahdi and to Jesus.

Like the Jews' Messiah, the Mahdi has not lost all his political potency in his postponement to the End Time. At various times in various places persons have come forth to announce that *they* were the awaited Mahdi. In modern times, the restoration of Islam has most often been pursued in the context of forming an Islamic state or throwing off foreign domination over a Muslim population. The most famous modern representative of the type remains Muhammad Ahmad, who revealed his identity as the Mahdi in the Sudan in 1881 and convinced enough Muslims of the truth of his claims to lead an insurrection against the British that destroyed one British army under General Charles Gordon at Khartoum in 1885 and required another under General Arthur Kitchener to put it down in 1889.

End Thoughts

People of the Book, and of the Covenant

THE THREE MONOTHEISTIC religious communities we call Judaism, Christianity, and Islam now constitute the single largest block of organized believers on earth. The figures are obviously little more than approximations, or perhaps guesses, but Christians of all persuasions are thought to approach 2 billion worldwide, Muslims somewhat more than 1 billion, and Jews nearly 15 million. To unify them under the name of monotheists is merely to begin to describe the ties that bind them. All worship what we may identify, with reservations, as the same God. All three believe this deity has intervened in human history on several occasions, in two very particular ways. First, this God concluded a pact or covenant with what is understood to be a historical personage, Abraham; and second, the same deity subsequently made his will known to his followers through a formal revelation that was eventually preserved in the form of a sacred book.

Thus, besides sharing a vast array of ideology, history, and traditions, each of the three communities we have looked at traces itself back to a sacred Scripture—Muslims properly call them People of the Book—a book that each believes was revealed by the One True God they all worship. Moreover, as already noted, all three may be called "Abrahamic" in the sense that (1) there is an Abraham story at the heart of their long-term memory (the Christians' long-term memory is actually the same as the Jews'—it is the Bible, though in a somewhat different form); (2) that story has to do with a promise, a covenant, a contract; and (3) each thinks it is the unique beneficiary of that promise, the sole genuine heir among Abraham's children.

Odium Theologicum

Jews, Christians, and Muslims do not seem to care much for one another, a perception as apparent from our own experience as from this brief survey of how these three have fared in the world. Everything from glowering silence to nasty polemic to unspeakable mayhem has marked their mutual relations when time, place, or circumstance has cast them together or, more accurately, has put one or two of them under political control of the third. There is no symmetry in their political relations, however. From the fourth century c.e. until 1948 Jews lived only at the political and religious sufferance of either Christians or Muslims, whereas the latter two have often exchanged places under each other from Spain to the Balkans to Palestine.

Why this ill-disguised hostility that at times has stopped just short of destruction? For in truth, each has recognized that the other two must be marked as inferior, though not, generally speaking, annihilated: a "final solution" has never been part of the calculus of any of the three monotheistic communities. But, there has been plenty of theological hostility, political contempt, and countless attempts at containment, control, and repression. The record is as plain as history. But why?

These three are all children of the same father, in a manner that is more than a mere metaphor. Although they may have had the same father, that father was thought, without a great deal of evidence, to recognize only a single genuine heir, which each now claims to be. The struggle among the monotheists is, then, one over inheritance—survival, vindication, exaltation, salvation, however it is parsed—and whatever grudging tolerance they grant one another is a recognition that they are, after all, siblings, offspring of the same father. God, the *same* God, is the Father Creator for Jews, Christians, and Muslims alike, but their true progenitor was the patriarchal sheikh called Abraham in the remote but still vividly remembered past.

The Religion of Abraham

The identity of monotheism's birth father and the problems he posed for his children come across with vivid clarity in western Arabia in the opening decades of the seventh Christian century. As Muhammad's message began to unfold in Mecca and Medina, some in those towns listened and heard something familiar in his words. This new call to monotheism, with its threat of judgment in the world to come, its stories of other prophets in other times—were these not of the faith of the Jews and the Christians? No, the new Arab prophet replied, "this is the religion of Abraham" (Quran 2:135).

Whether it was God speaking on that occasion, as Muslims believe, or simply an extraordinary Meccan preacher, the answer was accurate. This was indeed the religion of Abraham, this preaching bound up as revelation in the book called the Quran. Muhammad's insistent monotheism—the heart of the message pouring forth from his lips in Mecca and Medina—was Abrahamic in its urgency and its purity. For Muhammad, as for Jesus' follower Paul, Abraham was the prototypical monotheist, a man who had fought his way clear of the Middle Eastern idolatry of his fathers into a simple faith in the Creator God. But Abraham represented somewhat more. An additional argument is made in the Quran, as it was earlier by Paul. Abraham was *before* Moses and Torah, and *before* Jesus and the Gospel, and so he cannot be regarded as either a Jew or a Christian. The Quran's claim of affinity to Abraham was in effect a denial of dependence on, or derivation from, either Judaism or Christianity. But that prideful link to Abraham had, at the same time, made Islam, as the new community of believers came to be called, a brother to both of the other two. Together they were, and are, siblings, the family of Abraham.

Who Is the Heir?

The "Children of Abraham" summons up, then, the image of a family, of siblings of the same father. The portrait is both appropriate and accurate: the communities of Jews, Christians, and Muslims all claim to be in some sense the offspring of the Hebrew patriarch with whom God made his Covenant in the early days of the world. More properly, they all claim to be Abraham's sole rightful heirs since the Covenant God made with him carried a rich promise. In Genesis, where it is first reported, the inheritance that will pass to Abraham's children consists of numbers—they will be as numerous as the stars in the heavens and the sands on the seashore—and of land: they will survive, flourish, and, eventually be vindicated before all humankind.

For Jews, it is self-evident that they are Abraham's heirs because they are Abraham's descendants, both by blood kinship descent—in the Bible they are called by the tribal name "Children of Israel," Abraham's grandson—and by their fidelity to the terms of the Covenant. No one, neither Jews nor their non-Jewish contestants for the inheritance, has denied the first claim: the Jews are indeed descended from Abraham through Isaac and Jacob, the one later renamed Israel. Christians and Muslims have something else in mind, however. Some Jews, perhaps many, had taken up the issue that mere descent from Abraham was not enough to secure the inheritance; what more was required was a subject of lively sectarian debate at the turn into the common era. The Jesus movement was born in that contentious environment, and Jesus' followers eventually took the radical position that blood descent was not the issue at all—had not John the Baptist preached that God could raise up children of Abraham from the very stones if he chose (Matt. 3:9)?—nor was it *obedience* to the terms of the Covenant as a number of Jews were beginning to understand that term, as a scrupulous observance of the Law. It was his *faith* that made Abraham righteous in God's eyes, and now once again it would be faith—this time in Jesus as Messiah and Lord—that would constitute the new

Covenant that God had planned and the prophets foretold (Rom. 4:1–22). Thus the Christian, the Christ-believer, was the true heir to Abraham's faith and to the promise of God's Covenant.

The Muslim claim is somewhat similar. In the Quran's view, the Jews and Christians, both the recipients of a genuine revelation, proved unfaithful to the Abrahamic legacy. Their infidelity elicited another revelation, the Quran, delivered through the agency of a man signaled as "the seal of the prophets" (Quran 33:40), the final agent in God's providential revelations to humankind. Not only did the Quran both transcend and replace the Torah and Gospel; it commanded nothing less than a return to the "religion of Abraham" (3:68). What constituted this latter—what the Quran calls *islam* or "submission"— was strict monotheism and the practice of a purified version of certain of Abraham's ritual practices that had somehow managed to survive at Mecca and its vicinity.

The True Israel

On purely chronological grounds, the original cult of this God Yahweh, as the Jews were taught to call him (Exod. 3:13–16), appears as something pristine, without human origins or antecedents. It came about as the result of an unexplained, and perhaps inexplicable, act of belief and obedience on the part of a seminomadic Hebrew patriarch named Abraham (or Abram as he was then called) in "Ur of the Chaldees." Abraham's destiny lay not in what is today called Iraq, however, but in the sliver of territory squeezed, often in the manner of a captive in a trap, between Egypt on this side and Assyria and Babylonia on the other side of the Fertile Crescent. In the eyes of Abraham's descendants, their inherited common faith had no forerunners among the people of the Middle East, and its pretended successors are all regarded as misguided or malicious attempts to counterfeit the original. Or perhaps, in another, more liberal view, the other two would-be monotheists are a providential extension of the faith originally entrusted to and accepted by the Jews.

Neither Christianity nor Islam claims that it is pristine. They not only acknowledge their Jewish past; each openly proclaims its status as a supersessionist community. Each is in a sense the new, the true "Israel," the legitimate and authorized successor to the Covenant established with Abraham and his heirs. But just as the Jews contest this inheritance claim of the Christians, so too the Christians deny it to the Muslims: Jesus who is called the Christ closes the divine interventionist dispensation as finally for the Christians as Muhammad does for the Muslims.

When Christianity and Islam each claims that it has "succeeded" Judaism, the assertion is both theological and historical. Each announces its succession to the title of the Chosen People simply as such, but each succeeded to that title at a given moment in history, and the succession was conditioned by the evolution of the parent community. Jesus took flesh "in the fullness of time," as Paul put it (Eph. 1:10), and at a point in Israel's history determined from the beginning by God's eternal decree (Eph. 1:4), when the world "groaned" for its deliverance. The Christians, whose numbers soon included sophisticated intellectuals from the Gentile world of antiquity, were quick to discern signs of that expectant groaning among the pagan intelligentsia from Plato's meditations on the immortality of the soul to Virgil's New Age dreams in his fourth *Eclogue*.

Islam's election as the new Israel has the same type of vague specificity to it. The way the Muslims read history, both Judaism and Christianity had undergone a kind of degenerative evolution, a descent from the original revelation to a state of near-disbelief. Islam was not only a theological successor to the other two faith communities; as already noted, it was the historical revival of the original faith of Abraham and his family (Quran 2:135). The early Muslims' not terribly firm grasp of the history of the Jews and Christians, or of the secular history of the Middle East, did not, however, permit them to develop to any considerable extent the same type of historical argument of a *praeparatio quranica* that proved so useful to the Christians.

A Fractious Family

Both the Christians and the Muslims claim, as indeed do the Jews, that they are the unique heirs to Abraham's legacy. The exclusiveness of their claims has turned the three siblings into a notoriously fractious family since each doubts the legitimacy of the others, while at the same time acknowledging, often obliquely and always grudgingly, their mutual affiliation. The Christians, for example, when they have enjoyed the sovereignty that makes such action possible, decreed the annihilation of paganism and showed little toleration of its own heretics. At the same time they accorded the Jews living under their political control a measure of protective toleration. Muslims too, who showed no mercy toward pagans or apostates, decreed the Jews and Christians living under their sovereignty protected communities who lived under a covenant (*dhimma*) of security with the Muslims.

As has already been remarked, the peculiar animus of any of the three groups toward their fellow monotheists needs little documentation. The guaranteed protections were overlaid with centuries of oppressive polemic and mined with explosive bursts of persecutions and holy wars: pogrom and blood libel, crusade and jihad ring all too familiarly through the mutual communications of the Children of Abraham. The Jews stand somewhat aside in the equation, not because the fanaticism of their monotheism or the exclusivity of their claims is any less determined than that of the Christians and Muslims but because of the somewhat less extenuating reality that Jews have never, at least until 1948, exercised sovereignty over their theological rivals. Now, however, there exists a professedly Jewish state, the first perhaps since 6 C.E. when the Romans snuffed out the dying embers of a Jewish client monarchy in Palestine. Israel is a work in progress; is still attempting to find the balance between its secular origins and the growing religious sensibilities of its citizens. It has already enacted a law for "The Protection of the Holy Places" quite in the tolerant, rights-driven tradition of the now secular democracies of the West. At the same time the growth of religious fundamentalism there gives reason to think that this may not be the last word on the subject of the relationship of Jews and the other Children of Abraham in the State of Israel.

The three communities have parsed the Abrahamic promises of growth and land quite differently. Jews have always taken them quite literally. God's fidelity to his side of the Covenant is unmistakably demonstrated by the continued survival of the Jewish people, while their longtime rivals and antagonists, the Canaanites, Egyptians, Assyrians, and Babylonians, have been reduced to insubstantial historical memories. Even the promise of the land has been fulfilled, by the conquest of Canaan in the last years of the second millennium before the common era and again in these latter days, as some think, by the restoration of a Jewish state in that same land rendered holy by God's promise. Jews have always been Zionists in their attachment to the promised land, particularly when separated from its soil, as they were in the Exile of 597 B.C.E. or when barred from its holiest places, as they were after the insurrection of 132 C.E. That attachment was merely nostalgic, however, until it took on its first insubstantial flesh as a political dream in the last half of the nineteenth century and then as a full-bodied reality in the State of Israel in 1948.

For Christians and Muslims, whose community history was one of extraordinarily rapid growth, the issue of survival quickly seemed irrelevant. So did the territorial clause. The Roman Empire that became Christian three hundred-odd years after Jesus, exceeded the wildest dreams of imperial ambition, and Christianity had further shown its ability to leap both political and ethnic frontiers and extend into every corner of the globe. Islam too enjoyed extravagant political success: a mere hundred years after Muhammad, the Abode of Islam stretched from France to the borders of China. The attraction of a "promised land" was not so much overtaken as overwhelmed by events.

But both religious communities had another promise in their loins. The original preaching of Jesus and Muhammad had at its core a profound eschatological expectation of divine justice, of reward for the just and punishment for the wicked in the Afterlife. That justice would be meted out to individuals, to be sure, but their followers also understood it in a larger sense as the justification of the community. The dream was born of the original Israel but it had been rapidly appropriated by the two later claimants who no longer read out the promises of the Covenant in terms of numbers or land but as nothing less than the promise of eternal salvation.

The Rivals' Charms

The transparent hostility among Abraham's heirs seems often to have masked a common fear of each other's allure. Polemic among the three communities has in fact been produced mostly for home consumption, written to reassure its own believers that they, not their obviously (if we look closely) attractive rivals, were the Chosen People. If second- and third-century Jews anguished over the hemorrhaging of their members to the new, messianic form of their beliefs called Christianity, Christians were equally alarmed at the prospect that their new Gentile converts would revert to the trunk of the tree of which they were so evidently the branches. And although Muslim religious law permits the free practice of their religion to the Jews and Christians living in their midst, it makes very clear that their fellow Scripturalists should in no way attempt to seduce Muslims into embracing the faith of either of those two other worshipers of the One True God.

It is not easy to chart the interconfessional passage of believers from one faith community into another. All we can do is note that almost all the early converts to Christianity were Jews or Jewish satellite believers or Jewish sympathizers—those early Christian "fishers of men" cast their nets mostly in synagogue ponds—and that once Islam got past the pagan Bedouin of Arabia, the overwhelming number of new Muslims were made out of the ranks of the Jews and Christians. Like modern fundamentalists, ancient monotheists were chiefly bent on converting each other. Jews continued to convert to Christianity and Islam throughout the Middle Ages, though that fact must be read between the lines of polemic, and the same is true of Christians and Muslims with regard to each other, whether the motive was conviction, fear, or hope of advantage.

Always and everywhere there was a fear of the effects of that most potent of all missionaries, love. Jews and Christians strenuously preached and strenuously attempted to enforce endogamy. The medieval church legislation on the subject was as severe and interdictive as anything promulgated by Nehemiah in Jerusalem in the sixth century B.C.E. The hortatory efforts and legislative measures against marrying outside the faith were taken not from any sense of racial purity but because it was well understood that conversions were frequently made under the blankets, and that mothers would have their way with the heads and hearts of their little ones. The Muslims appear far more relaxed in this matter. The practice of polygamy and particularly of concubinage may have softened somewhat the bonds and bounds of matrimony, but more likely their complaisance in exogamy was attributable to the fact that Islam had spread in the wake of a male army of conquest, men who had left their wives and children, if any, long and far behind. They had married perforce with the conquered non-Muslim populations, an experience Jews and Christians never had. Christian missionaries were celibate; Islam's missionaries were bride-hungry.

Faith and History

The point of this study is not to underline the hostility (or the subliminal allure) that has existed and all too transparently still exists among the worshipers of the One True God, but to point to something equally in evidence among them, though only on somewhat more careful inspection. The claim of uniqueness is basic to Jewish ideology, and supercessionism, as we have seen, runs deeply into the self-identification of Christians and Muslims. But these three communities also grew up in each other's ideological and institutional shadow and, in premodern times, in quite similar social and political circumstances. So they bear not only genetic resemblances inherited from Abraham and the Covenant but a whole range of acquired and conditioned traits borrowed, stolen, or imitated—do the words really matter?—one from the other. This is, after all, a family portrait of siblings definitely not separated at birth. They lived together—side-by-side hardly does justice to their intimacy— through thick good times, in medieval Spain, for example, and in excruciatingly thin bad ones, as in early modern Jerusalem. That is why the present work is essentially a work of history. It is less concerned with events in heaven than with what transpired on earth; less with the *acta Dei* than with *gesta*, though with *gesta fidei*, the "deeds prompted by faith" rather than by the historian's more familiar *gesta hominum*.

If the three monotheistic communities seem to have integrated facts and faith, theology and history, without any great embarrassment, the present work enjoys no such easy confidence. The believers in the monotheistic faiths accept that faith precisely as such. Scripture is accepted as totally and simultaneously true—a great deal of effort was deployed in resolving its apparent contradictions—and the same acceptance is eventually granted to that expansive body of enlargement and explanation called "tradition." But the three communities are notable in that both their Scripture and their tradition unfold within the dimensions of time and place that we call history. Jews, Christians, and Muslims all have their cosmic moments and eschatological afterthoughts that escape history, but they are, for all that, merely moments. Both the acta Dei and the gesta hominum that make up the body of their Scriptures take place, we are given to understand, in discernible historical time.

If the internal acts of faith occur in some as yet undetected human organ, the instruments of the historian lie ready to hand, and since the eighteenth century they have been increasingly used in the West to attack, whether deliberately or as an unintended consequence of intellectual acuity, the foundations of religious faith. The events of Scripture—Moses' leading the Israelites from Egypt, Jesus before Pilate, Muhammad's defeat of the hostile Quraysh at Badr Wells—have all been presented as true history for the acceptance of believers, what I have just characterized as gesta fidei. But history, as it turns out, can be verified as well as accepted. By the nineteenth century, Europeans had not only managed to establish the absolute autonomy of the discipline—history neither is guided by nor answers to any higher truth—but had fashioned techniques of analysis and criticism that could be deployed on what had once been regarded as the Words of God. Scripture could now be treated as mere sources by the new breed of historians who had some hard questions to ask Moses in Egypt, Jesus before Pilate, and Muhammad at those famous western Arabian watering holes.

Index

Aaron, 169, 171, 308

Ab bet din, 67, 96. See also *Bet din*

Abbasids, Banu Abbas, 226; and Shiite messianism, 373–374

Abbot, 258

Abd al-Jabbar, 164

Abd al-Malik, caliph, 208, 223

Abd al-Qadir al-Jilani, 280

Abelard, 239

Abodah Zarah, 201

Abode of Islam, 56, 81, 95, 111, 114, 118, 133, 135, 174, 188, 219, 223, 236, 240, 283, 314

Abraham (Abram), xxi, 24, 27, 36, 88, 94, 133, 135, 181, 185, 201, 203, 293, 299, 308, 343, 354; intercessor, 368–369

Abraham ibn Ezra, 11, 57–58

Abrogation, 26, 33–34, 107, 166

Abu Bakr, caliph, 32, 86, 115

Abu Hanifa, Testament of, 229

Abu Hurayra, 82

Abu Said, 239

Abu Umar Hafs ibn Sulayman, 33

Abu Yusuf, 110

Abyssinia, Abyssinians, 219

Acquittal (from sin), 134–135. *See also* Atonement

Acquisition (*kasb, iktisab*), 165, 230

Acts of the Apostles, 1, 17, 34

Ada, pl. *adat* (custom), 121, 161

Adab (social and cultural etiquette), 161–162

Adam, 27, 42, 44, 54, 131, 133, 137–138, 142, 149, 293, 301–302, 311, 320

Adrianople, 119

Aeons, 320, 335, 352

Afghanistan, 282

Afterlife, 12, 28, 73, 135–136, 251, 349, 356–358. *See also* Eschaton

Agape, 177

Agent Intellect, 15, 244, 323

Agudath Israel, 361

Ahl al-hadith (partisans of tradition), 52–53, 120. *See also* Tradition; Traditionalist(s)

Ahl al-kalam (partisans of dialectical theology), 53–54

Ahmad ibn Hanbal. *See* Ibn Hanbal

Ahmadis, 54

Ahriman (god of darkness), 138

Aisha, wife of Muhammad, 82, 207, 310

Ajmer, 282, 283

Akbar, sultan, 282–283

Akhbar (accounts, prophetic reports), 120; Akhbari(s), 120

Akhlaq (ethics), 162

Akiba, rabbi, 41, 69, 296–297, 298

Alam al-Khayal (figured world), 249

Alawis, 320–321

Albania, Albanians, 284

Albigensians, 286

Alcalá, 24, 271

Alcantara, Knights of, 269

Alchemy, 220

Aleppo, 119, 123, 248, 256

Alexander III, pope, 193

Alexander the Great, 201, 213

Alexandria, 38, 44, 90, 176, 213, 217, 224, 226, 241, 243, 254, 256, 300

Alexis Comnenus, Emperor, 273

Alfonso I, king of Aragon, 269

Alfonso VII, king of Castile, 239

Alfonso X, king of Castile, 239

Alfonso di Ligouri, 157–158

Algeria, 123
Ali ibn Abi Talib, caliph, 34, 86, 115, 196, 222, 314, 320, 373. *See also* Alawis
Alim, pl. *ulama* (learned), 113. See also *Ulama*
Aliya ("going up," returning to Zion), 360
Aljamiado, 7
Allah, 27, 129, 197, 319; daughters of, 27, 34, 50, 353
Allegoria (other-referent), 40, 42. *See also* Exegesis, allegorical
Almohads (*al-muwahhidun*, "Unitarians"), 234
Almoravids (*al-murabitun, Ribat men*), 270, 279. See also *Ribat*
Alms-tithe. See *Zakat*
Alter, Yitshaq Meir Rothenberg, 290
Alumbrados, 306
Amina, mother of Muhammad, 195
Amoraim (speakers), 70, 71
Anabaptists, 368
Anachoresis (retreat), 254
Analogy. See *Qiyas*
Anamnesis, (remembrance), 176
Anan ben David, 72
Anaphora (bearing aloft), 176
Anastasis, Church of, 186. *See also* Holy Sepulcher, Church of
Anatolia, 118, 176, 204, 255, 283
Andalus, al-, 333. *See also* Spain
Andrew, apostle, 203
Andronicus II, emperor, 273
Angel(s), 131–132, 176, 351–354
Anglican(s), 103
Annunciation (to Mary), 189, 352; of Muhammad, 195
Anointing, Final or Last, 77, 142
Anthropomorphism, 53, 211, 212, 235, 297, 352, 354, 355
Antichrist, 365, 366, 373
Anti-god, 257
Antioch, 176, 213, 226, 241, 256
Antony of Egypt, 254–255, 300
Antun, Farah, 245
Apatheia (immune to affect), 277, 300
Apocalypse, apocalyptic, 106, 130, 298, 340, 363
Apocalypse of John. *See* John, Revelation of
Apocrypha, apocryphal, 3, 18, 19, 159, 295, 340–341, 342, 352, 359
Apophatic theology, 301
Apostasy, 221, 222
Apostles, 45, 74–75, 78, 89, 186, 203, 216, 263. *See also* Twelve, The

Apostolic, 17; succession, 75–76, 109, 290; tradition, 61, 75–76, 100
Apostolic Constitutions, 176, 177
Aqedah (binding [of Isaac]), 201
Aqida, 229. *See also* Creed
Aqsa, al-, mosque, 186, 268
Aquinas, Thomas, 21, 58, 143, 146, 148, 150–151, 154, 155, 156, 191, 195, 224, 241–242, 243, 246, 265, 305, 346, 354, 356, 368; and Islam, 242
Arab(s), Arabia, xxiii, 106, 122, 132, 184, 207
Arabesque, 209
Arabic, 2, 4, 6, 7, 27, 33, 36, 47, 49, 55, 161–162, 208–210, 219, 224, 239, 240, 287, 311. *See also* Quran, Arabic
Arafat, Mount, 181, 182
Aramaic, 4, 5–6, 16, 32, 38, 41, 46, 49, 56, 158, 172, 176, 209, 334
Aristotle, Aristotelianism, 58, 63, 128, 137, 143, 148, 150, 154, 156, 178, 212, 217, 219–220, 222, 227, 233–234, 237, 239, 240, 241–242, 246, 247, 248, 249–250, 322, 346, 347; in Arabic, 56, 161–162, 215, 219–220, 223–224, 225, 240–241; in Latin, 238–240, 241
Arius, Arianism, 218, 254
Ark of the Covenant, 168, 169, 184, 352
Armenia, Armenians, 219
Artaxerxes, shah, 18
Asceticism, 252, 254; Christian, 254, 257; Islamic, 275–278; Jesus', 253, 254; Jewish, 252–253; Muhammad's, 274, 275. *See also* Monasticism; Sufi
Ashari, al-, 165, 226–227; Asharite(s), 165, 227, 229, 234, 235, 357
Ashkenazi(s), 287, 336
Ashura, 135, 170, 196
Asr (afternoon prayer), 180
Assembly. *See* Synagogue
Assumption (of Mary), 189, 191, 193
Astrology, 220
Astronomy, 220
Athanasius, bishop, 254
Athanasius of Trebizond, 273
Athos, Mount, 273, 274, 303, 304
Atonement, 133–135, 141, 144, 169. *See also* Yom Kippur
Attributes, divine, 225, 229, 230, 236
Augustine, 22, 43, 77, 131, 137–138, 139–141, 143, 146, 148–150, 155–156, 190, 239, 241, 245, 246, 247, 258, 299, 343, 346,

355–356, 366–367; Canons of, 262; Hermits of, 262

Aurelian, Emperor, 179

Ave Maria, 189

Averah (crossing the line), 133

Averroes. *See* Ibn Rushd

Averroism, Latin, 244–245

Avicenna. *See* Ibn Sina

Aya; pl. ayat (signs, verses [of the Quran]), 25, 29, 356, 359; *Ayat Allah* (divine sign, Ayatollah), 121

Azazel, 134, 254

Baal Shem Tov, 289–290, 337, 338

Baalzebub, 130

Baba, Sufi leader, 283

Babylon, Babylonia, 70, 87, 92, 96, 172, 187, 248; Babylonian Exile, 10, 11, 25, 36, 68, 89, 95, 172, 209; Babylonian Talmud, 71, 112, 201

Badr, battle of, 353

Baghdad, 55, 81, 86, 111, 112, 199, 220, 224, 225, 226, 315–316

Bahais, 54

Bahya ben Paquda, 287

Baius (Michele de Bay), 156

Baldwin II, Latin king of Jerusalem, 268

Balkans, 118, 123, 283, 284

Baptism, 103, 104, 141, 142, 175

Baqa (subsistence in God), 312

Bar adam (a human), 158

Bar Kokhba, 20, 41, 296, 359, 373

Bar mitzvah (son of the Law), 137

Baraita (additional material), 69

Baraka, pl. *barakat* (blessings), 196, 254, 280–281, 282, 318

Barlaam, 304, 305

Barnabas, Letter of, 42, 43

Baronius, Caesar Cardinal, 79

Baruch, 19, 20, 24, 36

Barzakh ([cosmic] bridge), 331

Basil, bishop, 75, 101, 301, 303; Liturgy of, 176, 177; monastic rule, 257–258, 273

Basilica, 175, 176

Basque(s), 270

Batin (concealed, esoteric), 320, 324, 326

Baya (oath of allegiance), 281

Beatific Vision, 230, 301, 309–310, 347, 354–356

Beatitudes, 135

Bedouin, 109, 256

Bektashis, Bektashiyya, 283–284

Bellarmine, Robert, 152, 153

Belz, 240

Ben Sira. *See* Wisdom of Jesus ben Sira

Benedict XII, pope, 347, 354

Benedict XIV, pope, 194

Benedict, Benedictines, 257, 258–260, 268, 292

Benjamin al-Nihawandi, 72

Berber(s), 234

Bereshit, 4

Bereshit Rabba, 39

Berit (covenant), 16

Bernard of Clairvaux, 52, 191, 261, 268

Besht. *See* Baal Shem Tov

Bet din (religious court), 92, 95. *See also* Sanhedrin

Bet ha-knesset (house of assembly, synagogue), 172

Bet ha-midrash (house of study), 39

Bet ha- tefillah (house of prayer), 174

Bethlehem, 185

Beza, Theodore, 247

Bible, xxiv, 2–3, 4–5, 52, 87, 95, 131, 162–163, 170, 176, 243, 341, 352, 358; authorship, 10–11; Christian reading, 41; closure, 34; control, 61–62; debates, 57–60; quranic reading, 46–48; translations, 38, 55, 61

Bida (innovation), 195, 232, 287

Biel, Gabriel, 147–148

Bila kayf (without [asking] how]), 165, 230, 355

Biography, Muslim, 81

Birr (righteousness), 158

Bishop(s), 47–71, 75–76, 89, 99, 101, 103, 109, 112, 116, 124 , 218. *See also* Rome, bishop of

Bistami, Abu Yazid, 244, 310–311, 312

Black Death, 288

Black Stone, 182

Blood, bloodshed, 87–88, 170, 174–175

Bobova, 290

Boethius, 238–239

Bologna, university, 102, 240

Bonaventure, 191, 245, 267, 290

Boniface VIII, pope, 103, 145

Book(s), 4, 25, 106; heavenly, 15–16. *See also* Mother of the Book

Book of Life, 145–146, 371

Bosnia, Bosnians, 284

Breslau, 270
Brethren of Purity, 226, 248
Breviary, 259. *See also* Office, monastic
Britain, British, 188
Bruno, 260
Buddha, Buddhists, 139
Bulgaria, Bulgarians, 284
Bull, papal, 100–101. *See also* Decretals
Bultmann, Rudolf, 64
Burchard of Worms, 102
Bursa, 119
Byzantines, Byzantine Empire, 186, 204–206

Caimi, Bernardino, 190
Cairo, 59, 92, 119, 197, 325
Calatrava, Knights of, 269
Calendar, xxiv–xxv, 170, 183–184, 194, 196
Caligraphy, 209–210
Caliph, caliphate, 30, 109, 110, 112, 208, 222
Calvin, John, 22, 104, 150 , 178, 207,
    246–247; Calvinist(s), 103, 156
Cambridge, university, 7, 74
Canon(s), 17, 99–103; of authoritative texts,
    242–243; Biblical, 18–20; Christian, 34;
    New Testament, 17–18; Regular, 259, 261,
    264; of Scripture, 3, 5, 16–20
Capuchin (Franciscans), 267
Carmelites, 262, 306
Carthage, council of, 141
Carthusians, 260–261, 266, 273
Casimir, king of Poland, 289
Casuistry, 154–155, 156
Catechesis, catechism, 103–106, 153, 229,
    262
Catechumens, 176; Mass of, 175
Cathars (Pure Ones), Catharism, 138, 263,
    264
Catholics. *See* Church, Catholic
Celibacy, 101, 253, 256
Chalcedon, Council of, 190, 218–219, 220,
    257, 302
Chapter, general, 261, 285
Chariot, Mysteries, Work of, 238, 296. See
    also *Merkabah*
Chartreuse, La, 260–261
Chemnitz, Martin, 78
Cherubim, 168, 203, 352
Chilianism, 365–366. *See also* Millennialism
Chinese Rites, 284–285
Chishtis, Chishtiyya, 282–283
Chosen People, 13

Christians (*Christianoi*), Eastern Orthodox,
    189 ; Judeo- or Jewish, 67, 185, 216; Syr-
    ian, 224; popular devotions, 188–189. *See
    also* Church
Christmas, 66, 178–179
Christology, Christological, 20, 218, 256, 302
Chronicles, Books of, 10, 25, 57
Church, 196; building, 176; Catholic, 19, 20,
    64, 151, 153; Celtic, 142; confessional, 219;
    Eastern Orthodox, 142, 158, 189, 191, 193,
    194, 196, 205–206, 303, 304, 306; finances,
    73–74; Great, 103, 109, 141, 257; Latin or
    Western, 58, 62, 142, 144, 158, 171, 189,
    190, 191, 193, 281, 304, 306, 347; Militant,
    Suffering, Triumphant, 144 ; Roman,
    151–152, 191, 193, 259, 271; Shiite, 196.
    See also Reform
Cicero, 239
Circumcision, 11, 109, 166
Cistercians, 261, 268
Clement V, pope, 103, 269
Clement VIII, pope, 153
Clement XII pope, 285
Clement XIV, pope, 272, 286
Clement of Alexandria, 42–43, 215, 217, 237
Clergy, 123–124, 142, 153, 196, 199, 218,
    262, 263, 281, 288, 307
Cluny, 7, 260, 261
Coimbra, university, 153
Common good, 89, 101
Communion, 175
Companions of the Prophet, 45, 51, 82–83,
    86, 115, 208, 230, 232
Company of Jesus, 291. *See also* Jesuits
Concealment (of the Imam), 86, 115, 374. *See
    also* Imam
Confession (of sin), 134, 142
Confessor(s), 158, 193
Confirmation, 77, 142
Confucius, Cofucianism, 284–285
Consensus, 73, 75, 110, 114, 116–117,
    165–167, 232. See also *Ijma*
Constantia, sister of Constantine I, 202–203
Constantine I, emperor, 99, 123, 179,
    184–186, 193, 202 Donation of, 23
Constantine V, emperor, 204–205
Constantinople, 122, 123, 176, 226, 256, 274.
    See also Istanbul
Consubstantiation, 178
Conversion, Converso(s), 57–59, 235
Convivencia, 57

Copts, Coptic, 5
Cordovero, Moses, 337
Corpse impurity, 87–88
Corpus Christi, feast, 194–195
Cosmology, 347–348
Cossacks, 289
Council(s) of the Church, 45, 61, 76, 100, 103, 228
Counter-Reformation, 61, 151–152, 153, 191, 194, 307. *See also* Trent, Council of
Covenant, 16, 24, 36, 70, 88, 95, 133, 209, 299; New, 1, 35, 97, 170, 174. See also *Mithaq*
Creation, xxiv, 41, 155, 199, 214, 216, 301. *See also* Work of the Beginning
Creed(s), 104, 192, 228–230. See also *Aqida*
Crimes and punishments, 87, 107, 111–112; and sin, 128
Crucifixion, 185–186, 199
Crusades, crusaders, 144, 186–187, 263, 268
Custos Sanctae Terrae. See Holy Land, Custodian
Cynics, 136
Cyprus, 269

Dajjal, al- (the Deceiver), 373
Damascus, 119, 205, 228, 328
Damasus, pope, 23
Daniel, 294; Book of, 4, 6, 9–10, 41, 344, 365
Daniel al-Qumisi, 72
Dante Alighieri, 144, 244, 341, 348, 349, 350, 351
Dargah (Sufi convent [India]), 278, 282
David, king of Israel, 10, 13, 67, 184
Dawa (call, summons), 325
Dawla (government, state), 114
Dawud ibn Kalaf, 53
Dawwani, al-, 162
Dead Sea Scrolls, 89–90
Death, Muslim view, 369–370
Decretals, 100–103
Defilement. *See* Impurity
Delhi Sultanate, 282
Deposit of Faith, 74–75
Deuterocanonical, 19
Deuteronomist (D), 11
Deuteronomy, 4, 10, 19, 87, 89
Devotions, Christian popular, 188–189; Muslim, 195–196
Dhikr (recollection, Sufi liturgy), 279, 281, 319

Dhimma, dhimmi, (contract), 122, 124, 188, 210
Diabolos (devil), 130, 132
Diaspora, 4, 38, 75, 172, 213, 215
Didache, 176
Dietary laws, 11, 50, 73, 87, 147, 160, 276; monastic, 259
Dionysius the Areopagite, 302, 303
Diptychs, 176
Disputatio (discussion), 46
Divinization, 201. See also *Theiosis*
Divorce, 100, 101, 107, 161, 167
Dogma, 218
Dome of the Rock, 186, 223, 262
Dominic de Guzman, 262, 264–265
Dominicans (Order of Preachers), 58, 59, 70, 143, 152, 156, 157, 189, 191, 242, 244, 260, 261, 264–265, 271, 284–285, 286
Double truth theory, 244–245
Douleia (veneration), 192. See also *Hyperdouleia*
Dov Baer, 290, 291
Dress, monastic, 259, 290
Dualism, 129–130, 138–139
Duns Scotus, 191, 245

Early Catholicism, 99
Easter, 103, 178, 179, 186
Eck, Johann, 151
Edah Haredit, 361
Eden, Garden of, 44, 137, 342, 347, 348
Edessa, 176
Egypt, Egyptians, xxi, 12, 33, 56, 122, 176, 198, 217, 219, 224, 248, 254, 255, 263–264, 276, 279, 301, 336; pilfering from, 217
Eide (Forms, ideas of God), 155, 214, 239
Eighteen Benedictions (*Shemoneh Esreh*), 173, 345
Ekklesia (assembly, church), 17. *See also* Assembly; Church
Election (of the saved), 145–146, 150. *See also* Predestination
Elias, Brother, 266, 280
Elijah, 336, 341
Elohist (E), 10–11
Emperor worship, 201
En Sof, 335
End Time, 40, 42, 163, 230, 274–275, 294, 327, 363–364; scenario, 339–341
Energeiai (energies [of God]), 305, 356
England, 271, 272

Enlightenment, 52
Enoch, 241; Books of, 20, 36, 294, 295, 298, 340
Ephesus, Council of, 190
Ephraimites, 360, 361
Epiklesis (invocation), 176, 177
Epiphanius, bishop, 203
Episcopal, episcopate. *See* Bishop
Episkopos; pl. *episkopoi* (overseer), 75. *See also* Bishop
Epistemology, 14–16, 21, 244, 249, 322–323
Erasmus, Desiderius, 5–6, 246
Eremos (empty, alone, hermit), 255
Eretz Israel (Land of Israel), 59, 96, 172, 337, 344, 360–361
Eschaton, eschatology, 43, 74, 106, 136, 230, 253, 311, 339–376; realized and futurist, 363–364
Esdras, Books of, 19, 296, 365
Essenes, 39, 40, 90–91, 253, 295
Esther, 4, 10, 13
Ethics, 127, 128, 146, 161–162, 164
Ethiopic, 49
Eucharist, 16, 104, 142, 171, 174–175, 177–178, 179, 195, 198, 299; devotions, 194–195; Reform, 178
Eusebius, 79, 109, 202–203, 217
Evagrius Ponticus, 300–301
Eve, 44, 131, 133, 137, 139, 293
Evil, 129–130, 138–139, 251
Excommunication, 43, 142
Exegesis, 20, 35–64, 100, 107, 214–215, 246; allegorical, 40–41, 42–43, 214, 215, 229, 235, 237, 243, 326 ; biblical, 36–41, 214 ; humanist, 62–63; Islamic, 48–54; medieval Jewish, 56–57; messianic, 41; rabbinic, 5–56; Reform, 60–63, 246; Shiite, 54; typological, 42–43, 59, 64. See also *Midrash; Tafsir*
Exilarch, 124
Exile. *See* Babylon, Babylonian Exile
Exodus, 4, 10, 13, 34, 39, 87, 198
Ezekiel, 4, 10, 187, 294, 296, 298, 326, 342, 344
Ezra, 1, 4, 6, 10, 13, 16, 19, 25, 36, 37, 209, 294, 340

Faith, 148–149, 230 ; and good works, 140–141, 229, 230
Fajr (daybreak prayer), 180
Fakhr al-Din, 228
Fakir (mendicant), 277, 279

Falah (prosperity), 258
Falsafa, 220, 233, 235, 245, 256; and *kalam*, 238. *See also* Philosophy
Fana (self-extinction), 312, 325
Faqih, pl. *fuqaha* (jurisprident), 107, 123
Farabi, al-, 92, 221, 227, 232, 234, 237, 238, 240, 244
Fard (obligation), 160
Fasting, 105, 135, 142. *See also* Ramadan
Fathers, 23, 43, 45, 46, 61, 76–79, 203, 232, 243, 246, 247, 343
Fathers of impurity, 87
Fatiha (Opening), 180
Fatima, daughter of Muhammad, 86, 196, 314, 355, 373
Fatimids. *See* Shiism, Ismaili or Sevener
Fatwa (legal opinion, ruling), 112–113, 332
Faylasuf (philosopher), 220, 231, 233–235, 240, 248, 357
Filioque, 304
Fiqh (jurisprudence), 107, 160
Fiqh Akbar I, II, 229
Fitra (aboriginal, natural religion), 358–359
Flaccus Illyricus. *See* Vlacich, Mattias
Florence, Council of, 347
Forms. See *Eide*
Fourteen Pure Ones, 196
Francis de Sales, 288, 336
Francis of Assisi, 262–264, 266, 290; biography, 267
Franciscans (Order of Friars Minor), 58, 70, 189, 245, 260, 261, 262–264, 280, 285–286, 306; Conventuals and Observants, 267; poverty controversy, 266–267; Second Order (Poor Clares), 263, 267; Spirituals, 367; Third Order, 263, 267. *See also* Capuchin
Frankl, Jacob, 289
Free will, 129, 146, 162–165, 219, 223, 229. *See also* Predestination
French, 57
French Revolution, 272
Friars (*Fratres*, brothers), 262, 285. *See also* Dominicans, Franciscans, Mendicants
Friends of God, 254–255, 280. *See also* Saint(s), Muslim
Fudali, al-, 229
Fundamentalism/Revivalism, 118, 287
Furqan (criterion), 359

Gabriel, angel, 2, 14, 15, 26, 27, 84, 323, 352, 353

Galen, 162 , 220
Galicia, 289
Galilee, 22, 67, 70, 96, 174, 253, 286–287, 334
Gaon; pl. *geonim* (eminences), 112–113, 124
Garden Recital, 196, 199
Gayomart, 315
Gehenna, 106, 230, 342, 348, 349
Gemara (completion), 71, 92, 201
Gematria (science of letter-numbers), 299
Genesis, 4, 13, 39, 137, 298, 301
Genesis Apocryphon, 37
Geneva, 104, 150, 207, 247
Gentiles, 42, 136, 216–221
Ger, 290
Germany, Germans, 73, 287, 289
Gezerah, pl. *gezeroth* (rabbinic decree), 89, 94
Ghaybiyya (otherness), 330
Ghazali, al-, 160, 161, 165, 222, 227–228, 229, 231, 232–234, 237, 238, 244, 280, 323, 325–326
Ghazi (holy warrior), 122
Ghuluw (extremism), *ghulat* (extremists), 320
Glossa Ordinaria, 46, 51, 243
Gnosis (wisdom), 248, 314
Gnostic, Gnosticism, 3, 95, 130, 131, 221, 251, 295, 321, 325, 329, 333, 335, 352; and Sufism, 313–314, 320
Golden Legend, 189, 191, 270
Golgotha, 185
Good News, 1, 5, 75
Gospel(s), xxiv, 1, 5, 16, 34, 67, 77–78, 91, 130, 135, 145, 158–159, 172, 176, 179, 199, 209, 217, 294, 352
Grace (*charis, gratia*), 138, 140, 141, 142, 143, 152–153, 246; and mysticism, 318; and salvation, 147–148, 149, 150–151, 154–155, 356;. See also *Lutf*
Graphe, 13. *See also* Scripture
Gratian (jurist), 79, 102–103, 128
Greece, Greeks, 127–129, 136, 146, 161–162, 185, 201, 211–213, 248
Greek, 4, 16, 20–21, 24, 38, 49, 209, 215, 219, 224, 239
Gregory VII, pope, 102, 262
Gregory IX, pope, 103, 266
Gregory XIII, pope, 153
Gregory Nazianzum, 301
Gregory Palamas, 273, 304–305
Gush Emunim, 361

Habad, 291–292, 362–363
Habakkuk, 37
Haburah; pl. *haburoth* (brotherhoods), 135, 287–288
Hadd (quranic penalty), 111
Hadith (prophetic reports, traditions), 14, 48, 80–84, 108–109, 114, 116, 165–166, 208, 223, 231, 240, 308; collection, 83–84, 86; criticism, 82–83; and Jewish tradition, 83–84; as revelation, 83, 231–232; Shiite, 11, 85–86; types, 83–84
Hadrian, emperor, 185
Haeresis (choice, schools), 130. *See also* Heresy
Hafsa, wife of Muhammad, 32
Hag (pilgrimage), 170, 175
Haggadah, pl. *haggadoth* (homily), haggadic, 25, 37, 49, 59, 198, 200; haggadic midrashim, 38–39, 47, 49, 187, 357
Hagia Sofia, Council of, 305
Hagios (holy man), 254. *See also* Saint(s)
Hajj (pilgrimage), 105, 135, 180–183, 195, 328
Hakam (arbitrator), 109
Hakim, al-, Imam, 186
Halakah, pl. *halakoth* (legal material), halakic, 25, 37, 69, 72, 73, 88–89, 90–93, 94
Halal (permitted, kosher), 160
Halberstam, Shelomah, 290
Hallaj, al-, 249
Hamartia (missing the [moral] mark), 128
Hanafite(s), 114, 122–123
Hanbalite(s), 114, 197, 226–227, 229, 235–236
Hanhaqoth (rules of piety), 288, 336
Hanukkah, xxiii, 66
Haqq; pl. *huquq Allah* (claims, rights of God), 109
Haram, 160. *See also* Taboo
Haram (of Mecca), 181–182
Harawi, al-, 249
Harun al-Rashid, caliph, 110, 111
Hasan al-Basri, 223
Hasid, pl. *Hasidim* (pious, hasidic), 95, 124, 168, 188, 288–292, 333, 337–338; Zionism, 361
Hasmonaean(s), 67
Hattin, battle of, 269
Heaven, 143, 144, 145, 348; heavenly voyages, 294, 298, 308–309, 350–351
Hebrew (language), 4, 6, 16, 24–25, 32, 36, 37, 38, 49, 56, 57, 59, 60, 73, 74, 208–209, 210, 239, 287, 288

Hebrew Union College, 73
Hebrews, Letter to the, 171
Hebron, 185
Hegira (*hijra*), xxiv, 27
Hegoumenos (monastic superior), 273. *See also* Abbot
Heidegger, Martin, 64
Hell, 143, 144, 145, 294, 349–350
Hellenes, Hellenism, 15, 44, 90, 92, 95, 140, 211, 213, 215, 218, 219–220, 230, 240–241, 300; late, 247–248
Helvetius, 190
Henotheism, xxi
Heresy, 130, 262
Hermeneutics, 63–64
Hermes Trismegistos, 248
Herod, king of Israel, 169, 172, 179, 184, 185, 186, 187, 188
Herodians, 95
Hesychia (quietude), Hesychasm, 273, 301, 303–306, 319, 356
Het (missing the [moral] mark), 133
Hexateuch, 11
Heykaloth (palaces), 296, 297–298
Hikma (wisdom), 248, 314; *mashrqiyya* (illuminative or oriental), 248, 322; *mutaaliqiyya* (transcendent), 250
Hillel, 39, 40, 67, 69
Hindus, Hinduism, 283
Hitlahanut (divine transcendence), 291
Hokmah (wisdom), 248. *See also* Wisdom, divine
Holiness code, 91
Holocaust sacrifices, 169
Holy Days, 170
Holy Land, 263, 271; Custodian, 263
Holy man, 254, 256–257. *See also* Saint(s)
Holy of Holies, 89
Holy Orders, 142
Holy Saturday, 103
Holy Sepulcher, Church of, 186–187, 189, 262, 268
Holy Spirit, 21, 22, 74, 78, 100, 123, 151, 153, 176–177, 217
Homer, 40, 44, 213, 243
Homily, 172. *See also* Preaching
Homoousios (consubstantial), 217
Honorius III, pope, 264
Hosea, 170
Hospitalers, Knights, 268–270

Hugh of Payens, 266
Hujjat al-Islam (Proof of Islam), 121
Hungary, 290, 338
Hus, Jan, 368
Husayn ibn Ali, Imam , 196, 197; dramatization of his death, 199–200. *See also* Garden Recital; *Taziyeh*
Hyperdouleia (superveneration), 193
Hyponoia (under-thought), 40. *See also* Exegesis, allegorical
Hypostasis (existent being, individual), 217, 218

Ibadat (acts of worship), 161
Iblis, 132–133, 207
Ibn Abbas, 29, 50–51, 207–208
Ibn al-Muqaffa, 110
Ibn al-waqt (child of the moment), 278
Ibn Arabi, 52, 283, 324, 326, 327–332, 351, 356
Ibn Babaya, 86, 115, 320
Ibn Ezra, 237
Ibn Gabirol, 237
Ibn Hajar, 82
Ibn Hanbal, 53, 197, 225–226, 235
Ibn Hazm, 228
Ibn Ishaq, biographer of the Prophet, 159
Ibn Ishaq, Sufi, 282
Ibn Khaldun, 161, 227, 332
Ibn Miskawayh, 162
Ibn Nusayr, 321
Ibn Rushd, 231, 233–235, 237–238, 240, 244–245, 343
Ibn Sad, 81, 84
Ibn Sina, 54, 162 , 221–222, 227–228, 231, 232, 234, 238, 240, 244, 248, 249–250, 322–323, 329, 358
Ibn Taymiyya, 117, 197, 228, 231–232, 235–236, 331–332
Ibn Tufayl, 234
Ibn Tumart, 234, 235
Ibrahim ibn Muhammad, 123
Icons, 205–206; Iconoclasm, 204–206; Reform, 206–207
Id al-adha (Festival of Sacrfice), 171, 182
Idolaters, idolatry, 200–201, 204, 207
Idris (Enoch), 308
Ignatius, bishop, 75
Ignatius (Iñigo) of Loyola, 153, 270–271, 280, 288, 306–307, 336. See also *Spiritual Exercises*

Ihram (taboo state), 181–182

Ijma, 45, 109, 117, 165. *See also* Consensus

Ijtihad (personal effort or interpretation), 52, 107, 114, 116–118, 166, 220

Ikhwan (brethren), 281

Ilahiyyat (metaphysics), 249

Ilham (inspiration), 85

Illumination, 247–250, 300, 322. See also *Ishraq*

Images, 77, 200–208; Christians, 202–207; Islam and, 207–208; Jews and, 200–202

Imam, Imamate, 54, 86, 114, 115, 121, 196, 222, 227, 235, 280, 320, 352, 374

Imitation of Christ, 189, 307

Immaculate Conception (of Mary), 191

Impurity, 87–88

India, Indian, 138, 220, 278, 282–283

Indulgences, 143–145, 148, 246

Infallibility 62 , 76

Inimitability (of the Quran), 12, 29 , 209

Injil (Gospel), 2, 27, 55

Innocent II, pope, 261

Innocent III, pope, 263, 264

Innocent IV, pope, 70

Inquisition, Christian,133; Islamic, 225–226

Inspiration, 21, 76, 78. See also *Ilham*; Scripture, inspiration

Intellection *(episteme, ilm)*, 314

Intercalation, 170, 183–184, 195

Intercession, 193, 230; Abraham, 368–369; Muhammad, 371–372

Intercourse, 87–88

Interpolation, quranic, 33–34

Invincible Sun, 173, 179

Iran, 120, 122, 130, 138, 196, 220; Islamic Republic of, 6, 112, 375; Safavid, 249, 320

Iraq, 56, 70, 95, 112–113, 120, 122, 123, 196, 197, 219, 220, 223–224

Irenaeus, bishop, 75, 121

Irene, empress, 205

Isa ibn Miryam, 34. *See also* Jesus of Nazareth

Isaac, 203; sacrifice of, 94

Isabella, queen of Spain, 24

Isaiah, 4, 10, 13, 20, 201, 293, 340, 342

Isfahan, school of, 249–250

Isfahani, Abu Nuaym al-, 317

Ishmael, 27

Ishmael, Rabbi, 298

Ishraq, 221, 248, 322. *See also* Illumination

Isidore of Seville, 45

Islam (submission), xxiii

Isma (impeccability [of Muhammad]), 191–192

Ismaili(s). *See* Shiism, Ismaili or Sevener

Isnad (chain), 80, 83, 108–109

Isra. See Night Journey

Israel, State of, 188, 361

Israelite kings, 200–201

Israelites *(Benei, Banu Israel)*, xxi–xxii, 16, 37, 42, 87, 133, 168, 172, 184, 187, 198, 200–201, 251, 254, 293, 340

Istanbul, 119, 122

Istihsan (equity), 116

Istislah (public interest), 116

Ittihad (identity [with God]), 324

Ivo of Chartres, 10

Jacob (Israel), 203, 293

Jacob of Voragine, 189

Jafar al-Sadiq, Imam, 314

Jahannam, 145, 371

Jahiliyya, al- (the era of ignorance), xxiv, 106, 132

James, apostle, 75, 203, 294

James, "brother of the Lord", Gospel of, 18, 36, 190; Letter of, 17, 61; Liturgy of, 176–177

James I, king of Aragon, 58–59

Jami, 180. *See also* Mosque

Janazah (prayers for dead), 369

Janissaries, 285

Jannat Adan, 349, 355, 371. *See also* Eden, Garden of

Jansen, Cornelius, 156; Jansenism, 155–157

Japan, 271

Jehoshaphat Valley, 345, 347. *See also* Kidron Valley

Jeremiah, 4, 10, 13, 342

Jeroboam, king of Israel, 201

Jerome, 5–6, 24, 46, 60, 190

Jerusalem, 66, 70, 89, 119, 142, 144, 173, 179, 184–188, 198, 205, 223, 228, 263, 268, 301, 307, 336, 342, 350; Christian enshrinement, 184–187, 195; Christian quarter, 187; Jerusalem Talmud, 71; Moroccan quarter, 187–188

Jesuits, 124, 152, 156, 157, 258, 266, 270–272, 280, 284–285, 286

Jesus Movement, 41

Jesus of Nazareth, 1, 9, 20, 27, 39, 74, 99, 129, 130, 133, 139, 146, 158, 170, 172, 174–175, 185, 198, 209, 220, 328, 344, 359,

Jesus of Nazareth (*cont.*)
  363–364; asceticism, 253–254; birthday,
  178–179; high priest, 171; images,
  202–206, 207; last days (passion), 199; Logos, 216, 217; merits, 141–142; moral
  teaching, 135–136, 137; Mosaic law, 96–97,
  135–136; Passover sacrifice, 170–171;
  poverty, 255, 256; Quran, 47, 186, 308;
  temptation by Satan, 254; tomb, 185, 186,
  189 (*see also* Holy Sepulcher); transfiguration,
  294; and women, 253. *See also* Christology
Jesus Prayer, 302–303, 304, 307, 319
Jewish Theological Seminary, 74
Jimenez de Cisneros, Francisco Cardinal, 24
Jinn (demonic spirits), 13
Joachim de Fiore, 366–369
Job, 4, 10, 342
Joel, 340
John XV, pope, 193
John XXII, pope, 103, 347, 354
John, Apostle, 75, 203, 294, 365; Gospel of,
  17, 20, 34, 215–216; Revelation of, 3, 15,
  17, 61, 202, 354, 364–365
John, patriarch, 101
John Cassian, 300
John Climacus, 303
John of Damascus, 205
John Paul II, pope, 194
John the Baptist, 253, 295
Joseph, husband of Mary, 190
Joseph, son of Jacob, 47, 308, 360
Joseph ben Nathan Official, 58–59
Josephus, Flavius, 15, 18–19, 67, 90, 91, 134,
  169
Joshua, 4, 10, 11, 13, 34, 68, 71, 109
Josiah, king of Israel, 11, 19, 89
Juan de Capistrano, 267
Jubilee year, 145
Jubilees, Book of, 36
Judah Halevi, 237, 252, 360
Judah ha-Nasi, 68, 69, 70, 91–92
Judaism, Conservative, 73–74; Orthodox, 25,
  73, 200, 361; Reform, 73–74, 200; Ultra-
  Orthodox (Haredim), 361
Judas, 130
Jude, 17
Judges, 4, 10, 13, 34
Judgment, General, Last, 106, 132, 144, 230,
  342–343, 370; particular, 343, 370
Judith, 5, 19, 202
Junayd, 311–312, 315

Jus (right), 128. *See also* Justice
Justice, Islamic, 109–113; Jewish, 94–95, 342
Justification, 148–149, 150–151
Justin, martyr, 216
Justinian, emperor, 101–102, 106

Kaaba, 27, 171, 180, 181, 182, 207, 308
Kabbalah, kabbalists, kabbalistic, 52, 59, 93,
  168, 169, 287, 288, 289, 291, 296, 298,
  333–338, 351
Kabod (glory), 168
Kalam (dialectical theology), 160, 222, 223,
  233, 236–237; and *falsafa*, 238. See also
  Mutakallim; Theology, Islamic; Theology,
  Jewish
Kangxi, emperor of China, 285
Karaites, 56, 71–72, 91, 360
Karamat (gifts, graces), 197, 282
Karbala, 120, 196, 197
Karet (cutting off), 133
Karlstadt, Andras Bodenstein von, 206–207
Karo, Joseph, 336, 337
Kasani, al-, 125
Kasb, Iktisab (acquisition), 165
Kashf (unveiling), 321
Katechesis (instruction), 103, 175. *See also*
  Catechesis
Kayfiyya (howness), 355. See also *Bila kayf*
Kelal Israel (catholic Israel), 73
Kellia (monastic cells), 273
Kenoma (The Emptiness), 335
Kerygma, 105
Ketib, 32. *See also* Writing
Ketubim (Writings), 1, 4
Khadija, wife of Muhammad, 274
Khanqah (Sufi convent), 278–279, 280
Kharijism, Kharijites (seceders), 72, 222, 229
Khayal (imagined world), 331
Khayr, al- (the better), 158
Khomeini, Ayatollah, 375
Kidron Valley, 345
Kindi, al-, 220–221
King James Bible, 6
Kingdom of God (Messianic or End Time),
  75, 253, 363–364
Kings, Books of, 4, 10, 13
Kohen; pl. *kohenim* (priest), 171–172
Koine (vernacular [Greek]), 4
Koinobion (community), 255, 275
Komboskoinion (prayer rope, rosary), 303
Konya, 319

Kook, Abraham Isaac, 361; Zvi Yehudah, 361
Kufr (unbelief), 192
Kulayni, al-, 86, 115, 320

Lainez, Diego, 280
Laity, 153, 307
Lamb of God, 155, 170–171
Lamentations, 4, 10
Languages, 5–7
Last Supper, 16, 170, 174, 175, 177, 194, 199.
    See also Eucharist
Last Things. *See* Eschaton
Lateran IV, Council of, 131, 142, 178, 243
Latin, 2, 4, 5, 6, 7, 21, 23, 42, 176, 199, 218,
    219, 238–240
Latreia (worship), 193, 205
Laura, lavra (monastic compound), 273
Law, 20, 68, 70, 87, 128, 221, 240; biblical,
    88–89; canon, 99–103, 193, 218, 285;
    Christian, 98–99; customary, 121–122; Is-
    lamic (see *Sharia*); Jewish (*see* Mosaic Law;
    Torah); purpose, 94 ; statute, 121–123, 128.
    See also Natural law
Laxism, 154, 157
Lazarus, 343
Lectio (reading, study [of Scripture]), 46, 240
Lent, 10, 77
Leo III, emperor, 204, 205
Leo V, emperor, 205
Leo IX, pope, 267
Leontius, 203–204
Leviticus, 4, 28, 39, 87, 91, 134, 202
Lex, 128. *See also* Law
Light of Lights, 249
Lithuania, 269, 291, 338
Liturgy, liturgical, 168, 175–177, 188, 195;
    domestic Jewish, 172, 173, 188, 195; East-
    ern Christian, 176–177; Jerusalem,
    186–189; Mari and Addai, 126; Passover,
    198; Roman, 176; St. Basil, 176, 177; St.
    James, 176–177; St. Mark, 176, 177; West-
    ern Christian, 176
Logic, 223, 224
Logos, pl. *logoi* (word, reason), 211–213, 214,
    217, 218
Loquentes in lege Maurorum, 224, 242
Lord's Day, 173. *See also* Sunday
Lord's Prayer, 104, 176
Lord's Supper, 178. *See also* Eucharist, Reform
Lot, 4
Louis IX, king of France, 49

Louis XIV, king of France, 272
Louvain, university, 153, 156
Lubovitch, 290, 291
Lubovitcher. *See* Habad
Ludolph of Saxony, 270
Luke, Gospel of, 5, 10, 17, 20, 34, 67, 174,
    189, 190. *See also* Acts of the Apostles
Luria, Isaac, 336–337
Lutf (favor, grace), 164
Luther, Martin, 60–61, 76–77, 104, 145,
    147–148, 178, 194, 206, 246; Lutheran(s),
    103, 151
Lyons, Council of, 347

Macarius, 301
Maccabees, 96, 109, 192, 342; Books of, 5, 13,
    19, 24. *See also* Hasmonaean(s)
Madhhab (legal school), 109
Madonna, 189. *See also* Mary, cult
Madrasa(s) (law school), 114, 124–125, 227,
    228, 278, 281, 283; and university, 240
Maghrib (post-sunset prayer), 180
Magi, 138
Magic, 131, 132, 239, 248
Magisterium, 96, 112, 123, 151–152, 157
Mahdi (The Rightly-Guided), 234–235, 344,
    372–373, 375–376
Mahmud II, sultan, 119
Maimonides, Moses (Musa ibn Maymun,
    Rambam), 54, 58, 59, 92–93, 113, 215, 233,
    234, 235, 236–238, 356–357
Majlis (Sufi session), 281
Majnun (jinn-possessed), 132
Makruh (discouraged [act]), 161
Malachi, 36
Malik al-Kamil, sultan, 262
Malik al-Zahir, sultan, 248
Malikite(s), 114, 234
Malta, Knights of, 269
Mamluk(s), 111, 269
Mamun, al-, caliph, 224, 225
Mandaeans, 295
Mandub (recommended [act]), 160
Mani, 138–139
Manichaeans, Manichaeism, 130, 131,
    138–139, 278
Mansur, al-, caliph, 110
Marcion, 17, 43–44
Marienburg, 269
Marifa (gnosis, wisdom), 221, 314
Marja al-taqlid (exemplar for emulation), 121

Mark, Gospel of, 5, 10, 17, 20, 27, 174;
    Liturgy of, 176, 177
Marriaci, Ludovico, 7
Marriage, 95, 98, 99, 103, 107, 115, 118, 124,
    136, 142, 161, 195, 197, 256, 344. See also
    Muta
Martinique, 272
Martyrs, 158, 189, 204; cult, 192–193
Marwa, 182, 183
Mary, mother of Jesus, 186, 204, 207; cult,
    189–192, 193; perpetual virginity, 190;
    Quran, 47, 190
Mashaiyyun (Peripatetics), 248
Mashiah (Anointed One, Messiah), 359
Masjid, 180. *See also* Mosque
Masorah, Masoretes, 32–33, 46
Mass, sacrifice of, 171, 195; catechumens, 175
Mathematics, 220
Matn (text [of a *hadith*]), 80
Matthew, Gospel of, 5, 10, 17, 20, 41, 67,
    174, 190
Matzoh (unleavened bread), feast of, 198. *See
    also* Passover
Mawlid al-Nabi (Birthday of the Prophet), 66,
    195, 197
Mecca, xxiv, 8, 14, 22, 26–27, 49, 105, 132,
    135, 180, 181, 184, 198, 207, 274, 328, 350;
    Meccan Revelations, 328
Medicine, 220, 223, 240
Medina, xxiv, 14, 26–27, 49, 105, 135, 184,
    196, 274; Jews of, 170, 181, 198
Mehmed II, sultan, 118, 158–159
Mekilta, 39
Melanchthon, Philip, 368
Melkite (imperial) Church, 219, 220
Mendicants, 250, 262, 264. See also *Fakir;*
    Friars
Menstruation, 87–88, 105
Merkabah, 296. *See also* Chariot
Messiah, messianism, 20, 35, 41, 42, 59,
    158–159, 216–218, 289, 341, 357, 359, 361,
    362–363; Islamic, 372–376. See also
    Mashiah
Messina, Jesuit school, 271
Metanoia, 253. *See also* Repentance
Mevlevis, Mevlanas, 280, 284. *See also* Rumi
Michael, angel, 352, 353
Midrash (inquiry), 36, 37–40, 56. *See also*
    Exegesis
Midrash Lamentations, 39
Mihrab (qibla niche), 180

Mikraoth Gedaloth, 46
Millennialism, 365–368
Mina, 171, 181, 182–183, 195
Miqveh (ritual bath), 88
Mir Damad, 249, 250
Miracles, 12–13, 159, 197
Mishnah, 6, 7, 12, 16, 37, 68–71, 84, 91–92,
    108–109, 117, 169, 174, 201, 242, 296
Mishneh Torah, 1–3, 92–93, 113
Missionaries, 99, 271
Mithaq (covenant), 311, 315
Mitnaggedim (opponents), 291, 362
Mitzvah, pl. *mitzvoth* (commandment), 72, 88,
    99, 106, 141
Mizrachi(s), 361
Monachoi (solitaries, monks), 255
Monastery, monasticism, 141, 142, 143, 196;
    cenobitic and eremitic, 255; Christian,
    255–274; Christian and Muslim compared,
    285–286; Eastern, 258, 273–274; Eastern
    and Western Christian compared, 258;
    idiorhythmic, 274; Islamic (see *Tariqa*);
    Jewish, 287, 288; military, 267–270; reform,
    265–266; regulation, 257–258; suppression,
    286–287
Mongols, 122, 327
Monophysites, Monophysitism, 218–219
Monotheism, xxi–xxii, 105, 129, 130 , 186,
    214
Monte Cassino, 257, 258
Moor(s), 269
Morality, 88, 108, 127–167; Augustine's
    teaching, 139–141; Catholic, 153–158; con-
    sensus in, 165–167; and ethics, 127; Is-
    lamic, 158–162; Jesus' teaching, 135–136;
    Paul's teaching, 136–137
Morocco, 56, 234
Mosaic Law, 67, 89; administration, 94–96.
    See also Torah
Moses, xxi–xxii, 1–2, 10, 11–14, 15, 18, 21,
    27, 39, 66, 68, 87, 88, 89, 94, 96, 128, 169,
    174, 200, 203, 214, 215, 293, 294, 308, 328
Moses de Léon, 333, 334
Mosque, 105–106, 111, 279, 281
Mother of the Book, 16, 48
Muadhdhin (caller, muezzin), 180
Muamalat (transactional acts [between human
    agents]), 161
Mudejars, 7, 188
Mufti, 112–114, 119
Mughuls, 282–283

Muhaddith, pl. *muhaddithun*, 231. *See also* Traditionists
Muhammad ibn al-Hanifiyya, 373
Muhammad ibn Tughluq, sultan, 282
Muhammad, 1–2, 9, 11–14, 15, 20, 21, 22, 26, 27, 29–30, 47, 80, 105, 106, 113, 132, 135, 169, 170, 179, 180–181, 197, 207, 257, 314, 328, 355; ascension, 192, 294, 308, 309, 350–352; asceticism, 274–275, cosmic, 320; impeccability, 191–192; knowledge of the Bible, 47; life or biography, 49–50, 83, 154; messenger, 12, 26; moral exemplar, 158–160, 165, 192; opening of breast, 192, 308; poet, 28, 44, 55, 132; quranic exegete, 48, 230; seal of the prophets, 34, 35, 54, 139; tomb at Medina, 183, 196, 198; wives, 275
Muhammad Light, 86, 195
Muharram, 135, 196, 197, 200
Muhtasib (market inspector), 122
Muin al-Din, 202, 283
Mujahid, pl. *mujahidun* (holy warrior), 122
Mujtahid (interpreter), 120; *mujtahid mutlaq* (absolute interpreter), 118, 121
Mulla Sadra al-Shirazi, 249–250
Mullah, 119, 196
Munkar and Nakir, 270, 370
Muqallid (follower), 121. See also *Taqlid*
Musa, 34. *See also* Moses
Muslim, pl. *muslimun* (submitter), xxiii, 115, 359. See also *Islam*
Muslim, hadith expert, 83
Mustarabim (Wanna-be Arabs), 287
Muta (temporary marriage), 115
Mutakallim, pl. *mutakallimun* (dialectical theologians), 224, 226, 228, 231, 232, 236; Shiite, 250. See also *Kalam*
Mutawakkil, caliph, 226
Mutazilite(s), 53–54, 72, 164, 192, 225–227, 228, 229, 235, 236, 305, 357
Muzdalifa, 182
Mysticism, 293–338; Christian, 299–307; Islamic, 308–332; Jewish, 294–299, 333–338. *See also* Kabbalah; Sufi
Mythos (story, account), 211–212, 214

Nadir Shah, 120
Nahman of Breslau, 290
Nahmanides (Moses ben Nahman, Ramban), 59–60, 334, 360
Najaf, 120

Najran, 50
Names, Beautiful (of God), 230, 319
Nasi (prince), 67, 96. *See also* Patriarch
Natural law, 102, 128
Nature(s), 241
Nawawi, al-, 169, 170
Nazareth, 41, 253
Nebiim (Prophets), 4, 25
Nebrija, Antonio de, 24, 60
Nehemia, 4, 10, 13, 25
Neophythagoreanism, 226
Neoplatonism, 226, 227, 237, 314, 329, 352
Nestorians, Nestorianism, 218, 219
Neturei Karta, 361
New moon, 169, 170
New Testament, xiv, 1–3, 7, 13, 15, 16–18, 21, 42, 45, 46, 52, 64, 67, 100, 131, 135, 218, 246, 254, 343, 358; closure, 34; quranic reading, 46–48. *See also* Covenant, new
Nicaea I, Council of, 45, 99, 184–185, 218
Nicaea II, Council of, 193, 204, 205
Nicholas of Lyra, 60
Night Journey, 192, 307, 350
Niyya (intention), 161
Nizam al-Din, 282
Nizam al-Mulk, 228
Noah, 47
Noahic or Noahide Laws/Commandments, 292
Number mysticism, 298–299. See also *Gematria*
Numbers, Book of, 4, 28, 39, 87
Nusayris, 320. *See also* Alawis

Obedience, monastic, 255–256, 258
Oberammergau, passion play, 199
Occasionalism, 115, 232–233, 235, 241
Office, monastic, 257, 259, 260, 262, 271
Olam ha-ba, 349, 356. *See also* World to Come
Old Testament, xxiv, 19, 24–25, 42, 46, 63, 100, 199; Protestant and Catholic, 19, 24–25. *See also* Bible
Olives, Mount of, 185, 187
Omphalopsychikoi (navel-gazers), 304
Oral, orality, 28, 31
Orange, Council of, 141, 143
Orders, religious. See Monastery, monasticism; *Tariqa*
Origen, 22, 24, 42–43, 45, 64, 215, 217, 227, 237, 300
Original Sin, 44, 129, 137–138, 141, 146, 148–149, 155, 191, 251, 358

Orthodoxy, 66, 251, 305; Feast of, 205–206; Islamic, 225–226, 235–236, 305; Jewish, 237, 345

Orthopraxy, 66, 237

Ottomans, Ottoman Empire, 110, 118–120, 124, 269, 274, 280, 283

Ousia (essence, substance), 217, 218

Oxford, university, 7, 240

Pablo Christia (Paul Christiani), 59

Paganus, pl. *pagani* (outbackers, pagans), 99

Paidaia (culture), 16

Palestine, 8, 38, 59, 92, 95, 96, 136, 172, 179, 185, 201, 213, 255, 268, 287, 334, 360–361; Mandate, 188; Talmud, 71, 201

Pantokrator (all-ruling), 189, 198

Papacy. *See* Pope

Papal decrees, bulls, 156, 199; *Antiquorum fida relatio*, 145; *Decet Romanum Pontificem*, 149; *Exsurge Domine*,149; *Ite vos*, 267; *Quo elongati*, 266, 267

Parable (*parabole*), 136, 141

Paradise, 106, 230, 348, 349–351; Muslim, 355

Paradosis (handing down), 65, 74. *See also* Tradition

Paraguay, 271, 272

Paris, 58, 70; university, 153, 240, 245, 271

Parousia (presence), 180, 364, 365–366. *See also* Second Coming

Paschal, Blaise, 157

Paschasius Radbertus, 191

Passover, 130, 171, 174–175, 179, 198; haggadah, 198, 200

Patriarch, 96, 123, 124, 233. *See also Nasi*

Paul (Saul), 4, 20, 21, 42, 61, 97, 100, 130, 131, 140, 146, 171, 174, 176, 203, 209, 215–216, 217, 294, 299, 327, 344, 352, 363; letters, 9, 16, 17, 246, 299; moral teaching, 136–137; Torah, 97–98, 251

Paul V, pope, 153

Pelagius, Pelagianism, 138, 140–141, 143, 147, 148, 156

Penance (penalty), 142–143; sacrament, 138, 141–143

Pentateuch, 4, 10, 13, 19, 24, 36, 57, 91, 169, 334

Pentecost, 74, 82. See also *Shabuoth*

People(s)of the Book, 3–4, 8, 35, 48

Persia, Persian, 162, 220, 248, 278

Person, 218; see *Hypostasis*

Perushim, 67. *See also* Pharisees

Pesach, 170, 185, 198. *See also* Passover

Peshar, pl. *pesharim* (explanation), 37

Peshat (literal sense), 56, 67, 90

Pesiqta (section), 38

Pesiqta Rab Kahhana, 39

Pesiqta Rabbati, 39

Peter, Apostle, 75, 203, 253, 294, 295; Letters of, 17

Peter Lombard, 79, 243, 246

Peter the Venerable, 7, 260

Phainomena, 218

Pharaoh, 12, 47

Pharisees, Pharisaism, 39, 40, 67–68, 70, 71, 74, 89, 90–91, 94, 95, 99, 135, 252, 296, 344

Philip IV, king of France, 269

Philo of Alexandria, 4, 5, 40–41, 52, 53, 90, 155, 169, 209, 227, 235, 299, 315; theology, 213–215, 216

Philosophy, philosopher, 39, 52, 54, 56, 78, 92, 127, 177, 212, 213, 333; in Islam, 220–222, 233–235; late antique, 247–248. See also *Falsafa*

Pilgrimage, 27, 105; Christian, 185–187; of farewell, 181, 183; Jewish, 198 (see also *Hag*); Muslim (see *Hajj; Ziyara*); penitential, 142

Pillars of Islam, 105–106, 180

Pilpul, 154–155

Pisa, Council of, 105–106

Pittsburgh Platform, 73, 74

Pius V, pope, 104

Pius IX, pope, 191

Plato, Platonic, 41, 44, 58, 92, 128, 136–137, 139, 143, 155, 156, 162, 212, 214, 215, 217, 221, 239, 241–242, 245, 247, 248, 284, 300, 301, 313, 322; Arabic, 56, 161, 215, 220; Latin, 239, 240

Plays, Miracle, Morality, Passion, 199. See also *Taziyeh*

Pleroma (The Plenitude), 335, 337

Plotinus, 221, 300, 314, 315

Plutarch, 159

Pococke, Edward, 8

Poetry, poets, 49, 56, 57, 132, 243. *See also* Muhammad, as poet

Poland, 73, 269, 289, 338

Polycarp, 192

Polygamy, 118

Polyglot Complutense, 24

Pombal, Marquis de, 272

Poor Clares. *See* Franciscans, Second Order

Pope, papacy, 57, 100–101, 103, 115, 123, 149, 151–152, 193, 258, 271. *See also* Rome, bishop of

Porphyry, 162

Port Royal, 157

Portugal, 153, 286

Poverty, monastic, 256, 262, 263, 264, 265, 272; controversy, 266–267

Praedicatio (preaching), 46

Prayer, 134, 142, 160, 168, 172, 173, 257, 307; liturgical, 30, 170; monastic, 257, 259; Muslim, 179–180; mystical, 301, 302–303, 305, 319. See also *Salat*

Preaching, 264, 265

Predestination, 129, 146, 162–165, 219, 223; double, 149–150

Presbyteros (elder), 75. *See also* Priest

Priest, priesthood, 142 ,177, 258; Jesus as, 170–171; Jewish, 169–170, 171–172; Priestly Source (P), 11. See also *Kohen*

Primal, primordial man, 315

Probabilis (demonstrable), probabilism, 154–155, 166

Proofs of Prophecy, 159

Propagation of the Faith, Congrgation for, 285

Prophet(s), prophecy, 1, 4, 14–16, 20, 25, 36, 41, 54, 109, 134, 170, 172, 221, 236, 250, 292, 330

Prophetic report. See *Hadith*

Proskynesis (reverence), 205

Protestant, 286. *See also* Reform

Provence, 239

Proverbs, 4, 10, 13

Providence, 216

Psalms, 4, 10, 37, 176, 246

Pseudepigrapha, 36

Ptolemy, 220, 347

Pumbeditha, 112

Purgatory, 77, 143–145

Purity, 87–88, 135, 172

Pythagoras, Pythageanism, 162, 239, 247, 248, 298

Q (Quelle, "source"), 5

Qada (judgment, eternal decree), 163

Qadar (measure [of being]), 163

Qadi (judge), 108, 110–112, 113–114, 122, 124; qadi al-qudat (chief justice), 111; qadi asker (military judge), 118

Qadiriyya, 280. *See also* Abd al-Qadir al-Jilani

Qanun (statutes), 119, 121–123; *Qanun-name* (law code),123; Qanuni, al-, 123

Qarmatians, 315, 316

Qere, 32. *See also* Recitation

Qibla (prayer direction), 173, 179–180

Qiyama (resurrection), 327

Qiyas (analogy), 53, 107, 116

Qizilbash, 283

Qodashim (holy things), 169. *See also* Sacrifice(s)

Qohelet (Ecclesiastes), 4, 213

Qorban. See Taboo

Quakers, 306

Qubba (domed tomb), 197

Qumran, 37, 38, 40, 41, 89–90, 130, 253, 295

Qunawi, Sadr al-Din al-, 330

Quran, xxiii, 2–3, 12–13, 15–16, 20, 23–34, 46–54, 105, 106–107, 108–109, 113, 115, 116, 145, 158–160, 162–164, 165–166, 170, 179, 201, 219, 223, 244, 274–276, 308–310, 348, 350, 357–358; Arabic, 7, 28, 49, 56, 209; arrangement, 25–27 ; collection, 30–32; composition, 27–28, ; created or uncreated, 53, 225–226, 229–230; editing, 29–30; legal matter, 107; style, 28, 31, 49, 55, 209; text, 33; and tradition, 84–85, 108–109, 184; translation, 7–8

Quraysh, 8, 207

Qurra (readers, reciters), 33

Qushayri, al-, 317

Qutb (pole [saint]), 322

Rabbis, rabbinic, 6, 10, 18, 24, 25, 39, 40, 52, 66–74, 95–96, 144, 168, 172–174, 201, 296, 351; and *ulama*, 123–126

Rabia, 310

Rahbaniyya, 277. *See also* Monastery

Raka (bowing), 179

Ramadan, 94, 105

Raphael, 352

Rashi, 46, 57–58, 60, 93, 243

Rationes aeternae (moral ideals), 140

Rasul (messenger, envoy), 26

Ray (opinion), 116

Raymond du Puy, 268

Raymond of Penaforte, 242

Razi, al-, 221, 238, 316

Reaya (flock), 123

Rebbe(s), (Hasidic *zaddik*), 337

Recitation, 32–33

Red heifer ritual, 88

Redemption, 97, 98, 155, 158, 218

Reductions (*Reducciones*), 272

Reform, Reformers, Reformation, 5, 19, 20, 22, 45, 64, 71, 103, 104, 123, 146, 149, 151, 153, 155, 171, 193, 196, 206–207, 271; theology, 246–247

Reinterment in Eretz Israel, 345

Relics, 169, 189, 193, 197

Religion (*religio, din*), 41, 179

Renaissance, 62–63

Renan, Ernest, 245

Repentance, 253

Responsa, 93, 101, 112–113. *See also* Decretals

Resurrection, 173, 186, 192, 199, 342, 364; bodily, 343–346

Revelation, 11–14, 66, 213, 230, 236 (*see* also *Wahy*); Book of (*see* John, Revelation of); closure, 35–36; occasions, 49–50, 55; and reason, 230–232, 244–245

Rhetoric, 39

Rhodes, 269

Ribat (fortified monastery), 168–170

Ricci, Matteo, 284

Roman Catechism, 104

Roman College, 154

Roman Empire, Romans, 70, 95, 123, 127–129, 136, 138, 169, 184, 201

Rome, 43

Rome, bishop of, 100, 115. *See also* Pope

Roqeah, Shalom, 290

Rosary, 189, 303. See also *Subha*

Rum, 204. *See also* Anatolia

Rumi, Jalal al-Din, 280, 319

Russia, 73, 272, 274

Ruth, 4, 10, 13

Ruyat Allah (vision of God), 355. *See also* Beatific Vision

Saadya ben Yusuf, gaon, 55–56, 58, 72, 215, 236

Sabbatai Zvi, 289, 333, 359, 363

Sabbath, 36, 38, 89, 90, 94, 97, 133, 172, 173. *See also* Shabbat

Sabians of Haran, 314

Sacrament(s), 77, 103, 104, 123, 138, 141–143, 147, 196, 206, 282

Sacrifice(s), 88, 134–135; community, 169; Islamic, 171, 181, 182, 195; Jesus, 170–171; shared, 170; sin, 169; temple, 168–169, 172. See also *Id al-adha; Mina*

Sadaqa (charity), 125. See also *Waqf*

Sadducees (Sons of Zadok), 39, 40, 71, 344

Safa, 182, 183

Safad, 93, 287–288, 333, 336–337

Sahaba, 82. *See also* Companions of the Prophet

Sahl al-Tustari, 315

Saint(s), 204; canonization, 193–194; Christian veneration, 192–193; Muslim, 195, 197–198, 254–255, 312–313, 321–322, 329–330, 332

Sakina, 169. See also *Shekinah*

Salaf, 45, 252. *See also* Fathers

Salah al-Din (Saladin), 186, 248, 269, 279

Salamanca, university, 153, 271

Salat (ritual prayer), 105, 179–180, 195, 281

Sale, George, 8

Salerno, university, 240

Salonika, 119, 223

Salvation, 28, 140, 147–148, 156, 213, 358–359; in wisdom, 248. *See also* Election; Predestination

Sama (hearing, spiritual concert), 319

Samaria, Samaritans, 19, 295

Samuel, 4, 10

Sanhedrin, 67, 94, 96, 344

Santiago, Knights of, 269–270

Sarajevo, 284

Satan, Satanas, Shaytan, 130–133, 181, 207, 254; stoning, 181, 192

Satanic verses, 34

Satmar, 290

Saud, House of, Saudis, 196, 197–198

Saudi Arabia, 112

Scapegoat, 134, 254

Schechter, Solomon, 74

Schism, 19

Schleiermacher, Friedrich, 64

Schneersohn, Schneerson, 290–291; Joseph Isaac, 362; Menachem Mendel, 362

Scholasticism, 23, 106, 113, 148, 154, 242–243, 246–247

School, legal, 111, 114, 117; philosophical, 224. See also *Madhhab*

Scribe(s), 28, 32, 33, 37, 38, 68. See also *Sofer*

Scriptor (writer), 21

Scripture, Scripturaries, xxiv, 1–34, 74, 76, 90–91, 103, 151, 155, 218; conditioning, 21–23 ; criticism, 8–11, 23–24; inspiration, 20–21; recitation cycles, 172; senses, 42–43; tampering, 34, 47; and tradition, 65–66. *See also* People of the Book

Second Coming, 199, 364. *See also* Parousia
Second Temple Judaism, Second Temple times, 36, 68, 169, 170, 195, 213, 296, 298, 340, 348
Sects, sectarianism, 36, 95
Sedarim (orders [of the Mishna]), 69
Seder, 198
Sefarad, ha-, 333, 337. *See also* Spain
Sefer ha-bahir (Book of Brilliance), 333
Sefer ha-zohar (Book of Splendors), 333, 334–336
Sefiroth (elementary principles, the decad), 168, 298, 335–336, 352
Semika (ordination), 71, 94, 96
Sephardic, Sephardi(s), 56, 59, 287. *See also* Sefarad, ha-
Septuagint, 4–5, 16, 24, 36, 38, 40, 71, 209, 214
Seraphim, 252
Shabbat, 173. *See also* Sabbath
Shabuoth (Weeks), 170, 185. *See also* Pentecost
Shadhili, al-, Shadiliyya, 280
Shafaa, 372. *See also* Intercession
Shafii, al-, 85, 108–109, 114, 115, 116, 117; Shafiites, 114, 208
Shahada (profession of faith), 12, 105, 229
Shammai, 67, 69
Sharia (Islamic law), 80, 106–107, 110, 113, 119, 121, 124, 238, 279; Shiite, 114, 115–116, 120–121
Shaykh al-Islam (chief mufti), 119
Shaytan; pl. shayatin. See Satan
Sheikh, xxi, 281, 282, 285–286, 318
Shekinah (spirit, presence [of God], 168–169, 187, 335, 337, 357. See also *Sakina*
Shema, 173
Shemoneh Esreh (Eighteen Benedictions), 173, 345
Sheol, 341–342, 349
Shiat Ali (Party of Ali), 120. *See also* Shiism
Shiism, Shiites, 34, 115, 120, 122, 162, 225, 229, 230, 235; exegesis, 54; Imami or Twelver, 115, 118, 249–250; Ismaili or Sevener, 54, 111, 226, 227, 248, 279, 314, 324–325, 327; popular devotions, 196, 199–200; Sufism, 314–315
Shimon bar Yohai, 334
Shiur gomah, 297
Shulkhan Aruk, 93, 113, 291
Shurta (police power), 111
Sicily, 239

Sifra, 39
Sifre Zuta, 39
Sijistani, Abu Sulayman al-, 226
Silsila (spiritual chain), 281
Simeon, the New Theologian, 303
Simeon Stylites, 256
Simon, Richard, 62, 63
Simon Magus, 295
Sin, 128, 141–145; grave and light, 133, 192; in Israel, 133–135; mortal and venial, 133, 144; sin offerings, 88, 134, 170
Sinai, Mount, xxi, 22, 39, 42, 66, 68, 88, 109, 128, 171, 174, 185, 293
Siyasa (policy, governance), 121–122
Slave(s), slavery, 161
Slavic, Slavonic, 5
Slavs, 274
Smyrna, 119
Society of Jesus. *See* Jesuits
Socrates, 212
Sofer, pl. *soferim*, 37, 89. *See also* Scribe
Sola Scriptura, 61, 76–78
Solomon, king of Israel, 67, 132, 184, 297; Wisdom of, 5, 19, 20, 24. *See also* Song of Songs
Solomon ben Isaac. *See* Rashi
Son of God, 20, 97, 155, 158, 217–218 (*see also* Christology); sons of gods, 131
Song of Songs, 4, 10, 57, 297
Sophia, 248, 335. *See also* Wisdom, divine
Sozomen, 7
Souls of the spheres, 322
Spain, 7, 24, 56, 57, 59, 116, 152, 153, 159, 198, 234, 237, 239, 269–270, 270–271, 272, 286, 287, 306, 327, 333, 334, 337
Spinoza, Baruch, 63
Spiritual Exercises, 306–307
Stations and States, 317–318
Stations of the Cross, 190
Stoics, Stoicism, 40, 128, 137, 213, 223, 239, 247, 277, 300
Subh (daybreak prayer), 180
Subha (counting beads, rosary), 281, 303
Substance, 218. See also *Ousia*
Sufi, Sufism, 1, 195, 227, 249, 276, 284; and Gnosticism, 313–314; methods, 318–319; and Shiites, 314–315; theory, 317–319. *See also* Mysticism; *Tariqa*
Suhrawardi, Shihab al-Din, 248–249, 323–324, 326, 329
Sukkoth (Tabernacles), 170, 185, 187

Sulami, al-, 317
Sulayman, sultan, 119, 123
Sultan (power, authority, sultanate), 110, 111, 122
Sunday, 101, 173, 178, 179
Sunna (customary behavior, tribal law), 107; and the Quran, 84–85; *sunnat al-nabi* (custom of the Prophet), 80–82, 105, 107, 108, 116, 179, 181, 227, 231
Sunni(s), Sunnism, 120, 122, 123, 195, 196
Sura (Iraq), 55, 112
Sura(s) (of the Quran), 25–27, 29–32, 105, 180; editing, 29–30; Meccan, 26, 27, 28, 29–30, 106, 158; Medinan, 26, 27, 28, 106; titles, 31
Symbolon, 176. *See also* Creed
Synagogue, 41, 59, 172–174, 175, 198, 201–202; Great Synagogue, Assembly, men of, 10, 109
Synaxis (prayer service), 175, 176
Syndikon of Orthodoxy, 205. *See also* Orthodoxy, Feast of
Syria, Syrians, 8, 122, 126, 219, 224, 255
Syriac, 5, 24, 49, 176, 219, 220, 224

Tabari, al-, 50–51
Taboo, 16, 19, 87–88, 171, 183. See also *Haram; Ihram*
Tabor, Mount, 294, 304, 305
Tafsir (explanation), 36, 51–52. *See also* Exegesis
Tajalli ([divine] self-manifestation), 331, 356
Tajsim (corporeality), 310, 354
Talim (infallible teaching), 227, 324
Talmud, 6, 52, 59, 60, 67, 70, 91–92, 117, 174, 243, 289, 291; trial of, 58–60, 70. *See also* Babylon, Babylonian Talmud; Palestine, Talmud
Tamid (daily community sacrifice), 169
Tanak, 4, 18–19, 25, 44, 46
Tanasukh (metempsychosis), 321
Tanhuma, 39
Tannaim (reciters), 69, 92
Tanzih (stripping [God of imperfection]), 331, 332
Taqiyya (dissembling), 115–116
Taqlid (adherence, acceptance on authority), 117, 121. See also *Muqallid*
Taqqanah, pl. *taqqanoth* (rabbinic enactments), 89, 94, 106, 116

Targum(s) (Aramaic translation of Bible), 4, 38, 46, 172, 209; Targum Jonathan, 202
Tariqa (Muslim religious order), 278, 279–284; compared to Christian, 284–285; rule, 280–282; suppression, 287
Tarsus, 136
Tasawwuf, 278, 279–280. *See also* Sufi
Tashbih (comparing [God]), 330, 331, 354
Tannenberg, battle, 269
Tawaf (circumambulation [of the Kaaba]), 182–183
Tawakkul (trust in God), 277
Tawhid (unity of or with God), 311, 320
Tawil (allegorical exegesis), 51–52, 54
Tawrat (Torah), 27, 35. *See also* Torah
Taziyeh (consolation, passion play), 197, 200
Teitelbaum, Michael, 290
Tekke (Sufi convent [Turkish]), 278, 283, 284
Tempier, Stephen, bishop, 245
Templar, Knights, 268–270, 286
Temple, Jerusalem, 66–67, 95, 169–170, 171–172, 187, 198, 203, 252; tithe, 169
Temple Emanu-El, 73
Temple mount, 89, 186
Templum Domini (Dome of the Rock), 268
Templum Solomonis (Aqsa mosque), 268
Ten Commandments, 10, 42, 87, 104
Tent of Presence, 203
Tertullian, 45, 216, 217
Teshubah (return), 253. *See also* Repentance
Tetzel, John, 148
Teutonic Knights, 269
Theios (godlike), 201. *See also* Divinization
Theiosis, 304. *See also* Divinization
Theodicy, 136
Theodora, empress, 205
Theodosius, emperor, 203
Theologoumena, 219
Theology, theologians, 76, 78, 92, 143, 147, 148, 177–178, 211–250; Christian, 240–247, 333; Islamic, 222–233, 241; Jewish, 236–238; portrait of God, 212–213; sacred, 216, 227, 240–241; systematic, 217
Theology of Aristotle, 314, 315
Theophany, 293–294
Theophilus, emperor, 205
Theoria (contemplation), 300
Theosophy, 248, 299, 321–324
Theotokos (God-bearer), 190
Thomas, Gospel of, 5, 17, 36
Thomas à Kempis, 189, 307

Tiberias, 67, 71
Tikkun (aboriginal harmony of humankind, restoration), 337; *tikkun ha-olam*, 337
Timothy, 14, 99
Tirmidhi, al-, 159, 312–313; 315, 319
Titus, 99
Tobit, 19
Toledo, 239–240
Tomb, torments of, 144, 230, 370
Torah, 1, 14, 10, 15–16, 33, 34, 37, 68, 71–72, 168, 169, 171, 214, 236, 238, 251, 252, 289, 334; Christians and, 96–98; oral, 39, 57, 64, 68–69, 71–72, 73, 88, 89, 90, 93, 109, 133, 141, 174; written, 39, 57, 66, 68, 174
Tosefta (supplement), 69
Tradition, 65–66, 71–72, 73; Christian, 74–76; Islamic, 80–86, 231; Jewish, 66–74, 76; prophetic (see *Hadith; Sunna*); Reform, 76–80
Tradition from the elders, fathers, 74, 90–91
Traditionalist(s), Islamic, 231–232, 234–236
Traditionist(s), 228–231
Transfiguration, 75, 294, 301, 305, 326
Translation, 4, 7–8, 38, 47–48, 161–162, 209, 215, 219–220, 223–224, 238–240, 244; effects, 240–241. *See also* Septuagint; Targums
Transubstantiation, 171, 175, 177, 178
Trent, Council of, 6, 22, 61, 78, 79, 104, 150–152, 155, 156, 191, 194, 271, 307
Trinity, 218, 219, 242
Troyes, Council of, 268
Tunis, Tunisia, 118, 234
Turk(s), 118, 122, 274, 283. *See also* Ottoman(s)
Turkish Republic, 6, 287
Türkmen, 120
Tusi, al-, 86, 115
Tusi, Nasir al-Din al-, 162
Twelve, the, 74–75, 174. *See also* Apostles
Twelve Tribes of Israel, 75
Two Swords, 123
Typoi (archetypes), typology, 42–43

Ukraine, 73, 289, 290, 338
Ulama (the learned), 113–114, 118–121, 144, 196; and rabbis, 123–126; Shiite, 120–121, 196
Umar ibn al-Khattab, caliph, 32, 84, 110, 115
Umayyads, Banu Umayya, 110, 197, 222–223
Umma (community), 86, 105, 109, 116, 158

Umra (Meccan spring festival), 182, 183
United States, 73, 74
Universals, 239
University, 93, 143, 215, 240, 265; and *madrasa*, 240
Urban IV, pope, 194
Urf (custom), 121
Usul (roots, foundations [of the Sharia]), 120, 121, 160; Usuli(s), 120–121
Uthman, caliph, 32, 49, 115
Uzayr (Ezra?), 50

Valdes, Pierre (Waldo), 76. *See also* Waldensians
Valla, Lorenzo, 5, 25, 60
Valladolid, university, 153
Varallo, 190
Vatican I, Council of, 22
Vatican II, Council of, 195
Veiling, 167
Vergil, 144
Verna, Mount, 190
Via negativa, 301–302
Vlacich, Mattias, 63, 79
Voltaire, 157
Voluntarism, 146, 165
Vows, monastic, 259, 271
Vulgate, 5–6, 23, 24, 46, 60, 71

Wahdat al-wujud (oneness of being), 331–332
Wahhabis, 197–198
Wahidi, al-, 50
Wahy (revelation), 85
Walaya (sainthood), 312, 330
Waldensians, 76, 79
Wali; pl. *awliya* (friend [of God]), 197, 255. *See also* Saint(s), Muslim
Waqf (pious foundations), 114, 120, 125, 281, 286
Wasi (deputy, vicar), 54
Wellhausen, Julius, 11
Western Wall, 169, 187–188
Will, divine, 127, 128, 146, 160, 162–164, 230; absolute and ordained, 146–147, 163–164
William of Moerbeke, 244
William of Ockham, 147–148, 163, 246
Wine prohibition, 50, 270
Wird (Sufi prayer formulary), 281, 319
Wisdom, divine, 216
Wisdom of Jesus ben Sira (Ecclesiasticus), 5, 13, 19, 24, 39, 137, 213

Wittenberg, University, 148, 206, 246
Women, 75, 82, 105–106, 111, 118, 197, 253, 262, 274, 279, 328
Work of the Beginning, Creation, 238, 298
World to Come, 356–357. *See also* Afterlife
Writing, scripts, 28, 31–32, 32–33
Writings (*Ketubim*), 1, 19, 25, 36, 172
Wycliffe, John, 76

Xvarneh (Light of Glory), 323

Yabneh (Jamnia), 67–68
Yahweh, xxi–xxii, 88, 129, 217, 251, 293, 340
Yahwist (J), 10–11
Yawm al-din (Day of Judgment), 369, 371
Yawm al-juma (day of assembly, Friday), 173, 180
Yenisehir, 119
Yeshiva(s), 92, 112–113, 124
Yihud (unification), 336
Yohanan ben Zakkai, 67, 296
Yom Kippur, 134–135, 169, 170

Zaddik, 124, 254, 336, 337, 338
Zadok, Jewish high priest, 71; Sons of, 90

Zahir (evident, exoteric), 53–54, 116, 320, 326; Zahiris, 53, 116
Zakat (obligatory tithing), 105, 124
Zalman, Schneur, 290, 291
Zamakhshari, 53
Zamzam, 183
Zandaqa (heresy), 248, 316
Zawiya (Sufi convent), 279, 281. See also *Dargeh*
Zayd ibn Thabit, 32
Zaynab, daughter of Ali and Fatima, 196
Zealots, 39
Zechariah, 36
Zephaniah, 340
Zionism, Zionist, 73; political, 360–361; religious, 359–360
Ziyara (pious visit), 185
Zoroaster, Zoroastrians, 139, 315, 323, 340
Zohar. See *Sefer ha-zohar*
Zuggoth (pairs [of presiding rabbis]), 67
Zuhr (noon prayer), 180
Zurabbabel, 187
Zurich, 77, 207
Zwingli, Ulrich, 77, 178, 207